BUSINESS
ENVIRONMENT
AND
PUBLIC POLICY

ROGENE A. BUCHHOLZ

University of Texas at Dallas

BUSINESS ENVIRONMENT AND PUBLIC POLICY

Implications for Management

PRENTICE-HALL, INC., Englewood Cliffs, New Jersey 07632

Library of Congress Cataloging in Publication Data

BUCHHOLZ, ROGENE A.
   Business environment and public policy.

   Includes bibliographies and index.
   1. Industry and state—United States.
2. Industry—Social aspects—United States.
3. Management—United States. I. Title.
HD3616.U47B76   658.4'062   81-19967
ISBN 0-13-095554-X   AACR2

Printed in the United States of America

10 9 8 7 6 5 4 3 2 1

Editorial/production supervision and interior design by Paul Spencer
Cover design by Miriam Recio
Manufacturing buyer: Ed O'Dougherty

ISBN 0-13-095554-X

Prentice-Hall International, Inc., *London*
Prentice-Hall of Australia Pty. Limited, *Sydney*
Prentice-Hall of Canada, Ltd., *Toronto*
Prentice-Hall of India Private Limited, *New Delhi*
Prentice-Hall of Japan, Inc., *Tokyo*
Prentice-Hall of Southeast Asia Pte. Ltd., *Singapore*
Whitehall Books Limited, *Wellington, New Zealand*

Contents

v

Part Two

ENVIRONMENTAL INFLUENCES ON PUBLIC POLICY

Part Three

PUBLIC POLICY ISSUES

Preface

Throughout most of its history, the corporation has been viewed solely as an economic institution, with only economic responsibilities. These responsibilities include producing goods and services to meet consumer needs, providing employment for much of the nation's work force, paying dividends to shareholders, and making provision for future growth. If these economic responsibilities were fulfilled, business was considered to have discharged its obligations to society and made its maximum contribution to society's wealth.

The last fifteen years, however, have seen a dramatic change in the environment in which business functions. New roles have been defined for business to perform in society. Society has devoted an increasing amount of attention to issues such as pollution control, workplace health and safety, equal opportunity, and product quality and safety. Many of these concerns have resulted in a proliferation of new laws and regulatory agencies that restrict business activities as they affect society. The long-term effect of these issues and restrictions is a dramatic change in the "rules of the game" by which business is expected to operate.

Thus the economic functions of business are no longer as dominant as they traditionally have been, and they must be seen in relation to the social and political roles that business is being asked to assume. The business institution is being reshaped to meet these new responsibilities, which are growing in importance.

This changing role of business in society has, of course, made an impact on the managerial task within corporations. Managers have had to incorporate social and political concerns into their decision-making. Increasingly, these concerns are becoming part of routine business operations in many corporations. Many managers have changed the way in which they view their responsibilities to society. Recent years have seen the emergence of new philosophies of business that incorporate social and political concerns and are thus broader than any narrow economic interpretation of the firm and its responsibilities.

Business schools have responded to this changing role of business in society by introducing courses with titles like Business and Society, Business and Its Environment, Business and Public Policy, and The Legal Environment of Business. Other schools have integrated environmental material into their business policy and/or functional courses. Still others have developed courses dealing with government regulation of business. In addition, traditional courses in business and government, public policy, and current economic problems have been continued.

A recent survey of 450 schools of business and management in the United States showed that 382 or 85% had what they considered to be a separate course that dealt with environmental matters related to the changing role of business in society.[1] This study recommended that a comprehensive course devoted exclusively to environmental matters should be part of the required curriculum in schools of business and management.[2] Another survey of business executives unanimously supported this recommendation. They believed that the subject matter is so important to management education that it deserves to be a fundamental piece of the core curriculum.[3] Typical of the response of these executives is the following quote:

> Learning to understand the external environment, and to consider its impact in making management decisions, has become a most necessary skill for every successful manager. . . . No business decision today can be based solely on traditional business rationale and be successful.[4]

Thus the field of business environment/public policy, as it has come to be called, is of crucial importance to management education. Over the years of its existence, the field has become more rigorous, analytical, and management oriented. It has developed more substance and formalization than previously, a greater self-confidence, and an extensive body of literature. Yet the field still has a great deal of diversity, reflected in the course titles mentioned previously, which is both a strength and a weakness. It is a strength in that the complexity of the field calls for different approaches to cover the material adequately, but a weakness in that the lack of a clear focus threatens to disintegrate the field as it goes chasing off in many different directions.

Many leading scholars believe there is an emerging consensus regarding a definition of the field, that as the field has matured it has developed a clearer focus and claimed its own territory. These scholars define the field in terms of the external environment of business, those economic, legal, social, political, technological, and other forces and factors that impinge on business from the outside and give shape to its behavior. This external focus, it is said, deals with issues that are of central concern to management and distinguishes the field from other areas of the business school that focus more strictly on internal aspects of corporate management.

[1]Rogene A. Buchholz, *Business Environment/Public Policy: A Study of Teaching and Research in Schools of Business and Management* (St. Louis: Washington University Center for the Study of American Business, 1979), p. 98.

[2]*Ibid.*, pp. 125–126.

[3]Rogene A. Buchholz, *Business Environment/Public Policy: Corporate Executive Viewpoints and Educational Implications* (St. Louis: Washington University Center for the Study of American Business, 1980), pp. 26–30.

[4]*Ibid.*, p. 29.

While this external focus does indeed provide some boundaries for the field, the crucial element in tying the various parts of the field together is an underlying integrative concept. The concept of social responsibility was used for this purpose in the early years of the field's development, but it was subsequently criticized as being too moralistic, philosophical, and difficult to operationalize and thus make relevant in a business and management context. As the field became more rigorous, analytical, and management oriented, the concept of corporate social responsiveness came into vogue. It was believed that this concept provided a better underpinning for the field that could tie all the various environmental forces and factors together with a managerial orientation.

Most, if not all, of the existing textbooks in the field are written with this focus on the external environment, with some mixture of social responsibility and responsiveness as an integrative concept to tie the material together. It is believed by many, however, that neither of these concepts provides an adequate integrating framework for the field. Thus a new concept called public policy is emerging. This is reflected in the title of the previously mentioned AACSB/CSAB study, in the title of some new research centers in the field, and in the change of department title at one of the schools that has an extensive program in the area.

This textbook is the first in the field to use this concept of public policy throughout as an integrative concept. Environmental influences are discussed in terms of their impact on public policy rather than on the corporation directly, issues are discussed as public policy issues rather than social issues, and management's response to the changing environment of business is seen as participation in the public policy process rather than being viewed from the perspective of social responsibility.

It is believed that this concept provides a much more firm base for the field and allows for much better integration of topics that belong to the field. The public policy concept is much more consistent with what has actually happened in our society with respect to government regulation and other public policy measures. It also provides clearer guidelines for management in terms of the behavior presently required as well as the courses of action management has open to help shape the environment in which business functions. Thus the public policy concept is managerially oriented and provides a much better framework to discuss the impact of the external environment on business and management's response to these external influences.

The book is designed to equip a business manager or student with the knowledge and skills that are necessary to handle the public policy dimension of the job effectively. Part One introduces the subject of public policy and its relationship to business management. The first chapter attempts to point out the importance of public policy to management. The second chapter continues this task by describing the market system and the public policy process, specifying the major differences between these two ways of allocating society's resources. In Chapter 3, a historical view of business and public policy is presented, noting where major shifts in public policy have taken place in American history. The last chapter in this section discusses the social origins of public policy.

Part Two deals with some of the important environmental factors that are relevant to public policy. While there are many environmental influences on public policy, the main influences seem to arise from the social-cultural and political environments. The social-cultural environment includes values, ideologies, and social movements that precipitate social change; the realm of ethics and the influence of the ethical standards of society on business; and broader social-cultural influences in society related to the basic question of corporate governance. The political environment includes the current state of business-government relations, government regulation of business, and the manner in which business participates in the political system.

Part Three discusses the development, current status, and future outlook of specific public policy issues related to the society as a whole, the workplace and the marketplace in particular, and the physical environment. Management needs to understand these issues in all their complexity—how they affect the management task and how they can be responded to effectively.

Part Four deals specifically with management responses to the public policy dimension. This section includes chapters on the development of a management philosophy that incorporates the public policy dimension, changes in the corporate organization that have resulted from the impact of public policy, the importance of public issues management in developing responses to public policy issues, and developments in social measurement and reporting. The final chapter considers the future of business management and public policy.

This book is intended for use in a comprehensive course dealing with environmental matters of concern to business and management; it treats the political, social, economic, legal, ethical, and other environments of business. The book can also be used in more specialized courses dealing with government regulation or business-government relations. Because of its management focus, it should also be of value to managers of business corporations, serving as a handbook of public policy requirements and business involvement in public policy formulation. Finally, the book can also be useful to schools of public administration that have courses with a public policy orientation.

The intellectual debt of any author is enormous. One's thinking is the product of countless associations that have been engaged in over the years. Yet a few such associations that have been particularly influential in the writing of this book should be mentioned. Lee E. Preston and James E. Post deserve a great deal of credit for introducing me to the concept of public policy. Their book, *Private Management and Public Policy,* was very influential in shaping my own thinking and providing an acceptable integrative concept for the field. Equally influential was Murray Weidenbaum, with his emphasis on government regulation and the impacts regulation has made on business and management. Working with Murray at the Center for the Study of American Business for three years was an invaluable experience. Finally, the American Assembly of Collegiate Schools of Business, who along with the CSAB sponsored the study of the Business Environment/Public Policy field, deserves credit for giving me the opportunity to do the study. This work gave me a thorough acquaintance with what is going on in the field and allowed me to meet a great number of people both in academia and in business who are concerned about environmental matters.

James E. Post and John F. Mahon, of Boston University, and Richard

Cuba, of the University of Baltimore, deserve thanks for reviewing the book at an early stage and making many suggestions for its improvement. Frank Manning, of Washington University, provided invaluable assistance in tracking down references and providing other research assistance. The people at Prentice-Hall whom I worked with provided a great deal of assistance and encouragement. I am also indebted to Ruth Scheetz, Pamela Cutter, and Rhonda Tobin for having typed the various versions of the manuscript, and to Margo Bryant for assistance in preparing the index.

Portions of chapters have previously appeared in *Harvard Business Review*, *Business*, and *Business Horizons*. The editors of these journals kindly consented to the use of these materials. Other publications also cooperated by giving their permission to use tables, illustrations, quotes, and other material.

PART ONE

Introduction to Business Environment and Public Policy

1

The Changing Role of Business in Society and the Changing Management Task

This whole area is new to business, our ability to manage it is not as good as in other areas.[1]

These were the words of James F. Towey, outgoing chief executive officer of Olin Corporation, a Stamford-based industrial giant manufacturing chemicals, brass, cigarette papers, Winchester firearms, and other products. The area referred to in this statement is public policy, because in 1978 Olin found itself involved in two legal actions with the United States government.

One action concerned a charge that Olin had filed false reports with the Environmental Protection Agency that vastly understated the amount of mercury an Olin plant had dumped into the Niagara River between late 1970 and mid-1977. The plant apparently had been discharging an average of almost four pounds per day during this period while the reports showed no discharges above the government limit, which was first set at 0.5 pound and then changed to 0.1 pound. On one occasion, the plant had discharged 330 pounds in one day. This discrepancy was discovered by the company itself and reported to the Environmental Protection Agency. In addition, the

[1]Hugh D. Menzies, "The One-Two Punch That Shook Olin," *FORTUNE*, June 5, 1978, p. 122. Quoted with permission.

company conducted an internal investigation that led to the firing of two employees who were later indicted along with a third who had retired.[2]

The second action concerned the illegal shipment of $1.2 million in sporting arms and ammunition to South Africa. According to the *Fortune* article, the "Winchester salesmen who participated in the deal circumvented a ban on all weapons sales to South Africa by telling the U.S. Office of Munition Control that the material was bound for Austria, Greece, Mozambique, and Spain."[3] Again, falsification of documents filed with a United States agency was involved, uncovered by a U.S. Customs investigation.

In neither of these situations was the financial gain to the company large enough to have been the primary motivating factor. In the Niagara situation, the initial goal may have been to cover up what were believed to be only temporary variations from government standards that could soon be brought under control. Once it became clear to plant personnel that the plant could not be brought under control with existing equipment, it was too risky to go to top management and ask for increased spending for pollution control equipment for an aging plant. Olin management had previously shut down a chemical plant in Virginia that proved too costly to bring into compliance. The Niagara employees involved in the falsification may have feared that their plant would also be shut down if the facts about noncompliance were known to top management.

The South African sales did have an effect on the bonus of at least one employee. But the other employees involved in this deception may have done so because they believed the ban on the sales of sporting arms to South Africa was unreasonable. Most of the weapons involved were shotguns and .22 rifles, hardly military hardware, and the ban, which the employees may have believed served no worthwhile purpose, shut the company out of a good market.

There is no evidence in either of these situations that top management knew of these actions before they were uncovered, so it appears that top management was not directly involved. Yet, as the *Fortune* article points out, top management was involved more than they might have imagined. They had complained, as have many managers, about the unreasonableness or inanity of many new government intrusions on their business. This complaining, even if appropriate, might have created a climate that encouraged outright evasion of the law by subordinates.[4]

Another factor concerns the lack of controls in public policy matters. Management in any company has to concentrate on financial matters. Olin was no different. Apparently many financial reports and controls were available to top management, but there were virtually no controls capable of detecting evasions of government regulations pertaining to the environment and other public policy areas. The words of one executive are instructive: "It never really occurred to us that we would need such controls."[5]

The impact of situations like this on management and on the business is significant. Almost half of Olin's 1978 annual meeting, held in Godfrey, Illinois, was devoted to an explanation of these two matters. The incoming

[2]*Ibid.*, pp. 120–122.
[3]*Ibid.*, p. 121.
[4]*Ibid.*
[5]*Ibid.*, p. 122.

chief executive officer, John M. Henske, was reported to be spending 40 percent of his time on regulatory matters, and even when these two situations were settled, he expected such problems to take up to 20 to 30 percent of his time.[6] The reason for this may be that business has not learned how to handle these public policy matters as part of routine business operations.

The most serious impact of all is that violations such as these only tend to further erode the credibility of business and may eventually lead to more government controls in response to public pressure (see box). Thus James Towey's statement at the beginning of this chapter makes a key point. Management at all levels of the company needs to learn how to manage public policy issues as effectively as they manage other parts of the business. It is to this end that this book is dedicated.

THE ORIGINS OF DISTRUST

Businessmen concerned about widespread public distrust of business can only be dismayed at the long, sorry history now coming to light concerning Occidental Petroleum Corp.'s chemical subsidiaries and their persistent mishandling of toxic chemicals.

Past dumping practices of Hooker Chemicals & Plastics Corp., for example, have been held responsible for driving 239 families from their homes near the Love Canal in Niagara Falls, N.Y. Company officials first responded that the dumping occurred 40 years ago, using techniques thought to be safe. How could they be blamed now, they asked. But as the facts emerge, Hooker officials early on realized the extent of the problem and chose to remain silent. Had Hooker notified authorities, the chemicals might have been contained and the public suspicion of all chemical companies averted. Now the Justice Dept. is preparing a suit against the company, and the House Commerce Committee is investigating its past activities.

Beyond that, as recently as 1977, officials at Occidental Chemical Co. knowingly polluted underground water in Lathrop, Calif. with toxic pesticides and also knowingly violated air pollution limits at a Florida plant.

Ironically, when Congress passed the Resource Conservation & Recovery Act in 1976 to prevent hazardous materials from being disposed of improperly, industry officials argued that it was unnecessary and would place an undue burden on companies. After the revelations about Occidental's subsidiaries that argument would carry even less weight with Congress and the public.

Recently, in fact, Yankelovich, Skelly & White took a poll of attitudes toward business. Some 50% said they believed the chemical industry is doing a poor job of controlling air and water pollution. Occidental's irresponsibility goes far to explain such attitudes.

From *Business Week*, September 3, 1979, p. 164. Reprinted by permission.

The Changing Role of Business

The need for management of public policy issues arises out of the changing role of business in society. Throughout its history, a corporation's primary responsibility has been economic, to produce goods and services to

[6]*Ibid.*, p. 121.

meet consumer needs, to provide employment for much of the work force, to pay reasonable dividends to shareholders, to meet its debt obligations on time, and to make provisions for future growth.

In the sixties and seventies, however, an additional set of responsibilities was added to this list, generally called social responsibilities. These responsibilities included doing something about cleaning up and eliminating pollution, promoting equal opportunity for minorities and women, protecting the health and safety of workers, producing products that are safe and honestly represented in the marketplace, doing something to alleviate poverty in disadvantaged areas of the country, and similar responsibilities. These were not meant to supplant a corporation's economic responsibilities, but were added to them, and have been referred to as a new social contract that society was working out with business.

These new expectations of society in regard to business institutions were well stated some years ago by William C. Frederick, writing in the *California Management Review.* Social responsibility, Frederick implied, demands that business do more than perform its traditional economic functions. Production and distribution, he said, should enhance the total socioeconomic welfare of the country, and resources should be "utilized for broad social ends and not simply for the narrowly circumscribed interests of private persons and firms."[7]

The same point was made by the Committee for Economic Development, an independent research and educational group of leading business executives and educators.

> Today it is clear that the terms of the contract between society and business are, in fact, changing in substantial and important ways. Business is being asked to assume broader responsibilities to society than ever before and to serve a wider range of human values. Business enterprises, in effect, are being asked to contribute more to the quality of American life than just supplying quantities of goods and services.[8]

Business responded to these social expectations in a number of ways—building plants in disadvantaged areas of the country, creating organizations such as the National Alliance of Businessmen to promote the hiring and training of disadvantaged people, lending employees to staff such organizations as the NAB or to work in local communities, redesigning products to be less polluting, developing aid programs for needy people, and similar measures.

The bulk of these social responsibilities, however, became mandated by law—laws related to health and safety in the workplace, pollution control, equal opportunity, product safety, toxic substances, and other areas. These laws resulted in proliferation of new government agencies (Occupational Safety and Health Administration, Environmental Protection Agency, Consumer Product Safety Commission, Equal Employment Opportunity Commission) that are concerned with social regulation, as distinguished from the older type of industry regulation (Interstate Commerce Commission, Civil

[7]William C. Frederick, "The Growing Concern over Business Responsibility," *California Management Review,* Vol. 2, No. 4 (Summer 1960), p. 60.

[8]Committee for Economic Development, *Social Responsibilities of Business Corporations* (New York: CED, 1971), p. 12.

Aeronautics Board, Federal Communications Commission). These newer regulatory agencies have produced a volume of regulations affecting business that is unprecedented in our history.

Thus the social responsibilities of business have largely become matters of public policy. While there seems to be something of a respite of late regarding new legislation that would create whole new areas of regulation, the recently created areas that are not yet fully implemented (toxic substances, hazardous waste disposal, and others) will keep new regulations coming for some years to come. Thus, pressures from government in the area of social responsibilities will continue.

These changes in the environment of business and the resulting impact on business and management have changed the way many managers think about the corporation and the way they view their responsibilities to society. Recent years have seen the emergence of a new philosophy of business that incorporates social and political concerns and is thus broader than a narrow economic interpretation of the firm and its responsibilities. This broader perspective is reflected in the statements of many business leaders, such as the following:

> And no longer are society's wants and needs vis-à-vis business measured strictly in terms of marketplace demand. Instead, the corporation is now viewed as having a wide variety of responsibilities transcending the marketplace. Some of those responsibilities are to society at large. Whether a business has social responsibilities, is, I know, a subject of widespread debate. But to my mind, it is a debate that continues long after the argument is over. Today I know of no leader of business who sees his function as limited to the pursuit of profit. I know of none who does not realize that the business that for profit's sake ignores the impacts of its actions on society is not likely to make a profit very long.[9]

> Beyond its classical functions, business has a responsibility to contribute in appropriate ways to the overall well-being of the community in which it operates. Resolution of many social and human relations problems requires the active and intelligent participation of all elements of society—individuals, government, and institutions—including business."[10]

Not everyone in the corporate world, of course, agrees with this philosophy or with this view of the changing environment and its impact on business. The environment, in some cases, affects large and small businesses quite differently, thus making a difference in sensitivity to these changes. Even within large corporations, not everyone subscribes to this philosophy or would agree that the rules of the game have changed all that dramatically. Other managers, while agreeing that the environment has changed, do not view this change with great enthusiasm and personally still hold to the classical economic view of business and its responsibilities to society.[11]

Yet, there is a growing body of evidence that indeed the environment of business has changed and that this change calls for new philosophies and

[9]John D. deButts, "A Strategy of Accountability," *Running the American Corporation*, William R. Dill, ed. (Englewood Cliffs, N.J.: Prentice-Hall, 1978), p. 146.

[10]Irving S. Shapiro, "Business in Today's Society," remarks made at the University of Richmond, March 12, 1974.

[11]See, for example, George Cabot Lodge, "Business and the Changing Society," *Harvard Business Review*, Vol. 52, No. 2 (March–April 1974), pp. 59–72.

operating strategies on the part of the management of corporate organizations to meet the challenges such changes present. While the regulatory trend may indeed have reached a plateau as far as whole new areas of regulation are concerned, the long-term effect is a dramatic change in the rules of the game by which business is expected to operate. Economic responsibilities are no longer so dominant and must be seen in relation to the social and political roles business is being asked to assume. The business institution is being reshaped to meet these new responsibilities as society continues the process of developing a new social, political, and economic order.

The Changing Nature of Business Management

This changing role of business in society has, of course, affected the managerial task within corporations. Managers have had to incorporate social and political concerns into their decision-making. Increasingly, these concerns are becoming part of routine business operations in many corporations. George A. Steiner, Harry and Elsa Kunin Professor of Business and Society at the University of California, Los Angeles, describes the change in the management task as follows:

> Top managers of corporations spend a preponderant part of their time today dealing with environmental problems. These include addressing social concerns of society, complying with new social legislation, communicating with legislators and government executives concerning new proposed laws and regulations, meeting with various self-interest groups concerning their demands and/or grievances, and administering their organizations in such a way as to respond to the new attitudes of people working in the organization. This is in sharp contrast to the top executive of a major corporation twenty years ago whose attention and decision-making was focused almost wholly on economic and technical considerations. The increased attention of top management time to social and political questions results, of course, in different allocations of time of lower-level managers than in the past. They, too, are spending more of their time on social and political issues and are being measured more and more on their performance in these areas.[12]

This new dimension of management was foreseen some years ago by Walter G. Held, formerly Director of Advanced Management Programs for the Brookings Institution.[13] Writing in the *Columbia Journal of World Business*, Held stated that management theory at that time revealed a striking penchant toward introspection with relatively little attention being paid to the world in which business was challenged to survive and grow. That external world involved a changing relationship between business and government. Many of the major problems confronting a business executive, Held asserted, were becoming less business and more societal in one or another of their aspects, and, increasingly, societal problems were becoming governmental in nature.

[12]George A. Steiner, "An Overview of the Changing Business Environment and Its Impact on Business," paper presented at the AACSB Conferences on Business Environment/Public Policy, Summer 1979.

[13]Walter G. Held, "Executive Skills: The Repertoire Needs Enlarging," *Columbia Journal of World Business*, Vol. 2, No. 2 (March–April 1967), pp. 81–87.

Thus, in addition to technical, administrative, and human relations skills, the manager of a modern corporation must also learn and develop skills that are relevant to the public policy dimension of the manager's task. Research is needed, Held said, to define more precisely the nature of these skills and the proficiency required in them, but at a minimum the manager must be "sensitized to the importance of public policy, the processes by which it is made, and the factors that are relevant to public policy issues and their impact on business"[14]

More recently, Henry Tombari, Assistant Professor of Management Sciences at the California State University at Hayward, has described the role of management in modern society as "politico-economic" in nature.[15] Such a role requires management to become involved in the public policy process as well as the market process. Management must reshape the nation's primary economic institution, the corporation, into one that is politico-economic and will fit with society's values and its political system.

The author has recently completed research designed to define more precisely the new management skills that are relevant to public policy.[16] This research was conducted by interviewing a number of business executives at corporations that were believed to be on the forefront of understanding the changing role of business in society and had thus made corresponding changes in corporate and managerial behavior. These executives were able to identify a number of skills that they believed were important for management as they sought to understand the public policy dimensions of their job and make effective responses to public issues of concern to society.

The first skill mentioned was that the manager of today needs a *broadened awareness* of external influences on the corporation. He or she must consider many additional factors in decision-making beyond commercial considerations to run a successful business—a broader range of potential consequences must be considered before a final decision can be made. The modern business organization must serve other constituencies besides those interested in profit to survive. Managers at all operational levels must be aware of these important nonfinancial or nontraditional objectives, which can adversely affect profits. They must develop the instincts to be aware of external relations.

Some people described this change as incredible. Being a good technical specialist was sufficient for managing yesterday's corporation. Today, however, one must also be a good general manager who knows how to deal with more parameters and more publics and be better informed on a wide range of issues. Managers must understand how to interact with government and have a better knowledge of public affairs and an increased sensitivity to public issues. Their management philosophy must incorporate the belief that social responsibility is part of the corporate charter. In short, they need to be specialists who are also generalists.

[14]*Ibid.*, p. 85.
[15]Henry A. Tombari, "The New Role of Business Management," *The Collegiate Forum*, (Fall 1979), p. 12.
[16]Rogene A. Buchholz, *Business Environment/Public Policy: Corporate Executive Viewpoints and Educational Implications* (St. Louis, Mo.: Center for the Study of American Business, Washington University, 1980).

This broadened awareness imposes a new skill requirement on management, but it also implies a change of attitude. Some of the executives interviewed, however, recognized a real problem in finding or developing managers with this attitude. Business managers have traditionally been somewhat narrow in their training and focus. Since social objectives have never been taken very seriously in many companies, they have been evaluated throughout their careers on profit objectives. Thus when confronted with external issues, they sometimes handle them badly, and have to go through an education process to learn how to manage public policy issues that arise from pressures in the external environment.

Another factor mentioned was the need for modern management to have an *integrative ability*. The management task was believed to be more complicated today than before; the considerations are more varied. Managers are required to make decisions in a shorter time frame, often with less information than before. This makes the element of judgment all the more important, and good judgment rests on the ability to integrate the concerns of the traditional business areas with the concerns of the external environment into some kind of a comprehensive decision-making framework based on an understanding of the mission of business and its role in society. A narrow specialization does not necessarily encourage one to develop these integrative skills nor does it give one a holistic view of business and its relationship to the larger society in which it functions.

This skill is described by Harry Tombari as one that is required to integrate the corporation's political and economic activities into what he calls unified strategies to achieve both social and economic objectives. The manager of the future, he says, must understand both the public policy process and the management process and know how to integrate them into a unified system. Such integrated strategies also call for altered organizational structures and operating procedures to be consistent with this system.[17]

The ability to develop a *political sense* was mentioned by many interviewees as important for modern management. The existence of multiple constituencies to which the manager must respond makes the company more difficult to manage than before. The manager of today's corporation must be concerned about the "bottom lines" of these different stakeholder groups—the various publics that have a stake in the corporation.

Thus management becomes the resolution of competing interests among these different constituencies. But as mentioned before, the bottom line of many of these groups is nonfinancial, and the analytical skills the manager has learned throughout the years to run the business may not serve him or her well in balancing these different interests. This ability to resolve competing interests calls for political skills in the best sense of the word: the ability to see the various political (not economic) concerns of constituent groups and understand their bottom line, the ability to adopt a nonideological approach to issues, the ability to compromise and negotiate with groups that have different interests, the willingness to form coalitions with other groups on the same side of an issue even if these groups are not the traditional friends of business.

This is an uncomfortable arena for most business people, who would

[17]Tombari, "The New Role of Business Management," p. 12.

probably like to remain apolitical. Some interviewees thought managers were poor at functioning in a political arena and had not developed political sensibilities. Their training and experience had not prepared them to function in this kind of a more public capacity. Nonetheless, the modern business environment, it was believed, made this kind of skill or ability a necessity because it is important for business to participate in the public policy process and help shape the policy directives that are the outcome of that process. Business needs to adopt a more active stance in regard to public policy issues. It does not have to be negative and oppose every issue nor does it have to accommodate itself passively to every concern that is expressed. There is a middle ground where business can be active in both responding to and shaping the public policies that affect its behavior. Fundamental to any political involvement of this sort is a recognition of the public policy aspect of the management task, a dimension that must be taken seriously, and a knowledge of the public policy process so management will know where to effectively and appropriately intervene to influence the outcome.

Coupled with this is the need for modern managers to be skilled *communicators*; to be able to *articulate* a business position on complex public issues and *persuade* people not under the manager's control that this position is in their best interests and in the interest of society as a whole. One person characterized it as the skills of persuasion versus those of command. Some saw this as a major change in management behavior, but one that was necessary to deal effectively with the external environment.

These communication skills are necessary to function effectively in the public arena; be it testifying before Congress, speaking to a community group, or dealing with public interest group leaders. The business manager must learn how to handle public exposure comfortably and how to be effective on television and in other public roles where he or she will be discussing issues of concern to the public. The credibility of the message depends to some extent on the ability to communicate ideas effectively.

But the content of the message is also crucial, and this implies that a business executive must have the intellectual skills to analyze and understand complex public issues. These skills will become even more important as business adopts a more activist stance and participates more effectively in the debate about public issues. Business executives must be able to *think clearly* about complex public issues and must be able to *exchange ideas* with the various business publics. Thoroughness of preparation is important, as facts and opinions will be challenged by these publics, something managers may not be used to in their dealings with employees. Credibility depends on having something important to say that is well thought out, factually correct, and analytically sophisticated.

These attitudes and skills are summarized in Exhibit 1.1. What these comments imply about changes in the managerial task that have resulted from the impact of the external environment is that the corporate manager of today is a much more public figure and needs the skills and attitudes which go with this role. The distinction between elected public officials and the management of private corporations is blurring as far as both public accountability and public exposure are concerned. This is a very significant change that has important implications for management education in the 1980s and beyond.

EXHIBIT 1.1

Management Attitudes and Skills Important
in Relating to the External Environment

- A broadened awareness of influences in the external environment that affect the corporation and management decision-making
- The ability to integrate traditional business concerns with influences from the external environment into a comprehensive decision-making framework based on a holistic view of business and its relationship to the larger society in which it functions
- The development of political skills (compromise, negotiation) to resolve the conflicting interests among different constituencies that have diverse values and objectives
- The need for communication skills to articulate a business position on a very complex public issue and persuade people that this position has merit and deserves serious consideration
- The development of intellectual skills to analyze and understand complex public issues—the ability to think clearly about these issues and exchange ideas with the various business publics

Consistent with this view of the changed managerial task is the perception of what actually goes on in the modern corporation. The great majority of the people interviewed stated that top management, particularly the chief executive officer, was most concerned with public policy matters, both in terms of the time involved and the range of issues covered. Estimates of the amount of time that the chief executive officer spent on external matters ranged from 20 to 75 percent, with an average of 40 percent. The most frequently mentioned figure (mode) was 50 percent of the chief executive officer's time spent on external matters.

Almost everyone interviewed believed that top management's understanding of the external environment was quite sophisticated, that through experience and hard work they had managed to acquire many of the skills and attitudes necessary to handle external relations effectively. However, this was not necessarily true of all management levels.

A few executives mentioned that they thought concern about external matters was more diffused throughout the organization, involving corporate counsel, planning, consumer relations, and other areas. Some companies also had a large, well-developed public affairs staff that engaged in research into public issues and developed positions and strategies on issues. In these companies, the public affairs department was deeply involved in public policy issues, serving as idea people, providing a support system for top management, and in some cases developing environmental forecasts that were eventually merged into the company's overall strategic plan.

Other people mentioned that managers at all levels had to be concerned about external matters, because their performance ratings were partly dependent on reaching objectives of this type as well as the traditional profit objectives. In any event, there seemed to be general agreement that the front office must be replaced as the *only* place where external relations are considered. Nor should the public affairs department try to insulate operating management from external concerns so that operating management can devote full attention to its normal functions.

The external dimension must somehow be diffused throughout the organization and become a part of every manager's modus operandi. In fact, it might not be inaccurate to say that the reason top management has to spend so much time on external matters is because concern for these matters has not been widely diffused throughout the organization to become a routine and accepted part of business planning and operation.

Questions for Discussion

1. What were the contributing factors to the problems Olin Corporation was experiencing in the public policy area? What role did management play in aggravating or alleviating the situation?
2. What impact did public policy have on Olin Corporation? How did public policy change their way of doing business? Be as specific as possible.
3. What would you recommend that Olin do given the situation described in the text? How should they deal with their problems ? What should they do to prevent such problems from occurring in the future?
4. How has the role of business in society changed in the last twenty years? How have new roles for business been defined? How have these changes affected management's thinking about corporate responsibilities?
5. Why have these changes occurred? What factors can you specifically identify that have caused a redefinition of the role of business in society?
6. What does Henry Tombari mean by describing the role of management in modern society as "politico-economic"? Does the role that Olin's management played illustrate this concept?
7. Comment on the specific management skills relevant to the public policy dimension that are mentioned in this chapter. How can these skills be taught in a business school curriculum?
8. How can public policy concerns be integrated with traditional business concerns in corporate decisions? Think about the various levels of decision-making in the corporation and identify where public policy concerns are relevant.

Suggested Readings

Buchholz, Rogene A. *Business Environment/Public Policy: A Study of Teaching and Research in Schools of Business and Management.* St. Louis, Mo.: Center for the Study of American Business, Washington University, 1979.

———— *Business Environment/Public Policy: Corporate Executive Viewpoints and Educational Implications.* St. Louis, Mo.: Center for the Study of American Business, Washington University, 1980.

Davis, Keith, Frederick, William C., and Blomstrom, Robert L. *Business and Society: Concepts and Policy Issues,* 4th ed. New York: McGraw-Hill, 1980.

Eells, Richard, and Walton, Clarence. *Conceptual Foundations of Business.* Homewood, Ill: Richard D. Irwin, 1961.

McGuire, Joseph W. *Business and Society.* New York: McGraw-Hill, 1963.

Sawyer, George C. *Business and Society: Managing Corporate Social Impact.* Boston: Houghton Mifflin, 1979.

Steiner, George A., and Steiner, John F. *Business, Government, and Society,* 3rd ed. New York: Random House, 1980.

Sturdivant, Frederick W. *Business and Society: A Managerial Approach.* Homewood, Ill: Richard D. Irwin, 1977.

2

The Market System and Public Policy

. . . the scope of managerial responsibility can be defined in terms of a comprehensive model of the management-society relationship, and the goals to be served—which then become criteria for appraising the managerial unit's social performance—are determined through the public policy process, as well as the market mechanism.[1]

The reshaping of the business institution and the consequent changes in the management of business are being accomplished primarily through public policy measures that are related not only to the social responsibilities of business, but also to the more traditional antitrust concerns and newer concerns about corporate governance. Thus public policy is becoming an even more important determinant of corporate behavior, as market outcomes are being increasingly altered through the public policy process.

These changes are making it increasingly clear that business functions in two major social processes through which decisions are made about the allocation of corporate resources. These are the market system and the public policy process. Both processes are necessary to encompass the broad range of decisions that a society needs to make about the corporation. The market mechanism and public policy are both sources of guidelines and criteria for managerial behavior.[2]

Business has not had to concern itself throughout most of its history with the public policy process because it could assume with some confidence that the basic value system of American society was economic, and thus whatever public policies resulted were generally supportive of business interests.

---

[1]Lee E. Preston and James E. Post, *Private Management and Public Policy* (Englewood Cliffs, N.J.: Prentice-Hall, 1975), p. 13. Quoted with permission.
[2]*Ibid.*, p. 55.

There are exceptions to this, of course, but throughout most of American history public policy has by and large been designed to promote business rather than interfere with its functioning.

People believed in the market mechanism and were willing to abide by most of its outcomes. If some people in society became extremely wealthy and others remained desperately poor, so be it—equality of wealth and income was not a goal of the market system, or of society as a whole for that matter. If polluted air and water resulted from the production process, so be it—air and water were considered to be free goods available to business management for the disposal of waste material.

This has changed. With the advent of social responsibilities, business can no longer assume that public policy will be supportive of its interests. In fact, most, if not all of the social responsibilities of business that are now public policy measures interfere with normal business operations and result in nonproductive investments from a strictly economic point of view. Public policy measures directed toward pollution control, safety and health, and the like interfere with the ability of business to fulfill its basic economic mission.

Thus it is important for business management to understand the important conceptual differences between the market system and the public policy process. The differences referred to here are more basic than a description of functional elements. Exhibit 2.1 shows the important conceptual elements of each process, which will be discussed in the sections that follow.

Conceptual Elements of the Market System

The Exchange Process. In the market system, the values assigned to particular goods or services and the decisions that result with respect to those

EXHIBIT 2.1 —————————————————————————————

Conceptual Elements of the Market System and the Public Policy Process

Market System	Public Policy Process
Exchange Process	Political Process
Private Goods and Services	Public Goods and Services
Economic Value System	Diverse Value System
Self-Interest	Public Interest
The Invisible Hand	The Visible Hand
Economic Roles (Producers-Consumers-Investors-Employees)	Political Roles (Politicians-Citizens-Public Interest Groups)
Consumer Sovereignty	Citizen Sovereignty
Profits as Reward	Election as Reward
Business as the Major Institution	Government as the Major Institution
Operating Principles: efficiency, productivity, growth	Operating Principles: justice, equity, fairness

goods or services are made through an exchange process; that is, something is exchanged between the parties to a transaction. In a strictly barter type of situation, goods and services are exchanged directly for other goods and services. In a money-based economy, money serves as a sort of intermediary store of value in that goods and services are sold for money and then the money can be used to purchase other goods and services.

Thus, in the market system, all kinds of exchanges between people are continually taking place. People exchange their labor for wages and salaries, and in turn exchange this money for goods in a retail establishment. Investors exchange money for stock in a corporation and corporations exchange this money for purchases of raw materials or new plant and equipment.

Decisions as to whether or not to exchange one thing for another are made by and large by individuals acting in their own self-interest as defined by them and are based on the particular values they attach to the entities being exchanged. That is, people decide whether the item they want is of sufficient value to warrant the sacrifice of something they already have that is of value to them. Based on these individual decisions in the market, then, the resources of society are allocated according to the preferences of individuals for one kind of merchandise over another, one job over another, the stock of one corporation over another, and so forth through the entire range of options the market offers.

Private Goods and Services. The second element of the market system, which follows from the first, concerns the nature of the goods and services that are exchanged. These goods and services are *private* in the sense that they can be purchased and used by individual persons or institutions. They become the private property of the persons who attain them and are of such a nature that they do not have to be shared with anyone else. The goods and services exchanged in the market are thus *divisible* into individual units and can be totally used and consumed by the people who obtain the property rights to these goods and services.

Thus one can buy a house, a car, or a piece of furniture, and these items become one's property to enjoy and use in one's own self-interest. People can also contract for or purchase services and have a right to expect that the service will be provided. The legal system supports this concept of property rights and enables people to enforce these rights if necessary to protect their own property from illegal encroachment by others. This social arrangement provides a degree of security for people regarding their own property and forces them to respect the property rights of others. Private property is a "practical" social arrangement because of the nature of the goods and services involved.

Common Economic Value System. All of these entities that are exchanged in the market system are able to be expressed in a common, underlying value system. The worth of an individual's labor, the worth of a particular product or service, or the worth of a share of stock can be expressed in economic terms. This economic value system serves as a common denominator in that the worth of everything can be expressed in a common economic unit of exchange (dollars and cents in our society, rubles in another). This fact facilitates the exchange process and makes it possible for individuals to assess trade-offs much easier than if such a common denominator were not available, and allows people to perform an informal cost-benefit analysis when making a decision. People enter a store with money in their pockets or bank accounts that they have earned and assess the prices of the goods and services available by comparing their benefits to the real costs (the effort involved in earning the money) of attaining them. Since both sides of this equation are expressed in the same units, this assessment can be made rather easily.

This common value system allows a society to allocate its resources accordingly. If a particular product is not valued very highly by great numbers of people, its price will have to be low for it to be sold, if it can be sold at all. Thus, not many resources will be used for its production. Depending on general economic conditions, if a particular job is not valued very highly by society, its wage or salary will be relatively low, which isn't likely to attract many people to perform that job. Thus resources are allocated according to the values of society as expressed through the exchange process. They will go where the price, the wage and salary, or the return on an investment is the highest, all other things being equal.

Self-Interest. The fourth element of a market system is the element of self-interest. People are free to use their property, choose their occupation, and strive for economic gain in any way they choose, subject, of course, to a respect for the rights of others to do the same thing. The pursuit of self-interest is assumed to be a universal principle of human behavior, with a powerful advantage, as far as motivation is concerned, over such other forms of human behavior as altruism. The pursuit of one's own interest is believed to elicit far more energy and creativity than would the pursuit of someone else's interests. Not only is it difficult to determine what the interests of other people are in all cases, it is also difficult to find a way to sustain motivation if much of the effort one expends goes for the benefit of other people.

The definition of self-interest is not provided by a government, nor a king, but is defined by each individual. Otherwise the concept would not mean what it implies. Yet within a market system, the definition of self-interest is not completely arbitrary. If there is a common underlying economic value system in society, the definition of self-interest takes on a certain economic rationality.

Thus the self-interest of a producer becomes one of maximizing the return on his or her investment. The same holds true of an investor in the stock market. Sellers of labor are expected to sell their services at the most advantageous terms to themselves. Consumers are expected to maximize the satisfaction to themselves through their purchases of goods and services on the marketplace. And so it goes through all the roles performed in a market system.

The Invisible Hand. Resources are allocated in a market system by an invisible hand. There is no supreme government authority that makes decisions about the goods and services produced in society and allocates resources accordingly. These decisions are made by individuals in society as they express their preferences, based on their self-interest in the market. These preferences are aggregated, and if strong enough, elicit a response from the productive mechanism of society to supply the goods and services desired.

Thus the invisible hand consists of the forces of supply and demand that result from the aggregation of individual decisions by producers and consumers in the marketplace. Resources are allocated to their most productive use as defined by these individuals. According to Adam Smith, more good results from this kind of a resource allocation process than if someone were to consciously determine the best interests of society. Pursuit of one's own selfish ends, without outside interference, results in the greatest good for the greatest number.

> As every individual, therefore, endeavours as much as he can both to employ his capital in the support of domestic industry, and so to direct that industry that its produce may be of the greatest value; every individual necessarily labours to render the annual revenue of the society as great as he can. He generally, indeed, neither intends to promote the public interest, nor knows how much he is promoting it. By preferring the support of domestic to that of foreign industry, he intends only his own security; and by directing that industry in such a manner as its produce may be of the greatest value, he intends only his own gain, and he is in this, as in many other cases, led by an invisible hand to promote an end which was no part of his intention. Nor is it always the worse for the society that it was no part of it. By pursuing his own interest he frequently promotes that of the society more effectually than when he really intends to promote it.[3]

Economic Roles. Individuals perform certain roles in the market system, all of which have an economic character. They can be producers who take raw materials and give them utility by producing something that will sell on the market, consumers who buy these goods and services for their own use, investors who provide capital for the producers, or employees who work for producers and receive wages and salaries for their efforts in the production process. All of these roles are important in a market system and are economic roles in the sense that people are pursuing their economic self-interest in performing them.

Consumer Sovereignty. The most important role in a market system, however, is performed by the consumer. At least in theory, consumers through their choices in the marketplace are supposed to provide guidance for the productive apparatus of society. When there is enough demand for a product, resources will be allocated for its production. If there is not enough demand, the product will not be produced.

Consumer sovereignty is not to be confused with consumer choice. In any society, consumers always have a choice to purchase or not purchase the products that confront them in the marketplace. Consumer choice exists in a totally planned economy. But consumer sovereignty implies that the range of products with which consumers are confronted is also a function of their decisions, and not the decisions of a central planning authority. Thus consumers are ultimately sovereign over the system.

There are those who would argue that consumer choice in today's marketplace is a fiction, that consumers are manipulated by advertising, packaging, promotional devices, and other sales techniques to buy a particular product. Sometimes this manipulation is said to be so subtle that the consumer is unaware of the factors influencing his or her decision. Thus the demand function itself has come under control of corporations and consumer sovereignty is a myth.[4]

[3] Adam Smith, *The Wealth of Nations* (New York: Modern Library, 1937), p. 423.
[4] See, for example, John Kenneth Galbraith, *The New Industrial State* (Boston: Houghton Mifflin, 1967).

While there may be some truth to these views, it is hard to believe that consumers are totally manipulated by these techniques. They still have to make choices among competing products, and undoubtedly many factors, besides the particular sales techniques employed by a company, influence the purchase decision. And despite all the manipulation a company may attempt, if the product still will not sell, and many do not, it will disappear from the marketplace.

Profits as Reward. The reason products disappear when they do not sell is because there is no profit to be made. Profits are a reward to a company for the risks they have taken in producing something. These risks include, among other things, assessing consumer demand correctly. If the management of a business guesses wrong, and produces something people really do not want, the market system is a hard taskmaster, as no rewards will be received. Profits are also a reward for combining resources efficiently to be able to meet or beat the competition that may exist or come into existence. Thus if management makes a wrong assessment about consumer preferences or produces inefficiently, it is out of business, at least as far as that particular product is concerned.

Business as the Major Institution. The major institutional force in the market system is the business organization. Business is not the only institution active in the market system: hospitals buy goods and services, government is a producer of goods and services. But the business organization is the primary productive institution in a market economy, and in a strictly market arrangement, most of the decisions about the allocation of society's resources for the production of private goods and services are made within the walls of the business institution.[5]

Operating Principles. The operating principles of a market system are concepts such as efficiency, productivity, and growth. These are, of course, economic concepts, and have a specific meaning in the context of a market system. There are quantitative measures for these concepts, however crude, so that at least some idea exists as to how well the market system is functioning. These principles are thus crucial to the operation of a market system, since they support the functioning of the system and make its outcomes acceptable to society.

Conceptual Elements of the Public Policy Process

Political Process. Instead of an exchange process, values are assigned to particular entities in the public policy process and decisions are made about the allocation of resources through a political process. This is not to say that exchanges do not take place in the public policy process. Politicians can exchange a vote on one bill for some other politician's vote on another. Favors can be exchanged between elected public officials or between them

---

[5] If one were to argue strictly from the principle of consumer sovereignty, one would have to say that the productive institutions are guided by consumers as they make choices in the marketplace, and that management decisions are merely responses to the choices made by consumers. The viewpoint taken here is that business institutions are not merely passive entities in the market system, and that real decisions are made in these organizations that, of course, take consumer preferences into account, along with many other factors.

and members of their constituencies. Public interest groups can exchange a hearing on one issue in exchange for reducing their pressure on another.

Thus the political process also involves individuals pursuing their self-interest through an exchange process, but the way this takes place is much different than in the market system. The exchanges that take place in the political process are not directly related to the goods and services provided, that is, they are not directly related to each other nor is there an intermediary store of value such as money. The outcome of the political process is not under the control of an individual as is the outcome of an exchange process, where the individual knows that his or her decision is directly connected to the outcome as far as his or her self-interest is concerned.

If people decide to part with a sum of money, they do so only because they know they will receive a product or service they want in return.[6] But if those same people voted for a candidate they believed would support the issues they favored, and that candidate was elected, the candidate might not carry out his or her campaign promises, or their vote might count for nothing in the final outcome if few others voted the same way on the issues.

Thus any one individual's control over the outcome of the political process is much more nebulous than in the exchange process. Individual preferences cannot always be matched, the outcome of the transactions is not instantaneous as it is in many market transactions, and values cannot be expressed as directly, particularly in a representative democracy. Yet resources for the attainment of public policy objectives are allocated through some kind of a political process that has certain characteristics, depending on the kind of government a society has and the pluralistic or hierarchical structure of that society.

Public Goods and Services. The reason public policy decisions have to be made through a political process is the nature of the goods and services that are provided through the public policy process. These goods and services can appropriately be referred to as public goods and services (see box) as distinguished from the private goods and services described in the market system.

Public goods and services are *indivisible* in the sense that the quantity produced cannot be divided into individual units to be purchased by people according to their individual preferences. For all practical purposes, one cannot, for example, buy a piece of clean air to carry around and breathe wherever one goes. Nor can one buy a share of national defense over which one would have control. This indivisibility gives these goods their *public* character because if people are to have public goods and services at all, they must enjoy roughly the same amount.[7] No one owns these goods and services individually—they are collectively owned in a sense and private property rights do not apply. Thus there is nothing to be exchanged and the values people have in regard to these goods and services and decisions about them cannot be made through the exchange process.

[6]There are exceptions, of course, where risk is involved. Investors in a particular stock, for example, do not always get the return they want, they may get more or less, depending on the circumstances. But most exchanges in the market system are relatively certain and risk-free in this regard.

[7]John Rawls, *A Theory of Justice* (Cambridge, Mass.: Harvard University Press, 1971), p. 266.

The concept of public goods and services needs further explanation. The literature about this subject usually refers to national defense as the best example of a public good—something tangible provided by government for all its citizens that cannot be provided by the citizens for themselves.

Pollution is generally considered to be an example of an externality, defined as either a beneficial or detrimental (pollution is detrimental) effect on a third party (homeowner who lives close to a polluting factory) who is not involved in the transaction between the principals (customer and producer) who caused the pollution because of their activities in the marketplace. Yet the results of pollution control (clean air and water) can also be called a public good as they are entities with beneficial physical characteristics that are widely shared in different amounts by people in society.

Something like equal opportunity might be called a social value in that it is a particular goal of our society that is important for many of its members because of their individual values or ethical sensibilities. Yet if these values are widely shared or an important part of a society's heritage, policies designed to promote equal opportunity also produce a public good in that it is good for a society to implement its basic values.

Thus the concept of public goods and services as used here is an all-inclusive concept that refers to all these various outcomes of the public policy process. This broader use also includes the maintenance of completion when this is a basic value of a society and the maintenance of economic stability that makes it possible for people to find employment and maintain or improve their material standard of living.

One might argue, however, that even though public goods and services have these characteristics, they could still be provided through the market system rather than the public policy process. Suppose, for example, the market offered a consumer the following choice: two automobiles in a dealer's showroom are identical in all respects, even as to gas mileage. The only difference is that one car has pollution control equipment to reduce emissions of pollutants from the exhaust while the other car has no such equipment. The car with the pollution control equipment sells for $500 more than the other.

If a person values clean air, it could be argued that he or she would choose the more expensive car to reduce air pollution. However, such a decision would be totally irrational from a strictly self-interest point of view. The impact that one car out of all the millions on the road will have on air pollution is infinitesimal—it cannot even be measured. Thus there is no relationship in this kind of a decision between costs and benefits—one would, in effect, be getting nothing for one's money unless one could assume that many other people would make the same decision. Such actions, however, assume a common value for clean air and a concern for the public interest far beyond anything we see in human behavior at present. Thus the market never offers consumers this kind of choice. Automobile manufacturers know that pollution control equipment won't sell in the absence of federally mandated standards.

There is another side to the coin, however. If enough people in a given area did buy the more expensive car so that the air was significantly cleaner, there would be a powerful incentive for others to be free riders. Again, the impact of any one car would not alter the character of the air over a region. One would be tempted to buy the polluting car for a cheaper price and be a free rider by enjoying the same amount of clean air as everyone else and not paying a cent for its provision.

Because of these characteristics of human behavior and the nature of public goods and services, the market system will not work to provide them for a society that wants them. When goods are indivisible among large numbers of people, the individual consumer's actions as expressed in the market will not lead to the provision of these goods.[8] Society must register its desire for public goods and services through the political process because the bilateral exchanges facilitated by the market are insufficiently inclusive.[9]

Diverse Value System. The third element in the public policy process is the existence of a diverse value system. There is no common denominator by which to assess trade-offs and make a decision about resource allocation based on comparable information that can be analyzed in view of some relatively clear, single objective, such as improving the material standard of living or increasing the nation's gross national product.

What is the overall objective, for example, of clean air and water, equal opportunity, job safety and health, national defense, and other public goods and services? One could say that all these goods and services are meant to improve the quality of life for the members of society. But if this is the objective, what kind of common value measure underlies all these goods and services so that benefits can be assessed in relation to costs, and trade-offs analyzed in view of this common objective of improving the quality of life.

The costs of air pollution control equipment can be determined in economic terms. The benefits of this equipment should be positive in the sense of reducing the amount of certain harmful pollutants that people have to breathe. The ultimate benefits could be an increased life span, less chance of getting certain diseases, the good feeling some people might have from living in a clean as opposed to a dirty environment. Even assuming that these beneficial effects can be linked directly to the costs, that is, X number of dollars have to be spent to reduce a certain pollutant by X amount which in turn increases the chance of living three more years by X amount, what is the value of these three years? What is the value of not incurring cancer from being exposed to a cancer-causing or suspected cancer-causing agent? What is the value of not losing one's hearing because money has been spent to reduce the noise emitted by machinery in the plant where one works?

The basic question here is what is the value of human life? How can the value of human life be expressed appropriately? What dimensions of human life are most important? What trade-offs should be made regarding one aspect of human life versus another?

It seems clear in an a priori sense that these kinds of questions cannot be answered in the abstract for all people at all times in all places. People are going to value their lives differently from each other. Some may accept an economic valuation like the present value of future earnings. Others will scoff at such a notion. People's valuation of their own lives will also change

[8]Gerald Sirkin, *The Visible Hand: The Fundamentals of Economic Planning* (New York: McGraw-Hill, 1968), p. 45.

[9]James Buchanan, *The Demand and Supply of Public Goods* (Chicago: Rand McNally, 1968), p. 8.

with age and with other circumstances. Some people may believe they are worth any economic expenditure, no matter how great; others may feel their lives are relatively worthless. The answers to these questions about human life are subjective and relative rather than objective and absolute.

When people are making individual choices about private goods and services, this diverse value system presents no problems. They are forced to translate their values into economic terms and make choices accordingly. But dealing with public goods and services is another matter. Should more money be spent reducing the emissions from coke ovens than on improving highway safety with better signs, barriers, lighting, and the like? How much should society spend on improving the quality of air and water? For these kinds of questions, the political process seems to be a reasonable way to determine the diversity of people's values and make decisions when there is no common value system to use for more rational calculations.

The Public Interest. The universal motivating principle operative in the public policy process is the public interest, rather than self-interest. At least this principle is invoked by those who make decisions about public policy. Elected public officials often claim to be acting in the interests of the nation as a whole or of their state or congressional district. Public interest groups also claim to be devoted to the general or national welfare. This behavior makes a certain degree of sense. When politicians have to make a decision about the provision of some public good or service, they cannot claim to be acting in the self-interest of everyone in their constituency. When goods and services are indivisible among large numbers of people, it is impossible for individual preferences to be matched. Some more general principal such as the public interest has to be invoked to justify the action.

However, is this claim legitimate? Can any public policy-maker escape his or her own self-interest and really act for the general good of society? The public interest may represent nothing more than the aggregation of the various self-interests of those who are in positions of decision-making about the provision of public goods and serices. Politicians want to get reelected and will vote for those goods and services they believe have an appeal to the majority of their constituency. Public interest groups want to extend their power and influence in society, and might more appropriately be called special interest groups.

Getting into an extended philosophical discussion about the meaning of the public interest is beyond the scope of this book.[10] Perhaps there is a general principle such as the public interest that can be appealed to, perhaps certain things are of benefit to humankind in general regardless of people's individual preferences. But the point to be made is that the definition of the public interest is problematical, and cannot be entirely divorced from the self-interest of those who are doing the defining.

The Visible Hand. Whatever concept of the public interest is invoked, it is clear that resources are allocated in the public policy process by a visible hand. That visible hand is, of course, the decision-makers in the public policy process who are in a position of responsibility. They are the ones who consciously allocate resources to produce the public goods and services they

---

[10]See Douglas G. Hartle, *Public Policy Decision Making and Regulation* (Montreal: The Institute for Research on Public Policy, 1979), pp. 213–218.

believe the public wants, that is, those goods and services they believe serve the public interest.

Something of a supply and demand process occurs here in that if enough citizens demand something, the political process, at least in a democratic system, will eventually respond. But the decisions about resource allocation are visible in that certain people in the public policy process—elected public officials, government bureaucrats—can be held responsible for those decisions. The market system does not fix responsibility so precisely, as decisions about resource allocation are made by many people participating in the marketplace. The concept of the invisible hand is appropriate for a market system but not for the public policy process.

Political Roles. People play different roles in the public policy process than they do in the market system. These roles, of course, have a political character. Elected public officials are directly involved in the public policy process, but they are few in number relative to the total population. The same can be said of other government people such as those who serve on congressional staffs or regulatory agencies and have a real influence on public policy outcomes.

The average person simply plays the role of citizen by voting for a representative of his or her choice, contributing money to a campaign, writing elected public officials on particular issues, and similar measures. At the extreme, this role could involve driving one's tractor to Washington, D.C. and clogging the city streets in protest of certain governmental actions. Joining large social movements such as the civil rights movement is another way for the average person to exercise political influence. Widespread support for issues such as this has an effect on the voting of elected public officials. Finally, people can join public interest groups or support them with contributions and fulfill a political role in this fashion.

Citizen Sovereignty. Citizens are supposedly sovereign over the public policy process as consumers are supposedly sovereign over the market system. The vote is the ultimate power that citizens have in a democratic system. A public official can be voted out of office if he or she does not perform as the majority of citizens in his or her constituency would like. The citizens can then vote someone else into office whom they believe will make decisions about allocation of resources for production of public goods and services that are more consistent with the citizens' preferences. In the interim period between votes, citizens can express their preferences and try to influence the outcome of the public policy process either individually, through contact with public officials, or collectively, through interest groups.

The same comments apply to citizen sovereignty as apply to consumer sovereignty—the citizen vote can be manipulated through advertising and packaging of the various candidates for office. Misrepresentation of candidates is also possible as is misrepresentation of products. But citizens still have to make choices among competing candidates, not all of whom can be elected. And again, many factors undoubtedly enter into the voting decision in addition to the advertising and packaging of the candidates for office.

Election as Reward. The reward for a public official or potential public official is to be reelected or elected to office. If an incumbent has done a good job and assessed citizen preferences correctly and been able to supply the public goods and services the citizens in his or her constituency want in something approaching an efficient manner—in other words, if the official delivers—he or she will most likely be reelected. If there is some dissatisfaction with the incumbent, and a newcomer comes along who appears to be more responsive to citizen preferences and makes promises that people believe, that new person may be elected to office.

Government as the Major Institution. The major institutional force operative in the public policy process is government, primarily the federal government and to a lesser extent state and local government. Other institutions are, of course, also active in the public policy process. Business, for example, has always been and will continue to be an institutional force in the public policy process. Public interest groups are another institutional force.

But government is the principal institution involved in formulating public policy that shapes the behavior of business organizations. Government promotes business through tariff protection, subsidies, tax credits, and tax breaks. In some situations, government becomes a guarantor of business survival. It regulates business in four aspects: competitive behavior, industry regulation, social regulation, and labor-management relations. Government is a buyer of goods and services from private business, and in this capacity can promote such public policy goals as equal opportunity through the terms of the contract it makes with private business. It manages the economy through the use of fiscal and monetary policies. In all of these activities government is engaged in the public policy process and shapes and guides business behavior. Most of the decisions about the allocation of resources for the production of public goods and services are made in and through the institution of government.

Operating Principles. The operating principles of the public policy process are justice, equity, and fairness. These concepts are often invoked to justify the decisions that are made about resource allocation. There are no quantitative measures for these concepts, but nonetheless, society has some idea as to how well they are being implemented in public policy decisions. These principles are important to the operation of the public policy process and are part of the underlying value system that makes the outcome of the public policy process acceptable to society.

Questions for Discussion

1. What does it mean to say that the basic value system of American society has been economic throughout most of its history? In what ways has the value system changed? What implications does this change have for public policy?
2. Distinguish between the conceptual elements of the market system and the public policy process. Be critical of the author's distinctions. Eliminate those you believe are either false or unimportant, and add others you believe are more relevant to an understanding of the differences between the market system and the public policy process.
3. What deficiencies exist in having a common economic value system? Can the "true" worth of goods and services be evaluated in this manner? What advantages are inherent in this arrangement?
4. Define the concept of self-interest. Do you believe self-interest is a universal principle of human behavior? How does one determine what is in his or her self-interest? Are there any other kinds of "interests" that motivate people?

5. Do you believe in the concept of the invisible hand? Do you believe such a concept is relevant in today's economy? How would you define this concept more precisely?
6. Does consumer sovereignty exist in our modern economic system? What evidence can you find to support your case? What research is relevant to answer this question?
7. Is the distinction between private goods and services and public goods and services valid? List all the public goods and services you can think of and describe how they are different from private goods and services.
8. Describe the concept of the free rider. Can you think of instances where you have been a free rider? Does being a free rider have any moral implications?
9. What is the value of human life? What is the price of an arm, a leg, hearing, sight, etc.? How much is another three years added on to your life worth? How much would you pay to avoid cancer?
10. What definition of "the public interest" do you agree with most strongly? What implications does your choice have for public policy?
11. Are citizens sovereign over a democratic system? Why or why not? Does an individual's vote really count? Is there any logic to this kind of collective action?
12. Define the concepts of justice, equity, and fairness. How would you determine how well these concepts are being implemented in our society? Pick a recent public policy decision and discuss it with reference to these concepts.

Suggested Readings

Buchanan, James. *The Demand and Supply of Public Goods.* Chicago: Rand McNally, 1968.

Galbraith, John Kenneth. *Economics and the Public Purpose.* Boston: Houghton Mifflin, 1967.

————. *The New Industrial State.* Boston: Houghton Mifflin, 1967.

Hartle, Douglas G. *Public Policy Decision Making and Regulation.* Montreal: The Institute for Research on Public Policy, 1979.

Olson, Mancur. *The Logic of Collective Action.* Cambridge, Mass.: Harvard University Press, 1977.

Preston, Lee E., and Post, James E. *Private Management and Public Policy.* Englewood Cliffs, N.J.: Prentice-Hall, 1975.

Rawls, John. *A Theory of Justice.* Cambridge, Mass.: Harvard University Press, 1971.

Sirkin, Gerald. *The Visible Hand: The Fundamentals of Economic Planning.* New York: McGraw-Hill, 1968.

Smith, Adam. *The Wealth of Nations.* New York: Modern Library, 1937.

3

The Historical Origins of Public Policy

In retrospect, 1929 was the watershed year of the 20th century: the start of the Great Depression, which swept away all that had gone before and which forever changed the economic face of not only America but the world.[1]

The historical origins of public policy are those periods in history when new areas of public policy are developed in response to problems society is experiencing. The market is not trusted either because people believe it cannot respond to these problems effectively, or because they are not willing to accept the outcome that would result if the market were left alone to work things out according to its own dictates. Thus it could be said that public policy arises out of deficiencies in the market system, either real or perceived, that appear from time to time in our history.

At the risk of oversimplification, the historical origins of public policy will be discussed by identifying those periods of history that gave rise to major areas of public policy that are still with us today. This perspective will give the reader some idea of the way public policy affects the economy and business, the origins of public policy, and some of the major shifts in both content and magnitude of public policy throughout the growth of our country into a modern industrial nation. This knowledge provides an important foundation for many of the chapters which follow. To understand the nature of public policies in effect today one must understand something of the past.

[1]"The End of the Industrial Society." Reprinted from the September 3, 1979 issue of *Business Week* by special permission, © 1979 by McGraw-Hill, Inc., New York, NY 10020. All rights reserved.

The Nature of the Competitive Process

The first market deficiency appeared in the late 1800s, when large business enterprises came to dominate certain industries and began to act contrary to the interests of some groups in society. Regardless of the historical reasons behind the development of these large enterprises, there is a certain logic to the competitive process that would lead one to expect this kind of outcome. Competition, followed to its logical conclusion, means that some person or organization of people will eventually win out over all the others. The reason for engaging in competition in the first place is to win as big as possible.

The sports world can be looked to for an example of competition followed through to its logical conclusion. In baseball or football, for example, the season eventually comes to an end and one team emerges a winner over all the others and is crowned the World Series or Super Bowl Champion.

The same is not true of the economy. The season can never end, and if any one business or group of businesses begins to look like a big winner over others in its industry, the competitive process is threatened. The history of business and the sports world both show that without rules, competitive behavior sinks to the lowest common denominator. If one competitor begins to use unfair methods of competition (a spitball or predatory pricing practices), and these methods give it an advantage over its competitors, they will have to do the same to survive. The market system does not automatically ensure that competition will continue indefinitely or that it will be fair. The most likely outcome of a completely unregulated competitive process is control by one or a few firms in most industries. This is not good for society because of the evils associated with a monopolistic or semimonopolistic position.

Industrial Development. The American economy grew rapidly during the period between the founding of the nation and the beginning of the Civil War. Between 1790 and 1840, the population rose from 3.9 million to 17.1 million, and the total volume of goods produced and distributed increased enormously.[2] Inventions such as the cotton gin helped to establish whole new industries, like the textile industry. Iron-making dominated the metalworking industries. Other industries important during the period included leather products, lumber production, spirits and malt liquors, animal and vegetable oil processing, copper and brass works, carriages of all kinds, and gunpowder.[3]

In spite of this growth, however, the size and nature of business enterprises in all these industries changed little. According to Alfred Chandler, writing in *The Visible Hand,* the business enterprises producing and distributing these goods continued to be traditional single-unit enterprises managed by the owners and employing fewer than fifty workers.[4] Thus the economy

---

[2]Robert R. Russel, *A History of the American Economic System* (New York: Appleton-Century-Crofts, 1964), p. 113.

[3]Alex Groner, *The American Heritage History of American Business and Industry* (New York: American Heritage Publishing Co., 1972), pp. 68–70.

[4]Alfred Chandler, *The Visible Hand: The Managerial Revolution in American Business* (Cambridge, Mass.: Belknap Press, 1977), p. 14.

was comprised of many small businesses in competition with each other. There was little institutional innovation to create larger organizations.

The major constraint on the size of business organizations was not public policy, however, but the sources of energy available to business. Again according to Chandler, as long as the processes of production depended on traditional sources of energy such as people, animals, and wind power, there was little incentive for businesses to create large organizations. Such sources of energy could not generate a large enough volume of output in production and number of transactions in distribution to require the creation of large business organizations. The low speed of production and slow movement of goods meant that the maximum daily activity at each point of production and distribution could be easily handled by small personally owned and managed enterprises.[5]

The big story regarding industrial development during this period was the development of an infrastructure—the web of transportation, communication, and basic industries that are essential to advanced forms of industry and trade. Between 1783 and 1801, more than 300 business corporations were chartered by the states to build roads, bridges, canals, and water systems. The corporate form of organization was used primarily for these "public utility" purposes.

Roads such as the Philadelphia-Lancaster turnpike were built. Rivers such as the Hudson, Delaware, and Susquehanna became important for transporting goods. Canals such as the Erie, linking Albany and Buffalo, were built. Then the railroad industry picked up steam, and by 1840 more than 400 companies were operating almost 3,000 miles of track, more than the total mileage in all of Europe. Finally, the communications industry flourished with the invention of the telegraph and use of other forms of communication, such as newspapers and books.[6] The development of this infrastructure was crucial for further economic growth and was supported by public policy through land grants to railroads, the use of the corporate form of organization, and similar measures.

After the Civil War was over, the United States experienced an unprecedented period of economic growth. Statistics related to per capita wealth and income, shown in Table 3.1, tell the story. There was scarcely a millionaire in the country in 1790—in 1850 there were twenty-five millionaires in New York City alone, eighteen in Boston, and another nine in Philadel-

TABLE 3.1 **Per Capita Wealth and Income 1850–1880**

Year	Per Capita Wealth	Per Capita Income
1850	$822	$254
1860	$1,239	$280
1870	$1,295	$289
1880	$1,953	$330

Adapted from: Robert R. Russel, *A History of the American Economic System* (New York: Appleton-Century-Crofts, 1964), p. 277. Used with permission of the author.

[5]*Ibid.*, p. 17.
[6]Groner, *American Heritage History,* pp. 83–106.

phia. People in most parts of the country were generally experiencing rising standards of living with respect to food, housing, clothing, health care, and education.[7]

If one accepts the definition of an industrialized country as one in which 50 percent or more of the occupied males are engaged in nonagricultural pursuits, in about 1880 the United States achieved this distinction.[8]

There are a number of reasons for this rapid growth. First, the existence of an effective transportation system meant that finished goods and raw materials could be moved around the country fairly easily. Factories could be located where labor was available and built large enough to take advantage of economies of scale. Second, changes in agriculture made it possible for a smaller and smaller proportion of the population to feed the rest of the country. This released millions of workers to take jobs in the newly developing industries and other occupations.

A third reason was the development of a cheap source of energy to support economic growth. The opening of the anthracite coal fields in eastern Pennsylvania removed the technological constraint that Chandler claims kept business enterprises small for many years. Cheap coal provided heat for large-scale production in foundries, became the source of steam power for railroad locomotives, and became an efficient fuel for generating steam power for driving machines in factories. Coal allowed new technologies to be developed that speeded up production of goods and services, and led to the rise of the modern business enterprise.[9]

The fourth factor in this growth was a group of entrepreneurs who were able to build large-scale business enterprises to take advantage of these potentials. There were people like Commodore Vanderbilt, Jay Gould, Daniel Drew, and Jim Fisk in railroads, Andrew Carnegie in steel, Charles Pillsbury in flour milling, John D. Rockefeller in oil, and John Pierpont Morgan in banking and the steel industry. Although historians either condemn these people as robber barons or praise them as captains of industry, it seems clear that they and others like them understood the potentials of the changes taking place around them, took up the challenge, and created huge industrial enterprises that formed the foundations of our modern business system. They recognized the strength of the new foundations of business, and successfully put capital and resources to work to make large business enterprises possible. They were an important ingredient in America's becoming an industrial society and the productive use of the capital they were able to accumulate created unprecedented economic growth for the country.[10]

Thus the modern business enterprise was born in response to a number of changes taking place in American society. The corporate form of organization increasingly began to be used to make these enterprises even larger, as it allowed more capital to be accumulated and spread the risk across large numbers of stockholders. These large enterprises enabled mass production techniques to be used, which created a high rate of throughput and permit-

[7]Russel, *American Economic System*, p. 277.

[8]See Russel, *American Economic System*, pp. 338–39; Groner, *American Heritage History*, p. 157.

[9]Chandler, *The Visible Hand*, pp. 75–78.

[10]Groner, *American Heritage History*, pp. 155–182, 193–224.

ted a relatively small working force to produce an ever increasing output. Machinery was placed and operated in such a way that several stages of production were integrated and synchronized technologically and organizationally within a single industrial establishment.[11]

With the growth of these large individual enterprises, however, came other organizational innovations in the late nineteenth century that were eventually believed to have anticompetitive effects on the economy and society. As competition between businesses became more severe, some of these businesses tried different industrial arrangements to reduce or at least control this competition. Some of these innovations are briefly discussed below.

Gentlemen's Agreement: An informal unwritten contract among competitors in an industry to set uniform prices for their products or to divide territories so as not to compete in the same geographic markets.

Pools: A more formal arrangement by all competitors in a given industry regarding standardized prices and operations. Decisions in a pool were governed by votes, which were allocated to pool members on the basis of market share.

Trust: An actual change of ownership for a given company. Stockholders of many competing firms turned their shares (and voting rights) over to "trustees" who became directors of one large supercorporation. This large corporation then issued trust certificates back to the original stockholders.

Holding Company: Supported by state laws which allowed companies to hold stock in other companies. Several competitors would each buy stock in a firm whose only apparent function was to set policy for the owning companies.

The use of these devices led to a high degree of concentration in some industries. Table 3.2 shows the percentage of output produced by the dominant firm in some key industries at the turn of the century. The years between 1897 and 1904 saw a great surge of business combinations and concentration in certain industries. There were 318 industrial combinations in this period that included 5,300 plants with a combined capitalization of more than $7 billion. More than 1,000 different railroad lines were consolidated into six major systems that controlled almost $10 billion in capital. The trust device was particularly useful for combinations, and the trusts that were created in petroleum, cottonseed oil, linseed oil, sugar, whiskey, and lead processing came to dominate their industries for decades.[12]

TABLE 3.2 **Concentration in Selected Industries**

International Harvester	1900	85% of harvesting machines
National Biscuit	1902	70% of biscuit output
American Can	1901	90% of industry output
Corn Products	1902	80% of industry capacity
U.S. Leather	1902	60% of leather output
Distillers Securities	1902	60% of whiskey output
International Paper	1902	60% of all newsprint
American Sugar Refining	1900	100% of refined sugar

[11]Chandler, *The Visible Hand*, pp. 240–241.
[12]Groner, *American Heritage History*, pp. 197–200.

Public Policy: Three Theories. Eventually society, through its government, took action against these industrial combinations with specific public policy measures. Two forms of government regulation were born during the late 1800s—regulation of competitive behavior and regulation of a specific industry.

The latter was begun in 1887 with the creation of the Interstate Commerce Commission to regulate the railroads and prevent unfair rebates to large firms and other anticompetitive practices. Regulation of competitive behavior was begun with the Sherman Antitrust Act of 1890, which made restraints of trade and attempts to monopolize an industry illegal. This area was strengthened in 1914 with the passage of the Federal Trade Commission Act to outlaw unfair methods of competition, and the Clayton Antitrust Act, which dealt with stockholdings of one competitor by another and interlocking directorships.

There are at least three theories as to the primary motivation behind these public policy measures. The first is the standard theory found in most American history textbooks, which holds that these measures were the result of a strong populist movement in the country led by the farmers and others who were fearful of the power of these big business combinations. Many people in society apparently believed that the huge industrial combinations that were created were nothing more than the result of a few industrial leaders' greed and lust for power. The problem was that as these people accumulated more and more capital, they began to dictate the terms of trade to the rest of society rather than being subject to the pressures of competition. Something had to be done to break up these combinations and restore more competition in the economy or regulate them in the public interest, as in the case of the railroads. The government responded to these desires and passed the necessary legislation, supported by the executive branch under President Theodore Roosevelt, who became known as "the trust-buster." This was a case of the little guys against the big guys, with the little guys winning at least a partial victory.[13] One must say partial victory, because even though these antitrust measures were passed, the courts remained pro-business. In 1895, for example, the Supreme Court ruled that American Sugar Refining was not a monopoly in restraint of trade and therefore not in violation of the Sherman Act. A year earlier, the court had issued an injunction against the union in the Pullman strike on the basis that it was a conspiracy in restraint of interstate commerce. In the Danbury Hatters case of 1908, the striking union was declared financially liable for damages resulting from a boycott. The Justice Department lost seven of the first eight cases it brought under the Sherman Act. Finally, in 1911, two trusts (Standard Oil and American Tobacco) were found guilty of violating the Sherman Act and ordered dissolved into several separate firms.[14]

The second theory was developed by a group of revisionist historians in the 1960s who rewrote certain periods of American history.[15] This theory

---

[13]Russel, *American Economic System,* pp. 363–370.

[14]Groner, *American Heritage History,* pp. 214–215.

[15]See Gabriel Kolko, *The Triumph of Conservatism* (New York: Free Press, 1963); Paul Conkin, *The New Deal* (New York: Thomas Y. Crowell, 1967); Ellis W. Hawley, *The New Deal and the Problem of Monopoly* (Princeton, N.J.: Princeton University Press, 1966).

holds that certain key business leaders themselves realized they had no vested interest in a chaotic industry and economy in which not only their profits but their very existence might be challenged by cutthroat competition and other evils of a completely unregulated competitive system. The various anticompetitive arrangements that business leaders worked out among themselves were voluntary attempts to gain control over this situation and develop a more rational and stable system. But these voluntary attempts failed for one reason or another. Thus some business leaders came to believe that perhaps political means might succeed where voluntary means had failed, and actively supported government regulation. If government could stabilize the system by establishing certain rules of competition that everyone had to follow and enforcing them uniformly, corporations would be able to function in a predictable and secure environment, permitting reasonable profits to be earned over the long run.

The third theory holds that competition disappeared not because of the lust for power of a few business leaders but because of the technological possibilities inherent in large-scale enterprise. The efficiency of the production and distribution system could be increased dramatically when all the stages of production and distribution, from mining of raw materials to delivery of a finished product to the consumer, could be combined in a single business enterprise under the direction of a single management. Thus administrative coordination of these various stages became more efficient and more profitable than market coordination.[16]

Society also benefited from these large enterprises in that more goods were produced at lower prices than would otherwise be possible. But what also happened from the growth of these large, "integrated" enterprises was that the visible hand of the management of these enterprises replaced the invisible hand of market forces. This happened when and where new technology and expanded markets permitted a historically unprecedented high volume and speed of materials through the process of production and distribution. These enterprises grew into powerful institutions and came to dominate major sectors of the economy, and the managers of these enterprises became the most influential group of economic decision-makers. But it was not good to allow such power to go completely unregulated. If competition as a regulator had disappeared, the government had to assume the role through public policy measures.

Whatever theory one believes, the fact of the matter is that these measures represented a new departure for public policy at the turn of the century. Two new areas of public policy were created at this time that are still with us today. This is important to keep in mind in further discussions about public policy and its importance to business management.

The maintenance of competition became a function of public policy. The antitrust area developed as a response to a problem that the market was not allowed to solve. The most likely outcome of a completely unregulated market system was not acceptable to society. Ever since the late 1800s government has been in the business of maintaining what could be called a "workable" competition through passing and enforcing laws related to unfair trade practices and the structure of industries. Certain anticompetitive

[16]Chandler, *The Visible Hand*, p. 8.

practices such as price fixing, restriction of output, division of territories, stock ownership of one competitor by another, interlocking directorships, and price discrimination have been made illegal. Trusts have been broken up, the attainment of a monopoly or semimonopoly position has been attacked even if attained by honest industrial methods, mergers between companies in the same industry have been prevented or dissolved, and even oligopoly itself has been attacked by some agencies in government.

In addition, the regulation of competition in various industries, beginning with the railroads, became a matter of public policy. After the Interstate Commerce Commission came the Federal Power Commission, the Civil Aeronautics Board, and the Federal Communications Commission, all examples of what could be called industry regulation. There are many reasons for industry regulation, but the basic one is the belief that competition does not work very well in certain industries to protect the public interest, and thus prices, entry, and other economic matters in these industries must be regulated by a government commission. Recent years have seen a partial deregulation of these industries and a movement toward the introduction of more competition.

The Depression Era and Public Policy

The depression era saw the emergence of a number of new areas of public policy. Because of its severity and the basic questions this catastrophe raised about the market system, such a result is not surprising. The major public policy areas that stemmed from the depression were economic management, where government assumed responsibility for correcting such economic downturns, labor-management relations, with government support for the right of labor to bargain collectively, and the beginnings of a welfare system, originally designed to relieve the distresses of the depression.

Pre-Depression. After 1900, the modern multiunit industrial enterprise became a standard for managing the production and distribution of goods in America. By 1917, most American industries had acquired their modern structure. Companies like United States Steel, Standard Oil, General Electric, and Westinghouse were founded. For the rest of the century, large industrial structures such as these continued to cluster in much the same industrial groups and the same enterprises continued to be the leaders in the concentrated industries in these groups.[17]

During the twenties, these modern business enterprises came of age. They continued to flourish and spread in those sectors of the economy where administrative coordination proved more profitable than market coordination. The entrepreneurs who had built these enterprises hired professional managers to administer them. The new technologies and expanded markets called for more and more administrative coordination to take advantage of the opportunities and increase the flow of goods and services. This created a need for business schools to train these professional managers and equip them with the administrative skills necessary to run a large, integrated business enterprise.[18]

[17]*Ibid.,* p. 345.
[18]*Ibid.,* pp. 455–468.

Whole new industries were founded during the early years of the twentieth century. One leading entrepreneur in the early years of this period was Henry Ford. He brought together concepts of mass production, interchangeable parts, and central assembly with great effectiveness. The production process he put together enabled him to produce a cheap form of mass transportation—he kept his costs low enough to price his product for the lowest or largest possible mass market (see box). In 1909, Ford build 10,660 cars. By 1919 there were 6.7 million cars on the road, by 1929, 27 million. The phenomenal growth of the auto industry stimulated road construction and commercial construction, led to the formation of many new auto dealerships, and was of tremendous benefit to the rubber and steel industries.[19]

In 1916, Ford announced a price cut from $440 to $360 on the basic Model T automobile. The stockholders brought suit against the company, claiming that Ford was unjustified in giving their money away in this fashion. Ford's defense was that the company was clearing $2 to $2.5 million a month, which is all any firm ought to make in his opinion. The court, however held for the stockholders, ruling that it was not within the lawful powers of a corporation to conduct a company's affairs for the merely incidental benefit of shareholders and for the primary purpose of benefiting others.

© 1972 American Heritage Publishing Company, Inc. Reprinted by permission from *The American Heritage History of American Business and Industry* by Alex Groner.

The period following the First World War until the depression was one of unprecedented prosperity. Many people became new millionaires, the stock market soared, and production increased dramatically. There were many reasons for this burst of growth. The United States emerged from World War I economically and physically undamaged, giving it an advantage in world markets. Mass production methods became widely applied in many industries, increasing production of goods and services. Several major new products, such as automobiles and electric power, created or stimulated many new jobs and markets. Installment buying became popular and, coupled with the widespread use of advertising and sales techniques, stimulated consumption of these products. Finally, there were enormous profits to be made in stock market speculation, and low margin requirements made it possible for many people to participate (see box on next page).[20]

The Great Depression. Then came the crash. It is very difficult for those who did not live through this period of American history to grasp the full impact of the depression. Statistics such as those in Table 3.3 tell only part of the story. Unemployment soared to almost 25 percent of the labor force— over 12 million people out of 52 million workers in a nation of 122 million. Breadlines, clusters of tarpaper shacks called "Hoovervilles," and gray armies of job hunters became symbols of the period. Consumption spending slid by one-fifth and investment collapsed entirely. Waves of panic struck the

---

[19]Groner, *American Heritage History*, pp. 218–220, 275–278; "America in 1929: The Prosperity Illusion," *Business Week*, September 3, 1979, p. 6.

[20]"America in 1929: The Prosperity Illusion," *Business Week*, September 3, 1979, pp. 6–10.

banking system from late 1930 through 1933, forcing more than 9,000 banks with deposits of $7 billion to close their doois. More than nine million savings accounts were lost, and thousands of businesses went bankrupt because they could not take their money out of the bank.[21] Panic selling hit the stock market and paper fortunes were lost overnight when the crash began.

There is a great deal of debate over the cause of such a drastic change in the fortunes of the country, but the following seem to emerge as some of the major causes. First, the soaring stock market was more the result of speculation than increases in real physical wealth. Low margin requirements en-

TABLE 3.3 **Key Statistics of the Depression of the 1930s**

Index	1929	1932
Gross National Product (billions)[a]		
Current dollars	103.1	58.0
Farm income	12.0	5.3
Corporate profits	9.8	−3.0
Industrial production (1935–1939 = 100)[b]	110.0	57.0
Durable goods production (1934–1939 = 100)[b]	132.0	41.0
Steel production as percent capacity[c]		20.0
New private construction activity ($ billion)[d]	8.3	1.7
Automobile sales (millions of cars)[e]	5.4	1.3
Industrial stock prices (average dollars per share)[f]	311.0	65.0
Unemployment (millions)[g]	1.5	12.1
Percent of labor force	3.2	23.6
Farm products, wholesale price index (1957–1959 = 100)[g]	64.0	29.0

[a] U.S. Department of Commerce.
[b] Federal Reserve Board.
[c] American Iron and Steel Institute.
[d] U.S. Bureau of the Census.
[e] Automobile Manufacturers Association.
[f] Dow Jones.
[g] U.S. Bureau of Labor Statistics.

Source: George A. Steiner, *Business and Society* (New York: Random House, 1971), p. 59. Reprinted with permission.

[21] "A Debate That Rages On: Why Did It Happen?" *Business Week*, September 3, 1979, p. 12.

couraged such speculation. People borrowed heavily to buy stocks and participate in the rise of the market. Thus when the psychology of the market changed and investors sensed it had reached a peak, they began selling to get their profits and run. Panic quickly set in and the whole speculative structure collapsed rapidly.

Second, the prosperity of the late twenties was not shared by the agricultural sector. Farm purchasing power steadily deteriorated throughout this period, aggravated by the inelastic demand for farm products. Coupled with this was a bad and worsening distribution of income. Most of the money in the twenties went to those who were already wealthy rather than to workers with lower incomes. Smaller proportions of total income went toward wages and salaries. Much of the money that was received by the wealthy was reinvested in new productive facilities, causing an overextension of factory capacity. Workers simply could not buy all that the economy was producing.

Then the Smoot-Hawley tariff was passed, which only futher aggravated the situation. It was a very restrictive tariff structure that caused other countries to pass retaliatory tariffs of their own. This action curbed our exports to foreign countries just at the time such markets were badly needed.

Finally, the Federal Reserve System adopted a restrictive monetary policy during the late twenties, which some scholars believe was the major cause of the depression.[22] This action cut off credit to business and resulted in lagging business investment through the end of the period just before the crash, which only further aggravated an already deteriorating situation.

One can take his or her pick as to the real causes of the depression. The long-term effects, however, are quite clear. New areas of public policy were created. Franklin Delano Roosevelt won the election of 1932 promising a new deal for the American people. This New Deal consisted of a series of public policy measures (Exhibit 3.1) that was unprecedented in American history. The federal government assumed responsibility for stimulating business activity out of an economic depression and for correcting abuses in the economic machinery of the nation. It sought to relieve the distresses of businesses, farmers, workers, homeowners, consumers, investors, and other groups brought on by the adverse economic situation. In the famous 100 days that followed Roosevelt's swearing in, the president asked for, and Congress speedily granted, an unprecedented list of emergency legislation that plunged the federal government deeply and unalterably into the affairs of society and the economy. In all, during Roosevelt's first two years, 93 major pieces of legislation were passed that directly affected banking, business, agriculture, labor, and social welfare. This flow of legislation set the stage for the role government would be playing a generation later and dramatically increased the importance of public policy to the society as a whole and business in particular.[23]

Post-Depression. Whether all these public policy measures really pulled the economy out of the depression is again a matter of debate. The record, as shown in Table 3.4, is spotty. Unemployment never recovered its 1929 low, and gross national product in 1939 had barely recovered its 1929 high. Some

[22]See Milton Friedman and Anna J. Schwartz, *A Monetary History of the United States* (Princeton, N.J.: Princeton University Press, 1963).

[23]"Interventionist Government Came to Stay," *Business Week,* September 3, 1979, p. 39.

EXHIBIT 3.1 ——————————————————————————

Public Policy Measures of the New Deal Period

Year	Measure	Explanation
1932	Emergency Banking Relief Act	Reopened banks under government supervision
1932	Civilian Conservation Corps	First federal effort to deal with unemployment (youth) through direct public works
1932	Federal Emergency Relief Act	Required Washington to fund state-run welfare programs
1932	Reconstruction Finance Corporation	First use of government credit to aid troubled private companies
1933	Agricultural Adjustment Act	First system of agricultural price and production supports
1933	Tennessee Valley Authority Act	First direct government involvement in energy production and marketing
1933	Glass-Steagall Banking Act	Created bank deposit insurance Divorced commercial and investment banking Prohibited interest on checking accounts
1933	National Industrial Recovery Act	First major attempt to plan and regulate the entire economy through the use of industry and trade associations and codes of competition. First act to allow collective bargaining and wage and hour regulation. Portions were declared unconstitutional.
1934	National Housing Act	Provided for federal mortgage insurance and for regulation of housing standards
1935	Wagner Act	Promoted collective bargaining and prohibited unfair labor practice by employers
1935	Social Security Act	Created a system of social insurance and a national retirement system
1938	Agricultural Adjustment Act	Extended price supports, instituted parity payments, and launched wide federal management of agriculture
1938	Fair Labor Standards Act	Provided for minimum wage, 40-hour week, overtime, and control of child labor

historians believe that there were three parts to the depression that in effect lasted until the Second World War. These were: (1) the long, nearly uninterrupted decline for three and a half years to the low point of March 1933; (2) a gradual upturn for another three and a half years until August of 1937; and (3) a final plunge and ascent leading to the war production period.[24]

President Roosevelt, in the late thirties, became disappointed with the performance of the economy and turned on business. He called for an investigation of economic concentration, forming a Temporary National Economic Committee to do the investigation, declaring that free enterprise was ceasing to be free enterprise. Parallel with this development was the efforts of Thurman Arnold, the Assistant Attorney General, to enforce the

[24]Groner, *American Heritage History*, p. 302.

TABLE 3.4 **Employment and Production 1929–1942**

Year	Unemployment as a Percentage of the Labor Force[a]	Gross National Product per Capita in Dollars[b]	Year	Unemployment as a Percentage of the Labor Force	Gross National Product per Capita in Dollars
1929	3.1	696	1936	12.7	650
1930	8.7	619	1937	9.7	682
1931	15.8	563	1938	13.2	647
1932	23.5	478	1939	12.3	702
1933	24.7	485	1940	10.1	760
1934	20.7	537	1941	7.6	903
1935	17.6	561	1942	4.4	1024

[a]People on work relief and people in the armed forces are counted as employed.
[b]Dollars all of the same purchasing power.

Source: Robert R. Russel, *A History of the American Economic System* (New York: Appleton-Century-Crofts, 1964), p. 564. Reprinted with permission.

antitrust laws more vigorously.[25] These efforts became more or less academic with the advent of the war years, which called on the nation's productive capacity as never before, and ended concern about the depression for some time.

Public Policy Areas. *Economic Management.* The most basic problem, of course, was how to get the economy moving in the right direction again and restore the nation's economic health. The classic view of the market before the depression was that it was self-correcting—that with the onset of unemployment, wages and prices would fall, demand would begin to increase, albeit slowly, companies would respond by expanding output and hiring more workers, these workers would begin to buy more products, and thus an upward spiral would be set in motion that would eventually pull the economy out of the depression.[26]

But the depression was such a shock to the self-confidence of the nation and the distress was so widespread that people came to fear that self-correction would not happen or they were not willing to sit around in their Hoovervilles waiting for the market system to right itself. In any event, this traditional view of an inherently self-correcting economy proved bankrupt to deal with the problems of the depression. The unregulated market was too unstable and too slow-moving to be trusted. People, including business leaders, wanted action, and they wanted action immediately. The Roosevelt administration promised it to them.

It should be pointed out that the public policy measures that came out of the early part of the New Deal were part of a social welfare program designed to help victims of the depression. The idea that public works programs, among others, should be designed to stimulate the economy through deficit spending had not yet taken root. The immediate problem was to relieve the widespread distress the depression had caused. Only later

[25]*Ibid.*
[26]"The Scars Still Mark Economic Policy," *Business Week*, September 3, 1979, p. 22.

did economic theory develop to support the notion of an ongoing government involvement to manage the economy through countercyclical spending.[27]

These new theoretical developments came primarily from John Maynard Keynes and his followers in the form of what has since been called Keynesian economics. Keynes pointed out that classical theory was wrong on two counts: (1) in the real world prices and wages did not fall as expected, because of rigidities built into the system; and (2) a reduction in wages of sufficient magnitude to enable business to begin hiring workers lowers a worker's income drastically and therefore reduces even further the total demand for goods in the economy. The fundamental problem, according to Keynes, was this deficiency in demand, especially the demand for investment goods by business, which kept the economy at low levels of output and employment. Thus if no one else could spend money, government should, and prime the pump by putting money back into the economy to stimulate demand for goods and services.[28]

Eventually, these notions took root, culminating in the Employment Act of 1946, in which government was given the responsibility of managing the economy on an ongoing basis rather than simply to stimulate it in crisis situations like a depression. As the Second World War drew to a close, there was a great deal of concern that a new period of inflation would ensue because people had earned and saved a good deal of money during the war which they were not able to spend. Many goods and services were not generally available. After the war, it was believed, there would be a tremendous jump in demand as people took this money and moved into the marketplace. The productive facilities would not be able to keep up with this surge in demand, resulting in too much money in the economy chasing after too few goods, a classic cause of inflation. It was feared this high inflation would eventually lead to another serious downturn in the economy.

To prevent this from happening, the government was given the responsibility of managing the money supply through fiscal and monetary policies. Government was to even out business cycles by pumping money into the economy when necessary, dampening demand by raising taxes, stimulating investment, becoming the employer of last resort, and using other measures designed to maintain a stable economic environment in which business and the society at large could prosper. The idea that the market was self-regulating in this regard was rejected. It was believed that a completely unregulated market system was excessively prone to waves of over-investment and excess capacity, and deficient spending and underemployment of resources. Such boom and bust periods as had been experienced throughout much of American history were simply unacceptable. Management of the economy by government to promote stability of employment and purchasing power became a matter of public policy. Rather than trusting the market and succumbing to the ups and downs of normal cyclical behavior, government was given the responsibility of keeping inflation and unemployment under control and creating the conditions for continuing economic prosperity.

[27]*Ibid.*
[28]*Ibid.*

Labor-Management Relations. Another area of public policy that came out of the depression era was in the area of labor-management relations. The ordeal of the working class in those years ignited a militance that swept the country and revolutionized the industrial relations system. This militancy forced the federal government to intervene in labor-management relations and to adopt a national labor policy designed to protect the rights of workers to unionize. Out of this intervention came a revived labor movement, the development of collective bargaining as it is known today, and the end of management's unilateral control of the workplace.[29]

Workers found that the market system, particularly during periods of recession and depression when jobs were not readily available, was unable to deal with problems they were experiencing with the workplace—long hours, poor working conditions, low wages, and arbitrary hiring and firing practices. They began to form unions to counter the power of management with organized labor, but before the depression, management held an overwhelming advantage over the unions. The courts upheld the right of employers to do just about anything to prevent unionism. Companies could fire workers for joining unions, force them to sign a pledge not to join a union as a condition of employment, require them to belong to company unions, and spy on them to stop unionization before it got started. The attempt to form unions without government help was not very successful, and before the depression, the workers interest in unionism was declining.[30]

The National Industrial Recovery Act rekindled this interest. The NIRA authorized businesses to form trade associations to regulate production, and a few union leaders insisted that the bill also give employees the right to organize and bargain collectively. With the support of public policy and with job security at the forefront of workers' minds because of the depression, labor leaders found it easier to organize segments of the labor force. When the NIRA was found unconstitutional in 1935, a more comprehensive labor relations law called the Wagner Act was passed. The Wagner Act not only extended the right to organize and bargain collectively to workers, it also proscribed employer actions that interfered with that right, and established the National Labor Relations Board as the enforcement mechanism. Over the next few years, the NLRB created the rules which govern labor-management relations today.[31] Thus another area of public policy was born out of the depression, when market outcomes were unacceptable to a large segment of society.

The Welfare State. The depression was also responsible for the beginning of another series of public policy measures that can be grouped loosely under the title of welfare. The initial public policies of the New Deal era, as stated previously, were designed to alleviate distress. Many people were the victims of circumstances beyond their control. They were willing and able to work but there simply were no jobs available. Society conceded that the unemployed were not necessarily to blame for their situation and was willing to accept a government responsibility to help such victims. People were not

---

[29]"The Ruins Gave Rise to Big Labor," *Business Week*, September 3, 1979, p. 26.
[30]*Ibid.*
[31]*Ibid.*, pp. 27–28.

allowed to starve while waiting for the market to correct itself and make jobs available again.

So began a philosophy of entitlements, in which people believe they have rights to a good job, decent food, clothing, and shelter. The government has a responsibility to guarantee these rights—if the market will not respect them the government should. This philosophy has led to a whole series of measures, such as social security, aid to families with dependent children, Medicare and Medicaid, and food stamps, designed to help people whose basic needs have not been met, for one reason or another, by the market system.[32]

Social Goods and Services

The postwar period, at least until the Arab oil embargo in 1974, was yet another period of prosperity for the United States. By later standards, inflation was very low throughout most of this period. Unemployment was also low, and there were only minor recessions until that of 1974–1975. Cities and suburbs alike grew, people became wealthier, and more and more goods and services were produced until the gross national product topped the trillion-dollar mark. People were overwhelmed with new products, new services, and new inventions to make their lives easier. As more and more people moved into the middle class and came to own homes, buy cars, and acquire all the other amenities, society became referred to as a postindustrial society.[33]

A postindustrial society generally has three characteristics, and the United States had all three of them. The first was the affluence that became widespread throughout much of the population. The second was a service-based economy, one in which most of the labor force is engaged in service industries, such as banking or insurance, rather than manufacturing. The third characteristic was a knowledge-based society—one in which people became better and better educated and in which education was crucial to getting and keeping a good job. Unskilled jobs declined as society became more technologically sophisticated, demanding more highly skilled people.

If Maslow's hierarchy of needs concept is applied to a society, it seemed that throughout the 1950s and early 1960s American society fulfilled its basic economic needs. Thus it could move up the ladder to the next level, so to speak, and devote attention and resources to solving some of society's social problems. This it did, first in the civil rights movement, when an attempt was made to assure equal rights to blacks and other minorities who had been treated as second-class citizens at best throughout our history. Soon after this movement had peaked, the feminist movement developed to press for women's rights in all areas of American life, from equal job opportunities to equal treatment in the armed services. Then came a serious concern with pollution, air and water pollution at first, then noise and visual pollution, and later toxic substances and hazardous waste disposal. Soon

[32]"A Watershed in American Attitudes," *Business Week*, September 3, 1979, pp. 46–50.
[33]Daniel Bell, *The Coming of Post-Industrial Society: A Venture in Social Forecasting* (New York: Basic Books, 1973).

after that came a war on poverty, to eliminate it in American society. Then came a new wave of consumerism, touched off by Ralph Nader, which dealt with product safety and quality, warranties, truth in advertising, packaging, and other aspects of the marketplace. At the end of the decade, a new concern about safety and health in the workplace surfaced. And, finally, ethical concerns, stimulated by illegal campaign contributions in this country and foreign payments in other countries, came in for a great deal of attention.

Thus society experienced one social movement after another in the middle and late sixties, movements that changed the face of the country and altered fundamental values that had guided this country for years. Out of this change in values new public policy measures arose which have become of increasing concern to business because many of these measures, as we shall see in later chapters, have interfered with the basic economic mission of business.

Business attempted to respond to this change in values out of a sense of social responsibility, but its ability to meet these needs of society voluntarily proved to be very limited. In a competitive system, it is impossible for any one company to devote a great deal of money to pollution control equipment or to efforts to protect the safety and health of workers, because these are nonproductive investments from an economic standpoint. They do not contribute anything to the output of goods and services that can be sold on the market and earn a profit for the company. Yet the cost of these efforts will have to be reflected in the prices of products or the dividends paid to shareholders.

The company that goes very far in providing society with these social goods and services will simply price itself out of the market and/or become a very unattractive investment opportunity. The only way this situation can be corrected is for all the competitors in a given industry to make roughly the same level of voluntary efforts, a highly unlikely possibility.

Again the market proved deficient in responding to these problems and meeting the social needs of society. A new area of public policy ensued with the passage of much legislation directed at these problems and the creation of a new form of regulation called social regulation. Congress passed all kinds of social legislation related to environmental cleanup, consumer concerns, and other social issues, outdoing the New Deal Congress of Franklin D. Roosevelt. Government also created new regulatory agencies, such as the Environmental Protection Agency, the Equal Employment Opportunity Commission, the Consumer Product Safety Commission, and the Occupational Safety and Health Administration, and gave expanded powers to such existing agencies as the Food and Drug Administration. This new type of regulation affects every industry in the country rather than a particular industry, as was the old style of regulation patterned after the Interstate Commerce Commission model. These regulatory agencies set and enforce standards, in the case of pollution control and job safety and health, for example, which all companies are expected to meet. Every company is thus left in the same competitive position and at the same time social goods and services are supposedly provided to the society. The normal outcomes of the market system were unacceptable to society and a whole new area of public policy was created.

Post-Arab Oil Embargo and National Economic Planning

In the mid-1970s, American society experienced the worst recession since the great depression, an economic shock brought on primarily by the Arab oil embargo. While the country survived that recession, double-digit inflation, soaring energy costs, relatively high levels of unemployment, and declining real income for many people have become the order of the day. These factors, many of which seem out of our control, confronted American society with a whole new set of challenges as it entered the 1980s, challenges which may call for new business-government and business-society relationships.

The biggest challenge is inflation, which erodes people's incomes and destroys confidence in the future. Throughout the 1950s and 1960s, there were many years when inflation averaged only one percent for the entire year. During the late 1970s, the country was fortunate if inflation could be held to a one percent level for a month. This situation is not likely to be brought under control quickly. Perhaps the most important reason is because the price of oil, which is so basic to our economy, is not under our control. Members of the Organization of Petroleum Exporting Countries (OPEC) seem bent on a policy of continued increases to try and maintain the value of their dollar holdings and increase the value of their oil in the ground.

But there are other reasons for continued inflation. The huge buildup of private sector indebtedness presents a major obstacle to the Federal Reserve System's efforts to control inflation. As long as credit is available, attempts to control the money supply may have little effect on demand. People are motivated to buy now before inflation gets worse. Business has also been amassing debt with a view to paying it off at some future time in inflation-cheapened dollars. Workers seek a hedge against inflation with higher wage demands that are unchecked by government guidelines. Yet at the same time, productivity of American industry is declining. Much of the economy is indexed to inflation. Social security benefits rise automatically with increases in consumer prices. The same is true of wages that have a cost of living adjustment (COLA) as part of the contract. Inflation has built up such momentum that it will be hard to wring out of the economy.

With regard to these problems, a new area of public policy seems to be emerging, that of national economic planning. The government has been struggling to come up with a comprehensive energy policy for some time, for example, and a general semblance of one seems to have taken shape. The basic need for a policy of this kind is that energy resources, particularly oil, have become much more scarce than even a few years ago relative to the demand for these resources. The fundamental question here is whether the market can effectively allocate vital resources that are in short supply, or whether this allocation has to become a function of public policy. Will the unregulated market allocate these resources in an acceptable fashion? Does this allocation have to be directed by public policy measures?

Perhaps oil is only the first of such resource shortages.[34] The United States has used up a good many of its basic resources to the point where it is

[34]See "Now the Squeeze on Metals," *Business Week*, July 2, 1979, pp. 46–51.

dependent on foreign sources for many of its raw materials (Figure 3.1). This makes the country vulnerable to more OPEC-type cartels, although as yet none have appeared that have the organization and power of the oil producers. Nonetheless, the future holds more uncertainty about the cost and availability of raw materials crucial to the continued survival and operation of a sophisticated industrial and technological society.

Figure 3.1 U.S. Net Import Reliance on Selected Minerals & Metals as a % of 1978 Consumption

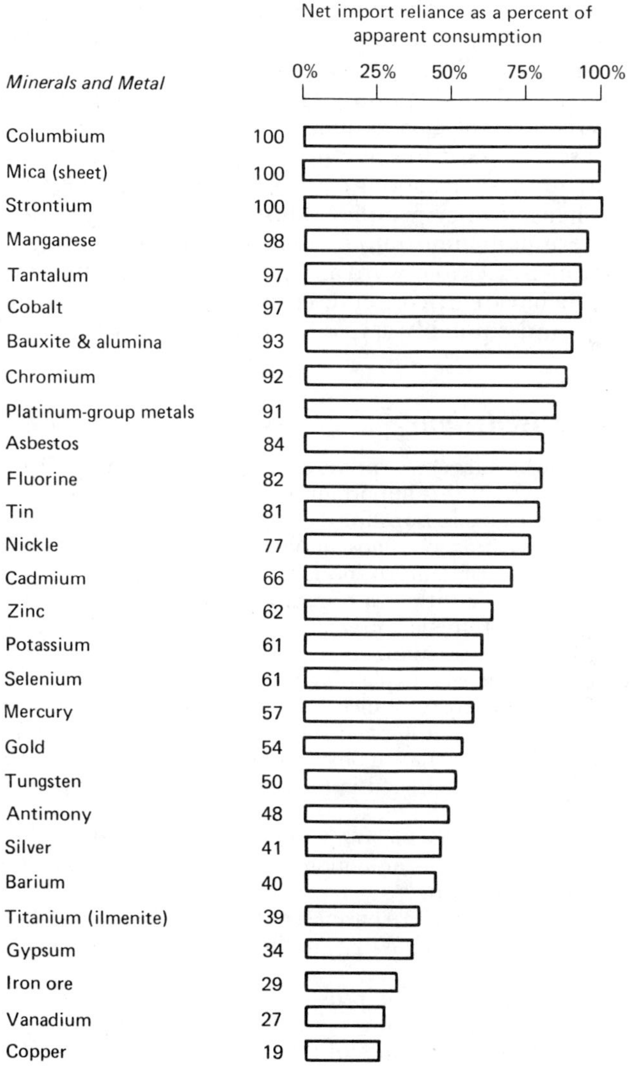

Net import reliance as a percent of apparent consumption

Minerals and Metal		0%	25%	50%	75%	100%
Columbium	100					
Mica (sheet)	100					
Strontium	100					
Manganese	98					
Tantalum	97					
Cobalt	97					
Bauxite & alumina	93					
Chromium	92					
Platinum-group metals	91					
Asbestos	84					
Fluorine	82					
Tin	81					
Nickle	77					
Cadmium	66					
Zinc	62					
Potassium	61					
Selenium	61					
Mercury	57					
Gold	54					
Tungsten	50					
Antimony	48					
Silver	41					
Barium	40					
Titanium (ilmenite)	39					
Gypsum	34					
Iron ore	29					
Vanadium	27					
Copper	19					

Source: Bureau of Mines, U.S. Department of Interior (import-export data from Bureau of the Census)

From Dale Singer, "Critical Minerals: Is the U.S. over a Barrel?" *St. Louis Post Dispatch,* July 27, 1980, p. 1I. Reprinted with permission.

One question about the allocation of critical resources concerns future generations. Do they not have a right to these resources? Does a market system, which encourages immediate consumption and exploitation rather than conservation, adequately respect those rights? With respect to the present generation, when these critical resources become more and more expensive, is it right that those at the low end of the income scale should suffer more than others? Does not everyone have a basic right to be warm in winter and have enough gasoline for normal driving?

These are the kinds of questions being asked about current resource shortages. The market works well when resources are relatively abundant, but public policy may have to intervene when resources necessary to basic survival become scarce. These critical resources may, in some sense, become public goods. The market responds to the short-run interests of people who have access to the market, but some people question whether this arrangement works best in regard to the long-run interests of society.

The answers to these questions are not yet clear, but the current debate over a comprehensive energy policy is just the beginning. The future may indeed see government enter into national economic planning with a series of public policy measures to reward and punish business and consumers and to shape their behavior to conserve certain resources, and allocate these resources fairly and equitably across the whole society.

Questions for Discussion

1. Why were most business enterprises small prior to the Civil War? What is an infrastructure? Why is this important to business growth?
2. Enumerate the various reasons for the rapid growth of industry after the Civil War. Which do you think were most important? Were Commodore Vanderbilt et al. robber barons or captains of industry? Why?
3. Distinguish among the different organizational innovations that appeared on the economic scene in the late nineteenth century. Were they anticompetitive? What motivated their creation?
4. Describe the three theories explaining the development of public policy during the late nineteenth century. Which theory do you agree with most strongly?
5. Did the Sherman Antitrust Act and Interstate Commerce Act represent significant departures from the state of business-government relations previous to that time? Is this period a watershed in terms of the role public policy plays in the economy?
6. Do you agree with the view of competition expressed in the text? Why or why not? Is the maintenance of competition a proper function of public policy? What is a "workable" competition?
7. Describe the growth of modern business enterprises. What were the major forces behind their development? Why was there a need for trained professional managers?
8. What were the reasons for the prosperity in the early years of the twentieth century? Were there any ominous signs on the horizon that seemed to indicate a change in the economic fortunes of the country?
9. List the major reasons for the depression. Which do you believe were most significant? Could the depression have been avoided? How? What should business and/or government have done which might have avoided this dramatic turnaround?

10. Describe the New Deal of Franklin Delano Roosevelt. Why did the American public believe in these promises from government? Was all this government intervention necessary? Why or why not? Did it do any good? What legacy did it leave?

11. What is the classic view of the market system? Why was this view rejected during the depression years? What theoretical developments underpinned government involvement in managing the economy?

12. Is a market system inherently unstable? Can business cycles be evened out by government policy? Why was the Employment Act of 1946 passed? Was government policy largely responsible for the many years of relative stability until the Arab oil embargo? What has happened since then—why isn't government policy effective in controlling inflation?

13. Why was it difficult for workers to unionize prior to the depression? What did the NIRA do with respect to labor-management relations? Is supporting the right of labor to bargain collectively a proper function of public policy? Why or why not?

14. Describe the philosophy of entitlements referred to in the text. How did this philosophy get started? Do you believe that you are entitled to a good job, adequate health care, and the like? Does the unregulated market system respect these rights?

15. What is a postindustrial society? Has the United States truly become this type of society? Why or why not? What implications does your answer have for the management of business institutions?

16. How did society change during the 1960s? How did this change affect business? Is this change permanent or only a temporary aberration brought on by unprecedented levels of affluence?

17. Is the market deficient in producing what are called social goods and services? Why or why not? What form has government intervention in this area taken? Are there other ways social goods and services could have been provided?

18. What is national economic planning? How does it differ from economic management? Is planning necessary with respect to critical resources? When these resources become scarce, do they in effect become public goods?

Suggested Readings

Allen, Frederick Lewis. *The Lords of Creation*. New York: Harper & Row, 1935.

Bonnifield, Matthew P. *The Dust Bowl: Men, Dirt, and Depression*. Albuquerque: University of New Mexico Press, 1979.

Chamberlain, John. *The Enterprising Americans*. New York: Harper & Row, 1963.

Chandler, Alfred. *The Visible Hand: The Managerial Revolution in American Business*. Cambridge, Mass.: Belknap Press, 1977.

Chandler, Lester V. *America's Greatest Depression, 1929–1941*. New York: Harper & Row, 1970.

Cockran, Thomas C., and Miller, William. *The Age of Enterprise*. New York: Harper & Row, 1942.

Degler, Carl N. *The New Deal*. Chicago: Quadrangle Books, 1970.

Galbraith, John Kenneth. *The Great Crash—1929*. 3rd ed. Boston: Houghton Mifflin, 1972.

Graham, Otis, L. *The New Deal: The Critical Issues*. Boston: Little, Brown, 1971.

Groner, Alex. *The American Heritage History of American Business and Industry*. New York: American Heritage Publishing Co., 1972.

Hacker, Louis M. *The Triumph of American Capitalism.* New York: Simon & Schuster, 1940.

Heilbroner, Robert L. *Beyond Boom and Crash.* New York: Norton, 1978.

Hendrick, Burton. *The Age of Big Business.* New Haven: Yale University Press, 1919–1921.

Josephson, Matthew. *The Robber Barons.* New York: Harcourt Brace Jovanovich 1934.

Mitchell, Broadus. *Depression Decade.* New York: Holt, Rinehart & Winston 1947.

Moody, John. *The Masters of Capital.* New Haven: Yale University Press, 1921.

Morison, Samuel E., and Commager, Henry S. *Growth of The American Republic.* Oxford: Oxford University Press, 1937.

Norton, Hugh Stanton. *The Employment Act and the Council of Economic Advisers, 1946–1976.* Columbia: University of South Carolina Press, 1977.

Russel, Robert R. *A History of The American Economic System.* New York: Appleton-Century-Crofts, 1964.

Schactman, Tom. *The Day America Crashed.* New York: Putnam, 1979.

4

The Social Origins of Public Policy

Centuries ago business was a rather uncomplicated relationship involving only a few interest groups, and it had been that way throughout history. There were owners who supplied the small amount of capital needed, employees who performed the work, and customers who purchased the products . . . During the last two centuries, revolutions in science, education, productivity, and culture developed in a way that expanded institutions and interest groups until the social system became significantly more complicated.[1]

The social origins of public policy refers to the structure of society—the way in which our society goes about identifying problems and developing policies to solve these problems. The structure of a society is important for many reasons, but for purposes of this chapter, the most important reason is that the problems a society decides to deal with and the public policies it eventually adopts with respect to those problems are largely a function of the structure of that society. The structure of the social-political process has a great deal to do with the kinds of problems that get attention and the response to those problems at any given point in history. Two different ways of looking at the structure of American society will be considered in this chapter.

The Power-Elite Model

The composition of society in this model is shown in Exhibit 4.1. According to this model, there are three major classes in society: the ruling elite, often referred to as the establishment; the middle class, sometimes referred

[1]Keith Davis and Robert L. Blomstrom, *Business and Society: Environment and Responsibility*, 3rd ed. (New York: McGraw-Hill, 1975), p. 57. Quoted with permission.

EXHIBIT 4.1 ———————————————————————

The Power-Elite Model of Society

I. The Ruling Elite or Establishment
   - Small in numbers
   - Upper-class background
II. The Middle Class
   - Large
   - Conflictual
   - Limited Importance
III. The Lower Class
   - Large
   - Indifferent
   - Alienated

to as the silent majority; and the lower class, those at the bottom end of the income scale with little wealth in their possession.

The ruling elite or establishment is a class that is small in numbers relative to the total population. Members of this class share an upper-class background: they are most likely listed in the social register of the community in which they live, they most likely attended one of a fairly small number of preparatory schools, they are probably members of what used to be called men's clubs, and they have a good deal of wealth, much of which may have been inherited. Because of these characteristics, the establishment is a homogeneous class in that its members share similar attitudes, values, and goals for themselves and the country as a whole.

The middle class is large, much larger than the establishment. And, taken as a whole, the middle class has control over a great deal of wealth. But it is composed of many different kinds of people with diverse backgrounds. It is a heterogeneous class in that its members do not share similar attitudes, values, and goals, and are always in conflict with one another over what issues are important and what policies should be adopted. The middle class can thus never organize itself as a whole and exercise the power in society it theoretically possesses, and therefore its importance in making public policy for society is limited.

The lower class is again large in numbers, but its members have little or no wealth; in fact, many of its members may have negative wealth. Many members of the lower class are indifferent toward and alienated from the rest of society. Most of their energies are taken up in seeking out an existence in what is perceived to be a basically hostile environment. Many members of this class, particularly the poorest ones, probably believe their lives do not count for much in society, that they are a forgotten class with few or no avenues through which to express their needs and opinions. Thus this class too is not very influential as far as making public policy is concerned.

The major point about this particular model of society is that the establishment largely "runs" society. The members of the ruling elite are the gatekeepers, so to speak, of the issues that society considers. Unless a particular problem is identified by this class as important and holds their interest, it is not given consideration (see box). Once a problem is identified, the public

A good example of this process is the War on Poverty, which had its beginnings during the Kennedy administration. Poverty has been a fact of life for many people since the beginning of history, but American society made a concerted effort to eradicate poverty during the Kennedy and Johnson administrations. It is said that Kennedy's first acquaintance with poverty was in reading Michael Harrington's book, *The Other America,* which pointed out that severe pockets of poverty existed in an otherwise affluent country. This issue captured his imagination enough that he then personally visited some areas of Appalachia, where some of these pockets existed. Thus was the interest of the establishment in this issue started, an interest which eventually developed into a full-scale war on poverty with such public policy measures as the creation of an Office of Economic Opportunity, Head Start programs, Volunteers In Service To America, and similar measures.

policy response to that problem is also largely under the establishment's control, since according to this model they exercise a broad scope of decision-making power in the major institutions of society. The members of the ruling elite are at the head of many of these institutions and thus can shape the behavior of the institution through the power to employ and reward the other people in the institution who work for them.

There was a good deal of literature in the 1950s and 1960s suggesting that this structure was basically representative of our society. Books with such titles as *The Protestant Establishment, Who Rules America?* and *America, Inc.* appeared, which tried to establish that a ruling elite did in fact exist that by and large controlled society and ran it in their interests.[2]

William G. Domhoff, for example, in *Who Rules America,* tried to show with some empirical evidence that there is an upper class in America that is also a governing class primarily through the control it exercises over major institutions. Membership in the national upper class was dependent on meeting the following criteria:

1. Being listed in any social register other than the Washington edition. The Washington Social Register is an index of the "political elite" as much as it is an index of the social upper class.

2. Attendance at any one of the private preparatory schools listed in the book. The list included, Groton, Middlesex, St. Andrew's, and similar schools.

3. Membership in any one of the "very exclusive" gentlemen's clubs found in major cities.

4. Having a father who was a millionaire entrepreneur or a $100,000-a-year corporation executive or corporation lawyer, and (a) attendance at one of the 130 private schools listed in Kavaler's *The Private World of High Society,* or (b) belonging to any one of the exclusive clubs mentioned by Baltzell or Kavaler.

[2]Edward Digby Baltzell, *The Protestant Establishment* (New York: Random House, 1964); William G. Domhoff, *Who Rules America?* (Englewood Cliffs, N.J.: Prentice-Hall, 1967); Morton Mintz and Jerry S. Cohen, *America, Inc.: Who Owns and Operates the United States?* (New York: Dial Press, 1971).

5. Marriage to a person defined as a member of the upper class by criteria 1 to 4 above. Cooptation by marriage is one of the ways by which the upper class infuses new brains and talent into its ranks.

6. Having a father, mother, sister, or brother who was listed in the social register, attended one of the exclusive private schools listed in criterion 2, or belonged to one of the exclusive gentlemen's clubs listed in the third criterion. This allowed for the reticence of some individual members of the upper class who might, for example, refuse to be listed in the social register.

7. Being a member of one of the old and still wealthy families chronicled by Amory in *Who Killed Society?* or *The Proper Bostonians.* Domhoff admitted that this criterion assumes that Amory is an accurate ethnographer of the American upper class.[3]

Domhoff then went on to show that this upper class was also a governing class in America, defining governing class as "a social upper class which owns a disproportionate amount of the country's wealth, receives a disproportionate amount of a country's yearly income, and contributes a disproportionate number of its members to the controlling institutions and key decision-making groups of the country."[4] He argued that the institutions in which the majority of decisions are made about American society (corporations, foundations, universities, the executive branch of the federal government, and the federal judiciary) are dominated by upper-class members, who can therefore be assumed to control the policies that flow from these institutions. Thus, according to Domhoff, the American upper class is also a governing class that by and large runs society, especially in light of the wealth owned and the income received by members of that exclusive social group.[5]

The Pluralist Model

This model differs from the power-elite model of society in that there are no reasonably well-defined classes, with one class exercising by far the most influence on public policy. A pluralistic society instead is composed of a number of organizations, all of which to varying degrees wield influence. These organizations can quite properly be called interest groups because they form around shared interests. People organize such groups and join or support them because they share common attitudes on a particular problem or issue and believe they can advance their interests better by organizing themselves into a group rather than pursuing these interests individually.

In a pluralistic society such interest groups are conveyers of certain kinds of demands that are fed into the public policy process. They fill a gap in the formal political system by performing a representation function beyond the capacities of the formal representatives chosen by the voters. At times they perform a watchdog function by sounding an alarm whenever policies of more formal institutions, such as corporations or governments, threaten the interests of their members. They generate ideas that may become formal

[3]Domhoff, *Who Rules America?* pp. 34–37.
[4]*Ibid.*, p. 5.
[5]*Ibid.*, p. 11.

policies of these and other institutions and in this manner these ideas become part of the public policy agenda.

Americans seems particularly inclined to form groups to pursue their common interests. There were 13,583 national associations in the United States in 1976, devoted to a variety of interests including religion, education, science, and business.[6] One study reported that 75 percent of all American adults belonged to at least one organization and 57 percent were active in at least one group.[7] The importance of associations in American life was recognized by Alexis de Tocqueville many years ago in his famous book on American democracy.

> Americans of all ages, all conditions, and all dispositions, constantly form associa- tions. They have not only commercial and manufacturing companies, in which all take part, but associations of a thousand other kinds—religious, moral, serious, futile, extensive or restricted, enormous or diminutive. The Americans make associations to give entertainments, to found establishments for education, to build inns, to construct churches, to diffuse books, to send missionaries to the antipodes, and in this manner they found hospitals, prisons, and schools.[8]

Functions of Interest Groups. These interest groups perform a variety of functions for their members. Groups may perform a *symbolic* function simply by giving members the opportunity to express the interests or values they hold. Such activity serves to reinforce one's identity or provide legiti- macy for certain ideas, a valuable function in and of itself. Closely related is an *ideological* function, whereby groups may provide an outlet for people who hold strong beliefs about a particular aspect of American life, such as free enterprise, and need a way to appeal to these strongly held principles. A common function of interest groups is to promote the *economic* self-interest of their members, a function most often associated with business and labor groups. Groups also provide members with *information*, ranging from politi- cal information related to particular causes the group may be pursuing to more technical information in which members may be interested, such as information about stamps, coins, or antique cars. Most groups collect, analyze, and disseminate information to their members to some extent. Finally, groups can perform *instrumental* functions for their members—con- crete goals that are noneconomic in nature. This goal can include the efforts of antiwar groups to end American participation in Vietnam or the right to life groups that seek to outlaw abortions.[9]

Classifications of Interest Groups. Interest groups can be classified according to their primary functions. *Economic interest groups,* formed to promote the economic self-interest of their members, may not have been formed with political activity in mind, but eventually find such activity necessary to promote or protect their interests. Economic interest groups

[6]*Encyclopedia of Associations*, Vol. I, National Associations of the U.S., 20th ed. (Detroit: Gale, 1976).

[7]Samuel H. Barnes, "Some Political Consequences of Involvement in Organizations," paper presented at the 1977 annual meeting of the American Political Science Association, quoted in Raymond E. Wolfinger, Martin Shapiro, and Fred I. Greenstein, *Dynamics of American Politics*, 2nd ed. (Englewood Cliffs, N.J.: Prentice-Hall, 1980), pp. 229–230.

[8]Alexis de Tocqueville, *Democracy in America* (New York: Schocken, 1961), Vol. II, p. 128.

[9]Norman J. Ornstein and Shirley Elder, *Interest Groups, Lobbying and Policymaking* (Washington, D.C.: Congressional Quarterly Press, 1978), pp. 29–34.

include business groups such as the National Association of Manufacturers or Business Roundtable, labor unions, and professional associations such as the National Education Association.

Solidarity groups draw on feelings of common identity based on a shared characteristic such as race, age, or sexual orientation. The basis of the group is a sense of kinship. Examples of this classification include ethnic groups, composed of members from a particular part of the world, and women's groups, formed to promote women's rights. These groups may have economic interests at stake, but their primary function seems to be in maintaining or promoting an identity or consciousness related to a common characteristic shared by all members of the group.

A third category is the *public interest* group that claims to speak for the public. Whether such groups should be called "public" interest groups or "special" interest groups is academic to this discussion. The fact is that such groups do not necessarily appeal to the economic self-interest of their members, nor do they share common characteristics such as a solidarity group, but exist to promote noneconomic interests, such as the environment or equal opportunity. Thus they are somewhat ideological in nature but also have concrete goals in mind. Some of these groups tend to advance overall value positions covering a wide range of issues (liberalism or conservatism); others are strictly single-issue groups. Examples of public interest groups are the Nader Network (see box) and Common Cause.[10]

The Nader Network includes many specialized organizations (see Figure 4.1), among which are the following. The Center for the Study of Responsive Law, the original Nader unit started with the money from the General Motors settlement, has conducted many studies, including exposés of the Federal Trade Commission and Interstate Commerce Commission, a study of corporate concentration called *The Closed Enterprise System*, and others. It also serves as a clearinghouse for other consumer groups. Congress Watch is the network's lobbying organization. The Public Interest Research Group (PIRG) serves as a coordinating and resource center for the many state PIRGs, which are staffed largely by student volunteers. The state PIRGs concern themselves with state and local consumer problems.

Interest Group Tactics. Interest groups have a number of tactics they can use to focus attention on the issue they are concerned with and win widespread support. *Boycotts* are one such tactic. Boycotts were particularly useful in the civil rights movement in the South because the black population was large and could be organized. When the blacks refused to ride the buses in Montgomery, Alabama, and boycotted white merchants in parts of the South, they had an effect because of the large numbers involved. Boycotts of lettuce in support of the California farmworkers were less successful.

Another tactic is for interest groups to hold *public demonstrations* in support of an issue or a cause. The purpose of these demonstrations, particularly peaceful protests, is to show that a significant number of people feel very

---

[10]Wolfinger, Shapiro, and Greenstein, *Dynamics of American Politics*, pp. 233–248.

Figure 4.1. The Nader Network

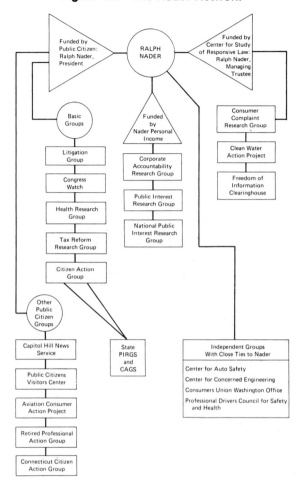

strongly about an issue, and have not been able to make their voices heard through the normal political process. When such demonstrations attract thousands of people, as did some of the civil rights demonstrations and protests against the war in Vietnam, they attract widespread public attention and often induce official action through normal governmental channels. Such demonstrations can also turn violent and involve the destruction of life and property. Most public demonstrations, however, have limited political objectives and do not aim to upset the normal functioning of government and society.

The use of *terrorism* as a tactic to advance a particular interest or cause is fortunately not as widespread in the United States as it is in some parts of the world. But it is not entirely unknown. Terrorism can involve the taking of hostages, hijacking of airplanes, killing of government officials, slaying of people with opposite interests, destruction of property, and similar measures. Much terrorist activity is directed against "the system" and is intended to upset and interfere with the normal functioning of a society or its government.

Interest groups can also attempt to win public support through advertisements in newspapers, distributing leaflets to large segments of the population, buying time on television, and other *uses of the media.* Sometimes they become quite skillful in using the media to their advantage. The events that transpired in Selma, Alabama, at the height of the civil rights movement were no accident. This particular city was chosen by civil rights groups because all the ingredients were there to make the use of nonviolent demonstrations successful. The sight of dogs attacking humans and police beating people provoked moral outrage all across the country as people sat in front of their television screens and watched. This generated a great deal of support for the movement.

When the concern of an interest group gets picked up by the political process, it can then, of course, *lobby* to help shape the public policies that are being developed to deal with the problem. Some of the larger groups have enough of a membership that provides adequate financial support to be able to support full-time paid lobbyists in Washington, D.C. and in some state capitals.

The word "lobbying" has a rather negative connotation in many people's minds, eliciting images of behind-the-scenes arm-twisting and money changing hands under the table. But looked at in its best light, lobbying can be defined as communication with public officials to influence their decisions in a manner that is consistent with the interests of the individual or group doing the communicating. The lobbyist's purpose is a selfish one in that a lobbyist seeks to persuade others that his or her position on an issue is meritorious. Lobbying behavior is thus designed to bring about favorable outcomes from government for the group represented by the lobbyist.

The lobbyist performs a number of functions. One activity is to provide members of Congress with information. Such information, of course, tends to put the position of the group represented by the lobbyist in the best possible light, but it must also be accurate enough to be acceptable to members of Congress. Lobbyists also keep their constitutents informed about developments in Congress or in the executive branch that may affect their interests. This information may stimulate grass roots efforts from the membership to contact their local Representatives or Senators. Finally, lobbyists can also use publicity to support or oppose a particular bill or to put pressure on the administration or Congress.[11]

Lobbying is presently regulated by the Regulation of Lobbying Act of 1946, which defines lobbyists as those individuals whose principal purpose is to influence legislation by direct contact with members of Congress. These legally defined lobbyists must register with Congress and give quarterly reports on their spending for lobbying activities. Lobbying in the executive branch is not currently regulated by statute.

This definition allows many people who do a great deal of lobbying to avoid registering because lobbying is not necessarily their principal purpose.

---

[11]*Ibid.,* pp. 252–253.

People who run Washington offices of corporations, for example, are not required to register because lobbying is not their primary job, even though they may lobby on various occasions. There were attempts in 1978 to change the law and make the reporting and registering requirements more stringent. However, these reform efforts failed.

In 1978, fewer than 2,000 lobbyists were registered with Congress, while the actual number was estimated at 15,000, an increase from 8,000 five years previously.[12] Most large corporations probably employ lobbyists, who are located in the Washington office of the company. More than 500 corporations, including some small companies, have such offices. Many general business and industry and trade associations have their headquarters or offices in Washington for lobbying purposes.

Finally, an interest group can use *litigation* to advance its interests. This has proven to be a very useful tactic for groups to use, so much so that recent years have seen a tremendous increase in litigation. Interest groups can sue the government or private parties they believe are violating the law. They can file "friend of the court" briefs, which are attempts to influence the courts through supplementary arguments. The Bakke case, regarding preferential admission of minorities to medical school, elicited more such briefs on both sides of the issue than any Supreme Court case in history.

Business groups file suit against government agencies blocking the issuance of new regulations. Environmental groups file suit against the Environmental Protection Agency pressuring it to speed up the issuance of regulations for hazardous waste disposal. Conservationists file suit against the government challenging a federal construction project, using the required environmental impact statement as the basis for their suit.

Because of the increase in litigation, the courts are deciding more and more public policy matters through interpreting laws, establishing precedent, and trying to discern the intent of Congress. As will be seen in later chapters, the courts play a crucial role in public policy-making that is likely to continue.

The Operation of a Pluralistic System. The way a problem gets identified in a pluralistic system, then, is for people who are concerned about the problem to organize themselves or join an existing organization to pursue their particular interests in the problem. If the problem is of widespread concern, and the group or groups dealing with it can attract enough financial and other kinds of support, the problem may eventually become public as people become aware of it and show varying degrees of support. Eventually government or other institutions may pick up on the problem and translate the issues being raised into formal legislation or other policy actions. These interest groups then continue to exercise influence in helping to design public policies to deal with these problems.

Thus in the pluralist model, problems are identified and policies designed in a sort of bottom-up fashion—concern about a problem can begin anywhere at the grassroots level in society and eventually grow into a major public issue that demands attention. This is in contrast to the power-elite model, a sort of top-down process in which the upper class identifies the problems, designs public policy, and forces it on the rest of society. One

---

[12]"The Swarming Lobbyists," *Time*, August 7, 1978, p. 15.

could see the pluralistic process at work during the social revolutions of the 1960s. Various interest groups, such as the Southern Christian Leadership Conference, Nader's groups, and the Sierra Club, were active in identifying the problems of civil rights, consumerism, and pollution and in helping to shape public policies on these problems.

In theory, a pluralistic system is an open system. Anyone with a strong enough interest in a problem can pursue this interest as far as it will take him or her. Membership in a particular social or income class or of a particular race does not shut one out from participating in the public policy process. Power is diffused in a pluralistic system and dominant power centers are hard to develop in such a competitive arrangement. The existence of many interest groups also provides more opportunities for leadership, making it possible for more people with leadership ability to exercise these talents.

But interest groups themselves, particularly as they become large, tend to be dominated by their own leadership. This leadership usually formulates policy for the group as a whole, and the public stance of an interest group often represents the views of a ruling elite within the interest group itself rather than all of the rank and file membership. Interest groups in many cases also draw most of their membership from better educated, middle- or upper-class segments of society. Many minorities and particularly the poorer elements of society are not adequately represented. Their problems are likely to be ignored and some groups cannot advance their interests even in a pluralistic system unless championed by other people who are more likely to participate in public policy-making.

Improved public policy decisions should also result from such a structure, since more people, particularly those who are closest to the problem, have an input in decision-making. Yet a pluralistic system is a system of conflict because interest groups compete for attention and influence in the public policy process, and such competing interests do not necessarily result in the best public policy decisions. Conflict can get out of control and result in social fragmentation, making a policy decision for society difficult to reach. This is particularly true when interest groups are unwilling to compromise, in which case reaching a public policy decision for society as a whole may be impossible. Furthermore, some interests, as stated above, are not adequately represented.

However, a pluralistic system does seem to allow for more interests to be represented than does a society structured along the power-elite model. More people should have a chance to promote their particular values and interests and have a chance to govern society. This is a mixed blessing, however, as the more pluralistic a society becomes, the more diverse will be the interests represented, and the less clear will be the direction in which society is moving. The lack of central direction for society, which an elite provides, can be a disadvantage of pluralism as society is pulled to and fro by the competition of many different interests with varying degrees of power and influence.

Any society is undoubtedly a mixture of both these models, with elements of an establishment and interest groups helping to identify problems and develop public policies to deal with them. Yet it could be argued that societies tend to lean toward one model or the other at various points in their history. If this is true, a great deal of evidence suggests that our society is leaning toward the pluralistic model at present. Interest groups have proliferated in the last decade and have become sophisticated in the use of various tactics to wield influence in the public policy process far beyond what their actual numbers would suggest. Many people active in these groups know how to pursue their own interests effectively. Few, if any, books are written about an "establishment" anymore, suggesting that if one did exist it either has disappeared or is not influential enough to worry about. Congress itself is fragmented, without the power-brokers of past years, and is thus more subject to grass-roots lobbying. This kind of structure has implications for business and public policy-making which will be discussed in subsequent chapters.

Questions for Discussion

1. Describe the power-elite model of social organization. How do issues or problems become identified and dealt with in this kind of society? What are its advantages and disadvantages?
2. How does the power elite govern society? What instruments of power does it possess? Think of some examples either at the national level or in your local community where such power has been used by a power elite.
3. What is a pluralistic society? What are the advantages and disadvantages of this kind of society? How are issues raised and policies formulated?
4. How are interest groups formed? What purposes do they serve as far as society is concerned? What functions do they perform for their members?
5. Describe the categories of interest groups presented in the text. Do these categories adequately cover all the interest groups of which you are aware? Do some interest groups overlap the categories? Are there some groups that do not fit in anywhere?
6. What tactics can interest groups use to advance their concerns? Under what circumstances can each tactic be effective? Which tactics are questionable from the standpoint of your own sense of ethics and values?
7. Is a pluralistic society a truly open society? Is it more consistent with democratic values than the power-elite structure? Which kind of a society would you rather live in? Why?
8. Which form of organization predominates in our society at the present time? From a strictly business standpoint, which model of society is preferable? Why? What implications does your answer have for your management task?

Suggested Readings

Baltzell, Edward Digby. *The Protestant Establishment.* New York: Random House, 1964.

Berry, Jeffrey M. *Lobbying for the People: The Political Behavior of Public Interest Groups.* Princeton, N.J.: Princeton University Press, 1977.

Dahl, Robert A. *Democracy in the United States: Promise and Performance.* Chicago: Rand McNally, 1972.

Domhoff, William G. *Who Rules America?* Englewood Cliffs, N.J.: Prentice-Hall, 1967.

Gamson, William A. *The Strategy of Social Protest.* Homewood, Ill.: Dorsey Press, 1975.

Kelso, William A. *American Democratic Theory: Pluralism and Its Critics.* Westport, Conn.: Greenwood Press, 1978.

Meyers, William, and Rinard, Park. *Making Activism Work.* New York: Gordon & Breach, 1972.

Mintz, Morton, and Cohen, Jerry S. *America, Inc.: Who Owns and Operates the United States?* New York: Dial Press, 1971.

Nicholls, David. *The Pluralist State.* New York: St. Martin's Press, 1975.

Ornstein, Norman J., and Elder, Shirley. *Interest Groups, Lobbying and Policymaking.* Washington, D.C.: Congressional Quarterly Press, 1978.

Wolfinger, Raymond E., Shapiro, Martin, and Greenstein, Fred I. *Dynamics of American Politics,* 2nd ed. Englewood Cliffs, N.J.: Prentice-Hall, 1980.

PART TWO

Environmental Influences on Public Policy

5

Social Change and Business

The roots of life in the United States are changing. Significant changes are occurring in personal styles and values, technological innovations, and social institutions. . . . Technological and intellectual changes have in turn fostered a new sensitivity and awareness of social problems and a desire to cope with them.[1]

Any society is a very complex mixture of many elements that influence social change. Some of these elements are values and the role they play in social change, ideologies that are common to a society, attitudes that people hold, and social movements that appear from time to time in the life of a society. Many of these elements are difficult to define conceptually, let alone measure empirically with a high degree of precision. There are several concepts or definitions of value and ideology, for example, and some of these concepts or definitions seem relatively close to each other. How do attitudes and values differ? What is a social movement and what role do values play in these movements?

When it comes to empirical measurement the questions become even more difficult. What connection is there between values and human behavior? Can values be measured independently of behavior? What techniques are appropriate for attitude measurement? There has been a good deal of research into these and similar questions, but, as one might guess, there are no definitive answers. There are also many different techniques for measuring values and ideologies, with no one technique having become generally accepted as appropriate. Each method has its own strengths and weaknesses.

[1]From *Creating Social Change*, edited by Gerald Zaltman, Philip Kotler, and Ira Kaufman. Copyright © 1972 by Holt, Rinehart and Winston, Inc. Reprinted by permission of Holt, Rinehart and Winston.

Even more difficult is to fit all these elements together into some kind of generalized model of social change that explains why and how change takes place and thus might even have predictive value in anticipating future social change. There are many such models with varying explanatory power and appeal.

This chapter does not offer a comprehensive treatment of the subject. The particular concepts and studies that have been selected for discussion were chosen because they are believed to be of particular interest to business as it attempts to understand its changing role in American society. This changing role resulted from widespread social change, and thus it is important to understand something about the elements that make up that change.

Social Values

Values are a critical element in social change. When a relatively homogeneous value system exists in a society over a period of time, that society is stable and experiences relatively little social change. When a homogeneous value system begins to break up and significant segments of society begin to express nontraditional values, social change of some kind seems inevitable. That process brings about changes in the major institutions of society to incorporate these new values.

The concept of value can be thought of as a particular quality that human beings associate with specific forms of human behavior, principles, institutions, or material goods and services. When something is valued, it is considered to be worthwhile, good, desirable, important, and esteemed or prized. Something that is valueless is worthless and not desired or prized. When one makes a value judgment about something, one is attributing a value (worthwhile, good, desirable) to a certain action or entity.[2]

Whether values are inherent in certain entities, that is, that an entity is worthwhile regardless of human judgment about it and thus value is absolute, is an interesting philosophical speculation. But from a human point of view, there is a certain relativity about values. Human beings do assign values to entities and make value judgments. The desirability and worthwhileness of entities also change over time.

When many people believe the same way about something, their values may spread to include the entire society. They then become social values, in that many if not most people in the society come to share the same values, that is, desire the same kinds of things. These values show up in principles the society believes in, the institutions that are most highly esteemed, the behavior that people believe is appropriate, the material goods that people pursue. These values are held in common because it is believed that certain principles, institutions, behavior, and material possessions will produce a desirable state of affairs for all members of that society.

Values can be measured along several dimensions that give some idea of how widespread they are and how strongly they influence a society's behavior. These are shown in Exhibit 5.1. If these dimensions can be measured

[2]*Webster's New Collegiate Dictionary* (Springfield, Mass.: G. & C. Merriam Company, 1977), p. 1292.

EXHIBIT 5.1 —————————————————————————————————

Value Dimensions

1. *Extensiveness* of the value in the total activity of the system. What proportion of a population and of its activities manifest the value?
2. *Duration* of the value. Has it been persistently important over a considerable period of time?
3. *Intensity* with which the value is sought or maintained, as shown by effort, crucial choices, verbal affirmation, and reactions to threats to the value—for example, promptness, certainty, and severity of sanctions.
4. *Prestige* of value carriers—that is, of persons, objects, or organizations considered to be bearers of the value. Culture heroes, for example, are significant indexes of values of high generality and esteem.

From Robin M. Williams, Jr., *American Society: A Sociological Interpretation,* 3rd ed. (New York: Knopf, 1970), p. 448. Reprinted with permission.

accurately, one can get some idea of the dominant value system in a society and where other values fall in a scale of preferences.

Values can also be classified into certain categories, such as those shown in Exhibit 5.2. Values that fall in the same category form a value system; they relate to each other in a cluster. Many would argue, for example, that American society is dominated by an economic value system, that we believe that those items which can be bought and sold on the marketplace are the most worthwhile things about our existence. Others argue that religious values are most important, that the ideals embodied in the Judeo-Christian tradition are the most desirable things in life to pursue.

Values change in response to many influences in society. Technology is one such influence that makes it possible for some things to be done that could never have been done before or to do something easier or cheaper than before, thus changing the cost-benefit ratio. The invention of the

EXHIBIT 5.2 —————————————————————————————————

Value Systems

Theoretic: The pursuit of knowledge for its own sake—the desirability of attaining knowledge because of the pleasure this brings to an individual.

Economic: The pursuit of those material goods and services that can be bought and sold on the marketplace whose value is determined through the exchange process.

Aesthetic: The importance of beauty in all aspects of existence, particularly in nature.

Social: The desire to associate and interact with other people either individually or as members of a group and affirm one's existence in this manner.

Political: The desire to make decisions that affect many people in society and exercise power over them.

Religious: The pursuit of the ideas and precepts of a particular religious system.

Ethical: The desire to do the right thing, take the right action, make the right decision in accordance with a particular ethical system.

Adapted from Keith Davis and Robert L. Blomstrom, *Business and Society: Environment and Responsibility,* 3rd ed. (New York: McGraw-Hill, 1975), p. 175. Quoted with permission.

airplane, for example, eventually made it possible to travel long distances with relative ease and at increased speeds, making accessible more and distant places. Most people probably desire good physical health, and modern medical technology makes it possible for more people to enjoy good health than before.

Information changes the importance of certain things in our society. When it became known that using the environment to dump our wastes into was having some disastrous side effects and might even change the climate of the world, the importance of the environment increased dramatically and more resources were allocated to cleaning it up.

Shifts in population have an effect on the dominant value systems in society. If the aged come to constitute an increasing proportion of the population, the values they hold as a group will tend to exercise more influence over the society as a whole. The same will hold true if young people come to constitute an increasing proportion of the population, as was true of American society in the 1960s. Their values tended to dominate many segments of American society in those years.

Another factor influencing values is education. As people attain more formal education, they may question their desires and the things they were raised to believe were important. They may come to reject these traditional values appropriated from their families and adopt a new set of desires and goals to pursue. Education supposedly broadens one's horizons and acquaints one with new sets of possibilities. Education gives people access to different dimensions of life and thus may change the things they believe are worthwhile.

Changes in basic institutions also affect values, institutions such as the family and religion. These institutions, particularly the family, play a crucial role in the socialization of children and the transmitting of values from generation to generation. Much evidence suggests that these institutions are changing. Increasing numbers of women are employed outside the home, leaving their children in day care centers or nursery homes. The increasing divorce rate breaks up more and more families. Attendance at religious institutions has declined and the authority of these institutions is severely questioned. As these institutions play a reduced role in value transmission, there is less continuity of values from one generation to the next.

Affluence also causes value changes. Society can be looked at from the standpoint of a Maslowian hierarchy of needs. As more and more people in society become affluent and thus fulfill their basic economic needs, they can move up the ladder, so to speak, to fulfill a higher order of needs. Other things become important to them that were not within the range of possibility before. They desire other goods and services besides economic ones and pursue other goals related to self-fulfillment or improving the quality of life for the whole society.

Rescher provides an interesting model that is of use in analyzing value change (Exhibit 5.3). At the extremes, a value can be newly *acquired* or *abandoned* completely. Such extreme changes are always possible, but some kind of value transformation between these extremes is more likely. A value may be upgraded by *redistribution* when it comes to be more widely held throughout society or downgraded when it becomes less widely held by people. A value may be *emphasized* or *deemphasized* due to changes in our life

EXHIBIT 5.3

Analysis of Value Change

Modes of Upgrading		Modes of Downgrading
value acquisition	1	value abandonment
increase redistribution	2	decrease redistribution
rescaling upwards	3	rescaling downwards
widening redeployment	4	narrowing redeployment
value emphasis	5	value deemphasis
restandardization by a raising of standards	6	restandardization by a lowering of standards
retargeting by adding implementation targets or by giving higher priority to existing ones ·	7	retargeting by dropping implementation targets or by giving lower priority to existing ones

environment. A value may also be altered by *rescaling;* it may move up or down our hierarchy of values, it may become the subject of greater or lesser investment of energy and resources, or it may be associated with different sanctions. If we change the source of our identity and self-worth, a rescaling is taking place.

The *redeployment* of a value may lend it more importance by extending the scope of its application to more groups or situations. *Restandardization* can represent a significant change in the impact of a value. The standard or norm for evaluating the attainment of a value can be heightened or lowered. Finally, *retargeting* may affect the influence of a value. When we subscribe to a value, we set objectives and targets for its implementation. These targets may be upgraded or downgraded from time to time. Upgrading of the target will require greater investment of energy and resources, downgrading of the target will have the opposite effect.

This framework can be used to analyze the significance of a value to an individual and to a society. If a value, such as equal opportunity, is associated with only a vague objective, is measured by low standards of attainment, is narrowly applied throughout the society, does not receive much investment of people's energy and society's resources, is rarely emphasized through concrete action, and is not in practice widely observed with respect to all social groups in society, that value lacks significance in the society, regardless of all the rhetoric which may be expended in its behalf.

Identifying specific value changes in American society is a risky proposition, but a good deal of evidence suggests that certain value changes have taken place in recent years. These changes have not occurred throughout the entire society, but are significant enough to have appeared in much of the literature related to American society. Some of these major changes are briefly described in the paragraphs that follow.

1. One traditional value is the importance that American society has attached to work and a corresponding disrespect for laziness. The traditional notion was that work had value in and of itself regardless of the nature of the work, because it was done for the glory of God (religious meaning) or

to make a contribution to the wealth of society (secular meaning). Thus work had a transcendent meaning that made all jobs of equal value and made work a serious duty of humankind. This has changed for many people. Work has lost this transcendent meaning and is valued more for what it contributes to the individual's personal enjoyment and fulfillment. Many people want a job that is fulfilling and challenging and shun jobs that involve drudgery and boredom. If they cannot find this kind of job, they try to gain more leisure time away from the job to do what interests them.

2. Related to the importance of working hard in the present was the traditional importance of deferring personal gratification until the future. There was value in providing for one's security in retirement, saving for a rainy day, building an estate for the children, and having such virtue rewarded in heaven rather than on earth. The credit card has destroyed this value, as it encourages instant gratification. Why wait? One can enjoy a particular product or service right now and pay later. Homes can be purchased with long-term mortgages. The future is taken care of with social security or institutional retirement plans.

3. Americans have traditionally believed that opportunity for success should be—and is in fact—equal for all people in society. America was the land of opportunity to which people came from all over the world. This led to the conclusion that the successful are differentiated from the unsuccessful only by their moral virtue, their willingness to work hard and save, and their innate abilities. Recent years have seen the recognition that equal opportunity has never existed for certain segments of society, most notably minorities and women. It has been discovered and admitted that systemic discrimination against these groups is built into the hiring, transfer, and other employment practices of our major institutions.

4. Since there was so much opportunity, Americans have always believed that it was important to make it on one's own in the world—that the world did not owe one a living but that one had to earn his or her own place in society by working hard to make a success of something. The depression years saw the beginnings of a philosophy of entitlement that has grown stronger. People have a right to an income, a job, good health, etc., but despite one's best efforts the marketplace doesn't always provide these. If the market system cannot respect these rights, the government should by becoming the employer of last resort, providing in effect a guaranteed annual income, or providing health care for all its citizens.

5. The tendency to pursue material wealth as a solution to many problems and a national belief in the desirability of economic growth and improved material living standards has been a social goal of the highest priority. This value was questioned in the 1950s and 1960s by many people who dropped out of the system for one reason or another to pursue something more meaningful for themselves than material wealth. It is also under question today because inflation is eroding the standard of living for many people and making it difficult for the nation to maintain a consistent growth in real gross national product.

6. The traditional American attitude toward the natural environment was that it is basically a hostile force to be subdued and exploited as a readily available source of economic growth. Our land and resources were believed to be infinite, and indeed, as the first pioneers saw the vast expanse of the

western region of the country, this belief was a reasonable response. This is so no longer. We know our resources are finite, since we have nearly exhausted some of them. We also know we have to live in harmony with nature and that our environment has deteriorated from many years of exploitation and neglect.

7. Technological progress is closely related to growth—a faith in the ability of science and technology, supported by money and economic resources, to ultimately solve all our problems. New technologies were introduced rapidly into society as a way to sustain growth and make life better. The side effects of many technologies, however, have now become all too apparent, and some technologies, such as nuclear power, are currently being questioned as to whether the risks involved make them worthwhile. Technology is seen as the source of many of our problems.

8. Finally, and in a sense summarizing all the rest, has been the predominance of economic values in our society. This predominance is reflected in the high priority and social approval granted to the economic institutions in our society and the men and women who manage them. Recently, the term "quality of life" has come into vogue as a concept used to broaden people's conception of the kind of life they desire for themselves. Within this conception, social values play an important part along with economic values, which in a sense lose their dominance. From this change comes the pressure to make the corporation respond to social values, to make it into a socioeconomic institution.

These changes in values are not, of course, spread throughout the entire society. They tend to be concentrated among younger people, people with college educations, and people in the middle- and upper-income groups. This concentration may reflect differences in formal education or it may indicate that people are not willing to abandon traditional values until they have attained the material success inherent in the old value system. But it is important to note that values seem to be changing fastest among people who one would expect to have the greatest influence over society's future.

It must also be noted that American society is not in the process of exchanging one set of values for another. But it is changing from a nation with relatively homogeneous values to one in which a variety of values is tolerated and encouraged. This change is consistent with the movement toward a pluralistic society, as such a social structure allows a greater diversity of values to be expressed.

Ideology

The concept of ideology can be understood as a shared set of beliefs that are representative of an individual, group, or an entire society. An ideology is the framework of ideas that integrates and synthesizes all aspects of an individual's, a group's, or a society's being—political, social, economic, and cultural. Ideology legitimizes the institutions of a society and helps make their functions acceptable.[3]

[3]William F. Martin and George Cabot Lodge, "Our Society in 1985—Business May Not Like It," *Harvard Business Review*, Vol. 53, No. 6 (November–December 1975), pp. 149–150.

Others view ideology as a shared belief system that provides a blueprint or map of social reality which serves to guide human behavior in the midst of social and cultural confusion. This view of ideology is held by Clifford Geertz, who focuses on the symbolic significance of ideology and sees ideology as a symbol system that provides information and meaning to a particularly confusing cultural situation. This importance of symbolic activity as a cultural phenomenon is described in the following manner by Geertz:

> They [symbol systems] are extrinsic sources of information in terms of which human life can be patterned—extrapersonal mechanisms for the perception, understanding, judgment, and manipulation of the world. Culture patterns . . . are programs; they provide a template or blueprint for the organization of social and psychological processes, much as genetic systems provide such a template for the organization of organic processes. . . . The reason such symbolic templates are necessary is that, as has been often remarked, human behavior is inherently extremely plastic. Not strictly but only very broadly controlled by genetic programs or models—intrinsic sources of information—such behavior must, if it is to have any effective form at all, be controlled to a significant extent by extrinsic ones.[4]

Cultural symbol systems, then, serve as an external guide or road map for human behavior. Ideologies are symbol systems of this sort that perform such a function. Ideological activity arises in times of strain, and ideologies are crucial to guide behavior when the normal institutional guides for behavior are lacking. Ideologies help people make sense of an otherwise incomprehensible social situation, enabling them to comprehend their rights and responsibilities and act purposefully.[5]

Thus ideologies are a system of shared beliefs expressed symbolically that are a response to cultural, social, and psychological strain, all of which influence each other. The loss of cultural orientation is particularly crucial, because the institutions of that culture can provide no guidelines with which to deal with the strains. Ideologies then arise to fill the gap, and provide guidelines for behavior during a cultural upheaval or transformation when people find themselves in very unfamiliar territory.[6]

While new ideologies may arise during periods of strain, they may actually function all the time, even during periods of relative cultural stability. There is always a certain amount of cultural confusion and thus a need to rely on symbolic meaning systems for guides to behavior. Ideologies that have served well during periods of strain and have brought meaning and purpose to incomprehensible social situations are likely to be relied upon to pattern human behavior for some time.

Ideologies may go through a series of stages such as the following: (1) they arise in response to cultural disorganization and strain and organize this confusion into some new and meaningful whole through a symbolic template that provides a pattern for purposive human behavior; (2) this

---

[4]Reprinted with permission of Macmillan Publishing Co., Inc. from Clifford Geertz, "Ideology as a Cultural System," in *Ideology and Discontent*, David E. Apter, ed., page 63. Copyright © 1964 by The Free Press of Glencoe, a division of Macmillan Publishing Co., Inc.

[5]*Ibid.*, pp. 63–64.

[6]Other writers hold similar views of ideology and its function: Anthony F. C. Wallace, "Revitalization Movements," *American Anthropologist*, Vol. 58 (April 1956); and José A. Moreno, *Barrios in Arms* (Pittsburgh: University of Pittsburgh Press, 1970), especially Chapter 7.

symbol system proves adequate to deal with the situation and becomes widespread throughout the culture; and (3) as the culture becomes settled and reorganized and new institutions develop·to provide guidelines for behavior, the ideology itself becomes routinized and part of the cultural system providing institutional support. At this stage an ideology is no longer attempting to effect change but rather becomes a means of legitimizing a new cultural system and becomes a bulwark used to support the status quo culturally and institutionally.

George Cabot Lodge of Harvard Business School has done some research into the nature of American ideology. He describes five key ideas that comprise the traditional American ideology, based primarily on Lockean notions of private property and individualism. This ideology was new at the time of the founding of the nation but became routinized and formed a widespread set of beliefs providing support for the existing economic and social system. These five key ideas, however, are being challenged by new ideas in contemporary times, giving rise to a new ideology. Exhibit 5.4 shows these two different sets of ideas or beliefs.

EXHIBIT 5.4

Ideological Changes

Five Great Ideas of American Society

1. *Individualism:* This is the atomistic notion that the community is no more than the sum of the individuals in it. It is the idea that fulfillment lies in an essentially lonely struggle in what amounts to a wilderness where the fit survive—and where, if you do not survive, you are somehow unfit. In the political order in this country, individualism evolved into interest group pluralism, which became the preferred means of directing society.

2. *Property Rights:* Traditionally, the best guarantee of individual rights was held to be the sanctity of property rights. By virtue of this concept, the individual was assured freedom from the predatory powers of the sovereign.

3. *Competition:* Adam Smith most eloquently articulated the idea that the uses of property are best controlled by each individual proprietor competing in an open market to satisfy individual consumer desires.

4. *The Limited State:* In reaction to the powerful hierarchies of medievalism, the conviction grew that the least government is the best government. We do not mind how big government may get, but we are reluctant to allow it authority or focus. And whatever happens the cry is don't let it engage in planning. Let it just be responsive to crises and to interest groups. Whoever pays the price can call the tune.

5. *Scientific Specialization and Fragmentation:* This is the corruption of Newtonian mechanics which says that, if we attend to the parts, as experts and specialists, the whole will take care of itself.

New Ideas

1. *Individual Fulfillment Occurs Through Participation in an Organic Social Process:* The community as conceived today is indeed more than the sum of the individuals in it. It has special and urgent needs, and the survival and the self-respect of the individuals in it depend on the recognition of those needs. There are few who can go it alone. Individual fulfillment for most depends on a place in a community, an identity with a whole, a participation in an organic social process.

2. *Rights of Membership Are Overshadowing Property Rights:* This is the right to survive—to enjoy income, health, and other rights associated with membership in the American community or in some component of that community, including a

corporation. The utility of property as a legitimizing idea for the corporation has eroded. Other options to legitimize the corporation are evolving.

3. *Community Need to Satisfy Consumer Desires Is Replacing Competition as a Means for Controlling the Uses of Property:* If in the name of efficiency, of economies of scale, and of the demands of world markets, we allow restraints on the free play of domestic market forces, then other forces will have to be used to define and preserve the public interest.

4. *The Role of Government Is Inevitably Expanding:* It is becoming the setter of our sights and the arbiter of community needs. Inevitably, it will take on unprecedented tasks of coordination, priority setting, and planning in the largest sense. It will need to become far more efficient and authoritative, capable of making the difficult and subtle trade-offs with which we are now confronted.

5. *Reality Now Requires Perception of Whole Systems, Not Only the Parts:* Specialization has given way to a new consciousness of the interrelatedness of all things. Spaceship earth, the limits of growth, the fragility of our life-supporting biosphere have dramatized the ecological and philosophical truth that everything is related to everything else. Harmony between the works of man and demands of nature is no longer the romantic plea of conservationists. It is an absolute rule of survival, and thus it is of profound ideological significance.

Lodge eventually put these ideas together into two paragraphs, which he appropriately labeled Ideology I and Ideology II (see box) and asked a series of questions of *Harvard Business Review* readers about these two ideologies. Responses were received from 1,844 readers in several countries. Most of

IDEOLOGY I

The community is no more than the sum of the individuals in it. Self-respect and fulfillment result from an essentially lonely struggle in which initiative and hard work pay off. The fit survive and if you don't survive, you are probably unfit. Property rights are a sacred guarantor of individual rights, and, to satisfy consumer desires in an open market, the uses of property are best controlled by competition. The least government is the best. Reality is perceived and understood through the specialized activities of experts who dissect and analyze in objective study.

IDEOLOGY II

Individual fulfillment and self-respect are the result of one's place in an organic social process; we "get our kicks" by being part of a group. A well-designed group makes full use of our individual capacities. Property rights are less important than the rights derived from membership in the community or a group—for example, rights to income, health, and education. The uses of property are best regulated according to the community's need, which often differs from individual consumer desires. Government must set the community's goals and coordinate their implementation. The perception of reality requires an awareness of whole systems and of the interrelationships between and among the wholes. This holistic process is the primary task of science.

the people responding were managers of corporations (76 percent), but some were nonmanagement personnel in business (12 percent) and others were professionals, such as doctors and lawyers (10 percent). Only 2 percent of the respondents did not give their occupation.[7]

The most significant findings of this survey are interesting. More than two-thirds of the respondents preferred Ideology I, however many respondents sensed its replacement by a new set of value definitions based on the communitarian principles of Ideology II. Sixty-two percent of the readers regarded Ideology I as the more dominant ideology in the United States at present, whereas 73 percent anticipated that Ideology II would dominate in 1985.[8]

Many readers thought that the transformation from Ideology I to II could lead to social disaster, with burdensome government interference causing the disintegration of business and loss of personal freedom. A minority accepted the change with cautious optimism, acknowledging that many perplexing problems, such as resource shortages, explosive population growth, and environmental degradation, could only be resolved within the framework of Ideology II. Interestingly, while two-thirds of the American respondents regarded Ideology I as the more effective ideological framework for solving future problems, the same proportion of foreign respondents believed Ideology II was more desirable.[9]

Since this survey was done in 1975, the respondents who personally favored Ideology I and believed it was then dominant expected a major ideological transformation in just ten short years. Such a view is well nigh inexplicable on the part of so many managers. It may be, as Lodge suggests, that while Ideology I appeals to a personal level, advocating individual responsibility and personal freedom, Ideology II actually provides a more legitimate basis for modern corporate institutions which are, in effect, communitarian institutions struggling for survival in a world of limited resources, ecological problems, and the like (see box on page 74).[10]

Attitudes

Attitudes are another element of social change. Attitudes have been defined as a mental position with regard to a fact or state of being.[11]
Thus people hold attitudes about all sorts of things just as they do values, but attitudes are probably easier and faster to change in many instances. Particularly important are the American people's attitudes toward business, as current surveys show that business has lost a good deal of credibility in the eyes of the American public.

Surveys taken by the firm of Yankelovich, Skelly, and White, for example, show that confidence in American business has declined steadily in the last

---

[7]Martin and Lodge, "Our Society in 1985," p. 144.
[8]*Ibid.*, p. 145.
[9]*Ibid.*
[10]*Ibid.*, p. 150.
[11]*Webster's New Collegiate Dictionary*, p. 73.

decade, from a high of 70 percent in the late 1960s to a low of 15 percent in recent years. Polls taken by Louis Harris show the same kind of decline.[12] Other polls show that people believe business makes too much profit and that the concentration of power represented by big business is inherently dangerous and untrustworthy.[13]

This decline in confidence must be put in context, however, as business is not the only institution suffering such a decline. The same phenomenon shows up with labor unions and government. The business community has been caught in a downdraft that has swept over much of the social landscape.[14]

Further analysis of the survey data also shows that people have not lost confidence in the economic system. The notions of a market economy and a free enterprise system are still widely supported (see box). People believe the government should not run the economy, but should serve as a regulator-referee, a protector of the public interest. The American public still shows a basic ideological confidence in the system in which business functions.[15]

What the survey data do reflect is a decline in the moral legitimacy of business and other institutions. People question the honesty, dependability, and integrity of some institutional leadership (see box) and believe that business in particular serves its own self-interest by profiteering rather than

[12]Seymour Martin Lipset and William Schneider, "How's Business? What the Public Thinks," *Public Opinion* (July–August 1978), p. 41.

[13]See Alan F. Westin, "Good Marks But Some Areas of Doubt," *Business Week,* May 14, 1979, p. 14, for a somewhat different viewpoint.

[14]Lipset and Schneider, "How's Business?" p. 44.

[15]*Ibid.*, p. 47. See also Daniel Yankelovich, "On the Legitimacy of Business," *Issues in Business and Society,* 2nd ed., George A. Steiner and John F. Steiner, eds. (New York: Random House, 1977), pp. 76–79.

A survey by the Cambridge Survey Research Center in 1976 found that 62% of the people (58% of those identified as liberals) were opposed to socialism. Even Ralph Nader is quoted as saying that "the only thing worse than having a car built by General Motors is to have one built by the government." In 1976 and 1977, Yankelovich, Skelly, and White found that 74% of the public disapproved of the view that the country would be better off if big business were taken over by the government, 62% rejected the proposition that we all would be better off if the government had more control of the economy, and 60% said they would be willing to sacrifice, if need be, to preserve the free enterprise system.

From Seymour Martin Lipset and William Schneider, "How's Business? What the Public Thinks," *Public Opinion,* July–August 1978, pp. 41–42. (*Public Opinion* magazine published bimonthly and held in copyright by the American Enterprise Institute for Public Policy Research, Washington, D.C. 20036.) Quoted with permission.

the legitimate function of profit-making. Profiteering is when business is believed to benefit at the expense of the rest of society, profit-making is when the whole of society benefits.[16] In general, what seems to bother the public is the apparent growth of concentrations of power and the seemingly cynical, self-interested abuse of that power by those at the summits of government, labor, and business.[17] Since 1972, these three institutions have received below average confidence ratings (Figure 5.1).

These attitudes form a rather hostile environment for business as far as public policy is concerned. These attitudes are reflected in questions concerning the governance of corporations, increasing regulation of business, continued attacks on big business including oligopoly and conglomerate mergers, passage of windfall profits tax on the oil companies, efforts to institute some kind of plant closing controls on business to enhance job

U.S. NEWS AND WORLD REPORT RATINGS (1976)

Institution	Ability to Get Things Done	Honesty, Dependability, Integrity
Banks		
Medical profession	High	High
Science and technology		
Corporate business		
Labor leaders	High	Low
Lawyers		
Media		
Political institutions (except Supreme Court)	Low	Low

From Seymour Martin Lipset and William Schneider, "How's Business? What the Public Thinks," *Public Opinion,* July–August 1978, p. 45. Reprinted with permission.

[16]Yankelovich, "On the Legitimacy of Business," p. 78.

[17]Lipset and Schneider, "How's Business?" p. 47.

Figure 5.1. Percent Expressing "A Great Deal of Confidence" in People in Charge of Running Nine Institutions

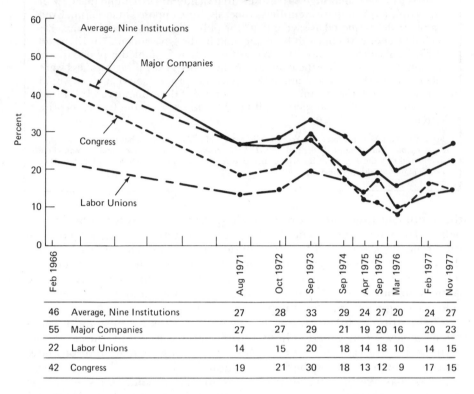

	Feb 1966	Aug 1971	Oct 1972	Sep 1973	Sep 1974	Apr 1975	Sep 1975	Mar 1976	Feb 1977	Nov 1977
Average, Nine Institutions	46	27	28	33	29	24	27	20	24	27
Major Companies	55	27	27	29	21	19	20	16	20	23
Labor Unions	22	14	15	20	18	14	18	10	14	15
Congress	42	19	21	30	18	13	12	9	17	15

From Lipset and Schneider, "How's Business? What the Public Thinks," *Public Opinion*, July-August 1978, p. 45. Reprinted with permission.

security, trends in product liability settlements, and other public concerns. This environment presents challenges to the management of business corporations to understand the society in which business functions and how the public policy process functions so that they can participate in making public policy and develop effective responses to the changing needs and expectations of society.

Social Movements

This element of social change occurs when a number of people come to share a particular value that they believe is worthwhile and ought to be a value of the society as a whole. They organize themselves in some fashion to pursue this objective and precipitate social change. Social movements have been defined as large-scale, widespread, and continuing elementary collective action in pursuit of an objective that affects and shapes the social order in some fundamental aspect.[18] There are certain stages in the development of a social movement, as described below.

1. Dissatisfaction of a group
2. Dramatic events
3. Strategies to obtain social change
4. Emergence of strong leadership.[19]

While social movements have appeared at various times throughout American history, they seemed to proliferate in the 1950s and 1960s. The result was a great deal of social change. The period started with the civil rights movement, which was based on the dissatisfaction of blacks with their status in American society. The dramatic event which precipitated the movement was the refusal of a black woman, Rosa Parks, to move to the back of a bus in Birmingham, Alabama, a customary practice in southern states with Jim Crow laws. This refusal led to her arrest and ignited a social movement throughout the South in support of civil rights for blacks. The strategies of boycotts, nonviolent demonstrations, and marches were used with great success. Leadership was provided by Martin Luther King in particular, along with other prominent people, both black and white. The movement resulted in the passage of new federal laws and a significant change in the opportunities for blacks and other minorities to pursue their interests throughout American society.

The feminist movement grew out of the civil rights movement as many women became dissatisfied with their lot in society. This movement has also used the strategies of boycotts and demonstrations, and its current focus is obtaining passage of the Equal Rights Amendment.

The consumer movement resulted from consumers' dissatisfaction with the quality of products available on the marketplace, the response of companies to complaints, the meaninglessness of warranties, the number of product-related accidents, and similar problems. The dramatic event which sparked the movement was the publication of Ralph Nader's *Unsafe at Any Speed*. Nader also became the most prominent leader of the movement. The strategy used by the consumer movement was primarily exercising pressure in the political system to help pass an enormous amount of consumer legislation.

The same stages are evident in the ecology movement—the writing of books that focused attention on the problem, the use of protests and demonstrations, the use of lobbying tactics to get legislation passed, and the emergence of strong leadership. All of these movements have changed society as a whole, and business behavior in particular, as the end result has been a whole series of social regulations related to the values these movements were pursuing.

[18]Kurt Land and Gladys Engel Lang, *Collective Dynamics* (New York: Thomas Y. Crowell, 1961), p. 490, quoted in Frederick D. Sturdivant, *Business and Society: A Managerial Approach* (Homewood, Ill.: Richard D. Irwin, 1977), p. 100.

[19]Sturdivant, *Business and Society*, p. 101.

General Theories of Social Change

Typing all these elements together into a comprehensive or general theory of social change is a challenge. One such theory, however, which provides an interesting framework for the analysis of social change, is called the mythic/epic cycle of social change. This theory or model grows out of the post-Enlightenment critical study of the history of religions.[20] As the name suggests, this theory consists of two major cycles. The mythic cycle addresses itself to the problem of maintaining a shared sense of meaning and continuity in a society. The epic cycle deals with radical change from essentially one society to another.

According to this theory, societies maintain a shared sense of meaning and a particular vision of reality through myth. Myth is that collection of shared stories which mediate ultimate reality to a given society, and is, therefore, directed toward psyche, internal reality, personal transformation, and process. Societies undergo radical change, however, through the process of an epic struggle of a cultural hero. Epic focuses on history, human relationships, and events. Together these cycles provide a model for a society in equilibrium and a society undergoing radical change.[21]

Applied to a capitalistic system (Figure 5.2), the primal mythical reality is Adam Smith's notion of the invisible hand, a mythical view of reality regarding how a society provides itself with material goods and services. The invisible hand is a secularized version of God, who promises abundance to

Figure 5.2. Mythic/Epic Cycle Applied to Capitalism and Socialism

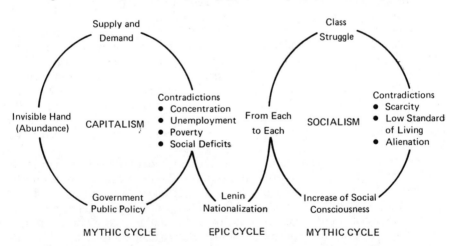

[20]See Owen Barfield, *Poetic Diction: A Study in Meaning* (New York: McGraw-Hill, 1964); Joseph Campbell, *The Hero with a Thousand Faces,* 2nd ed. (Princeton, N.J.: Princeton University Press, 1971); Edward F. Edinger, *Ego and Archetype* (Baltimore, Md.: Penguin Books, 1974); Mircea Eliade, *Patterns in Comparative Religion* (New York: Sheed & Ward, 1958); and Claude Lévi-Strauss, *Structural Anthropology,* translated by Claire Jacobson and Brooke Grundfest Schoepf (New York: Basic Books, 1963).

[21]Ken Kochbeck "The Mythic/Epic Cycle and the Creation of Social Meaning," unpublished paper (St. Louis, Mo.: Washington University, 1979), p. 3.

his people. If the invisible hand is left alone to do its work (laissez faire) and competition prevails, everyone's cup will run over with wealth and riches. People can pursue their own self-interest and society as a whole will benefit. Thus stories of free enterprise and entrepreneurship are all part of this primal reality.

This primal reality is eventually differentiated into a more scientific concept that provides a structural view of the way the system works. This view was provided by the mechanistic concept of supply and demand, that these forces are in effect the invisible hand and allocate resources to the appropriate places and provide full employment for all the members of society willing and able to work.

Eventually, however, contradictions appear that challenge the primal view of reality. The competitive free-enterprise system, left to its own devices, tends towards oligopoly or even monopoly. Thus imperfections of competition appear. Unemployment also appears, particularly during recessions or depressions, which cannot be blamed on the people themselves. Many are not able to share in the abundance a capitalistic society produces and live out the Horatio Alger story. Instead they remain hopelessly rooted in poverty. Social deficits appear in the form of pollution or toxic wastes not disposed of properly.

These contradictions require some sort of mediation if the primal vision of reality on which society rests is to be maintained. In American society, the government becomes the primary mediator to deal with these contradictions through public policy measures, to enable the system to continue functioning. The mythic cycle is profoundly conservative, and as long as adequate mediating terms can be found the society will remain stable. Change will have occurred, of course, but it will not be perceived as such because the change has been incorporated into the original mythic structure.

If these contradictions cannot be successfully mediated or reconciled, however, the epic cycle starts and the old order begins to break apart. The people who are affected by the contradictions express their alienation and oppression in what has been called a lament—a legal petition to the powers governing the universe to intervene. Eventually, a hero appears who delivers the people from their alienation and despair and becomes the leader of the new social order. That order then proceeds to maintain itself through the mythic cycle.[22]

Something like this must have happened in Czarist Russia during the Bolshevik revolution. The contradictions of the capitalistic system could not be reconciled. Eventually a hero appeared (Lenin) who promised to deliver the oppressed people from their despair by abolishing the institutions of a capitalistic society (private property) and founding a new order based on a vision of reality appropriated from Marxist theory.

The primal vision of reality in this order is the myth "to each according to his need, from each according to his ability." The differentiating principle to describe how the system works is the notion of a class struggle. Contradictions that appear include scarcity and a lower standard of living when compared with many nations of the world, but these contradictions are

[22]*Ibid.*, p. 4.

successfully mediated by increasing the social consciousness of the people through purges or propaganda.

Ordinarily, then, societies operate in the mythic mode. Only when the underlying vision of reality on which the social order rests breaks down because of unreconciled contradictions does true epic appear. The epic cycle always deals with radical social change. Usually the outcome of an epic cycle is the establishment of a new social order. Should this not happen, people can face generations of oppression and anarchy. One destroys old myths and gods only at the risk that no new ones may appear to give life meaning and order.

Clearly the time frame for this model is unpredictable. The process of mythic stability can go on for generations, even thousands of years, without serious disruption. Even when the alienation stage is reached, the epic cycle may not take place for generations, or the hero figure essential to triggering rapid and radical social change may appear overnight and the revolution be accomplished in a matter of hours. The model gives no basis for estimating the time parameters for any stage or movement.[23]

Questions for Discussion

1. Distinguish between values and value judgments. What values do you hold? What are some value judgments you have recently made? Where do your values come from?
2. Referring to the value dimensions in Exhibit 5.1, discuss your personal values in relation to the four dimensions of extensiveness, duration, intensity, and prestige of value carriers. Are your values also social values?
3. Which value system (Exhibit 5.2) is dominant in America today? What changes have taken place in the last decade? Which systems have increased in importance? Which have decreased?
4. Discuss the changes identified in the above question in relation to the factors that influence value change. Which factors were most influential in causing these changes?
5. Analyze the specific value changes mentioned in the chapter, using Rescher's model for analyzing value change. Which values have been acquired or abandoned, which have been redistributed, which have been redeployed, etc?
6. What is an ideology? Which definition in the chapter do you like best? Describe the traditional business ideology. Is this also widespread throughout society?
7. What are the implications of Lodge's ideological changes for American business? What problems are inherent in personally holding one ideology and yet believing another will be dominant in society within a few years? How do you explain this phenomenon?
8. What is the difference between attitudes and values? Are values more deeply held? How do attitudes change? What can business do to change American attitudes to make them less hostile to business?
9. Why are Americans hostile toward business? Is this attitude logical? Is it deserved? What specific factors have contributed to the decline of confidence in business leadership? How can this decline be arrested and reversed?
10. Identify some recent social movements and trace them through the four stages of development? Can the impact of social movements be predicted when the movement is beginning? What criteria are relevant for this prediction?

[23]*Ibid.*, p. 7.

11. Describe the mythic/epic cycle. Apply it to other aspects of our society, such as the civil rights movement. Did this movement successfully mediate some contradictions in our political system? What myths are important to this system?
12. Is public policy a mediator for the contradictions that appear over time in a capitalistic society? Besides those mentioned, what other contradictions exist? Which are most important in today's world? Will the government be able to deal with them? If not, will other mediators appear?

Suggested Reading

Allport, G., Vernon, P., Lindzey, G. *Study of Values, Test Booklet and Manual,* 3rd ed. Boston: Houghton Mifflin, 1960.

Baier, Kurt, and Rescher, Nicholas. *Values and the Future: The Impact of Technological Change on American Values.* New York: Macmillan, 1969.

Boulding, Kenneth E. *The Meaning of the Twentieth Century: The Great Transition.* New York: Harper & Row, 1964.

Cavanagh, G.F. *American Business Values in Transition.* Englewood Cliffs, N.J.: Prentice-Hall, 1976.

Ellul, Jacques. *The Technological Society.* Trans. John Wilkinson. New York: Knopf, 1964.

Harvard University, Program on Technology and Society: 1964 to 1972, A Final Review. Cambridge, Mass.: Harvard University Press, 1972.

Lodge, George Cabot. *The New American Ideology.* New York: Knopf, 1978.

McCready, W.C., Greeley, A.M. *The Ultimate Values of the American Population.* New York: Russell Sage Publications, 1976.

Mesthene, Emmannuel G., ed. *Technology and Social Change.* Indianapolis: Bobbs-Merrill, 1967.

Reich, C. *The Greening of America.* New York: Random House, 1970.

Rokeach, M. *The Nature of Values.* New York: Free Press, 1973.

Schumpeter, J.A. *Capitalism, Socialism, and Democracy,* 3rd ed. New York: Harper & Row, 1950.

Sutton, F.X. et al. *The American Business Creed.* Cambridge, Mass.: Harvard University Press, 1956.

Toffler, Alvin. *Future Shock.* New York: Bantam Books, 1970.

6

Business Ethics

We can learn a good deal about the nature of business by comparing it with poker. While both have a large element of chance, in the long run the winner is the man who plays with steady skill. In both games ultimate victory requires intimate knowledge of the rules, insight into the psychology of the other players, a bold front, a considerable amount of self discipline, and the ability to respond swiftly and effectively to opportunities provided by chance.

No one expects poker to be played on the ethical principles preached in churches. In poker it is right and proper to bluff a friend out of the rewards of being dealt a good hand. . . . Poker's own brand of ethics is different from the ethical ideals of civilized human relationships. The game calls for distrust of the other fellow. It ignores the claims of friendship. Cunning deception and concealment of one's strength and intentions, not kindness and openheartedness are vital in poker. No one thinks any worse of poker on that account. And no one should think any the worse of the game of business because its standards of right and wrong differ from the prevailing traditions of morality in our society.[1]

Ethics refers to a conception of "right" and "wrong" in relation to human behavior; thus business ethics refers to "right" and "wrong" behavior in business decisions, such as whether to hire or fire someone, market a new product, or build a new plant or close an old one. While ethical considerations are not necessarily a part of every business decision, they are undoubtedly a part of a good many. Perhaps some decisions are purely technical, but any time human judgment is called for, standards of right and wrong enter into the picture. The ethical part of these decisions generally refers to habits of honesty, compassion, truthfulness, trust, fairness, and other such virtues believed to be valuable traits for a civilized people.

[1]Reprinted by permission of the *Harvard Business Review*. Excerpt from "Is Business Bluffing Ethical?" by Albert Z. Carr (January–February 1968). Copyright © 1968 by the President and Fellows of Harvard College; all rights reserved.

The question raised by Albert Z. Carr in the article from which the lengthy quote was taken to begin this chapter is whether business ethics are different from the ethics of society at large. The answer to this question will set the basic direction for a discussion of business ethics. Carr argues that the ethics of business are game ethics, which are different from the ethics of religion and society. Business has the impersonal characteristics of a game—a game that demands both a special strategy and an understanding of its special ethics.

Business executives, Carr states, are compelled to practice some form of deception. This deception could take the form of conscious misstatements, concealment of pertinent facts, or exaggeration; behaviors that Carr believes are all forms of bluffing. The need to bluff is a central fact of life for business executives, according to Carr: if they feel obligated to tell the truth in all situations, they will be ignoring many business opportunities and putting themselves at a heavy disadvantage in many business dealings.[2]

From this view of business comes the analogy of business with poker. The ethics of poker are different from the ethical ideals of civilized human relationships. Poker calls for distrust, cunning deception, and concealment of one's strengths and intentions. The game of poker ignores the claim of friendship and does not involve kindness and openheartedness. But no one thinks any worse of poker on that account. Such behavior is accepted as part of the game. Thus, if the analogy holds, no one should think any worse of business either because its standards of right and wrong differ from those of society at large.

Business is the main area of competition in our society and it has been ritualized into a game of strategy. The basic rules of this game are set by the government, which attempts to detect and punish outright fraudulent behavior. But as long as a company does not transgress the rules of the game set by law, it has the right to shape its strategy without reference to anything but its profits, and this strategy will sometimes run counter to the ethical ideals of society.[3]

Carr's article, when it first appeared, received a good deal of comment. Some agreed with his basic thrust. One executive, after citing several examples that supported Carr's view of business as being realistic, stated: "What is universal about these examples is that these managers, each functioning on a different corporate level, are concerned with one thing—getting the job done. Most companies give numerous awards for achievement and accomplishment, for sales, for growth, for longevity and loyalty, but there are no medals in the business world for honesty, compassion or truthfulness."[4]

Others disagreed with the thrust of the article, however, and argued that the comparison of business to poker was unfair and inaccurate, that business is too important an area of human endeavor to be regarded as a game. Other readers complained that the article condoned unethical business practices, that a business executive cannot separate the ethics of his or her business life

[2]*Ibid.*, p. 428.

[3]*Ibid.*, p. 433.

[4]Timothy B. Blodgett, "Showdown on Business Bluffing," *Harvard Business Review*, Vol. 46, No. 3 (May–June 1968), p. 163.

from the ethics of his or her home life, and that the article is one-sided and extreme in its description of what goes on in business.[5]

Another criticism stated that the article did not point out that if business fails to raise the moral level of its practices, it invites eventual reprisals from the public and the government. In response to this criticism Carr replied: "This thought was not within the scope of the article, but I could not agree with it more. As the article plainly conveys, sound long-range business strategy and ethical considerations are usually served by the same policy."[6]

This latter point could be the most important of the entire article, and Carr's response seems to undercut the foundations of his argument. For if business is subject to reprisals from government and the public, as Carr admits, and the rules of the game can be changed through law to raise the moral level of business practices, then indeed business ethics are not separate from the ethics of society as a whole. That this is in fact what happens—that the ethics of society influence public policy—will be illustrated by a brief review of the foreign payments controversy, an issue that had many ethical overtones.

The Foreign Payments Controversy

This controversy erupted in the early 1970s as a result of the Watergate investigations into illegal political contributions by corporations to the 1972 reelection campaign of then President Richard Nixon and of the Security and Exchange Commission's investigation into the death of the Chief Executive Officer of United Brands Corporation, who had committed suicide by jumping from the fortieth floor of the Pan American building in New York City, where United Brand's offices were located.

These investigations eventually uncovered the fact that not only had many large corporations made contributions to political campaigns in this country, but the same had been done abroad. And not only were these contributions to politicians for political campaigns, but many payments were also made to agents or government officials to win contracts or win favors of one sort or another. The terms that appeared in the media to refer to these payments were varied, but one frequently used was "questionable," because of the ethics involved.

Foreign payments have been defined as "any transfer of money or anything of value made with the aim of influencing the behavior of politicians, political candidates, political parties, or government officials and employees in their legislative, administrative and judicial actions."[7]

These payments can be classified by legal type, by type of foreign recipient, by mode of payment, and by purpose of payer (see Exhibit 6.1). Regarding legal type, lawful payments include contributions to political parties or candidates in countries where this behavior is not illegal, as it is in this country. Many countries allow corporations to make such contributions.

[5]*Ibid.*, pp. 163–166.
[6]*Ibid.*, p. 170.
[7]Neil H. Jacoby, Peter Nehemkis, and Richard Eells, *Bribery and Extortion in World Business* (New York: Macmillan, 1977), p. 86.

EXHIBIT 6.1 ───────────────────────────────

Classification of Foreign Political Payments by U.S. Multinational Corporations

1. *By Legal Type*
   A. Lawful payments
   B. Bribery
   C. Extortion
   D. Hybrids of bribery and extortion
2. *By Type of Foreign Recipient*
   A. Major government officials—legislative, executive, or judicial
   B. Minor government employees
   C. Employees of government-owned corporations
   D. Political organizations
   E. Candidates for government offices
   F. Politically affiliated news media
   G. Agents, finders, consultants, or representatives
3. *By Mode of Payment*
   A. Cash
   B. Deposits in numbered foreign bank accounts
   C. Overbilling of sales with kickback to the buyer
   D. Gifts of property (watches, jewelry, paintings, "free" samples)
   E. Gifts of services (use of automobiles, aircraft, hunting lodges, payment of rent on homes, country club dues, etc.)
   F. Payment of travel and entertainment expenses
   G. Making unsecured loans—never collected
   H. Putting relatives on the payroll as "consultants"
   I. Providing scholarships and educational expenses for children
   J. Making contributions to charities of the payee's choice
   K. Purchasing property from the payee at an inflated price
   L. Selling property to payee at a deflated price
4. *By Purpose of Payer*
   A. Obtain or retain business
   B. Reduce political risks
   C. Avoid harassment
   D. Reduce taxes
   E. Induce official action

Even where such payments were unlawful, it does not seem appropriate to call them bribes, as they were not meant to abuse government authority.[8]

A bribe is a payment made to induce the payee to do something for the payer that is improper and is an inducement to any person acting in an official or public capacity to violate or forebear from his or her public duty. Extortion, on the other hand, is a situation in which the recipient of the payment is the initiator and the motivating force behind the payment is a threat of harm to the payer. Sometimes it is difficult to tell the difference between a bribe and extortion, and some actions, such as facilitating payments to customs officials to speed customers' clearances, are a little of both or hybrids.[9]

[8]*Ibid.*, p. 89.
[9]*Ibid.*, pp. 90–91.

Such transfers of value were made to a variety of recipients, as shown in Exhibit 6.1, and by various modes of payments. The most frequent purposes of such payments were to obtain or retain business in the foreign country, reduce the political risks by having a government favorable to foreign business in power, avoid harassment by governments, reduce taxes on exports or facilities, and induce official action such as customs clearances for goods or health clearances for employees of the company.[10]

Once a few companies were discovered to have made payments of these types, the SEC developed a voluntary disclosure program to, among other things, discover how widespread this action was among American corporations. In March 1974, the SEC announced that any company which had made illegal political contributions or other foreign payments should disclose that fact to its shareholders and to the commission. This program was based on the SEC's mandate to protect shareholders' interests and enforce their right to full disclosure of "material" information, defined as encompassing all those matters of which an average prudent investor ought reasonably to be informed before purchasing securities. With respect to foreign payments, materiality was defined as (1) cases where the payment itself was large, (2) situations where the payment itself was not necessarily large but where it related to large transactions or where the deals were an important part of the firm's total business, or (3) cases where the payoff reflected on the lack of integrity of management, especially top management, in setting up overseas slush funds and secret bank accounts from which the payments were made but which investors knew nothing about.[11]

Under this program, news stories appeared day after day describing yet another corporation that had discovered such payments and was making this fact public knowledge. The SEC made investigations of its own and pressured companies to make some kind of settlement. Eventually 527 companies, including some of the largest corporations in the country, were alleged to have made foreign payments over a six-year period to foreign governments and agents. Some of the largest payments were attributed to Exxon ($59.4 million), Lockheed ($55.0 million), Boeing ($50.4 million), and General Tire and Rubber ($41.3 million).[12]

Business tried to defend these practices by explaining that these payments were a necessary cost of doing business—that payments of this kind were an accepted practice in other countries. Business was transacted in many of these countries through agents who collected high fees for their services and passed some of this money on to government officials. In other cases, government officials were paid directly to award favors to companies. Customs officials were paid low salaries or wages with the expectation that their income would be supplemented by payments from foreign corporations. When in Rome, one had to do as the Romans, and we should not impose our ethical standards on other countries. In addition, if companies in this country did adhere to "higher" standards, the business would simply go to a non-American corporation that was not so virtuous and we would be shut

[10]See *Ibid.*, pp. 92–122.
[11]Richard L. Baravick, "The SEC Unleashes a Foreign Payoffs Storm," *Business and Society Review,* No. 19 (Fall 1976), pp. 48–50.
[12]"Business without Bribes," *Newsweek,* February 19, 1979, pp. 63–64.

out of many foreign markets. One company, for example, defended its payments with these words:

> The discontinuance of such payments at this time would needlessly hamper the conduct of the business of the company in numerous foreign locations, would contravene local practices, in some cases would imperil the safety of Company employees on the protection of its property, and would be detrimental to the best interests of the stockholders.[13]

The public's concern about these payments was based, on the one hand, on the belief that such payments corrupted the free enterprise system, under which the most efficient producers with the best products are supposed to prevail. As put by one treasury official: "When the major criterion in a buyer's choice of a product is the size of a bribe rather than its price and quality and the reputation of its producers, the fundamental principles on which a market economy is based are put in jeopardy."[14] Such payments were believed to subvert the laws of supply and demand and result in free markets being replaced by contrived markets.

On the other hand, the public's concern for these payments stemmed from our beliefs about the proper relationships between the economic and political systems, and the behavior of public officials and private managers. The idea that official power vested by the state in a government official can be bought and sold on the marketplace is repugnant to the American mind. We make a clear separation between business and government, between the commercial and the political, and draw a boundary line between marketable goods and services and nonmarketable political rights, duties, and authority.[15]

Despite the pleas of business for an acceptance of special ethics in this case, the government continued its relentless pursuit. The SEC continued to apply pressure for disclosure of these payments. The Internal Revenue Service developed a special audit program of companies suspected of having slush funds. It was believed that some companies may have committed tax fraud by deducting payoffs as expense on income-tax returns. The Federal Trade Commission investigated possible antitrust violations in countries where only American competitors were involved. The Treasury Department accused one company of violating the Bank Secrecy Act, which requires anyone transporting more than $5,000 between the United States and a foreign country to file a report with the government.[16]

Eventually, a new public policy measure was passed by Congress and signed by the President, the Foreign Corrupt Practices Act of 1977. This law makes it illegal to pay money or give anything of value to a foreign official, foreign political party, or any candidate for foreign political office for purposes of (1) influencing any act or decision of such foreign official or foreign political party or party official or candidate in his or its official capacity (including a decision to fail to perform his or its official functions) or

---

[13]Gordon Adams and Sherri Zann Rosenthal, *The Invisible Hand: Questionable Corporate Payments Overseas* (New York: The Council on Economic Priorities, 1976), p. 5.

[14]*Ibid.*, p. 3.

[15]Jacoby et al., *Bribery and Extortion*, p. 127.

[16]*Ibid.*, pp. 45–85.

(2) inducing such foreign official or political party or party official or candidate to use his or its influence with a foreign government (or instrumentality thereof) to influence any act or decision of such government or instrumentality. The law does not cover facilitating or so-called grease payments that are intended merely to move a matter toward an eventual act or decision not involving discretionary action, such as payments or gifts to a customs duties officer of a foreign government to facilitate the passage of material to a plant. The penalties for violations of these provisions are up to $1 million for a corporation, and up to $10,000 and five years in jail for individuals found guilty of violations.[17]

Separate and apart from these antibribery provisions, this law also amends the Securities Exchange Act of 1934 to require registrants to maintain reasonably complete and accurate books and records and to devise sufficient systems of internal accounting controls to prevent payments from being hidden through the use of "creative" accounting methods. Failure to comply with these accounting provisions could also result in fines and imprisonment.[18]

Conceptions and Misconceptions About Business Ethics

The subject of business ethics is a complicated one, and there are no easy answers to questions about ethics. But as the foregoing discussion attempted to indicate, ethics is an important dimension of management and has a definite influence on public policy. The foreign payments controversy had many clear ethical implications related to honesty and fairness, and while business tried to plead that special ethics were involved which should be accepted by the American public, such an argument did not prevail as far as public policy was concerned.[19] The Foreign Corrupt Practices Act makes American business subject to the ethical standards of American society in its business dealings abroad.

Some believe that ethics, particularly honesty, provides the moral foundation for a free enterprise system. According to this view, ethics involves more than being honest, but honesty is the beginning point of ethics and is a basic working social principle and not just a moral guideline. Ethics should be equated with fairness and justice as well as honesty, but the conditions for

[17]An Analysis of the Foreign Corrupt Practices Act of 1977 (Chicago: Arthur Andersen & Co., 1978), pp. 3–5.

[18]Ibid., pp. 7–11.

[19]The argument that foreign countries adhered to a different set of ethical standards than ours in regard to business dealings was somewhat spurious anyway. As a result of corporate political contributions, Italy enacted new legislation to provide for government financing of political campaigns as well as to require public disclosure of all contributions of more than $1,600. Honduras considered nationalization of the banana-growing lands of United Brands. Threats of nationalization were also heard in Costa Rica and Peru. Former Japanese Prime Minister Kahuei Tanska, along with other business and government leaders, was accused of accepting $1.7 million from Lockheed Corporation in payoffs. These disclosures shook Japanese politics to its foundations. Prince Bernhard of the Netherlands was stripped of many of his official duties because of allegations of accepting payoffs from Lockheed to influence the decision about fighter aircraft in its favor. The ultimate in dealing with bribery comes from the Soviet Union (see box).

HOW THE RUSSIANS DEAL WITH BRIBERY

Reprinted from *U.S. News & World Report*

The Soviet Government has just served notice that bribery in connection with Russia's growing trade with the Western countries is risky business.

The death sentence has been meted out to a Soviet official who was found guilty of soliciting and receiving bribes in return for placing contracts with a foreign supplier. And the Swiss businessman who was convicted of making the payments has been sentenced to 10 years in prison.

News of the bribery case—said to be the first of its kind involving foreign trade—appeared in a Government weekly magazine, *Nedelya,* which gave these details—

Yuri S. Sosnovsky, director of a Russian Government furniture-manufacturing organization, approached the businessman, Walter Haefelin, at a trade exhibition in the Soviet Union in 1973. They agreed that the Russian agency would purchase machinery through Haefelin and that Sosnovsky would receive payments concealed in the price of the equipment.

On the first contract, Sosnovsky received about $140,000 in rubles plus about $7,000 worth of goods.

In July, 1974, Haefelin was arrested at the Moscow airport on a flight from Prague, Czechoslovakia. He was carrying about $65,000 in rubles as a first payment to Sosnovsky on another contract.

Merely bringing rubles into the country is itself a crime under Russian law.

Haefelin reportedly co-operated with the police in order to improve his own chances of being expelled instead of imprisoned.

Altogether, the magazine article indicated, millions of dollars in contracts were involved in the dealings of the two men, and the Government, in effect, paid about a half million dollars extra as a result of the bribes.

Both men appealed their sentences. Further word of their fates has not yet appeared.

From "Why Americans Pay Bribes to Do Business Abroad," *U.S. News & World Report,* June 2, 1975, p. 58. Copyright 1975 U.S. News & World Report, Inc.

fairness and justice derive from honesty. According to this viewpoint, "the first and most basic principle necessary to make a private enterprise economy work is to keep the game honest. The illicit payments by international companies strike at the ethical foundations of capitalism, under which all decisions are to be made on their economic merits, and further undermine the credibility of the free enterprise system in countries where it is already suspect or under attack."[20]

Such a strong view of ethics seems to assume a direct connection between ethics and economics, that good ethical behavior is consistent with rational economic behavior. Such an easy identification of ethics with economics is suspect. Being ethical does not always lead to profitability. The inability to pay foreign officials and agents to win contracts has hurt some American companies overseas, and some exporters complain that the new law will further increase the U.S. trade deficit. On the other side of the coin, there

[20]Jack N. Behrman, remarks in brochure describing the Ethics Resource Center founded under the auspices of American Viewpoint, Inc., p. 19.

are undoubtedly many instances when unethical behavior has led to business success. Being ethical is not always good business.

The reason for this is simple. Ethical behavior is not necessarily rewarded in the marketplace. Consumers and investors do not have ethical information about the companies from which they buy products or in which they invest. Employees and the general public are in the same position. Consumers do not know if the prices they pay were set honestly and fairly. Investors do not know if the company in which they hold stock has always engaged in honest competition, either in this country or abroad. Prospective employees do not know if the management of a company has been honest and fair in its dealings with the work force. And the general public does not know if companies follow the law in all regards. Even if this information were available, it may have no bearing on the purchase or investment decision anyway.

Many situations in management present ethical dilemmas. Should one make a decision based on one's own sense of ethics or make a decision that may violate those ethics but make good business sense? This dilemma was stated some years ago by Benjamin and Sylvia Selekman as the technical must versus the ethical ought. Ethical considerations are only oughts, they stated, while technical business considerations are always musts or necessities. Technical business matters are the ultimate values—a technical business necessity is a must that always takes precedence over an ethical ought that would be nice to follow but is simply not practical.[21]

This way of stating the ethical dilemma finds a modern expression in a book by Arthur Okun, which deals with the egalitarian emphasis in current society. Okun states that equality in the distribution of incomes as well as rights is a humanistic ideal that represents his ethical preference. But, given the realities of the modern business system, which depends on inequality of income to motivate people, equality is not practical. "Any insistence on carving the pie into equal slices," he says, "would shrink the size of the pie. That fact poses the tradeoff between economic equality and economic efficiency. . . . Although the ethical case for capitalism is totally unpersuasive, the efficiency case is thoroughly compelling."[22]

Related to these views is that of William C. Frederick, who argues that ethical ideals will not provide answers to problems of finance, personnel, production, and general management decision-making. The businessperson's role is defined largely, though not exclusively, in terms of private gain and profit, and to suggest that this can be set aside for adherence to a set of ethical principles which may conflict with that role is startlingly naive and romantic. The businessperson, says Frederick, is locked into a going system of values and ethics that largely determine the actions that can be taken. There is little question that at any given time individuals who are active within an institution are subject in large measure to its prevailing characteristics.[23]

[21]Benjamin and Sylvia Selekman, *Power and Morality in a Business Society* (New York: McGraw-Hill, 1956).

[22]Arthur M. Okun, *Equality and Efficiency: The Big Tradeoff* (Washington, D.C.: The Brookings Institution, 1975), pp. 48, 64.

[23]William C. Frederick, "The Growing Concern over Business Responsibility," *California Management Review*, Summer 1960, pp. 58–59.

These views seem to err in the opposite direction from an easy identification of ethics and good business, and make ethics seem unimportant and irrelevant in business and economic considerations. There must be a middle ground somewhere. Society can change the rules under which institutions operate and define new rules for business management. This has happened throughout American history as society has made certain kinds of practices—price fixing, division of territories, price discrimination, and now foreign payments—illegal because they were deemed to be unfair and hence unethical methods of competition. Thus the ethical dimension is an important consideration for management, along with many other dimensions, because of its implications for public policy. Business management can step out of bounds, so to speak, regarding society's ethical standards, and society will take action through the public policy process to bring business back into line.

Ethics, as pointed out by Roland McKean, become public policy concerns because ethics are in some sense public goods. Habits of trust, friendliness, neatness, fairness, generosity, and nonviolence are to some extent public goods that are produced by the observance of behavioral traditions.[24] But as public goods, ethical behavior is subject to the free rider and other problems associated with these goods. Foreign companies are now profiting in some countries at the expense of American companies who can no longer legally make payments to agents or foreign government officials. The only answer to this situation is some international ban on payments that establishes uniform rules of the game for all business and thus keeps everyone in the same competitive position.

Studies of Business Ethics

Some recent studies of ethics in American business have been completed that may give insight into the state of business ethics today. An article in the *Harvard Business Review,* written by Brenner and Molander, entitled "Is the Ethics of Business Changing?" was based on a questionnaire survey of 1,227 HBR readers, most of whom were managers of business corporations. This study was compared to a similar study conducted in 1961 by Raymond C. Baumhart, to see what changes, if any, had occurred.[25] The following general conclusions emerged from the Brenner and Molander study.

1. With regard to ethical dilemmas, the respondents were asked if they had ever experienced a conflict between what was expected of them as efficient, profit-conscious managers and what was expected of them as ethical persons. In 1961, three out of four respondents reported they had experienced such conflicts, compared with only four out of every seven respondents in the 1977 study. While this is only a slight decrease, the nature of the conflicts had changed. Honesty in communication was much more of a

---

[24]Roland N. McKean, "Collective Choice," *Social Responsibility and the Business Predicament,* James W. McKie, ed. (Washington, D.C.: The Brookings Institution, 1974), pp. 120–122.

[25]Steven N. Brenner and Earl A. Molander, "Is the Ethics of Business Changing?" *Harvard Business Review,* Vol. 55, No. 1 (January–February 1977), pp. 57–71.

contemporary problem, while conflicts associated with firing and layoffs and pricing practices were not as important as before. Most of the contemporary ethical dilemmas occurred in relations with supervisors, customers, and employees. That such dilemmas existed in these studies lends empirical support to the idea that ethical standards and business practices do come into conflict in many situations.

2. Another question dealt with generally accepted business practices that the respondents regarded as unethical. While nearly four-fifths of the respondents indicated that such practices existed in 1961, only two-thirds responded affirmatively to this question in the 1976 survey. Again, the nature of these practices had changed. There was a substantial drop in concern over price discrimination and unfair pricing, price collusion, dishonesty in contracts, and dishonest advertising, and a sharp increase in concern over unfairness to employees and prejudice in hiring, and cheating customers. The authors concluded that these changes are probably attributable to government enforcement and higher legal standards.

3. If these studies can be legitimately compared, the results might be taken to show a slight improvement in business ethics, but such a statement must be made very cautiously. There was substantial disagreement among the respondents themselves as to whether ethical standards had changed from what they were 15 years previously. Fifty percent of the respondents in the 1976 survey believed that ethical conduct is not necessarily rewarded in the business organization, that their supervisors often did not want to know how results were obtained, as long as the desired outcome was achieved. Another 43 percent felt that competition was stiffer than ever, resulting in practices that were considered shady but necessary for business survival.

4. The factors influencing ethical standards are shown in Table 6.1. Public disclosure and concern about unethical business practices are the most potent forces for improvement in ethical standards. These were quite obviously important factors in the foreign payments controversy. The general decay in social standards is by far the most important factor causing lower ethical standards in business. None of these factors are under the control of business, which reflects the earlier point made about the influence of ethical standards in society as a whole over ethical standards in business.

5. The respondents to the 1976 survey were somewhat more cynical about the ethical conduct of their peers than was true of the earlier survey. This attribute was measured by asking the respondents to deal with four case situations. Half the sample was asked what *they* would do in the situation, the other half was asked what they thought the *average executive* would do.

The responses of these two groups to the four cases in the 1976 survey differ more than the responses of the earlier Baumhart study to similar questions. One of these cases dealt with the making of a foreign payment that could help land a large contract. Forty-two percent of the respondents said they would refuse to make such a payment no matter what the consequences, while only 9 percent felt that the average executive would do the same. Furthermore, seven-eighths of the respondents who reported that the average executive would see such payments as unethical believed that he or she would go ahead and make them anyway.

This tendency to view oneself as more ethical than one's peers has also

TABLE 6.1 **Factors Influencing Ethical Standards**

Factors Causing Higher Standards	Percentage of Respondents Listing Factor
Public disclosure; publicity; media coverage; better communication	31%
Increased public concern; public awareness, consciousness, and scrutiny; better informed public; societal pressures	20
Government regulation, legislation, and intervention; federal courts	10
Education of business managers; increase in manager professionalism and education	9
New social expectations for the role business is to play in society; young adults' attitudes; consumerism	5
Business's greater sense of social responsibility and greater awareness of the implications of its acts, business responsiveness; corporate policy changes; top management emphasis on ethical action	5
Other	20
Factors causing lower standards	
Society's standards are lower; social decay; more permissive society; materialism and hedonism have grown; loss of church and home influence; less quality, more quantity desires	34%
Competition; pace of life; stress to succeed; current economic conditions; costs of doing business; more businesses compete for less	13
Political corruption; loss of confidence in government; Watergate; politics; political ethics and climate	0
People more aware of unethical acts; constant media coverage; TV; communications create atmosphere for crime	9
Greed; desire for gain; worship the dollar as measure of success; selfishness of the individual, lack of personal integrity and moral fiber	8
Pressure for profit from within the organization from superiors or from stockholders; corporate influences on managers; corporate policies	7
Other	21

Note: Some respondents listed more than one factor so there were 353 factors in all listed as causing higher standards and 411 in all listed as causing lower ones. Categories may not add up to 100 due to rounding errors.

Reprinted by permission of the *Harvard Business Review.* Exhibit from "Is the Ethics of Business Changing?" by Steven N. Brenner and Earl A. Molander (January–February 1977). Copyright © 1977 by the President and Fellows of Harvard College.

been found in other studies.[26] Apparently, this is a common phenonome-non, but the crucial question is which response is more realistic—the way people believe they would act or the way they believe their peers would behave in a given situation.

Another survey recently completed dealt with the purchasing function in corporations rather than with management in general. The purchasing function often finds itself in the center of concern about business ethics. Some believe that purchasing departments are largely responsible for im-

[26]See John W. Newstrom and William A. Ruch, "The Ethics of Management and the Management of Ethics," *MSU Business Topics,* Winter 1975, pp. 29–37.

proper payments in the form of bribes, kickbacks, gratuities, and other white-collar crimes.[27]

The purchasing function, operating between a firm and outside suppliers, is to a large extent a guardian of the company's reputation for honesty and fair dealing. Purchasers—both the purchasing managers and buyers—spend millions of dollars of their company's money each year. They wield tremendous economic power and receive considerable attention from suppliers. They are normally under significant pressures, particularly in a gray area such as ethics, to bend the rules a bit for their company's or their own benefit.

This survey was based on results obtained from 66 senior industrial purchasing managers and 136 industrial purchasers from manufacturing companies who were members of the Minneapolis-St. Paul area chapter of the National Association of Purchasing Management.

Gifts, entertainment, and trips plus preferential treatment for certain suppliers were the two main kinds of ethical questions that concerned senior purchasing managers, no matter what size their firm (Table 6.2). On the question of gifts, accepting free sales promotion prizes or "purchase-volume incentive bonuses" is seen as an ethical issue by just over 80 percent of the purchasing managers, and nearly 60 percent consider free trips, free meals, and other free entertainment as ethically significant. Distinctions are made here, though. One manager said, "A trip to Hawaii and a fishing trip by car to a lake 100 miles away are two different situations."

Preferential treatment for certain suppliers is also considered ethically relevant. Informing a supplier of a competitor's quote and allowing him or her to rebid was noted as an ethical question by nearly 80 percent. And about two-thirds of the purchasing managers saw ethical questions in practices of preferring suppliers who are good customers, exaggerating the seriousness of a problem to gain concessions, and favoring suppliers preferred by their own firm's higher management. Over 60 percent of the managers also are concerned about the personality of the seller entering into the supplier selection process. Some think the personality makes no difference, while others feel it can determine how the order will be serviced.

Many of the practices listed in the survey were considered to be merely part of the negotiating game: using buying power leverage to obtain concessions, inventing a second source to gain an advantage, and asking suppliers for information about competitors.

The managers are also relatively unconcerned about the ethics of "back-door selling" (circumventing the purchasing department), soliciting quotations from suppliers who have little chance of success, and cancelling a purchase order in progress while also trying to avoid cancellation charges.

Closely related to these ethical issues are the key relationships that underlie them. Purchasers work as individuals, as part of their purchasing departments, as members of the entire organization, and with suppliers. These relationships and the conflicts they engender probably make purchasing personnel more powerful than their salaries or positions on the organization chart indicate. This second part of the survey shows how the larger

[27]William Rudelius and Rogene A. Buchholz, "What Industrial Purchasers See as Key Ethical Dilemmas," *Journal of Purchasing and Materials Management,* Vol. 15, No. 4 (Winter 1979), pp. 2–10. Quoted with permission.

TABLE 6.2 Respondents' Attitudes Toward Certain Purchasing Practices

Practices	*Percent Replying "Definitely Yes" or "Probably Yes"*		
	An Ethical Problem?	*Have Stated Policy Now?*	*Want a Stated Policy?*
1. Acceptance from a supplier of gifts like sales promotion prizes and "purchase volume incentive bonuses."	83%	71%	89%
2. Giving a vendor information on competitors' quotations, then allowing him to requote.	77	55	86
3. Acceptance of trips, meals, or other free entertainment.	58	70	83
4. Preferential treatment of a supplier who is also a good customer.	65	45	68
5. Discrimination against a vendor whose sales people try to deal with other company departments directly rather than go through purchasing.	35	38	62
6. Solicitation of quotations from new sources, when a marked preference for existing suppliers is the norm, merely to fill a quota for bids.	23	37	59
7. To a supplier, exaggerating the seriousness of a problem in order to get a better price or some other concession.	68	28	57
8. According special treatment to a vendor who is preferred or recommended by higher management.	65	28	56
9. Attempting to avoid a cancellation charge when the cancellation involves an order already being processed by the source.	40	22	52
10. Allowing personalities—like of one sales representative or dislike of another—to enter into supplier selection.	63	24	46
11. Use of the company's buying power to obtain price or other concessions from a vendor.	22	29	46
12. To obtain a lower price or other concession, informing an existing supplier that the company may use a second source.	34	26	42
13. Seeking information about competitors by questioning suppliers.	42	19	34

Source: William Rudelius and Rogene A. Buchholz, "Ethical Problems of Purchasing Managers," *Harvard Business Review,* Vol. 57, No. 2 (March–April 1970), p. 12. Copyright © by the President and Fellows of Harvard College.

group of purchasing managers at several levels, buyers, and assistant buyers interpret these relationships and the ethical questions that arise from them.

The buyers see their most important relationships as those with present and potential suppliers, and, equally, with their purchasing or materials managers, as is indicated in Figure 6.1. Next in importance are their relationships with other company departments, with higher levels of management, and with other buyers, in that order.

Ethical questions emerge from these relationships in different degrees.

Figure 6.1. Five Key Relationships for Industrial Buyers

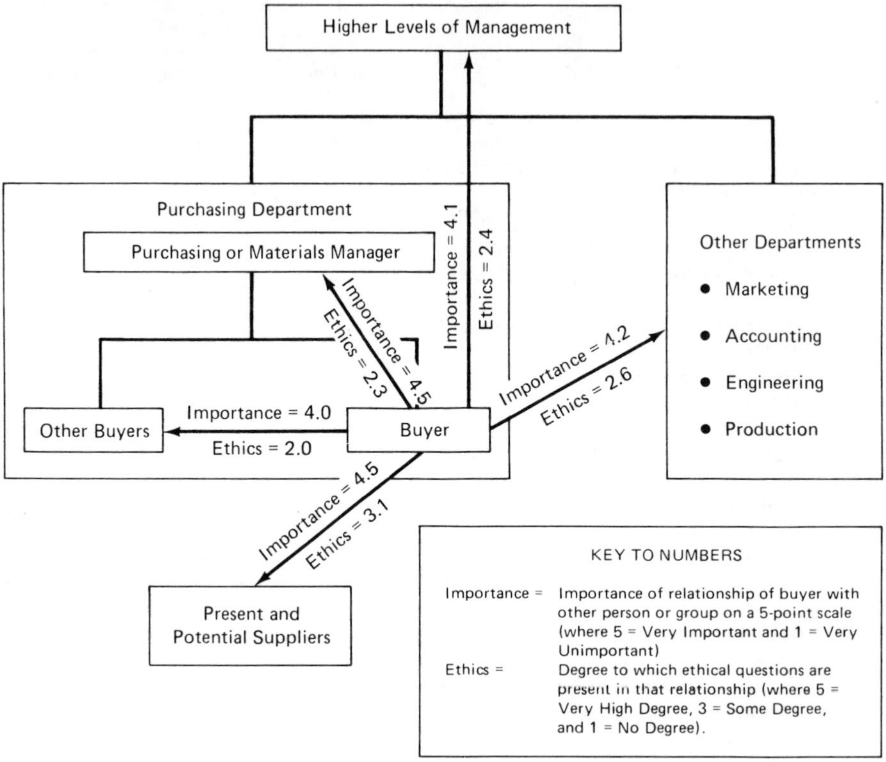

From William Rudelius and Rogene A. Buchholz, "What Industrial Purchasers See as Key Ethical Dilemmas," *Journal of Purchasing and Materials Management,* Vol. 15, No. 4 (Winter 1979), p. 8. Reprinted with permission.

The problems occur most often in the purchaser-supplier relationship. But ethics also appear relevant in the purchaser's relationships with the marketing, accounting, engineering, and production departments. Engineering may prefer that a contract be awarded to a high quality but expensive supplier, while the purchaser's own department is trying to meet a 5 percent cost reduction target, for example.

Ethical issues with management are only slightly less significant, according to the purchasing personnel. Unrealistic management goals, for example, are thought ethically important by many of the purchasers, whether the goals come from purchasing managers or from higher levels of management. And having new suppliers added, especially minority or foreign vendors, is also considered an ethical question by some purchasers.

The fewest ethical problems, not surprisingly, were noted in the purchasers' relationships among themselves. A few cited the example of a buyer not devoting enough time to train and assist new buyers.

Ethical Codes as a Response

In response to ethical conflicts, many companies have adopted ethical codes. Some companies have had such codes for some time, others were developed in response to the Watergate crisis and the foreign payment controversy. A study by Coopers and Lybrand examined the ethics code of twenty-one major corporations in a variety of industries. The topics covered in these statements are shown in Exhibit 6.2. In general, the study concluded that many of these companies were broadening and updating their codes to include a wider range of issues.

Some of the functional areas in companies, such as purchasing, have their own code of ethics related to specific practices in that function.[28] In addition to determining what specific purchasing practices presented ethical dilemmas, the Rudelius and Buchholz study also asked whether the respondent's companies had a stated policy on certain purchasing practices, and whether the respondents wanted a stated policy.[29]

EXHIBIT 6.2 ————————————————————————————

Topics Covered in Ethics Policy Statements

Most Frequent
Basic guidelines
Conflicts of interest
Proprietary information
Political contributions and activities
Outside activities
Off-book transactions
Improper transactions and payments
Relations with the community
Antitrust compliance
Treatment of company property
Equal opportunity

Less Frequent
Policy extends to subsidiaries and affiliates
Obligation to and relations with shareholders
Compensation is restricted solely to salary and stated benefits

Role of internal auditors
Role of independent auditors
Role of board of directors
Working conditions, basis of promotions, and other employee relations
Espionage and sabotage
Prohibition of loans to personnel
Fidelity bond coverage
Influencing foreign exchange markets
Product safety
Dealings with news media

Implementation Matters Covered Within the Policy Statement
Dissemination and administration of ethics policy
Procedures for reporting and dealing with ethics violations
Signed acknowledgment of policy

From "Corporate Ethics," *Coopers & Lybrand Newsletter,* Morton Meyerson, ed., Vol. 20, No. 6 (June 1978), p. 6. Reprinted with permission.

As shown in Table 6-2, explicit ethical policies for purchasing are most common in coverage of gifts, entertainment, and trips; about 70 percent of the senior managers mentioned company policies here. One of them com-

[28]See Rogene Buchholz and William Rudelius, "Purchasing Standards Revisited," *Journal of Purchasing and Materials Management,* Vol. 14, No. 3 (Fall 1978), pp. 23–26.
[29]William Rudelius and Rogene A. Buchholz, "Ethical Problems of Purchasing Managers," *Harvard Business Review,* Vol. 57, No. 2 (March–April 1979), pp. 12, 14.

mented, "The best guideline I ever heard was: If you want it, don't accept it, because it could influence your decision. If you don't care whether you have it, don't take it, because someone will think you wanted it."

Less common an area for management policy is allowing certain suppliers inside information on quotes and an opportunity to requote. About 55 percent of the companies regulate this practice. One purchaser views the problem this way: "I want quoters to know where they stand. However, I do not believe in allowing requotes just so the quoter can get the order. Only if there are mistakes do I allow a requote."

None of the other practices listed is covered by stated policy at a majority of the companies surveyed. Nearly all of the very largest companies, however, have standard policies on such practices as reciprocity and soliciting vendors for information on competitors. Clearly, the bigger companies feel a compulsion to "get it in writing."

A striking aspect of the responses to the questionnaire is the degree to which the purchasing managers desire a stated policy. This desire is so even in regard to practices they don't consider unethical, such as retaliation against a supplier who tries to circumvent the purchasing department. In part this may be attributed to "yea saying" in reaction to situations where the ethical problem is not obvious.

Perhaps more important, purchasing managers see themselves as caught between suppliers, with whom they try to develop good relations (and who are sometimes favored by management), and their own superiors, who expect them to maintain, if not reduce, their cost levels. It is not surprising that purchasers want top management to make the tough, ethically uncertain decisions for them by establishing blanket policy.

Preferential treatment of certain suppliers probably presents the most complex challenge. This is clearly an ethical issue that lacks the underpinning of management policy and involves the pulls of loyalties and disloyalties among people and their organizations rather than merely the elemental tug toward a free dinner.

Purchasing managers also are asking for more direction in three areas of organizational protocol and procedure, even though they do not generally see them as ethical issues—backdoor selling, soliciting "extra" quotations, and conditions of cancelling purchase orders.

Purchasing officials do not want management to dictate policy affecting certain aspects of their jobs. According to the vote on question 10, the majority feels that the personal relationship between seller and buyer cannot be legislated. The same holds true with regard to the power politics of their positions, as evidenced by the responses to the last three questions listed. One manager called them "good purchasing practices anyway."

The Brenner and Molander study also asked questions about codes of ethics. Twenty-five percent of the respondents said they favored no code at all. Of those who did favor a code of ethics, 58 percent preferred one dealing with general precepts while only 17 percent preferred one dealing with specific industry practices. Despite this low percentage favoring codes, the majority of respondents believe that such a code would help executives to raise the ethical level of their industry, define the limits of acceptable conduct, and refuse unethical requests.

The respondents in the 1976 survey were less certain of a code's usefulness than were the respondents in Baumhart's 1961 survey. They generally believed that a code is limited in its ability to change human conduct, as 61 percent believed that people would violate the code whenever they thought they could avoid detection, and only 41 percent believed the code would reduce underhanded practices.

The ethical dilemmas people in business experience and the factors that have the greatest impact on business ethics suggest that ethical codes alone will not substantially improve business conduct. One of the major problems with such codes is their enforceability (what group within the corporation should have the power and authority for enforcement), the difficulty of getting information about violations, and the problem of uniform and impartial enforcement.

Clearly, a written policy cannot be drawn up to cover every ethical difficulty faced by corporate employees. Yet, in general, written policies can help employees handle the usual situations (and the vast majority of situations are usual) in a consistent way that helps achieve the organization's goals.

Among key advantages of written policies are that they (1) focus management and employee attention on vital problems to provide sounder, more logical solutions, (2) communicate the importance of the policy to those affected by it as the collective standard of the organization ("If it's in writing, it's got to be important"), (3) provide a degree of legal protection for the organization, (4) provide justification for a person to act the way he or she really wants to act anyway ("Of course I'd like to go fishing with your group in Canada, but we have a company policy that says no"), (5) set limits on an individual who might be tempted, and (6) identify the penalty for not following the policy.

But there are also disadvantages associated with written policies. For example, they (1) can require substantial amounts of time and money to develop and communicate to employees, (2) are often difficult to operationalize—to tie general policy statements to specific problems, (3) can suggest, by implication, that everything not explicitly covered is acceptable practice, when it is not, and (4) compel management action to penalize offenders for violations.[30]

Management must weigh the benefits and costs of written policies dealing with ethical problems in business. When policies become too detailed, they run the dual dangers of being increasingly inflexible and of going unread. Perhaps the most realistic statement about the usefulness of ethical codes is the following quote from the Brenner and Molander study. After analyzing the data concerning the dilemmas encountered, the practice respondents would most like to eliminate, and the factors causing shifts in standards, they asked where ethical codes could have an impact.

> In general the responses suggest that codes can be most helpful in those areas where there is general agreement that certain unethical practices are widespread and undesirable. Ethical codes do not, however, offer executives much hope for either controlling outside influences on business ethics or resolving fundamental ethical dilemmas. This is not to minimize the potential for codes to have an impact

[30]Rudelius and Buchholz, "Key Ethical Dilemmas," p. 15.

in narrow areas of concern. It is to emphasize that regardless of form they are no panacea for unethical business conduct.[31]

Questions for Discussion

1. What is the thrust of Albert Z. Carr's argument concerning ethics and business? Do you agree with his position? Why or why not?
2. What are foreign payments? For what purposes were they made? Who received them? Were they necessary to do business in foreign countries?
3. Why was the Securities and Exchange Commission concerned with these payments? What authority did it have to get involved in this controversy? What kind of a program did it develop?
4. How did business attempt to defend these payments? Was this defense justified? Do you agree with the position taken by business? Why or why not?
5. Why didn't the public accept the "necessity" of such payments? What basis did the public have for concern? What was the result of the controversy?
6. What were the ethical issues raised in the foreign payments controversy? Why did businesspeople ignore these issues? What kind of a control system would you set up to prevent such payments from being made in the future?
7. The statement is made in the text that being ethical is not always good business. What argument is used to support this position? Do you agree or disagree with this position?
8. What is an ethical dilemma? Think of some recent situations where you faced such a dilemma. How was it finally resolved? What factors influenced your behavior? Which factors were dominant?
9. In what sense is ethics a public good? How does the free rider apply? What is the best way for society to provide itself with this good?
10. What important points are raised by the Brenner and Molander article? Have the ethics of business changed? For better or for worse? What evidence is relevant to your answer?
11. Why do people generally view themselves as more ethical than their colleagues? What behavioral characteristics are important in this phenomenon? Which view do you believe is the most realistic?
12. What ethical problems do purchasers face? Are these important problems? How would you resolve them? What relationships have the most potential for ethical problems?
13. Why do businesspeople want ethical policies? What function do these policies perform? Are they useful? Write a code of ethics for students. How should this code be enforced?
14. What is the difference between a general precept code and one dealing with specific industry practices? Which do you prefer? Which is likely to be most effective?

Suggested Reading

Adams, Gordon, and Rosenthal, Sherri. *The Invisible Hand: Questionable Corporate Payments Overseas.* New York: The Council on Economic Priorities, 1976.

Baumhart, Raymond. *An Honest Profit: What Businessmen Say about Ethics in Business.* New York: Holt, Rinehart & Winston, 1968.

Clark, John W. *Religion and the Moral Standards of American Businessmen.* Cincinnati: South-Western Publishing Co., 1966.

[31]Brenner and Molander, "Ethics," p. 68.

DeGeorge, Richard T., and Pichler, Joseph A., eds. *Ethics, Free Enterprise, and Public Policy.* New York: Oxford University Press, 1978.

Frankena, William K. *Ethics,* 2nd ed. Englewood Cliffs, N.J.: Prentice-Hall, 1973.

Hill, Ivan. *The Ethical Basis of Economic Freedom.* Chapel Hill, N.C.: American Viewpoint, 1976.

Jacoby, Neil H., Nehemkis, Peter, and Eells, Richard. *Bribery and Extortion in World Business.* New York: Macmillan, 1977.

Selekman, Benjamin, and Selekman, Sylvia. *Power and Morality in a Business Society.* New York: McGraw-Hill, 1956.

Silk, Leonard, and Vogel, David. *Ethics & Profits.* New York: Simon & Schuster, 1976.

Sufrin, Sidney C. *Management of Business Ethics.* London: Kennikat Press, 1980.

Towle, Joseph W., ed. *Ethics and Standards in American Business.* Boston: Houghton Mifflin, 1964.

Walton, Clarence C. *Ethos and the Executive: Values in Managerial Decision Making.* Englewood Cliffs, N.J.: Prentice-Hall, 1969.

———, ed. *The Ethics of Corporate Conduct.* Englewood Cliffs, N.J.: Prentice-Hall, 1977.

7

Corporate Governance

It is essential to the conduct of business operations to have a decision process which can adapt quickly, flexibly and boldly to changes in the marketplace and in competitive behavior. This process functions best when there is a substantial degree of decentralization of initiative and operating decision-making to the level of management with the best access to the facts.

Moreover, an effective decision process requires an hierarchical organization so that there will be clear lines of authority to resolve differences and clear accountability for results. Again this process requires strong leadership at the top—a strong chief executive officer—to select, assign and motivate people and to set overall standards and directions.

However, despite its crucial role, operating management does not stand in an independent relationship either to the owners of the enterprise or to the corporation's constituencies in the larger society. Operating management derives its authority and legitimacy from the board of directors.

We think it appropriate that most of the discussion in the last few years on improvements in the system of corporate governance has focused on the functioning of the board of directors. This focus is undoubtedly based on a widespread appreciation of the practical obstacles to enlarging the role of share owners in the conduct of corporate affairs.[1]

Environmental influences are currently at work in society that are directed right at the very heart of the corporation itself—the internal control or governance of the corporation. The term *corporate governance* refers to the process by which decisions are made within the corporation itself as to the allocation of corporate resources. Many critics of business question the

---

[1] *The Role and Composition of the Board of Directors of the Large Publicly Owned Corporations* (New York: The Business Roundtable, 1978), pp. 6–7. Quoted with permission.

legitimacy of this process and see the corporate form of organization, at least as it has evolved over the years, as a public policy problem in and of itself, and have advocated various types of reform measures.

These measures undoubtedly stem at least in part from abuses of power by those who run the modern corporation—illegal campaign contributions in this country, the maintenance of secret slush funds for payments to foreign officials, the seeming unconcern of the management of some corporations for the safety of their products. But there is good reason to believe that even if such abuses had not occurred, the issue of corporate governance would still have emerged.

In a sense, corporate governance has been a latent issue since the growth of the large industrial corporation with power over vast resources. Such large corporations are not run democratically: the one man, one vote principle does not apply to corporations as it does to government (instead voting rights are based on share ownership), most employees have no say in the major decisions that are made by the corporation, and the public at large, many of whom may not own any stock at all but whose lives are affected by corporate decisions, are even further removed from having any internal control. There has thus existed for some time a fundamental conflict between the way in which our economic organizations are governed and the democratic principles upon which our government is based. It seems inevitable that this conflict should have surfaced at some time, and that it has at this particular time may be due more to the educational level of the population and other factors than to any specific abuses of power.

Before we deal with reform measures directed at the corporate form of organization, it will be useful to take a closer look at who actually does control the modern corporation. What people or groups make most of the major decisions in the corporation? What evidence or theories exist that would help us answer these questions?

Control of the Modern Corporation

Shareholders. Theoretically, the shareholders control the corporation. They own the property and have certain legal rights to see that this property is used to further their interests. Figure 7.1 shows how this process is supposed to work. The shareholders meet once a year in an annual meeting to listen to a review from management of corporate performance and to elect a board of directors. This board of directors, in turn, elects the management and officers of the company to run the corporation on a day-to-day basis. The board meets periodically to receive reports from management and exercise an overseer function to protect the interests of the shareholders. Management, in turn, exercises a derived authority over the rest of the employees to direct their activities to accomplish corporate objectives.

The ultimate control over the corporation thus rests in the property rights held by the stockholders. Stockholders have legal rights to exercise their control through the voting mechanism described above, and if desired and necessary, by challenging actions of corporate management in the courts when circumstances leave them no other feasible alternative. The final right

Figure 7.1. The Formal Legal System of Control

of shareholders, of course, is to dispose of the property they own by selling their ownership certificate.

That this system does not work out in practice as spelled out by theory should come as no surprise to anyone acquainted with the modern corporation. Share ownership of most major corporations is widely dispersed throughout society so that no one person owns a large enough block of the stock to make a difference in the voting outcome at an annual meeting. This dispersion, with many people holding a small amount of shares, means that they do not think of themselves as owners of the corporation but as investors who hope to make an adequate return on their investment. If they feel this return is not adequate, they do not go to the management of the company or the board of directors and demand better performance. They go to their stockbroker and sell the stock and get into something else that seems to hold more promise. As far as voting rights are concerned, investors simply send their signed proxy statements back to the company, perhaps without even reading them.

Because of this dispersion of stock ownership, there has been a change in the way stockholders perceive themselves. This change has been described by the well-known thesis of Berle and Means regarding the separation of ownership and control in the modern corporation.[2] The owners of the large corporations do not have control over corporate resources. Individually, they have little or no power to affect change. Because of the change in stockholders' perceptions of themselves, it is difficult to organize them in significant numbers even to attend an annual meeting and exercise the collective power they have in theory.

[2] Adolf A. Berle and Gardiner C. Means, *The Modern Corporation and Private Property* (New York: Macmillan, 1932).

These facts about the modern corporation were documented by Berle and Means in their 1932 classic (see Exhibit 7.1). Using data about share ownership obtained from various sources, and establishing certain categories of control, the crucial one being the 5 percent cutoff point, they determined that 44 percent by number and 58 percent by wealth (assets) of the largest 200 nonfinancial corporations at that time were under control of the management. No dominant stock-interest owned even so much as 5 percent of the stock in these corporations, which Berle and Means concluded was the minimum needed to exercise some influence.

This kind of study was updated in 1971 by Robert Larner, who at that time had access to different sources of stock ownership (Exhibit 7.2). Larner also changed the critical cutoff point from 5 percent to 10 percent, concluding that it took at least a 10 percent interest by an individual or compact group that would vote as a unit to exercise any influence. Under these assumptions, Larner found that as of 1963, 85 percent of the top 200 corporations were controlled by management. Thus there is some evidence to support the idea that stock ownership is widely dispersed in many corporations, providing an

EXHIBIT 7.1

Berle-Means Study

I. Sample

The 200 largest nonfinancial corporations ranked according to assets as of around January 1930. Used estimated asset figures. Data collection period: 1928–29, 1930–31.

II. Sources

Standard's Corporation Records (1929–31)
Moody's Manuals (1930)
The New York Times (1928–30)
The Wall Street Journal (1928–30)

III. Classifications

Private: ownership of 80% or more of the stock by a compact group of individuals
Majority: ownership of 50–80% of the stock
Minority: ownership of 20–50% of the stock
Legal Device: pyramiding arrangement which led to a considerable separation of ownership and control
Management: dominant stock interest of less than 5%. From 5–20% classed as joint minority-management control

IV. Findings

	Number	Wealth
Private Ownership	6%	4%
Majority Ownership	5%	2%
Minority Ownership	23%	14%
Legal Device	21%	22%
Management Control	44%	58%

Adapted from Adolf A. Berle and Gardiner C. Means, *The Modern Corporation and Private Property* (New York: Macmillan, 1932). Used with permission.

EXHIBIT 7.2

Robert Larner Study

Sample: The 200 largest nonfinancial concerns ranked by assets as of 1963.

Sources: Corporate proxy statements
Stock ownership information submitted annually to the SEC on the 10K Form
Reports filed with the FPC and ICC

Classification: Control defined as the holding of 10% or more of the voting stock. Otherwise the same as the Berle-Means study.

Findings:

	Number	Wealth
Private Ownership	0%	0%
Majority Ownership	2.5%	1%
Minority Ownership	9%	11%
Legal Devices	4%	3%
Management Control	84.5%	85%

	Nonmanagerial Interests
Manufacturing and Mining	27% of top 290
Merchandising Concerns	39% of top 33
Transportation Companies	13% of top 45
Public Utilities	2% of top 120

Adapted from Robert J. Larner, *Management Control and the Large Corporation* (New York: Dunellen, 1971). Used with permission.

empirical foundation for the theory about the separation of ownership and control.

Management. If one accepts this evidence and buys the theory of the separation of ownership and control, management not only runs the company on a day-to-day basis but also exercises ultimate control over corporate resources. Critics of the corporation are quick to point out that management controls the proxy machinery; they select the proxies that appear on the ballots sent to shareholders and naturally will select proxies who will elect directors who will in turn reappoint the existing management. Thus management becomes self-perpetuating in this sense.

Furthermore, it is alleged that the board of directors is ineffectual in protecting stockholder rights. Many companies have boards composed of a majority of inside directors (officers of the company). Those outside directors who are on the board are "buddies" of management—officers of other corporations, investment bankers, and the like—who share the same values as management and are not likely to raise any serious opposition to management's policies. Since the chief executive officer of the company is in many cases also chairman of the board, he or she sets the agenda for board meetings and controls information going to the board members. There were instances, such as in Lockheed Corporation (see Chapter Eight), where the board members were supposedly unaware of the financial plight of the company and were as surprised as anyone when the real condition of the company became public knowledge.

From these allegations comes the image of a small group of unknown managers controlling the resources of the large corporations in our society, and thus exercising vast powers over almost every facet of American life. These managers, so the image goes, are beholden to no one but themselves, going through the ritual of directors meetings and annual meetings that have no real purpose other than to perpetuate a myth of stockholder control. Whether this image is true or not is unimportant: the crucial point is that many people believe it is true, and out of this rather marked contrast with a democratic system of control come pressures for reform of corporate governance.

Family Control. Challenging the notion of a widespread diffusion of stock ownership is the rather common knowledge that in some corporations, at least, a large block of stock is held by a prominent wealthy family, such as the Mellon family. Presumably, these families can control a corporation in which they have substantial holdings because they can be expected to vote their stock more or less uniformly and take an active interest in the running of the company because they have such a large stake in its performance. Thus they would seem to have the power to influence management policies and even replace management, if necessary, with people more to their liking.

This phenomenon was studied by Robert Sheehan in a 1967 *Fortune* article. The sources of his information were not disclosed in the article, which raises a question of validity, but in any event he determined that 17 percent of the top 200 corporations in the country were controlled by wealthy families who owned a substantial block of stock (Exhibit 7.3). In

EXHIBIT 7.3 ──

Robert Sheehan Study

Sources: Not identified. Failed to identify either Gulf or Alcoa as being under family control, which raises a serious question of validity.

Classification: Corporations ranked according to volume of sales as of 1966. Control defined as holding of 10% or more of voting stock.

Findings:

Family Control
11% of top 100
17% of top 200
24% of top 300

Ford family holds 11% of Class B Shares (3.492 votes per share), which in terms of votes means 39% of the company.

DuPont family owns 30% of Christiana Securities, which in turn owns 29% of E.I. duPont de Nemours.

The four Firestone brothers own 15% of Firestone Tire and Rubber.

The Danforth family controls 22% of Ralston Purina.

The Pitcairn family holds 26% of Pittsburgh Plate Glass.

The Pews and their family trusts maintain 44% of Sun Oil Company.

addition, he identified some of the corporations that were controlled by families.

The most complex of any of these studies that deal with stock ownership was done by Philip Burch in a 1972 book entitled *The Managerial Revolution Reassessed.* Using a variety of information sources, employing a cutoff point of 4 to 5 percent (the same as Berle-Means), and looking at representation on the board of directors in addition to stock ownership, Burch concluded that 39.5 percent of the top 200 industrial corporations in 1965 were probably under family control, and another 17.5 percent were in the possible family control category (Exhibit 7.4). That left 43 percent ostensibly under management control, with no significant stock ownership or board representation to indicate family control. Burch also examined ownership for the top 50 banks, transportation companies, and merchandising establishments.

EXHIBIT 7.4

Philip Burch Study

Sample: Used *Fortune*'s 1965 list of the top 500 industrial corporations, concentrating on the first 300. Also appraised the top 50 merchandising firms, top 50 transportation companies, and the top 50 commercial banks.

Sources:

Standard and Poor's Corporation Records
Fortune (1950–71)
Time (1955–71)
Business Week (1955–71)
Forbes (1955–71)
The New York Times (1960–71)
Moody's Manuals
1963 House Select Committee on Small Business Report

Classification:

Probably Family Control: (1) 4–5% of stock held by family, group of individuals, or an individual; (2) inside or outside representation on the Board of Directors.

Possibly Family Control: definite signs of family influence but insufficient data to make a reliable assessment.

Probably Management Control: no significant stock ownership or representation on board to indicate family control.

Findings:

	Probably Management	Possibly Family	Probably Family
Top 50 Industrials	58%	22%	20%
Top 100 Industrials	44%	20%	36%
Top 200 Industrials	43%	17.5%	39.5%
Top 300 Industrials	41.3%	16%	42.7%
Top 50 Merchandising	28%	14%	58%
Top 50 Transportation	46%	18%	36%
Top 50 Banks	48%	22%	30%

Reprinted by permission of the publisher, from *The Managerial Revolution Reassessed* by Philip H. Burch, Jr. (Lexington, Mass.: Lexington Books, D. C. Heath and Company, 1972; copyright D. C. Heath and Company)

Thus there is some evidence to indicate that families do exercise control by owning large blocks of stock in some companies or being represented on the board of directors. But this potential for control may not be exercised. Perhaps the members of the family have no particular interest in overseeing the running of a business but are more interested in enjoying their wealth. Unless there is someone in the family with a good business sense and an active interest in business, the potential for control may never be exercised. And even if one desires to do so, it is not always easy to exercise influence over an entrenched management.

Institutional Share Ownership. Anyone acquainted with the stock market knows that financial and other kinds of institutions own substantial blocks of stock in many major corporations. One of the first people to point out this phenomenon argued that already in 1970, financial institutions, not individual investors, were the dominant influence in the stock market. Thus the market had entered the era of the institutional investor.[3]

As of 1970, Barber noted, mutual funds, pension funds, and insurance companies, all with varying degrees of bank involvement, owned more than a third of all stocks listed on the New York Stock Exchange. At that time, some 10 million people were purchasing $5 billion worth of shares a year of over 200 mutual funds. In 1967, these funds reported assets of over $50 billion, which was fifty times their 1948 holdings. In 1940, only four million jobholders were covered by pensions, and the reserves for these pensions totaled less than $2.5 billion. But in 1970, more than 28 million people were covered by pensions, and the assets had swollen to $80 billion, half of which was invested in common stock.[4]

Much of this institutional money became concentrated in bank trust departments. In 1973, it was estimated that bank trust departments controlled $330 billion of the $500 billion worth of securities held by all institutional investors. Two banks, Morgan Guaranty and Bankers Trust, held more stocks and bonds than all the 500 mutual funds in existence at the time. By 1980, another $150 billion of investment money was expected to flow into their coffers. Much of this money was invested in a few dozen growth stocks, which meant that these banks came to have significant holdings in some major American corporations. There was some concern about this because it meant that many corporations not considered "blue chip" companies were finding it difficult to raise equity capital.[5]

A more recent study dealing with all financial institutions, not just banks, shows the potential clout these institutions can exercise (see box). Couple the holdings of these financial institutions with the holdings of universities, churches, and foundations, and institutions indeed have the potential to

---

WHERE THE BIG BLOCKS ARE

Way back in 1932, Adolf A. Berle and Gardiner C. Means showed in *The Modern Corporation and Private Property* that one can control a corporation by controlling even a minority of its shares. Hence it is no surprise that today's

---

[3]Richard J. Barber, *The American Corporation* (New York: Dutton, 1970).
[4]*Ibid.*, pp. 54–59.
[5]"The Storm over the Billions that Trust Officers Invest," *Business Week,* September 15, 1973, pp. 161–166.

institutional investors—bank trust departments, pension funds, insurance companies and the like—exert great influence over companies and securities markets. Just how concentrated, however, is such influence? In 1975 Congress ordered the SEC and other regulatory bodies to supply it with new information on who owns what. Armies of lawyers descended upon the capital, arguing that such disclosure would be costly and difficult, and so far only one agency (the ICC) has compiled a report.

But Montana Democratic Senator Lee Metcalf asked Senate Aide Victor Reinemer last June if he could not do better. With the help of two assistants and a research firm called Corporate Data Exchange, Reinemer drug through tons of information, most of it on the public record, involving 122 major corporations. Last week the study was published. Of the firms, 56 either had more than 5% of their shares voted by a single institutional investor, had more than 10% controlled by five or fewer such investors, or had 10% owned by a single family. Among the top five stockholders in each of the 122 companies, twelve investors showed up more than half the time. New York's Morgan Guaranty Trust was the No. 1 stockholder in 27 corporations. Morgan, Citibank, Chase Manhattan and other top investors also appeared as the principal shareholders in each other.

Morgan Guaranty was quick to respond. Said a spokesman: "Where are the examples of abuse?" Indeed, the study shed a lot more light on the extent of stock-power concentration than on its effects, good or ill.

Investor	No. companies in which it has the most stock votes	No. companies in which it is among the top five stockholders
Morgan Guaranty Trust	27	56
Citibank	7	25
Teachers Insurance & Annuity	2	24
Capital Research & Management	2	19
Prudential Insurance	4	18
Dreyfus Corporation	4	17
National Bank of Detroit	5	17
Kirby Family Group Alleghany Corp.	4	16
BankAmerica Corp.	1	15
Fidelity Management & Research Corp.	2	13
Manufacturers Hanover	1	12
Bankers Trust	0	11
First National Bank of Chicago	2	11
Lord, Abbett & Co.	2	11
Equitable Life Assurance	2	10
First National Bank of Boston	0	10
Harris Trust & Savings	2	10
Chase Manhattan Corp.	3	8
Continental Ill. Natl. Bank & Trust	3	8

exercise control over many corporations. But until a few years ago, this potential was apparently not exercised, as the institutions themselves acted much like individual investors. Their major concern was financial return, and if they did not like one stock, they shifted out of it into another. They rarely opposed management on any issue, and apparently routinely sent in their proxies as did individual investors.

Employees. Employees in this country exercise control primarily through labor unions. Elected representatives of the employees' choosing bargain with management every three years over wages and working conditions. There is thus far no direct representation of employees on boards of directors in this country on any significant scale, as is true of some countries in western Europe. Unions seemed unconcerned about having representation at the board level to exercise some influence over corporate policies as a whole, not just those concerned with wages and working conditions.[6] The collective bargaining process, in those companies where unions exist, gives employees an indirect influence over the allocation of corporate resources.

John Kenneth Galbraith, however, has developed an interesting theory about the modern corporate organization and its structure.[7] He invented a new term, "technostructure," to describe decision-making within the corporation. The technostructure refers to all persons who contribute specialized information to group decision-making in the organization. This technostructure consists of management, technical specialists, scientists, and other people, depending on the type of decision.

Galbraith's point is that the complexity of modern technology makes it impossible for top management to possess enough knowledge to make a decision that will work in the corporation's best interests. They have to rely more and more on specialists within the organization and include them in the decision-making process. This need for information from numerous individuals derives from the technological requirements of modern industry. Decision-making and control have moved from the top of the organization down into lower levels, involving more and more employees. Power has thus shifted to some degree to those who possess knowledge rather than just status or position.

Foreign Control. Recently another aspect of control over American corporations has appeared on the scene, that of foreign ownership. This is of particular concern since so much money is being transferred to OPEC countries in payment for oil, and much of that money finds its way back to this country, which provides better investment opportunities than elsewhere. According to W. T. Grimm & Co., the Chicago-based merger specialists, there were 199 acquisitions of American concerns by overseas companies in 1978, up 23 percent from 1977, and that increase came during a year when the number of mergers overall declined by 5 percent.[8]

---

[6]Douglas Fraser, head of the United Auto Workers union, did obtain a seat on Chrysler's board of directors in 1980. This seems due to the unique Chrysler situation, however, rather than the beginning of a trend.

[7]John Kenneth Galbraith, *The New Industrial State* (Boston: Houghton Mifflin, 1967).

[8]"Foreign Firms Continue Buying U.S. Companies," *New York Times*, February 25, 1979, 111, p. 1.

For all of 1979, foreign direct investments in the United States by number increased to 1,070 transactions from only 334 in 1978. The total value of these transactions increased to $12.5 billion in 1979 from $6.1 billion in 1978, as estimated by the Commerce Department. The chief foreign investors were Britain, France, the Netherlands, West Germany, Switzerland, and Canada.[9]

Whether this foreign ownership will become a major factor in corporate control remains to be seen. Nonetheless, Congress from time to time has expressed concern with rumors of requiring corporations to disclose their major shareholders so any foreign influence can be seen, and putting a limit on the proportion of shares of any one U.S. corporation that can be owned by foreign sources. The obvious solution, should a foreign source come to own a substantial share of an American corporation, is to nationalize the company and confiscate the property. This is said tongue-in-cheek and is not advocated as a serious policy. However, such action is not outside the realm of possibility (see box).

Reform of Corporate Governance

The structure of corporate governance and the opportunities provided for input from various segments of society is apparently not sufficiently democratic for many critics of corporations. One of the basic questions asked by reformers is whether decisions made in large corporations are sufficiently representative of society as a whole so that not only are the private interests of the corporation a factor but that the broader public interest is also taken into account. From these concerns comes a good deal of activity to reform the internal structure of corporations and open up the process of decision-making to a wider set of influences.

The U.S. Senate in 1978, under the leadership of Senator Howard M. Metzenbaum (D-Ohio), held hearings to explore "what, if anything, the American people should be doing to make corporations more accountable to their stockholders and to the public." The Securities and Exchange Commission in the same year held public hearings to reexamine the commission's rules relating to shareholder communications, shareholder participation in the corporate electoral process, and corporate governance generally. The Federal Trade Commission formed a task force on corporate accountability to study the inside decision-making processes of the corporation.[10] With all this activity questioning the legitimacy of the private corporation, it would be useful to take a closer look at the major areas of reform.

Increased Disclosure. The purpose behind increased disclosure is to make the corporation more responsible to stockholders' interests, and perhaps secondarily to society as a whole. Reforms in this area, in fact, could be seen as attempts to make the present system work better by providing shareholders with more information on which to base their investment

[9]"Foreign Investors Doubled Investment in U.S. during 1979," *The Wall Street Journal,* April 9, 1980, p. 2.
[10]"New Fire in the Drive to Reform Corporation Law," *Business Week,* November 21, 1977, pp. 98–100.

ALIEN CORPORATIONS CAN'T OWN PROPERTY IN OKLAHOMA, ITS ATTORNEY GENERAL RULES

Special to *The Wall Street Journal*

OKLAHOMA CITY—The state's attorney general ruled that alien corporations can't own property here, raising the specter that millions of dollars of foreign-owned property could be confiscated without recompense.

The new opinion results from an investigation of alien ownership ordered by the state legislature and both says nonresident corporations can't own property and spells out that the law requires the attorney general and district attorneys to start legal proceedings to confiscate the property.

It isn't known how much property is involved or precisely what companies own it, but Attorney General Jan Eric Cartwright said 45 corporations are included, based in Canada, Italy, Switzerland, West Germany, The Netherlands, Britain and the Arab nations.

The properties include farmland, motels, shopping centers, industrial parks, apartments and office buildings. The attorney general has indicated that he expects to take action soon to divest alien owners of their Oklahoma holdings.

But another official who would be involved, Oklahoma County District Attorney Andrew M. Coats, said the ruling raises some legal questions, such as:

"What percentage of a corporation has to be foreign, and what happens when an American corporation is formed by Oklahomans in the Bahamas for tax reasons? There is also a problem of foreign ownership of corporate stock, for example, in General Motors. What about a minority stockholder or people from other countries who form Oklahoma corporations?"

Mr. Coats says his understanding is that aliens wouldn't be reimbursed if their property were confiscated, and that while that mightn't be fair, "it is a matter of what the law is."

There are exceptions allowing alien ownership, such as an alien resident or one who inherits land or gains it through foreclosure. But if the resident leaves, he must dispose of his holdings within five years, and those who hold it through inheritance or foreclosure have five years to get rid of it, too.

In addition to the new ruling, the attorney general is asking the legislature to tighten the rules further by requiring purchasers of land for somebody else to swear that the buyers aren't aliens or to indicate who the final owners will be. It had been ruled earlier that alien individuals couldn't own property, and the latest move extends that to corporations.

decisions. The chairman of the SEC, Harold Williams, warned business that it must tell its shareholders more to make the corporate accountability process work in its present form, or the pressures may become irresistible for the more radical reform measures related to federal chartering, federal standards, or some other kind of federal governance of the American corporation.[11]

The primary force for increased disclosure in recent years has been the

[11]"Business Must Tell Holders More or Face Tougher U.S. Controls, SEC Chief Warns," *The Wall Street Journal*, September 30, 1977, p. 10.

SEC, but the establishment of the Financial Accounting Standards Board (FASB) in 1973 continues the effort at self-regulation in establishing uniform standards of disclosure. Recently, for example, the FASB unveiled an inflation accounting proposal that would require most large companies to present a new kind of income statement as a supplement to the familiar earnings statement. Items such as cost of goods sold and depreciation would be based on current cost in order to measure the impact of inflation. In addition, companies would be asked to provide a five-year summary of such major financial items as sales, income, assets, and dividends to enable investors to see just how much of an impact inflation was making. If this proposal is eventually accepted by industry, it could replace the SEC replacement-cost requirement for 10-K annual reports issued in 1976, which ordered the nation's top corporations to restate their assets on a replacement-cost basis and refigure the additional depreciation expense.[12]

Thus one area of disclosure of current interest is adjustment of financial statements for the effects of inflation to show profits more accurately. Another requirement for increased disclosure of recent origin is line of business reporting, a requirement imposed by the SEC that was unsuccessfully fought in the courts by business for some years. This type of disclosure requires business to report sales and earnings for each component of a company with over 10 percent of total sales and earnings. Supposedly, this information would help investors determine which lines of business are most profitable and be a factor in their investment decisions.

Other areas of disclosure include an SEC ruling in 1974 requiring companies to disclose a five-year history of financial statistics, a 1978 SEC requirement that all proxy statements disclose the economic and personal relationship of members of boards of directors, the requirement of the Foreign Corrupt Practices Act of 1977 for disclosure of foreign payments, and new SEC rulings pertaining to disclosure of executive compensation to include not only salaries and bonuses, but also deferred compensation, fringe benefits, and nonsalary compensation, which are commonly referred to as "perks" and are usually buried in the footnotes of annual reports. Besides inflation accounting, another area currently being discussed by the SEC is the disclosure of profit projections, management forecasts, management plans and objectives, and future capital structure and dividend policies.

Thus the SEC has been particularly active in the last decade in revolutionizing the disclosure rules of American corporations. An interesting question regarding this increased disclosure, of course, is whether all the new information is really of use to stockholders. More research is needed on this question, but at least one study concluded that stockholders did not find the majority of proposed disclosures truly useful in their investment decisions. The additional effort required by reporting companies to provide this additional information may exceed the potential use to stockholders.[13]

Boards of Directors. Another attempt to make the current governance process work better is the effort to reform the board of directors to make it more responsive to the interests of the owners. Three trends toward reform

---

[12]"More Fine Tuning for Inflation Accounting," *Business Week,* June 11, 1979, pp. 93–94.

[13]Larry B. Godwin, "CPA and User Opinions on Increased Corporate Disclosure," *The CPA,* July 1975, pp. 31–35.

of boards began in the late 1970s. The first was a change in the composition of boards to include more outside directors. In some cases this change went so far as to change the board from a majority of inside directors to a majority of outside directors. This is accomplished by either expanding the board or simply dropping some inside members from it. The Chairman of the SEC, Harold Williams, once suggested that the ideal board should have just one management director and he should not be the chairman.[14] While companies are not likely to go that far, Korn/Ferry International, a New York based executive search concern, predicts that the number of inside directors will continue to drop until the average at medium-size and large corporations is two or three compared with the current average of four to seven.[15]

The second trend is that these new outside directors are rarely quasi-insiders such as the company's legal counsel, banker, major supplier, or retired officer. Instead they usually have no ties to the company itself that would make them beholden to management. They are more likely to be college professors, executives of unrelated concerns, professional directors, or representatives of civil rights and consumer groups. The representation of women and minority-group members has also increased.[16] The use of independent outside directors once advocated by Chairman Williams seems to be occurring.

The third trend is the development of board committees to perform various functions. Perhaps the most important committee is the audit committee, composed entirely of outside directors. The purpose of this committee is to monitor the company's accounting procedures and ensure the accuracy of information appearing in the annual report. There is some question about the usual process of formal auditing being able to provide this assurance if management has the power to hire and fire the auditors. The foreign payments controversy also played a role here, as the auditing firms failed to turn the payments up in the annual review. The new SEC proxy disclosure rules require that companies disclose the existence of audit committees and that they disclose the number of meetings held annually and the composition of the committee.[17]

Another very important committee is the nominating committee, which takes the power of nominating new board members away from management. Thus management cannot control the composition of the board by continuing to nominate its own friends. When these nominating committees are also made up of outside directors, management has even more difficulty in controlling the new board members and limiting the role it can play in supervising management.[18]

[14]"Management Should Fill Only One Seat on a Firm's Board, SEC Chairman Urges," *The Wall Street Journal,* January 19, 1978, p. 3.

[15]"Firms Add More Independent Directors but Find Doing So Can Mean Headaches," *The Wall Street Journal,* May 26, 1978, p. 38.

[16]"Composition, Duties of Corporate Boards Are Changing, Korn/Ferry Study Shows," *The Wall Street Journal,* February 21, 1978, p. 8.

[17]R. Joseph Monsen, "Directions in United States and European Corporate Governance," paper presented at the AACSB Conferences on Business Environment/Public Policy, Summer 1979, pp. 4–5.

[18]"Independent Panels of Corporate Boards to Tap New Directors Are Proliferating," *The Wall Street Journal,* February 15, 1979, p. 14. See also "Survey Finds Board Nominating Panels Help Determine Management Succession," *The Wall Street Journal,* January 28, 1980, p. 10.

These efforts all move in the direction of making the board a truly independent body between the shareholders and management that is not under the control of management, allowing the board to perform its true function of reviewing management's actions to determine if it is acting in the stockholders' best interests. Many see this as a very healthy development in the area of corporate governance, but others are not satisfied with these developments and would like to see further reform.

Special Interest Directors. One proposed reform is for boards of directors to have *special interest* directors who would represent the interests of other constituent groups besides shareholders. These special interests could include consumers, minorities, women, environmentalists, and others who would have a board member to represent their interests. The purpose of including these members on the board would be to broaden the board's perspectives to consider other interests affected by corporate decisions besides those of shareholders and management.

A good example of such a director is the Reverend Leon Sullivan, who in 1971 was chosen to serve on the board of General Motors. Sullivan claims that he represents the interests of blacks, not stockholders, and boasts that during his years on the board, GM has increased its advertising in black publications, increased its purchases of parts and supplies from black manufacturers, opened an account in every one of the nation's black-owned banks, and other measures.[19]

Many problems with this idea, however, make it difficult to implement on a large scale. For one thing, where does one draw the line on what special interests should be represented? Why should the interests of blacks be represented on GM's board, for example, and not women's interests as well? What about the interests of left-handed people, short people, and other such groups? How could adequate representation be assured for all the groups in society whose interests are affected by the corporation and the board still function?

Second, obvious conflicts of interest arise for special interest directors as well as for the entire board. Regarding the former, under law directors owe their loyalty to the corporation. To whom would special interest directors owe their primary loyalty? There is some indication that women experience this conflict. Is their role to look out for women's interests or the interests of the stockholders?[20] Regarding the entire board, the representation of many diverse interests would obviously politicize the board and make every issue an interest group controversy. Whether such a board could be very effective in governing a corporation is questionable.[21]

Public Directors. Instead of special interest directors, others propose a public director. Robert Townsend, the former head of Avis Corporation, for example, advocates that all manufacturing companies with over a billion dollars in assets should have such a public director. This director would have an office in the company headquarters, have access to all company files, and receive notice of all company meetings, which should be open for his or her

---

[19] "The Black on GM's Board," *Time,* September 6, 1976, pp. 54–55.
[20] See "A Big Jump in the Ranks of Female Directors," *Business Week,* January 10, 1977, pp. 49–50.
[21] Monsen, "Directions in Corporate Governance," p. 9.

attendance. This public director would be required to call at least two press conferences a year to report on the company's progress or lack of progress on issues of interest to the public. These directors would be chosen by an ad hoc legislative committee of Congress from a pool of candidates previously screened and approved by the committee. They would be assigned to specific corporations by lottery. These public directors, according to Townsend, would have a catalytic effect on board meetings, enhancing management's perception of public values.[22]

Employee Directors. Many European countries allow employees to serve on the board of directors along with the traditional shareholder representatives. After the Second World War, for example, West Germany passed a codetermination law that required companies in the coal, iron, and steel industries to have employee representation on the board of directors. Later this principle was extended to other industries. Other countries, such as Denmark, Norway, and Sweden, now also require firms to have employee directors elected either by unions or by the employees themselves.

Whether this idea will catch on in the United States is a question that will only be answered with the passage of time. Some feel the idea will not catch on because of the ideological and cultural differences between Western Europe and the United States.[23] Others believe the idea will eventually cross the Atlantic, because they believe trends in Western Europe foreshadow what will eventually happen in this country. But as of now, these notions of industrial democracy or self-management have been almost entirely a European phenomenon.

Activist Shareholders. The activist shareholder movement began in the 1960s, as small shareholders interested particularly in pursuing social goals found a way to make their voices heard at annual meetings. The SEC amended the proxy rules to allow small shareholders to place resolutions concerning social responsibility issues on corporate proxy statements. Thus the door was opened for public interest groups and others to buy a few shares of stock in a company and introduce resolutions dealing with social issues. These resolutions have increased to the point that in 1979, public interest activists presented at least 112 corporations with 130 shareholder resolutions raising questions of social responsibility and corporate governance.[24]

Table 7.1 shows the composition of these resolutions for the 1979 proxy season. Twenty-eight resolutions were withdrawn following discussions and agreement between the proponents and the companies involved. That left 102 resolutions that were brought to a vote at the annual meeting, with 46 surviving to be considered again the next year. To survive, these resolutions have to receive 3 percent of the vote to come up again the second year, 6 percent for the third year, and 10 percent for subsequent years.

The main concerns, as shown in Table 7.1, were investments in or doing

---

[22]Robert Townsend, "A Modest Proposal: The Public Director," *Corporate Power in America,* Ralph Nader and Mark J. Green, eds. (New York: Grossman Publishers, 1973), pp. 257–259.

[23]Monsen, "Directions in Corporate Governance," pp. 1–3.

[24]Theodore V. Purcell, "Management and the Ethical Investors," *Harvard Business Review,* Vol. 57, No. 5 (September–October 1979), p. 24.

TABLE 7.1 **How 130 Shareholder Resolutions in 19 Areas Fared**

Subject	Total presented*	Total withdrawn	Resolutions brought to vote	
			Total	Survivors†
South African issues	34	8	26	9
Trade with other repressive governments	14	2	12	4
Former government officials	16	0	16	5
Nuclear weapons and power plants	12	5	7	6
Corporate governance	11	0	11	8
Redlining and community reinvestment	8	4	4	2
Domestic political activities and contributions	7	0	7	4
Domestic labor practices and EEO	6	2	4	2
Military conversion to peacetime uses	4	1	3	1
Questionable foreign payments	4	2	2	1
Children's TV: food advertising and violence	3	2	1	0
Infant formula	3	0	3	2
Overseas operations and labor practices	2	1	1	0
Domestic media policies	1	0	1	0
Foreign military sales criteria	1	0	1	1
Low alcoholic beer production	1	1	0	0
Maritime lobbying	1	0	1	0
Price fixing	1	0	1	0
Western irrigated land sales	1	0	1	1
Total	130	28	102	46

*As of July 1, 1979.
†Getting 3% for the second year, 6% for the third year, and 10% for subsequent years.
Note: Actually, the American Society of Corporate Secretaries, Inc. found nearly 800 proposals for the period July 1, 1978 to July 1, 1979, but most of these were not strictly public interest resolutions.

Reprinted by permission of the *Harvard Business Review*. Exhibit from "Management and the Ethical Investors" by Theodore V. Purcell (September–October 1979). Copyright © 1979 by the President and Fellows of Harvard College; all rights reserved.

business with South Africa, trade with repressive governments other than South Africa, resolutions against nuclear power plants, redlining and community reinvestment, domestic political activities, employment of former government officials, domestic labor practices, and proposals asking military contractors to convert their business to peacetime production.

Most of these shareholder resolutions in 1979 were coordinated and inspired (though not formally sponsored) by the New York based Interfaith Center on Corporate Responsibility. This organization is related to the National Council of Churches, and while mainly a Protestant group, it also includes 170 Roman Catholic religious orders and dioceses. These church shareholders alone filed more than 82 resolutions in 1979 to 61 U.S. corporations, including 30 regarding South Africa. The ICCR also sought support from other institutional investors for the resolutions introduced by its members.[25]

The resolutions introduced by these activist shareholders never received anything approaching a majority of the shareholder vote. But occasionally they receive the support of the large institutional investors. While mainly interested in financial return, they do support certain social resolutions. The chairman of the Teachers Insurance and Annuity Association, William C. Greenough, justified this action with the following statement: "In its supporting and nudging role, the institutional investor has a potent lever to move the American corporation—the voting of corporate shares. Failure to use this lever leaves a vacuum in the responsible exercise of corporate power."[26]

The Purcell study indicated how some financial institutions voted on six major issues in 1979 in regard to specific corporations. These issues included infant formula (American Home Products and Bristol-Meyers), management-employee review committee (J. P. Stevens), stopping of loans to South Africa (Bank America), reporting on loans to South Africa (Citicorp and J. P. Morgan), stopping of sales to South African government if repressive use intended (Eastman Kodak), and stopping of sales to South African military and police (Ford Motor Co. and General Motors). Some financial institutions supported the public interest resolutions for all six issues. Banks tended to vote against these resolutions and in favor of management's positions more than any other financial institution, while pension funds and insurance companies were most supportive of these resolutions.[27]

The SEC appears to be strengthening this movement toward investors' responsibility. In February 1978, it reversed its earlier "one percent rule," which permitted a company to omit a resolution that was not "significantly related" to the company's business, that is, if it concerned less than one percent of the company's business. In reversing this rule, Chairman Williams said, "There are some issues that are so important that quantitative tests are irrelevant." The commission also ruled that a company must forward to the sponsors of the resolution a copy of its statement opposing the resolution ten days before the preliminary filing of the proxy with the SEC so that the sponsors have a chance to challenge any alleged factual misstatement in the company's response.[28]

Despite these favorable developments, the activist shareholder movement is likely to remain limited in its influence over corporate policy. The influence on public policy, however, has been more significant. In the words

[25]*Ibid.*, p. 26.

[26]"Institutions and Antisocial Management," *Business Week*, January 19, 1974, pp. 66–67.

[27]Purcell, "Management and the Ethical Investor," p. 26.

[28]*Ibid.*, p. 44.

of David Vogel, a business school professor with a political science background at the University of California at Berkeley:

> Clearly, what is least important about citizen pressures has been their direct, substantive effect on corporate decisions. These have been, and are likely to remain, marginal. Their impact on public policy has been more substantial. They have played a relatively important role both in bringing a number of issues before the political process, and in increasing the effectiveness of government controls over business.[29]

Federal Chartering. The previous reforms are actually conservative attempts to make the present system of corporate governance function more effectively—disclosure of more information to shareholders, changes in the board of directors to make it more independent of management, and activist shareholders promoting the idea of investor responsibility with regard to social issues of importance to society. Nothing in these reforms suggests radical change in the present system of corporate governance.

The proposals advocating federal chartering, however, are different. This concept means just what the term implies, that corporations would be required to obtain their charter from the federal government rather than from the states, as is the current practice. The Nader proposal, which was the most comprehensive federal chartering proposal to date, involves a law that would require all industrial, retail, and transportation corporations which sold over $250 million in goods or services or employed more than 10,000 people in the United States in any one of the previous three years to obtain their charter from the federal government. The law would bypass the 15 million smaller business associations, yet would reach some 700 industrial, retail, and transportation companies whose size clearly indicates a national impact.[30]

The arguments advanced in favor of federal chartering include the following. First, according to Nader, state incorporation makes no sense as state boundaries are not the relevant boundaries for corporate commerce. State chartering makes about as much sense, says Nader, as 50 state currencies or 50 state units of measurement.[31]

Second, control of national and multinational power requires at least national authority, and federal chartering would go far toward an accessible framework for shaping and monitoring corporate power. Such an authority could remind the corporation that the charter is a compact between the government and itself to ensure business behavior in the public interest. It can also remind the corporation that it holds the charter in trust for public benefit, and if it violates that trust, it can forfeit the charter and the right to do business.[32]

The third argument advanced by Nader is that state incorporation laws are a major impediment to proper ground rules and the functioning of

---

[29]David Vogel, *Lobbying the Corporation: Citizen Challenges to Business Authority* (New York: Basic Books, 1978), p. 226.

[30]Ralph Nader, Mary Green, and Joel Seligman, *Taming the Giant Corporation* (New York: W. W. Norton & Co., 1976), pp. 240–241.

[31]Ralph Nader, "The Case for Federal Chartering," *Corporate Power in America*, Ralph Nader and Mark J. Green, eds. (New York: Grossman Publishers, 1973), p. 79.

[32]*Ibid.*, p. 80.

corporations as public citizens. Powerful corporations can threaten to run away to a different state if such items as incorporation fees, regulatory laws, and charter provisions are not to their liking. Federal chartering could equalize the varying burden and benefits corporations obtain due to the vagueness of the different state authorities.[33]

The competition between states for chartering of corporations began with the General Revision Act of 1896 in New Jersey. This act permitted unlimited corporate size and concentration (thus corporations chartered in New Jersey could merge or consolidate at will), allowed for the purchase of stock of other corporations by payment of the corporation's own stock, and permitted stockholders to be classified as preferred and common, with unequal power given to them. These were such attractive provisions that, by 1900, 95 percent of the major corporations were incorporated in New Jersey. The state raised so much money from incorporation fees that in 1902 it abolished property taxes and paid off the entire state debt, and by 1905 had $2,940,918 surplus in the treasury.[34]

It did not take other states long to see the benefits involved in this arrangement and some began to pass similar incorporation provisions. New Jersey, in fact, was the only state to ever reform its incorporation laws. Under Woodrow Wilson in 1913, the state passed provisions to outlaw the trust and the holding company. These provisions were later repealed, but big business would never trust New Jersey again.[35]

Delaware took over the lead. Its self-determination provision allowed the corporation to be a lawmaker unto itself. The certificate of incorporation could contain any provision the incorporaters chose to insert for the management of the business and the conduct of the affairs of the corporation, and any provision creating, defining, limiting, and regulating the powers of the corporation, the directors, and the stockholders, provided such provisions were not contrary to the laws of the state. Previous to this, the corporation could only exercise powers explicitly provided or necessarily implied in the charter. Further liberal provisions were created in the 1967 revisions.[36]

By 1971, franchise taxes and related corporate income comprised 23 percent of the state revenues. Between 1967 and 1974, 134 of the 1,000 largest companies reincorporated or incorporated in Delaware, and by 1974, Delaware was home for 448 of the largest 1,000, 251 of the largest 500, and 52 of the largest 100 corporations. This competition has rendered state incorporation ineffectual as a regulator of corporate behavior.[37]

> State corporation law—both statutory and case law—has seen its day. Statutes have become so broad and sweeping that they let a corporation do just about anything it wants. A modicum of legal skill and common sense enables management to do its will, and to plan around—not to say evade—what few restrictions state law contains. State law does not and cannot exert any real controls. Corporation statutes

---

[33]*Ibid.*

[34]Nader, *Taming the Giant Corporation,* pp. 44–47.

[35]*Ibid.,* p. 49.

[36]*Ibid.,* p. 52.

[37]*Ibid.,* p. 57.

and most judicial decisions largely tend to reflect the interests and orientation of management, or, to use another popular term, insiders.

In short, state law has abdicated its responsibility. As a result, so the argument must run, only federal law can handle the situation, and a massive infusion of federal legislation is needed.[38]

The federal chartering concept would provide such control because corporations who wanted to headquarter in this country would have nowhere else to go to incorporate. The federal government could insist on certain provisions regarding the corporation's structure and behavior. The provisions in the Nader proposal deal with internal governance of the corporation, corporate dealings with the public, company relations with employees, and industrial structure.

Internal Governance. Management autonomy would be greatly restricted by directing federally chartered companies to establish nine-member boards of directors with specific duties to approve a variety of actions that management now routinely takes without even consulting the directors. In addition to their general responsibilities, each director would be assigned a specific area of responsibility, such as employee welfare, consumer protection, shareholder rights, environmental protection, or community relations. Management would also be subject to harsh penalties for violating laws related to corporate operations. For example, an executive found guilty of such violations would be barred from holding an executive job in any federally chartered corporation for five years.[39]

Dealings with the Public. This provision would require corporations to publish a detailed list of economic and social data in a new government publication called the *Corporate Register.* This information would include where and how a company is polluting and the remedies it is undertaking, toxic substances used in each plant location, employment statistics analyzed by race, sex, and income, substantiation of advertising claims, and corporate lobbying efforts. Corporations would also have to disclose the names of the 100 largest owners of its stock, the extent of corporate holdings in other companies, the income and benefits of the thirty highest paid executives, and financial reporting by product line.[40]

Relations with Employees. This provision would provide employees with a "bill of rights" for their protection. The corporation can presently dismiss employees for good cause, no cause, or even for a cause morally wrong without being legally wrong. The bill of rights would prevent a corporation from firing, penalizing, or intimidating an employee in violation of constitutional rights to freedom of expression, equal rights, or privacy. This constitutionalizing of the corporation would force it to observe first amendment requirements for freedom of religion, freedom of the press, freedom of speech and peaceable assembly, to respect rights of privacy, and not to discriminate on account of race, religion, creed, sex, or national origin. Thus employees could not be dismissed for "blowing the whistle," nor could companies use polygraph tests or other invasions of privacy as a condition of employment.[41]

[38]*Ibid.,* p. 61.
[39]"A Step toward the Federal Corporate Charter," *Business Week,* June 21, 1976, pp. 80, 82.
[40]*Ibid.,* pp. 82, 84.
[41]Nader, *Taming the Giant Corporation,* pp. 194–197.

Industrial Structure. The final provision would be a version of an industrial deconcentration bill introduced into Congress at various times, under which the mere existence of a concentrated industry, defined in quantitative terms as a certain percentage of sales by the top four firms, would trigger antitrust action to split the largest firms into smaller companies, regardless of whether or not there had been any evidence of corporate wrongdoing.[42]

These provisions are just one example of the form the federal chartering concept might take to control corporate structure and behavior. The concept is radical because it raises some fundamental questions about the proper relationship between the state and a private corporation. What gives a corporation a right to exist? If that right derives from the marketplace, that is, that a corporation gets the right to exist by serving the needs of consumers, chartering takes on a different character. Chartering, as suggested by Robert A. Hessen, research fellow at the Hoover Institution, then "merely records the existence of corporations and [is] not at all essential to their creation, any more than the registrar of births is essential to the conception of a child."[43] The federal chartering process implies that corporations get their right to exist from the state and that the state has the right to control private corporations in the "public interest."

Questions for Discussion

1. Do you agree with the proposition that questions about corporate governance arise more from fundamental conflicts with democratic values than specific abuses of power? What specific conflicts exist between the way in which a corporation is run and the principles of a democratic society?
2. What has happened to the role of shareholders in the modern corporation? What legal rights do they have in relation to the corporation? What is the ultimate basis of these rights?
3. How does management control the corporation? Do you think management control is as widespread as some studies indicate? What percentage of stock ownership does it take to have influence over corporate policies?
4. Identify some important families in the nation or in your region who own a large number of shares in some corporations. Find some evidence that indicates they have actually used the power that such share ownership would imply. How have they influenced corporate policies?
5. Do you think employee representation on the board of directors will catch hold in this country to any significant degree? What ideological and cultural differences exist between the United States and Western Europe? Are you in favor of employee representation at the board level? Why or why not?
6. Do you believe the ownership of American corporations by foreign sources will increase? Should this be a cause of concern to Congress and the American public? What can be done about it?
7. What kinds of disclosure do you believe are most beneficial to shareholders? Why? Will increased disclosure satisfy critics of the corporate governance process to any significant degree?
8. What, in your opinion, is a truly "outside" director? Should corporate boards be composed of a majority of these outside directors? Are they better able to look out after shareholders' interests? Why or why not?

[42]*Ibid.,* pp. 233–236.
[43]New Fire in the Drive to Reform Corporation Law," *Business Week,* November 21, 1977, p. 100.

9. What is the difference between a special interest director and a public director? What are the advantages and disadvantages of each of these proposals? Which, if any, do you favor? Would this aid the governance process? How?
10. Do institutional shareholders have a moral obligation to take social concerns into account when making investments or voting their shares? Or should their concern be limited strictly to the financial return of their portfolio?
11. Why is federal chartering a radical proposal as far as corporate governance is concerned? What is the purpose of the chartering process? Do you believe the provisions in the Nader proposal would enhance corporate responsibility? In what ways?
12. What other reforms, besides those mentioned, can you think of that relate to the governance of corporations? Which reforms do you believe are most likely to take place? What impacts will these have on the management task in future years?

Suggested Reading

Barber, Richard J. *The American Corporation.* New York: Dutton, 1970.

Berle, Adolf A., and Means, Gardiner C. *The Modern Corporation and Private Property.* New York: Macmillan, 1932.

Blumberg, Philip I. *The Megacorporation in American Society.* Englewood Cliffs, N.J.: Prentice-Hall, 1975.

Brown, Courtney C. *Putting the Corporate Board to Work.* New York: Macmillan, 1976.

Burch, Philip H. *The Managerial Revolution Reassessed.* New York: Lexington Books, 1972.

Burnham, James. *The Managerial Revolution.* Bloomington: Indiana University Press, 1941.

Galbraith, John Kenneth. *The New Industrial State.* Boston: Houghton Mifflin, 1967.

Larner, Robert J. *Management Control and the Large Corporation.* New York: Dunellen, 1971.

Nader, Ralph, and Green, Mark J., eds. *Corporate Power in America.* New York: Grossman Publishers, 1973.

———, ———, and Seligman, Joel. *Taming the Giant Corporation.* New York: W. W. Norton & Co., 1976.

The Role and Composition of the Board of Directors of the Large Publicly Owned Corporation. New York: The Business Roundtable, 1978.

Stone, Christopher D. *Where the Law Ends: The Social Control of Corporate Behavior.* New York: Harper & Row, 1975.

Vogel, David. *Lobbying the Corporation: Citizen Challenges to Business Authority.* New York: Basic Books, 1978.

8

Business-Government Relations

Today, nearly everyone agrees that the business-government relationship in the United States is in trouble. A faulty interaction between these two most important institutions of our society has resulted in a piling up of unresolved social problems. Effective cooperation between government and business is a sine qua non of sustained social progress; the fact that during recent years the forward momentum of our society has faltered—and occasionally stalled—suggests an unsatisfactory interface between the public and private sectors. Add to this a disturbing lack of confidence by the American people in both business and government, and it becomes clear that improvement of the relationship between them—and thereby in the performance of both—is a matter of primary importance, and even of urgency.[1]

The relationship between business and government is so complex that it would take volumes to describe it thoroughly. All that can be done in a single chapter is to explore the business-government relationship at the federal level from a number of important dimensions. This will at least introduce some conceptual approaches that may help the reader to understand the business-government relationship more precisely. These approaches should also be relevant to understanding the business-government relationship at state and local levels.

Before doing this, however, something needs to be said about the growth of the federal government. There are various ways to describe this growth. One method is to look at the size of the federal budget. It took 186 years for the federal budget to reach the $100 billion mark, a line that was crossed in

[1] Neil H. Jacoby, ed., *The Business-Government Relationship: A Reassessment* (Pacific Palisades, Calif.: Goodyear, 1975), p. 3. Quoted with permission.

1962, but in only nine more years the $200 billion mark was reached. Four years later, the $300 billion barrier was broken.[2] The budget for 1981 was first estimated at $615.8 billion, to be cut later in an attempt to bring inflation under control. In Figure 8.1, the growth of the federal budget from 1920 through 1980 is shown in constant 1972 dollars, removing the effects of deflation during the 1930s and inflation at most other times.

Another way to look at the growth of the federal government is to express these budget amounts as a percentage of gross national product. In 1930, prior to the New Deal, government spending at all levels accounted for just 12 percent of gross national product. In 1975, government spending accounted for 32 percent of gross national product, and if such trends were to continue until the year 2000, government would account for as much as 60 percent of gross national product.[3]

In terms of people employed, by 1975 one out of every six working men and women in the country worked directly for either federal, state, or local government.[4] In 1976, there were 11 cabinet departments at the federal level, 59 independent agencies, 1,240 advisory boards, committees, councils, and commissions, 1,026 aid programs, and some 34,000 federal offices scattered across the country employing thousands of people.[5] Senate staff

Figure 8.1. Federal Budget Outlays

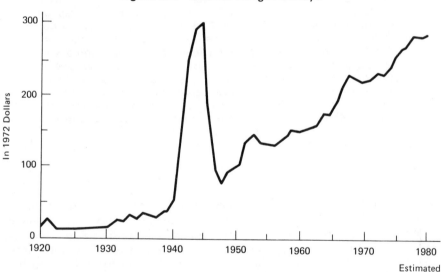

From Arlen J. Large, "Depression Was a Spur to Big Government, but Surge Came Later," *The Wall Street Journal,* October 10, 1979, p. 1. Reprinted with permission.

[2]Darryl R. Francis, *Public Policy for a Free Economy* (St. Louis, Mo.: Washington University Center for the Study of American Business, 1975), p. 2.
[3]*Ibid.*
[4]*Ibid.*
[5]Lawrence Hebron, "Why Bureaucracy Keeps Growing," *Business Week,* November 15, 1976, p. 23.

members averaged 68 staffers per senator in 1979, double that of a decade before, and the combined House and Senate staff grew from 11,700 in 1968 to 18,400 in 1979.[6]

Finally, one can look at the growth of government from the standpoint of the growth in regulatory activities, the major growth area of government in recent years. The budget of the numerous federal regulatory agencies increased from $2.2 billion in fiscal 1974 to $4.8 billion in 1979, a 115 percent increase in just five years. Besides these budget outlays, the typical regulatory agency generates private compliance costs far in excess of its own outlays (see Chapter 9).

It is interesting to reflect on this phenomenal growth in view of the principle of laissez faire upon which this country was founded. The colonists believed that the government in England was running the colonies too much and feared centralization of power. They sought to limit the power of the federal government by delegating it specific powers in the constitution and reserving all other powers to the states. In addition, power was dispersed among the three branches of government, which were to act as a check on each other. Eventually, a bill of rights was added to the constitution to prevent the government from interfering with the rights of individual citizens. How, then, is the growth of government to its present size explained?

One reason behind this growth is simply the growth of military expenditures. As is shown in Figure 8.1, the outlays required by World War II topped anything that has yet appeared in terms of real government expenditures. While many might argue that the seeds of big government were sown during the depression years, it appears that big government really arrived during the 1940s as the war progressed. The legacy of that war against Germany and Japan was the ensuing cold war with the Soviet Union and its allies. The two shooting wars in Korea and Vietnam put detectable clips on the growth chart. As the United States grew into a world power and its international responsibilities increased, the need for an increasing amount of the public good called military expenditures or national defense went right along with this role.

The depression era did, however, result in the beginning of some new areas of government spending that continue today. The idea that the government should relieve the distresses of an economic downturn and then later become responsible for the ongoing health of the economy took root in those years. Later years have seen the government commit itself to a more equal distribution of income, a goal shared by many in our society and supported by the philosophy of entitlements that began during the depression. In fact, the largest share of the federal budget is currently devoted to transfer payments which support programs mainly designed to help low-income people.

Then, in the 1960s, the government responded to the change in social values by passing a plethora of new legislation and creating new regulatory agencies or adding additional functions to old agencies. Many believed that

[6]"A Bureaucracy Grows in Congress as Panels and Staffs Mushroom," *The Wall Street Journal,* December 18, 1979, p. 1.

the government could do the best job in attaining these socially desirable objectives by forcing business to conform to laws and regulations.

Thus the growth of government is explained by the growth of public policy. As society increasingly turns to the public policy process instead of the market to allocate resources, the government has to grow since it is the institution largely responsible for formulating public policy for the society as a whole. As public goods become more important and market outcomes less and less acceptable, society turns more to the public policy process, and government grows bigger.

Some believe that the roots of this growth go deeper into the psyche of American society. Lawrence Hebron, for example, writing in *Business Week,* believes that the real problem in our society is not the size or costs of the federal bureaucratic establishment, but the philosophy that allowed it to be created. It is illogical and irresponsible for the citizens of the United States to complain about big government, he says, while still demanding more and more benefits and programs from the government.

> There will be no reform of our bureaucracies so long as the prevailing theory of open-ended government responsibility continues to hold sway over our legislators. The government does not owe anyone a living. It is not a proper function of the state to see that everyone is fed, clothed, and housed. It is a proper function of the state to see that everyone has an opportunity to feed, clothe, and house himself. We must reaffirm such values as self-help, individual initiative, and personal and community responsibility. We must acknowledge that it is the individual and the family that bear responsibility for personal failure—not the society or the state.[7]

A similar view recently appeared in the *Wall Street Journal* (see box). These views, of course, decry the growth of government and see it as a detrimental factor in our society. Whether one agrees with these views or not, however, they do point to some deeper roots behind the growth of government that deserve to be taken into account. The question of whether government is too big or not is, of course, a value question, as the factors behind the growth of government involve a change of values that have altered the nature of the relationship between business and government.

The federal government, however, cannot grow and intervene in the economy without some constitutional basis. The government cannot be completely arbitrary in terms of how and where it can affect business, and the constitution helps to ensure that decisions by the federal government reflect the will of the people rather than the autocratic authority of despots. Most of the economic powers granted to the federal government are contained in Article 1, Section 8 of the constitution, the most important of which are the following:

- The power to regulate interstate and foreign commerce
- The power of taxation—the authority to levy and collect taxes, duties, imports, excises, and to pay the debts of the country
- The power to coin money and regulate the value thereof

[7]Hebron, "Why Bureaucracy Keeps Growing," p. 24.

THE BURDENS OF CUTTING BACK ON GOVERNMENT

By Randall R. Rader

On a recent night I suffered one of those introspective moments when I was compelled to reevaluate if a philosophy of limited government is worth the worry.

I had just returned from an exhausting choir practice. My conscience felt a pang when my eyes fell on the unanswered letter from my parents. Lisa, my adopted black daughter, was loudly vocalizing her displeasure with the circumstances of the moment. Larke, the world's cutest four-year-old blonde, would not wait another minute for her nightly bedtime story. The open Sunday School manual on the kitchen table was a grim reminder that my lesson was not yet prepared. Tomorrow my softball team entered the all-day playoffs in the morning and the evening featured another choir rehearsal.

Each of these demands is an integral part of my effort to live according to principles of limited government. If an individual really shares Jefferson's view ("That government is best that governs least"), he must have provisions in his own life to take responsibility for essential services that government should not be allowed to monopolize.

No charitable society will allow the aged to suffer deprivations when they can no longer care for themselves. Therefore if we do not care for our own parents or the elderly in our greater family units, the government will tax everyone (force us) to set up massive nursing home programs. But forced government programs cannot meet the real needs of the aged. Love cannot be forced; the elderly need the love and respect of their posterity as much as they need food and shelter. Hence, I must strengthen my ties to my own parents.

No self-respecting society will deny that all men are of equal worth and deserve equal respect. Therefore, if we do not openly welcome all qualified citizens regardless of race into our civic associations, schools, and clubs, the government will tax everyone (force us) to bus students and institute civil rights lawsuits. But government cannot eliminate racial discrimination because by taking sides in any racial conflict it is giving the force of law to, and thereby perpetuating, distinctions based on race.

No humane nation wants to leave others to endure poor health, the specter of a life with pain. Therefore, if we do not eat correctly, exercise regularly, avoid harmful agents (cigarets, narcotics and the like) to remain healthy, the government will tax everyone (force us) to create an unwieldy national health program. Hence, softball season will be followed by basketball for me.

I am not suggesting that government has no role in meeting individual and social needs. Instead it should have a very limited role. It should be a last line of defense.

If we profess a philosophy of limited government we profess in the same breath a faith in unlimited personal responsibility. When I arrived home last night that thought made me tired. Yet everything worth having in life must be earned: health, respect, creativity, friendship and so forth. Government cannot meet the need because in most instances the need is for personal effort or activity or growth. If we do not believe in pervasive government, we must believe in pervasive individual, family, church and community responsibility.

- The power to establish tariffs and regulate foreign affairs and military matters
- The power to establish laws related to bankruptcy, copyrights, and patents

These few constitutional provisions do not seem to provide much of a base for the vast power the federal government has over the economy today. It must be remembered, however, that these clauses are subject to interpretation by the courts, reflecting changes in society. At one time, for example, the definition of "interstate commerce" was interpreted so narrowly that a company which sold its products nationwide but produced them in only one state was not considered to be engaged in interstate commerce. Similarly, the debate about the establishment and continuance of the First and Second Bank of the United States hinged on the meaning of "regulate the value thereof." Thus the way these constitutional provisions are interpreted can restrict the growth of government or allow it to expand.

The State of Business-Government Relations

Before we look at some specific ways in which business and government are related to each other, it might be useful to try and describe the relationship as a whole. In some sense, the business-government relationship is like the relationship between two people, and many of the terms used to describe a human relationship can also be used to describe the business-government relationship.

Numerous references in the literature describe the nature of this relationship, but perhaps the best place to look is to the experts and what they say about it. Such a group of experts gathered at a conference on the subject in 1974 at the Graduate School of Management of the University of California at Los Angeles.

A summary of the conference was written by Neil H. Jacoby, who concluded that the participants generally agreed that the word "adversarial" most accurately characterized the present state of the business-government relationship.[8] This word is frequently used to refer to the relationship between business and government, so it comes as no surprise. Adversarial means having antagonistic interests, two parties acting against each other or in a contrary direction, opposite in position.[9] The interests of business and government in an adversary relationship are thus opposed to each other and often move in opposite directions.

Government officials are not seen as friends of business with common interests, but are viewed as probers, inspectors, taxers, regulators, and punishers of business transgressions. Businesspeople view government agencies as obstacles, constraints, delayers, and impediments to economic progress. Each lacks knowledge and understanding of the role, motivation, problems, and modes of action of the other.[10]

[8]Jacoby, *The Business-Government Relationship*, pp. 167–176.
[9]*Webster's New Collegiate Dictionary* (Springfield, Mass.: G & C Merriam Co., 1977), p. 17.
[10]Jacoby, *The Business-Government Relationship*, p. 167.

Furthermore, Jacoby concludes, the relationship is deteriorating. The goals and values of our burgeoning, affluent, urbanizing, and technological society have become more numerous, complex, interrelated, and harder to reconcile. Conflicts among interest groups have multiplied, trade-off relationships are harder to measure, social priorities are more difficult to establish, and social consensus is harder to achieve. We have many unresolved issues related to energy, environment, transit, housing, poverty, drug use, and crime, all of which are mounting.[11]

The wellsprings of this malfunctioning are to be found in society at large and in the institutions of business and government themselves. As far as society as a whole is concerned, a national society has emerged that is also a communal society, placing a greater emphasis on public goods. The society also has experienced rising expectations related to a concern for the quality of life, not just the quantity of goods and services produced by the private sector. These value changes have multiplied the number of political decisions that have to be made relative to the number of decisions made in markets. Consequently, the political system has become clogged. The political system translates public preferences into operational programs in a very halting, inaccurate manner, and the structure of government is often contradictory to the imperatives of business efficiency.[12]

But business by and large has shown an insensitivity to social values. In the past, says Jacoby, business has opposed most social legislation instead of helping to design regulations. Furthermore, business has an ignorance of government and lacks an understanding of the problems and constraints under which government officials labor. Business espouses individualism while government operates on a collectivist ethic. Business rewards or punishes individual inequalities whereas a collectivist ethic emphasizes the equality of individuals. This lack of understanding contributes to the malfunctioning of society, along with public ignorance of the respective responsibilities of business and government.[13]

This adversarial relationship is believed to be true of business and government by many commentators, but is not necessarily believed to be in the best interests of society. Various other terms have been used to describe a more ideal relationship including cooperation, mutually beneficial coexistence, or peaceful coexistence. The conference of experts, however, rejected any idea of unity or even of confederation or partnership. They advocated social pluralism as an ideal—a certain amount of tension and arms-length dealing in the government's relationship with business.[14]

The Roles of Government

Instead of looking at the business-government relationship as a whole, another way to describe the relationship is to look at the various roles government plays in the economy—how it relates to business in terms of

[11]*Ibid.*, p. 168.
[12]*Ibid.*, pp. 168–169.
[13]*Ibid.*, pp. 169–170.
[14]*Ibid.*, p. 173.

things it does to or for business. These roles include promoter, regulator, guarantor, buyer, owner, manager of the economy, and planner. These roles will be discussed briefly in the following pages, except for the role of regulator. This role has become so extensive and pervasive in its influence on business that it deserves an entire chapter.

Government as Promotor of Business. Government is a major promoter of business with a vast array of subsidies, tax credits, tariffs, etc., which are designed to promote various regions of the country, certain industries, or even specific business organizations. Some of these forms of promotion are widely accepted, others are more controversial. The purposes of these forms of promotion are as varied as their number. These purposes include stabilizing the economy, maintaining a favorable balance of trade, stimulating innovation, and maintaining balanced growth throughout the economy. Some of these major forms of promotion are described in the following paragraphs.

Tariff Protection or Import Quotas. Tariffs or quotas on imports are an attempt to promote certain industries or companies by protecting them from foreign competition. Since the federal government was given the constitutional right to establish tariffs, this has become a major promotional device that is sought by many industries. A current example is the trigger price mechanism designed to stem the increase of steel imports from foreign countries and help the domestic steel industry earn sufficient profits to modernize its facilities and become more competitive in world markets. The steel industry is believed to be vital to our domestic economy, and therefore must be protected from foreign "dumping" that would severely cut its earnings.

Subsidies. The government has provided subsidies to various parts of the economy, including agriculture, airlines, and other sectors and industries. The agriculture sector has been given subsidies at various times to take land out of productive use, maintain stable prices for crops, and provide for storage of crops when necessary. Airlines have been subsidized to service smaller cities that were unprofitable to service on a strictly profit and loss basis. New subsidies will undoubtedly proliferate in the energy area to promote the development of alternative energy sources.

Besides these direct subsidies, there are also indirect subsidies that are not so readily apparent. For some years, the price of fourth class mail was apparently set below the actual cost of delivery. This was, in effect, a promotion of the publishing industry. When these rates were increased to reflect the actual costs of delivery more closely, many magazines, such as *Fortune* and *Esquire,* were cut in size to the standard 8½ × 11 to reduce the mailing costs because of the increased rates.

Research and Development. Government spends a great deal of money to promote research and development in certain industries, such as aerospace and energy. Such promotion is based on a presumed failure of private industry to put enough money into these areas that are considered vital to the nation's well-being. This form of promotion is particularly true of industries with complex technology, where the costs of research and development are very high and the payoffs uncertain. The energy area may receive a good deal of research and development money to promote the development of alternative forms of energy, such as solar power and coal gasification.

Tax Credits and Tax Breaks. Tax credits refer to items like the new investment tax credit designed to promote investment in new plants and equipment. Companies that expand or modernize are given a credit on their total tax bill to the federal government. Tax breaks refer to United States policy on taxes of multinational companies, who are not required to pay taxes on income earned abroad until that income has been returned to the United States as dividends. Some scholars have argued that this policy has encouraged multinationals to invest in expanding facilities overseas to avoid paying United States taxes. This expansion overseas is done, at least partially, at the expense of domestic expansion, costing this country losses of jobs and productivity.[15]

Government as Guarantor of Business. This role of government first came in for widespread public attention when Lockheed Corporation faced serious financial problems in the late 1960s and early 1970s. Because the company wanted to reduce its dependence on the military market, it decided to enter the commercial jet aircraft market by building a three-engined, wide-bodied jet airplane called the L-1011. The company spent about $400 million on fixed assets to produce this commercial transport, with the money coming from internal cash flows generated by other projects, bond issues, and advance progress payments from airlines who ordered the airplane. In May 1969, a group of banks extended a credit line of $400 million to the company.[16]

The engines were to be built by Rolls Royce of Britain, but Rolls Royce soon ran into technological problems with the fan blades. The solution to these problems resulted in a heavier engine as well as huge cost overruns for the company, which was more than Rolls Royce could bear without declaring bankruptcy. Lockheed was faced with having no engines for the L-1011, and could not, at that late date, switch to another company and meet its delivery schedules. Because of this problem and settlement with the government on alleged cost overruns of its own, cancellations, and failure to meet performance standards related to defense contracts, Lockheed itself was faced with bankruptcy. The company had a net loss after taxes of $86.3 million for 1970 and a net worth that was reduced from $371 million at the end of 1968 to $235 million by the end of 1970.

Lockheed needed help, and its only recourse was to turn to the federal government. The risk was too great for banks and other creditors to extend any more money to Lockheed under normal guarantees. This help came in the form of Emergency Loan Guarantee Legislation, introduced into Congress to guarantee loans up to $250 million specifically for Lockheed. With the federal government standing behind the loans to pick up the tab in case of default, banks and other creditors would then be willing to extend Lockheed the cash it needed to continue operations.

[15]See Robert Gilpin, *U.S. Power and the Multinational Corporation* (New York: Books, 1975).

[16]The information for the Lockheed case came from George A. Steiner, *Casebook in Business and Society* (New York: Random House, 1975), pp. 165–173.

The debate about this bill was extensive. Those who opposed the bill did so mainly on the principles of a free enterprise economy. Subsidizing a failing company, they argued, would undermine the very purpose of a competitive economy, which is to ensure that the resources of society are used efficiently. The management of Lockheed was inefficient, it was charged, and to save the company from bankruptcy would be rewarding poor management. If government played the role of guaranteeing the survival of inefficient companies, the incentives for big business to be efficient would be removed.

Those who favored the bill pointed out that the bill would cost government nothing since it had first claim on the company's assets should it fail. These could be sold at well over the guaranteed figure. Also, 60,000 jobs would be lost if the company closed its doors, including those who worked directly for Lockheed as well as its suppliers, many of which were small businesses that would also go bankrupt. These people would then go on the unemployment rolls until they found another job, resulting in additional expenses to the government. Losses in income taxes to the federal government could reach $500 million a year according to Treasury Department estimates. In addition, the company was providing much military equipment to the government that could not readily be picked up by another manufacturer, making the company essential to national defense. Finally, there were international implications, as the British government wanted assurances that Lockheed was not going to collapse, as it had created a new nationalized company out of Rolls Royce and wanted to continue development of the engines for the L-1011.

These more practical arguments carried the day over the arguments from principle related to a free enterprise economy. The loan guarantee bill was passed. The end of the story is good. Lockheed survived and eventually became profitable, the L-1011 is flying, and the government earned $26.6 million on the deal in fees received in return for the guarantee and another $5.4 million by investing the proceeds.

More recently, Chrysler Corporation faced a similar situation. Its share of the domestic car market had shrunk from 25.7 percent in 1946 to 9 percent in 1978. It had reacted too slowly to the decline in the market for standard-sized cars, and in 1979 had an unsold inventory valued at $700 million, which was mostly large cars. Chrysler initially set its 1979 loss at $800 million, one of the biggest losses in U.S. corporate history. When the final figures were tallied, the loss for 1979 exceeded $1 billion. Thus Chrysler was faced with imminent shutdown in early 1980 unless someone helped.

The solution was again a federal loan guarantee so creditors could safely extend the money Chrysler needed to continue operations. The arguments were much the same as in the Lockheed situation. Some 360,000 jobs were at stake, taxes would be lost to the government, people would be forced on the unemployment rolls, and so forth. Opponents of the guarantee blamed Chrysler's problems on bad management that had made a series of wrong decisions and therefore should not be helped out in a state of emergency.

The government came through again, this time to the tune of $1.5 billion in loan guarantees. Chrysler lobbied hard for these guarantees (see box); management appealed to Congress and the public for federal help. The company also had to find additional financing outside the guarantees, and

CHRYSLER DESERVES FEDERAL HELP

By Lee Iacocca

Chrysler Corp's request for federal loan guarantees to help get us through a bad patch has not reached sympathetic ears in some parts of the business community.

I can understand why. There is the sound principle that the marketplace should be the final judge of success or failure, and if the government started routinely bailing out failing firms, there would be a breakdown of market discipline.

Chairman Proxmire of the Senate Banking Committee has based his entire argument against aid for Chrysler on this principle, saying, "A bailout for Chrysler would open the floodgates. And the United States would thereby have put into effect a sure-fire system for insuring incompetence . . . achieved at colossal new cost to the federal government."

On paper, this is a terrific principle, a free enterprise standard. But what happens when the real life cause of a company's trouble is not market discipline? What happens when one company—because of the industry it's in, because of its size, because of its relative position—is driven into the ground by the unequal effects of government regulation?

As a newcomer to Chrysler, but not to the auto industry, I'm in an unusual position to assess the causes of Chrysler's problems. As a competitor at Ford, I could see what was happening to the industry as a whole, and how Chrysler in particular was being squeezed by the heavy cost of government regulation. It wasn't management mistakes (although there were some), or superior competition in the marketplace (there was some of that too), that brought the company to its knees. It was the relentless hammer of more and more government regulation.

Degree of Burden. True, every industry is regulated by the federal government to one degree or another. Some, like pharmaceuticals, may be regulated even more. But nothing comes close to the U.S. automobile industry when you measure the degree of the burden imposed over a short period of time.

Fifteen years ago, there was almost no government regulation of the auto industry.

In 1965 the government set the first auto emissions standards. The government has steadily tightened those standards to the point that today's cars are virtually pollution-free. We have now reduced emissions by 90% from uncontrolled levels. By 1981 we have to reduce emissions by another 5%—for a total reduction of 95%. Removing the last 5 grams of pollutant will add $250 to the price of a new car—ten times as much as it cost to remove the first 60 grams.

In 1967, automobile safety standards started pouring out of Washington. Today we have to meet a total of 44 separate safety standards. In 1982 we have to begin putting passive restraints, such as air bags, on passenger cars. Air bags will cost $600 to $800, even though today's belts give better protection.

In 1975, fuel economy regulations were added. By 1985, we will have doubled the average fuel economy of our passenger cars over 1977 models.

The crucial element is time—we have only about five years to do a job that would normally take 15 to 20 years.

It's not only that you have to raise 15–20 years' worth of capital in five years, but also that you have to compress 15–20 years' worth of management and engineering talent into five years in order to get the job done. Even people who on principle are firmly opposed to government assistance to Chrysler can see that General Motors and Ford, with much greater financial and management resources, have had to shoulder a relatively lighter regulatory burden.

Regulations amount to a regressive tax that hits the smallest company the hardest. They are not responsible for all of Chrysler's problems. But without this heavy tax, Chrysler would not be in trouble today—and consequently we wouldn't be asking the U.S. government for help.

I am not suggesting that we ought to abolish all forms of government regulation. Regulations may be the most efficient way to finance social objectives, when it becomes clear that car buyers, on their own, are unwilling to pay for socially desirable features that give us cleaner air, safer highways and better fuel economy. I am suggesting that helping Chrysler get through a financial crunch resulting from these regulations is itself a socially desirable thing to do.

It should be made clear that there are no suitable alternatives to the help we seek. Those who offer glib assurance about the desirability of bankruptcy proceedings ignore one basic fact. Chrysler's problem is not one of paying off creditors. It is the need to raise massive amounts of new capital to meet federal law. We cannot raise that capital while going through bankruptcy.

The final alternative of liquidation is absolutely not acceptable. According to estimates that are not our own, there are as many as 600,000 jobs at stake in communities across the country. Every state would be affected by a Chrysler failure, as hundreds of thousands of jobs moved overseas.

Who will pay the pension guarantees of $1.1 billion, the $2.7 billion of social costs estimated by the Secretary of the Treasury if Chrysler fails? The businessmen of America will, and it will be a bad deal. Any businessman should know that it's a far better investment to guarantee loans to Chrysler. The risk is small, and the payout is great. It is a simple case of good business judgment.

Because the problem for Chrysler has not been "bad management" or superior competition, but the compression of 15–20 years of regulatory burden into five, the problem is not a perpetual one. Getting through the bad patch gets Chrysler back to a profitable footing, avoids colossal costs to the several hundred thousand people whose livelihoods are tied to Chrysler, and brings on stream several new lines of highly fuel-efficient cars built by American workers.

The issue we have raised by going to the government is not free enterprise. We are not asking for a handout. We are asking government to guarantee loans that we intend to pay back in full. We really don't think a loan guarantee to Chrysler is in any sense a reward for failure, nor would it lead to a breakdown in market discipline. Our request breaks no new ground. Right now the federal government has $409 billion of loans and loan guarantees currently outstanding.

Nor is the immediate issue the need for regulatory reform—even though certain reforms are clearly desirable.

People and Jobs. Rather, the central and critical issue at stake in Chrysler's survival is people and jobs. If government wants to do something about unemployment, if it wants to keep the nation's urban areas and cities alive, if it wants to prevent increased welfare dependency and government spending, if it wants to offset an $8 billion imbalance of automotive trade with Japan, let it approve Chrysler's legitimate and amply precedented request for temporary assistance.

Senator Proxmire, for one, says he believes we will get the help we seek. But he says it will be due to the brute force of our lobbying "clout." I believe we will get the help we need, too. But if we do, it will be due to the "clout" of some 600,000 American workers who have a direct interest in our success, combined with the responsible action of a Congress that places the national interest above high-sounding, but misapplied doctrine.

Mr. Iacocca is chairman of Chrysler Corp.

From *The Wall Street Journal*, December 3, 1979, p. 24. Reprinted by permission of *The Wall Street Journal*, © Dow Jones & Company, Inc., 1979. All rights reserved.

the union had to make concessions to keep Chrysler going. But the crucial element that gave the company a reprieve was federal aid in the form of a loan guarantee.

Thus the federal government is playing a new role in the economy, guaranteeing the survival of big companies that get in trouble. Apparently, some companies get so large that the impact of their failure on the economy would be too severe and therefore they must be kept alive (see box). Such loan guarantees have also been extended to steel firms facing bankruptcy—the Commerce and Agriculture Departments decided in 1979 to guarantee 90 percent of the $150 million worth of loans to Wheeling-Pittsburgh Steel Corporation. The amount of these guaranteed loans rose sharply in the late 1970s. There is concern to put a lid on these guarantees and keep them under control.[17]

WHEN COMPANIES GET TOO BIG TO FAIL

By John Cobbs

In the years before World War I, Germany invested so heavily in battleships that, when the war came, it did not dare let them fight. As the U.S. economy slides deeper into recession, the federal government finds itself in a similar position. The huge U.S. corporations have become such important centers of jobs and incomes that it dare not let one of them shut down or go out of business. It is compelled, therefore, to shape national policy in terms of protecting the great corporations instead of letting the economy make deflationary adjustments.

As many scholars have pointed out, the corporation is the institution that the capitalist nations have chosen to translate rapidly increasing scientific knowledge into jobs, goods, incomes, and consumption. Adolph A. Berle, Jr., lawyer, teacher, businessman, and part-time politician, perhaps said it best in his thoughtful little book *The 20th Century Revolution*, published just over 20 years ago. His theme was that the corporation was doing for the U.S. and other advanced countries what the Russians were trying to achieve with Communism.

Primitive nations such as Russia, said Berle, had to choose Communism as "an instrument by which a vast backward country could be mauled into industrialization." But "the capitalist revolution in which the United States was the leader found apter, more efficient, and more flexible means through collectivizing capital in corporations."

Losing control. The past two decades have confirmed Berle's argument

[17]See "Slapping a Lid on Federal Loan Guarantees," *Business Week*, October 1, 1979, p. 130.

that "it is justifiable to consider the American corporation not as a business device but as a social institution in the context of a revolutionary century." In the last five years, however, something has gone badly wrong. Caught in an explosive inflation and wracked by two painful recessions, an increasing number of giant corporations can no longer claim either flexibility or efficiency. They have lost control of their costs, lost their access to capital, misjudged their markets, and diversified into lines of business they do not understand. In desperation they turn to Washington for help, and if they are big enough and shaky enough, they get it. Neither the Administration nor Congress dares allow a major employer to go down the drain—any more than the Kaiser dared to risk one of his expensive battleships.

The mounting number of bailouts—loans, tariffs, import quotas, and tax cuts—blurs the distinction between the capitalist revolution and the Marxist version. A visitor from Mars might see little difference between the government and the ailing corporation it is propping up.

More important, the willingness of the government to shelter a big corporation from the pain of retrenchment takes the flexibility out of the system. A game in which there are no losers puts no premium on good management or good economic policy. This is one reason the U.S. has developed a chronic inflationary bias.

In the days when there were several hundred ambitious auto producers, it did not hurt the economy greatly if a Stutz or a Franklin dropped out. The market could ruthlessly penalize bad judgment, and the system emerged stronger than ever.

There are still industries—electronics is one—where competition can prune out the weak operators and force the strong ones to hustle. But each dropout increases the relative importance of the surviving companies, and in the end, each producer will be so important that its collapse would be an economic disaster.

Rescue operations. When Lockheed Aircraft lost control of its costs and teetered on the edge of bankruptcy, Congress saved it with a $250-million loan guarantee. And when the bankrupt Eastern railroads ran out of cash and threatened to stop running trains, the government bankrolled a federal corporation to take over their essential operations.

And now the auto industry—reduced to three huge companies and one small one—is stuck with acres of 1975 cars that the public does not want. It is following the well-trodden path to Washington. It suggests relaxing emissions and safety requirements, and vigorous stimulation of the economy. Chrysler has called for a cut in income taxes and easier credit for car buyers.

A bad year for autos is a bad year for everyone. But if the government guarantees a no-lose game for autos, it will have to provide some other mechanism by which the economy can correct the mistakes of management and government alike. When a big company brings out a bad product, or when it yields to a powerful union and writes an inflationary wage contract, its management should not end up just as well off as good management. If it does, the economy will have no built-in discipline, no way of confirming good decisions and revising bad ones.

The answer of the dedicated antitrusters is to break up the big companies, but the U.S. probably has gone far beyond the point where that could be done without paralyzing the economy. The real problem, therefore, is to make big corporations more resilient, more capable of correcting mistakes. Ideas for achieving this result are strangely scarce.

Perhaps the trouble is that Berle's forecast was wrong in another respect. "There is solid ground," he said in 1954, "for the expectation that 20 years from now the men of greatest renown in the United States will be the spiritual,

Government as a Buyer. The government buys goods and services from the private sector, including everything from paper clips to sophisticated military hardware. Out of a 1974 gross national product of $1,385 billion, government at all levels purchased $305 billion worth of goods and services, with $117 billion purchased by the federal government alone. Many companies, such as Lockheed, depend on the government for much of their business. Many other businesses benefit either directly or indirectly from government procurement.

As a buyer, and such a large one at that, government can force, or at least attempt to force, companies to meet public policy goals in addition to meeting the specifications and other terms directly related to the product. Contractors must file affirmative action plans with the federal government that must meet with approval before they can be awarded the contract. Contractors have also been encouraged to use minority business as subcontractors and suppliers, hire more handicapped people, comply with wage and price guidelines, and other public policy goals. The awarding of a contract partially depends on meeting these public policy objectives and sometimes contracts are cancelled if these objectives are not met satisfactorily.

Government Ownership. Although nationalization of industries has not been a goal of government in this country as it has in Western Europe, in some cases the government does come to own outright and control some parts of the economy. Since the 1930s, for example, the government has often participated in the generation and distribution of electric power. By 1968, the federal government was producing about 13 percent of all electric power in the United States, with another 10 percent generated by municipally owned utilities. One of the best examples of this form of government ownership is, of course, the Tennessee Valley Authority, a large-scale program of river basin development and electrical power generation begun in the 1930s.[18]

Government also came to take over most of the passenger rail service in the country. In 1971, a federal corporation called the National Railroad Passenger Service, or Amtrak, was created to take over and operate passenger service from railroads that decided to join. Thus the government got into the business of providing intercity rail service which apparently was no longer profitable for private transportation companies to provide.[19]

Besides these forms of outright ownership, the federal government also participates in mixed enterprises—those which are a mixture of private and

[18]James W. McKie, "Government Policies to Control and Assist Private Business," *Business and Society 74-75*, William D. Evans and Robert A. Wagley, eds. (Morristown, N.J.: General Learning Press, 1974), pp. 117–118.

[19]*Ibid.*, p. 116.

governmental ownership and control. Examples are the Communications Satellite Corporation (COMSAT), which draws its capital from both public and private sources, the Federal Deposit Insurance Corporation (FDIC), the Export-Import Bank, and the Post Office. These agencies resemble private enterprise to a degree unknown in regular government offices and departments.[20]

The reasons for these kinds of government ownership are complex. During wartime, private industry may not have enough capacity to provide war material on the scale needed. The government may have to build and operate facilities, as it did with aluminum production during the Second World War, and then later sell them off to private industry. The government also gets involved when the risks are too high for private investors or the capital requirements too large and too complex, as in the case of such large projects as the TVA endeavor. In the case of Amtrak, government becomes the owner when it is no longer privately profitable to operate something, yet it seems socially beneficial to continue the service at taxpayers' expense.

Government as Manager of the Economy. This role was assigned the federal government by the Employment Act of 1946, which passed the Senate without a dissenting vote and received little opposition in the House of Representatives. The government was given the responsibility to ensure full employment of resources, while at the same time pursuing the goal of price stability (see box). Full employment generally means that qualified people can find jobs at prevailing wage rates in productive activity without excessive delay. While no specific goals were set in the act itself, widely used targets before the Arab oil embargo of 1974 were that unemployment should not exceed 4 percent of the workforce, and that price rises of 1.5 percent and 2 percent per annum were within the goal of price stability. Since 1974, what full employment and price stability mean in a quantitative sense is anybody's guess.

THE EMPLOYMENT ACT OF 1946

The Congress hereby declares that it is the continuing policy and responsibility of the Federal Government to use all practicable means consistent with its needs and obligations and other essential considerations of national policy, with the assistance and cooperation of industry, agriculture, labor, and State and local governments, to coordinate and utilize all its plans, functions, and resources for the purpose of creating and maintaining in a manner calculated to foster and promote free competitive enterprise and the general welfare conditions under which there will be afforded useful employment opportunities, including self-employment, for those able, willing and seeking to work, and to promote maximum employment, production, and purchasing power.

The act contained three major provisions creating a mechanism to meet the purposes specified in the legislation. The first provision required an Economic Report of the President to be delivered to Congress each year specifying the levels of employment, production, and purchasing power

[20]*Ibid.*, pp. 118–119.

obtaining in the United States at that time. The report is to contain current and foreseeable trends in levels of employment, production, and purchasing power, discuss the economic conditions affecting employment, and review the economic program of the federal government for carrying out a full employment policy together with such recommendations for legislation as the President may deem necessary or desirable.

The second provision of the act created a Council of Economic Advisors to assist and advise the President in preparing the economic report. The council gathers information about current economic trends and development, interprets economic data and submits studies to the President, appraises federal programs in view of the objectives of the act, and recommends national economic policies and legislation to the President.

The Joint Economic Committee of Congress, the third part of the mechanism, makes continual studies of matters pertaining to the economic report and coordinates programs to carry out the provisions of the act. The committee files the results of its hearings, findings, and recommendations with Congress to act as a guide for the various congressional committees as they take up specific legislative proposals related to the economy.

The tools that the federal government has at its disposal to accomplish the purposes of the act are broadly defined as fiscal and monetary policy. The former includes tax cuts or increases to put more money into the economy or take it out if necessary, and increases in government spending to stimulate the economy. Monetary policy involves the efforts of the Federal Reserve Board to control the amount of money in circulation by changing reserve requirements for member banks, engaging in open-market operations to buy or sell securities, and changing the rediscount rate it charges members of the system.

It should be noted that both fiscal and monetary policy are generally directed toward the management of aggregate demand in the economy. Starting in 1979, a good deal of attention was given to what was called supply-side economics, that is, more direct attempts to deal with productivity problems through stimulating business investment in new plants and equipment, encouraging saving and private investment by lowering the capital gains tax and perhaps making a certain amount of interest tax-free, and reducing the regulatory burden on business, which hampers productivity. The basic assumption behind supply-side economics is that our fundamental problem is not one of deficient demand but one of declining productivity and growth because of aging plants and equipment, increased resource prices, particularly energy, and insufficient incentives for new investment.[21]

The benefits of the Full-Employment Act have been substantial. Prior to 1974, the record of stable economic growth was much better than before the existence of the act, as the period since the Second World War has largely been one of price stability and full employment. The act set some goals for the economy and forced the executive branch and Congress to develop a set of public policies to attain them. The result was a stimulus to comprehensive and coordinated long-range planning in government and business. The

[21]See "Why Supply-Side Economics Is Suddenly Popular," *Business Week,* September 17, 1979, pp. 116–117.

administration of the act, the Economist Report of the President, and hearings before the Joint Economic Committee of Congress have also provided a forum for and stimulated education about economic theory and practice.

Government as Planner. Two planning bills were introduced into Congress in the 1970s. The first, sponsored by Senator Hubert Humphrey (D-Minn.) and Jacob Javits (R-N.Y.), was introduced into the first session of the 94th Congress (S. 1795) to amend the Employment Act of 1946. The bill advocated the development and adoption of a balanced economic growth plan for the country. The Humphrey-Javits bill, as it came to be called, provided a mechanism for more formal government planning by setting up an Economic Planning Board in the Office of the President, assisted by an Advisory Committee and a Council on Economic Planning. The President, with the help of the Economic Planning Board, would be required to submit a Balanced Economic Growth Plan to Congress every two years. Provisions were contained in the bill for congressional review of the plan and for establishing procedures for broad public participation in the planning process.

The functions of the Economic Planning Board, which was the key agency in this planning process, were imposing. These functions included: (1) anticipating the nation's economic needs; (2) measuring the available national economic resources; (3) insuring an adequate supply of industrial raw materials and energy; (4) outlining economic goals for the nation as a whole; (5) developing a proposed Balanced Economic Growth Plan; and (6) recommending policies to achieve the objectives of the plan. The plan itself, submitted by the President, would contain the following elements.

- an examination of long-run economic and social trends and objectives
- a recommended six-year economic and social plan, embodying coherent and realizable economic and social goals, including specific goals for each major sector of the economy
- identification of the resources required for achieving the stated goals and objectives and a statement of the governmental policies and programs needed
- a review of economic and social goals contained in existing legislation, with analysis of the progress toward meeting such goals that can reasonably be expected in the six-year period
- identification of the resources, policies, and programs necessary to achieve such progress, and the extent to which the achievement of such progress will compete with other goals and objectives that the President considers of equal or greater importance
- pertinent data, estimates, and recommendations which the Office considers useful to the President, Congress, or the public.[22]

Figure 8.2 shows how this planning process would work. The Economic Planning Board, as stated, would create the plan using various inputs, to be modified and approved and eventually submitted to Congress by the Presi-

[22]"Notes from the Joint Economic Committee," Congress of the United States, Vol. 1, No. 19 (July 1, 1975), p. 6.

Figure 8.2. Development and Flow of the Balanced Economic Growth Plan

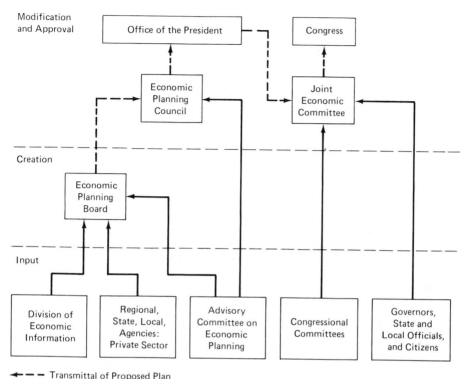

From "Notes from the Joint Economic Committee," Congress of the United States, Vol. 1, No. 19 (July 1, 1975), p. 7.

dent. Governors would be encouraged to hold hearings in their states on the plan to provide the widest possible public participation. They would be able to file a report with the Joint Economic Committee of Congress, which would take these inputs, along with inputs from congressional committees, and develop recommendations to Congress about the plan submitted by the President. The Congress would have to act within 135 days of its submission to adopt, modify, or reject in whole or in part the plan submitted by the President. Depending on the action taken by Congress, the President could revise or submit a new plan until approval was obtained and the plan put into effect.

The second bill, formally called the "Full Employment and Balanced Growth Act of 1976" (the Humphrey-Hawkins bill), was introduced into the House (H.R. 50) and Senate (S. 50) in March 1976. The general purposes of this bill, shown below, were more sweeping than those of the Employment Act of 1946.

> To establish and translate into practical reality the right of all adult Americans able, willing, and seeking to work to full opportunity for useful paid employment at fair rates of compensation; to combine full employment, production, and purchasing power goals with proper attention to balanced growth and national

priorities; to mandate such national economic policies and programs as are necessary to achieve full employment, production, and purchasing power; to restrain inflation; and to provide explicit machinery for the development and implementation of such economic policies and programs.[23]

Specifically, the bill defined full employment as a rate not in excess of 3 percent of the adult Americans in the civilian labor force to be attained as promptly as possible within four years after the bill's enactment. If a gap should exist between the levels of employment achieved through aggregate fiscal and monetary policies and the employment goals specified in the act itself, the act provided for a system of comprehensive flexible employment policies to create jobs in both the private and public sectors of the economy. These policies were designed to encourage the optimum contribution of these sectors toward achievement of the purposes of the act. These countercyclical employment policies could include the following:

    (A) countercyclical public service employment;
    (B) accelerated public works, including the development of standby public works projects;
    (C) State and local countercyclical grant programs as specified in section 203;
    (D) the levels and duration of unemployment insurance;
    (E) skill training in both the private and public sectors, both as a general remedy, and as a supplement to unemployment insurance;
    (F) youth employment programs as specified in section 205;
    (G) a community development program to provide employment in activities of value to the States, local communities, and the Nation; and
    (H) augmentation of other employment and manpower programs that would prove helpful in meeting high levels of unemployment from cyclical causes.[24]

The Humphrey-Javits bill never passed Congress. The Humphrey-Hawkins bill finally did pass Congress, but in a watered-down version of the original. The final version requires the President and the Federal Reserve Board to report to Congress each year on how their programs will lead to full employment by 1983. It contains goals of 4 percent unemployment for all workers and 3 percent for adults over 20, and in this sense attempts to breathe new life into the Employment Act of 1946 by enshrining what the 1946 Act simply codified.[25]

These bills indicate an interest in a more formal planning system for government, the revival of a debate that began with the National Industrial Recovery Act in the depression years. The debate continues as to whether more formal planning is a proper role for government in the struggle to establish some kind of a comprehensive energy plan for the country to attain the goal of energy independence. In a sense, the government does plan already, but it is ad hoc and uncoordinated, consisting of bits and pieces located in various agencies and departments that affect various sectors of the economy. The kind of planning described here is a more comprehensive formal approach that would specify social and economic goals for the society as a whole and attempt to coordinate all the efforts of the public and private

[23]"The Full Employment and Balanced Growth Act of 1976," *Challenge*, May–June 1976, p. 56.
[24]*Ibid.*, p. 62.
[25]"The Sanitizing of Humphrey-Hawkins," *Business Week*, November 28, 1977, p. 41.

sectors toward the attainment of these goals. This is a new role the government has not as yet attempted.

One argument for national planning is simply that if government management of aggregate demand has had such success for most of the period since the Second World War, more such planning on an even more comprehensive basis must be better. Others argue that the difficulties we have experienced since 1974 with high inflation and unemployment make planning a necessity. We have moved into an era of resource shortages, it is said, where the market can no longer allocate resources to their best uses. The market must be supplemented by national economic planning to allocate these scarce resources in a fair and just manner so all members of society can maintain a decent quality of life.

Others point to the success corporations have had with planning and argue that government should be using some of the techniques that corporations have developed to set goals, objectives, and strategies for all its agencies. "Our government suffers from the absence of (1) an overall sense of direction, (2) well-defined national goals and objectives, (3) an integrated strategy for achieving such goals and objectives, and (4) a process for answering difficult 'What if?' questions that cut across department lines within the government."[26] The answer is a comprehensive planning system which would solve the problems of energy, national defense, environment, and other problems of this scope.

Another argument in favor of planning is that business itself would benefit from it; our present haphazard approach to problems like inflation and unemployment does not create an environment in which business can function effectively. A more coordinated and planned response to problems would create a more stable environment for business and help it to gain credibility.[27] Finally, the planning exercise, some argue, would itself be beneficial. There has been a tendency for the nation to charge off after a variety of social and economic goals, all of them desirable but not necessarily compatible with one another. Planning might introduce some realism and discipline to this process.

The arguments against planning are many and formidable. Some fear that this role would inevitably result in more government control over business and eventually produce such a concentration of economic and political power in the hands of the federal government as to threaten our pluralistic system. Such a role involves a further shift in power to government bureaucrats and gives them greater control over the daily lives of citizens.

Another argument against planning is that the sheer size and complexity of the socioeconomic system is simply beyond the capability of people and machines to coordinate effectively. Too many variables and too many decisions would have to be made centrally to take into account all the various interests of society. Critics of planning need only point to the efforts of the

[26]Thomas H. Naylor, "The U.S. Needs Strategic Planning," *Business Week*, December 17, 1979, p. 18.
[27]Robert Lekachman, "A Cure for Corporate Neurosis," *Saturday Review*, January 21, 1978, pp. 30–34.

Department of Energy to allocate energy resources, and the dislocations and problems these efforts caused.

Finally, the comparison of government planning with planning by business is questioned. There is a fundamental difference, some point out, between the two processes. Business planning is based on the assumption that the ultimate decisions as to the allocation of society's resources are made by individual consumers. Thus business planning is geared to the corporate purpose of attempting to persuade consumers to buy the firm's goods or services. If the company's planning is wrong, it will suffer the consequences.

Government, on the other hand, will determine through a planning process what is in the best interests of society as a whole. If the public does not respond accordingly, the government can use its power to achieve the results it desires. This power includes promotion, procurement, regulation, ownership, taxation, and other roles it plays in the economy. Unlike a private organization, government may not only plan, it can also command. While a business firm can set goals only for itself, government can establish goals for society as a whole and see that they are followed through some form of government control.[28]

Questions for Discussion

1. What are the different ways by which the growth of government can be measured? Which is most significant from a business point of view?
2. Discuss the reasons behind this growth. Which, in your opinion, are most important in explaining the growth of government? Which reasons are likely to be a continuing influence behind big government? Which will decrease in importance? Based on the assessment, is government in the next decade likely to get larger, smaller, or stay about the same?
3. Do you agree with the experts about the current state of business-government relations? What problems does this cause for society? What would you suggest as an alternative relationship?
4. What roles does government play in the economy? Which of these roles has increased most significantly in importance during the past decade? Have any of these roles decreased in importance?
5. Should government guarantee loans to companies like Chrysler that get in trouble? Why or why not? Are some companies indeed too big to be allowed to fail?
6. Why is government allowed to own some pieces of the economy? Is there anything like a trend in our country toward nationalization of more industries? Why or why not? Why hasn't the United States nationalized more of the economy as some countries in Europe have done?
7. Describe the mechanism created by the Employment Act of 1946 to carry out the purposes of the act. What is the difference between fiscal and monetary policy? Which is more effective in stimulating the economy?
8. Discuss the new supply-side economics. How does this approach differ from past economic policy of the federal government? Would more attention to the supply-side solve our current economic problems?
9. Describe the two planning bills discussed in the chapter. How do they differ? Which do you like best? Why? Be as specific as possible.

[28]Murray L. Weidenbaum and Linda Rockwood, "Corporate Planning versus Government Planning," *The Public Interest*, No. 46 (Winter 1977), pp. 59–72.

10. What are the arguments for and against government planning? Are you in favor of some type of government planning? What do you think the future holds in this regard? What implications does your answer have for business organizations?

Suggested Reading

Anderson, James E., Brady, David N., and Bullock, Charles III. *Public Policy and Politics in America.* North Scituate, Mass.: Duxbury Press, 1978.

Anderson, Ronald A. *Government and Business,* 3rd ed. Cincinnati: South-Western, 1966.

Jacoby, Neil H. *The Business-Government Relationship: A Reassessment.* Santa Monica, Calif.: Goodyear Publishing Co., 1975.

Liebhafsky, H. H. *American Government and Business.* New York: John Wiley, 1971.

Schnitzer, Martin. *Contemporary Government and Business Relations.* Chicago: Rand McNally, 1978.

Solo, Robert A. *The Political Authority and the Market System.* Cincinnati: South-Western, 1974.

9

Government Regulation

No business, large or small, can operate without obeying a myriad of government rules and restrictions. Costs and profits can be affected as much by a directive written by a government official as by a management decision in the front office or a customer's decision at the checkout counter. Fundamental entrepreneurial decisions—such as what lines of business to go into, what products and services to produce, which investments to finance, how and where to make goods and how to market them, and what prices to charge—are increasingly subject to government control.[1]

The regulation of business by the federal government is so pervasive and comprehensive that it deserves a chapter by itself. This role of government has expanded more in recent years than any of the other roles discussed in the previous chapter, so much so that it is difficult to find an area of business that is untouched by government regulation. This growth of regulation has been referred to as a second managerial revolution, involving a shift of decision-making power and control over the corporation.[2]

The first revolution was based on the idea of a separation of ownership and control, first advocated by Adolph A. Berle and Gardner C. Means.[3] They argued that decision-making power in the modern corporation had shifted from the formal owners to a class of professional managers. The second managerial revolution is a shift of decision-making power from the managers of corporations to a vast cadre of government regulators who are influencing, and in many cases controlling, managerial decisions of the

[1] Murray L. Weidenbaum, "Government Power and Business Performance," *The United States in the 1980s,* Peter Dunignan and Alvin Robushka, eds. (Palo Alto, Calif.: Stanford Univeristy, Hoover Institution, 1980), p. 200. Quoted with permission.

[2] Murray L. Weidenbaum, *Business, Government and the Public* (Englewood Cliffs, N.J.: Prentice-Hall, 1977), p. 285.

[3] Adolph A. Berle and Gardner C. Means, *The Modern Corporation and Private Property* (New York: Macmillan, 1932).

typical business corporation. These types of decisions, which are increasingly subject to government influences and control, are basic to the operation of a business organization. According to Murray Weidenbaum, Chairman of the Council of Economic Advisors in the Reagan administration, these decisions include the following:[4]

- What lines of business to go into?
- What products can be produced?
- What investments can be financed?
- Under what conditions can products be produced?
- Where can they be made?
- How can they be marketed?
- What prices can be charged?
- What profit can be kept?

Government regulations affect every department or functional area within the corporation and every level of management. Top management in particular, as illustrated by the Olin case in the first chapter, can spend a great deal of time on public policy matters that are regulatory in nature. They also face varying and rising penalties under federal statutes.[5] Some of the impact that regulation makes on the functional areas of a corporation includes the following:

Research and development has been affected by a host of safety and health regulations. Thus a good deal of R&D effort now goes into what is called "defensive" research directed toward meeting the requirements of government regulatory agencies rather than toward the development of new and/or improved products.

The manufacturing function has been affected by a host of regulations dealing with safety and health in the workplace and pollution control. Depending on the industry, some companies have to allocate a significant portion of their capital expenditures toward meeting these regulatory requirements.

Marketing is affected by regulations that deal with deception in advertising, disclosure of product characteristics believed to be of interest to the consumer, requirements for warning labels on certain products, and regulations pertaining to packaging. The marketing department is also responsible for the reverse distribution mechanism—product recalls that can be ordered by a government agency.

The personnel function is affected by regulations pertaining to equal opportunity for women and minorities, regulations related to age discrimination, and efforts of government agencies to promote the hiring of handicapped people. These regulations affect all aspects of the personnel function: hiring, firing, transfers, promotions, and the like.

---

[4]Murray L. Weidenbaum, *The Future of Business Regulation* (New York: AMACOM, 1979), p. 34.
[5]S. Prakash Sethi, "Who Me? Jail as an Occupational Hazard," *The Wharton Magazine*, Vol. 2, No. 4 (Summer 1978), pp. 19–27.

The finance department is affected by demands for increased disclosure of information to shareholders and the Securities and Exchange Commission, as well as having to respond to increased demands for information from other government agencies.[6]

The volume of regulations that affect business is so large that no corporation in the country can comply with all the laws and regulations to which it is subject. Small companies in particular are probably not even aware of all the regulations affecting them. The National Council on Wage and Price Stability, for example, made a study in 1976 that listed 5,600 regulations from 27 different agencies with which steelmakers must comply. In 1976, a total of 83 federal agencies were regulating business.[7]

Types of Regulation

It might be useful at the outset to look at the various types of government regulation in existence, since the regulatory activities of government are not all the same. Different types of regulation have different objectives, use different methods to accomplish these objectives, affect different segments of business, and involve different costs to society. The major types of government regulation are regulation of competitive behavior, industry regulation, social regulation, and regulation of labor-management relations. The list of agencies in Exhibit 9.1 is by no means exhaustive, but is representative of these different types of regulation.

Competitive Behavior. Since the Sherman Antitrust Act of 1890, the government has been regulating competitive behavior by investigating such illegal practices as price fixing and price discrimination and the structure of industries when they become highly concentrated. The agencies of the federal government involved in regulating competitive behavior are the Antitrust Division of the Justice Department and the Bureau of Competition in the Federal Trade Commission. This type of regulation will be discussed in Chapter 11, which deals specifically with this area of public policy.

Industry Regulation. This type of regulation is the oldest, beginning with the Interstate Commerce Commission of 1887, which was established to provide continuous surveillance of private railroad activity across the country. While some states had practiced such regulation before the federal government, the inability of the states to regulate railroads effectively led to the passage of this act, which set the pattern for additional regulatory commissions of this type. Thus followed the Federal Power Commission, the Civil Aeronautics Board, and the Federal Communications Commission, all examples of industry regulation.

One reason for this type of regulation is the belief that certain natural monopolies exist where economies of scale in an industry are so great that the largest firm would have the lowest costs and thus drive its competitors out of the market. Since competition cannot act as a regulator in this situa-

---

[6]See Weidenbaum, *The Future of Business Regulation,* pp. 33–54.

[7]George A. Steiner, "An Overview of the Changing Business Environment and Its Impact on Business," paper presented at the AACSB Conferences on Business Environment/Public Policy, Summer 1979, pp. 7–8.

EXHIBIT 9.1 ───────────────────────────────

Types of Government Regulation

I. Competitive Behavior
  A. Justice Department
  B. Federal Trade Commission

II. Industry Regulation
  A. Utilities—FERC
  B. Communications—FCC
  C. Air Transportation—CAB
  D. Surface Transportation—ICC
  E. Finance and Securities—SEC

III. Social Regulation
  A. Occupational Safety and Health—OSHA
  B. Equal Opportunity—EEOC
  C. Advertising and Deceptive Practices—FTC
  D. Product Safety—CPSC
  E. Physical Environment—EPA
  F. Food and Drugs—FDA
  G. Auto Safety and Economy—NHTSA

IV. Labor-Management Relations
  A. National Labor Relations Board
  B. Labor-Management Services Administration

tion, the government must perform this function to regulate these industries in the public interest.

Another reason for industry regulation is that an agency may be needed to allocate limited space, as in the case of the airlines and broadcasters. The threat of predatory practices or destructive competition is another rationale for regulation that is often used to justify regulation of the transportation industry. Regulation may be needed, it is often argued, to provide service to areas that would be ignored by the market. An example is the provision of railroad and airline service to small towns and cities. Finally, some argue that regulation is needed to prevent fraud and deception in the sale of securities.

Thus utilities are regulated at the federal level by the Federal Energy Regulatory Commission (FERC), whose purpose is to regulate interstate aspects of the electric power and natural gas industries. This agency, associated with the new Department of Energy (DOE), succeeded the Federal Power Commission (FPC) in 1977. Where federal regulation of utilities does not apply, state regulatory commissions have been created.

The Federal Communications Commission (FCC) regulates domestic and foreign communications by radio, television, wire, cable, and telephone. The Civil Aeronautics Board (CAB) promotes and regulates the civil air transport industry. Surface transportation, including trucking, railroads, buses, oil pipelines, inland waterway and coastal shippers, and express companies are regulated by the Interstate Commerce Commission (ICC). The Securities and Exchange Commission (SEC) regulates the securities and financial markets to protect the public against malpractice.

This type of regulation focuses on a specific industry and is concerned about its economic well-being. While the original impetus for regulation may have come from consumers who believed they needed protection, the so-called capture theory suggests that these agencies eventually become a captive of the industry they are supposed to regulate. This happens because of the unique expertise possessed by members of the industry or because of job enticements for regulators who leave government employment. The public or consumer interest is often viewed as subordinate as the agency comes to focus on the needs and concerns of the industry it is regulating.

Social Regulation. This new wave of regulation, as Murray Weidenbaum calls it, appeared in the 1960s and 1970s in response to the change in the social values and concerns of society. This type of regulation is a radical departure from the industry type of regulation. Health and safety regulation, for example, affects virtually all of business, not just a particular industry, and thus is far broader in scope. The effects of CAB regulation are largely limited to air carriers and air passengers, while safety and health regulations apply to every employer engaged in a business affecting commerce.[8]

Furthermore, this new style of regulation affects the conditions under which goods and services are produced and the physical characteristics of products that are manufactured rather than focusing on markets, rates, and the obligation to serve. The Environmental Protection Agency (EPA), for example, sets constraints on the amount of pollution a manufacturer may emit in the course of its operations. The Consumer Product Safety Commission (CPSC) sets minimum safety standards for products.[9]

These agencies are concerned with noneconomic matters and sometimes pay little or no attention to an industry's basic mission of providing goods and services to the public. Their impetus comes from social considerations related to improving the quality of life, and they often ignore the effects of their regulations on such economic matters as productivity, growth, employment, and inflation.[10]

Social regulation often means that the government becomes involved with very detailed facets of the production process, interfering with the traditional prerogatives of business management. For example, the Occupational Safety and Health Administration (OSHA) sometimes specifies precise engineering controls that must be adopted. The CPSC mandates specific product characteristics that it believes will protect consumers from injury. The Federal Trade Commission (FTC) deals with specific advertising content in some cases. These activities involve the government in many more details of business management than industry regulation.[11]

The pressures for this new type of regulation primarily come from a variety of interest groups concerned with the social aspects of our national life—environmentalists, consumer groups, labor unions, and civil rights organizations. The traditional capture theory—the idea that the industry captures its regulators—does not apply to this type of regulation. Industry, by and large, has shown no enthusiasm for social regulation because it interferes with the basic economic mission of business. If anyone comes to

---

[8]William Lilley III and James C. Miller III, "The New Social Regulation," *The Public Interest*, No. 47 (Spring 1977), p. 53.

[9]*Ibid.*

[10]See Weidenbaum, *The Future of Business Regulation*, pp. 116–140.

[11]Lilley and Miller, "Social Regulation," pp. 53–54.

dominate these new functionally oriented agencies, it will be the special interest concerned with the agency's specific task of regulation.[12]

One reason for this type of regulation is related to the nature of today's workplace and marketplace. It is often argued that when goods and technology are complex and their effects largely unknown, consumers are incapable of making intelligent judgments of their own, and workers may not know the risks they face on various jobs or may not be able to acquire the necessary information. Expert judgment is needed in these areas to protect consumers and workers from unnecessary risks that they cannot assess for themselves.[13]

Another reason for this type of regulation is the existence of externalities when the actions of a firm have a harmful effect on others. The cost of external diseconomies such as air and water pollution cannot be voluntarily assumed by firms unless a government agency exists to enforce standards equally across all firms in an industry. Voluntary assumption by some firms would place them at a competitive disadvantage; regulation is needed to make all companies meet the same standard, leaving them in the same competitive position.[14]

Agencies dealing with social regulation include the Occupational Safety and Health Administration (OSHA), whose purpose is to enforce worker safety and health regulations. The Equal Employment Opportunity Commission (EEOC) enforces the antidiscriminatory provisions of the Civil Rights Act and other related laws that have recently come under its jurisdiction. The Consumer Product Safety Commission (CPSC) was created to protect the public from unreasonable risks of injury associated with consumer products. Protection and enhancement of the physical environment is the responsibility of the Environmental Protection Agency (EPA). The Bureau of Consumer Protection in the Federal Trade Commission (FTC) deals with false or deceptive advertising of consumer products. The purpose of the Food and Drug Administration (FDA) is to protect the public against impure and unsafe food, drugs, and cosmetics, and to regulate hazards associated with medical devices and radiation. Finally, the National Highway Traffic Safety Administration (NHTSA) sets standards for motor vehicle safety and fuel economy.

Labor-Management Relations. This area of regulation grew out of the depression years, when the Wagner Act established the right of employees to form unions and collectively bargain with management over wages and working conditions and other aspects of labor-management relations. A full discussion of this aspect of regulation is more properly the subject of an industrial relations course. But the two principal agencies involved in this aspect of regulation are the National Labor Relations Board (NLRB), which was created by the Wagner Act to administer the laws related to collective bargaining between companies and labor unions, and the Labor-Management Service Administration, which regulates certain aspects of union activ-

[12]Murray L. Weidenbaum, "The Changing Nature of Government Regulation of Business," paper presented at the AACSB Conferences on Business Environment/Public Policy, Summer 1979, p. 14.

[13]Robert E. Healy, ed., *Federal Regulatory Directory 1979–80* (Washington, D.C.: Congressional Quarterly, Inc., 1979), p. 5.

[14]*Ibid.*

ity and shares, with the Internal Revenue Service, the administration of legislation pertaining to benefit plans of corporations.

Description of Regulation

Given this diversity of types of regulation, it is difficult to come up with an all-encompassing definition of regulation. The following definition from the State Governmental Affairs Committee, however, comes close to encompassing this diversity of composition and function. In a January 1977 report, the committee described a federal regulatory office as "one which (1) had decision making authority, (2) establishes standards or guidelines conferring benefits and imposing restrictions on business conduct, (3) operates principally in the sphere of domestic business activity, (4) has its head and/or members appointed by the president . . . [generally subject to Senate confirmation], and (5) has its legal procedures generally governed by the Administrative Procedures Act."[15]

Some agencies are independent in the sense that they are not located within a department of the executive branch of government. Since they are not part of the legislative or judicial branch either, a fourth branch of government seems to have emerged that combines the functions of the other three in the making, interpreting, and implementing of legislation. These independent agencies include the CAB, CPSC, EEOC, EPA, FCC, FERC, FTC, ICC, NLRB, and the SEC. In creating these agencies and making them independent, Congress sought to fashion them into an arm of the legislative branch and insulate them from presidential control. But many Presidents have considered these commissions to be adjuncts of the executive branch and have argued that they should be able to coordinate and direct the independent agencies.[16]

Critics of this structure argue that the independent character of these commissions can hinder political monitoring by the executive branch and Congress that would make the agencies more responsive to social and economic change. Since Congress in particular does not exercise its oversight function very well in some cases, the agencies can become complacent in their functions. On the other hand, these agencies can also become too zealous in their efforts, requiring new congressional action to reign them in, such as recent efforts directed toward the FTC and its rule-making authority.[17]

Another criticism is that the independent character of these agencies has weakened them by removing the benefits of more direct congressional and presidential support. In the case of industry regulation, this makes the agencies more vulnerable to pressure from the regulated industries. They become timid in defending the public interest and developing effective regulatory programs. In the case of social regulation, the independence of the agencies makes them subject to pressures from various interest groups, which may make them ignore the economic impact of their actions.[18]

[15]Healy, *Regulatory Directory*, p. 3.
[16]*Ibid.*, p. 25.
[17]*Ibid.*
[18]*Ibid.*, p. 26.

Other agencies are located within the executive branch in one of the cabinet departments. These agencies include the FDA as part of the Department of Health and Human Resources, the Antitrust Division of the Department of Justice, the Labor-Management Services Administration and OSHA in the Department of Labor, and NHTSA in the Department of Transportation. Even here, however, there is some question whether these agencies are subject to presidential influence and guidance or whether they are free to use the regulatory authority granted them by Congress. Some believe that the President's power to appoint and dismiss cabinet officers carries with it an implicit authority to direct actions by regulatory agencies within the executive departments. Others argue that these agencies may accept White House advice, but that ultimately they are as independent as the separate regulatory commissions.[19]

Regulatory activities may be pursued in a number of ways—rate-making, licensing, granting of permits, establishing routes, establishing standards, requiring disclosure of information, and pursuing formal litigation against violators of federal standards. In general, however, the traditional industry-oriented agencies have used adjudication procedures more than rule-making procedures to carry out their functions. Rates and routes for air carriers, for example, are set in trial-like circumstances, where interested parties present their oral arguments and are cross-examined. After a lengthy process of review, the agency eventually reaches a decision, which may be appealed in the courts.

The rule-making procedure is generally preferred by the newer social agencies. Under this process, an agency must publish a proposed regulation in the Federal Register and provide an opportunity for public comment. It is up to the agency itself to decide whether to hold hearings, but if they are held, they are different from the adjudication hearings. They are not presided over by an administrative law judge, nor are witnesses subject to cross-examination. The final regulation is then published in the Federal Register along with a summary of comments received and responses to them. This regulation can be challenged in court, but if not challenged or if upheld by the court, it has the force of law and violators of the regulation can be fined or otherwise punished, depending on the enabling legislation of the agency.[20]

The Growth of Regulation

There is little doubt that regulation was a growth industry during the 1970s, with the leading product being the newer areas of social regulation. While many of the more traditional industry regulatory agencies were created during the New Deal era, the 1970s saw a surge in federal regulation with the creation of many new agencies dealing with social regulation. Figure 9.1 shows the growth in the number of agencies.

This growth is also shown in Tables 9.1 and 9.2, which list the expenditures on federal regulatory activities from 1970 to 1979 (administrative costs contained in the federal budget) and the increases in the staff of these

[19]See *Ibid.*, p. 31.
[20]*Ibid.*, p. 22.

Figure 9.1. A Historical Perspective to Agency Growth

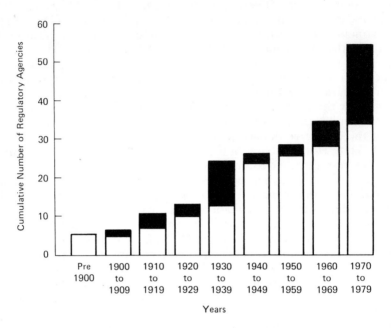

From Kenneth Chilton, *A Decade of Rapid Growth in Federal Regulation* (St. Louis, Mo.: Washington University, Center for the Study of American Business, 1979), p. 5. Reprinted with permission.

agencies over the same time period. Overall regulatory expenditures in 1979 were six times the 1970 level, while staff had increased nearly three times the 1970 level. These tables also show that the major growth has taken place in the newer forms of social regulation (consumer safety and health, job safety and other working conditions, and environment and energy).

During the decades of the 1960s and 1970s, Congress enacted over a hundred laws regulating business activity. Some of these are shown in Exhibit 9.2. In addition, existing or new federal agencies issued thousands of rules and procedural requirements. The number of pages in the Federal Register grew from 20,036 in 1970 to 42,422 in 1974. In March 1979, the Office of the Federal Register reported that 61,000 pages of government regulations had been issued, a 305 percent increase in eight years.[21]

Costs of Regulation

This phenomenal growth has led to a concern about the costs of all this regulation to the American economy. The problem with these costs is that they are largely hidden. The most visible costs of regulation are the costs of running the agencies themselves, which are contained in the federal budget.

[21] Healy, *Regulatory Directory*, p. 10.

GOVERNMENT REGULATION

TABLE 9.1 **Expenditures on Federal Regulatory Activities (Fiscal Years, Millions of Dollars)**

Area of Regulation	1970	1971	1972	1973	1974	1975	1976	1977	1978	1979	Growth Factor (1979 ÷ 1970)
Consumer Safety and Health	$369	$587	$771	$1042	$1266	$1326	$1557	$1857	$2512	$2592	7.0
Job Safety and Other Working Conditions	62	104	124	227	310	379	447	492	550	620	10.0
Environment and Energy	94	154	47	213	370	445	628	772	941	1064	11.3
Financial Reporting and Other Financial	22	23	27	31	36	45	52	56	68	67	3.0
Industry-Specific Regulation	125	151	166	140	203	220	251	286	290	293	2.3
General Business	73	81	92	100	115	122	145	166	186	190	2.6
Total	$745	$1100	$1227	$1753	$2300	$2537	$3080	$3629	$4547	$4826	6.5
Annual % Increase		48%	12%	43%	31%	10%	21%	18%	25%	6%	

Source: Marcia B. Wallace and Ronald J. Penoyer, *Directory of Federal Regulatory Agencies* (St. Louis, Mo.: Washington University, Center for the Study of American Business, 1978), p. ii. Reprinted with permission.

TABLE 9.2 **Staffing of Federal Regulatory Agencies**

Area of Regulation	1970	1971	1972	1973	1974	1975	1976	1977	1978 (Estimated)	1979 (Estimated)	Growth Factor (1979 ÷ 1970)
Consumer Safety and Health	5768	6212	27755	27567	27991	27943	29010	32618	32110	32699	5.7
Job Safety and Other Working Conditions	3921	4337	5100	9946	10820	11857	12563	13278	13578	14883	3.8
Environment and Energy	0	54	5119	5138	7055	7421	7834	8899	9114	9863	∞
Financial Reporting and Other Financial	7635	8073	8388	8703	9006	9640	10473	10934	11427	11852	1.6
Industry-Specific Regulation	5874	5771	5798	6112	6583	7216	7538	6140	6179	6275	1.1
General Business	4445	4472	1675	1852	4951	5094	5282	5236	5275	5293	1.2
Total	27643	28919	53835	59318	66406	69171	72700	77105	77683	80865	2.9
Annual % Increase		5%	86%	10%	12%	4%	5%	6%	1%	4%	

Source: Marcia, B. Wallace and Ronald J. Penoyer, *Directory of Federal Regulatory Agencies* (St. Louis, Mo.: Washington University, Center for the Study of American Business, 1978), p. ii. Reprinted with permission.

EXHIBIT 9.2

Significant Regulatory Legislation, 1960–1979

Civil Rights Act of 1960
Federal Hazardous Substances Labeling Act of 1960
Fair Labor Standards Amendments of 1961, 1966, and 1974
Federal Water Pollution Control Act Amendments of 1961
Oil Pollution Act of 1961 and Amendments of 1973
Food and Agriculture Act of 1962
Air Pollution Control Act of 1962
Antitrust Civil Process Act of 1962
Drug Amendments of 1962
Clean Air Act of 1963 and Amendments of 1966 and 1970
Equal Pay Act of 1963
Civil Rights Act of 1964
Food Stamp Act of 1964
Automotive Products Trade Act of 1965
Federal Cigarette Labeling and Advertising Act of 1965
Water Quality Act of 1965
Clean Water Restoration Act of 1966
Fair Packaging and Labeling Act of 1966
Federal Coal Mine Safety Act Amendments of 1966
Financial Institutions Supervisory Act of 1966
Oil Pollution of the Sea Act of 1966
Age Discrimination in Employment Act of 1967
Air Quality Act of 1967
Flammable Fabrics Act of 1967
Wholesome Meat Act of 1967
Agricultural Fair Practices Act of 1968
Consumer Credit Protection Act of 1968
Natural Gas Pipeline Safety Act of 1968
Radiation Control for Health and Safety Act of 1968
Cigarette Smoking Act of 1969
Child Protection and Toy Safety Act of 1969
Federal Coal Mine Health and Safety Act of 1969
Tax Reform Act of 1969
National Environmental Policy Act of 1970
Bank Holding Act Amendments of 1970

Bank Records and Foreign Transactions Act of 1970
Economic Stabilization Act of 1970 and Amendments of 1971 and 1973
Environmental Quality Improvement Act of 1970
Fair Credit Reporting Act of 1970
Investment Company Amendments of 1970
Noise Pollution and Abatement Act of 1970
Occupational Safety and Health Act of 1970
Securities Investor Protection Act of 1970
Water and Environmental Quality Improvement Act of 1970
Export Administration Finance Act of 1971
Consumer Product Safety Act of 1972
Equal Employment Opportunity Act of 1972
Federal Environmental Pesticide Control Act of 1972
Noise Control Act of 1972
Agriculture and Consumers Protection Act of 1973
Emergency Petroleum Allocation Act of 1973
Highway Safety Act of 1973
Water Resources Development Act of 1974
Energy Policy and Conservation Act of 1975
Toxic Substances Control Act of 1976
Resource Conservation and Recovery Act of 1976
Clean Air Act Amendments of 1977
Water Pollution Control Act Amendments of 1977
Endangered Species Act Amendments of 1978
Amendments to the Age Discrimination in Employment Act of 1978
Emergency Energy Conservation Act of 1979
Safe Drinking Water Act Amendments of 1979

But these administrative costs are only the tip of the iceberg. The bulk of the costs of regulation are the compliance costs that are imposed on business.

The Center for the Study of American Business estimated these compliance costs for 1976 by taking the most reliable estimates for the various areas of regulation that were available at the time.[22] For example, figures

[22]Murray L. Weidenbaum and Robert DeFina, *The Rising Cost of Government Regulation* (St. Louis, Mo.: Washington University Center for the Study of American Business, 1977).

from the Council on Environmental Quality were used for estimating compliance costs for pollution abatement. The paperwork figure came from the Commission on Federal Paperwork study. This procedure was believed to be conservative because when a range of costs was involved, the lower end was generally chosen. In some cases, no cost estimates at all were available.[23]

> The basic approach followed in the study was to cull from the available literature the more reliable estimates of the costs of specific regulatory programs, to put those estimates on a consistent and reliable basis, and to aggregate the results for 1976. Where a range of costs was available for a given regulatory program, the lower end of the range was generally used. In many cases no cost estimates were available. Thus, the numbers in this study are low and surely underestimate the actual cost of federal regulation in the United States.[24]

Table 9.3 shows the results of this procedure. For 1976, the study showed approximately $3.2 billion in administrative costs and $62.9 billion in compliance costs.[25] This study clearly shows that the costs imposed on the private sector are much greater than the cost of running the agencies themselves. The estimated compliance costs in 1976 were twenty times the administrative costs for that year. Applying this multiple of twenty to the amounts budgeted for regulatory activities in subsequent years, approximations were generated, as shown in Table 9.4, for the total dollar impact of government regulation from 1977 to 1979.

TABLE 9.3 **Annual Cost of Federal Regulation, by Area, 1976 (Millions of Dollars)**

	Administrative Cost	Compliance Cost	Total
Consumer safety and health	$1,516	$ 5,094	$ 6,610
Job safety and working conditions	483	4,015	4,498
Energy and the environment	612	7,760	8,372
Financial regulation	104	1,118	1,222
Industry specific	484	$19,919	20,403
Paperwork	—	25,000	25,000
Total	$3,199	$62,906	$66,105

[23]No cost estimates were available for the following regulatory activities: Animal and Plant Health Inspection Service, Packers and Stockyards Administration, Department of Housing and Urban Development, Antitrust Division, Drug Enforcement Administration, Federal Railroad Administration, Bureau of Alcohol, Tobacco and Firearms, Customs Service, Consumer Product Safety Commission, National Transportation Safety Board, Mining Enforcement and Safety Administration, Department of Energy, Federal Maritime Commission, Commodity Future Trading Commission, Nuclear Regulatory Commission, Comptroller of the Currency, Federal Deposit Insurance Corporation.

[24]Murray L. Weidenbaum and Robert DeFina, *The Cost of Federal Regulation of Economic Activity* (Washington, D.C.: American Enterprise Institute, 1978), p. 1.

[25]This total of $66 billion is equivalent to: 4 percent of the gross national product; $307 per person living in the United States: 18 percent of the federal budget; twice the amount that the federal government spends on health; 74 percent of the amount devoted to national defense; over one-third of all private investment in new plants and equipment. *Ibid.,* p. 3.

TABLE 9.4 **Estimated Cost of Federal Regulation of Business (Fiscal Years, in Billions of Dollars)**

	1977	1978	1979
Administrative costs	$ 3.7	$ 4.5	$ 4.8
Compliance costs	75.4	92.2	97.9
Total	$79.1	$96.7	$102.7

The Business Roundtable subsequently completed a study of the compliance costs imposed on part of its membership by six regulatory agencies or programs.[26] This study, which was managed by the accounting firm of Arthur Andersen and Company, claimed to be different from other regulatory cost studies because of its specificity. It dealt only with incremental costs, defined as "the direct costs of those actions taken to comply with a regulation that would not have been taken in the absence of that regulation. These incremental costs were based upon (1) information drawn from companies' accounting, engineering and other business records, and (2) informed judgement as to which actions would have taken in the absence of regulation."[27]

These incremental costs were classified into operating and administrative costs, research and development, product related costs, and capital costs. Not only were the costs distributed into these classifications, they were also broken out by specific regulations. The study omitted so-called secondary costs of regulation, such as productivity losses, construction delays, inflation, and misallocation of resources.

The study, released in March 1979, covered 48 companies in more than twenty industries. All of these participants were considered to be large corporations. Many of them were multinational, although only their domestic operations were included. The six government agencies and programs included in the study were the Environmental Protection Agency, Equal Employment Opportunity Commission, Occupational Safety and Health Administration, Department of Energy, Employee Retirement and Income Security Act, and the Consumer Protection Bureau of the Federal Trade Commission.

The incremental cost for the 48 companies to comply with regulations from the six agencies and programs for 1977 was $2.6 billion. Figure 9.2 shows the breakdown of this cost by the four classifications mentioned previously. Operating and administrative costs compose the bulk (42 percent) of the total. The costs by agency (Figure 9.3) show that fully 77 percent of the total incremental costs is attributable to the Environmental Protection Agency alone.

[26]Arthur Andersen and Company, *Cost of Government Regulation Study* (New York: The Business Roundtable, 1979).
[27]*Ibid.*, p. ii.

Figure 9.2. Incremental Costs Summarized in Four Classifications

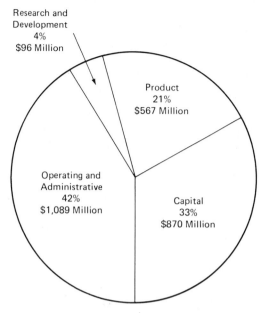

Total Incremental Costs $2.6 Billion

From Arthur Andersen and Company, *Cost of Government Regulation* (New York: The Business Roundtable, 1979), p. 15. Reprinted with permission.

Figure 9.3. Incremental Costs for Each Agency

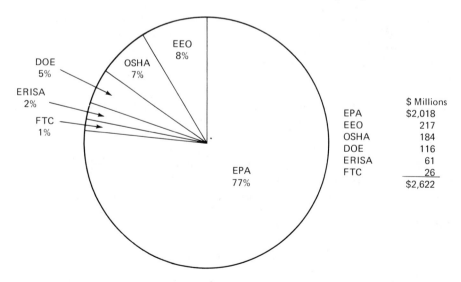

From Arthur Andersen and Company, *Cost of Government Regulation* (New York: The Business Roundtable, 1979), p. 19. Reprinted with permission.

The impact of regulation showed a wide variation among industries. For example, the incremental cost of OSHA rules averaged $6 per year per worker in the banking industry, but $220 per worker per year in the chemical industry. The study also identified attributes of regulation that had a high incremental cost, which would hopefully be useful in reform efforts.

Besides these comprehensive studies covering the entire economy or a select number of companies, some corporations have estimated regulatory costs for themselves. Caterpillar Tractor Co., for example, estimated that its regulatory costs for 1976 were $67.6 million, of which $21.5 million was administrative and operating costs, $22.0 million went for capital costs, and $24.1 million was related to product costs.[28] Of the total cost, over 90 percent resulted from regulations issued by two agencies (EPA and OSHA) that before 1970 did not even exist (Table 9.5). To put these figures in perspective, the following comparisons were made by the company:

- Expended almost one-fourth as much on government regulation as for purchase of rough steel
- Expended almost as much on government regulation as for world-wide energy needs
- Expended more for government regulation than for Social Security: and about the same on government regulation as on all medical benefits in the U.S.
- Expended more than one-third as much for government regulation as the company paid in U.S. federal income taxes
- Expended half as much on government regulation as for dividends paid to shareholders.[29]

The Impact of Regulation on Small Business

Some believe that government regulation has had a disproportionate adverse impact on small business as compared with the large corporation. The small firm has a limited ability to pass along regulation-induced costs or to generate investment capital to finance regulation-induced expenditures. As stated by Kenneth W. Chilton, Associate Director of the Center for the Study of American Business: "Large capital expenditures to meet environmental or job safety standards above those that would be followed voluntarily may represent merely an uneconomical application of resources for a large firm, but it may literally be a matter of the enterprise's life or death for the small firm."[30]

The foundry industry is a case in point. Before 1968, there were approximately 4,200 foundries in the industry. Eighty-two percent of these firms employed fewer than 100 people and 75 percent employed fewer than fifty. The total industry employed 375,000 workers. Around 1968, this industry began to lose some of its small plants due to a combination of the recession and EPA regulations. The size of the mandated EPA emission control

[28]*Government Regulation,* Caterpillar Governmental Affairs Bulletin, July 5, 1978, pp. 2–3.
[29]*Ibid.,* p. 4.
[30]Kenneth W. Chilton, *The Impact of Federal Regulation on American Small Business* (St. Louis, Mo.: Washington Center for the Study of American Business, 1978), p. 2.

TABLE 9.5 **Regulatory Costs for 1976, Caterpillar Tractor Co. (U.S. Regulation Only)**

Agency or Department	Total Costs Due to Regulations
Environmental Protection Agency	$32,168,709*
Occupational Health and Safety Administration	31,090,895**
Equal Employment Opportunity and Affirmative Action	1,198,334
Federal Trade Commission and Department of Justice	821,973
Department of Transportation	768,164
Interstate Commerce Commission	306,635
Department of Defense	259,841
Department of Commerce	220,740
Department of Treasury	197,787
Civil Aeronautics Board	150,243
Department of Labor	91,618
Securities and Exchange Commission	84,891
Department of Interior	74,356
National Labor Relations Board	41,627
Federal Communications Commission	32,943
Federal Energy Administration	19,986
Federal Power Commission	13,751
Consumer Product Safety Commission	10,301
All Others	52,554
Total	$67,605,348

*Of which $10,258,709 is administrative/operating cost; $21,800,000 capital cost; and $110,000 product cost.
**Of which $6,936,445 is administrative/operating cost; $167,450 capital cost; and $23,987,000 product cost.

Source: Government Regulation, Caterpillar Governmental Affairs Bulletin, July 5, 1978, pp. 2–3. Reprinted with permission.

TABLE 9.6 **Causes of Foundry Closings 1968–1975**

Year	EPA in Part or Total	Labor or Skills	Bankrupt or Economics	Consoli-dations	Death of Principal	Unknown	Total
1968–69	1	1	7	1	4	22	36
1970	6	3	8	4	2	52	75
1971	14	1	22	5	1	74	117
1972	14	9	13	3	2	28	69
1973	7	1	5	2	—	4	19
1974	11	1	5	2	—	9	28
1975	1	—	1	1	—	3	6
Total	54	16	61	19	9	192	350
% of Total Excluding Unknown	34%	10%	39%	12%	6%	—	—

Source: Kenneth W. Chilton, *The Impact of Federal Regulation on American Small Business* (St. Louis, Mo.: Washington University Center for the Study of American Business, 1978), p. 4. Reprinted with permission.

expenditures for many of these foundries exceeded their net worth, forcing them to close down their operations. From 1968 to 1975, there were 350 verified foundry closings, and, as shown in Table 9.6, many of these were due to the impact of EPA regulations.[31]

A study by Charles River Associates examined the impact of proposed OSHA standards for air-lead exposure levels. The total compliance cost for business was estimated at $416 million (1976 dollars), with annual operating costs of $112 million. The impact on the battery industry alone, which was composed of 143 firms, was estimated as follows:

> . . . OSHA lead regulations would result in much larger per unit production costs for smaller plants than for larger plants. Because of large differential costs and the fact that battery prices would only rise to cover the unit costs of the larger firms . . . smaller plant operators would be forced to absorb the differential in costs. In many cases the amount absorbed would . . . eliminate entirely the plant's profitability and about 113 single plant battery firms would be forced to close. . . . [This] would eliminate half of the productive capacity not operated by the five major battery companies.[32]

Besides these capital expenditures, the paperwork associated with government regulation often commands large segments of the entrepreneur's time and effort. The Commission on Federal Paperwork reported that the five million small businesses in the country spend between $15 and $20 billion per year, or an average of over $3,000 each on federal paperwork. The commission went on to say that "small businesses are relatively harder hit by federal information requirements than larger firms and often lack the necessary expertise to comply."[33]

Besides these effects, regulatory agencies can sometimes hurl devastating blows at a small company by releasing incorrect information about a product on which the company is dependent.[34] Some government regulations adversely affect the ability of small business to attract investment. Finally, many pension plans of small business have gone out of existence because of the increased costs of meeting pension law requirements.

Other Costs of Regulation

The cost studies previously cited dealt mainly with the direct or first-order costs of regulation—the cost to the economy and the firm of directly complying with government regulations. There are also what Murray Weidenbaum calls the indirect or second-order effects of regulation.[35] The most serious of these costs, according to Weidenbaum, is losses in productivity. Edward Denison of the Brookings Institution, for example, estimated that business

---

[31]*Ibid.*, p. 3.

[32]"CRA Examines the Cost of Meeting OSHA Lead Standards," *Charles River Associates Research Review,* February 1978, p. 2.

[33]Commission on Federal Paperwork, *Final Summary Report* (Washington, D.C.: U.S. Government Printing Office, 1977), p. 66.

[34]See the Marlin Toy Products case in Murray L. Weidenbaum, *Business, Government and the Public* (Englewood Cliffs, N.J.: Prentice-Hall, 1977), pp. 213–219.

[35]Weidenbaum, *The Future of Business Regulation,* pp. 16–23.

productivity in 1975 was 1.4 percent lower than it would have been if business had operated under the regulatory conditions existing in 1967. Of that amount, one percent was due to pollution abatement requirements and 0.4 percent to employee safety and health programs. That productivity loss, according to Denison, amounted to a reduction of about $20 billion in the level of gross national product for that year.[36]

Besides this indirect effect on productivity, regulation can also affect employment. Older, marginal facilities may have to be closed down because they cannot meet regulatory standards and remain profitable.[37] The minimum wage law also affects employment by pricing teenagers out of the market. Other plants that were proposed have been cancelled because of the difficulty of obtaining all the regulatory permits from federal, state, and local agencies.[38]

A final category of regulatory costs are the induced, or third-order effects. These are the actions that the firm takes to respond to the direct and indirect effects of regulation. Weidenbaum believes that these "difficult to measure impacts may, in the long run, far outweigh the more measurable costs resulting from the imposition of government influence on private sector decision making."[39]

One of these third-order effects is the impact regulation has on capital formation. This situation arises from the closing down of plants that cannot remain economically viable and meet government standards. The closing of the foundries mentioned in the previous section is an example. The other side of the coin is the difficulty in obtaining all the necessary permits and clearance necessary to construct new facilities, as the Dow Chemical case illustrates. The effect of many of these regulations is to halt or limit new capital formation and hence economic growth.

Government regulation also has an effect on innovation in some industries. In the drug industry, for example, the volume of new drug products and new chemical entities has declined since the 1962 amendments to the Pure Food and Drug Act. These amendments required extensive premarket testing of new drugs. This drop in innovation has been accompanied by increases in the cost, duration, and risk of new product development. The results have been a sharp reduction in the rate of return on R&D investment in the drug industry and an erosion of American technological leadership in new drug development.[40]

Finally, regulation diverts management attention from its basic function of running the enterprise. As the Olin case in Chapter 1 illustrates, management sometimes has to devote a significant portion of its time to dealing with the impacts of regulation on the economy. The net result of these

---

[36]Ibid., p. 20. See also Healy, *Regulatory Directory*, p. 40.

[37]See Chapter One, the Olin Case.

[38]Dow Chemical Company cancelled plans in January 1977 for building a $300 million petrochemical complex in California. After two years and a $4 million expenditure, Dow had obtained only four of the 65 permits that were needed from federal, state, local, and regional regulatory agencies in order to build the facility. Weidenbaum, *The Future of Business Regulation*, pp. 19–20.

[39]Ibid., p. 23.

[40]Jerome E. Schnee, "Regulation and Innovation: U.S. Pharmaceutical Industry," *California Management Review*, Vol. XXII, No. 1 (Fall 1979), pp. 23–32.

third-order effects, Weidenbaum says, "can be seen in the factories that do not get built, the jobs that do not get created, the goods and services that do not get produced, and the incomes that are not generated."[41]

The Benefits of Regulation

Regulation supposedly produces many benefits, such as better customer service, cleaner air and water (which may contain fewer pollutants which can cause disease), more economic opportunities for minorities and women, fewer accidents on the job, and safer and higher quality products for consumers. The costs of regulation are difficult enough to quantify, but when it comes to the benefits, the task is much more difficult. The benefits are much more diverse and are not necessarily translatable into economic terms so that a direct comparison with the costs can be made.

Some believe that it is impossible to quantify the benefits of regulation. How can a dollar value be put on human life? What is the dollar value of preserving wilderness areas for future generations? What is the correct value to society for providing all its citizens with equal opportunities for employment? What is the value of preserving competition?

Mark Green of Congress Watch, for example, asks: "What is the price tag for lives saved by avoiding future diseases, since asbestos and other substances in our lives today cause cancer in 30 years? How much will you pay for a 6-year-old who is not disfigured from flammable sleepware? How do we calculate the exact benefits of being able to see across the Grand Canyon, of avoiding needless destruction of our recreation areas?"[42]

Despite these criticisms, studies have been made which attempt to quantify the benefits. In 1970, for example, the EPA estimated that it would cost $650 million to repaint surfaces damaged by air pollution. In support of its cotton dust standards, OSHA estimated that these standards would save more than $500 million a year in medical costs by preventing 1,749 cases of brown lung. A study conducted by Data Resources, Inc. of Cambridge, Mass., calculated that environmental controls would actually decrease unemployment by 0.2 to 0.3 percent annually and would increase the inflation rate by only 0.1 to 0.2 percent a year over the next eight years. Job losses caused by pollution controls would be more than offset by the need to hire workers to construct, install, and service mandated antipollution devices and sewers.[43]

The General Accounting Office in 1974 estimated that some 28,000 lives were saved between 1966 and 1974 because of motor vehicle safety standards. The National Highway Traffic Safety Administration estimated that the societal costs of motor vehicle accidents in 1975 and 1977 were $38 billion and $43 billion respectively, including income lost, medical care, insurance administration, and legal expenses. Thus there were substantial benefits to be gained if accidents could be reduced.[44]

[41]Weidenbaum, *The Future of Business Regulation*, p. 30.
[42]Healy, *Regulatory Directory*, p. 43.
[43]*Ibid.*, pp. 45–46.
[44]*Ibid.*, p. 46.

GOVERNMENT REGULATION

More recently, Ralph Nader completed a study that showed government safety and health regulations provided Americans with more than $35 billion in benefits in 1978 and in 1985 will produce $80.6 billion in benefits. The agencies studied were the EPA, NHTSA, FDA, and CPSC, and in all but the EPA, so the study claimed, the costs of regulation were outweighed by the benefits. Environmental regulation cost $.5 billion more than the benefits it provided to society.[45]

Besides these kinds of studies where some attempt is made to quantify benefits in economic terms so direct comparisons with costs can be made, attempts have been made to estimate benefits along other dimensions. The EPA, for example, in its original estimate of environmental costs and benefits for the 1970s, said that the estimated $287.1 billion cost would reduce illness and premature death from bronchitis by 25 to 50 percent, produce a 20 percent reduction in morbidity and mortality from heart disease and a 25 percent reduction in respiratory diseases, cause a 25 percent reduction in deaths from lung cancer, and add three to five years to the life expectancy of the average adult in urban centers.[46] Even these kinds of estimates, if reasonably accurate, are useful in at least providing some idea of what benefits regulation is providing so that a crude cost-benefit analysis can be performed. Obviously, however, much more work needs to be done in this area to develop an appropriate methodology to assess benefits.

Problems of Regulation

Cost is the most obvious problem with regulation and the regulatory process. Many regard this cost as excessive, that the economy is over-regulated in the sense that the costs exceed the benefits to society. Another common complaint is that the regulatory agencies are too often indifferent to the burdensome costs of their interventions, sometimes even displaying an arrogance toward business and toward economic analysis.[47]

But there are other problems with regulation. Many regulations are unclear and vague, requiring a good deal of effort in interpretation and clarification. Regulations are often adopted on the basis of inadequate information, not only about the costs, but also about the status of affected groups. Another problem is the haphazard enforcement of government regulations.

Kangun and Moyer point out that the regulatory agencies are dominated by lawyers, which means there is a lack of quantitative skills for analysis, inattention to priorities regarding the cost and benefits of actions, and an overemphasis on the adversary system in making economic decisions. External review of the agencies is also hampered by industry dominance and bias, underfunding of the agencies dealing in industry regulation, thereby forcing the agencies to place a heavy reliance on industry-generated data,

[45] Mark Green and Norman Watzman, *Business War on the Law: An Analysis of the Benefits of Federal Health/Safety Enforcement* (Washington, D.C.: Corporate Accountability Research Group, 1979).

[46] *Environmental Quality: The Third Annual Report of the Council on Environmental Quality* (Washington, D.C.: U.S. Government Printing Office, 1972).

[47] See Weidenbaum, *The Future of Business Regulation*, pp. 116–117.

and the tendency of regulatory bodies to make less than socially optimal decisions in order to avoid strong challenges to their mandates.[48]

John T. Dunlop, former U.S. Secretary of Labor, provides a useful list of problems in an article entitled "The Limits of Legal Compulsion." An abbreviated version of this list is presented below.[49]

1. Simplistic thinking about complicated issues is encouraged.

2. Designing and administering a regulatory program is an incredibly complicated task.

3. Often policies that appear straightforward will have unintended consequences which can create problems as severe as those with which the regulations were intended to deal.

4. The rule-making and adjudicatory procedures of regulatory agencies tend to be very slow, creating conflicts among the different groups involved, and leading to weak and ineffective remedies for the people the programs aim to help.

5. The rule-making and adjudicatory procedures do not include a mechanism for the development of mutual accommodation among the conflicting interests.

6. Regulatory efforts are rarely abandoned even after their purpose has been served.

7. Legal game-playing occurs between the regulatees and the regulators.

8. Small and medium-size firms encounter difficulty in complying with the regulations of the various agencies, and the government has problems in trying to enforce compliance.

9. As the rule-making and compliance activities of regulatory agencies become routine, it grows increasingly difficult for the President and the agency to attract highly qualified and effective administrators to leadership positions.

10. Uniform national regulations are inherently unworkable in many situations because the society is not uniform.

11. Regulatory overlap, where a number of different regulatory agencies share some of the same responsibilities, causes problems.

The latter point deserves further comment. There have been many instances of agencies that have required two diametrically opposed actions on the part of business (see box). This would seem to be inevitable when two or more agencies have responsibility for the same area and no effective coordinating mechanism exists. Some effort has been made to deal with this problem with the formation of interagency committees when jurisdictional responsibilities overlap among two or more agencies.

Finally, there is the problem that more and more decision-making in society is being turned over to the "experts" in government agencies. These experts are being relied upon to make critical decisions affecting all of

[48]Norman Kangun and R. Charles Moyer, "The Failings of Regulation," *MSU Business Topics,* Spring 1976, p. 13.

[49]John T. Dunlop, "The Limits of Legal Compulsion," *The Conference Board Record,* March 1976, pp. 24–26. © 1976 The Conference Board.

COORDINATING REGULATION

The internal structures of regulatory agencies are diverse and the quality of their performance varied, as is the scope of their oversight. Each has its own congressional mandate and governing statutes and varied degrees of independence from presidential control.

This diversity has led to some overlapping of jurisdictions, which in turn has resulted on occasion in confusing or contradictory regulations. For example, an Occupational Safety and Health Administration (OSHA) regulation stipulated that butcher shops have grated floors to reduce the risk of employees' slipping, while the Department of Agriculture mandated that the floor be smooth because grates increased the hazards of contamination. In 1977 OSHA directed that the Made-Rite Sausage Co. of Sacramento, Calif., place protective guards on its meat-blending machine, but it turned out that the guards violated Department of Agriculture rules because they made cleaning the machines too difficult.

Some of the contradictions are inherent. Standards issued by the Environmental Protection Agency (EPA) designed to reduce auto and industry pollution involve costs that could fuel inflation and mechanisms that could reduce mandated fuel efficiency.

Fragmented authority can lead to instances where it is difficult to implement or alter policies or for Congress and the president to exercise effective oversight. On the other hand, as the Senate Committee on Government Operations noted in its December 1977 study on regulatory organization,

> Certain instances of apparent duplication are . . . often situations where different agencies are considering separate aspects of a problem and separate review may be useful. . . . [A]certain degree of "redundancy" is not only natural, but also necessary for sound regulatory administration. . . . Our study reveals that . . . in certain instances this redundancy has reduced errors, resulted in greater reliability for the system as a whole and that the process of eliminating redundancy through agency consolidation would impose unacceptable political costs compared with any foreseeable administrative advantages.

Some efforts to improve coordination have been made. For an example, in 1977 an Energy Department was created, consolidating into one agency energy programs that had been spread among 40 agencies. In May of that year the Food and Drug Administration, Consumer Product Safety Commission and the EPA joined to impose a ban on fluorocarbons with a single timetable.

From Robert E. Healy, ed., *Federal Regulatory Directory 1979–80* (Washington, D.C.: Congressional Quarterly, Inc., 1979), p. 5. Reprinted with permission.

society and are becoming much more powerful in the process. In the words of James C. Miller III of the American Enterprise Institute:

> Another institutional matter is that we are relying more and more on "experts" to make critical decisions. What is the role of these experts and to whom do they answer? Nowhere are they more clearly in positions of power than in government regulatory agencies. Irving Kristol calls them the "new class," and his descriptions remind me of Eric Hoffer's characterizations of "intellectuals." Fundamentally, these people are zealots in the pursuit of *justice as they see it.* They are prone to view polluters, not as rational businessmen responding to what may be a perverted set of incentives, but as "sinners" to be punished. And since by definition all have

sinned, there is much punishment to be meted out. The simple truth of the matter is that the people who have the most to say about a particular rule or regulation are the GS-12s, 13s, and 14s who prepare the initial drafts. For once a proposed rule or regulation appears in the *Federal Register*, seldom is it changed to any significant degree. Of course, even the government should look with favor on employees who like their work; it raises productivity. But in so many cases these experts are not pursuing well-defined tasks but are in a real sense serving the role of judges, and the prejudices many of them being to the job should be cause for concern.[50]

Regulatory Reform

The costs and other problems of regulation have stimulated many efforts at reform. These reform measures have taken different forms, depending on the type of regulation and the objectives of reform measures and proponents. Some of the most popular methods of reform are considered in the following paragraphs.

Deregulation. The most obvious type of reform regarding industry regulation is simply to deregulate the industry and allow it to function on a more competitive basis. Congress passed such a deregulation bill aimed at air passenger service in 1978, which facilitated the offering of new services by the airline companies themselves and granted them a measure of flexibility in raising and lowering their fares. The bill contained an automatic route entry program which granted unused route authority to air carriers willing to serve those routes.

The bill was not passed without opposition, however, even from the airlines themselves. Many in the industry feared that deregulation would lead to predatory competitive practices, driving the smaller airlines out of existence or bringing about increased concentration through mergers. Small communities feared they would lose service as airlines concentrated on the more lucrative major markets. The immediate results of deregulation were promising, as both ridership and profits increased.

A study by the Bureau of Pricing and Domestic Aviation in the CAB showed that in the twelve-month period ending February 1979, scheduled service measured by aircraft departures had increased 8.4 percent nationwide. Some smaller airports, however, had experienced declines as predicted. At the smallest airports, service had risen or held steady at 459 points, while departures dropped an average of 21 percent at 218 others.[51]

Similar measures were proposed for the trucking industry, but met with fierce opposition. The large trucking firms as well as the Teamsters Union were content with the status quo, as regulation limited new entry and kept rates and profits high. The Teamsters viewed deregulation as a threat to jobs and safety on the road. The railroad industry, however, welcomed deregulation, and in 1979 railroads were given the right to charge as little or

[50]James C. Miller III, "Regulation and the Prospects for Reform," *Regulation, Competition, Deregulation—An Economic Grab Bag*, Charles F. Phillips, Jr., ed. (Lexington, Va.: Washington and Lee University, 1979), p. 113.

[51]"Airline Deregulation Is Increasing Service, CAB's Study Shows," *The Wall Street Journal*, March 23, 1979, p. 2.

as much as they pleased for hauling fresh fruits and vegetables instead of following ICC approved rates. The FCC also proposed in 1979 to abolish much of its control over commercial radio broadcasting. Clearly, for some industries, deregulation in 1979 gathered a great deal of momentum.

The Legislative Veto. While Congress is supposed to exercise oversight of regulatory agencies, particularly those independent agencies it created, there are many obstacles to the fulfillment of this oversight function. These obstacles include the overlapping jurisdiction between the many committees of Congress, leading to fragmented oversight, the difficulties these committees have in getting information from the agencies, and the disparity in size between congressional staffs and the agencies they oversee.[52]

To remedy this situation, a legislative veto has been proposed to give Congress more direct control over agency actions. Some versions of this idea provide that a ruling would take effect unless disapproved by Congress within a certain period of time. Other versions require Congress to take affirmative action before an agency ruling or new regulation could go into effect. In 1979, this idea was used as a means of curbing the power of the FTC, particularly in regard to its industrywide trade rule writing authority granted by Congress in 1975, which many believed had been used irresponsibly.

Advocates of the legislative veto believe it would provide Congress with a clear means of approving or disapproving a proposed regulation. Even the threat of a legislative veto might make the agencies more responsible to congressional sentiments. Critics point out, however, that such a mechanism would result in additional delays in the regulatory process, and represent an added burden to Congress's already heavy workload.[53]

Sunset Legislation. Another idea which would enhance congressional oversight is a periodic review and reauthorization of federal agencies and programs. Time limits would be placed on a program's existence, and if no justification for its continuation could be found, it would be discontinued. Hence the term sunset. One bill would require that an executive branch agency's budget and mission would have to be justified every five years (S. 2), another would require a systematic review of all independent regulatory agencies on an eight-year schedule (S. 600).

Such reauthorization is already required for the CPSC and FTC (three years) and the SEC (two years). Advocates argue that this process requires Congress to evaluate the need for regulation and eliminate waste and duplication. Again, the threat of termination could put pressure on the agencies to be more responsive to congressional sentiments. Critics point out, however, that an effective review of all the agencies, or even the most important ones, would not only be expensive, but would severely increase individual committee workloads. Such review would also lead to congressional bargaining for support of favored programs.[54]

Presidential Intervention. In March 1978, President Carter issued Executive Order 12044, which established a new procedure for development of regulations by executive agencies. The order could not, of course, be

[52]Healy, *Regulatory Directory,* p. 28.
[53]*Ibid.,* p. 29.
[54]*Ibid.,* p. 30.

extended to the independent commissions. Under the order, agencies were required to publish semiannual agendas of anticipated regulatory actions, write regulations in language as simple and clear as possible, seek approval of agency heads for all significant regulations before they are published for public comment, perform a "regulatory analysis" on each significant regulation, outlining the economic consequences of the proposal and its major alternatives, and periodically review all major existing regulations to determine whether they are achieving goals consistent with the order. In addition to the order, the President established a Regulatory Analysis Review Group to assess significant proposed rules and a Regulatory Council to prepare a calendar of new rules prepared by the agencies.[55]

When President Reagan took office, a Task Force on Regulatory Relief was established to review major regulatory proposals by regulatory agencies in the executive branch, especially those proposals that have a major policy significance or that appear to involve overlapping jurisdiction among agencies. The task force is also to assess executive branch regulations already in effect, oversee the development of legislative proposals, and codify President Reagan's views on the appropriate role and objectives of regulatory agencies. These are examples of what the President can do to exercise oversight of the agencies in the executive branch.

Regulatory Budget. The regulatory budget idea would provide a ceiling on the compliance costs that could be imposed on the private sector during any fiscal period as well as limiting the operating costs of the agencies themselves. Such a budget process would introduce some measure of control, say advocates, over compliance costs in particular. It would require that total regulatory costs be incorporated into the federal government's annual budgetary and program review mechanism (see box).

Analytical Techniques. Many advocate the use of more analytical techniques for all agencies before a new regulation is issued. Some assessment of the cost and benefits, it is argued, should be required of all new regulations to justify on a more rational basis the imposition of regulations. But the mere performance of a cost-benefit analysis is not enough. As stated by Murray Weidenbaum: "The key action needed by Congress is to pass a law limiting the regulations of all federal agencies to those instances where the total benefits to society exceed the costs. Government regulations should be carried to the point where the added costs equal the added benefits, and no further. Overregulation—which can be defined as regulation for which the costs exceed the benefits—should be avoided."[56]

Cost effectiveness analysis is another analytical technique that might be useful, particularly in conjunction with a regulatory budget. This technique is useful in determining where a given level of expenditure can be used most effectively. Thus if $400 million is all that can be spent by an agency on new regulations, the question of where this money can be used to save the most lives or improve the qualify of life by the greatest amount, however this is measured, is the crucial question to answer.

On February 17, 1981, President Reagan issued an Executive Order to

[55]*Ibid.,* pp. 52–53.
[56]Murray L. Weidenbaum, *Reducing the Hidden Cost of Big Government* (St. Louis, Mo.: Washington University Center for the Study of American Business, 1978), pp. 9–10.

$100 BILLION IS MISSING

When the President announces his budget later this month, $100 billion will be missing. That is the amount Washington forces private citizens to spend to comply with its rules and regulations. Whereas some good comes from this regulation, much harm does too, and few people believe it contributes $100 billion to the national welfare.

But whether you think federal regulation is on balance helpful or harmful, the cost of it should be included in the federal budget because it preempts private expenditures just as do federal taxation and borrowing. Moreover, since regulation is not an item in the budget, there is no control over the amount of resources spent in this way.

In effect, federal agencies have acquired de facto the power to tax. They use this power to supplement their appropriated budgets to the tune of $100 billion a year.

The Budget Act of 1974 was supposed to close "off-budget" spending loopholes, but somehow this massive one escaped the attention of the Congress. Now Rep. Bud Brown (R., Ohio) and Senator Lloyd Bentsen (D., Texas) want to amend the Budget Act to include an annual regulatory budget to set a limit on the regulatory costs that each agency can impose on the economy.

Presently there is no effective control over the vast majority of the federal regulatory agencies. The President can't set limits because most of the regulatory agencies are independent commissions or administrations. Congress occasionally intervenes to rein in some of the more outlandish regulatory initiatives, but without a regulatory budget it has no systematic way of controlling the taxing power of the federal bureaucracy.

The result is entirely predictable. The agencies have no incentive to consider the cost of compliance when they develop regulations. Lacking a budget restraint on their activities, they push them to the hilt and over-regulate.

A regulatory budget would bring cost-benefit considerations into the picture, and it would also provide a more accurate picture of the federal government's total impact on the economy. Moreover, as Senator Bentsen points out, a regulatory budget would aid the Congress in choosing between regulatory and spending programs and help the government establish priorities in pursuing regulatory objectives.

Until the Congress establishes a regulatory budget, neither a spending limitation, a tax limitation, nor a balanced budget amendment will put a meaningful lid on government spending.

replace E.O. 12044 that required agencies in the executive branch to prepare a Regulatory Impact Analysis for each major rule being considered. This analysis should permit an accurate assessment of the potential costs and benefits of each major regulatory proposal. In addition, the Executive Order required that the agencies choose regulatory goals and set priorities to maximize the benefits to society, and choose the most cost-efficient means among legally available options for achieving the goals.

Alternatives to Regulation. Finally, there may be areas where alternatives to regulation may work more effectively to achieve the objectives of regulation than the regulatory process itself. This area of reform is in effect a form of deregulation applied to the social regulatory area. Most social regulation presently involves a command and control system where laws and rules are used to more or less force people and business to meet certain objectives. The reinforcement mechanism is negative in that business and individuals are subject to penalties or lawsuits if they do not comply. Alternatives to this process involve the use of indirect methods of encouraging business to meet the same objectives.[57]

The use of a market approach to achieve regulatory objectives stresses incentives, not duties or rights. Changes in business and individual behavior can be accomplished by modifying the incentives that induce people to act in a certain way as dictated by their self-interest. Government can provide these incentives through its taxing power, for example; pollution control taxation may provide a more effective and less costly mechanism to achieve ecological objectives than the standards approach. Business would be induced to reduce the size of the tax by installing pollution control devices of its own choosing. Similarly, provision of more accurate information to consumers on a wide range of potential product hazards may be more effective in providing safe products than outright bans or setting of safety standards which require expensive alterations.[58]

Questions for Discussion

1. How does government regulation affect business? What functional areas does regulation affect? What changes has it made in the management function?
2. Distinguish between industry and social regulation. What are the objectives of each type of regulation? What reasons can you think of to explain the development of industry and social regulation?
3. What does regulation mean as used in this chapter? In what specific ways is regulation pursued? What procedures are used to regulate business?
4. Distinguish between independent and executive agencies. Give examples of each. In what respects are they different? Is there any reason to believe one type is more effective than another? Should business prefer one type of agency to the other? Why?
5. Describe the difference between compliance costs and administrative costs of regulation. How can compliance costs be measured? Pick a specific agency, such as the EPA, and work out a methodology to measure the compliance costs in a specific business organization.
6. Is Murray Weidenbaum's multiplier of twenty a valid method of estimating compliance costs for future years? What assumptions are made in using this figure? What other methods could be developed to estimate future compliance costs?
7. Define the concept of incremental costs. Discuss implementation of this concept. Are the Roundtable guidelines specific enough? Is use of this concept valid in determining the true cost of regulation?
8. What is the usefulness of comprehensive cost studies of this nature? Are they precise enough to be used by public policy-makers in making decisions? Should such studies continue to be performed regularly?

[57]See Charles L. Schultze, *The Public Use of the Private Interest* (Washington, D.C.: Brookings Institution, 1977).
[58]Weidenbaum, *Reducing the Cost of Government*, pp. 11–12.

9. Are the effects of regulation on small business any different from those on large corporations? In what ways? Should small business be exempt from regulation? If not, what can be done to reduce the impact?
10. Distinguish between second- and third-order effects of regulation. Give examples of each type. In your opinion, is this distinction valid? If so, which are the most serious costs as far as society is concerned?
11. Do you believe the benefits of regulation can be quantified? In what terms? Think of a methodology to measure the benefits of consumer regulation. What value assumptions have to be made?
12. Define overregulation of business. Is business currently overregulated? In what respects? In what ways is overregulation bad for society?
13. Discuss other problems with regulation besides the cost burden. Can these problems be alleviated with the proper procedures? What procedures would you recommend to deal with each of the problems mentioned in the Dunlop article?
14. Discuss the problem of experts and decision-making. What role should experts play in public policy formulation? What should be the relationship between citizens and experts in the public policy process?
15. Discuss the various reform measures. Which hold the most promise for meaningful reform? What would be the beneficial and detrimental effects of each measure? For business? For society?
16. Can the regulatory process be reformed? What alternatives to regulation exist? How can these be implemented? Why haven't alternatives been seriously considered in our society? Why regulation?

Suggested Reading

Bernstein, Marver H. *Regulating Business by Independent Commission.* Princeton, N.J.: Princeton University Press, 1955.

Kohlmeier, Louis M., Jr. *The Regulators.* New York: Harper & Row, 1969.

Regulating Business: The Search for an Optimum. San Francisco: Institute for Contemporary Studies, 1978.

Schultze, Charles L. *The Public Use of the Private Interest.* Washington, D.C.: Brookings Institution, 1977.

Shepard, William G., and Gies, Thomas G., eds. *Regulation in Further Perspective.* Cambridge, Mass.: Ballinger Publishing Co., 1974.

————, and Wilcox, Clair. *Public Policies toward Business,* 6th ed. Homewood, Ill.: Richard D. Irwin, 1979.

Simon, William E. *A Time for Truth.* New York: Reader's Digest Press, 1978.

Weidenbaum, Murray L. *Business, Government and the Public.* Englewood Cliffs, N.J.: Prentice-Hall, 1977.

————. *The Costs of Government Regulation of Business,* Subcommittee on Economic Growth and Stabilization of the Joint Economic Committee, Congress of the United States. Washington, D.C., U.S. Government Printing Office, 1978.

————. *The Future of Business Regulation.* New York: AMACOM, 1979.

10

Corporate Political Activities

> Our conclusions with respect to managerial participation in the public policy process, therefore, come down to a few very simple points. Such participation is inevitable and legitimate; and, as public policy becomes an increasingly important consideration in the process of management, such participation can be expected to become more widespread and significant.[1]

No discussion of the political environment of business would be complete without considering the various methods through which corporations participate in the political process. Corporations have many ways in which they can influence public policy and in this sense are an important environmental influence on public policy that must be taken into account. Corporations are active in helping to shape the rules of the game by which they must live, and this participation will undoubtedly become more important in the future as public policy becomes more important.

The methods that corporations have for participating in the public policy process will be discussed in a framework that corresponds with the various stages of the public policy process. The first stage concerns the formation of public opinion on specific issues that affect business or toward business in general. By helping to shape public opinion, corporations can exercise a broad influence in the society as a whole. The second stage is public policy formulation when Congress or the executive branch is considering specific legislative proposals, holding hearings on issues, or otherwise discussing various public policy issues of concern to business. The corporation has various ways by which it can participate in this stage of public policy formula-

[1] Lee E. Preston and James E. Post, *Private Management and Public Policy* (Englewood Cliffs, N.J.: Prentice-Hall, 1975), pp. 144–145. Quoted with permission.

tion. The last stage occurs after legislation is passed, when regulations are being written and court decisions made on specific issues that affect business.

Obviously these categories overlap—methods useful at one stage may also be effective at another—but certain methods seem more appropriate at one stage than another and will be discussed accordingly. The chapter will end with a short discussion of the appropriateness of corporate political activity in general, as many people are concerned about the kind of influence corporations can and do exercise in the public policy process.

Influencing Public Opinion

Many people in business believe it is important for business to identify key issues in society that may affect business and to engage in a debate about these issues before they are picked up by the formal political system. At such an early stage, the options that business has to deal with an issue are broadest, and thus involvement at this stage has the potential of being very effective. Some argue that when government gets involved with an issue, it is too late for business to have much effect on the outcome. Government is reactive, they believe, and when it does finally begin to consider an issue, such as hazardous waste disposal, society has already by and large made up its mind and the general outlines of policy on that issue have already been formed.[2] In any event, business has various methods at its disposal to participate at this stage and attempt to influence public opinion on a specific issue or business and the free enterprise system in general.

Speaking Out on Issues. One such method is the attempt of business to get involved in speaking out on issues that concern the company's interests. Management at some companies spends a good deal of time taking advantage of opportunities to speak to civic groups, participate in conferences, speak to high school and college classes, write articles for business journals or newspapers, meet with the media, and similar opportunities to get its viewpoint before the public. Some corporations have changed from a posture of keeping quiet on issues and working behind the scenes to one of raising their voices in public and becoming much more visible. This strategy not only involves top management at headquarters, but management at all levels in communities where company facilities are located.[3]

The success of this method of influencing public opinion depends a great deal on how well business has done its homework. The position that management takes on an issue must be factually correct and defensible, because those who "go public" can expect to be questioned, sometimes hostilely, by their audience. If the homework is done well, however, and the businesspeople involved have communications skills to articulate a business position and engage in debate, this can be an effective way to influence

---

[2]Rogene A. Buchholz, *Business Environment/Public Policy: Corporate Executive Viewpoints and Educational Implications* (St. Louis, Mo.: Washington University Center for the Study of American Business, 1980), p. 20.

[3]See Hugh D. Menzies, "Union Carbide Raises Its Voice," *Fortune*, September 25, 1978, pp. 86–89.

public opinion and gain credibility with the public. Increased communications with the public has to be a positive factor.

There are problems, however, with this approach. One problem is the speaker's credibility. For whom is the manager speaking? What group does his or her position represent? Who is the corporation? Agreement on a position may be reached by the management of a corporation, but is management alone the corporation? What about shareholders, customers, and employees? These constituencies, if indeed they are a legitimate part of the corporation, will undoubtedly have different views on an issue. How, then, can these diverse views be represented in a single "corporate" position?[4]

A second problem concerns the kinds of issues in which business gets involved. If these issues are only those in which the company has a significant stake, the company can be criticized as pursuing only its own narrow self-interest at the expense of the public interest, which may only contribute more to the credibility problem that business already has with the public. Some people argue that business should concern itself with a wide range of issues, many of which may not be directly related to the business itself but are of concern to society. To gain credibility, it is argued, business must concern itself with broader interests rather than just its own self-interest. It must seek to understand the concerns of other groups in society outside the business community and engage in debate about a broad range of issues that have a bearing on the quality of life.[5]

Finally, there is a question of how much influence business can have over public opinion with this method no matter how credible the message or the speaker. Most managers have a recognition problem, the same as many public officials. Who knows them? And worse yet, how many people seriously listen to their opinions? To overcome this problem, managers might direct their efforts to the opinion leaders in society or in a community—those people who are influential in molding public opinion on an issue.[6]

Advocacy Advertising. This method has been defined as a form of advertising in which business takes a public position on controversial issues of public importance, aggressively stating and defending its viewpoint and criticizing those of opponents. Advocacy advertising is "concerned with the propagation of ideas and elucidation of controversial social issues of public importance in a manner that supports the position and interests of the sponsor while expressly denying the accuracy of facts and downgrading the sponsor's opponents."[7] Advocacy advertising can deal with specific issues, such as divestiture policy toward the oil companies (see Figure 10.1), or general issues, such as public attitudes toward free enterprise or capitalism (see Figure 10.2).

Advocacy advertising might be engaged in for a number of reasons. One may be to counteract public hostility caused by ignorance or misinformation

[4]Buchholz, *Corporate Executive Viewpoints*, p. 21.

[5]*Ibid.*, p. 20.

[6]*Ibid.*, p. 21.

[7]S. Prakash Sethi, "Advocacy Advertising as a Strategy of Corporate Response to Societal Pressures: The American Experience," *Business and Its Changing Environment,* proceedings of a conference held at UCLA, July 24–August 3, 1977, p. 56.

Figure 10.1

IF THEY BREAK UP THE OIL COMPANIES, YOU'LL PAY THROUGH THE HOSE.

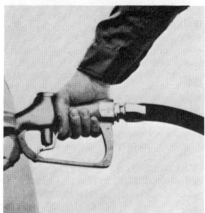

There are people who want to dismember America's integrated oil companies—those companies that do the whole job from exploration through marketing.

Today, more than 50 integrated oil companies compete for your business. Hundreds of firms compete in various phases of the industry—exploration, production, refining, transportation, and marketing.

What would happen if the oil companies were taken apart?

Ironically, prices would go up, not down. A so-called breakup would destroy the efficient integrated system and create a need for a new layer of costly and unnecessary "middlemen." Additionally, the chaos created by such a breakup would make it tougher for the industry to attract the capital it needs. Millions of Americans in oil and oil-related industries could lose their job security. Technical advances would be slowed down. Money needed to search for new supplies would dry up.

The result? *Less domestic oil would be available,* increasing our dependence on foreign oil. America could be weakened. You, the consumer, would be less certain of getting the oil—the automotive gasoline and home-heating fuel and other products you need—when you need it, *while paying more for what you get.*

Before it's decided to take apart the oil companies—let's find out just who would benefit. We firmly believe it wouldn't be *you.*

We're working to keep your trust.

From *Newsweek*, March 5, 1976. Reprinted with permission.

Figure 10.2

Capitalism: moving target

The list of things wrong with business in this country is almost endless. Nearly as long, in fact, as the list of what's right with it.

Perhaps the most frustrating thing about business, for those who keep trying to shoot it down, is this: Corporations are so tenacious that they will even do good in order to survive. This tenacity goes beyond the old maxim that man, in his greed for profit, often unavoidably serves the public interest. In times of crisis, business will even do good *consciously* and *deliberately*.

Nothing could be better calculated to confound business's critics than this underhanded tactic. The Marxist dialectic has it that capitalism must inevitably founder in its own inherent contradictions; that it contains the seeds of its own destruction. But business also contains the seeds of its own adaptation and survival.

Businessmen are pragmatists, and with their daily feedback from the marketplace, they readily abandon dogma whenever their survival instinct tells them to. It has become less and less a question of what they *want* to do or might *like* to do, but of what their common sense and survival instinct tell them they *have* to do.

Remember the Edsel? That was one of the fastest plebiscites in history. But it wasn't the American public that took the loss; it was the shareholders of Ford Motor Company. (Then, you'll recall, Ford changed course and bounced back with the Mustang, which quickly showed its tailpipe to the competition by breaking all sales records for a new make of car.)

Because it is keyed so closely to the marketplace and so responsive to it, private business is necessarily the most effective instrument of change. Some would call it revolutionary. Many of those who attack business fail to comprehend its constructive contributions to responsive change. And this sort of change is one of the basic reasons business manages to survive.

Not *all* businesses survive, of course. The record is replete with companies that expired because they didn't adapt rapidly enough to a new milieu.

While businessmen as a whole are not exactly social reformers, they do respond to criticism and to sustained social pressures. The alert businessman regards such pressures as a useful early warning system. The danger is that criticism can become a mindless reflex action that persists long after the basis for it has been dissipated.

Partly because of its ability to adapt—which is simply another word for responsive change—private business remains the most productive element in our society and on balance the best allocator of resources. If you decide to draw a bead on it, remember you're aiming at a moving target. Because, as we've said here before, business is bound to change.

about a particular issue. Another reason may be to counteract the spread of misleading information by business critics and fill the need for a greater explanation of a complex public issue of concern to business. Many advocacy advertisements are obviously seeking to foster the values of the free enterprise system. Finally, advocacy advertising may be used to counteract inadequate access to and bias in the news media.[8]

The right of corporations to speak out on public issues in this manner was upheld by the Supreme Court in a 1978 decision. This ruling struck down a Massachusetts law, upheld by a state court, that made it a criminal offense for any bank or business incorporated in the state to spend money to influence a vote on referendum proposals in the state other than those materially affecting the property, business, or assets of the corporation. The specific instance in the case concerned a referendum to win voter approval for a graduated, rather than a flat-rate, income tax, which the law stated did not materially affect corporations. This law was challenged by a few banks and corporations in Massachusetts. The majority of the Supreme Court held that the type of speech the companies wanted to engage in was at the heart of the protection offered by the First Amendment to the constitution, which was aimed at promoting a free discussion of public issues.[9]

The most important question concerning advocacy advertising may be the question of its effectiveness. A poll conducted by Yankelovich, Skelly, and White in 1978 showed that the advocacy advertisements of Mobil Oil Corporation had a high visibility among administration, congressional, and other government leaders, as 90 percent of the sample had read them. On the other hand, 66 percent of the government leaders said that the ads were of little or no use to them in understanding energy deregulation issues and did not have any influence on their opinion about policy matters. Only 33 percent found the ads useful in this regard, and 1 percent were unsure.[10]

As far as the public was concerned, only 6 percent considered public issue ads generally as "very credible" and as many as 53 percent said they were "not credible."[11] However, a Harris poll conducted in 1976 showed that Mobil in particular among the seven oil companies included in the survey ranked highest in public perception as a company that had consumer interests in mind, was helping to improve the quality of life, and was seriously concerned about the energy problem. Mobil was also viewed as being committed to free enterprise, working for good government, and being honest and direct in talking to consumers. The company believes that this reflects a real change in public attitudes.[12]

Some pitfalls in the use of advocacy advertising must be mentioned. The first concerns the level of intellectual integrity regarding treatment of the subject matter. A high level of intellectual integrity must be maintained if business expects opinion leaders in a community or government officials to

[8]*Ibid.*, pp. 59–74.

[9]*First National Bank of Boston v. Bellotti*, 435 U.S. 765. Rehearing denied 438 U.S. 907. See also "A Right-To-Speak Ruling Business May Regret," *Business Week*, May 15, 1978, p. 27; and "Corporation's Right to Disseminate View on Political Issues Backed by High Court," *The Wall Street Journal*, April 27, 1978, p. 4.

[10]"How Good Are Advocacy Ads?" *Dun's Review*, June 1978, p. 76.

[11]*Ibid.*

[12]"Industry Fights Back," *Saturday Review*, January 21, 1978, p. 21.

give serious consideration to what is admittedly a partisan position. To help accomplish a positive impact, Sethi recommends that the sponsoring corporation should openly identify itself with the message and not hide behind such innocuous sounding names as the "Citizens Committee for Better Economic Environment."[13]

Second, there must be a congruence between the message of advocacy advertising and business performance.[14] If, for example, a corporation's advertising is directed toward promoting the values associated with free enterprise, competition, and laissez faire, and then is subsequently found guilty of price fixing or making payments to government officials of a foreign country, its advertising efforts are very likely to be counterproductive and the company's credibility questioned even more severely.

Then there is the matter of how advertising expenditures are treated with regard to taxation. The Internal Revenue Service prohibits writing off expenditures to influence public opinion about legislative matters. Pure image advertising (see next section) would seem to fall outside this ruling, but sometimes the distinction between image advertising and advocacy advertising is not altogether clear. Sethi recommends that the emphasis in a corporation should not be on what ad expenses can be squeezed into the deductibility area, but on what expenses must stay out because they fall into the gray area and therefore may become controversial.[15]

Finally, there is a possible danger of shareholder suits over wastage of corporate assets by using corporate resources to further views with which some shareholders might disagree. Minority shareholders, for example, might resort to lawsuits to challenge corporate expenditures made for improper purposes or merely to further management's own interests.

Abuses of advocacy advertising would probably lead to some form of regulation or forced disclosure of money corporations spent to influence public opinion.[16] But properly used, "advocacy advertising can indeed serve the corporate objective of reducing public distrust of its actions and performance. It can also serve an important public purpose by contributing to a vigorous debate on controversial issues of social importance."[17]

Image Advertising. This type of advertising does not deal directly with public issues, but instead seeks to better the image of a particular company or industry by presenting it as being genuinely concerned about the environment, health and safety, or some other issue of social concern. The distinction between image ads and advocacy ads, as stated earlier, is not altogether clear in some cases. The real purpose of an oil-company ad trumpeting its commitment to environmental cleanup might be to influence public opinion about the windfall profits tax rather than to sell gasoline.[18]

Examples of image ads are the American Forest Institute ads on forest conservation and the Chemical Facts of Life ads of Monsanto Corporation (see Figure 10.3). The purpose behind these ads is to better the image of the

[13]Sethi, "Advocacy Advertising," p. 77.

[14]*Ibid.*, p. 79.

[15]*Ibid.*, pp. 78–79.

[16]See A. F. Ehrbar, "The Backlash against Business Advocacy," *Fortune*, August 28, 1978, pp. 62–68.

[17]Sethi, "Advocacy Advertising, p. 76.

[18]Ehrbar, "Backlash," p. 62.

Figure 10.3

Without chemicals, life itself would be impossible.

Some people think anything "chemical" is bad and anything "natural" is good. Yet nature is chemical.

Plant life generates the oxygen we need through a chemical process called photosynthesis. When you breathe, your body absorbs that oxygen through a chemical reaction with your blood.

Life is chemical. And with chemicals, companies like Monsanto are working to help improve the quality of life.

Chemicals help you live longer. Rickets was a common childhood disease until a chemical called Vitamin D was added to milk and other foods.

Chemicals help you eat better. Chemical weed-killers have dramatically increased the supply and availability of our food.

But no chemical is totally safe, all the time, everywhere. In nature or in the laboratory. The real challenge is to use chemicals properly. To help make life a lot more livable.

For a free booklet explaining the risks and benefits of chemicals, mail to:
Monsanto, 800 N. Lindbergh Blvd., St. Louis, Mo. 63166. Dept. A3NA

Name _____

Address _____

City & state _____ Zip _____

Monsanto

Without chemicals,
life itself would be impossible.

From *Monsanto Speaks Up About Chemicals,* (St. Louis, Mo.: Monsanto Company, 1977), p. 14. Reprinted with permission.

industry by educating the public about issues related to forestry and the use of chemicals in daily life. It is hoped that this information will have some positive influence on public opinion with respect to that industry in general and companies in the industry doing the advertising. Regarding the AFI ads, the Yankelovich poll found that 56 percent of the government leaders and 70 percent of the public said that the ads were useful in supplying them with information on forestry issues.[19] Monsanto spent $4.5 million on its ad campaign in 1977, and has since equalled or exceeded that amount each year seeking to improve the image of the company and the industry.[20]

Economic Education. This method of influencing public opinion is based on the assumption that much of the American public is economically illiterate. The credibility problem business has and the support given for regulation that adversely affects business performance is based on an ignorance of how business actually operates and how the economic system functions. People simply do not understand the role of profits, it is believed; concepts such as efficiency and productivity have no meaning, and the way a market system allocates resources is poorly understood. Many of the problems business has with the public and with government thus stem from an ignorance about business and the economic system rather than hostility toward business or the system.

Some companies have developed extensive educational programs directed at various segments of the public, including their own employees, educators, high school students, and shareholders.[21] These programs can include speakers dealing with various economic subjects, video tapes, and reading materials prepared by the company itself. The three major objectives of these programs are to (1) improve understanding of economic principles, (2) improve audience attitudes toward business in general, and (3) explain the free enterprise system.[22] The impact of these programs is difficult to measure and is usually done subjectively, making the success which is claimed for these programs in achieving their objectives open to question.[23]

Public Policy Formulation

Some business executives, as stated earlier, believe that involvement at this stage of an issue is more or less a rearguard action. If lobbying and other forms of political participation appropriate to this stage are necessary, business has already "blown it" as far as shaping policy with respect to that issue is concerned.[24] On the other hand, many business leaders also believe that business must identify those issues of concern to itself that are currently

[19]"How Good Are Advocacy Ads?" p. 77.

[20]"Cleansing the Chemical Image," *Business Week*, October 8, 1979, p. 73.

[21]Myron Emanuel, Curtis Snodgrass, Joyce Gildea, and Karn Rosenberg, *Corporate Economic Education Programs: An Evaluation and Appraisal* (New York: Financial Executives Research Foundation, 1979). p. xv.

[22]*Ibid.*, p. 338.

[23]*Ibid.*, p. xiv.

[24]Buchholz, *Corporate Executive Viewpoints*, pp. 21–22.

being discussed in the halls of government, and must get involved politically to try and influence the outcome of the discussion and engage in more formal public policy formulation. Because of the influence of government on business, business managers must become students of public affairs and learn their way around governmental circles. Various methods are appropriate at this stage of the public policy process.

General Business Associations. There are several nationwide organizations that are composed of corporate members representing all or most industries in the country. These groups can organize the resources of many business organizations across the nation to get involved in public policy formulation. They can help business organizations to identify issues being considered in government, gather information about issues, assess the political climate, coordinate the strategies of the various companies that are concerned about a given issue, lobby on behalf of their membership, and perform other functions related to this stage of public policy formulation. Individual business organizations can use these general associations to pursue their interests at the level of the federal government. The most prominent organizations of this type are the National Association of Manufacturers (NAM), the Chamber of Commerce of the United States, and the Business Roundtable.

The NAM moved its headquarters to Washington, D.C. in 1974, and reorganized itself in the process. The organization is currently structured into four divisions covering thirteen regions of the country. The functions of the NAM are to provide early information to its membership at the formative stages of legislative development and activate corporate grass roots programs. The NAM restructured its activities in Washington into nineteen committees, each of which is headed by a registered lobbyist who follows a major issue through all the branches of government. The organization also conducts meetings for member companies to bring together corporate executives with the legislators from their region of the country.[25]

The United States Chamber of Commerce has a membership of 79,500, most of whom are corporations, but which also includes municipal and state chambers of commerce and trade associations. The membership relies on the Chamber's assistance in the legislative field in testifying before Congress on behalf of business, lobbying or talking with government leaders, going to court for business, keeping track of the legislative agenda, and speaking out for business whenever possible. This latter function is accomplished through a number of publications, such as a *Washington Report,* the *Voice of Business,* and the *Nation's Business.* The Chamber also conducts a far-reaching grass roots program to mobilize its constituency with respect to an issue. Finally, the Chamber engages in business education by holding law workshops for corporate executives, conducting executive development programs, and offering a communications education program to teach executives how to use the media, especially television, effectively.[26]

The Business Roundtable was formed in 1972, but despite its youth when compared to the other general business associations it has had a tremendous

---

[25] Phyllis S. McGrath, *Redefining Corporate-Federal Relations* (New York: The Conference Board, 1979), pp. 85–86.

[26] *Ibid.,* pp. 86–87.

impact that in many ways has eclipsed the older organizations. The Roundtable was formed partly because many leaders of large business corporations believed their interests were not being adequately represented by the NAM or the Chamber because their membership was so diverse and consisted largely of smaller business corporations. Thus the Roundtable's membership is all heads of large companies. The organization presently has a membership of about 200 chief executive officers representing a wide diversity of industries and regions of the country.

The really unique feature of the Roundtable is the fact that the chief executive officer of a company is the person who is involved. These CEOs, of course, have direct personal access to the highest levels of government. The Roundtable has an office in both New York and Washington, but these offices have very small staffs in comparison to the other general business associations. The Roundtable occasionally hires outside help for research and public relations efforts, but the bulk of its work is done through task forces that cover such issues as taxation, consumer interests, energy users, environment, regulation, antitrust, and the like. Each task force is headed by the CEO of a member company (see Exhibit 10.1), who can draw on the research capabilities of his or her own company or the companies of the other task force members. This help is of no cost to the Roundtable itself.[27]

These task forces research issues in their domain and eventually draft a position paper. When the task force reaches a consensus, the issue then goes to a policy committee that works out what differences remain on the issue and then formally releases a position paper to the media, government officials, and other interested parties.[28] The positions of the Roundtable do not always reflect the interests of its entire membership. The Roundtable, for example, opposed the government loan guarantee for Chrysler Corporation, and Chrysler, of course, subsequently cancelled its membership.

The Business Roundtable has thus far been highly effective and its advice and counsel on a wide range of issues is sought by the administration and Congress alike. The enthusiasm of its membership is probably responsible for a large degree of its success, along with its resistance to becoming bureaucratized. This helps the organization to be flexible and respond to issues more quickly than larger organizations like the NAM and the Chamber, which have a great deal of organizational inertia to overcome.[29] Another reason for the Roundtable's success is its pragmatic and positive approach to problems and acceptance of government involvement. Two Roundtable guidelines are pivotal in this regard:

- A recognition that the adversarial relationship of business and government is exaggerated and counterproductive; that in most instances business and government seek the same ends; that the means to the end, not the end itself, is usually the principal concern; and that business and government must work together to find the best way to achieve agreed goals.

[27]"Business' Most Powerful Lobby in Washington," *Business Week*, December 20, 1976, pp. 60–61.

[28]McGrath, *Corporate-Federal Relations*, p. 88.

[29]Donald J. Watson, "The Changing Political Involvement of Business," paper presented at the Conference on Business and Its Changing Environment," UCLA, July 31, 1978, p. 16.

EXHIBIT 10.1

The Business Roundtable Task Forces, 1979

Accounting Principles	Thomas A. Murphy General Motors
Antitrust	George A. Stinson National Steel
Consumer Interests	James L. Ferguson General Foods
Corporate Constituencies	Rawleigh Warner, Jr. Mobil
Corporate Organization Policy	Alden W. Clausen Bank of America
Economic Organization	Robert S. Hatfield Continental Group
Energy Users	W. H. Krome George ALCOA
Environment	James H. Evans Union Pacific
Field Support	Robert S. Hatfield Continental Group
Government Regulation	Frank T. Cary IBM
Inflation	Donald V. Seibert J. C. Penney
International Trade	William S. Sneath Union Carbide
National Health	Walter B. Wriston Citicorp
National Planning and Employment	Lewis W. Foy Bethlehem Steel
Social Security	Robert A. Beck Prudential Insurance
Taxation	Theodore F. Brophy GTE
Welfare	Richard R. Shinn Metropolitan Life

From *The Business Roundtable,* June, 1979. Reprinted with permission.

- A recognition that the Roundtable will receive better support for its views, and make a greater contribution to society, if it registers "positive ideas and objectives," and avoids the negative posture on important issues that critics of American capitalism often present as the stereotype stance of the business community.[30]

Industry and Trade Associations. Industry and trade associations perform many functions for their membership, including development of industry standards, conducting educational programs, and industrywide advertising. But, increasingly, politics is becoming the major focus of these organizations, which perform many of the same political functions for their membership as do the general business associations mentioned earlier.[31]

---

[30]*Ibid.*, p. 7.

[31]"For Trade Associations, Politics Is the New Focus," *Business Week*, April 17, 1978, pp. 107–115.

Many members simply do not have enough strength of their own in Washington and must rely on their trade association for political activity. These political activities include testifying at congressional hearings on matters affecting the industry, appearing in proceedings before government agencies and regulatory bodies on issues of concern to the industry, contributing to precedent-setting cases before the courts, raising political contributions, making industry information available to the courts, and serving on various advisory committees.

The nation's capital now contains 1,500 association headquarters with more to come. Many of these have recently moved their headquarters from New York City to Washington, reflecting the focus on politics.[32] The budgets and membership of some of these associations are large (Table 10.1) and managers of these associations can make up to $150,000 a year, reflecting their increasing importance. These industry and trade associations stand between business and government, interpreting the government's actions and attitudes to their business constituency and bringing the interests of business before government officials.

TABLE 10.1 **Some Top Spenders Among Trade Associations**

Industry	Association	Annual Budget* (millions of dollars)	Corporate Membership
Energy	American Petroleum Institute	$30	350
	American Gas Assn.	30	300
Banking	American Bankers Assn.	20	13,254
Automotive	Motor Vehicle Manufacturers Assn.	11	11
	National Automobile Dealers Assn.	10	21,146
Housing	National Assn. of Home Builders	11	96,000
Utilities	Edison Electric Institute	11	200
Trucking	American Trucking Assns.	11	2,000
Steel	American Iron & Steel Institute	10	2,600
Beer	U.S. Brewers Assn.	8	37

*BW estimates

Source: "For Trade Associations, Politics Is the New Focus," Business Week, April 17, 1978, p. 107. Reprinted by permission.

Lobbying. Lobbying by business has both an offensive and a defensive function. The offensive function consists of getting a company's views on pending legislation across to senators, members of the House of Representatives, their aides, and committee staff members. Of late, these efforts have been largely geared to opposing or at least amending the rising flow of federal legislation that results in greater government control over business decision-making. The defensive function of lobbying is geared to avoiding embarrassing investigations of and attacks on a company or an industry. This function is accomplished by providing additional information and presenting the other side of the story at an early stage of, say, a committee's deliberations.

The nature of lobbying has changed from what it was in the past. The job

[32]Ibid., p. 107.

demands, as never before, homework on issues and legislators.[33] As reported by *Time* magazine: "Instead of cozying up to a few chairmen or a powerful speaker, the lobbyist must do tedious homework on the whims and leanings of all the legislators. . . . Lobbying now demands, as never before, highly sophisticated techniques, a mastery of both the technicalities of legislation and the complexities of the legislator's backgrounds, and painstaking effort."[34] Many yearn for the simpler, more splashier days of the trade. As stated by one longtime corporate lobbyist: "My job used to be booze, broads, and golf at Burning Tree. Now it is organizing coalitions and keeping information flowing."[35]

The success of lobbying depends a great deal on finding where the real power lies in government.[36] In past years, this was not too difficult since powerful committee chairmen existed and a few key congressmen exercised great influence over their colleagues. But while power in the aggregate has become centralized in Washington, it has also become more diffused with the change in the committee structure of Congress, which has weakened the power of committee chairmen, the election of independent-minded legislators who do not necessarily adhere to the party line, the increasing importance of congressional staffs in drafting legislation, and the growing regulatory bureaucracy that implements the legislation. Lobbying only in the nation's capital has its limitations, and corporations have turned increasingly to grass-roots lobbying on the assumption that rank-and-file legislators in this new political environment may be more sensitive to expressions of political sentiment from their home districts. Grass-roots lobbying takes place in the legislator's home district rather than in Washington.

Many companies have instituted grass-roots lobbying programs throughout the company in response to this change. They are putting a good deal of money and energy into organizing employees and shareholders into a concerted voice powerful enough to capture the attention of legislators. Table 10.2 shows the prevalence of such grass-roots programs by industry, and Table 10.3 shows that most of these programs have been introduced in the last few years, indicating that for many companies this is a new effort.

A company gets into grass-roots programs because such efforts represent a force in the community. Employees in particular are people who vote locally and may even have personal relationships with the local legislators. A great deal of political power within the corporation itself potentially can be mobilized to influence government.

These programs vary among corporations, but some of the typical elements of a grass-roots program include the organization of political education or discussion groups for employees, presentation of management's views on issues that concern the company, and mailings of political information along with the company's position on certain legislative issues to employees and stockholders (see Figure 10.4). The purpose of these efforts is to

---

[33]"The Swarming Lobbyists," *Time,* August 7, 1978, pp. 15–16.

[34]*Ibid.,* p. 16.

[35]"New Ways to Lobby a Recalcitrant Congress," *Business Week,* September 3, 1979, p. 148.

[36]See Dan H. Fenn, Jr., "Finding Where the Power Lies in Government," *Harvard Business Review,* Vol. 57, No. 5 (September–October 1979), pp. 144–153.

TABLE 10.2 **Prevalence of Grass-roots Programs by Industry**

Industry	Percent of Respondents
Food	56%
Lumber and Paper	70
Chemicals and Drugs	48
Petroleum	70
Metals	63
Machinery	51
Transportation Equipment	71
Other Manufacturing	76
Total Manufacturing	60%
Transportation	31
Utilities and Communication	64
Retail and Wholesale	52
Banks	32
Life Insurance	43
Diversified Financial	40
Total Nonmanufacturing	44%

Source: Phyllis S. McGrath, *Redefining Corporate-Federal Relations* (New York: The Conference Board, 1979), p. 37. Reprinted with permission.

TABLE 10.3 **Introduction of Grass-roots Programs**

Years	Percent of Programs*
1940–1969	12%
1970–1974	26
1975–1978	61

*Will not total 100% because of rounding.

Source: Phyllis S. McGrath, *Redefining Corporate-Federal Relations* (New York: The Conference Board, 1979), p. 37. Reprinted with permission.

develop a network of people who can readily be mobilized to respond to an issue by contacting their local elected officials and making their views heard.

Such efforts at both the Washington and grass-roots levels are believed to be effective and perform a useful function in the formulation of public policy by government. The professional lobbyist in Washington can supply a practical knowledge that is vital in the writing of workable legislation. He or she can point out potential consequences of certain provisions in the law that may otherwise be overlooked. The lobbyists in Washington are eager to point out such hazards and do so at no public expense. Grass-roots lobbying lets a congressional representative know what his or her immediate constituencies believe about an issue, and makes for a closer link of accountability between elected officials and the people they represent.

Campaign Contributions. Another way to exercise influence at the stage of public policy formulation is to contribute money to candidates for political office. This can be done to help elect people who will be favorable to business interests or who will then owe business some favors because of the help given

Figure 10.4. Public Affairs Dateline: International Harvester

Public Affairs Dateline

Legislative news for International Agricultural Equipment Dealers

ILLINOIS BULLETIN

Unemployment insurance bill passage urgently needed to avoid penalty

October, 1977

Private employers in Illinois face the imposition of a $175 per employe penalty if the Illinois Legislature does not approve House Bill 236.

This legislation will put Illinois unemployment insurance law into compliance with the federal U.I. law and thereby avoid the imposition of penalties on Illinois businesses. If the Legislature fails to pass H.B. 236, the U.S. Department of Labor has indicated private employers will lose the 2.7 percent credit they are now allowed toward their federal unemployment insurance tax rate. This credit—or federal offset—is granted to only those employers contributing to a state unemployment insurance system that is in compliance with federal law. If H.B. 236 passes, Illinois law will be in compliance and employers will be permitted to continue to take the credit.

Further, a quirk in the loan payback requirements the state faces for its U.I. trust fund would also raise 1977 taxes already paid, if the state law does not comply with federal statutes. This additional non-compliance penalty amounts to a retroactive .3 percent surtax on the 1977 payroll wage base.

Some experts have estimated the per employee cost of non-compliance penalties to be $174.60 per employee. To determine your own cost, use the following formula:

Number of Employees × $6000 × .027 = _____

Number of Employees × $4200 × .003 = +_____
Approximate total of penalties
for non-compliance   _____

Utilizing that formula, it has been estimated a small firm with 25 employees would be facing a penalty of $4,365 each year the state unemployment insurance law is not in compliance with federal law.

From Phyllis S. McGrath, *Redefining Corporate-Federal Relations* (New York: The Conference Board, 1979), p. 36. Reprinted with permission.

them in their campaigns. Society has been concerned about this kind of involvement since the beginning of the century, and has passed legislation to limit the financial participation of business in the election process.

The Tillman Act of 1907 made it illegal for business to make contributions to campaigns involving the election of federal officials. The objectives of this act were to (1) destroy business influence over elections, (2) protect stockholders from the use of corporate funds for political purposes to which they had not given their assent, and (3) protect the freedom of the individual's vote. The Corrupt Practices Act of 1925 broadened this concept by defining corporate contributions to include not only monetary contributions, but anything of value, a definition which markedly affected future contributions activities. The Labor-Management Relations Act of 1947 extended these same restrictions to labor unions.[37] Finally, in 1972, Congress passed the Federal Election Campaign Practices Act, which requires that candidates for federal office and their potential committees must make public the names and addresses of their supporters who contribute more than $100 to the campaign. The act also limits the contributions an individual can make to all candidates for federal office to $25,000 per year and $3,000 per candidate per campaign ($1,000 each in primaries, runoffs, and general elections).

Thus both business and labor unions are prohibited from making contributions to federal political campaigns from company or union funds. Some states also prohibit contributions to state elections. These laws, however, do not prevent such contributions from being made from time to time. During the Watergate era it was disclosed that a number of corporations had made illegal contributions to the campaigns of people in both parties. Most of the money, however, went to the Committee to Reelect the President (CREEP), with some companies alleged to have given as much as $100,000 to Nixon's campaign.

The new phenomenon that has appeared in recent years with respect to campaign contributions is Political Action Committees (PACs). From 1974 to 1979, the number of PACs tripled from 608 to 1,900 in number. In 1978, 1,828 PACs gave $35.1 million to House and Senate campaigns; in 1974, by contrast, the PACs then in existence contributed only $12.5 million. These figures include PACs not only from business, but also from industry and trade associations and similar organizations. Regarding business alone, in 1974 there were only 89 corporate PACs in the country. By 1976 there were 433, and by 1979, 812 in existence.[38] The phenomenal growth of PACs is explained by reforms in the nation's election laws, which encouraged business, industry and trade associations, and other organizations to engage in political action through committees, which before 1974 was largely a union strategy. In 1975, the Federal Election Commission issued a historic advisory opinion upholding the right of a corporation to establish and administer a separate, segregated fund out of which political contributions could be made. This opinion set forth rules and limitations for such funds, including the following:

1. General treasury funds can be expended for establishment, administration and solicitation of contributions to the PAC—if it is maintained as a separate segregated fund.
2. A company can make political contributions in a federal election, if made solely from PAC funds which are obtained voluntarily.
3. A company can control disbursement of funds from a separate segregated fund.

---

[37] Keith Davis and Robert Blomstrom, *Business and Society: Environment and Responsibility*, 3rd ed. (New York: McGraw-Hill, 1975), p. 210.

[38] *Business' Political Awakening: PAC Overview* (Washington, D.C.: Fraser/Associates, 1979), p. i.

4. A company can solicit contributions from its shareholders and employees.

5. A company can accept contributions to its PAC from any source that would not otherwise be unlawful.[39]

These PACs, of course, solicit money from individuals including employees, stockholders, and others, which is different from using corporate funds for contributions. A company, however, must not use coercion to solicit these contributions. An individual is not to be penalized for refusing to contribute or rewarded for participating. Should such incidents occur, the chairman and treasurer of the PAC would be subject to criminal prosecution. The operation of a PAC is usually monitored by the company's legal counsel.[40] The following methods are generally used to solicit contributions from employees:

- Letters from the CEO or PAC chairman
- Individual contacts
- Solicitation meetings
- Solicitation brochures
- Management newsletter[41]

The legal definition of a PAC is a fund that receives political contributions from more than fifty people and receives or spends more than $1,000 a year. Such organizations must file regular reports with the Federal Election Commission. The maximum annual contribution that an individual can make to a PAC is $5,000 per election. The ceiling on the contribution a PAC can make to any one candidate for federal office is also $5,000 per election. Such relatively small amounts are not likely to buy a candidate's vote for any corporation, but they can open the door to future corporate influence.

The typical PAC organization is shown in Figure 10.5. The law permits a company itself to pay the costs of administering the PAC, including expenses for salaries, rent, postage, and the like. Contributions to candidates, however, must be made out of the voluntary contributions of individuals. Each PAC is required to have a chairman and a treasurer, and a number have set up contributions committees. The officers of the PAC on these contributions committees must often decide where the money will go, but some companies allow the contributors to designate the party they wish their money to reach and most are open to suggestions from contributors.[42]

In 1978, corporate PACs contributed a total of $8.8 million to political campaigns, slightly behind labor's $9.4 million. Trade association PACs reported the highest total, $10.7 million, while PACs organized by other groups contributed $3.1 million.[43] The top ten corporate and association contributors are shown in Exhibits 10.2 and 10.3, while Figure 10.6 shows that the amount given by the top ten associations far outweighs the top ten corporate contributors.

During the first few years of contributions by business PACs, it was clear

---

[39]*Ibid.,* p. 6.

[40]McGrath, *Corporate-Federal Relations,* p. 49.

[41]*Ibid.*

[42]*Ibid.,* pp. 50–51.

[43]*PAC Overview* (Fraser/Associates), p. ii.

Figure 10.5. Typical PAC Organization

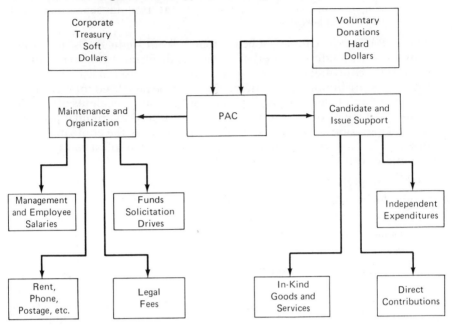

From *Business' Political Awakening: PAC Overview* (Washington, D.C.: Fraser/Associates, 1979), p. 16. Reprinted with permission.

EXHIBIT 10.2

Leading Corporate PAC Contributors to the 1978 Elections

1. Voluntary Contributors for Better Government
   (International Paper Company) $164,818
2. Amoco Political Action Committee
   (Standard Oil of Indiana and Sub.) $144,600
3. Non-Partisan Political Support Committee
   (General Electric Company) $107,320
4. American Family Political Action Committee
   (American Family Corporation) $106,450
5. Dartpac
   (Dart Industries, Inc.) $104,300
6. Union Camp Political Action Committee
   (Union Camp Corporation) $104,250
7. Eaton Public Policy Association
   (Eaton Corporation) $101,000
8. United Technologies Corp. PAC
   (United Technologies Corp.) $ 97,225
9. Political Awareness Fund
   (Union Oil Company of California) $ 96,380
10. Civic Involvement Program/GM
    (General Motors Corporation) $ 96,275

From *Business' Political Awakening: PAC Overview* (Washington, D.C.: Fraser/Associates, 1979), p. 68. Reprinted with permission.

EXHIBIT 10.3 ——————————————————————

Leading Trade/Membership/Health PAC Contributors to the 1978 Elections

1. American Medical Political Action Committee (American Medical Association)	$1,562,545
2. Realtors PAC (National Association of Realtors)	$1,168,378
3. Automobile and Truck Dealers Election Action Committee (National Automobile Dealers Association)	$ 968,775
4. American Dental PAC (American Dental Association)	$ 493,000
5. Life Underwriters PAC (National Association of Life Underwriters)	$ 351,263
6. NRA Political Victory Fund	$ 317,736
7. Attorneys Congressional Campaign Trust	$ 207,675
8. Conservative Victory Fund (American Conservative Union)	$ 238,654
9. Commodity Futures Political Fund (Mercantile Exchange, Chicago)	$ 221,125
10. Bank PAC (American Bankers Association)	$ 207,675

From *Business' Political Awakening: PAC Overview* (Washington, D.C.: Fraser/Associates, 1979), p. 69. Reprinted with permission.

that more money was being given to Democratic candidates than Republican candidates, a surprising development for many corporate leaders. The reason for this development seems to be that PACs were supporting incumbents more than challengers, and there simply were many more Democrats in that position.[44] In 1977, for example, business favored incumbents over challengers by a nine-to-one ratio.[45] The data for 1978 show a slight change in that trend (Table 10.4) as business and professional PAC contributions began to be weighted in favor of Republicans, indicating a shift to more ideologically supported efforts. Still, the labor PACs gave a significantly higher proportion of their money to Democratic candidates than business PACs did to Republican candidates. Even if a challenger is more closely aligned ideologically with a company's position, it is a fact of political life that incumbents win most elections.

There has been a good deal of concern in government about the growth and impact of PACs, especially those of business and professional organizations. The House voted to prevent any PAC from giving a House candidate more than $6,000: the previous limit was $10,000. The House also voted to bar any House candidate from accepting more than $70,000 from PACs in any two-year period between elections. The House measure also provides that candidates who dip into their own pockets to finance their campaign cannot later reimburse themselves from PAC funds for any more than $35,000. These measures do not affect the Senate, but they are indicative of

[44]McGrath, *Corporate-Federal Relations,* p. 54.
[45]*PAC Overview* (Fraser/Associates), p. 64.

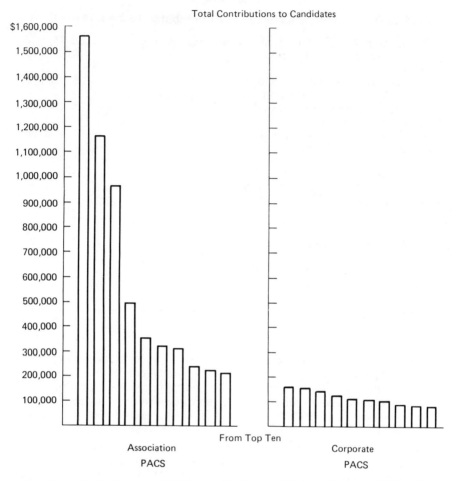

Figure 10.6

Total Contributions to Candidates

From *Business' Political Awakening: PAC Overview* (Washington, D.C.: Fraser/Associates, 1979), p. 69. Reprinted with permission.

the current trend to reduce the impact PACs are making on the political landscape.[46]

Post-Legislation Stage

There is not much to say about corporate involvement at this stage of the public policy process, because many options for business are closed after legislation is passed. Yet it is important to be involved at this stage because business may get a bill passed that they believe they can live with, and then

[46]"House, in a Defeat for Business Lobbyists, Votes to Curb Growing Influence of PACs," *The Wall Street Journal*, October 18, 1979, p. 6.

TABLE 10.4 **Committee Contributions to Federal Candidates (In Millions of Dollars)**

Types of Committees	Number of Active Committees	Number Making Contributions To Federal Candidates	Contributions To Federal Candidates	Senate	House	Democrat	Republican	Other	Incumbents	Challengers	Open Seats
Corporations	812	646	8.8	3.2	5.6	3.4	5.4	.009	5.4	1.8	1.6
Labor Or-ganizations	275	198	9.4	2.6	6.7	8.8	.5	.005	5.7	2.0	1.7
Non-Connected	257	111	2.2	.6	1.6	.6	1.6	.001	.7	.9	.6
Trade/ Membership/ Health	529	374	10.7	2.4	8.3	4.7	6.0	.023	6.6	1.9	2.2
Cooperatives	12	11	.8	.2	.6	.6	.2	0	.6	.1	.1
Corporations w/o Capital Stock	25	20	.1	.03	.1	.1	.04	.0005	.08	.01	.03

Source: Business' Political Awakening: PAC Overview (Washington, D.C.: Fraser/Associates, 1979) p. 75. Reprinted with permission.

see it modified beyond recognition as it is finally implemented by a government agency that issues regulations. Thus continual contact with government agencies is important, but much of this contact is technical rather than political, as experts in environmental affairs from the company, for example, work with EPA professionals to reach realistic compromises on pollution standards and the kind or amount of pollution control equipment the company has to install to be in compliance.

The primary political activity at this stage is court proceedings and hearings before regulatory agencies, more a judicial or legal kind of involvement. Business has tried to block many regulatory requirements in court, and has lost some of these proceedings and won others. Many of the standards proposed by OSHA, for example, have been the subject of court proceedings by business claiming that they were not determined appropriately or did not take economic costs into account. While managers may be involved at some point in these proceedings, these efforts are more legal in nature.

Concluding Remarks

There are many critics of business who would like to severely limit any sort of political activity of business because they believe business can wield too much political power and shape public policy in its own favor much more than other institutions, and, of course, any individuals in society. There is a great difference, they argue, in the size and power of the corporate "person" and other natural persons involved in the political process. The economic power of the corporation can be translated into political power quite readily. Another criticism of corporate political activity is that business managers lack political legitimacy, since they are not duly elected representatives of the public. They would be better off to stay at home and mind the store, so to speak, than to get involved in an area where not only their legitimacy but their competence as well is questionable.[47]

The arguments in favor of political participation are based on the belief that such participation is inevitable given the nature of our highly diverse and organized society. Corporations have legitimate political concerns, and should be placed on a par with other interests and recognized as legitimate political participants in the democratic process. Thus political participation by management and other employees of corporations is both inevitable and as legitimate as any other form of representation within a pluralistic decision-making process.[48]

> Our conclusions with respect to managerial participation in the public policy process, therefore, come down to a few very simple points. Such participation is inevitable and legitimate; and, as public policy becomes an increasingly important consideration in the process of management, such participation can be expected to become more widespread and significant. Our caveat is that such participation should be acknowledged for what it is—both with respect to source and with

[47]Preston and Post, *Private Management and Public Policy*, pp. 144–145.
[48]*Ibid.*, pp. 145–146.

respect to purpose—and that it not be conducted in such a fashion as to exclude other views and interests from equal participation in the process itself.[49]

Certain guidelines for managerial involvement in political activities may be useful. Such a set of guidelines has been suggested by Donald J. Watson of General Electric Company.[50] The first guideline mentioned by Watson is that management must be *proactive rather than reactive*. Anticipation of future issues, says Watson, buys lead time and encourages a more positive approach to issues. It gives business time to choose among a variety of options rather than being placed in a position where it can only react to events beyond its control. With a reasonably accurate agenda of future legislative initiatives, business can have time to analyze the elements of an issue and come up with constructive alternatives.

The second principle of management involvement is to be *constructive rather than destructive*. Business in the past has all too often simply opposed all legislation that affected it without proposing any constructive alternatives to help solve the problem the legislation was addressing. The problems, however, do not disappear. Society wants some kind of solution, and if government responds, however inefficiently, it at least looks like a good guy rather than a narrow-minded reactionary. A constructive approach to public policy problems might go a long way toward working out compromises that are acceptable to business and also helpful to society.

Third, Watson advocates a *nonpartisan approach* to political activity. There is only one President and one Congress at any point in time. It is in the best interests of business, says Watson, to work with them in bringing about constructive legislation and regulation regardless of their political make-up. To refuse to do so on partisan grounds may reduce business' role to that of spectator, where it again can only react to events.

The fourth principle or guideline is to limit political activity to areas in which management has *competence and credibility*. With so many issues on the public agenda, business must limit itself to those it can speak about with experience and knowledge. The manager must do his or her homework and be accurate so a legislator can use the manager's material with confidence. Competent staff work on a limited number of issues is crucial to maintain the credibility of business in the political process.

Finally, the chief executive officer must be *committed and involved* for corporate political activity to be successful. The CEO sets the tone for the entire organization, and without that commitment, the whole effort is much less likely to succeed. The success of the Business Roundtable can be attributed to the direct involvement of the top management of member corporations. This commitment and involvement is a must, according to Watson, for corporate political activity to be effective.

Questions for Discussion

1. Think of some examples where managers of corporations have spoken out in favor of business. Do you believe this was an effective means of influencing public opinion. Why or why not?

---

[49]*Ibid.*, p. 147.
[50]Watson, "The Changing Political Involvement of Business, pp. 5–10. Quoted with permission.

2. Does the manager have a credibility problem regarding the entity he or she represents? For whom does the manager speak? Who or what is the corporation? Is a "corporate" position on an issue possible?
3. What is advocacy advertising? How does it differ from image advertising? Are you in favor of advocacy advertising? What pitfalls exist in using this method to influence public opinion?
4. What do the studies in the chapter suggest to you regarding the effectiveness of advocacy advertising? What would you do to increase the effectiveness of this method? Pick an advocacy ad and rewrite it in a manner that you think would be more effective.
5. Is economic education based on realistic assumptions about the American public? How can this method of influencing public opinion be made less self-serving and more educationally sound?
6. Which of these methods of influencing public opinion do you believe is best? Is it possible for corporations to have a significant influence on public opinion? How would you measure success of any method? Are there other methods you can think of to influence public opinion?
7. What is the Business Roundtable? How does it differ from the National Association of Manufacturers and the United States Chamber of Commerce? Do you believe these differences give the Roundtable a distinct advantage over the older organizations?
8. Define "lobbying." How has lobbying changed both in Washington and overall? How would one go about finding where the real power lies in government?
9. Set up a grass-roots lobbying program for a company. What elements does it include? How would it work? How would you measure its effectiveness?
10. Why are campaign contributions by corporations illegal in this country? Why do companies sometimes make them anyway? What kind of analysis do you imagine executives engage in when deciding whether or not to make an illegal contribution?
11. What is a Political Action Committee? What functions does it perform? How does it work in the typical corporation? Are you in favor of PACs? Why or why not? Would you put any more stringent limitations on their activities than already exist?
12. List the arguments for and against political participation by business. Which side do you think carries the most weight? Think through the policy implications of your answer.
13. Should corporations be nonpartisan in their approach to political activity? What are the implications of this recommendation? Is business no longer tied to the Republican party as it has been in the past?
14. Discuss the guidelines or principles mentioned by Donald J. Watson for management involvement in political activity. Do they make sense? Would you recommend them for your company? Which are most relevant from your point of view?

Suggested Reading

Blumberg, A. *The Scales of Justice.* Chicago: Aldine-Transaction Books, 1970.

Buchholz, Rogene A. *Business Environment/Public Policy: Corporate Executive Viewpoints and Educational Implications.* St. Louis, Mo.: Washington University Center for the Study of American Business, 1980.

Business' Political Awakening: PAC Overview. Washington, D.C.: Fraser/Associates, 1979.

Christoffel, Tom, Finkelhor, David, and Gilbarg, Dan. *Up against the American Myth.* New York: Holt, Rinehart and Winston, 1970.

Edwards, Richard C., Reich, Michael, and Weisshopf, Thomas E. *The Capitalist System: A Radical Analysis of American Society.* Englewood Cliffs, N.J.: Prentice-Hall, 1972.

Emanuel, Myron, Snodgrass, Curtis, Gildea, Joyce, and Rosenberg, Karn. *Corporate Economic Education Programs: An Evaluation and Appraisal.* New York: Financial Executives Research Foundation, 1979.

Epstein, Edwin M. *The Corporation in American Politics.* Englewood Cliffs, N.J.: Prentice-Hall, 1969.

Hacker, Andrew. *The Corporation Take-Over.* New York: Harper & Row, 1964.

McGrath, Phyllis. *Redefining Corporate-Federal Relations.* New York: The Conference Board, 1979.

Mintz, Morton, and Cohen, Jerry S. *America, Inc.: Who Owns and Operates the United States?* New York: Dial Press, 1971.

Nader, Ralph, and Green, Mark J. *Corporate Power in America.* New York: Grossman Publishers, 1973.

Raymond, A., Pool, Ithiel De Sola, and Dexter, Lewis Anthony. *American Business and Public Policy: The Politics of Foreign Trade.* Chicago: Aldine-Atherton, 1972.

Rose, Arnold M. *The Power Structure: Political Process in American Society.* New York: Oxford University Press, 1967.

Schumpeter, Joseph A. *Capitalism, Socialism, and Democracy.* New York: Harper & Row, 1947.

Sethi, S. Prakash. *Advocacy Advertising and Large Corporations.* Lexington, Mass.: Lexington Books, 1977.

Truman, David. *The Governmental Process.* New York: Knopf, 1951.

PART THREE

Public Policy Issues

11

Antitrust Policies

> We do have great concentrations of economic power but there is no unanimity about what to do about them. There are those who wish to break them up into smaller units. Others say that it is inappropriate because we do have vigorous competition with all of its beneficial fruits.[1]

The field of antitrust is as complicated as any in public policy. Supposedly, this area of public policy began as a response to the large modern business enterprises that began to emerge at the close of the nineteenth century. Whatever one believes about the emergence of antitrust as a government policy, it did appear in those years that a completely unregulated system was leading to excessive concentration and eventual monopoly. Such power was unacceptable in American society, as it was believed that this power over markets would be used to ride roughshod over the public interest. Monopoly per se is bad, since a monopolist can set prices and output levels more or less at will, responding only to general economic conditions, not to the challenge of a business competitor.

The ideal form of competition is, of course, pure competition, where the structure of most industries exhibits a low concentration, where there are insignificant barriers to entry, and no product differentiation exists so that the firm has no other choice but to meet the competition. In this kind of competition, the buyers and sellers are so small as to have no influence over the market, thus ensuring that the forces of supply and demand alone determine market outcomes.

This kind of competition exists, however, only in the textbooks. Most industries in today's economy are oligopolistic, containing a few large firms. These firms recognize the impact of their actions on rivals and therefore on

---

[1]George A. Steiner and John F. Steiner, *Business, Government, and Society: A Managerial Perspective*, 3rd ed. (New York: Random House, 1980), p. 514. Quoted with permission.

the market as a whole. In oligopoly, firms deal with each other more or less directly and take into account the effect of their actions on each other. What they do depends very much on how their rivals are expected to react. Oligopolistic firms adjust prices in response to changing market conditions or to changes introduced by rivals in the industry.

Modern large corporations are not simply passive responders to the impersonal forces of supply and demand over which they have no control. The large firms do possess some degree of economic power and do have some influence in the marketplace. Economic power can be defined as the ability to control markets by the reduction of competition through concentration. The limitation of this power is the goal of antitrust policy. The role of government is to maintain a workable competition by raising questions about the size of corporations and the structure of the industries in which they function as well as mergers and other forms of combination, and promote fair competition by making certain forms of anticompetitive practice illegal.

American society has really never come to trust corporate power. Many people believe there is something inherently wrong with bigness, even though such bigness is a fact of life. The antitrust area keeps alive the American virtues of competition, in some sense, and provides a way for society to bring the giant corporations to heel, so to speak, and keep alive the notion of a purely competitive economy where economic power is limited. In *Northern Pacific Ry. v. United States,* Justice Black called the Sherman Act:

> . . . a comprehensive charter of economic liberty aimed at preserving free and unfettered competition as the rule of trade. It rests on the premise that the unrestrained interaction of competitive forces will yield the best allocation of our economic resources, the lowest prices, the highest quality and the greatest material progress, while at the same time providing an environment conducive to the preservation of our democratic political and social institutions.[2]

Public Policy Measures

The Sherman Act of 1890. The most important sections of the Sherman Act are Sections 1 and 2 (see box). Section 1 attacks the act of combining or conspiring to restrain trade. This section seems to make illegal every formal arrangement among firms aimed at curbing independent action in the market. It places restrictions on market conduct, in particular those means of coordination between sellers who use formal agreements to reduce the independence of their actions.[3]

Section 2 enjoins market structures where seller concentration is so high that it could be called a monopoly. But the wording of the section speaks not of monopoly (the state of market structure) but of monopolizing (the act of creating a high level of seller concentration). Taken literally, this could mean that monopolies that existed before 1890 could not be touched, or those that

---

[2]*Northern Pacific Ry. v. United States,* 356 U.S. 1, 4 (1958).

[3]Richard Caves, *American Industry: Structure, Conduct, Performance* (Englewood Cliffs, N.J.: Prentice-Hall, 1972), p. 57.

SHERMAN ACT OF 1890

Sec. 1. Every contract, combination in the form of trust or otherwise, or conspiracy, in restraint of trade or commerce among the several States, or with foreign nations, is hereby declared to be illegal. Every person who shall make any such contract or engage in any such combination or conspiracy, shall be deemed guilty of a misdemeanor, and, on conviction thereof, shall be punished by fine not exceeding five thousand dollars, or by imprisonment not exceeding one year, or by both said punishments, in the discretion of the court.

Sec. 2. Every person who shall monopolize, or attempt to monopolize, or combine or conspire with any other person or persons, to monopolize any part of this trade or commerce among the several States, or with foreign nations, shall be deemed guilty of a misdemeanor, and, on conviction thereof, shall be punished by fine not exceeding five thousand dollars, or by imprisonment not exceeding one year, or by both said punishments, in the discretion of the court.

somehow become monopolies in spite of Section 2 were immune from prosecution.[4]

Clayton Act of 1914. The Clayton Act attacks a series of business policies insofar as they would substantially lessen competition or tend to create a monopoly. The language of the Sherman Act is quite broad, and there was a good deal of uncertainty as to what specific practices were in restraint of trade and thus illegal. The Clayton Act was passed to correct this deficiency by being more specific. It also contained a section that was designed to slow down the merger movement that had resulted in the emergence of many large corporations in the years immediately preceding its passage. The most important sections as far as these purposes are concerned are the following:

Sec. 2: This section bars price discrimination (charging one buyer more than another for the same item) when it tends to lessen competition in any line of commerce.

Sec. 3: This section forbids sellers from requiring buyers of their line of goods to refrain from buying the goods of their rivals when such a policy tends to create a monopoly. There are two situations where this could happen: (1) a tying arrangement, where sellers give buyers access to one line of goods only if the buyers take other goods as well, and (2) an exclusive dealing arrangement, where sellers give buyers access to their line of goods only if the buyers agree to take no goods from any of the sellers' rivals.

Sec. 4: This section provides for treble damages in a private suit; it specifies that the successful claimant in an antitrust case shall recover "three-fold the damages by him sustained, and the cost of the suit, including a reasonable attorney's fee." This section thus encourages private parties such as corporations to pursue antitrust suits against alleged violators.

Sec. 7: This section forbids mergers which substantially lessen competi-

[4]*Ibid.*

tion or tend to create a monopoly. It is concerned with structure and size alone rather than specific anticompetitive practices. It reads as follows:

> . . . no corporation engaged in commerce shall acquire, directly or indirectly, the whole or any part of the stock or other share capital of another corporation engaged also in commerce where the effect of such acquisition may be to substantially lessen competition between the corporation whose stock is so acquired and the corporation making the acquisition or to restrain such commerce in any section or community or tend to create a monopoly of any line of commerce.[5]

While the language is somewhat fuzzy, this section clearly prevented the acquisition of the stock of one corporation by another in the same line of business when the effect was to lessen competition or tend to create a monopoly. The act did not say anything, however, about the purchase or sales of assets by one corporation of or to another, even in the same line of business. This proved to be a huge loophole in the law, which merger-minded companies exploited. The loophole was finally plugged by the 1950 Celler-Kefauver Amendments, which changed Section 7 to read: "no corporation . . . shall acquire, directly or indirectly, the whole or any part of the stock or . . . any part of the *assets* of another corporation . . . where . . . the effect of such acquisition may be substantially to lessen competition, or tend to create a monopoly."[6]

The Federal Trade Commission Act of 1914. This act created the Federal Trade Commission and gave it rather sweeping powers to investigate business organizations and examine business conduct, practices, and the management of companies engaged in interstate commerce. Section 5 provides the language relevant to the antitrust area: "Unfair methods of competition in or affecting commerce, and unfair or deceptive acts or practices in or affecting commerce are hereby declared unlawful."

Thus unfair methods of competition are declared unlawful, but it was up to the commission itself to define what was unfair. The FTC was allowed to attack practices it defined as unlawful even though such practices did not violate the established antitrust laws (*FTC v. The Sperry and Hutchinson Company*).[7] No right of private action exists under this section (*Carlson v. Coca-Cola Co.*).[8] In 1938, the Wheeler-Lea Act amended this section to read ". . . unfair or deceptive acts or practices in commerce," thus giving the FTC the authority to pursue deceptive advertising and other marketing practices.

Current Developments. Throughout most of the period since 1890 and the Sherman Act, violations of antitrust laws have been considered only misdemeanors, carrying very low penalties and jail terms (see Table 11.1) for corporations and individuals found guilty of violations. In 1955, the penalties were upgraded substantially, but the really significant development took place in 1974, when violations were declared a felony punishable by fines not exceeding $1 million for a corporation or $100,000 for an individual and imprisonment not exceeding three years.

---

[5] George A. Steiner, *Business and Society*, 2nd ed. (New York: Random House, 1975), p. 420.
[6] *Ibid.*, p. 423.
[7] *FTC v. The Sperry and Hutchinson Company*, 405 U.S. 233 (1972).
[8] *Carlson v. Coca-Cola Co.*, 483 F.2d 279 (9th Cir. 1973).

TABLE 11.1 **Penalties for Violations of Antitrust Laws**

Period	Maximum Penalty for Corporations	Maximum Penalty for Individuals	Maximum Jail Term
1890–1955	$5,000	$5,000	1 year
1955–1974	$50,000	$50,000	1 year
1974–Present	$1,000,000	$100,000	3 years

Another recent development in the antitrust area as far as public policy measures is concerned is the Hart-Scott-Rodino Antitrust Improvements Act of 1976. Title 1 of this act gave the Justice Department broadened authority to interview witnesses and gather other evidence in antitrust investigations. It gave broadened powers to obtain oral testimony and written interrogatories as well as documents from corporations that may be needed for an investigation. These provisions not only applied to formal cases actually filed by the Justice Department, but also to investigations mounted in connection with planned mergers and joint ventures.

Title II provided for premerger notification, requiring large companies planning mergers to give federal antitrust authorities advance notice of their plans. Under this provision corporations cannot complete the merger for 30 days after the report is filed. This gives the agencies time to study the proposal and take action to block the merger before it is consummated. Subsequent rules issued by the FTC specified that these reporting requirements applied to mergers of large companies and acquisitions of either 15 percent of the outstanding stock of a large concern or $15 million of the stock and assets of such a company. One of the companies involved must have assets of at least $100 million and the other must have assets of at least $10 million for the law to apply. The reporting requirement also applies to joint ventures when the joint venture has assets of at least $10 million and one company involved has at least $100 million in assets or annual sales and another has at least $10 million in assets or annual sales. The requirement also applies if the joint venture has assets of at least $100 million and each of the two companies involved has assets of at least $10 million.

Title III of the act allows state's attorneys general to sue antitrust violators in federal court for treble damages on behalf of overcharged consumers, on the assumption that each state may be a parent to its citizens. These suits may be initiated even though the state itself was not injured. The state can aggregate all the damages on behalf of all alleged victims without having to prove exactly how much each was overcharged. If the state should win, consumers would be able to claim a share of the money or the judge could also order the violator to cut prices for a while to benefit the injured class of consumers.

History of Antitrust Interpretation

The Sherman Act was first applied to unions (See Chapter 3), and it was not until 1911 that cases were decided on the Standard Oil Company and the American Tobacco Company, two giant trusts of the time. Both firms were found guilty of violating Sections 1 and 2 of the Sherman Act and ordered dissolved into several separate firms. But in doing so, the court invoked the so-called rule of reason—these firms were found guilty because they had restrained trade unreasonably, not just because they had restrained trade. This decision emphasized the vicious practices these companies had used against their competitors.

Thus Section 1 of the Sherman Act was interpreted by the courts to prohibit only "unreasonable" restraints of trade. Under this "rule of reason" test, courts would review all relevant facts and circumstances, including economic evidence, to determine whether a contract, combination, or conspiracy unduly restricts and hampers competition. A frequently cited statement of this rule of reason appears in *Chicago Board of Trade v. United States,* in which Justice Brandeis described the "true test of legality" to be whether the restraint merely regulates and perhaps promotes competition or whether it suppresses and even destroys competition.[9] Relevant facts identified by the court to be used in applying the rule of reason test included: (1) facts peculiar to the business, (2) the condition of the business before and after the restraint, (3) the nature of the restraint and its effects, (4) the history of the restraint, and (5) the reason and purpose for adopting the restraint.

Subsequent cases against Eastman Kodak Company, United Shoe Machinery, International Harvester Company, and United States Steel Company were found in favor of the firms because they had not visibly coerced or attacked rivals; in other words, had not restrained trade "unreasonably." Such actions as price fixing were even allowed *(Appalachian Coals Inc. v. United States)* if this was done so as to promote a "fair market" and end injurious competition.[10]

Eventually, however, the courts came to adopt a more or less consistent per se approach to violations of Section 1 of the Sherman Act; that certain kinds of conduct are so unreasonable that they cannot be excused by evidence that they do not adversely affect competition. In the Trenton Potteries Case *(United States v. Trenton Potteries Co.),* the court held that price fixing per se was illegal, whether reasonable or unreasonable. "The power to fix prices," the Court said, "whether reasonably exercised or not, involves power to control the market and to fix arbitrary and unreasonable prices. The reasonable price fixed today may through economic and business changes become the unreasonable price of tomorrow."[11]

Other practices besides price fixing were eventually treated in the same manner more or less consistently. The practices that are thus generally considered to be per se violations of Section 1 of the Sherman Act include (1)

---

[9]*Chicago Board of Trade v. United States,* 246 U.S. 231 (1918).

[10]*Appalachian Coals Inc. v. United States,* 288 U.S. 344 (1933). In this case 137 companies, producing a tenth of the bituminous coal mined east of the Mississippi River and around two-thirds of that mined in the Appalachian territory, had set up a joint agency to handle all their sales. The Court recognized that this arrangement established common prices for the firms involved, but it went on to find that the industry was seriously depressed, that competition in the sale of coal had been subject to various abuses, and that the selling agency did not control enough of the supply to enable it to fix the market price. On this basis, the arrangement was allowed to stand. William G. Shepherd and Clair Wilcox, *Public Policies toward Business,* 6th ed. (Homewood, Ill.: Richard D. Irwin, 1979), p. 202. Copyright © 1979 by Richard D. Irwin, Inc. All rights reserved.

[11]*United States v. Trenton Potteries Co.,* 273 U.S. 392 (1927).

price fixing, (2) restriction of output, (3) division of markets, (4) group boycotts, and (5) tying arrangements. With respect to these practices, proof can be limited to the fact and amount of damage. The establishment of a per se approach to these practices relieves the parties to the suit and the court from inquiring into the factors relevant to a rule of reason analysis.

With respect to Section 2, an attempt to monopolize can be defined as the employment of method, means, or practices which would, if successful, accomplish monopolization, or something so close as to create a dangerous probability of monopolization. To be guilty of actual monopolization, one must possesss (1) monopoly power in the relevant market, and (2) the intent and purpose to exercise that power. Monopoly power is the power to control prices or unreasonably restrict competition. Thus almost any combination or conspiracy to monopolize would also violate Section 1 of the Sherman Act, but unlike Section 1, which requires two separate entities for a "conspiracy," a violation of Section 2 can be based on the conduct of a single actor.

When the rule of reason doctrine was in effect, it was clear that the law did not make mere size or the existence of unexerted power an offense. Size could only be an offense if accompanied by certain predatory types of market conduct. This changed with the Alcoa case of 1945 (*United States v. Aluminum Co. of America*), where it was held that a high level of seller concentration in and of itself could constitute a violation. While there was no precise definition as to what share of the market constituted a monopoly, the court in this case remarked that 90 percent of the market, which apparently was Alcoa's market share at the time, "is enough to constitute a monopoly, it is doubtful whether sixty-four percent would be enough; and certainly thirty-three percent is not."[12]

The court could find no predatory conduct on the part of Alcoa; its 90 percent market share was obtained by an honest industrial effort. But Alcoa's monopoly was not thrust upon it, the court said, and by a series of normal and prudent business practices the firm had succeeded in discouraging or forestalling all would-be competitors. The Sherman Act forbade all such monopolies no matter how acquired. Furthermore, the court said, the existence of power to fix prices inherent in a monopoly position could not be distinguished from the exercise of such power. Such a distinction was purely formal, and when monopoly entered the market, "the power and its exercise must needs coalesce."[13]

Thus a standard centered on market structure replaced one which had previously depended essentially on market conduct. This decision comes close to making size in the sense of market share a per se violation of the Sherman Act, but the precedent established in this case, which was a departure from previous interpretations, has not been applied consistently in later years. The question of whether mere size in itself constitutes a violation of the antitrust laws is unanswered, and the "bigness is bad" debate continues (see next sections). This question is enormously complex, and is one of the reasons cases such as the IBM case, which is now (1981) in its twelfth year, drag on so long.

---

[12]*United States v. Aluminum Co. of America*, 148 F. 2d 416 (1945).
[13]*Ibid.*

The government must first of all prove that IBM dominates the market to show that it possesses monopoly power. The question of the relevant market is crucial to this proof. The government defines it narrowly as limited to the markets for general purpose computers and peripheral products that are compatible with IBM equipment. This definition gives IBM a 70 percent market share. The company, of course, defines the market differently and comes up with a much lower market share. The government must also prove that IBM had an intent to monopolize by driving competitors out of business. Thus the government must prove that IBM not only possesses "monopoly power," but also intended to acquire and maintain that power.

In the 1960s, a new type of merger appeared on the scene, the so-called conglomerate merger. These mergers are combinations of companies in completely different lines of activity; therefore, it is argued, these mergers have no anticompetitive effects and are not subject to antitrust litigation. Since the only case filed by the government against a conglomerate (ITT) was settled out of court, no precedent has been established on interpretation of antitrust laws and their application to these combinations. Some legislators, however, have attempted to answer this question with new legislation aimed specifically at mergers between firms in different industries. For example, the Kennedy bill entitled the "Small and Independent Business Protection Act of 1979" (S. 600) would amend Section 7 of the Clayton Act to: (1) prohibit mergers between firms with $2 billion in sales or assets, (2) restrict mergers between firms of $350 million, and (3) restrict the right of still smaller firms to sell out to companies of $350 million in sales or assets. The proposed law assumes that big companies, regardless of their make-up, have unfair advantages, since no showing of anticompetitive dangers would be required to bar these mergers.[14]

Finally, recent efforts by the FTC and Justice Department have attempted to extend the reach of antitrust laws to oligopoly itself. This structure has been referred to as a "shared monopoly," in the sense that the largest companies in some industries achieve consensus decisions on output and pricing that resemble those of a more traditional single-company monopoly. This consensus is reached through open communication, such as published price lists or news releases, that constitutes price-signaling to other companies. The Justice Department has proposed filing a suit on this basis to test the thinking of the Courts regarding this issue.[15]

The FTC also filed suit in 1972 against the four largest U.S. manufacturers of ready-to-eat breakfast cereal, charging violations of Section 5 of the Federal Trade Commission Act (FTC v. Kellogg et al.). The four were Kellogg, General Mills, General Foods, and Quaker Oats (Quaker Oats was subsequently dropped from the case because its market share was significantly smaller than the other three companies). The case is based on economic theories of localized competition first developed in 1929 by Harold Hotelling. This theory holds that in areas where products are clearly differ-

---

[14]See A. F. Ehrbar, "Bigness Becomes the Target of the Trustbusters," *Fortune,* March 26, 1979, pp. 34–40.

[15]"Taking Aim at Shared Monopolies," *The Wall Street Journal,* August 22, 1978, p. 18.

entiated, products compete with one or two others that share similar characteristics rather than with every other product on the marketplace.[16]

Thus companies in the cereal industry compete by introducing more and more brands. The result is brand proliferation, which gives little hope that new companies will get much of a foothold because they have to compete for ever smaller slices of the market. This is an unfair method of competition because it raises high barriers to entry for new companies and is, in a sense, a shared monopoly. The FTC is seeking to break up these companies into smaller firms, and institute a system of trademark licensing that would enable new companies to imitate existing brands.

In October 1980, however, the FTC issued a ruling that signaled a departure from its attack on bigness. The agency dismissed charges against DuPont Company for dominating the titanium dioxide market, and defended this ruling by stating that actions which could create a monopoly are not illegal if they resulted from aggressive competition based on technological advantage. The competitive process would not be served, the FTC argued, if antitrust was used to block aggressive competition that is solidly based on efficiency and growth opportunities. This change in thinking, coupled with a new administration that initially adopted a softer line on antitrust, may usher in a new era where bigness is seen to offer many advantages both domestically and in international markets.

Economic Concentration

The question of size and structure is a crucial one as far as the antitrust area is concerned. Does the size of some corporations and the concentration of production of certain goods in the hands of a few companies make competition ineffective as a regulator of business behavior? Should the government then regulate business further by the use of public commissions and act to curb corporate growth by law to protect the public interest in good products at reasonably low prices? If, however, competition can be effective in protecting the public interest, what should be done to enhance its vigor? Should the government fragment giant enterprises to introduce more competition in industries dominated by these giants?

The answers to these questions depend in part on the degree of economic concentration that exists in our economy. Is monopoly rising, declining, or staying about the same? Conversely, what about competition: is it increasing, decreasing, or remaining stable? How much economic power do corporations actually have in our society? It is useful to look at some studies of economic concentration that might give at least tentative answers to these questions.

Aggregate Concentration. One way to study the structure of the economy is to deal with it in the aggregate by measuring overall concentration in the economy. This is done by taking the top 100, 200, or 500

---

[16]"Too Many Cereals for the FTC," *Business Week,* March 20, 1978, pp. 166–167. See also Walter Kiechell III, "The Soggy Case against the Cereal Industry," *Fortune,* April 10, 1978, pp. 49–51; and Richard Schmalensee, "Entry Deterrence in the Ready-To-Eat Breakfast Cereal Industry," *The Bell Journal of Economics,* Vol. 9, No. 2 (Autumn 1978), pp. 305–327.

corporations in the country and determining whether their share of total corporate assets, sales, income, or value added has increased or decreased over some period of time. If the top corporations have increased their share of total corporate assets, sales, income, or value added, it can be concluded that aggregate economic concentration is increasing. If their share is decreasing with respect to the total, aggregate concentration is declining.

One study of this type was completed in 1932 by Adolph A. Berle and Gardiner C. Means.[17] This study dealt with the 200 largest nonbanking corporations as of January 1, 1930, with size being determined by taking gross assets less depreciation as reported in Moody's Railroad, Public Utility, and Industrial Manuals. They found that in 1929, the top 200 corporations controlled 49.2 percent of all nonbanking corporate wealth and received 43.2 percent of the income of all nonbanking corporations.

For the 1909–1928 period, the annual rate of growth of these 200 corporations had been 5.4 percent, for all corporations the growth rate was 3.6 percent per year, and for corporations other than the top 200 the growth rate was only 2.0 percent per year. Thus the 200 largest corporations were increasing in wealth 50 percent faster than all corporations and over two and a half times as fast as smaller corporations. At these rates they concluded, it would take only 40 years for all corporate activity and practically all industrial activity to be absorbed by the top 200 companies. The fact that this did not happen means that either there were deficiencies in their original trend data or that the trend toward increasing aggregate concentration abated.

Another study of this kind, completed in 1963 by a Senate Subcommittee on Antitrust and Monopoly, found that in 1958, the 50 largest manufacturing companies accounted for 23 percent of all the value added by manufacturing. The 200 largest companies accounted for 38 percent of value added. By 1963, these percentages had become 25 percent and 41 percent respectively. Also in 1958, the 100 largest firms in mining, manufacturing, and distribution owned almost 30 percent of all the assets in these industries.[18]

A Conference Board study completed in 1973 looked at the growth of the largest manufacturing firms by comparing the 1947–1958 and 1958–1967 periods. The study concluded that the share of U.S. manufacturing attributable to the top 50, 100, and 200 largest manufacturing firms in terms of total assets, sales, and value added had grown during both periods, but the rate of growth in each case was lower in the later period than in the earlier. Thus the largest corporations were not following a trajectory that would in the foreseeable future lead to the concentration of all manufacturing activity in a few hands, an opposite conclusion from the earlier Berle-Means study.[19]

Finally, Philip Blumberg reported sales, assets, employees, and net income for the largest 500 industrial corporations for 1955, 1960, 1965, 1970, and 1973 (see Table 11.2). These percentages show the proportion held by the top 500 companies with respect to total industrial sales, assets,

[17] Adolf A. Berle and Gardiner C. Means, *The Modern Corporation and Private Property* (New York: Harcourt Brace Jovanovich, 1932).

[18] U.S. Congress, Senate, Committee on the Judiciary, Subcommittee on Antitrust and Monopoly, *Concentration Ratios in Manufacturing Industry, 1963* S. Rept., 89th Cong., 2d sess., 1966, p. 2.

[19] Betty Bock and Jack Farkas, *Relative Growth of the Largest Manufacturing Corporations, 1947–1971* (New York: The Conference Board, 1973).

TABLE 11.2 **The Performance of the 500 Largest Industrials Relative to Total Industrial Performance for Selected Years**

Year	Percent of Total Sales	Percent of Total Assets	Percent of Total Employees	Percent of Total Net Income
1955	58.0%	64.2%	49.1%	77%
1960	59.2%	68.8%	52.6%	76%
1965	60.6%	70.1%	60.3%	78%
1970	65.4%	74.7%	73.1%	76%
1973	65.6%	82.9%	76.0%	79%

Adapted from Philip I. Blumberg, *The Megacorporation in American Society* (Englewood Cliffs, N.J.: Prentice-Hall, 1975), p. 25. Reprinted with permission.

employees, and net income. These figures show a consistent increase in all respects except for two years with regard to net income. The largest increases in concentration took place with respect to assets and employees.[20]

These are by no means all the significant studies that have been completed on aggregate concentration, but only a representative sample. It is difficult to draw any generalizations from these studies, since they were done at different times and used different sources of information. However, many scholars in this area seem to conclude that aggregate economic concentration has increased over the years, particularly with respect to assets; that is, the share of assets owned by the top corporations in the country has increased with respect to the assets of all corporations.

Market Concentration. Some scholars argue that studies of aggregate concentration tell nothing about competition and monopoly or about corporate economic power.[21] All that these data show is that some corporations are large with respect to the total economy when aggregated across certain aspects, such as sales or assets. But the large size of these companies in the aggregate says nothing about the rivalry they face individually, the kind of market in which they function, or their price-output patterns. Therefore a different kind of approach is recommended, one that deals with market concentration rather than aggregate concentration.

Market concentration can be defined as the percentage of total industry sales that are contributed by the largest few firms in an industry, ranked in order of market shares. The most common measure is the four-firm sales concentration ratio—the percentage of industry sales made by the leading four firms in the industry.

One study of this type is shown in Table 11.3 and Table 11.4. These data were presented by Dr. Betty Bock of the Conference Board in May 1977 to the Subcommittee on Antitrust and Monopoly of the Senate Judiciary Committee chaired by Senator Edward Kennedy of Massachusetts.[22] Table 11.3 shows only those 136 industries that are definitionally comparable over the 1947–1972 census years, based on the standard industrial classifications

[20]Philip I. Blumberg, *The Megacorporation in American Society* (Englewood Cliffs, N.J.: Prentice-Hall, 1975), p. 25.

[21]See M. A. Adelman, "The Two Faces of Economic Concentration," *The Public Interest*, No. 21 (Fall 1970), pp. 117–126.

[22]U.S. Congress, Senate, Committee on the Judiciary, *Oversight of Antitrust Enforcement, Hearings before the Subcommittee on Antitrust and Monopoly*, 95th Cong., 1st sess., 1977, pp. 160–180.

TABLE 11.3 **Number and Percent of Definitionally Comparable Industries by Value of Shipments Concentration Brackets, 1947–1972***

First-4 Company Value of Shipments Concentration Bracket	1947 (1)	1954 (2)	1958 (3)	1963 (4)	1967 (5)	1972 (6)
			Number of Industries			
90% or more	2	2	1	3	1	4
80% to 89%	8	7	8	6	8	5
70% to 79%	9	9	9	8	6	8
60% to 69%	9	10	9	8	14	9
50% to 59%	12	13	14	18	11	16
Less than 50%	96	95	95	93	96	94
Total	136	136	136	136	136	136
			Cumulative Percent of Industries			
90% or more	1	1	1	2	1	3
80% or more	7	7	7	7	7	7
70% or more	14	13	13	12	11	12
60% or more	21	21	20	18	21	19
50% or more	29	30	30	32	29	31
Less than 50%	71	70	70	68	71	69
Total	100	100	100	100	100	100

*Includes only those industry categories which are definitionally comparable in the years 1947, 1954, 1958, 1963, 1967, and 1972 and for which value of shipments concentration data are available in all years. Five categories were omitted because they are listed as not elsewhere classified or miscellaneous.

Source: U.S. Congress, Senate, Committee on the Judiciary, *Oversight of Antitrust Enforcement, Hearings before the Subcommittee on Antitrust and Monopoly,* 95th Cong., 1st sess., 1977, p. 174.

employed by the Census Bureau. Table 11.4 shows the data from all four-digit SIC industries.

The cutoff point of 50 percent is usually meant to indicate an oligopolistic market structure, one where the top four firms control 50 percent or more of the market. Both of these tables show a remarkable stability throughout the 1947–1972 period, indicating that market concentration is not a rising tide that threatens to engulf the American economy. The 50 percent and over category remained stable at around 30 percent of all industries.

One problem, however, is that while a study such as this may show more about competition in given industries, it assumes that all industries are equal in terms of their impact on the total economy. This is undoubtedly not the case; the industries that have concentration ratios of 50 percent or more may also account for a large percentage of all manufacturing assets, sales, income, or value added. If that were true, these findings would have to be seen in a quite different perspective.

Market concentration studies show nothing about aggregate concentration. There is, therefore, no easy answer to questions about the degree of monopoly and competition in the American economy. One needs to ask questions and conduct research at both the aggregate and market levels to

TABLE 11.4 **Number and Percent of All Industries by Value of Shipments Concentration Brackets, 1947–1972***

First-4 Company Value of Shipments Concentration Bracket	1947 (1)	1954 (2)	1958 (3)	1963 (4)	1967 (5)	1972 (6)
	Number of Industries					
90% or more	10	8	6	8	5	10
80% to 89%	18	21	15	10	17	10
70% to 79%	27	25	28	17	15	19
60% to 69%	31	30	29	25	30	25
50% to 59%	46	47	44	38	34	49
Less than 50%	254	253	255	248	240	254
Total	386	384	377	346	341	367
	Cumulative Percent of Industries					
90% or more	2	2	2	2	1	3
80% or more	7	8	6	5	6	5
70% or more	14	14	13	10	11	11
60% or more	22	22	21	17	20	17
50% or more	34	34	32	28	30	31
Less than 50%	66	66	68	72	70	69
Total	100	100	100	100	100	100

*Includes all industry categories for 1947, 1954, 1958, 1963, 1967, and 1972, respectively, except:

(1) industries for which value of shipments concentration data are not available due to large but unknown amounts of duplication in shipments figures;

(2) industries for which no concentration data are provided due to Census disclosure rules (D);

(3) industries which are combined to avoid disclosure of individual company operations; and

(4) industries listed as not elsewhere classified or miscellaneous.

Source: U.S. Congress, Senate, Committee on the Judiciary, *Oversight of Antitrust Enforcement, Hearings before the Subcommittee on Antitrust and Monopoly,* 95th Cong., 1st sess., 1977, p. 175.

arrive at even tentative conclusions about the structure of the American economy.

Structure versus Performance

The interest in these studies of economic concentration stems, of course, from a concern about size and its relationship to economic power. Such concerns give rise to the structural theory of industrial organization. This theory holds that the structure of the economy or an industry predetermines the behavior or performance of firms in the economy and in particular industries. The more concentrated are all corporate assets in the largest companies, and the more concentrated are the sales of an industry in the largest few firms of that industry, the more economic power exists in society. Such concentration is bad for society because this economic power can and will be used to control markets by fixing prices in some fashion, determining which products are put on the market, restricting volume, and maintaining high or excessive profits. There are a number of basic propositions in this structural theory, including the following:

1. If an industry not atomistic there is administrative discretion over prices.
2. Concentration results in recognized interdependence; no price competition in concentrated industries.
3. Concentration is not natural, due mostly to merger; for most efficient scale no more than 3 to 5% of industry required; high degree of concentration is unnecessary.
4. Positive correlation between concentration and profitability is evidence of monopoly power in concentrated industries—the ability to elevate prices and persistence of high profits; entry does not take place to eliminate excessive profits.
5. Aggravated by product differentiation and advertising; advertising is correlated with higher profits.
6. Oligopolistic coordination by signaling.[23]

The opposite point of view is the performance argument, which holds that concentration of economic power in large companies is due to underlying economic, sociological, and technological forces in society, and is not based on a desire of corporate managers to monopolize an industry. Massive and complex business organizations are the tangible manifestation of the advanced technology they employ.[24] In certain industries large companies and concentration are essential because of the heavy capital investment needed to do business and produce products. The nature of the technological processes involved provides advantages for an integrated large-scale enterprise which can coordinate all the stages of production to increase throughput.[25] Thus the large size of modern corporations is a function of technology more than of conscious attempts to monopolize an industry.

From a sociological point of view, Peter Drucker argues, American society has become a society of large, highly organized, and professionally managed institutions. The United States has become a society of large pluralistic institutions, including business, hospitals, educational institutions, and others. Bigness is here to stay, says Drucker, and an atomistic market structure would be quite out of step with the demands of modern society. People are in no mood to do without the fruits of modern, large-scale organizations. The essence of a modern, large organization is that within it, people of very diverse skills and knowledge can work together for a common purpose. The tasks that need to be accomplished in modern society require large-scale organizations. Thus the job of society is not to abolish them but to make them perform better for individuals, for communities, and for the society as a whole.[26]

Finally, it is argued that there are sound economic reasons behind the

[23]J. Fred Weston, "Big Corporations: The Arguments for and against Breaking Them Up," *Business and Its Changing Environment,* proceedings of a conference held at UCLA, July 24–August 3, 1977, pp. 232–233.

[24]See John Kenneth Galbraith, *The New Industrial State* (Boston: Houghton Mifflin, 1967).

[25]See Alfred Chandler, *The Visible Hand: The Managerial Revolution in American Business* (Cambridge, Mass.: Belknap Press, 1977).

[26]Peter F. Drucker, "The Concept of the Corporation," *Business and Society Review,* No. 3 (Autumn 1972), pp. 12–17.

growth of large organizations, such as (1) economies of large-scale production, (2) advantages of integrated and long-range planning, (3) advantages of large-scale purchasing and distribution economies, (4) ability to afford heavy research and development expenditures necessary for innovation, and (5) more effective competition in foreign markets.

Bigness is not necessarily bad, according to this view, but must be judged on its merits or performance. The performance of large firms must be examined independently and not inferred from the structure of the economy or the industry in which they function. Measures of performance could include product and process innovations, reductions in costs that have been passed on to consumers, whether profits are excessive or are more or less in line with other industries, or whether these large firms are operating efficiently with above average productivity gains.

Structuralists want to prevent or break up large concentrations of economic power and promote competition, and only then, they argue, will society get economically desirable performance. The performance view holds that structure is by and large irrelevant to the performance of corporations, and that society should concern itself more directly with performance rather than with the structure of the economy or of particular industries. This debate revolves around certain dimensions of the modern corporation.

Economies of Scale and Efficiency. The structuralist view holds that the efficiency arguments for large corporations are not valid, that economies of scale are significant only at the plant level and do not extend to the organizational level. Beyond a certain plant size, no further economies exist, and there are no economies that relate to the number of plants any one manufacturer controls. Giant companies are simply aggregations of plants scattered around the country, each of which may be small compared to the market. These companies could be broken up without in any way reducing efficiency at the plant level.

The performance view, however, holds that firms are large because they are more efficient than their smaller rivals. Economies of scale accrue to large firms, and this greater efficiency is of benefit to society. Such studies as the one completed by Arthur A. Thompson support this view, at least in part.[27] Thompson found that prices for 31 product categories dominated by large firms rose more slowly on the average over the 1947–1973 period than did the price indexes of 29 small-firm-dominated product groups (Figure 11.1). This finding could suggest that these larger firms were more efficient and were able to pass on cost savings to consumers. In another study of the relationship between concentration and profits, Harold Demsetz found a positive correlation between profits and concentration. However, these high profits may be associated more with efficiency than with exercise of monopoly power. Demsetz says his research "strongly suggests that the relatively large firms in concentrated industries produce at lower cost than their smaller rivals. The relative competitive superiority of large firms grows more significant as concentration increases."[28]

[27]Arthur A. Thompson, "Corporate Bigness—For Better or for Worse," *Sloan Management Review,* Vol. 17, No. 1 (Fall 1975), pp. 37–61.

[28]Harold Demsetz, *The Market Concentration Doctrine* (Washington, D.C.: American Enterprise Institute, 1973), pp. 22, 25–26.

Figure 11.1. Comparative Price Trends in Corporate-Dominated and Small-Firm-Dominated Markets

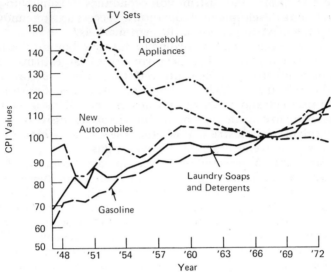

Corporate Price Trends as Reported in
BLS Consumer Price Index, 1947–1973

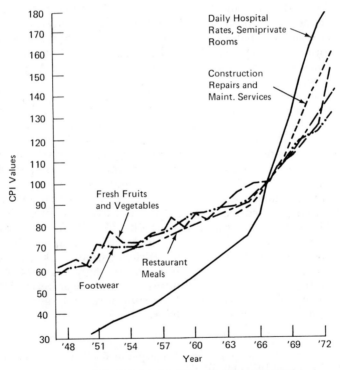

Price Trends in Small-Firm Markets as Reported
in BLS Consumer Price Index, 1947–1973

Reprinted from "Corporate Bigness—For Better or for Worse," by Arthur A. Thompson, *Sloan Management Review*, Vol. 17, No. 1, p. 53, by permission of the publisher. Copyright © 1975 by the Sloan Management Review Association. All rights reserved.

Technological Innovation. The performance view holds that large firms are able to operate a proficient research and development program that will keep these firms on the frontiers of technological innovation and supplied with a reliable stream of new products and product improvement. Most research and development expenditures take place in large firms that are part of oligopolistic industries. Furthermore, large firms are able to finance the development of technological innovations that will offset rising costs through increases in productivity.

The structuralist view says that empirical evidence does not support the argument that bigness provides the necessary environment for invention, innovation, and technological progress. For example, the Jewkes study of 61 important inventions made since 1900 showed that over half were the work of independent inventors who were disassociated from the industrial research laboratories of big enterprises.[29] Moreover, a substantial part of the research carried on by big firms is actually financed by the federal government, particularly in the aerospace, electrical equipment, and communications industries.

With regard to the introduction of new technology, the large company may actually be a barrier to technological progress rather than a facilitator. There is no competitive spur, it is argued, to productive efficiency. Large companies, particularly in heavy industries such as the steel industry, are slow to accept technological change. The cost of replacing existing capital equipment, which would then be rendered obsolete, would exceed any benefits that would result from the new technology.

The Nature of Competition. The structuralist view focuses on price competition, and deplores the price leadership phenomenon in olgopolistic industries and the price signaling that occurs between companies. Prices in a concentrated industry, it is argued, are set by administrative discretion rather than market forces, proving that competition is all but nonexistent in these industries. The relationship is one of "live and let live," based on a recognition that all companies in the industry will be better off charging uniformly high prices for similar products. Price competition will only destroy this relationship and eventually lead to lower profits for all companies in the industry.

The performance view is that there are many dimensions of competition besides price, including quality of product, differences in product characteristics, competition in sales or marketing strategies, advertising, service, and financing arrangements at various stages of the distribution process. As stated by Fred Weston:

> The processes of competition take place over so many dimensions and are so dynamic in their nature that they can't be reduced to neat and simple textbook diagrams or even well-behaved equation systems. But these dimensions of competition are nonetheless real, important and the actual content of real world industrial processes.[30]

---

[29] J. Jewkes, R. Sawers, and R. Sullerman, *The Sources of Invention* (New York: St. Martin's Press, 1968).

[30] Weston, "Big Corporations," p. 245.

Policy Implications

There are no easy answers to these questions about the relationship of structure and performance. There seem to be no definitive studies at the present time that would conclusively answer some of these questions and thus have relatively clear policy implications. Many studies deal with various aspects of this question—the preceding section presented only a few representative studies. One can find studies of varying degrees of quality to support either the structuralist or performance position. It might be not wholly inaccurate to say that the view one adopts and the policies supported depend on value preferences relative to a competitive structure versus a more concentrated one and value preferences for large enterprises versus smaller enterprises.

Thus the bigness is bad versus bigness is good issue may be more of a debate about values than about structure and performance as such, which means there can be no definitive answers to these questions. One's values are simply one's values, and if a person has a preference for small companies and a more competitive economy, there is no rightness or wrongness to this preference, it is simply a value choice. These preferences are worked out through the political process, where public policy decisions are eventually made.

Many believe, however, that the antitrust area needs reform. There are questions, as stated earlier, about the way current antitrust laws apply to conglomerates and the notion of a shared monopoly. Cases could be brought before the court on these issues, forcing the court to decide them, but many believe that legislative action should be taken to modernize the antitrust area and make the laws themselves more appropriate to a market system that has grown increasingly large, complex, and multinational in scope.[31]

One such reform measure is simply to abolish the laws altogether, either in whole or in part. Some economists, such as Yale Brozen of the University of Chicago, argue that antitrust laws are largely unnecessary, that both conduct and structure should be left up to market forces. Few businesspeople agree, however, that the antitrust laws should be abolished completely.[32] There is some support for at least limiting the antitrust area to business practices or conduct and abolishing the concern about size and structure stated in Section 2 of the Sherman Act and continued in later public policy measures. The laws could specify the rules of the game as far as fair and honest methods of competition are concerned and continue to rule out such practices as price fixing, division of markets, price discrimination, exclusive dealing arrangements, predatory pricing, and other types of anticompetitive conduct. Certain kinds of conduct would be illegal, but the size of corporations and the structure of the economy as well as the concentration of individual industries would be left up to market forces. As long as competition is honest and fair, so the argument goes, the emergence of large companies and concentrated industries should reflect genuine economic advantages related to efficiency and productivity increases.

Another reform measure would clarify more precisely in the legislation

---

[31]"Is John Sherman's Antitrust Obsolete?" *Business Week*, March 23, 1974, pp. 47–56.
[32]*Ibid.*, p. 49.

itself exactly what business practices are unlawful. Some people complain that the vagueness of the antitrust laws causes a great deal of uncertainty about how the laws will subsequently be interpreted. Specifying more precisely what practices are unfair methods of competition would help business to know exactly where it stands. The difficulty of doing this, however, stems from the task of identifying and foreseeing all such practices when business conditions and the economy are constantly changing. It would seem to be impossible to develop an all-inclusive list of anticompetitive conduct at any point in time. And even if certain practices, such as price fixing, were specified in the law, there would still be a debate over what practices constituted price fixing. There is uncertainty in any legislation, which is the reason legislation needs constant interpretation by the courts as conditions and society change.[33]

Replacing the antitrust laws with direct regulation is favored by some economists, including John Kenneth Galbraith, who believes that a competitive economy cannot be produced because of the technological imperatives behind the growth of large corporations. Others, such as George Stigler, point out that antitrust has not been able to bring about a more competitive economy, since the evidence shows there has been no long-term decline in concentration. Thus if bigness and concentration are inevitable, so the argument goes, regulation of the ICC type to reduce the effects of these "natural" or "shared" monopolies would seem a reasonable approach.[34]

Such a view, however, runs counter to the trend toward deregulation of some industries that have been regulated for years. Many economists now believe that this type of regulation only amounts to a government supported and maintained cartel, that regulated companies come to share monopoly power with the active cooperation of the government. Therefore the best thing to do with industry regulation is to abolish it in favor of competition.

Finally, there is an approach that would make size alone an offense by adopting a per se approach to the size of corporations, as has been taken in most instances toward certain forms of corporate conduct. One such bill, introduced into Congress in 1972 by Senator Phillip Hart of Michigan, called for the establishment of a federal commission with the power to break up large firms if any one of the following three conditions were present in an industry.

- An average rate of return on net worth after taxes in excess of 15% over a period of 5 consecutive years in the most recent 7 years preceding the filing of the complaint.
- No substantial price competition among two or more corporations in three consecutive years out of the most recent five years preceding the filing of the complaint.
- If any four or fewer corporations account for 50% or more of sales in any one year out of the most recent three years preceding the filing of the complaint.[35]

There have been other bills of this type, including the Kennedy bill

[33]Ibid.

[34]Ibid., pp. 49–50.

[35]U.S., Congress, Senate, Industrial Reorganization Act, 93rd Cong., 1st sess., 1973, S. 1167, pp. 2–3.

mentioned earlier that is directed specifically at conglomerates. This approach would specify in some quantitative fashion what size was illegal and would thus make it unnecessary for government to prove the existence of monopoly power or that there was an intent to attain and maintain this power. In addition to the limitations such a structuralist approach would place on corporate growth, such a policy might deprive the society of substantial economies. It has not yet been conclusively proven that society would be better off with smaller companies.

Managerial Implications

It seems safe to say that given the foregoing, there is a good deal of interest and activity in this area of public policy. While reform measures like the Kennedy bill may not pass, the federal government seems intent on pushing into new areas such as shared monopolies and using its new powers to block mergers and gather evidence. There is also a trend toward higher fines and longer jail sentences being assigned, thus treating violators of the antitrust laws tougher than has been true in the past. Experiments such as an antitrust hotline have been tried to encourage consumers and business to report violations (see box).

ANTITRUST HOTLINE EXPERIMENT IN PITTSBURGH IS CONSIDERED A SUCCESS

A toll-free telephone arrangement set up by the Justice Department's Antitrust Division to induce consumers and businesses to report antitrust violations produced 150 formal complaints in two months of operation. As a result, the government has begun 20 investigations and has scheduled another five or 10, says Bruce Wilson, an attorney for the antitrust unit.

John J. Hughes, chief of the Middle Atlantic office of the Antitrust Division, says public response "shows there's a substantial untapped interest in the antitrust laws and their enforcement." He says the project is being evaluated for possible use in other regions. Most of the complaints were lodged by consumers against retailers, although some small businesses were heard from. Discount stores, for example, charged that manufacturers unfairly stopped shipments because of the discounters' pricing.

In addition to all this federal activity, the states have also become increasingly active in antitrust litigation. Congress recently set aside $11 million to bolster state antitrust activity in addition to the appropriations that went with the 1976 law permitting states to sue on behalf of consumers for antitrust violations.[36] States have increased the number of suits filed, increased antitrust budgets, and hired more antitrust attorneys along with additional

---

[36]"State Prosecutors Crack Down on Business," *Business Week*, May 15, 1978, pp. 53–54.

ANTITRUST POLICIES

investigators, economists, and accountants to supplement the antitrust staff. Other states have passed new antitrust laws that provide for expanded jurisdiction, stiffer penalties, and more investigative powers.

All of this says nothing about private antitrust suits, which are also on the increase, and questions being raised about the application of antitrust laws to overseas activities of American firms. Thus the antitrust area can affect many areas of management. In response to this activity, some companies have adopted an antitrust compliance program. Such a program typically includes (1) education of company personnel about antitrust matters, (2) a statement of the company's antitrust policy, and (3) development of a documentation system for relevant company records.

Questions for Discussion

1. What are the origins of antitrust as an area of public policy? What were the problems that the antitrust laws were originally designed to address? Are those problems still present in the American economy today?
2. What are the goals of antitrust policy? Have these goals been attained? What data are relevant to answering this question?
3. What is economic power? Is the existence of such power bad or good for society? How does antitrust policy attempt to place limitations on this power?
4. What is the difference between the two sections of the Sherman Act? Which section, in your opinion, is more important? Which section could have the greatest impact on business? Why?
5. What is the purpose of the premerger notification provision of the Hart-Scott-Rodino Antitrust Improvements Act of 1976? Are you in favor of this provision? What is a good merger? What is a bad merger? What criteria are relevant to answering this question?
6. What is the "rule of reason" as applied to the antitrust laws? How is this different from a per se approach? Is there such a thing as a "reasonable" restraint of trade?
7. Is the size of a corporation in and of itself a public policy problem? Why or why not? What did the Alcoa decision say about this problem? Should the government drop its case against IBM?
8. Describe a shared monopoly. Is the government justified in pursuing this concept? What is the issue in the government's case against the cereal companies? What is the likely outcome of this case?
9. What is the difference between aggregate and market concentration? Which area is more relevant to the questions raised by antitrust policy? How are these two types of concentration related?
10. Distinguish between structure and performance as approaches to economic concentration. What are the key assumptions behind both approaches? Where do values enter into these arguments?
11. Discuss the different dimensions to the structure versus performance argument. Are there any definitive answers to these questions? Why or why not?
12. Which of the reform measures mentioned in the text do you like best? Which would be best from a business standpoint? Which would be best for society?
13. Is it possible for antitrust laws to be more precise? Would this reform help business to relate better to public policy in the antitrust area?
14. Examine the advice to managers on antitrust policy of a typical corporation. Can you understand these guidelines? Do you believe they are relevant to the job you are considering in business? In what ways?

Suggested Reading

Bain, J. S. *Barriers to New Competition.* Cambridge, Mass.: Harvard University Press, 1956.

———. *Industrial Organization,* 2nd ed. New York: John Wiley, 1968.

Blair, J. M. *Economic Concentration: Structure, Behavior and Public Policy.* New York: Harcourt Brace Jovanovich, 1972.

Blumberg, Philip I. *The Megacorporation in American Society.* Englewood Cliffs, N.J.: Prentice-Hall, 1975.

Bock, Betty, and Farkas, Jack. *Relative Growth of the Largest Manufacturing Corporations, 1947–1971.* New York: The Conference Board, 1973.

Caves, Richard. *American Industry: Structure, Conduct, Performance.* Englewood Cliffs, N.J.: Prentice-Hall, 1972.

Demsetz, H. *The Market Concentration Doctrine.* Washington, D.C.: American Enterprise Institute for Public Policy Research, 1973.

Kaysen, Carl, and Turner, Donald F. *Antitrust Policy.* Cambridge, Mass.: Harvard University Press, 1959.

Lustgarten, S. *Industrial Concentration and Inflation.* Washington, D.C.: American Enterprise Institute for Public Policy Research, 1975.

McGee, J. S. *In Defense of Industrial Concentration.* New York: Praeger, 1971.

Mueller, W. F. "Industrial Structure and Competition Policy, Study Paper Number 2," *Studies by the Staff of the Cabinet Committee on Price Stability.* Washington, D.C.: U.S. Government Printing Office, 1969.

Nelson, R. L. *Concentration in the Manufacturing Industries of the United States.* New Haven, Conn.: Yale University Press, 1963.

Scherer, F. M. *Industrial Market Structure and Economic Performance.* Chicago: Rand McNally, 1970.

Schmalensee, R. *The Economics of Advertising.* Amsterdam: North-Holland Publishing Company, 1972.

Shepherd, William C., ed. *Public Policies toward Business: Readings and Cases,* rev. ed. Homewood, Ill.: Richard D. Irwin, 1979.

Stelzer, Irwin M. *Selected Antitrust Cases,* 5th ed. Homewood, Ill.: Richard D. Irwin, 1976.

Weston, Fred J., ed. *Large Corporations in a Changing Society.* New York: New York University Press, 1974.

12

Equality of Economic Opportunity

The argument between those who think that poverty can best be eliminated by providing jobs and other resources and those who feel that cultural obstacles and psychological deficiencies must be overcome as well is ultimately an argument about social change, about the psychological readiness of people to respond to change, and about the role of culture in change. The advocates of resources are not concerned explicitly with culture, but they do make a cultural assumption: Whatever the culture of the poor, it will not interfere in people's ability to take advantage of better opportunities for obtaining economic resources. They take a *situational* view of social change and of personality: that people respond to the situations—and opportunities—available to them and change their behavior accordingly. Those who call attention to cultur**á**l (and psychological) obstacles, however, are taking a *cultural* view of social change, which suggests that people react to change in terms of prior values and behavior patterns and adopt only those changes that are congruent with their culture.[1]

The definition of equal opportunity is relatively simple, compared to many other concepts. Generally it means that people in American society should be free to compete for the opportunities that do exist in society on the basis of their abilities to do whatever it is that the opportunity requires. Merit is at the heart of this concept: the opportunity should go to those who merit it because they have the ability to take advantage of the opportunity to its fullest. Equality of opportunity means that everyone in our society should be able to compete fairly and honestly for the rewards society has to offer on the

---

[1]Herbert J. Gans, "Culture and Class in the Study of Poverty: An Approach to Anti-Poverty Research," *On Understanding Poverty,* Daniel Moynihan, ed. © 1968, 1969 by the American Academy of Arts and Sciences, Basic Books, Inc., N.Y., pp. 205–206.

basis of merit, where merit refers to the ability of an individual to perform in some capacity. Irrelevant considerations such as race, sex, religion, creed, or national origin are not supposed to be a factor in the distributive outcomes of our society. The rewards are supposed to go to those who perform the best and thus are able to compete most effectively.

This view of equal opportunity is consistent with a free enterprise philosophy, because the most efficient combination of resources should result if this freedom exists and those with the best abilities get the best economic opportunities—the best jobs, the best chances to start a new business, and the like. Society is better off because people will end up in positions where their abilities can be best utilized, and those who are unfit for that position will have to go elsewhere. The principle of equal opportunity helps to ensure that the best performers in society, no matter where they were born, what they believe, or what race or sex they are, have a chance to rise to the top based on their proven ability to use society's resources efficiently and wisely, or, in other words, to do something society wants done and is willing to reward commensurately. Equality of opportunity is a key value of such an economic arrangement, along with the concepts of individualism, private property, self-interest, and competition. Recent surveys attest to the continuing importance of the equality of opportunity standard in American society.[2]

This concept of equal opportunity never held that people would be of equal ability or that such free and open competition for existing opportunities would bring about equal results in terms of economic condition. The trend toward equality of results described in the next chapter is a more recent phenomenon. The concept of equal opportunity focuses on the immediate situation and accepts the fact that people have different abilities and does not raise moral questions about how they got them, as does the egalitarian movement. Nor does equal opportunity raise questions about the results of the competitive process, since it assumes that unequal results are morally right and just. People with superior ability will obviously get ahead and are morally justified in receiving a greater share of the rewards society has to offer if they use their abilities to the fullest and in this way contribute to their own as well as society's well-being. The important thing about equal opportunity is that people should be free to compete equally on the basis of merit for the rewards society offers and be free to go as far as their abilities, interests, ambition, and whatever else is relevant will take them.

It was obvious and acceptable to society that not everyone started from an equal position in terms of what they brought to a situation. But equal opportunity would ensure that no matter where people started from, they would have an equal chance to compete. Whatever outcomes resulted from this free and open competition on the basis of merit were believed to be fair and just. If the result was inequality in the distribution of rewards, so be it, as equality of results was never held to be a worthy social objective in and of itself.

Perhaps there were those who believed that equal opportunity for all races, sexes, and other groups actually did exist in this society. The argument might have been made that since this country had such abundant

[2]Everett C. Ladd, Jr., "Traditional Values Regnant," *Public Opinion*, March/April 1978, pp. 47–48.

opportunity—vast natural resources, a favorable climate, a democratic government—that if a person did not make it, so to speak, it must be because of individual or personal characteristics. Either that person had no abilities, not even potential that could be developed, or had no interest in succeeding in an economic sense, or perhaps was just lazy.

Many people, of course, realized that equal opportunity never existed in this country for some groups, since they recognized slavery for what it was, understood the effects of poverty, or may even have recognized the phenomenon of role stereotyping in regard to women. But in the 1960s, such beliefs became rather widespread and it was recognized that because of prejudice and stereotyping, something called systemic discrimination was built into our major institutions, preventing members of some groups, most notably minorities and women, from being free to compete on an equal basis with white males for available opportunities and to utilize or develop their abilities to go as far as they might. Barriers were built into the employment practices of businesses and other institutions, barriers to starting a new business, and barriers to an equal education that prevented members of these groups from gaining experience and training to become qualified and thus having a true equal opportunity to compete with the predominant white male culture.

The effects of poverty also came to be recognized during this decade. While discrimination helps produce poverty, many white people are also poor and suffer the same deprivation as minorities. Poverty can become a vicious cycle that is perpetuated from one generation to the next. Children born into conditions of poverty have a high probability of remaining in poverty because of a lack of good education, poor health, psychological depression, and more, all of which places them at a severe disadvantage to people born into better conditions.

Thus it came to be recognized that the market was not by itself effectively implementing the concept of equal opportunity and making it a reality for all members of society. The people in control of the market, those making the key decisions about who got what opportunities (employment decisions, loan decisions, purchasing decisions) were by and large white males, and not surprisingly, most of these decisions were made in favor of other white males who were in advantageous positions. Women and minorities were simply not "qualified" for the better positions in society. Disadvantaged people had nothing much to offer employers and thus the market placed a low value on their services.

The implementation of equal opportunity, then, which is much more difficult and complicated than its definition, became a matter of public policy. Many public policy measures were adopted in the 1960s and 1970s that were directed at rooting out systemic discrimination and overcoming the disadvantages of poverty to give members of these groups a fair and equal chance at the opportunities and rewards society has to offer. There are two general approaches to providing equality of opportunity to people who have been the victims of discrimination and poverty. One is to ensure that equal employment opportunity exists in the major institutions of society, including business, and eliminate racism and sexism in the decisions made about employment. The other approach, which is the focus of this chapter, is to provide help to disadvantaged people so they have something to offer employers or can start their own business to compete in the marketplace. This approach provides equality of economic opportunity to those who, perhaps through no fault of their own, have never had a chance to compete in the marketplace on anything like an equal basis.

The Nature of Poverty

Poverty can mean many different things depending on who is doing the defining. Poverty can mean a shortage of money to buy the essentials that people or families need to support themselves. The official poverty level established by the United States Government is based on an estimation of the level of income that it would take for various categories of people, such as a family of four, to provide themselves with a minimum level of food, clothing, shelter, and other essentials. These estimates are made for single people as well as for other size families, but the family of four is the most widely cited figure.

Others argue that to view poverty as merely a lack of income is much too unrealistic and simplistic. George L. Wilber, for example, views poverty as a system that has multiple properties capable of measurement. This system of poverty is defined by Wilber as the relative lack of resources and/or the inability to utilize resources.[3] The word "relative" is important, as Wilber also points out that poverty can be defined in either relative or absolute terms. When people's basic needs for food, clothing, shelter, and medical care are not met, these people are in need in an absolute sense. But whether or not these basic needs are taken care of, people may or may not feel "relatively deprived," as this feeling depends on one's position with respect to the relevant reference group in society at any particular time and place.[4]

Defining poverty solely in terms of income or subsistence levels does not seem to capture the entire meaning of the concept. Martin Rein, of the Bryn Mawr College School of Social Work, argues that even "subsistence measures of poverty cannot claim to rest solely on a technical or scientific definition of nutritional adequacy. Values, preferences, and political realities influence the definition of subsistence."[5] What is adequate for one person may not be adequate for another. Thus no absolute measurement of poverty in subsistence terms is possible either.

The idea that there is something called a culture of poverty is useful to some scholars and policy-makers. The culture of poverty, as described by Oscar Lewis, "is both an adaption and a reaction of the poor to their marginal position in a class-stratified, highly individuated, capitalistic society. It represents an effort to cope with feelings of hopelessness and despair that develop from the realization of the improbability of achieving success in terms of the values and goals of the larger society."[6]

[3]George L. Wilber, ed., "Introduction," *Poverty: A New Perspective* (Lexington: University of Kentucky Press, 1975), pp. 3–4.

[4]*Ibid.*, p. 37.

[5]Martin Rein, "Problems in the Definition and Measurement of Poverty," *Poverty in America*, Louis A. Ferman, Joyce L. Kornbluh, Alan Haber, eds. (Ann Arbor: University of Michigan Press, 1968), p. 130.

[6]Oscar Lewis, "The Culture of Poverty," *On Understanding Poverty*, Daniel Moynihan, ed. (New York: Basic Books, 1968), p. 188.

EQUALITY OF ECONOMIC OPPORTUNITY

People with a culture of poverty produce very little wealth and receive very little in return. They have a low level of literacy and education, do not belong to labor unions, are not members of political parties, generally do not participate in the national welfare agencies, and make very little use of banks, hospitals, department stores, museums, or art galleries. They have a critical attitude toward some of the basic institutions of the dominant classes, hatred of the police, mistrust of government and those in high position, and a cynicism that extends even to the church. These factors give the culture of poverty a high potential for protest and for being used in political movements aimed against the existing social order.[7]

This culture of poverty is not only an adaption to a set of conditions, but tends to perpetuate itself from generation to generation. Children born into the culture of poverty absorb the basic values and attitudes of this subculture and are not psychologically equipped even to take advantage of more favorable conditions or better opportunities that may occur in their lifetime. They tend to remain in the culture of poverty because it has become a way of life for them and not just a condition to be overcome.[8] This concept has important implications for public policy measures designed to eliminate poverty.

The other way to look at poverty is as a cycle, rather than in terms of a culture. The poor get sick more than other people, live in unhealthy conditions, have inadequate diets, cannot get decent medical care or a good education. Thus they cannot get and hold good paying jobs to earn a decent income, which means they cannot afford good housing, medical care, and a decent education. Poverty becomes a vicious cycle that tends to perpetuate itself, but the cycle can be broken into somewhere. If poor people could be given a good job, for example, and receive the extra training and attention necessary to keep it, they might be able to climb out of poverty, breaking out of the cycle.[9] This view of poverty has other policy implications.

There are many factors related to poverty, including national, regional, and personal factors. National factors include a downturn in the overall economy, which means that jobs, particularly unskilled jobs, are hard to find. Many people slip below the poverty line in periods of recession. A change in the nature of jobs available also relates to poverty, as unskilled jobs disappear with the advent of automation. The minimum wage law shuts out many teenagers from jobs that would otherwise be available.[10] Finally, long-term trends in society, such as the dissolution of family responsibilities, makes poverty a national problem that needs to be addressed by public policy.

Regional factors include slumps in a local economy that can be brought on when the major employer in the area fails to win a large government contract. Such contracts pump a great deal of money into a local or regional area. There may also be a decline in the demand for locally produced goods and services, such as a decline in the demand for textiles produced by factories in the northeastern part of the United States. This situation is aggravated by factories moving to the southern part of the country because of lower wages, and by foreign competition. Finally, plants that are major

[7]*Ibid.*, p. 190.

[8]*Ibid.*, p. 188.

[9]Michael Harrington, *The Other America* (New York: Macmillan, 1964), p. 15.

[10]It is estimated that the rise in the minimum wage law in 1978 meant that 90,000 people were not hired because it discouraged some employers from taking on additional employees. "Lifting the Minimum Wage," *Time*, October 31, 1977, p. 75.

employers in a region may have to close because they are too old or cannot meet EPA requirements and remain profitable.

Regarding personal factors, Wilber lists five kinds of poverty properties that accrue to individuals: (1) health, (2) capability, (3) motivation, (4) personality, and (5) socioeconomic status (Exhibit 12.1). Handicaps, either physical or mental, make it difficult for a person to get a job, as does having a disease or an injury. Lack of a decent education or training is a factor in earning a decent income. People may also suffer a poverty of motivation because of blocked goals and frustration. They may not have been socialized into the basic value system of society and thus may not share the same work habits as the dominant groups in society. Low social status relates to low mobility, which tends to keep a person on the bottom of the income scale. The ability of a person to utilize or mobilize whatever personal resources he or she has available in an effective manner will help to determine the nature and extent of relative poverty or prosperity.[11] These personal factors are related, of course, to national and regional factors, as these latter factors provide an environment that is conducive or not conducive to the utilization of individual resources.

Because of poverty, some people are disadvantaged from the start of the race for the rewards society has to offer. They have at least one hand tied behind their back. They are never able to compete effectively, and unless helped in some way, simply fall further and further behind to constitute an underclass that is rooted in severe deprivation. These people need some

EXHIBIT 12.1 ———————————————————————————————

Poverty Properties of Individuals

Resources	Mobilization	Poverty properties
Health	Actual use of health facilities and services Personal hygiene	Handicap: physical and/or mental Disease Injury
Capability capacities, abilities, skills	Education and training facilities and services Employment	Low education and/or training Unemployed; underemployed Low income
Motivation: drives, norms	Goal achievement process	Blocked goals Reduced goals Frustration
"Personality"	Socialization Maturation	Unsocialized Antisocial Social isolation
Socioeconomic status	Status achievement	Low mobility Low status

From George L. Wilber, ed., "Introduction," *Poverty: A New Perspective.* Copyright © 1975 by the University of Kentucky Press. Reprinted with permission.

———————————————————————————————————————

[11]Wilber, "Introduction," pp. 9–12.

basic kind of help if they are ever to become productive human beings, able to overcome the disadvantages of poverty. Only thus will equality of opportunity become a reality for them as well as for other, more fortunate, members of society.

Employment of the Disadvantaged

Disadvantaged people are shut out of many employment opportunities. Public policy measures aimed at eliminating discrimination in employment are not going to help them. Many disadvantaged people are white, so that racial discrimination is obviously not a factor. They simply do not have much to offer employers by way of skills or experience and thus find it difficult to obtain decent employment to provide for themselves or their families. This lack of skills and experience for some may indeed be due to past discrimination, but the reason they cannot get jobs is because the market places a very low value on what they have to offer, not because they are necessarily discriminated against in the selection process.

People with these characteristics were once referred to as "hard-core unemployed," a term with rather negative connotations. This term has subsequently been changed to simply disadvantaged. Disadvantaged people are those who, perhaps through no fault of their own, have never learned any skills that are marketable, may have poor health, undoubtedly have a poor education, or may never have learned appropriate work habits. Thus they simply are not qualified for most employment opportunities.

What is needed to bring them into the marketplace is some effort to help them obtain the skills and experience necessary to get and hold employment. The emphasis of public policy must be placed on equality of economic opportunity, with programs to equip them with the skills, abilities, and habits that are fundamentally necessary to compete for a job in the marketplace. There are both public and private sector programs directed toward this purpose.

Public Sector Programs. There are different kinds of public sector programs designed to increase the productivity of people, including (1) training programs that attempt to equip people with skills so they can enter the market with something to offer employers, (2) public works programs that provide people with actual work experience and enable them to earn an income, and (3) information services that are designed to help people find out what jobs are available.

An example of a public policy program that is both a training and a public works program is the Comprehensive Employment and Training Act (CETA). This act became law in 1973, replacing the federally controlled Manpower Development Training Act with a program that allows distribution of federal funds by local officials. This shift of control to prime sponsors at the county and municipal levels was based on the theory that local officials knew more about local conditions than federal bureaucrats.[12]

Except for general revenue sharing, CETA was the first federal, decentralized program to be created. CETA programs are funded through the

[12]Juan Cameron, "How CETA Came To Be a Four-Letter Word," *Fortune*, April 9, 1979, p. 116.

Department of Labor with money distributed to the local government prime sponsors on the basis of formulas to reflect local needs. These programs are operated by local governments of at least 100,000 in population, or by states for areas not otherwise covered. The prime sponsors plan and operate employment and training programs, following regulations established by the Department of Labor.

CETA was originally passed to provide new skills for the nation's disadvantaged people. This population was referred to as the "structurally" unemployed—those people who are left out of the competitive labor market for reasons of race, poor education, lack of opportunity, or other social and economic reasons.

Thus CETA money goes for vocational education, but in the late 1970s, an increasing share went to hire the unemployed into public service jobs. These jobs are only temporary. Their purpose is to tide some people over rough spots in the economy, while people without skills may be able to get some experience that would help them to get permanent jobs after their CETA stint. The public service employment part of CETA grew from $440 million in 1974 to about $6 billion in 1979, leaving approximately $4 billion for various job training programs.[13]

The program, however, has had its problems. According to Juan Cameron, writing in *Fortune,* the program has made no noticeable dent in the number of disadvantaged people unemployed, and billions of dollars have been wasted on ill-defined and hastily executed relief programs. In addition, the slackness of its management has been an invitation to widespread abuse and fraud. Many members of Congress and the Reagan administration believe it is time to scrap the program entirely. The problem is much more complex than anticipated and involves the psychology of the poor and their attitudes toward work.[14]

Information services are provided by State Employment Offices, which attempt to match people looking for work with employers who have job openings, at no cost to the job seeker. These offices are located in major cities around the country. At one time, there was talk about a federal data bank to match people looking for work with job openings on a nationwide basis.

Private Sector Programs. The National Alliance of Businessmen (NAB) was founded in 1968 in response to President Johnson's manpower message to Congress. In this message he announced a joint business-government effort to expand employment and training for what were then called the "hard-core" unemployed. The NAB, under the initial leadership of Henry Ford II, formed the Job Opportunities in the Business Sector (JOBS) program to carry out this objective. The rationale for the program was to bring the disadvantaged into the mainstream of the economy. The NAB claimed to be doing this not just for humanitarian reasons, but because it paid off in economic terms. Business gained a worker, the community gained a productive citizen, business gained a paying customer, and the government saved on welfare and gained a taxpayer. There was a claim that the program also had a pay-off for the free enterprise system by proving that business and

---

[13]"Why CETA Is in Trouble," *Business Week,* October 2, 1978, p. 124.
[14]Cameron, "CETA," p. 112.

private citizens could help solve an urgent social problem that had not been able to be solved by government alone.

The NAB was organized with a national headquarters in Washington and Metro offices in 120 cities across the country. These offices are staffed both nationally and locally by business executives who are loaned from their companies for a period of time (see box). The JOBS program itself operates through a system of pledges by employers, solicited by the NAB, to hire a certain number of disadvantaged people each year. The employer then seeks out the people to fulfill these pledges from employment agencies or other sources. The NAB has a follow-up routine to see that the employer actually does follow through on these commitments.

The program was initially financed by both government and business, with the government covering the extra costs of training the disadvantaged over and above what business normally spent on a newly recruited worker. These costs could include costs for extra training, medical attention, transportation, day care for dependent children, and costs associated with recruitment. Business found that disadvantaged people required different kinds of training than ordinary workers because of their deprived background. But business was also pleased to learn that many of these people, while not initially qualified for many jobs, were indeed qualifiable, and with proper training and attention, could become fully productive employees.

National policy direction, guidance and leadership is provided by a Board of Directors composed of business, industry and community service organizations.

The chief executive officer is the President, usually a senior executive loaned by the Chairman's corporation. The Chairman, as well as the Regional and Metro Chairmen, are volunteer business executives appointed by the President of the United States and elected by the Board.

NAB regional offices, which correspond to the 10 regions of the Department of Labor, maintain Metro Assistance Teams available upon request to help local Alliance offices in such areas as management, account executive training and pledge campaigns.

The local Metro carries out its activities under the direction of a local Chairman, who is usually a senior local business executive; an Advisory Board, composed of area business leaders; and a core staff under a Metro Director who reports to the local Chairman and to the local Advisory Board.

NAB largely relies on loaned executives and donated resources to conduct its activities—a characteristic fundamental to NAB since its inception. The Alliance receives a portion of its funding under Department of Labor contracts.

From "A Few Words about the National Alliance of Business" (Washington, D.C.: NAB, undated).

In 1977, the White House and Labor Department held discussions with leaders of NAB and other business organizations. There was a concern that the primary thrust of government employment programs at that time involved fully subsidized public jobs, with a very small fraction of government money supporting job training and hiring in the private sector. The decision was made to try and bring the government's workforce employment apparatus into closer collaboration with the private sector, including the universe of small businesses that were largely overlooked by past programs.[15]

Thus was born Title VII, an amendment to the 1973 Comprehensive Employment and Training Act. Enacted in October 1978, Title VII authorized $400 million for what was called a Private Sector Initiative Program (PSIP). This program called for the establishment of business-led organizational units called Private Industry Councils that would share with CETA prime sponsors—the local government units that operate CETA programs—the responsibility and authority for administering Title VII funds.[16]

The NAB was given leadership responsibility for organizing the private sector response, and began developing the professional staff expertise to fulfill this new assignment. It began working with the local prime sponsors through the Metro offices to assist in the organization of the Private Industry Councils, 300 of which were expected to have been organized by October 1979. Late in 1978, the NAB negotiated a $13 million contract with the Labor Department, $2.9 million of which was earmarked for PSIP. These funds were to make it possible for the NAB to pursue the following three tasks:

• *Leadership.* Marketing, selling, communicating the program to the business community and other important groups.

• *Technical Assistance.* Conducting a national program to assist business and prime sponsors in developing the most efficient programs, methods, and procedures "to motivate, rather than inhibit, the private sector participation in these programs."

In addition to existing staff, NAB is hiring forty-four technical advisors experienced in cooperative public-private programs to help local communities carry out this effort.

• *Information Clearinghouse.* With the help of other interested groups, NAB will establish a national clearinghouse for processing, analyzing, and disseminating information on results of local programs, successful demonstrations, and experimental programs. It will make sure that the best methods and information are made available to all interested groups.[17]

In addition to these efforts to hire and train the disadvantaged, the NAB since its inception has also developed programs for unemployed youth, Vietnam veterans, and exoffenders. The youth programs seek to provide students with the motivation, guidance, and on-the-job work experience that will enable them to pursue productive careers. Programs such as summer jobs for youth, vocational exploration, and youth motivation focus on the special problems of youth unemployment, which in 1978 stood at 16 percent of those who were of high school age and seeking work. For black urban males and females of high school age, the unemployment rate was more than 35 percent.[18] Finding jobs for Vietnam-era veterans became an objective of the NAB when it was noted that the unemployment rate of these veterans was substantially higher than that of their nonveteran peers. Many Vietnam veterans suffered the embittering experience of returning from an unpopular war to an unwelcoming society with too few job opportunities. Finally, in

---

[15]*National Alliance of Business: 1978 Annual Report* (Washington, D.C.: NAB, 1978), p. 8.
[16]*Ibid.,* p. 9.
[17]*Ibid.,* p. 10.
[18]*Ibid.,* p. 7.

1973, the plight of the exoffender was added to the Alliance's mandate. Programs in this area provide expertise and guidance to inmates so that prison does not become a revolving door for a person who knows nothing else but crime.

Since its inception, the NAB claims to have helped more than 2.7 million disadvantaged people find suitable employment. It has found more than 1.9 million summer jobs for needy youth. The veterans program has found jobs for 1.1 million veterans, and more than 70,000 exoffenders have found employment through the exoffender program. These opportunities have been provided by some 54,000 participating companies located throughout the nation.[19]

Minority Business Enterprise

Another approach to creating equality of economic opportunity is through the development of minority businesses. This approach involves giving minorities in this country special assistance in establishing businesses, forming capital, finding markets for their products, and building a managerial class. From this effort, the minority community should obtain a substantial measure of social and economic benefit. The goal of this approach is not to eliminate discrimination from the employment opportunities in the institutions of society run by the white majority, but to promote the development of more economic institutions owned and operated by minorities themselves. Disadvantaged areas of cities are much like developing nations and need similar assistance to begin the process of social and economic development. If this effort could be successful and minority businesses established on a wide enough scale throughout minority communities, equality of opportunity might become more of a reality and the effects of past discrimination overcome through the economic and social growth they would generate.

The need for this approach was recognized in the late 1960s, when statistics showed that there were few minority manufacturing firms in the country. The major reasons for this lack were the substantial amounts of capital needed to start such businesses and the lack of markets where the products produced by minority firms could be sold. In 1969, for example, minorities accounted for 17 percent of the total United States population, but they owned only 4.3 percent of the businesses, and these firms accounted for only 0.1 percent of business receipts. Well over 80 percent of these minority firms were in the services or retailing industries and thus were very small in comparison with most companies. Discrimination was, of course, a factor in these dismal figures. Minorities found it difficult to obtain financing from banks and other institutions, people were reluctant to buy products from minority firms because of concerns about quality and service, and aspiring minority businesspeople often found it difficult to get an education that would prepare them for an entrepreneurial position.

A new business needs capital, a market for its products, and managerial talent. The government became a supplier of capital for this effort at

[19]*Ibid.*, p. 1 facing.

promoting minority business enterprises. Executive Order 11625, issued in October 1971, formed the Office of Minority Business Enterprise (OMBE), whose purpose was to initiate programs in both the public and private sectors geared toward increasing minority-owned and -financed businesses. Since 1970, OMBE has spent $318 million funding over 200 "business assistance organizations" to counsel minority businesspeople, help them obtain financial assistance, and provide them with a variety of technical services.[20] The Small Business Administration also began a program called MESBIC (Minority Enterprise Small Business Investment Corporation), which provided direct and guaranteed loans to minority entrepreneurs. In 1978 these loans amounted to over $400 million.[21]

The larger business community itself has been active in providing a market for minority businesses. Many corporations voluntarily have instituted what is called a minoritiy purchasing program to increase their purchases from minority enterprises. An organization called the National Minority Purchasing Council (NMPC) was formed by business to coordinate and promote these efforts throughout the business community. According to the NMPC, corporate spending with minority businesses rose from a total of $87 million in 1972 to $1.1 billion in 1977. This trend is expected to continue, as NMPC has set a goal of $3.0 billion for 1980 with the support of the nation's largest corporations. About half of the Fortune 500 companies have established minority purchasing programs to contribute to this effort.[22]

The government has also begun providing markets for minority businesses. Winners of federal contracts of more than $500,000 have been required to do their best to find minority subcontractors. Efforts to locate them had to be recorded on forms filed with the federal government. Changes in this procedure (Public Law 95-507) now require contractors to work out a plan for subcontracting to minority businesses before the contract is awarded, rather than simply show they did their best to find them. These new regulations require contractors to spell out goals for the amount of business they expect to place with minority-owned small businesses. This procedure is very similar to the affirmative action requirement for federal contractors with respect to equal employment opportunities.[23]

Under the SBA's 8(a) set-aside program, government agencies like the Department of Defense or Transportation can pluck contracts from their competitive procurement channels and allocate them to the SBA, which then becomes the prime contractor and gives the work to minority firms on its roster. In fiscal 1978, 3,406 contracts were awarded under this program, totaling $767 million. This was an increase from eight contracts totaling $10.5 million awarded in 1968.[24]

Finally, Congress set a precedent in 1977 by writing into a $4 billion Commerce Department public works appropriation bill a clause that 10

---

[20]Irwin Ross, "The Puny Payoff from Affirmative Action in Small Business," *Fortune*, September 10, 1979, pp. 100–101.

[21]*Ibid.*, p. 101.

[22]Donald E. Gumpert, "Seeking Minority Owned Businesses as Suppliers," *Harvard Business Review*, Vol. 57, No. 1 (January-February 1979), p. 111.

[23]See "Minority Contracting Gets a Federal Overhaul," *Business Week*, February 5, 1979, p. 32.

[24]Ross, "Puny Payoff," p. 103.

percent of this total be reserved for minority contractors and subcontractors. This action did not make the construction industry very happy, and 27 suits were filed charging that this 10 percent set-aside was unconstitutional. The issue was one of reverse discrimination, that such a quota for minority business constitutes discrimination against nonminority enterprise. The Supreme Court agreed to hear one of these cases *(Fullilove v. Kreps)* and thus deal with this aspect of preferential treatment.[25]

The case was decided in July 1980 in favor of the federal government. The case was renamed *Fullilove v. Klutznick* because the head of the Commerce Department had changed. The court said that Congress, under the constitution, had special powers to make up for the effects of past discrimination and can legitimately require innocent whites to "share the burden" as long as that burden is not unreasonable. This decision will probably give civil rights advocates encouragement to press for affirmative action at all levels of government.[26]

Training for minority enterpreneurs, of course, can be done primarily by schools of business and management. Some schools have attempted to increase their percentage of minority students through a consortium arrangement with money raised from private business. Other schools have developed programs using MBA students to provide training in accounting, finance, marketing, etc., to minority businesspeople. The lack of management training is a serious problem in the effort to promote minority business enterprises that has been only partially addressed.

The effort to promote equality of economic opportunity in this manner is difficult. Large pools of equity funds must be made available under realistic conditions. Some black leaders have estimated that it would take an investment of $442 billion for minority businesses to reach economic equality. There are not enough minority clients to make some minority businesses profitable and white people are reluctant to patronize minority businesses. Large numbers of white-run organizations will have to do business with minority companies if they are ever to develop a market for their products. The business and technical skills of minorities must be developed if they are to compete successfully in the marketplace and move out from under the shelter of government and business.

Minority Purchasing Programs

A minority purchasing program is designed to increase the purchases of goods and services a corporation needs from minority-owned businesses. A minority-owned business is generally defined as one that is at least 51 percent owned by a member or members of a racial minority group. Some government definitions of a minority business have also included economically disadvantaged people, white or minority, and a few corporate programs have included women in the definition.

Development of a minority purchasing program can be a complicated exercise, particularly in finding qualified or qualifiable minority suppliers.

[25]*Ibid.*, p. 104.
[26]"Four Big Decisions," *Time*, July 14, 1980, p. 12.

The National Minority Purchasing Council maintains a Vendor Information Service that provides corporations with information about minority businesses that may be capable of supplying goods and services. In addition, the NMPC has published guidelines to assist corporations in developing minority purchasing programs. Some of the steps they advocate include the following:

- Commitment from the chief executive officer of the corporation to such a program.
- Appointment of a Minority Purchasing Coordinator to guide, direct, and monitor the program.
- Use of a goal-oriented approach to minority purchasing.
- Techniques to locate minority vendors and to assist them to become qualified suppliers. Examples of assistance include lending technical and managerial expertise and breaking large purchases into smaller quantities.
- Monitoring performance and recognition of achievement in minority purchasing.[27]

Setting goals to be accomplished is of crucial importance to the development of a minority purchasing program. These goals can be set in various terms, including total purchase dollars from minority vendors, percentage increase over prior year's purchase dollars, percentage of annual purchases from minority vendors, and number of new minority vendors developed. Research conducted by Larry C. Giunipero showed that those corporations which set minority purchasing goals at both the buyer and corporate level (see Exhibit 12.2) have more active minority purchasing programs spending more dollars with a larger number of minority vendors. Those corporations with a goal-oriented approach were also more likely to implement policies, procedures, training, and techniques about minority purchasing to assist in developing new minority vendors.[28]

Building Plants in Disadvantaged Areas

Another strategy to promote equality of economic opportunity is for corporations to build plants in economically depressed inner-city areas. The idea behind these plants is the same as the idea behind minority business enterprises, that they will provide an impetus for economic development of the immediate community. Priority for employment should be given to community residents so that jobs will be available to them. The plants should also provide a mixture of job levels to create opportunities for advancement, even into management levels. The availability of entry-level positions and training programs is an important ingredient for the success of these efforts.

[27]Larry C. Giunipero, "The Impact of Goal Setting on Minority Purchasing Programs," paper presented at 40th Annual Meeting, Academy of Management, Detroit, Michigan, August 9–13, 1980, p. 3.
[28]*Ibid.*, p. 8.

EXHIBIT 12.2

Control Data Corporation Minority Business Program

In 1973 Control Data established an affirmative action program for purchasing supplies and services from minority-owned or controlled businesses. Under this program, the company takes positive action to seek out, use and assist minority vendors. All purchasing operations set goals for minority business activity and report their progress quarterly to the Purchasing Council which has corporate responsibility for the program.

Control Data initiated the program to more effectively practice its social commitment by expanding the opportunities for minorities to become economically independent. Therefore, we emphasize assistance to minority businesses to help them become qualified suppliers. Among the ways we do this are supplying raw materials or components and providing engineering and technical assistance.

Accompanying charts show minority purchasing program activity for Control Data and Commercial Credit.

Minority Business Program for Purchasing: Summary of Activity

Control Data

	1976	1977	Percent Change
1. Number of New Minority Firms Identified	254	276	+9
2. Number of Minority Firms Contacted	554	457	−18
3. Number of Orders Placed with Minority Firms	1,673	2,283	+36
4. Total Dollars Committed to Minority Firms	$ 2,419,098	$ 4,286,466	+77
5. Total Dollars Committed to All Suppliers	$273,271,000	$391,755,266	+43
6. Percent of Total Commitments with Minority Firms	0.89%	1.1%	+24

Commercial Credit

	1976	1977	Percent Change
1. Number of New Minority Firms Identified	2	19	+850
2. Number of Minority Firms Contacted	22	59	+168
3. Number of Orders Placed with Minority Firms	192	330	+72
4. Total Dollars Committed to Minority Firms	$ 114,948	$ 147,456	+28
5. Total Dollars Committed to All Suppliers	$3,797,324	$4,682,146	+23
6. Percent of Total Commitments with Minority Firms	3%	3.1%	+0.03

From *Social Responsibility Report 1978* (Minneapolis: Control Data Corporation, 1978), p. 9. Reprinted with permission.

These facilities are built to provide jobs for inexperienced people and give them the opportunity to begin careers in the mainstream of industry.[29]

Control Data Corporation has adopted this strategy and has built four such inner-city plants (see box). These facilities are located in depressed areas of Minneapolis and St. Paul, Minnesota, Washington, D.C., and Wolfe County, Kentucky. A fifth facility is planned for northern Manitoba. When all these plants are completed, total employment will exceed 1,500 people. While not a very large number in comparison to the number of people living in depressed neighborhoods, that is at least 1,500 more jobs than previously existed. In 1978, the payroll from three of the plants totaled more than $6.5 million, a fairly substantial addition to the economic base of the communities where the plants are located.[30]

INNER-CITY OPERATIONS

Control Data has successfully established three inner-city plants. These facilities are located in economically depressed areas of St. Paul, Minneapolis and Washington, D.C. A fourth facility is under construction and a fifth is in the planning stages. When the fifth is completed, total employment of the inner-city plants will exceed 1500.

Control Data has succeeded in making the inner-city plants profitable at a level competitive with Control Data's other operations. At the same time, the inner-city facilities serves the interests of the surrounding communities . . . providing jobs for inexperienced persons and the means for inner-city residents to begin careers in the mainstream of industry. In 1978 the payroll from the three plants will total more than $6.5 million—a substantial addition to the economic base of these communities. And the presence of new facilities helps the communities rebuild.

The Selby plant, operating in the inner city of St. Paul, provides publication services that include collating, binding, and mailing for Control Data and other customers. It is the only plant in the country known to employ part-time workers for nearly all its work force. The part-time arrangement is an innovation that meets the needs of the community and has worked out well for Control Data.

Selby's work force is made up primarily of mothers with school age children and high school students. The part-time work schedule allows them the opportunity to work while meeting other obligations. The City of St. Paul has a 6.5% minority population; the employee population at Selby is 90% minority and management is 100% minority.

To accommodate Selby's growing business, construction of a major addition was begun in 1978. The addition will nearly double the size of the plant from its current 15,000 square feet.

A new Control Data worldwide parts distribution center is under construction in an inner-city area near the Selby plant. It will consolidate existing operations from several suburban locations. When the center opens in early 1979, it will employ 400 people. Some current Control Data employees will relocate to the new facility but priority for filling job openings will go to neighborhood residents.

From the experience in operating plants in depressed inner city com-

---

[29]*Social Responsibility Report 1978* (Minneapolis: Control Data Corporation, 1978), p. 5.
[30]*Ibid.*

munities Control Data has gained an understanding of how to plan and construct inner city facilities and operate them as successful business operations.

The commitment of the corporation and the support of the community leadership is fundamental and essential to success.

The community can define its needs and work with the company to achieve the mutual goal of a successful operation. Control Data also works in concert with local government especially in the siting and construction of the facilities. Because open land for building is usually scarce in inner city communities, the involvement of the city is needed to assist in site development. Control Data has found local governments to be enthusiastic partners.

What the plant produces is important too. Control Data strives to identify products for inner city facilities which are needed and can provide stable work. It is important that the products be central to the profitability and operation of the corporation or the plant will be vulnerable during times of economic recession.

Priority for employment should be given to community residents and the plant should provide a mixture of job levels to create opportunities for advancement from within. Availability of entry-level positions and accompanying training programs is an important ingredient.

After the plant is established, continued attention to the human resource is needed. Job skill development and ancillary services such as financial counseling, day care and other similar services may be necessary. At times this requires effort beyond that experienced at conventional plants, but Control Data's record shows that the extra effort pays off.

From *Social Responsibility Report 1978* (Minneapolis: Control Data Corporation, 1978), p. 5. Reprinted with permission.

The community works with the company to achieve the mutual goal of a successful operation. The company also has to work with the local government, especially in the siting and construction of facilities. The company attempts to identify products for these facilities that will provide stable employment, even during times of economic recession. This is important, to prevent employees from becoming discouraged and feeling let down after an initial promise of better times.

In 1978, Control Data helped form City Venture Corporation, a private concern that will plan and manage programs designed to improve conditions in economically depressed inner-city areas. Control Data was to initially manage the concern as its major shareholder, but other major corporations such as Dayton-Hudson Corporation and Northwest Bancorporation also bought equity positions. Initially capitalized at $3 million, the corporation's major effort was to bring jobs to the inner city by constructing and operating plants in poverty areas as well as other programs.

Results

The results of all these efforts to provide equality of economic opportunity are not very encouraging. The CETA program, as stated earlier, is alleged to be ridden with scandal and sloppy administration, and was recently cut by $3.8 billion through the 1984 fiscal year.[31] The JOBS program of the NAB, while placing a good number of disadvantaged people over the years, has not prevented the phenomenal growth of welfare programs. Plants built in depressed areas have employed but a handful of people when compared with the total number of unemployed.

The record for minority business enterprises is even more dismal. The last year for which firm statistics are available is 1972, and these figures show that while there were 382,000 minority businesses, they still constituted only 4.4 percent of all businesses in the country. The gross receipts of these enterprises totaled less than 0.1 percent of all business revenues. The reason for this lackluster performance is that most of these enterprises are small, undercapitalized, heavily concentrated in the retail and service industries, and in minority neighborhoods.[32] Minority business is selling to and serving other minorities. The picture is well illustrated by the following quotation from a *Harvard Business Review* article.

> An examination of the June 1978 issue of *Black Enterprise* magazine, which contains a list of the 100 leading black-owned companies, amply illustrates the situation. The top company has annual sales of only $61.4 million and the totals drop quickly, the tenth-ranked having only $13 million in sales. Moreover, 44 of the concerns are auto dealerships and only 11 are manufacturers. The list also indicates the volatility of even the largest minority companies—17 that were on the 1977 list are missing in 1978 thanks to bankruptcies, mergers into larger companies, and faltering sales.[33]

Thus minority businesses have yet to emerge as a major factor in the total business picture. Improving the skills and abilities of disadvantaged people has many obstacles. The success of all of these efforts depends to a large extent on the condition of the overall economy. When the economy is healthy and growing, equality of economic opportunity is easier to provide. When the economy is stagnant or in a decline, those at the bottom of the ladder who have just recently grasped the first rung are most likely to get pushed off (see cartoon). There is a cyclical nature to these efforts, with the major underlying force being the performance of the total economy. Economic growth may indeed be the factor that is most responsible for providing equality of economic opportunity.

Questions for Discussion

1. Define the concept of equal opportunity. How does this concept relate to a free enterprise system? What is the basis of equal opportunity?
2. Has equal opportunity ever existed in our society? Why or why not? Is it necessary that public policy be directed toward the provision of equal opportunity?
3. Distinguish between equality of employment opportunity and equality of economic opportunity. What is the primary cause of inequality in regard to economic opportunity?

[31]"Why CETA Is in Trouble," p. 124.
[32]Ross, "Puny Payoff," p. 99.
[33]Gumpert, "Seeking Minority Owned Businesses," p. 112.

Cartoon taken from *The St. Louis Post-Dispatch*, May 25, 1980, p. 28. Reprinted with permission.

4. Describe the nature of poverty. What are the different factors that contribute to a poverty condition? Which of these factors, in your opinion, are most significant? What are the effects of poverty?
5. Describe a disadvantaged person. What handicaps do disadvantaged people take with them into the marketplace? What can public policy do in general to help overcome these handicaps?
6. Describe the CETA program and the JOBS program of the National Alliance of Businessmen. What are the objectives of these programs? Which, in your opinion, has the most potential for success? What reforms, if any, would you suggest for both programs?
7. What is a minority business enterprise? How would the development of more of these enterprises promote equality of economic opportunity? What ingredients are necessary for their success?
8. Should the government help provide markets for these minority enterprises? Is this fair to the white businessperson? Is there an element of reverse discrimination in allocating a certain percentage of public works money to minority enterprises? How would you rule on this issue if you were a federal judge?
9. Describe a minority purchasing program. What elements are necessary for the success of these programs? Would you recommend such a program for your company if it does not already have one? How should it be administered?
10. Why are the results of all these efforts to promote equality of economic opportunity rather dismal? Is there no good solution to this problem, either through the market or public policy? What are the implications of your answer for the future of the free enterprise system?

Suggested Reading

Bell, Carolyn Shaw. *The Economics of the Ghetto*. New York: Pegasus Books, 1970.

Gelber, Steven M. *Black Men and Businessmen*. Port Washington, N.Y.: Kennikat Press, 1974.

Haddad, William, and Pugh, Douglas, eds. *Black Economic Development*. Englewood Cliffs, N.J.: Prentice-Hall, 1969.

Hill, A. David et al. *The Quality of Life in America: Pollution, Poverty, Power, and Fear*. New York: Holt, Rinehart & Winston, 1973.

Hund, James M. *Black Entrepreneurship*. Belmont, Calif.: Wadsworth Publishing Co., 1970.

Janger, Arthur R., and Shaeffer, Ruth G. *Managing Programs to Employ the Disadvantaged*. New York: National Industrial Conference Board, 1970.

Peren, Francis, and Cloward, Richard. *Regulating the Poor*. New York: Pantheon Books, 1972.

Sobin, Dennis P. *The Working Poor: Minority Workers in Low-Wage, Low-Skill Jobs*. Port Washington, N.Y.: Kennikat Press, 1973.

Zimpel, Lloyd, ed. *The Disadvantaged Workers: Readings in Developing Minority Manpower*. Reading, Mass.: Addison-Wesley, 1971.

13

Equality of Results

Egalitarianism is a vital counter-force to the traditional business philosophy for several reasons: (1) It has a great appeal to the masses, for it promises them their "rights" to a higher life style and greater positions of power; (2) The egalitarian thrust has necessitated (and will continue to demand) the strengthening of centralized power in order to reduce the privileges of the "haves" and the transfer of some of their largess to the "have nots"; (3) It is directly antithetical to the managerial ideology, for it tends to create a society wherein there are smaller numbers of winners and losers, and thereby reduces the capitalistic incentives, which, of course, depend upon the presence, and desirability, of inequalities; and, finally, (4) Egalitarianism confuses the notion of "progress," for its emphasis is on distribution rather than on production.[1]

What started out as an effort to relieve the distresses of the depression era grew into a full-fledged welfare system designed to relieve the deprivation of those who, for one reason or another, have not been able to provide for their own needs in a market economy. The market system offers large rewards, in some cases, to winners of the competitive race, but can also impose severe penalties on some of the losers. Those losers often fall so far behind that they end up in a seriously deprived condition. They have such small quantities and low qualities of resources at their disposal that the market places a very low value on what they do have to offer. As seen in the last chapter, attempts to provide equal economic opportunities for people in this situation fall far short of providing equal economic conditions.

Many times, people end up in this condition through no fault of their own. During the depression, for example, there were simply not enough jobs to go around even for skilled workers who were willing and able to provide for

---

[1] Joseph W. McGuire, "Today's Business Climate," *Business and Its Changing Environment*, George A. Steiner, ed. (Los Angeles: UCLA Graduate School of Management, 1978), p. 10. Quoted with permission.

themselves. Even in prosperous times, there are sometimes not enough jobs for young people and others who have not had a chance to develop skills and gain experience that is useful to employers. Discrimination plays a role in preventing some people from getting jobs commensurate with the skills and ability they do have. And there are never enough good paying jobs for people with severe physical and emotional handicaps who could still be productive to some degree. Finally, technological progress destroys the livelihood of many people almost overnight.

An unregulated market system can produce inhumane results, locking some people into a vicious cycle of poverty, and preventing them from ever really entering into the race for the rewards society has to offer. As Arthur Okun states: "Vast disparities in results—living standards, income, wealth—inevitably spawn serious inequalities in opportunity that represent arbitrary handicaps and head starts. . . . The children of the poor are handicapped in many ways—their nutrition, their education, their ability to get funds to start businesses and buy homes, and their treatment on many of the hiring lines for both private and public jobs.[2]

A commitment to equality of opportunity requires, says Okun, some correction of the inequality of results that an unregulated market system produces. Severe poverty cannot be accepted in a democratic society. Even if the race is fair, condemnation to a life of deprivation is not necessarily a fair penalty for the losers. Such a result is not consistent with the goals and values of a democratic society.[3]

> . . . [P]overty cannot be ignored by a society that proclaims democratic values, insisting upon the worth of all its citizens and the equality of their political and social rights. Our commitment to freedom of speech, equality of suffrage, and equality before the law rests on a broader commitment to human values that is violated by the persistence of economic misery in an affluent society. I cannot imagine how a sane society could decide deliberately to guarantee every citizen a fair trial before a judge and jury and at the same time permit some citizens to be condemned to death by the marketplace.[4]

Almost all modern industrial societies have some kind of welfare system designed to alter these unequal market outcomes through public policy measures. Such outcomes are unacceptable and are changed by a system of transfer payments that takes money from some groups in society through taxation and gives it to other groups in the form of benefits.

Public Policy Benefits

The types of benefits provided differ widely, but they can be categorized as in Exhibit 13.1 according to the type of benefits provided. There is a basic split between public policy measures that are designed to provide people with cash-income assistance and other forms of support referred to as in-kind assistance.

[2]Arthur M. Okun, "Our Blend of Democracy and Capitalism: It Works but Is in Danger" (Washington D.C.: The Brookings Institution, Reprint #351, 1979), p. 73.
[3]*Ibid.*
[4]*Ibid.*

EXHIBIT 13.1 —————————————————————————————

Income/Support Programs

I. Cash-Income Assistance
   A. Social Security
   B. Public Assistance to the Aged, Blind, and Disabled
   C. Veterans' Compensation and Pensions
   D. Aid to Families with Dependent Children
   E. Unemployment Compensation

II. In-Kind Assistance
   A. Medicare and Medicaid
   B. Food Stamp Program
   C. Student Aid
   D. Housing Subsidies and Public Housing
   E. Nutritional Programs for Children

Cash-income assistance includes payments made through the Social Security program, established in 1935 as a national insurance scheme. Since this program was set up on a pay-as-you-go basis, it is a simple transfer of money, year by year, from the working to the retired population. Payments into the system by wage earners and employers in 1977 reached $95 billion. Social Security accounts for more than 25 percent of all federal tax revenues and expenditures and provides benefits for one out of every seven Americans.[5]

In addition to Social Security, there are programs that provide public assistance to aged, blind, and disabled people, the Aid to Families with Dependent Children program (AFDC), which provides broad-scale public assistance, veterans' compensation and pensions, and unemployment compensation designed to tide people over while they are between jobs when the termination of their previous employment was involuntary.

The various benefit areas that provide in-kind assistance include Medicare and Medicaid: Medicare designed to provide medical care for the aged, and Medicaid for the nonaged poor. The food stamp program started out small in 1962 but escalated in the mid-1970s to become the second largest in-kind transfer program. Also included are various kinds of student aid programs to provide scholarships for higher education, housing subsidies or low-rent public housing, and free school lunches for elementary and secondary school children.

Growth of Benefits

The growth of these benefits can be looked at in two ways: (1) the growth of specific programs, and (2) the growth of transfer payments overall. Table 13.1 shows the growth of cash-income assistance and in-kind assistance for selected fiscal years from 1960 to 1975 by program. The graph that follows (Figure 13.1) shows the growth in selected program areas even more dra-

[5] Nathan Keyfitz, "Why Social Security Is in Trouble," *The Public Interest*, No. 58 (Winter 1980), pp. 102–119.

TABLE 13.1 **Federal Outlays on Programs for Cash Income Assistance and In-Kind Assistance, Selected Fiscal Years, 1960–1975**

Program	1960	1970	1973	1975
Cash Income Assistance				
Social security	11,018	29,685	48,288	64,351
Public assistance to aged, blind, and disabled	1,449	1,979	2,000	25
Supplemental security income	—	—	41	4,770
Veterans' compensation and pensions	3,312	5,229	6,401	6,548
Federal civilian retirement	1,821	4,192	6,954	10,229
Benefits for disabled miners	—	10	952	879
Aid to families with dependent children	612	2,163	3,922	4,322
Unemployment compensation	2,375	3,369	5,362	7,065
Total	20,587	46,927	73,920	98,189
In-Kind Assistance				
Medicare	—	7,149	9,479	14,191
Medicaid	—	2,727	4,600	6,508
Food stamps	—	577	2,208	3,926
Other food	324	833	1,433	1,744
Housing	279	1,279	1,420	2,292
Higher education student aid	498	1,625	3,880	4,556
Total	1,101	14,190	23,020	33,217

Source: Barry M. Blechman and others, *Setting National Priorities: The 1975 Budget* (Washington, D.C.: Brookings Institution, 1974), p. 168. Reprinted with permission.

Figure 13.1. The Growth in Public Welfare Expenditures by Federal, State and Local Governments 1967–1977
(In Billions of Dollars)

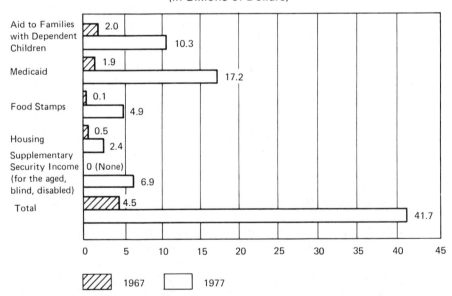

From Brookings Institution figures submitted to a House of Representatives subcommittee in 1977.

From *Free to Choose: Viewer Guide* (Erie, Pa.: Public Communications, Inc., 1979), p. 8. Reprinted with permission.

matically. The big gainers have been the AFDC and Medicaid programs, increasing by 515 percent and 905 percent respectively in a ten-year period. Finally, the information presented in Figures 13.2 to 13.5 shows the projected growth through 1983 in areas of education, health, income security, and veterans' benefits and services. These projections were made before the Reagan administration took office.

As far as the overall growth of transfer payments is concerned, fiscal year 1965 marks a clear dividing line between the moderate growth of these transfers during the first half of the decade and the much higher growth rates that began with fiscal 1966 and finally slowed in fiscal 1978 to their present level. Payments to individuals grew at an average annual rate of 15.3 percent during fiscal years 1966–1979, compared with 6.6 percent during fiscal 1961–1965. As a percent of GNP, these payments averaged 4.3 percent in fiscal 1961–1965, 5 percent in fiscal 1966–1969, 6.7 percent in fiscal 1970–1973, and 8.8 percent in fiscal 1974–1979 (Table 13.2).

Fiscal 1965 saw the beginning of a new "social activitism" period, according to Michael E. Levy of the Conference Board, when many new welfare programs were enacted (Figure 13.6). Those programs included the Economic Opportunity Act, the Permanent Food Stamp Act, and the Social

Figure 13.2. Outlays for Education

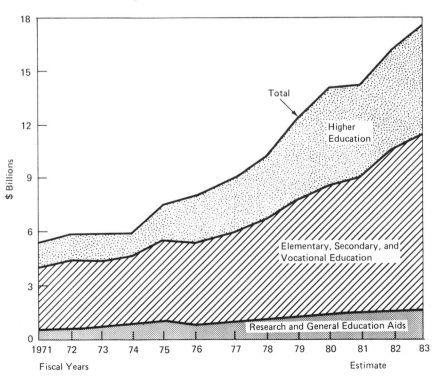

From *The United States Budget in Brief: Fiscal Year 1981* (Washington, D.C.: U.S. Government Printing Office, 1980), p. 44.

Figure 13.3. Outlays for Health

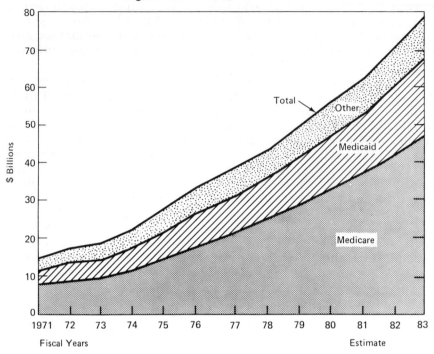

From *The United States Budget in Brief: Fiscal Year 1981* (Washington, D.C.: U.S. Government Printing Office, 1980), p. 50.

TABLE 13.2 **Growth in Payments for Individuals**

Measure	1961–65 Average	1966–79 Average	1961–65 Average	1966–69 Average	1970–73 Average	1974–79 Average
Annual Growth Rate	6.6%	15.3%	6.6%	16.1%	15.9%	14.5%
Percent of GNP	4.3%	7.1%	4.3%	5.0%	6.7%	8.8%

Note: Includes all direct and indirect transfer payments, except unemployment compensation, which was excluded here as the major cyclical component.

Source: Adapted from Michael E. Levy, "Federal Budget Policies of the 1970s: Some Lessons for the 1980s," *Stabilization Policies* (St. Louis, Mo.: Washington University Center for the Study of American Business, 1980), p. 167. Reprinted with permission.

Security Amendment of 1965, which created Medicare and Medicaid.[6] The growth of these programs contributed, of course, to the overall growth of transfer payments. Currently, 43 percent of the 1981 federal budget goes for direct benefit payments to individuals (see Figure 13.7).

[6]Michael E. Levy, "Federal Budget Policies of the 1970s: Some Lessons for the 1980s," *Stabilization Policies* (St. Louis, Mo.: Washington University Center for the Study of American Business, 1980), pp. 169–170.

Figure 13.4. Outlays for Income Security

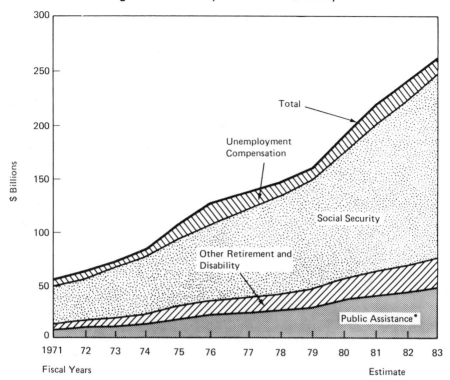

*Includes Other Income Assistance Such as Food Stamps, SSI, and AFDC

From *The United States Budget in Brief: Fiscal Year 1981* (Washington, D.C.: U.S. Government Printing Office, 1980), p. 53.

Impact of Benefits

What has been the impact of these programs in helping to alleviate the deprivation of poor people? Has poverty actually been reduced through these large-scale transfer programs? The official figures are rather depressing. In 1977, for example, the number of persons classified as poor was 24.7 million, almost the same as in 1968, although a smaller percentage of the population because of gains in the total population of the country. Yet with the enormous expansion of transfer payments through this period, one would have expected more gains to have been made in reducing the absolute number in poverty.

The reason for this, says Morton Paglin, is not a slowing growth rate in the economy as a whole or work disincentives in the welfare system, but the way poverty is defined and measured. The official poverty statistics are inadequate in measuring the real improvement which has taken place in low-income households.[7]

[7]Morton Paglin, "Poverty in the United States: A Reevaluation," *Policy Review*, No. 8 (Spring 1979), p. 8.

Figure 13.5. Outlays for Veterans Benefits and Services

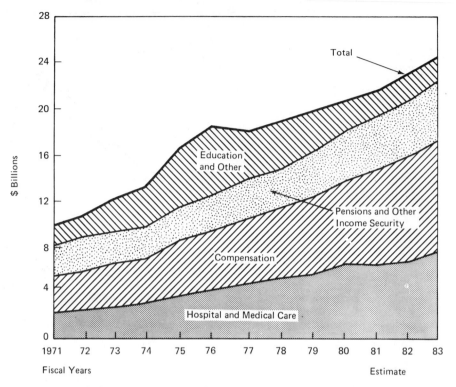

From *The United States Budget in Brief: Fiscal Year 1981* (Washington, D.C.: U.S. Government Printing Office, 1980), p. 55.

The official definition of poverty begins with the concept of a nutrition-ally adequate diet as estimated by the Department of Agriculture. This concept is then extended by a food-total-expenditure multiplier to cover a minimum adequate amount of other necessities. Families with money income that is insufficient to purchase this minimum amount of food and other necessities are officially considered low-income families and are included as such in the Current Population Surveys published by the Bureau of the Census.

The problem is that the measuring rod used in the Current Population Survey is only money income—no attempt is made to measure the impact of such in-kind programs as food stamps and Medicaid, which have been among the fastest growing part of transfer payments and now constitute about 60 percent of the transfer payment budget. When these in-kind programs were small, this omission was of minor consequence. Now, according to Paglin, their exclusion results in a gross distortion of the poverty problem.[8]

This problem has been taken into account in the Paglin study, which computed these in-kind transfers at market value. Table 13.3 shows the

[8]*Ibid.*, p. 9.

Figure 13.6. Payments for Individuals, Fiscal 1961–1979

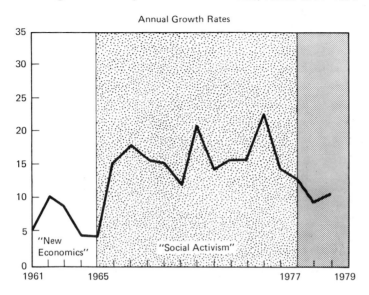

Annual Growth Rates

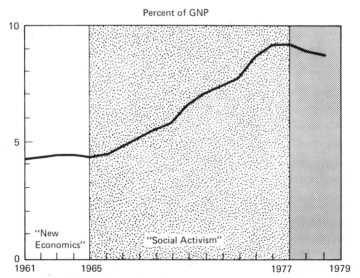

Percent of GNP

Note: Includes all direct and indirect transfer payments except unemployment
compensation, which was excluded here as the major cyclical component.

From Michael E. Levy, "Federal Budget Policies of the 1970s: Some Lessons for the 1980s," *Stabiliza-tion Policies* (St. Louis, Mo.: Washington University Center for the Study of American Business, 1980), p. 166. Reprinted with permission.

Figure 13.7. The Budget Dollar—Fiscal Year 1981 Estimate

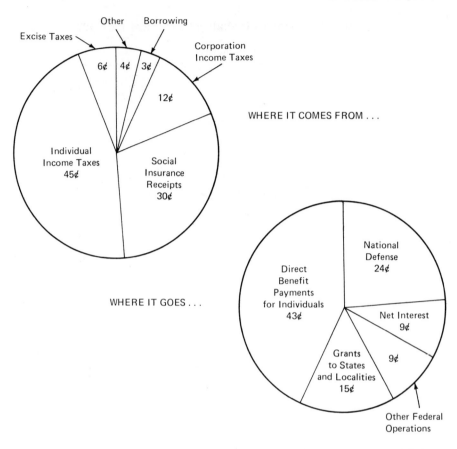

WHERE IT COMES FROM . . .

Excise Taxes

Other

Borrowing

6¢ 4¢ 3¢

12¢

Corporation
Income Taxes

Individual
Income Taxes
45¢

Social
Insurance
Receipts
30¢

WHERE IT GOES . . .

National
Defense
24¢

Direct
Benefit
Payments
for Individuals
43¢

Net Interest
9¢

Grants
to States
and Localities
15¢

9¢

Other Federal
Operations

From *The United States Budget in Brief: Fiscal Year 1981* (Washington, D.C.: U.S. Government Printing Office, 1980), p. 1.

value of these transfers for 1959–1975 for three program areas. When these estimates are factored into the final estimates of poverty, some dramatic differences show up when compared with the official poverty statistics.

Figure 13.8 shows that when in-kind transfers are taken into account, poverty continued to decline throughout the entire 1959–1975 period, instead of leveling off from 1968 to 1975 as the official CPS figures suggest. The 1968–1975 period was one in which the market value of in-kind transfers in the housing, food and nutrition, and medical areas went from $3.5 billion to $14.1 billion, making quite a difference in the final outcome. As shown in Table 13.4, the Census and final revised figures were much closer together in 1959 than in 1975, again reflecting the impact of in-kind programs. The Census cash-income measure of poverty, Paglin concludes, has departed further and further from reality.[9]

[9]*Ibid.,* p. 22.

Figure 13.8. Persons in Poverty: 1959–1975 (Official and Final Revised Estimates After All In-Kind Transfers Have Been Taken Into Account)

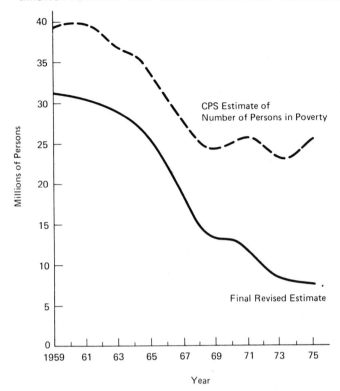

From Morton Paglin, "Poverty in the United States: A Reevaluation," *Policy Review*, No. 8 (Spring 1979), p. 23. Reprinted with permission.

This same phenomenon shows up in studies of income distribution. Table 13.5 shows a typical study based on the Current Population Reports that leaves out in-kind transfers and educational benefits. It shows the share of total money income received by families according to quintiles. Thus the lowest 20 percent of families in 1972 received only 5.4 percent of total money income. The highest 20 percent received 41.4 percent of the total income in that year. This table suggests that a great deal of inequality exists, and that the shares received by the various quintiles has changed little over the 1952–1972 period.[10]

The figures for Table 13.6, which are adjusted for in-kind transfers and education, present a much different picture. The distribution of income is more equal in each year than the Census figures indicate. The table also shows a marked trend toward equality over the 20-year period, particularly since 1962 when in-kind transfers grew faster than cash transfers. The share of the lowest quintile grew from 8.1 percent in 1952 to 11.7 percent in 1972,

[10]Edgar K. Browning, "How Much More Equality Can We Afford?" *The Public Interest*, No. 43 (Spring 1976), p. 92.

TABLE 13.3 Total In-Kind Transfers to the Poor: Housing, Food, and Medical Services*

Year	Housing	Food and Nutrition	Medical	Total Transfers to the Poor (Current $)	Total Transfers to the Poor (1975 $)
1959	103.1	137.6	299.6	540.3	997.6
1960	118.0	95.8	333.9	547.7	995.5
1961	146.1	170.2	384.5	700.8	1260.9
1962	169.3	240.2	481.7	891.2	1585.8
1963	199.2	231.7	567.8	998.7	1755.5
1964	232.6	241.9	645.3	1128.8	1958.7
1965	256.4	260.4	736.3	1253.1	2137.7
1966	267.6	207.1	1066.7	1541.4	2556.2
1967	299.0	213.7	2092.4	2605.1	4199.7
1968	333.9	288.5	2835.0	3457.4	5348.7
1969	386.6	452.2	3513.3	4352.1	6389.9
1970	502.4	816.8	4014.3	5333.5	7392.2
1971	617.6	1674.1	4624.9	6916.6	9191.5
1972	818.4	2060.1	5289.7	8168.2	10508.4
1973	1008.3	2245.5	5961.9	9216.2	11161.7
1974	1153.0	3140.1	6761.6	11054.7	12064.5
1975	1328.2	4243.2	8501.1	14072.5	14072.5

*In millions of dollars

Source: Morton Paglin, "Poverty in the United States: A Reevaluation," Policy Review, No. 8 (Spring 1979), p. 16. Reprinted with permission.

TABLE 13.4 Official and Final Revised Poverty Estimates (Rounded for Easy Reference)

Year	Poverty Deficit* (In Billions of 1975 $) (1) Census	(2) Final Revised	Persons in Poverty (In Millions of Persons) (3) Census	(4) Final Revised	(As % of Population) (5) Census	(6) Final Revised
1959	25.2	19.4	39.5	31.1	22.4	17.6
1960	25.2	19.0	39.9	30.7	22.2	17.1
1961	25.5	19.3	39.6	30.4	21.9	16.6
1962	24.1	18.3	38.6	29.9	21.0	16.1
1963	22.7	17.1	36.4	29.0	19.5	15.4
1964	21.6	15.7	36.1	27.8	19.0	14.5
1965	20.3	15.0	33.2	25.7	17.3	13.3
1966	18.0	12.8	30.4	22.3	14.7	11.4
1967	17.0	10.2	27.8	18.4	14.2	9.3
1968	15.2	7.2	25.4	14.5	12.8	7.3
1969	15.1	6.7	24.1	13.1	12.1	6.5
1970	16.0	6.9	25.4	13.1	12.6	6.4
1971	16.0	5.6	25.6	11.5	12.5	5.6
1972	15.5	5.0	24.5	9.7	11.9	4.7
1973	14.5	3.9	23.0	8.3	11.1	4.0
1974	14.5	4.1	23.4	8.0	11.2	3.8
1975	16.1	4.1	25.9	7.8	12.3	3.6

*The poverty deficit is the amount of money necessary to raise the incomes of all poor persons up to the poverty threshold.

Source: Morton Paglin, "Poverty in the United States: A Reevaluation," Policy Review, No. 8 (Spring 1979), p. 22. Reprinted with permission.

EQUALITY OF RESULTS

TABLE 13.5 **Relative Income Distribution (Expressed as Percentage Share of Total Money Income Received by Families, by Quintile)**

Year	Lowest Quintile	Second Quintile	Third Quintile	Fourth Quintile	Highest Quintile
1952	4.9	12.2	17.1	23.5	42.2
1962	5.0	12.1	17.6	24.0	41.3
1972	5.4	11.9	17.5	23.9	41.4

Reprinted with permission of the author, Edgar K. Browning, from *The Public Interest*, No. 43 (Spring 1976), p. 93. © 1976 by National Affairs, Inc.

TABLE 13.6 **Adjusted Relative Income Distribution (Expressed as Percentage Share of Income Received by Quintile)**

Year	Lowest Quintile	Second Quintile	Third Quintile	Fourth Quintile	Highest Quintile
1952	8.1	14.2	17.8	23.2	36.7
1962	8.8	14.4	18.2	23.1	35.4
1972	11.7	15.0	18.2	23.3	32.8

Reprinted with permission of the author, Edgar K. Browning, from *The Public Interest*, No. 43 (Spring 1976), p. 93. © 1976 by National Affairs, Inc.

an improvement of 44 percent in the relative position of low-income families. Concurrently, the share of the highest quintile declined from 36.7 percent in 1952 to 32.8 percent in 1972, a decline of 10.6 percent in the relative position of these families.[11]

Equality of Results

Studies such as the latter have helped to raise an important debate in our society about the meaning of equality and the objective of public policy relative to transfers of the sort just described. While the original intent of welfare may have been to relieve the distress and deprivation of low-income people, some now believe that the objective of these transfers is to produce a leveling of income in the country. This has been referred to as a move toward equality of results.

The idea of equality is now linked increasingly with this notion of result instead of opportunity, and such a linkage has a greatly different meaning. This linkage is the result of a new egalitarian thrust in our society that is most often characterized as a movement composed of blacks and other minorities, women, welfare workers, and leaders of new unions of government employees.[12] Some commentators have described the new egalitarianism as

[11]*Ibid.*, p. 93.

[12]John Cobbs, "Egalitarianism: Threat to a Free Market," *Business Week*, December 1, 1975, pp. 62–65; John Cobbs, "Egalitarianism: Mechanisms for Redistributing Income," *Business Week*, December 8, 1975, pp. 86–90; and John Cobbs, "Egalitarianism: The Corporation as Villain," *Business Week*, December 15, 1975, pp. 86–88.

a revolution instead of a movement, which implies a much more volatile and comprehensive change, involving the whole of society rather than just a few groups.[13]

Whether a movement or a revolution, however, the goal of the new egalitarians is to promote equality of income, or at least what could be called "equivalent income"—the cash value of goods and services people have at their disposal. Perhaps it would be more accurate to say that equality of results as defined by the new egalitarians means primarily equality of economic condition.

The new egalitarian movement or revolution is based on different notions of equality and justice than have been traditional in our society. Dow Votaw, for example, points out that the traditional concepts of "equality of opportunity" and "equality before the law" form a part of the very structure on which our society is built. But he goes on to say that these traditional notions of equality are neither major factors nor important goals in the new egalitarian movement. Equality has been redefined to refer to the creation of equal outcomes of income, status, and power for all persons in society.[14]

It appears that "equality of opportunity" and "equality before the law" are held to be delusions by the new egalitarians unless they produce equality of results. Thus they are asking society to alter the results of a market economy by giving more attention to those with fewer native assets and those born into less favorable social positions. The principle of justice that provides a philosophical underpinning for these demands comes from the Harvard philosopher, John Rawls. While only one statement from a lengthy and profound book certainly does not begin to do justice to the richness of his thought, a key principle mentioned by Rawls relates to these egalitarian demands. This so-called difference principle can be briefly stated as follows: "There can be no justification for differences in the condition of individuals unless it can be shown that the difference benefits the inferior more than the superior."[15]

The new egalitarian movement seems to assume that all people in our society have a right to an equal share of goods and services—they have a right to an adequate income, they have a right to good health, they have a right to retire in dignity, they have a right to a good education. These rights are held to accrue to individuals simply because they are members of society, or perhaps more accurately, human beings. These rights do not have to be earned in the marketplace.

The fact is, however, that some people are born with better and perhaps more native assets; they may also be born into more favorable positions where they have access to a better education and better opportunities to develop these assets. Some are naturally, or more or less by accident, going to be in a better position to compete and thus receive greater rewards based on their performance. A market system that allocates rewards based on individual performance and that encourages the pursuit of self-interest allows

[13]Herbert J. Gans, *More Equality* (New York: Vintage Books, 1974).

[14]Dow Votaw, "The New Equality: Bureaucracy's Trojan Horse," *California Management Review*, Vol. XX, No. 4 (Summer 1978), pp. 5–17.

[15]See John Rawls, *A Theory of Justice* (Cambridge, Mass.: Harvard University Press, 1971), especially Chapter 5.

the person who started the competitive race in a favorable position to take advantage of this position and get much further ahead than someone in a not-so-favorable starting position. To some extent a free enterprise or market economy depends on inequality to motivate or induce people to innovate and take risks and take all those other human actions necessary for material progress.

The egalitarian movement and Rawls's philosophy question the justice of this arrangement. Why should a person who, merely because of historical accident, is born into favorable circumstances be entitled to a greater share of the goods and services society has available than another person who, through no fault of his or her own, is born into poverty and does not have the advantages of a good education, may suffer from poor health, and may not have access to or knowledge of all the opportunities that are available? Why should a person who by a biological accident happens to be born with greater native assets be entitled to greater rewards than someone who was not so fortunate? In sum, why should merit, which is not earned but is the product of these native assets plus an environment in which these assets can be nurtured and developed, be the basis on which society distributes rewards?

> The new egalitarians are offended by the insistence on fundamental differences of capacity among human beings and by the assumption that the fostering and rewarding of superior ability are essential to the well-being of society as a whole.[16]

Rawls's principle of justice would try to correct for these differences in the condition of individuals by allocating a greater proportion of resources to those who are inferior in income, status, or power. This reallocation would be carried out to the point where the incentive of those who are in superior positions begins to be adversely affected. Rawls is not ignorant of the necessity to maintain the efficiency of the productive mechanism in society, nor is he unaware of the importance of material incentives. However, if this principle were to be implemented in society it would definitely narrow the gap between inferior and superior, and perhaps over time, even result in a complete leveling.

The Growth of Bureaucracy. This new emphasis on equality of results has a number of implications and raises a number of issues that are being discussed in the literature. One issue concerns the growth of government bureaucracy, an issue raised by Dow Votaw in his article appropriately entitled "The New Equality: Bureaucracy's Trojan Horse." The drive for equality of results contributes to strengthening centralized bureaucratic power, because government must allocate outcomes. At the same time, the egalitarian thrust weakens defenses against such a central despotism because of equality's widespread appeal.[17]

The goals of the egalitarian and the bureaucrat coincide, according to Votaw, in promoting uniformity and in eliminating centers of power and authority intermediate between the state and the citizen. This provides a powerful impetus to increased centralization. Also, the goal of equality is an attractive umbrella under which to extend bureaucratic power because of its emotional appeal. The objective of equality is also never reached, as it is

---

[16]Votaw, "The New Equality," p. 8.
[17]*Ibid.*, pp. 7, 12.

insatiable, and this provides a tremendous advantage for the bureaucracy. For these reasons, the bureaucracy itself comes to have a vested interest in egalitarianism.[18]

> In addition to the obvious need for bureaucracy and for increased centralization of power in order to implement equality of result, there is another role of bureaucracy that is particularly important to note: the interest which established bureaucracy itself has in equality. Not only does the implementation of egalitarian policies require a giant bureaucracy, but also that bureaucracy becomes active in increasing egalitarian pressure for its own ends. Thus, equality becomes the Trojan horse for a set of bureaucratic drives that have little or nothing to do with egalitarian motivations.[19]

Along these same lines, Meltzer and Richard argue that this push for equality is the greatest single force changing and expanding the role of the federal government.[20] Government grows because there is a difference in outcomes between the political process and the market process. The distribution of votes in our society is more equal than the distribution of income produced by the market. Those with the lowest income use the political process to increase their income. These voters, who become more numerous as the franchise is extended, can gain if incomes above the average are taxed.

Equality versus Efficiency. Another issue that has received attention is the impact on efficiency that egalitarianism involves. Some see this egalitarian trend as posing a serious threat to business and the economy. Arthur Okun, former chairman of the Council of Economic Advisors, for example, sees the issue as one of equality versus efficiency—that this is the big trade-off society faces. The American economy, which is based on private property, uses the market to determine rewards and allocate resources. Differences in wages and profits are essential, he says, to keep the economic machine running. Public efforts to promote equality represent a deliberate interference with the results generated by the marketplace. In pursuing equality, Okun states, society would forego any opportunity to use material resources or rewards as incentives to production. That would lead to inefficiencies which would be harmful to the welfare of the majority.[21]

Curiously enough, Okun supports the notion of egalitarianism on ethical grounds alone. He states, for example, that "equality in the distribution of incomes as well as in the distribution of rights would be my ethical preference. . . . [T]o extend the domain of rights and give every citizen an equal share of the national income would give added recognition to the moral worth of every citizen, to the mutual respect of citizens for one another, and to the equivalent value of membership in the society for all."[22] That is as fine a humanistic ideal as one could hope to find anywhere.

Okun rests his case, however, on the effects that such an ethical ideal would have on economic efficiency. "Any insistence on carving the pie into

[18]*Ibid.*, p. 7.

[19]*Ibid.*

[20]Allan H. Meltzer and Scott F. Richard, "Why Government Grows (and Grows) in a Democracy," *The Public Interest*, No. 52 (Summer 1978), pp. 111–118.

[21]Arthur M. Okun, *Equality and Efficiency: The Big Tradeoff* (Washington, D.C., The Brookings Institution, 1975), p. 48.

[22]*Ibid.*, p. 47.

equal slices," he says, "would shrink the size of the pie. That fact poses the tradeoff between economic equality and economic efficiency. . . . Although the ethical case for capitalism is totally unpersuasive, the efficiency case is thoroughly compelling to me."[23]

This efficiency versus equality issue bears further examination. The competitive marketplace, with its incentives for economic gain, has generally proven to be the best system of organizing production. As Okun states in an article entitled "Capitalism and Democracy: Some Unifying Principles":

> Every day for the past two centuries, our economy (as well as those of other advanced western countries) has confirmed the validity of Adam Smith's theory of the "invisible hand." The competitive marketplace transmits signals to producers that reflect the values of consumers, offering profits for the production of those goods whose value to consumers exceeds their cost to producers. Profitability becomes the magnet that pulls resources into their most productive use. Thus, in the competitive marketplace, economic self-interest becomes an engine of social welfare.[24]

On an institutional level, the relationship between efficiency and incentives is important to consider. While the decline in productivity in our country in recent years is a complex phenomenon that has many causes, including increased government regulation and higher prices for energy, perhaps a major contributing factor to this decline has been the lack of incentives in our society that a leveling effect produces.[25]

This relationship is especially crucial in an era of resource shortages. While resources may not be as limited as some claim, there is no doubt that they are not as cheaply abundant as they have been in the past years, particularly energy resources. Growth may indeed be slower for some time as a result of resource shortages and price increases, and the opportunities for an ever-rising standard of living may become limited for more and more people.

If this is what the future looks like, the egalitarian movement may take on added significance. Part of the tolerance for inequality may come from the opportunities that people have to better themselves. As these opportunities become limited and available to fewer and fewer people, more attention might be given to the distributive mechanism of society to allocate more equitably those goods and services that are available. Inequality may not be tolerated in a society of relative scarcity to the extent it is even today.

If such a scenario were to happen, however, it could be a disaster. As resources become harder to find and more difficult to extract, it is precisely the productive mechanism of society that needs increased attention. Society in this situation needs increased technological innovation, more incentives to find new sources of supply. To emphasize distribution of what is presently available at the expense of future production may invite disaster.

The experience of other countries that have adopted leveling as a public policy goal is perhaps instructive in this regard. Britain adopted a com-

[23]*Ibid.*, pp. 47, 64.

[24]Arthur M. Okun, "Capitalism and Democracy: Some Unifying Principles," *Columbia Journal of World Business,* Winter 1978, pp. 22–30.

[25]See Harold M. Williams, "Egalitarianism and Market Systems," *Columbia Journal of World Business,* Winter 1978, pp. 7–14.

prehensive system of social insurance after World War II by putting into effect the principles of the 1942 Beveridge Report. The system was essentially an insurance scheme that gave benefits up to a subsistence level as a matter of right. Currently, about 50 percent of the expenditures of the national government are on social welfare services, including free medical care, family allowances, old age pensions, maternity benefits, and the like. Meanwhile, the economy has floundered throughout most of the period since the Second World War with low growth rates and a persistent balance of payments problem.[26]

The culprit is not poor industrial productivity or destructive trade unionism, say Bacon and Eltis, two Oxford economists who have done a detailed study of the impact of specific public policies on the industrial sector.[27] There has been, they argue, a structural maladjustment in the country. The major increases in employment for many years have taken place outside the industrial sector, and this increase has been predominantly in the public sector, where the need for people to run all the government programs has been insatiable. This puts added pressure on industrial production because with more workers outside industry, more industrial production is required for those who play no part in production. This reduces the amount of product available to industrial workers as incentives and the amount available for investment, which produces low growth of industrial capacity and structural unemployment.

Individual Motivation. One of the basic defects in Rawls's philosophy is his lack of attention to incentives and motivation at the level of the individual. At this level, the egalitarian movement represents another step away from the protestant ethic tradition, a motivational philosophy that has been a part of our society since its inception. This philosophy is consistent with a free enterprise system and its method of distributing rewards. It holds that a person is to work hard at whatever place in life one is located, that he or she is called to a particular vocation. Success is linked to one's efforts; if one works hard enough, he or she will be rewarded for those efforts. Individual initiative is thus the way to get ahead and acquire more of the rewards society has to offer. People receive recognition and respect through making a productive contribution to society.

The protestant ethic produces a certain type of personality with a high motivation to achieve success in worldly terms by accumulating wealth and working diligently to overcome every obstacle. The self-discipline and moral sense of duty and calling which are at the heart of this ethic are vital to the kind of rational economic behavior that is required in a free enterprise system. The protestant ethic contributes to the development of a social climate favorable to individual human enterprise and the accumulation of wealth. Within this climate, people are motivated to behave in a manner that produces economic growth and material progress.

The trends toward more leisure time and increased consumption, which have been evident in our society for some time, suggest that this tradition may indeed be weakening, or at least that it does not provide the kind of

[26]James W. Nordyke and Martin C. Schnitzer, *Comparative Economic Systems* (Cincinnati: South-Western Publishing Company, 1977), pp. 229–257.

[27]Robert Bacon and Walter Eltis, "How Britain Went Wrong" (St. Louis, Mo.; Washington University Center for the Study of American Business, 1977), pp. 1–19.

meaning that it may have at one time. The egalitarian movement, then, may represent the culmination of the erosion of this tradition that began some time ago.

If the link between human effort and material rewards is broken, however, and if rewards in the form of income and other material benefits are distributed on the basis of assumed rights rather than individual effort, what implications does this have for human motivation? What is it that really motivates people? Are they so motivated by material rewards that their removal reduces performance? Can intrinsic factors such as the nature of the job itself replace the earning of income as an incentive?

A market economy assumes material incentives are the most powerful motivator, at least insofar as economic performance is concerned. Economists stress the exchange concept of money and say it is valued because it can be exchanged for goods and services that are desired. The material wants of human beings are numerous and varied and seldom satisfied. But several studies also show that pay is associated with some basic psychological needs, such as security, status, esteem, and recognition.[28] Money is an important determinant of status in our society, for example, and high status is valued because it usually leads to more respect, attention, and deference from others.

The importance of pay has been shown to vary among different groups. For example, managers have been shown to score lower on the need for financial reward than workers and supervisors.[29] Other studies show that the importance of pay decreases with advancing age.[30] Differences in basic needs may explain why pay has been rated of lower importance to females than to males.[31]

But in general, money is an effective incentive because it can contribute to the satisfaction of so many diverse needs and wants simultaneously. After making a survey of the existing literature on the subject, Lawler concludes that the evidence rather clearly suggests that pay can be instrumental in the satisfaction of a variety of needs and that it is likely to be seen as more instrumental with respect to some needs than to others.[32] Thus the literature shows that material incentives can be an important motivator and demonstrates the importance of performance-contingent reward systems.

The Moral Issues. Moral issues are involved in this egalitarian movement. Apparently the ethical case for capitalism is unpersuasive for the egalitarians as well as for Okun, as the former are unwilling to abide by the outcomes of a market system and want to alter these outcomes by public policy measures. The moral appeal of the equality of results philosophy helps make it such a strong force in our society. These moral issues therefore must be considered along with the bureaucratic, efficiency, and motivational issues.

As an economist, Okun can be forgiven for thinking an appeal to effi-

[28]See, for example, Edward E. Lawler III, *Pay and Organizational Effectiveness: A Psychological View* (New York: McGraw-Hill, 1971); Allan N. Nash and Stephen J. Carrall, Jr., *The Management of Compensation* (Belmont, Calif.: Wadsworth Publishing Co., 1975).

[29]E. E. Ghiselli, *Explorations in Managerial Talent* (Pacific Palisades, Calif.: Goodyear, 1971).

[30]Lawler, *Pay and Organizational Effectiveness*, p. 48.

[31]*Ibid.*, p. 47.

[32]*Ibid.*, p. 33.

ciency will carry all the weight, but as a human being with obvious ethical sensibilities, he cannot. To cite an old saying, man does not live by bread alone. Moral concepts such as justice, equity, or fairness have at least as much motivating power as do economic or more technical concepts like efficiency, cost, or allocation of resources. By making a sort of backhanded appeasement to ethics, and resting his case on economic grounds alone, Okun in a sense completely undercuts his own argument.

Is it really right and just that all members of a society have equal income, status, power, prestige, and other conditions of life? Would such equality really give added recognition to the moral worth of every citizen, to the mutual respect of citizens for one another, and to the equivalent value of membership in the society for all?

These moral questions are dealt with in an article by Marc F. Plattner, who is a consulting editor of *The Public Interest* and on the staff of the Twentieth Century Fund. The egalitarian philosophy implies that greater effort, like greater natural ability, has no moral claim to greater reward, instead, lesser effort, like lesser natural ability, is entitled to be compensated or rewarded. Thus the person who works harder is entitled to nothing more, or at least nothing near the full fruits of his or her labor, while the person who works less hard gains a greater claim over what others have produced. Plattner claims that the moral absurdity of this view is transparent. Furthermore, he maintains, all modern societies do hold that men and women who possess the capacity and opportunity for productive work and yet refuse to perform it have no moral claim upon the society's resources.[33]

It is difficult to see how equality would give added recognition to the moral worth of every citizen when it penalizes those who are most productive. Instead of mutual respect, such an arrangement would most likely lead to a great deal of jealousy and strife. And those who are productive and yet do not receive the fruits of their labors do not hold anything like an equivalent value of membership compared to those who are less productive and yet receive an equal share of the rewards.

Equality of results may not lead to the kind of perfect justice that is assumed by the egalitarians. It would seem that there is some kind of a moral connection between one's productive efforts and the rewards one is entitled to receive. To argue otherwise involves correcting the arbitrariness of nature in the distribution of natural abilities in a manner that in and of itself may be quite arbitrary.

Marvin Olasky, in a recent article appearing in the *Columbia Journal of World Business*, makes the point that pure efficiency arguments are not enough to challenge egalitarian ideals.[34] Business leaders, he argues, must not ignore equity values because people want more from life than the material prosperity the market system provides. Thus, he states, "corporate spokesmen have to challenge equality of result proposals on the basis of their impact on equity, not on the field of efficiency which practical-minded

[33]Marc F. Plattner, "The Welfare State vs the Redistributive State," *The Public Interest*, No. 55 (Spring 1979), pp. 36–37.
[34]Marvin Olasky, "Efficiency, Equity and Equality of Result: What Should Business Be Doing?" *Columbia Journal of World Business*, Winter 1978, pp. 15–21.

business people might prefer. They have been fighting the right war but assembling their troops on the wrong front."[35]

Reform Measures

The measures that one supports to reform the welfare system depend on the objectives one believes should be pursued. If welfare is viewed as a necessary overhead cost to a market system to relieve the deprivation of low-income people, then reform measures that remove some of the inefficiencies in the current system and reduce some of the economic distortions it causes will probably be supported.

The current welfare system has been criticized as being inequitable, providing inadequate benefits to some people, breaking up families, placing too heavy a burden on local governments, providing insufficient incentives to work, or being an inefficient tangle of separate programs.[36] The most obvious reform would be to replace the existing system with a comprehensive, well-thought-out program that addressed some of these problems. Every new administration seems to make an attempt of this kind, and ends up frustrated by its inability to get such a program through Congress. The reason, say Doolittle, Levy, and Wiseman, is that any suggestion of "total welfare reform" exposes every aspect of the existing system to debate, guaranteeing political stalemate. Somebody has a vested interest in every aspect of the current system and will argue it ought to be retained. Thus any administration is politically constrained to pursue an incremental strategy of reform.[37]

If, however, one views the welfare system and transfer payments as an instrument for pursuing equality of economic condition, the reform measures deemed appropriate are much different. One would then support such measures as national health insurance, which increase the share of income going to the lowest income brackets and provide more services to the people who cannot afford to pay for them. These reform measures are most likely to be supported by those who are gaining from the egalitarian trend in the form of increased income or services available to them for the same amount of effort they previously expended for some level of economic well-being. They are benefiting more than they are losing, at least in the short run, from any efficiencies that are being introduced into society by the shift to equality of results.

If income increasingly is being considered a common product or public good to be distributed by the political system, thought must be given to the long-term effects on the economy and society as a whole. Someone has to impose a discipline on government, according to Harold Williams, Chairman of the Securities and Exchange Commission, and force it to consider the impact of its actions to impose equality on the economy. An equilibrium is

---

[35]*Ibid.*, p. 19.

[36]Frederick Doolittle, Frank Levy, and Michael Wiseman, "The Mirage of Welfare Reform," *The Public Interest*, No. 47 (Spring 1977), p. 62.

[37]*Ibid.*, p. 77.

needed to balance the enormous energies of the market with the compassion and social justice associated with democracy, so that the free market is not prevented from providing a healthy, growing economy necessary to achieve the promises of democracy.[38] This principle of balance or trade-offs is also enunciated by Arthur Okun:

> This is an area of particularly vexing trade-offs. No objective dollar price tag can be placed on the benefit of reducing deprivation and misery; the valuation is a matter of individual judgment and ethical assessment, on which citizens will disagree. And with few exceptions, efforts to shift resources to the poor and disadvantaged have their costs. As I like to put it, society can transport money from rich to poor only in a leaky bucket. The leakages are of two distinct types: direct administrative and compliance costs of the tax and transfer programs; and indirect economic costs of the distortions of incentives to work, save, invest, and innovate. The cost of the leakages must be balanced against the benefits obtained from what is left in the bucket. A program cannot be damned just because it has some leakage, nor can it be blessed simply because something is left in the bucket. Correcting deprivation and preserving economic efficiency are both desirable goals, which unfortunately sometimes conflict with each other. Of necessity, we must live with compromises between the two. We cannot aid low-income groups to the point of destroying the incentive system of the market that marshals the effort and economic activity to fill the bucket. Nor can we tolerate kids with empty stomachs, adults selling apples, and oldsters with begging cups in the name of a greater aggregate of real GNP. There are serious, legitimate grounds for debate and controversy among informed citizens about how much assistance should be provided and how it can be handled with minimum leakage. We need those constructive dialogues and debates, not ideological shouting matches, to formulate policies in this perplexing and crucial area.[39]

The Reagan administration which took office in January 1981, saw its election as a mandate to reverse the egalitarian trend by enacting deep budget cuts in some of the entitlement programs. The programs due for the biggest cuts include food stamps, Medicaid, aid to families with dependent children, student aid, and unemployment insurance. These budget cuts, coupled with a proposed 10 percent tax cut over each year of a three-year period, are supposed to bring government spending under control, bring inflation down, stimulate increased saving and investment, and promote economic growth. These proposals, if enacted, will drastically alter the nature of the trade-offs, as the cut in entitlement programs will disproportionately affect lower income groups because they receive most of the benefits from these programs, and the tax cut will disproportionately benefit the upper and middle income groups because they receive the most income. These policies, then, will result in a transfer of money back to the middle and upper income groups who have provided most of the support for the entitlement programs. If these proposals are enacted and prove to be of long duration, 1981 could indeed prove to mark another watershed in this area of public policy.

[38]Williams, "Egalitarianism and Market Systems," pp. 7, 12.
[39]Okun, "Democracy and Capitalism," p. 74.

Questions for Discussion

1. Describe the origins of the welfare system. Does the market system, indeed, condemn some people to death? Are the rewards and penalties that the market allocates fundamentally arbitrary?
2. Does a democratic government owe its citizens some form of aid if they have not been able to provide for themselves through the market system? Are transfer payments a legitimate area of public policy?
3. Distinguish between cash-income assistance and in-kind assistance. If you were a recipient of assistance, which form would you rather have? Is there any basic difference in these forms of assistance from society's point of view?
4. Study the Social Security system in more detail. What was the rationale for making it a mandatory system for most people in the country? Why was it designed as a pay-as-you-go system? Should the benefits be indexed to keep up with inflation? How will or do you feel about supporting the aged—seeing some of your paycheck directly transferred to the Social Security system for the benefit of other people?
5. Think of some alternative methods to provide for the needs of the aged in this country. Which are most feasible? Should the mandatory retirement age be removed entirely? How would this affect your job or prospects of finding a job?
6. Explain the growth of transfer payments throughout the late 1960s and early 1970s. Does this growth represent a fundamental shift in the thinking and values of the American people? What implications do your answers have for the free enterprise system?
7. Examine closely the studies that take in-kind transfers into account. Do you agree with the methodology used to cash-out these transfers? Are the conclusions valid? Is there less poverty than the official figures would lead us to believe? Has income distribution changed significantly?
8. If in-kind transfers have such an impact, then why haven't policy-makers taken these into account? What would you recommend be done to make the figures more realistic?
9. Is the distinction between equality of opportunity and equality of results valid? Which concept is currently receiving more emphasis in our society? Why?
10. Is the notion of merit a fair and just concept on which to base the distribution of rewards in a society? What are the moral foundations of an equality of results approach? Do you agree with any of the arguments justifying this approach?
11. Is there a trade-off between equality and efficiency? What measures are relevant in trying to determine the nature of this trade-off? What guidelines could you suggest for policy-makers who are concerned about taking this trade-off into account in their decision-making?
12. Is business fighting the battle on the wrong front? Will efficiency arguments carry the day or do the moral issues have to be dealt with more directly, as Olasky suggests? Why or why not?
13. Do you agree that welfare reform is likely to be only incremental at best? Why? What are the political realities?
14. In general, is the notion of egalitarianism the most serious threat to the market system? Is it more of a threat than government regulation? If pursued further, where is the equality of results movement likely to lead?

Suggested Reading

Abernathy, George L., ed. *The Idea of Equality.* Richmond, Va.: John Knox Press, 1959.

Gans, Herbert J. *More Equality*. New York: Vintage Books, 1974.

Hawkins, David. *The Science and Ethics of Equality*. New York: Basic Books, 1977.

Okun, Arthur M. *Equality and Efficiency: The Big Tradeoff*. Washington, D.C.: The Brookings Institution, 1975.

Rawls, John. *A Theory of Justice*. Cambridge, Mass.: Harvard University Press, 1971.

Tawney, Richard H. *Equality*. London: Unwin Books, 1964.

Vartikar, V. *Equality and Free Enterprise*. Waynesburg, Pa.: Kitaab Press, 1977.

Ward, Michael Don. *The Political Economy of Distribution: Equality vs. Inequality*. New York: Elsevier, 1978.

Weale, Albert. *Equality and Social Policy*. Boston: Routledge & Kegan Paul, 1978.

Wilensky, Harold L. *The Welfare State and Equality: Structural and Ideological Roots of Public Expenditures*. Berkeley: University of California Press, 1975.

14

Equality of Employment Opportunity

Preferential programs may only reinforce common stereotypes holding that certain groups are unable to achieve success without special protection. . . . There is [also] a measure of inequity in forcing innocent persons in [Bakke's] position to bear the burdens of redressing grievances not of their making (Supreme Court Justice Lewis Powell writing for the majority in the Bakke decision). I suspect that it would be impossible to arrange an affirmative action program in a racially neutral way and have it successful. To ask that this be so is to demand the impossible. In order to get beyond racism, we must first take account of race. There is no other way. And in order to treat some persons equally, we must treat them differently (Supreme Court Justice Harry Blackmun in a dissenting opinion on the Bakke decision).[1]

This approach to equal opportunity focuses on the workplace, and is aimed at rooting out the kind of discrimination that prevents members of certain groups, most notably minorities and women, from having an equal chance at the job opportunities that are available. The basic issue here is not necessarily one of poverty or disadvantages that make it difficult to compete in the marketplace because of the lack of fundamental skills or work habits. It is one of prejudice and discrimination that prevent certain groups from utilizing to the fullest the skills and abilities they already possess, or from gaining the experience and training that is necessary to become qualified for the opportunities society has to offer. Since the focus of equal employment opportunity is on prejudice and discrimination, some discussion of what these concepts mean is important.

[1]*Regents of the University of California v. Bakke*, 98 S.Ct. 2752, 2807 (1978).

271

The Nature of Prejudice and Discrimination

This is not the place to go into an extended treatment of these concepts, but something at least needs to be said about prejudice and discrimination and how they enter into people's decisions. The nature of prejudice is such that it produces a tendency to evaluate individuals on the basis of their identity with a group rather than their individual characteristics. Group membership becomes a primary and ruling consideration when making judgments about people. All the characteristics that are believed to be true about that group are automatically assigned to individuals who are members of that group, whether or not they actually possess those characteristics. The individual is seen through the veil of the group stereotype, since prejudice does not allow the assumptions made about individuals to be tested against reality.[2]

People thus become stereotyped. Every black person is believed to be inferior to every white person on many dimensions related to job performance, because this is what is believed about the black population as a whole. When it comes to making decisions about job opportunities, whites are assumed to have naturally superior ability to perform. Every woman is believed to be too emotional to make rational decisions required of a manager, because this is believed about women as a whole. When decisions are made about management opportunities, men have the inside track because it is believed they have superior ability to perform this function.

This kind of stereotyping builds barriers around members of a group that are very difficult to break through. Not only are these characteristics about individuals in a group believed true by people outside the group, they often come to be believed by members of the group itself. Thus prejudice and stereotyping have a transactional aspect—they are cultural phenomena. Whites use blacks to build a superior identity. Blacks internalize this identity and reinforce the pattern. The behavior of these two groups becomes a function of each other and the identities of individuals in the groups become a social product.

The same can be said of the relationship between men and women. This is what makes prejudice and stereotyping so difficult to deal with for both those doing the discriminating and those being discriminated against. These concepts are related to people's basic identity and understanding of themselves. When this identity is threatened or changed in any way, severe resistance can be expected.

The way characteristics originally become assigned to certain groups is not clearly understood. These characteristics, however, are not entirely a figment of imagination. Some black people do have less ability to perform certain tasks than some white people. Some women are too emotional to handle the demands of a management function. The point is, however, that some white people also have less ability to perform certain tasks than some black people. Some men are also too emotional to perform effectively in a management role. Prejudice enters in when these characteristics are assumed to be true of an entire group—that a whole race of people is believed to be condemned by God or by nature to hereditary inferiority and that

[2]Philip Mason, *Race Relations* (London: Oxford University Press, 1970), p. 52.

another group has been destined to be superior for all times and places because of native endowment; or that an entire sex has been assigned to stay at home to be good wives and mothers, and if they want to enter the business world, they have to be content with lower-paying, nonprofessional, non-managerial jobs because they are not inherently equipped for the better-paying, more interesting opportunities that are available.[3]

The roots of racism and sexism are deep and the dynamics complex. There are economic, social, psychological, cultural, and other reasons for prejudice and stereotyping. Factors such as jealousy, frustration, guilt, fear, and power enter into the development and maintenance of prejudice and stereotypes. They are passed from generation to generation by complex and subtle mechanisms that are often very difficult to unveil. Sometimes it almost seems as if prejudice is in the air and is assimilated by the process of osmosis.

Nonetheless, the effects of prejudice and stereotyping are quite visible in discriminatory behavior against certain groups in our society. The relationship between prejudice and discrimination is shown in Figure 14.1, which shows the different kinds of relationships that can take place between groups on a continuum from friendly to hostile.

A cooperative relationship implies that both groups accept each other and interact in a color-blind and sex-blind manner in most job-related endeavors. They work and play together in a mutually fulfilling manner with little or no exploitation of each other. Respect does not necessarily mean that the groups will interact much; in fact, they may stick very much to themselves. But they at least do recognize each other's rights to share equally in the opportunities and rewards of society.

The word tolerance implies that there may be some kind of hostility already present, but the groups at least allow each other a certain degree of coexistence and do not engage in open warfare or overt discrimination.

Figure 14.1. Continuum of Social Relations Among Human Groups

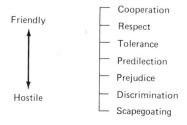

[3]The author recognizes that there has been much scientific work—some bogus to be sure, but also some that is more respectable—to prove the inherent inferiority of races. The black race in particular has been questioned with respect to native intelligence (see "The Return of Arthur Jensen," *Time*, September 24, 1979, p. 49). The assumption made here, however, and it is admitted to be an assumption, is that nature does not distinguish between groups with respect to native ability or intelligence, and that whatever differences between groups do exist are due to environmental or cultural factors, such as climate, social mores, economic condition, educational opportunities, or similar factors. It is assumed that ability and intelligence are randomly distributed throughout all the people of the world, and that no genetic or other inherent factors favor one group over another. This assumption is also behind affirmative action programs, which deem that minorities and women should appear in all occupational categories in proportion to their numbers in the relevant population.

Predilection is defined as the simple preference of an individual for members of one culture, color, sex, or language as opposed to another. While this kind of preference may be seen as inevitable and natural, it opens the door to prejudice, since group interaction is minimal and knowledge of what individuals in other groups are really like is not readily available.

Prejudice arises when a predilection becomes rigid, inflexible, and exaggerated, and myths arise because of the strangeness of the groups to each other. Each group in isolation may overrate its own virtues and exaggerate the vices of the other. These beliefs become very strongly held and form part of an individual's identity. An act of discrimination is an act of exclusion based on these prejudices. Those who make decisions about individuals in the group do so on the basis of characteristics assumed to be true of the group rather than on an individual's intrinsic characteristics. Scapegoating is the ultimate form of hostility, involving full-fledged aggression in word or deed where the victim of discrimination is abused verbally or physically, or in more severe cases, killed.

While scapegoating is certainly not unknown in our country, the public policy measures to be considered in this chapter are directed at rooting out discrimination in employment opportunities. The difficulty in attaining this objective, however, is not only caused by the deficiencies of government regulation, inept or inexperienced administration, poorly designed regulations, and the like; it is also rooted in the nature of prejudice and discrimination itself, which is the reason some time was devoted to explaining these concepts. These dynamics have to be better understood in order to develop effective public policy measures or to reform the present ones in ways that will produce the desired results.

Public Policy Measures

One of the first efforts to promote equal employment opportunity as a matter of public policy was Executive Order 8802, issued in 1941 by President Franklin D. Roosevelt. This order prohibited racial discrimination by companies under federal contract and established the first Fair Employment Practices Committee. The effect of this order was significant, as most companies had some kind of a federal contract because of the war effort. This order plus the severe workforce shortage provided many job opportunities for blacks and women that would otherwise not have been available. After the war ended, however, many blacks were fired because they were no longer needed, and many women left the workforce to return to their traditional role as homemaker.

Then, in 1961, President John F. Kennedy issued Executive Order 10925, which established a President's Commission on Equal Employment Opportunity with the power to investigate complaints by employees and enforce a ban on discrimination by federal contractors. The Commission had the power to terminate contracts if necessary or prevent companies from obtaining new contracts from the government. The order also required government contractors to take affirmative action to make certain that minority group members were treated equally in terms of job opportunities and informed of job openings. This was the first time the word "affirmative action" was used in a public policy measure.

States also passed what are called Fair Employment Practice (FEP) Acts to prohibit discrimination in employment. Most of these acts are aimed at employers, unions, and employment agencies, forbidding them to discriminate in any term or condition of employment. The first such act was passed by New York in 1945, and since that time most other states have adopted such measures. These statutes generally take one of three forms: (1) statutes that provide for an administrative hearing and judicial enforcement of orders of an administrative agency or official, (2) statutes that do not provide for any type of administrative agency or enforcement of orders but do make employment discrimination a misdemeanor, and (3) statutes that call for voluntary compliance only and have no enforcement provisions.

Thus there was some action on the equal employment opportunity front prior to the 1960s, but it was during the sixties that major public policy measures were passed in response to the civil rights movement and the feminist movement. These measures deal primarily with discrimination against minorities and women, although other groups, such as the handicapped and aged, are also victims of discrimination. Efforts to promote equal treatment of these groups are, however, not the primary subject of this chapter.

The Civil Rights Act of 1964. The cornerstone of public policy regarding equal employment opportunity is Title VII of the Civil Rights Act of 1964, which forbade discrimination in employment by an employer, employment agency, or labor union on the basis of race, color, sex, religion, or national origin, in any term, condition, or privilege of employment. The law forbids discrimination in hiring and firing practices, wages, fringe benefits, classifying, referring, assigning, or promoting employees, extending or assigning facilities, training, retraining, apprenticeships, and other employment practices.

The ban on employment discrimination based on sex was inserted as an amendment during the debate about the bill on the floor of the House. Presumably this was done in an effort to defeat the bill. There is little legislative history to clarify congressional intent with respect to sex discrimination, and as a result the Equal Employment Opportunity Commission and the courts have had difficulty in applying the sex provision.[4] This may be part of the reason that many women deem the Equal Rights Amendment to be so important.

The Civil Rights Act established the Equal Employment Opportunity Commission (EEOC) as the administrative agency to implement the act, but it gave the Commission no enforcement powers. Prior to 1972, the EEOC only had authority to investigate complaints filed by individuals and to attempt to settle them by conciliation. For an employer to be taken to court, the EEOC had to convince the Justice Department that the case was worth considering. Consequently, not many cases were pursued through litigation.

---

[4]Howard J. Anderson, *Primer of Equal Employment Opportunity* (Washington, D.C.: The Bureau of National Affairs, Inc., 1978), p. 25.

An important provision of the act, called the "quota" provision, expressly forbade preferential treatment of groups discriminated against, emphasizing that the intent of the act was to promote equal opportunity for individuals. Section 703 (j) of Title VII stated that "nothing in the title should be interpreted to require an employer, an employment agency, a union or a hiring hall, to grant preferential treatment to any individual or to any group because of the race, color, religion, sex, or national origin of such individual or group on account of an imbalance which may exist in such employment as compared with the total or percentage of such persons in any community, state, section, or other area, or in the available work force in any community, state, section, or other area."[5]

Equal Employment Opportunity Act of 1972. This act was an amendment to Title VII, broadening its coverage and giving the EEOC power to bring enforcement action in the courts. This amendment also provided that discrimination charges may be filed by organizations on behalf of aggrieved individuals, as well as by employees and job applicants themselves. As amended, Title VII now covers the following main categories of employers:

- All private employers of fifteen or more persons. Bona fide, tax-exempt private clubs, however, are excluded from this definition.

- All educational institutions, public and private. Title VI of the Civil Rights Act also applies to educational institutions.

- Public and private employment agencies, defined as any person regularly undertaking with or without compensation to procure employees for an employer or to procure for employees opportunities to work for an employer.

- Labor unions with fifteen or more members, including not only local unions, but national and international unions and collateral bodies.

- Joint labor-management committees that control apprenticeship or other training and retraining programs. There is an exception when religion, sex, or national origin is a bona fide occupational qualification for employment. This exception does not apply to race or color.

The Equal Pay Act of 1963. This act prohibits discrimination because of sex in the payment of wages, including overtime, for equal work on jobs that require equal skill, effort, and responsibility, and that are performed under similar working conditions. This law was aimed at the long-established practice of paying women lower wages than men for essentially the same work, including differential rates of pay set by union contracts. The law specifically prohibits employers from reducing the wage rates of any employee to equalize pay between the sexes. The act originally covered employees subject to the minimum wage requirements of the Fair Labor Standards Act, but in 1972 coverage was extended to include executive, administrative, and professional employees and outside salespeople.

The Age Discrimination in Employment Act. As originally passed, the act prohibited employers, employment agencies, and labor unions from discriminating, on the basis of age, against people between the ages of 40 and

[5]*Ibid.*, p. 35.

65 in hiring, firing, and promotion, or other aspects of employment. The law applies to employers of 20 or more employees, labor unions of more than 25 members, and also covers public employees. In 1978, this act was amended to raise the top age to 70 effective April 6, 1978, for employees then under 65, and effective January 1, 1979, for employees then between the ages of 65 and 69, subject to an exemption for employees covered by collective bargaining contracts.

Executive Orders. Executive Order 11246 (as amended by E.O. 11375), issued by President Lyndon B. Johnson in 1965, forbade employment discrimination based on race, color, religion, sex, or national origin by prime contractors and subcontractors who had government contracts in excess of $10,000, and called for them to develop affirmative action plans in "good faith" for the hiring and training of minorities. Originally, no administrative machinery was set up to define what "affirmative action" meant or ensure its implementation. Eventually, it became apparent that rules and regulations were needed to guide contractors as well as compliance officers to fulfill the spirit of the order.

Thus Revised Order No. 4 was issued by the Office of Federal Contract Compliance in 1970, requiring employers with contracts of over $50,000 and 50 or more employees to develop written affirmative action programs identifying areas of minority and female underutilization and establishing goals and timetables to correct existing deficiencies in the employment of minorities and women. Underutilization was defined as having fewer minorities or women in a particular job classification than would reasonably be expected by their availability. The goal of this order was to increase the utilization of minorities and women at all levels and in all segments of the workforce where such deficiencies existed. Failure to meet these provisions satisfactorily could lead to cancellation of a contract and being barred from issuance of future government contracts. This order is an example of the government using its power as a buyer to promote social goals and values.

The Rehabilitation Act of 1973. This act again applies only to federal contractors and requires them to take affirmative action to employ and promote qualified handicapped persons. The act applies to employers with federal contracts over $2,500, and while no numerical goals are specified, the act does require than an employer take steps to accommodate a handicapped worker unless such accommodation imposes an undue hardship on the employer. The act defines a handicapped person as one "who has a physical or mental impairment which substantially limits one or more of such person's major life activities."[6] Failure to comply with these regulations can again result in contract termination, debarment from future contracts, or withholding of contract payments as necessary to correct any violations.

The Vietnam Era Veterans Readjustment Assistance Act. Applying to employers with government contracts of $10,000 or more, this act requires these contractors to take affirmative action to employ and advance disabled veterans and qualified veterans of the Vietnam era. In addition to this affirmative action requirement, the act also imposes an obligation on all covered employers to list all suitable job openings with an appropriate public or private local employment service. Priority for referral will then be given to

---

[6]*Ibid.,* p. 60.

Vietnam era veterans. Enforcement of the act is by complaint to the Veteran's Employment Service of the Department of Labor.

Equal Rights Amendment. While not yet a public policy measure, the Equal Rights Amendment was approved by Congress in 1972 and submitted to the states for ratification. If ratified by three-fourths (38) of the states, this amendment would become the twenty-seventh amendment to the constitution two years after the final date of ratification. The states originally had seven years to complete the approval process. This was subsequently extended for two more years after approval was not granted by enough states during the original ratification period. In 1981, the amendment was still three states short of passage. The amendment itself consists of the following three sections:

> Section 1: Equality of rights under the law shall not be denied or abridged by the United States or by any State on account of sex.
> Section 2: The Congress shall have the power to enforce, by appropriate legislation, the provisions of this Article.
> Section 3: This amendment shall take effect two years after the date of ratification.

The effects of the ERA are subject to a number of misconceptions, including broken families and unisex toilets. The possibility of women being drafted into the armed forces and serving in combat is a subject of concern when there is talk about reviving the draft system. The U.S. Code might have to be rewritten, as the U.S. Civil Rights Commission has identified more than 800 sections as sex-biased. Other effects of a national ERA would probably be similar to what has happened in states that have written equal rights for women into their own constitutions. These effects include abolishing the assumption that all household goods belong to the husband and allowing wives to share control of family assets, providing women prisoners with rehabilitation programs previously available only to men, extension of rape laws to protect both men and women against sexual assault, and equal application of antiprostitution laws, which has resulted in the arrest of male patrons in some states.[7]

Administrative Structure

The Equal Employment Opportunity Commission. Established by the Civil Rights Act of 1964, the EEOC is a five-member commission (including the chairperson) appointed by the President with the advice and consent of the Senate. The responsibilities of the EEOC include: (1) issuing guidelines on employment discrimination, (2) investigating charges of discrimination, and (3) settling cases where discrimination exists through conciliation or, if necessary, litigation (see Exhibit 14.1). Prior to the 1972 Amendments to the Civil Rights Act, the EEOC could pursue cases where it found evidence of discrimination only through conciliation aimed at reaching an agreement between the parties concerned to eliminate aspects of discrimination revealed by the investigation. The 1972 Amendments gave the EEOC power to take a case to court itself if conciliation fails. Since that time, the number of

[7]"Evolution, not Revolution," *Time*, March 26, 1979, p. 25.

EXHIBIT 14.1

EQUAL EMPLOYMENT OPPORTUNITY COMMISSION
2401 E Street NW, Washington, D.C. 20506
Telephone: (202) 643-6930

Purpose: To enforce antidiscrimination provisions of the 1964 Civil Rights Act (Title VII) as regards discrimination based on race, sex, color, religion, or national origin in hiring, promotion, firing, wages, testing, training, apprenticeship, and all other conditions of employment.

Regulatory Activity: The EEOC (1) issues guidelines on employment discrimination, (2) investigates charges of discrimination and makes public its decisions, and (3) litigates non-compliance cases. (The U.S. Attorney General in the Department of Justice brings suit when a state government, governmental agency, or political subdivision is involved in a charge of employment discrimination.) Under Reorganization Plan No. 1 of 1978, EEOC is also responsible for all compliance and enforcement activities relating to equal employment opportunity among federal employees, including handicap discrimination.*

Established: 1964

Operational: July 2, 1965

Legislative Authority:
Enabling Legislation: Title VII of the Civil Rights Act of 1964 (78 Stat. 241), as amended by the Equal Employment Opportunity Act of 1972 (86 Stat. 103; P.L. 92-261) and by the Pregnancy Discrimination Act of 1978 (P.L. 95-555)
The EEOC is also responsible for the administration of:
Equal Pay Act of 1963 (77 Stat. 56), as amended
Age Discrimination in Employment Act of 1967 (81 Stat. 602), as amended
Rehabilitation Act of 1973 (87 Stat. 355)
Executive Orders relating to equal employment opportunity
Reorganization Plan No. 1 of 1978

Organization: This independent agency is headed by five commissioners who are appointed by the President with the advice and consent of the Senate.

*These EEO activities were transferred from the Civil Service Commission and the Department of Labor.

Budgets and Staffing
(Fiscal Years 1970-1981)

	70	71	72	73	74	75	76	77	78	79	(Estimated) 80	81
Budget ($ millions)	12	16	21	28	42	56	59	72	74	92	120	135
Staffing	780	910	1325	1909	2416	2384	2584	2487	2705	3752	3779	3891

From Ronald J. Penoyer, *Directory of Federal Regulatory Agencies,* 2nd ed. (St. Louis, Mo.: Washington University Center for the Study of American Business, 1980), p. 28. Reprinted with permission.

cases taken to court has substantially increased and the EEOC has established litigation centers around the country with a substantial legal staff to provide rapid and effective court action.

The EEOC has had a rather spotty history. It has had eight chairpersons, including acting chairperson Ethel Bent Walsh, over the course of its sixteen-year history. Some of these heads lasted less than a year, overwhelmed by the agency's problems. One of the major problems facing the agency is the huge backlog of unresolved cases it has managed to accumulate.[8] The chairperson during the Carter administration, Eleanor Holmes Norton, inherited a backlog of about 125,000 complaints. She generally won good marks for reducing this backlog through developing new charge processing systems rather than proceeding on a case-by-case basis, and by integrating some of the agency's litigation, investigation, and compliance functions. Some of these cases are so old that by the time they are investigated, the original complainant cannot even be found. The activities of the EEOC from 1975 to 1981 are shown in Figure 14.2.

In July 1979, a reorganization plan submitted by the President and approved by Congress transferred administration and enforcement of the Equal Pay Act and the Age Discrimination In Employment Act to the EEOC. These had formerly been the responsibility of the Wage-Hour Division of the Labor Department. The EEOC also has authority to require covered employers, employment agencies, and labor unions to keep and preserve records, and to file the following reports:

Figure 14.2. Equal Employment Opportunity Commission Activities

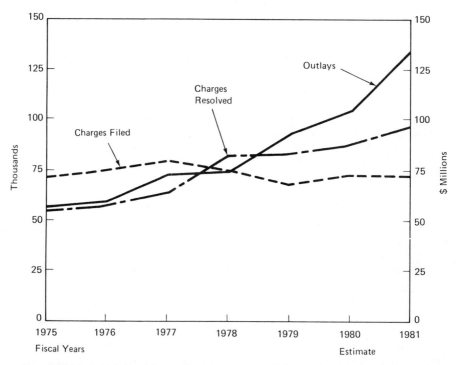

From *Special Analysis: Budget of the United States Government, Fiscal Year 1981* (Washington, D.C.: U.S. Government Printing Office, 1980), p. 295.

[8]See "EEOC: Has It Really Worked?" *Black Enterprise,* September 1977, pp. 21–24; Dorothy Rabinowitz, "The Bias in the Government's Anti-Bias Agency," *Fortune,* December, 1976, pp. 138–148.

- EEO-1 must be filed by all employers covered by Title VII that have 100 or more employees and by government contractors covered by Executive Order 11246 that have 50 or more employees and government contracts of $50,000 or more.
- EEO-2 must be filed annually by joint labor-management committees that have five or more trainees in their programs and at least one employer and union sponsor covered by Title VII.
- EEO-2-E must be filed annually by employers operating unilateral apprentice-ship programs. But programs with four or less apprentices need not be reported. The form must be filed by each employer who has a companywide employment of 100 or more employees and who conducts and controls an employer-operated apprenticeship program with four or more apprentices.
- EEO-3 must be filed annually by local unions that have 100 or more members at any time since the previous December 31. An international union is not required to file a report unless it operates a local union under a trusteeship or other arrangement.
- EEO-4 must be filed annually by state and local governmental jurisdictions with 100 or more employees.
- EEO-5 must be filed annually by public and secondary school systems, districts, and individual schools with 15 or more employees.
- EEO-6 must be filed biennially by every institution of higher learning with 15 or more employees.[9]

The Office of Federal Contract Compliance Programs. The OFCCP (formerly OFCC), which is located in the Labor Department, is responsible for administration of Executive Orders 11246 and 11375, the Rehabilitation Act of 1973, and the Vietnam Veterans Readjustment Assistance Act of 1974, all programs requiring equal employment opportunity and affirmative action by federal contractors and subcontractors. This compliance authority was consolidated in the OFCCP in 1978; previously, the Labor Department had shared this authority with eleven other governmental departments and agencies. The reason for this consolidation was to establish accountability, and to promote consistent standards, procedures, and reporting requirements.

The basic enforcement tool of the OFCCP is a comprehensive review process encompassing all aspects of a contractor's hiring and promotion policies for handicapped workers, veterans, minorities, and women. During 1980, the OFCCP was expected to carry out 7,000 such compliance actions. Some of these could result in the termination of government contracts (see box).

Implementation of Public Policy Measures Aimed at Providing Equal Employment Opportunity

The implementation of these public policy measures has been very difficult, given the nature of prejudice and the complexities involved in attempting to interpret the meaning of key concepts in the legislation and determining the intent of Congress in writing and passing legislation related

[9]Anderson, *Primer,* p. 108.

to equal opportunity. There are questions about affirmative action, reverse discrimination, retroactive seniority, pattern or practice cases, the meaning of equal pay for equal work, and testing procedures. These issues will be treated in this section.

UNIROYAL BARRED FROM HANDLING FEDERAL ORDERS

Move Results From Finding That Firm Discriminated Against Female Workers

By a *Wall Street Journal* Staff Reporter

WASHINGTON—Uniroyal Inc., the big tire and rubber manufacturer, was barred from doing business with the federal government as the result of a job-discrimination case.

Labor Secretary Ray Marshall barred Uniroyal from holding federal contracts after affirming a Labor Department hearing officer's finding that the company discriminated against female workers at its Mishawaka, Ind., plant. Mr. Marshall also affirmed the hearing officer's finding that the company violated its contractual obligations to the government by refusing to cooperate with an investigation into charges of discrimination at the company.

In New York, Uniroyal, which has about $40 million of government contracts, said it would file a motion in U.S. district court in Washington, for a temporary restraining order and a stay pending review of the Department of Labor's final administrative order. The company, whose 1978 sales totaled $2.7 billion, said it also will file in the same court for a declaratory judgment and review of the Secretary's debarment order.

The department's action was taken under a 1965 presidential order that prohibits companies doing business with the government from discriminating against workers on the basis of race or sex. A Labor Department official said Uniroyal is the largest government contractor to be barred from federal contracts under the order.

Military Contracts

According to Defense Department tallies, Uniroyal received $36.7 million in military contracts during the fiscal year ended Sept. 31, 1978. Labor Department officials said these represented the bulk of the company's federal contracts.

The Labor Department official said government agencies doing business with Uniroyal will be able to decide whether to terminate existing contracts with the company or to let them run to their normal expiration dates. These decisions will be based on whether terminating existing contracts would prove burdensome to the government, he said.

The case dates back to 1975, when the Labor Department's Office of Federal Contract Compliance Programs began an investigation into allegations of job bias at the Mishawaka plant. The office in July 1976 issued an administrative complaint against the company, charging that it failed to provide equal job opportunities to minority and female workers and that it favored male employes through a sex-segregated work force and in conducting layoffs and worker recalls.

Hearing Requested

According to documents in the case, the company then requested a hearing to present its side of the case but later refused to permit federal inspection of company records or to cooperate in allowing workers to be interviewed. Uniroyal unsuccessfully challenged in federal court many of the Labor Department's procedures for getting information from the company.

The company's actions during the information-gathering process prompted the hearing officer's recommendation that it be barred from federal contracts. Although his recommendation was based primarily on those actions, he also concluded that the company falsely claimed during these proceedings that it had ended certain discriminatory practices in 1968.

Thus, he said, findings of fact supported the allegation of discrimination.

Uniroyal has continued to assert that the allegations of discrimination aren't true. The company said that "the Secretary's final order doesn't address or find the company discriminated against its female employes at the Mishawaka plant." Rather, a spokesman said, "the order seeks to bar Uniroyal for not complying with the Department of Labor's pretrial discovery rules and regulations."

He said that the company's position on this matter is that the Labor Department "has exceeded the authority given to it by the Congress to make and enforce these rules and regulations and, therefore, the order should be set aside."

Labor Secretary Marshall was sued last week by 26 former and present female Uniroyal employes who charged that he had "violated his obligations as secretary" by delaying action on the hearing officer's recommendation. The recommendation was issued on April 11, 1978.

The Labor Department's action against Uniroyal came a day after the White House Council on Wage and Price Stability ruled that the company and three other rubber concerns are in "probable noncompliance" with President Carter's voluntary wage guideline.

The government said the companies faced losing their federal contracts if that determination survives final scrutiny, but some officials had expressed concern that indiscriminate termination of rubber-industry contracts could hurt the country's military preparedness.

From *The Wall Street Journal,* July 2, 1979, p. 6. Reprinted by permission of *The Wall Street Journal,* © Dow Jones & Company, Inc., 1979. All rights reserved.

Affirmative Action. The Civil Rights Act of 1964, taken literally, ruled out any form of preferential treatment, thus forbidding such devices as quotas, and seemed to treat discrimination as an intentional, deliberate act of exclusion. It ignored both the moral question of whether groups that had been discriminated against in the past were owed something more than simply an equal chance to complete with those who had benefited from discrimination, and the more practical question of how discriminated groups were supposed to get the education and experience necessary to qualify themselves for jobs—particularly those professional and managerial jobs that commanded the most money and status—without some kind of preferential treatment that would make up for deficiencies in education and experience that were the result of discrimination.

It was recognized early in the federal contracting procedure that a passive approach to implementing the concept of equal opportunity would not work. What was needed was some kind of an "affirmative action" program where positive steps would be taken to hire more minorities and women and promote them into better-paying positions. Federal contractors were required to analyze their workforce to determine where deficiencies existed, and then file an affirmative action plan with goals and timetables to show how these deficiencies were going to be corrected.

There are various approaches to affirmative action (see box), but the use of quotas became fairly widespread as the most useful device to ensure compliance with the executive order as applied to federal contracting. Eventually, the courts came to regard the Civil Rights Act as requiring similar procedures to implement the intent of Congress. The use of quota systems became a preferred means of correcting deficiencies where they were known to exist and to demonstrate to the government that a company was making a "good faith" effort to comply with equal rights legislation. Even though the guidelines for affirmative action programs speak about goals, the difference between goals and quotas is difficult to determine in practice.

TYPES OF AFFIRMATIVE ACTION PROGRAMS

1. *Passive nondiscrimination* involves a willingness, in all decisions about hiring, promotion, and pay, to treat the races and sexes alike. However, this posture may involve a failure to recognize that past discrimination leaves many prospective employees unaware of present opportunities.

2. *Pure affirmative action* involves a concerted effort to expand the pool of applicants so that no one is excluded because of past or present discrimination. At the point of decision, however, the company hires (or promotes) whoever seems most qualified, without regard to race or sex.

3. *Affirmative action with preferential hiring.* In this posture, the company not only ensures that it has a larger labor pool to draw from but systematically favors women and minority groups in the actual decisions about hiring. This might be thought of as a "soft" quota system, i.e., instead of establishing targets that absolutely must be met, the top officers of the company beef up employment of women and minority-group members to some unspecified extent by indicating that they want those groups given a break.

4. *Hard quotas.* No two ways about it—specific numbers or proportions of minority-group members must be hired.

From Daniel Seligman, "How Equal Opportunity Turned Into Employment Quotas," *FORTUNE*, March 1973, p. 162.

The difficulty of proving intent to discriminate is obvious. One would have to find some internal memoranda that clearly indicated race or sex was a factor in the employment decision or find someone who was in on the decision who would testify in court to that effect. It is much easier to infer that discrimination exists from the composition of the workforce, by comparing the percentage of minorities and women employed overall with some relevant population parameter such as the percentage of minorities or women in the labor force from which the company could be expected to draw its employees and by comparing the percentage of minorities and women in various occupational categories within the company itself. Where there was an obvious lack of women or minorities in the total workforce, or where they were obviously concentrated in lower-paying occupations, discrimination was inferred to exist. The best way to correct these deficiencies was through the use of a quota system, which in effect gave preferential treatment to women and minorities to bring them up to some kind of statistical parity. The assumption behind this approach, of course, is that skills and abilities are randomly distributed throughout the population.

This result-oriented approach was upheld by a Supreme Court decision that not only dealt with the effects of certain hiring practices rather than intent, but also had implications for testing procedures. In *Griggs v. Duke Power Co.*, the Supreme Court upheld the EEOC and overruled a court of appeals decision.[10] The Duke Power Company had been requiring applicants for certain jobs to have a high school diploma and also to score at a certain level in an aptitude test. The effect of this procedure was to disqualify black applicants at a higher rate than white applicants. The company argued that it was using these standards to improve the overall quality of its labor force, but it could not demonstrate that these standards had a direct relationship to job performance. The Supreme Court ruled that such an action or policy, while neutral on its face, was discriminating in effect unless there was a substantial business justification for the policy. There was no contention that Duke Power had intended to discriminate, but the focus was on the effect of the policy. The burden was placed on the company to show that a requirement of employment had a manifest relationship to the employment in question.

Thus the concepts of equal opportunity and affirmative action are not the same. Equal employment opportunity means that everyone gets an equal chance at a job or promotion. Affirmative action implies a set of specific result-oriented procedures designed to achieve equal employment opportunity at a pace beyond that which would occur normally. The objective of an affirmative action program is to achieve within a reasonable period of time an employee workforce which in all major occupational categories reflects the makeup of the relevant external labor market. Affirmative action programs establish specific goals (quotas) and timetables designed to accomplish this objective.

Reverse Discrimination. The widespread use of goals or quotas to implement affirmative action meant that inevitably reverse discrimination would be a factor. This phenomenon occurs when a minority or a woman is equally qualified with a white male and is given preference over the latter for a job or promotion, or where quotas resulted in hiring minorities or women who are actually less qualified than white male applicants for the same position. While the phenomenon was tolerated for a while, cases of reverse discrimination began to receive attention, and eventually the courts began to rule that civil rights laws applied to whites as well as blacks and preferential treatment was a violation of these laws.

One of the first cases of this kind was brought by two white employees of the Santa Fe Trail Transportation Co. who were accused of misappropriating a shipment of antifreeze and subsequently fired. A black worker, who was also accused of being involved in the misappropriation, was retained. The Supreme Court ruled against this procedure, stating that the 1964 Civil Rights Act banned employment discrimination against whites as well as blacks.[11]

[10]*Griggs v. Duke Power Co.*, 401 U.S. 424 (1971).
[11]*McDonald v. Santa Fe Trail Transportation Co.*, 427 U.S. 273 (1976).

Then a lower court ordered AT&T to pay damages to a male employee who was passed over for promotion in favor of a less experienced woman with lower seniority.[12] This promotion had apparently been made to fulfill the terms of a 1973 federal consent decree in which AT&T agreed to hire and promote thousands of women and minorities into jobs previously held mostly by white males. The male employee bringing the suit alleged that he had suffered sex discrimination when he was denied a promotion. Federal Judge Gerhard A. Gesell agreed and awarded damages to the employee. He stated that AT&T "relied upon and properly applied the consent decree" in promoting the woman but that Mr. McAleer, the male employee who was passed over, was "an innocent employee who had earned promotion." The judge felt that the courts should attempt to protect innocent employees by placing this burden on the wrongdoing employer wherever possible. Thus, he concluded, "AT&T should bear the principal burden of rectifying its previous discriminatory conduct. An affirmative award of some damages on a rough justice basis is therefore required and will constitute an added cost which the stockholders of AT&T must bear." Rather than appeal this decision, AT&T settled out of court to prevent this ruling from becoming a legal precedent that could be used by other passed-over employees.[13]

Next, the California Supreme Court, in a six-to-one ruling, banned minority quotas in the graduate schools of California's state university system.[14] The case was brought by Allan Bakke, who contended that he was denied admission to the medical school at the University of California's Davis campus in 1973 and 1974 because of reverse discrimination. Of the 100 openings for entering classes in those two years, 84 places went to those selected by normal admissions standards, which emphasized college grades and entrance examination scores. The other 16 openings were filled under an admissions program giving preference to nonwhite applicants.

The university acknowledged that it admitted minority applicants it rated substantially below Bakke. The court said the medical school's reserved places for minority students who did not necessarily score as high as white students violated the constitution's Fourteenth Amendment guarantees of equal protection to all persons regardless of race. Universities could consider factors other than grades and test scores in admitting students—such as the needs of society—but without regard to race. The University of California appealed this ruling to the U.S. Supreme Court, which agreed to hear the case. Many people thought the country would finally have a definitive ruling on preferential treatment and reverse discrimination.

Such a definitive ruling, however, was not the result. The court split five-to-four on the decision, which essentially had two parts.[15] On the one hand, the court affirmed by a five-to-four margin the lower court order admitting Bakke to medical school at the University of California at Davis, because its special admissions program for minorities did violate Title VI of

[12]*Daniel McAleer and Local #2350, Communications Workers of America v. American Telephone and Telegraph Co.,* 416 F. Supp. 435 (1976).

[13]Carol J. Loomis, "AT&T in the Throes of Equal Employment," *Fortune,* January 15, 1979, p. 56.

[14]*Allan Bakke v. the Regents of the University of California,* 553 P.2d 1152 (1976).

[15]*Regents of the University of California v. Bakke,* 98 S. Ct. 2733 (1978).

the Civil Rights Act of 1964, which forbade racial discrimination in any program or activity receiving federal financial assistance. Quotas based entirely on race where no previous discrimination had been found were held to be illegal. This provision left open the use of quotas to correct deficiencies as part of a settlement where previous discrimination had been found.

On the other hand, a majority of the court, again by a five-to-four margin, with Justice Lewis Powell being the swing vote in both cases, ruled that a university could continue to take race into consideration in admissions. Exactly how this was to be done was unstated, but Justice Powell referred to the admissions policies at Harvard as a possible model. Race is a factor that is considered at Harvard along with geographical location or athletic or artistic ability. Other factors Justice Powell mentioned that could be considered along with race included unique work or service experience, leadership potential, maturity, demonstrated compassion, or a history of overcoming disadvantage.[16]

The Justices of the Supreme Court wrote six different opinions, reflecting their own diversity as well as that of the nation as a whole. This case attracted more briefs than any other case that had ever been considered by the Court. Yet the decision was hardly the landmark decision many had hoped for—the court ruled narrowly and delicately, trying to find a middle ground. The decision was not definitive, and left room for further development, which on the whole may have been a positive approach to such a complex situation.

The last case to deal with this issue was the so-called Weber case, in which an employee of Kaiser Aluminum and Chemical Corporation sued his employer and the Steelworkers Union, claiming that he had been illegally excluded from a training program for higher-paying skilled jobs in which half the places had been reserved for minorities. The Fifth Circuit Court of Appeals agreed with Weber, observing that the quota system used by the company improperly favored blacks who had not been the subject of prior unlawful discrimination.[17] The Supreme Court disagreed, however, and by a five-to-two vote ruled that employers can give blacks special preference for jobs that had traditionally been all white.[18] Whether or not it has had discriminatory job practices in the past, the Court said, a company can use affirmative action programs of this type to remedy "manifest racial imbalance" without fear of being challenged in these efforts by the courts. Thus, the Supreme Court backed job preference programs for minorities that had been voluntarily set up and were not the result of a previous settlement.[19] This ruling was consistent with EEOC guidelines issued in 1978 dealing with affirmative action programs.

Last In, First Out. While affirmative action programs have been helpful in getting minorities and females into jobs, during a recession the problem becomes one of keeping them in jobs they may have only recently acquired. Because of the last in, first out (LIFO) principle, many of the gains that minorities and women may have made during prosperous times are wiped out by a declining economy. The issue here, of course, is one of seniority.

---

[16]"Bakke Wins, Quotas Lose," *Time*, July 10, 1978, p. 11.

[17]*Weber v. Kaiser Aluminum Corp.*, 563 F.2d 216 (5th Cir. 1977).

[18]*United Steelworkers of America v. Weber*, 99 S. Ct. 2721 (1979).

[19]"What the Weber Ruling Does," *Time*, July 9, 1979, p. 48.

Should retroactive seniority be granted to women or minorities or some kind of a quota system be adopted for layoffs so the effects of a declining economy are spread across all groups? Or do women and blacks without seniority have no protection?

Section 703(h) of Title VII seems to exempt bona fide seniority systems and insulate them from discrimination charges, even though the system may be discriminatory in effect. The courts have upheld this exemption as long as the system is not a guise for unlawful discrimination.

One of the first cases dealing with seniority involved black truck drivers who were hired for city driving only and were kept there because of a discriminatory transfer policy that prevented them from transferring to over-the-road trucking. Finding that blacks had been denied over-the-road jobs because of this discriminatory policy, the Supreme Court held that granting retroactive seniority back to the date of application was an appropriate remedy.[20]

In 1977, the Supreme Court added some qualifications to the doctrine. In the Teamsters Case, the Court ruled that even if a seniority system perpetuated pre-act or even post-act discrimination, its bona fide status was not affected.[21] Section 703(h) immunizes all bona fide seniority systems. The key as to whether a system is bona fide is whether or not it was adopted without a discriminatory motive. This doctrine was upheld in another case involving an employee who was discharged and later rehired, and then sued to obtain seniority back to the date of her original employment even though the seniority system of the company was based solely on current employment. She was originally discharged because of the company's policy of not hiring married stewardesses, a policy that was later abandoned, enabling her to be rehired. The court, however, again said that the seniority system was bona fide and insulated from attack.[22] Lower courts have applied the same interpretation to the application of executive orders, which may not be interpreted as making a bona fide seniority system unlawful.[23]

Thus the LIFO principle seems to apply in the case of layoffs, and seniority systems that may in effect discriminate are legitimate. Nothing like an affirmative action program on the layoff end of the employment cycle can be adopted. Unions, of course, are not going to give up hard-won seniority provisions to keep new employees on the payroll. But civil rights advocates claim that the Weber decision allows companies and unions to change the seniority system without fearing charges of reverse discrimination. About 75 percent of the nation's workforce is not covered by union contracts, however, and companies not involved with unions are not legally bound to use seniority as a basis for layoffs. If layoffs in these companies are shown to be discriminatory in effect, they may be open to charges of discrimination.

Pattern or Practice Cases. The Civil Rights Act of 1964 gave the Attorney General authority to seek an injunction when he had "reasonable cause" to believe that a "pattern or practice" of discrimination existed in an organization subject to Title VII of the Civil Rights Act. The 1972 amendment to

[20]*Harold Franks v. Bowman Transportation Co.*, 419 U.S. 1050 (1976).

[21]*Teamsters v. U.S.* (T.I.M.E.–D.C., Inc.), 14 FEP Cases 1514 (1977).

[22]*United Airlines v. Evans*, 14 FEP Cases 1510 (1973).

[23]Anderson, *Primer*, p. 87.

Title VII transferred this authority to the EEOC, which became effective two years later. This transfer gives the EEOC sweeping authority to investigate discrimination throughout an entire company and file suit against the company if it finds sufficient evidence of systemic discrimination. This procedure is much broader in attacking discrimination than a case by case approach, and the settlements much more complex and major in their impact on the company.

The first case of this kind involved AT&T, the nation's largest private employer. After investigating the company, the EEOC alleged that women were represented only at the bottom levels of the company and that equal pay problems also existed. After more than two years of negotiation, the company entered into a consent decree which was signed on January 18, 1973. This decree did not require AT&T to confess that it had violated any laws or practiced discrimination. Compliance with the decree would put the company in compliance with Title VII and the OFCC's revised Order No. 4, thus wrapping up all government equal-employment actions outstanding against the company. The decree required AT&T to pay compensatory damages to women and minorities where there was a possibility of discrimination (possibility because the company did not admit discrimination) and to make sweeping changes in its hiring and promotion practices to advance the cause of women and minorities. Specifically, the agreement required the company to do the following:

> Approximately $15 million—by far the largest single back pay award ever made—in one-time payments to thousands of employees charged to have suffered from discriminatory employment practices.
>
> An additional estimated $50 million in yearly payments for promotion and wage adjustments to minority and female employees.
>
> Affirmative actions to include:
>
> > Specific hiring and promotion targets, including goals to significantly increase utilization of women and minorities in every job classification. These targets will be reviewed regularly by EEOC and the Office of Federal Contract Compliance.
> >
> > Goals for employing males in previously all-female jobs.
> >
> > Women and minorities now in nonmanagement noncraft jobs will be able to compete for craft jobs based on their qualifications and company seniority.
> >
> > Promoted employees will be paid, generally, on the basis of their length of service.
> >
> > All female college graduates hired since 1965 will be assessed to determine interest and potential for higher level jobs and a specific development program will prepare these women for promotions[24]

This decree involved goals and timetables, and a controversial override provision to allow preferential treatment of women and minorities and override the seniority provisions of the union contract. Under terms of the override, "AT&T became obliged, when satisfaction of its targets required the deed to be done, to override the provisions of the union contract and promote a basically qualified person rather than the one best qualified or

---

[24]U.S. Equal Employment Opportunity Commission, *Affirmative Action and Equal Employment,* Vol. 1, pp. 10–11.

most senior."[25] The definition of basically qualified varied from job to job, but tended to apply to a person performing satisfactorily in his or her present job and who could pass various tests.

In mid-1975, a supplemental order was signed because of allegations by the decree oversight body, called the Government Coordinating Committee, that many managers in the company had not taken the decree seriously. This order required AT&T to make up most of its deficiencies in meeting targets approved in the original decree and do it in ways that would produce fast results. After that, AT&T became a superachiever.[26] The decree finally expired in January 1979, when the GCC informed the U.S. District Court in Philadelphia that the Bell system operating companies were found to be in substantial compliance with the original decree (see box).

Other such pattern and practice agreements were reached with the major steel companies and General Electric Company. The latter settlement was one of five such complaints issued by the EEOC in 1973, one being issued against Sears Roebuck and Company which is currently being pursued in the courts.[27] More such companywide complaints came in 1979, as the EEOC increased the staff in what it calls its systemic charge processing system. The head of EEOC estimated that each of the twenty-two district offices should be able to file one such companywide or systemic complaint a month.[28]

Equal Pay for Equal Work. The Equal Pay Act made it unlawful for an employer to pay wages "at a rate less than the rate at which he pays employees of the opposite sex in such establishments for equal work on jobs the performance of which require equal skill, effort, and responsibility, and which are performed under similar working conditions."[29] Thus skill, effort, responsibility, and working conditions were tests to be applied in judging the equality of work. Equal work did not mean, however, that jobs had to be identical or performed with the same frequency. The controlling factor in applying the equal pay standard was job content—actual job requirements and performance—not job titles or classifications.

Perhaps a case will help to clarify the meaning of this standard. Several years ago, Northwest Airlines was found guilty of violating the law by a federal appeals court in Washington.[30] The airline had been paying its 137 male cabin pursers 20 percent to 55 percent more than its 1,746 female stewardesses. The men also received such fringe benefits as a laundry allowance for their uniforms and better hotel rooms than the women. The court held that despite the differences in job classification, there were no essential differences in duties between the job of purser and stewardess.[31]

After some years of civil rights laws, however, there is still a great disparity between the median incomes of men and women, primarily because women are still channeled into lower-paying jobs, such as secretarial or clerical work.

[25]Loomis, "AT&T," p. 48.

[26]*Ibid.*, p. 50.

[27]See Lawrence J. Teel, "EEOC's Secret Struggle with Sears," *Business and Society Review*, No. 30 (Summer 1979), pp. 29–34.

[28]"Firing Up the Attack on Job Bias," *Business Week*, June 25, 1979, p. 64.

[29]Anderson, *Primer*, p. 65.

[30]*Laffey v. Northwest Airlines*, 13 FEP Cases 1068 (1970).

[31]Lee Smith, "The EEOC's Bold Foray into Job Evaluation," *Fortune*, September 11, 1978, p. 59.

AT&T HAS COMPLIED WITH ANTIBIAS DECREE
U.S. ATTORNEYS SAY

By a *Wall Street Journal* Staff Reporter

WASHINGTON—Government civil-rights attorneys said American Telephone & Telegraph Co. has "substantially complied" with the anti-discrimination provisions of a 1973 consent decree and recommended against any extension of the decree.

The recommendation was made in a "final report" on AT&T's compliance with the decree filed with the federal district court in Philadelphia. Because the government plaintiffs—the Labor Department, the Equal Employment Opportunity Commission and the Justice Department—argued against extending the decree. It expired late last night.

The report offered statistical evidence of what it termed "substantial progress" by AT&T and its 23 operating units in reducing job discrimination based on sex, race or ethnic factors. Women currently hold 28.5% of all management jobs in the Bell system compared with 22.4% in 1973, the report said. The percentage of top management jobs held by women has risen to 6.9% from 2.1% in 1973, and the percentage of craft jobs held by women has jumped to 9.5% from 2.8% over the six-year period of the decree, it added. The most dramatic increase in women's employment was in outside-the-office craft jobs, where the percentage of women jumped to 4% from 0.2%.

According to the report, total employment of blacks by the Bell system increased to 12% from 10.6%, and their representation in management jobs increased to 5.5% from 2.2%. Hispanic employment increased to 3.9% of the Bell system's total from 2.5%, and their share of management jobs increased to 2.1% from 0.7%, it said.

The report stated that to meet its obligations under the decree, the Bell system has made more than $12 million in one-time payments to employees who suffered discrimination and has spent more than $40 million on other pay adjustments.

"The consent decree didn't solve all of the equal employment opportunity problems within the Bell system operating companies," the report cautioned. But it said any continuing problems "wouldn't constitute a violation of the decree." The report also noted that the Bell system's gains in utilizing minorities in positions where they were previously subject to discrimination might have been greater if total employment had increased at the operating companies.

The consent decree, which has signed Jan. 18, 1973, settled a discrimination suit. The decree was hailed as the most far-reaching corporate civil-rights agreement ever negotiated. Since then, periodic compliance reports have indicated gains similar to those the government cited in its final report on the case.

One way to correct this situation would be for women to step into higher-paying jobs, a process that is taking place, albeit very slowly. A faster way of reducing this gap would be to stretch the meaning of the equal pay standard to mean equal pay for work of comparable worth.[32]

[32]*Ibid.*, pp. 58–59.

Women's groups argue that job evaluation systems themselves are discriminatory, that jobs held primarily by women, such as secretarial and electronics assembly positions, are just as important to a company as jobs held primarily by men, such as supervision, engineering, sales, and the like. Thus these traditional women's jobs should receive equal pay because they are of equal worth. Rather than let the market determine pay scales, jobs ought to be evaluated according to their intrinsic worth, a concept with social as well as economic meaning.[33]

Such a concept, if implemented, would have quite an impact on the way jobs are evaluated and pay scales developed. Content would be rejected as the basis for pay differentials and worth would be substituted. Presently, the EEOC has commissioned the National Academy of Sciences to study whether it is feasible and desirable to develop job evaluation systems that are "fair, objective, comprehensive, and bias-free." If the report is favorable, the EEOC will then presumably develop a system of job evaluation and induce all businesses to adhere to it and pay employees accordingly.[34]

Testing. Under Title VII, it is not unlawful "for an employer to give and to act upon the results of any professionally developed ability test, provided that such test, its administration or action upon the results is not designed, intended, or used to discriminate because of race, color, religion, sex, or national origin."[35]

The standards the EEOC developed in its first years for validating tests, however, were very difficult to meet, so much so that many companies abandoned testing programs entirely. The Supreme Court ruling in *Griggs v. Duke Power Co.* stated that any test having an adverse effect on women or minority-group applicants must be job related, whether or not the employer intended to discriminate. The burden of proof was on the employer to prove job relatedness.

The same position is maintained in the Uniform Guidelines on Employee Selection Procedures issued in 1978, a 14,000 word catalogue of do's and dont's for hiring and promotion. These guidelines use a four-fifths rule of thumb to determine what adverse impact is significant: if the company can show that it hires members of minority groups or women at a rate at least 80 percent of the rate at which it hires from the group that provides most of its employees (usually white males) the federal government will let it alone.[36] As to whether each step of the selection procedure must be studied for adverse impact, or whether employers will be judged on the final overall tally (referred to as the bottom line), the guidelines say: "If . . . the total selection process for a job has no adverse impact, the federal enforcement agencies . . . generally will not take enforcement action based upon adverse impact of any component of that process. . . ."[37]

If the company's hiring rate is below 80 percent for minorities and

---

[33]D. Quinn Mills, "Human Resources in the 1980s," *Harvard Business Review,* Vol. 57, No. 4 (July–August 1979), p. 157.

[34]Smith, "EEOC's Bold Foray," p. 60.

[35]Anderson, *Primer,* p. 16.

[36]Lee Smith, "Equal Opportunity Rules Are Getting Tougher," *Fortune,* June 19, 1978, pp. 152–153.

[37]Anderson, *Primer,* p. 18.

women, it may be asked to prove that its screening procedures are related to the job that has to be performed. There are three methods of validating tests to be sure they are job related. The new guidelines allow all three methods to be used, with some restrictions on the use of construct validity validation. These three methods are:

- By conducting a study to determine if those who do well on the test also do well on the job, and if those who do poorly on the test do poorly on the job. This is called "criterion-related validity."
- By determining that it is a representative sample of important or critical job behaviors, such as a typing test used to hire a typist. This is called "content validity."
- By showing that it measures the degree to which candidates have identifiable characteristics which have been determined to be important for successful job performance, such as a test for emotional stability used to hire a police officer. This is called "construct validity."[38]

In addition, companies are required to show that no other procedures could have been used which would have been just as effective in selecting suitable employees and yet not have as much adverse impact on minorities or women. This is known as a "cosmic search," and the question facing employers is how far they have to go in searching for alternative selection procedures. Companies are encouraged, however, to form consortiums where they have similar job classifications and devise tests to be used throughout the industry or even to be extended to other industries.[39]

Other Forms of Discrimination

While race and sex discrimination have received the most attention, there are, of course, other forms of discrimination, two of which are receiving increasing attention. In the 1972 amendments to Title VII, Congress added a definition of religion to aid the courts in applying the prohibition of discrimination because of religion. The definition states:

The term "religion" includes all aspects of religious observance and practice, as well as belief, unless an employer demonstrates that he is unable to reasonably accommodate to the employee's or prospective employee's religious observance or practice without undue hardship on the conduct of the employer's business.[40]

A key Supreme Court case in 1977 introduced a great deal of confusion into this area of interpretation. The case involved Larry G. Hardison and Trans World Airlines.[41] Hardison was a member of the Worldwide Church of God, whose day of worship was Saturday. The court said that TWA could not be required to violate a seniority provision in its collective bargaining agreement with its union to accommodate Hardison's refusal to work on Saturdays. Nor could TWA be expected to pay overtime wages on a regular

[38]*Ibid.*
[39]Smith, "Equal Opportunity," p. 154.
[40]Anderson, *Primer*, p. 42.
[41]*Trans World Airlines, Inc. v. Hardison,* 14 FEP Cases 1697 (1977).

basis to another employee or create a serious shortage of necessary employees in another department.

Thus the right to refuse to work on Saturdays because of religious reasons was struck down by the Court. This ruling led to many problems for Seventh Day Adventists and others whose religion prohibited them from working on Saturdays. Subsequent investigations by the EEOC encountered a number of other religious practices that were not respected by employers. These included the following:

- The frequent prayer breaks required by some religions, notably Islam.
- Dietary requirements that might require that an employee have access to a kitchen.
- Extended periods of mourning for a deceased relative.
- Prohibition against medical examinations, which are usually required by a prospective employer to limit his liability for workman's compensation claims.
- Practices regarding dress or other personal grooming habits.[42]

The EEOC has proposed a set of guidelines to afford protection for these practices. One controversial aspect of the guidelines is that religion is defined so broadly as to invite abuse. Critics argue the guidelines would protect smoking marijuana before lunch, listening to inspirational music at all times, burning incense at one's desk, and other such practices. The agency considers religious practices to include "moral or ethical beliefs as to what is right and wrong, which are sincerely held with the strength of traditional religious views."[43]

The proposed guidelines would also put the burden on the employer to accommodate an employee's religious practices. The employer would be required to "explore all possible methods of reasonable accommodation." The guidelines make it a violation to fail to accommodate the practice unless the method of accommodation "would result in undue hardship," which is left undefined. The guidelines would also prohibit an employer from asking a job applicant whether he or she would be available to work at all times as well as allow a person who has religious objections to joining a labor union to escape membership by devoting a sum equal to the union dues to a charity.[44]

Handicapped discrimination is also receiving increasing attention, as the OFCCP is stepping up its enforcement of the Vocational Rehabilitation Act. A recent survey by the Labor Department found that 91 percent of businesses were not in compliance. These findings elicited a great deal of criticism from businesspeople and vocational rehabilitation specialists as well as from the handicapped people themselves and their advocates. In 1977, close to $750,000 was received in settlements nationwide and in 1978, six major contractors were cited for violations. Some people believe these efforts indicate that employment of the handicapped will be a major issue in society as well as a focus of increasing government attention.[45]

[42]Martha Shirk, "Religion at Work: EEOC Tackles Growing Problem of Bias," *St. Louis Post-Dispatch*, January 31, 1980, p. 30.

[43]*Ibid.*

[44]*Ibid.*

[45]Gopal C. Pati and John I. Adkins, Jr., "Hire The Handicapped—Compliance Is Good Business," *Harvard Business Review*, Vol. 58, No. 1 (January–February 1980), pp. 14–22.

Thus not only are minorities and women the object of concern regarding employment discrimination, but other groups are receiving increasing attention as well. An interesting question concerns how far society wants to go in identifying groups that experience some kind of discrimination. Many groups could claim they have been discriminated against in one way or another and deserve some kind of attention—left-handed people, fat people (see box), short people, and others. As long as groups of people have certain characteristics that constitute some kind of deficiency as far as competing in the marketplace is concerned (at least a deficiency as perceived by the group controlling the marketplace and making decisions about qualifications for employment opportunities), some kind of discrimination is likely to be found.

Impact on Personnel Policies

The impact on the employment practices of employers has been enormous. As can readily be seen, if an employer sincerely wants to implement equal opportunity in his or her workplace, the questions that need to be considered are endless. The composition of the workforce in any company is less and less a function of the marketplace where all one had to worry about was qualifications for the job, and more and more a function of public policy where one must ask questions about discriminatory intent in making decisions about qualifications, and discriminatory effect in looking at the results of employment decisions. One must strive for some kind of racial and sexual balance in the overall workforce and across occupational categories, unless there are bona fide occupational qualifications that justify otherwise, to be in compliance and avoid potential lawsuits.

But in many cases an employer must find himself or herself between a rock and a hard place, with no clear guidelines as to what path to take. Designing an affirmative action program to meet all the requirements that now exist as a matter of public policy would seem to be impossible. Indeed this is what Sears Roebuck and Company claimed in a class action lawsuit it filed against ten federal agencies, including the EEOC. Sears contended that contradictory government policies made it impossible for employers to follow all the guidelines. The government forced employers to favor white males through veteran preference laws, Sears said as an example, but now accuses employers of discriminating against women and minorities. Thus conflicting federal policies and poor statistical data frustrated the firm's efforts to comply with EEOC laws.[46] This suit has since been dismissed in federal court (see box).

Various suggestions have been made to help employers in designing affirmative action programs. To cope with white male backlash, Rosen and Jerdee suggest that managers (1) reappraise affirmative action policies and practices periodically to insure that guidelines established to create opportunities for one group do not unfairly discriminate against other groups, (2) survey employees' reactions to affirmative action to pinpoint units or de-

---

[46]"Sears Roebuck Charges U.S. Actions Hurt Firm's Efforts to Hire Women, Minorities," *The Wall Street Journal,* January 25, 1979, p. 2.

BUDDING MOVEMENT IS SEEKING TO STOP
'FAT DISCRIMINATION'

Group Says Society Penalizes Obese People, Especially When It Comes to Hiring

By Robert N. Webner
Staff Reporter of *The Wall Street Journal*

When Joyce English walked into an interview at Philadelphia Electric Co. on a brisk spring day in 1977, she hoped to walk out with a job. She was unemployed, and a harsh winter had gobbled up her meager savings. "I needed to work to make ends meet," she says.

But Miss English flunked a physical examination when she tipped the scales at more than 300 pounds. The company rejected her application.

"I was really heartbroken to find that weight could reflect on my ability," she recalls.

Then Miss English began to get angry. On April 26, 1977, she took her case to the Pennsylvania Human Rights Commission, charging Philadelphia Electric with "fat discrimination" under a state law protecting the rights of the handicapped. The commission held a hearing last August, and attorneys for both sides are to submit briefs in the next few weeks. A decision may be rendered before the year-end.

Fat-Rights Movement

Miss English is a pioneer in a budding fat-rights movement. The movement hasn't got very far yet, mostly because people expect a punch line when they first hear about it. But to many of the estimated 65 million overweight Americans, being fat isn't a laughing matter. They argue that society is penalizing them merely for their shape, and some are trying to convince America that fat isn't bad.

"If anyone is treated as handicapped, it's fat people," says Lisbeth Fisher, the 270-pound executive secretary of the National Association to Aid Fat Americans, a nonprofit organization with 2,000 members. "Fat people don't want to be considered handicapped but if that is our only chance to gain equality, we'll take it."

This inequality is most evident in the employment area. Companies say they have good reasons for refusing to hire or promote fat people. For many jobs that involve physical labor or that require an employe to stand all day, thin people tend to perform better than fat employes. For jobs that require a great deal of contact with the public, thin people get better results than fat people. And ultimately, the companies say, thin people aren't as big a health risk as fat people.

Most companies, including Philadelphia Electric, use charts developed by insurance companies to determine who's overweight. Philadelphia Electric, in its defense against Miss English's discrimination charge, contends that by using the charts, it is able to judge potential employes' health. The company adds that some obese applicants who were rejected have lost weight and later been accepted.

Legal Precedent

The companies also have legal precedent on their side. In 1973 a federal judge in Florida ruled that companies' weight standards aren't discriminatory because it is reasonable to conclude that obese people are "more likely to become disabled during employment." And in 1975 the Wisconsin Labor and Industry Review Commission ruled that a fat individual who sought a job at a

Milwaukee company wasn't handicapped because his weight was within his control rather than, for instance, the result of a glandular problem.

Still, there have been a few successes for the fat-rights movement. Recent television exposure has given it publicity, and clothing manufacturers are beginning to market more king-sized fashions.

The most encouraging development so far is a five-year study of fat discrimination in Maryland that began last year. The resolution establishing the study urges "work toward ending all unjust discriminatory practices against fat people," Fat-rights advocates hope other states will follow Maryland's lead.

partments where negative reactions are particularly intense and to identify areas where improved communication about the affirmative action policy is needed, (3) increase understanding and awareness of the legal and social issues surrounding an affirmative action program, and (4) involve employees in the development and revision of affirmative action guidelines.[47]

In an article entitled "Affirmative Action and Guilt-Edged Goals," Neil Churchill and John Shank argue that instead of analyzing past and planned rates of hiring and promoting women and minority group males as a basis for setting goals, management should use a model that shows the "flow" of women and minority group men through each management level. "Such a model," they state, "may suggest quite different answers from those provided by conventional methods of analysis."[48] The former method is a "balance sheet" approach that looks at cumulative hiring and promotion performance, while the latter is more of a "flow of funds," or more appropriately, a "flow of people" approach. Thus, they conclude, "the phrase employment opportunity should be defined in terms of current hiring rates and current promotion rates rather than in terms of the current management mix."[49]

Alice G. Sargent, writing in the *University of Michigan Business Review*, argues for a total systems approach to affirmative action. Most affirmative action programs during the past decade have focused on the victim of discrimination, which has the potential for increasing the negative self-image of the disadvantaged person and evoking guilt and frustration from white male managers. Furthermore, such efforts are designed to take minorities and women into the white male mainstream without doing much to question the mainstream system itself. What is needed, she argues, is a reappraisal and restructuring of the corporation to include values that are feminine as well as masculine and minority as well as majority. Rather than socializing minorities and women into white male managerial styles, it may be time to socialize white male managers into alternate management styles.[50]

[47]Benson Rosen and Thomas H. Jerdee, "Coping with Affirmative Action Backlash," *Business Horizons,* Vol. 54, No. 2 (March–April 1976), p. 111.

[48]Neil C. Churchill and John K. Shank, "Affirmative Action and Guilt-Edged Goals," *Harvard Business Review,* Vol. 54, No. 2 (March–April 1976), p. 111.

[49]*Ibid.,* p. 116.

[50]Alice G. Sargent, "Affirmative Action: Total Systems Change," *University of Michigan Business Review,* Vol. XXX, No. 5 (September 1978), pp. 18–19.

In another article, Arnold R. Deutsch points out the importance of practicing affirmative action in company communications.[51] And so it goes. There is no end of suggestions on how to design and implement affirmative action programs. Nonetheless, the management task remains difficult in view of the shifting policies of the EEOC and OFCCP, conflicting or confusing court rulings, the pressure from women's and civil rights groups, and the changing attitudes of employees. All of these ambiguities reflect the ambiguities about equal employment opportunity that are in the society at large.

Results

The results of all this effort to promote equal employment opportunity are inconclusive. Some studies based on the last census showed that the median family income of blacks remained about 55 percent to 60 percent of white family income and that the unemployment rate of black males was still about twice that of white males, with the gap in teenage unemployment even worse. While some blacks may have benefited from affirmative action programs and moved into the middle class, many are left behind to constitute a significant underclass in severe deprivation.[52] Other studies showed that even though more and more women were entering the labor force, the median income of women as a percentage of median income of men went

[51] Arnold R. Deutsch, "Does Your Company Practice Affirmative Action in Its Commnications," *Harvard Business Review*, Vol. 54, No. 6 (November–December 1976), pp. 16, 188.

[52] U.S. Department of Commerce, Bureau of the Census, *The Social and Economic Status of the Black Population in the United States* (Washington, D.C.: U.S. Government Printing Office, 1975).

down because women still tended to be concentrated in the lower-paying jobs (less rank and more file).[53]

Still other studies indicate that opportunities for black executives are increasing[54] and that women are shaking up the workforce, with even more changes to come as business schools graduate more and more women with MBA degrees (see box). Perhaps the next census will show much more progress toward the goal of equal opportunity. One suspects, however, that much depends on the state of the economy, and that to some extent, the progress of minorities and women varies with the growth of the economy in general.

WOMEN SHAKE THE WORK FORCE

By Marshall Loeb

Marina Whitman, the newly appointed chief economist of General Motors, claims that she can almost cite the fateful day when the men who run New York City's banks declared: "O.K., fellas, we've got to let *them* in." *Them* are American women, and it was only half a dozen years ago that they began to be admitted, little by little, to the executive establishment. Whitman knows because when she meets groups of bankers, she sees more and more women junior executives, poised for that big leap up to higher management. But almost all are age 32 or 33 or younger—and practically none are older.

Throughout corporate America, male managers are awaking to the reality that women are rising all around them—challenging them, changing their companies and generally shaking things up. Men at the very top are pressing this revolution. Even in the most encrusted industries, chief executives like Bethlehem Steel's Lewis Foy. Equitable Life's Coy Eklund, Du Pont's Irving Shapiro and many others are telling their troops to find and hire and promote women. Resistance persists down in the middle-management trenches, but it is crumbling.

For all the publicity surrounding this significant social development, several essential points probably deserve more emphasis. For instance:

The rise of young women executives will fairly soon accelerate. In U.S. graduate schools of business, one in five students working toward an M.B.A. degree is a woman. The percentage is larger in the elite universities. The share of women M.B.A. recipients in last spring's graduating classes was Stanford 24%, Dartmouth 25%, Wharton 26%, M.I.T. 28%, Northwestern 30%, Columbia 33%. And the percentage is growing. In the incoming first-year classes this autumn, the share was 38% at Yale and 44% at New York University.

Even more important is the rapid growth of women in the blue-collar force. Over three-fifths of all U.S. women aged 20 to 64 hold jobs and are tremendously affecting the current economy. One example: productivity is flat, in some part because many women are holding first-time jobs and are not so well trained as men. But as the newcomers gain experience, productivity will rise.

[53] U.S. Department of Commerce, Bureau of the Census, *A Statistical Portrait of Women in the United States* (Washington, D.C.: U.S. Government Printing Office, 1976).
[54] "Profiling the Typical Black Executive," *Business Week*, January 21, 1980, p. 32.

Policymakers are radically changing their views about unemployment. Even liberal economists no longer consider "full employment" to be a 4% rate of unemployment, but a 5.5% rate. That means, compared with the past, the U.S. is prepared to accept 1.5 million more Americans out of work before Washington policymakers start pumping up the economy in an inflationary way to fight unemployment. A higher level of joblessness is tolerable today because so many more people are at work, and thus, if one family member loses his or her job, there is a better than 50% chance that another family member is collecting a paycheck and can take up the slack. This is a reason why the Federal Reserve Board felt prepared a month ago to put on extremely tight credit clamps, risking a jump in unemployment just as a recession appeared to be developing.

Future recessions will be milder and briefer than they otherwise would have been. Even in hard times, the family's spending power will not collapse. If Dad is laid off, Mom will bring home the bread and bacon, although she still earns less than the average man. Because of her extra paycheck, total family income now is up, even though individual real income is down. So most consumer spending rolls merrily along, delaying and defying the much heralded recession.

From the blue-collar assembly line to the white-bloused executive aerie, quite a few more changes are ahead as the women's revolution not only continues but expands. As workers, decision makers and big money spenders, women will continue to affect cmpanies and markets in ways that can scarcely be imagined. Most important, in an increasingly competitive world, they will significantly enhance the nation's richest asset: its pool of talent.

Reprinted by permission from *TIME*, The Weekly Newsmagazine, November 19, 1979, p. 86; Copyright Time, Inc., 1979.

In any event, the difficulties of implementing equal opportunity should be readily apparent. The concept is fraught with questions of justice, equity, and fairness in addition to being tied up with power and control. There seems to be no praeto optimum solution to this problem, where groups that have suffered discrimination can gain without causing a loss on someone else's part. This is particularly true in a stagnant economy experiencing little or no growth. The privileged position that white males have enjoyed for years is not surrendered easily. If it is just to give women and minorities preferential treatment because there have been sexist and racist barriers to education and employment opportunities, is it just that some white males who may have individually discriminated against no one bear the brunt of this preferential treatment?

The issues get terribly complex as society struggles for answers and attempts to give meaning to equal opportunity in employment. Perhaps the most beneficial result of all this effort is that business has been forced to define more precisely just exactly what qualifications are necessary for performance of a job and how these qualifications can be measured. If this can be done effectively and without bias, so that merit is truly the primary consideration in employment decisions, society will then have benefited through the enhancement of productivity and efficiency as well as implementation of one of its most cherished values.

Questions for Discussion

1. Define prejudice. How does prejudice differ from stereotyping? Enumerate different places where prejudice can enter into employment decisions. What does it mean to say that prejudice and stereotyping have a transactional aspect?
2. What are the roots of racism and sexism? Are prejudice and stereotyping a figment of the imagination? What do you believe about theories of inherent inferiority, say, with respect to intelligence?
3. What is discrimination? How does it differ from the other kinds of social relationships that can exist among human groups? Where does the relationship change from one of being friendly to hostility?
4. What are Fair Employment Practice Acts? Why were they not effective in providing equal employment opportunity? Was there a need, then, for some other kind of approach?
5. Describe the important provisions of the Civil Rights Act with respect to business. What was the general philosophy behind the legislation? What important provisions were added by the 1972 amendments?
6. Describe how Executive Order 11246 and Revised Order No. 4 are examples of the power government has in its role of buyer. Do you think this is a legitimate use of government power? Why or why not? As a taxpayer and as a citizen, how would you vote on this issue?
7. Why is the equal rights amendment important to many women? If it were to pass, what likely effects would it have? Why has it run into such difficult problems in receiving ratification from only three more states at the time of writing?
8. What are the main functions of the Equal Employment Opportunity Commission? What have been some of its major problems? What changes would you recommend to make the EEOC more effective?
9. What is the difference between equal opportunity and affirmative action? What types of affirmative action programs or approaches are there? Why did quotas come into widespread use? Is there a difference between goals and quotas? What is the objective of affirmative action programs?
10. Is preferential treatment of minorities and women morally justified? How can preferential treatment be awarded without reverse discrimination? Does reverse discrimination violate the civil rights laws?
11. Describe the difference between proving intent to discriminate and a result-oriented approach? Which approach seems to be currently favored by the courts? Why?
12. Describe the Bakke case. Was it a definitive case in its implications for business organizations? Did the Weber case provide more guidance for employers? Where do affirmative action programs now stand?
13. What is the relationship between equal employment opportunity and seniority systems? What are the issues that the courts had to consider? Would you be in favor of retroactive seniority for women and minorities? How would this be determined?
14. What is a pattern or practice case? How does this differ from approaching discrimination on a case by case basis? Are these cases a legitimate objective for the EEOC to be pursuing?
15. What was the original meaning of equal work? What does work of comparable worth mean? Are job evaluation systems in and of themselves discriminatory? What makes one job worth more than another?
16. Do you agree with the EEOC guidelines on testing? What kind of approach have they taken? What are the assumptions behind this approach? What alternative forms of validating tests exist?
17. What other forms of discrimination exist? How far should public policy go in

protecting the rights of groups that have been discriminated against? Where would you draw the line? Why?

18. Did you think Sears Roebuck and Company had a legitimate case against the government? Why or why not? Should more companies adopt this strategy?

19. Which of the various suggestions mentioned in the text on affirmative action programs did you like best? Why? What is a total systems approach to affirmative action? Do you agree with this approach?

20. Why haven't the results of the emphasis on equal opportunity been more promising? Will it take more time for the results to manifest themselves? Is the public policy approach to equal employment opportunity basically flawed? Is there a market approach?

Suggested Reading

Allport, Gordon. *The Nature of Prejudice*. Cambridge, Mass.: Addison-Wesley, 1954.

Anderson, Howard J. *Primer of Equal Employment Opportunity*. Washington, D.C.: The Bureau of National Affairs, Inc., 1978.

Bittker, Boris. *The Case for Black Reparations*. New York: Random House, 1973.

Brownlee, W. Elliot, and Brownlee, Mary M. *Women in the American Economy: A Documentary History, 1675 to 1929*. New Haven, Conn.: Yale University Press, 1976.

Bureau of National Affairs, Inc. *The Equal Employment Opportunity Act of 1972*. Washington, D.C.: U.S. Government Printing Office, 1973.

Chafe, William H. *The American Woman: Her Changing Social, Economic, and Political Roles, 1920–1970*. New York: Oxford University Press, 1972.

Foner, Philip. *Organized Labor and the Black Worker, 1619–1973*. New York: Praeger, 1974.

Glazer, Nathan. *Affirmative Discrimination: Ethnic Inequality and Public Policy*. New York: Basic Books, 1975.

Goldman, Alan H. *Justice and Reverse Discrimination*. Princeton, N.J.: Princeton University Press, 1979.

Gordon, Francine E., and Strober, Myra H., eds. *Bringing Women into Management*. New York: McGraw-Hill, 1975.

Gross, Barry, ed. *Reverse Discrimination*. Buffalo, N.Y.: Prometheus, 1976.

Kreps, Juanita. *Sex in the Marketplace: American Women at Work*. Baltimore, Md.: Johns Hopkins University Press, 1971.

Mason, Philip. *Race Relations*. London: Oxford University Press, 1970.

Purcell, Theodore V., and Cavanaugh, Gerald F. *Blacks in the Industrial World: Issues for the Manager*. New York: Free Press, 1972.

Sobin, Dennis P. *The Working Poor: Minority Workers in Low-Wage, Low-Skill Jobs*. Port Washington, N.Y.: Kennikat Press, 1973.

15

Occupational Safety and Health

A means of egress is a continuous and unobstructed way of exit travel from any point in a building or structure to a public way and consists of three separate and distinct parts; the way of exit access, the exit, and the way of exit discharge. A means of egress comprises the vertical and horizontal ways of travel and shall include intervening room spaces, doorways, hallways, corridors, passageways, balconies, ramps, stairs, enclosures, lobbies, escalators, horizontal exits, courts, and yards.

Exit access is that portion of a means of egress which leads to an entrance to an exit.

Exit is that portion of a means of egress which is separated from all other spaces of the building or structure by construction or equipment as required in this subpart to provide a protected way of travel to the exit discharge.

Exit discharge is that portion of a means of egress between the termination of an exit and a public way.[1]

Sometimes it seems as if safety and health problems in the workplace did not exist until relatively recently. This is obviously not the case, since accidents have always occurred in the workplace. Even before the use of power machinery was widespread, people still suffered injuries from falls, dropped equipment or materials, and horse bites. Some of these injuries were all the more serious then because inadequate medical attention often turned a minor injury into a serious one or in some cases even a permanent physical impairment.[2]

[1]*Federal Register*, Vol. 37, No. 202 (October 18, 1972), p. 22130.
[2]See Rollin H. Simonds and John V. Grimaldi, *Safety Management* (Homewood, Ill.: Richard D. Irwin, 1963), pp. 17–24; and Frank E. Bird, *Management Guide to Loss Control* (Atlanta, Ga.: Institute Press, 1974), pp. 1–14.

The coming of industrialization and the increased use of power machinery ushered in a new era of occupational hazard and danger. "The introduction of machinery with its moving gears, cutting blades, and power operation that continued until shut off, regardless of fingers or hands that might be caught, brought a new type of hazard and a tremendous number of work injuries."[3] Industrialization brought a rapid expansion of facilities and jobs where new hazards (power machinery, chemicals, heat, electricity) were brought together with large numbers of workers (without much training or experience) working long hours. The results were predictable.

While the possibility of accidents was most prevalent during the early years of industrialization, problems of occupational health were not entirely unknown. Such problems as "brass chills," "painters colic" (from lead poisoning) and "grinders consumption" (from inhaling dust) were known to exist. Other problems, such as those exhibited by hat makers who used mercury in curing beaver furs, were also fairly common.[4]

Society, however, gave little or no thought to the notion of occupational safety and health. The dramatic oversupply of labor in the late 1800s and early 1900s made workers so cheap that labor was thought of as a commodity to be secured at the lowest possible price rather than a human resource to be carefully husbanded for humanitarian or economic reasons. Because much of the work done was unskilled, investment in training and experience was low, making replacement of injured workers much cheaper than efforts to protect them from hazards in the workplace.

Safety efforts were seen as directly conflicting with the maximization of profits, and many owners and managers tended to take an extremely cavalier attitude toward them. Statements such as "I don't have money for frills like safety. We're not in business for safety" or "some people are just accident prone and no matter what you do, they'll hurt themselves in some way" were representative of employers' feelings on the subject.[5]

Interestingly enough, employees' attitudes were often similar. Accidents were accepted as simply part of working for a living and it was believed they could not be eliminated. This attitude may have been fostered by the protestant ethic, which contained a certain sense of fatalism and created the expectation of a life full of adversity.

The attitude of the courts toward workplace injuries reflected this social climate. The prevailing doctrines of the time were "assumption of risk," "contributory negligence," and the "fellow servant." The courts generally held that employees accepted all the customary risks associated with an occupation when they took a job, and that if injured they could sue and collect damages from an employer only if (1) they could prove the employer was negligently at fault, (2) they could prove that they had not contributed to the accident through their own negligence, and (3) none of their fellow employees contributed to the accident through their negligence.[6]

[3]Simonds and Grimaldi, *Safety Management*, p. 17.

[4]Frederick D. Sturdivant, *Business and Society, A Managerial Approach* (Homewood, Ill.: Richard D. Irwin, 1977), p. 158.

[5]Bird, *Management Guide*, pp. 2, 3.

[6]George Klemm, "Workplace Safety and Health," unpublished paper (St. Louis, Mo.: Washington University, April 13, 1978), pp. 5–6.

Given the difficulty of making these proofs, suits against employers were uncommon and awards to employees rare. Employees were understandably reluctant to risk their jobs to sue an employer, and fellow employees were similarly reluctant to risk their jobs to testify on the injured party's behalf. Even if an injured employee should be brave enough to sue and fortunate enough to win, legal fees usually ate up a good portion of any award. Thus the liability law of these early years failed to protect employees, proved wasteful of time and money (for legal action), and failed to stimulate any action toward accident prevention.[7]

The first substantial effort to promote safety and health in the workplace came from the states in the form of workman's compensation laws. These laws required the employer to either carry insurance to cover damages or to pay out of pocket damages to employees injured on the job regardless of who was at fault. There was at first some question about the constitutionality of such laws since they did in effect seize property without any determination of guilt or fault, but it was held that in view of the public interest involved, it should be a matter of public policy that the employer be liable for injuries occurring to employees on the job. Medical care or compensation for workers should be one of the costs of doing business.[8]

These laws left business free to deal with the safety problem as it saw fit. If business could reduce accidents and lower its insurance premiums (usually based on a three-year moving accident average) and operating costs and thus save money overall, it was free to take this course of action. If, on the other hand, measures to reduce accidents would be prohibitively costly, business was not forced to undertake them with subsequent loss to itself and society through higher costs, lower production, and economic inefficiency. Business, however, would be required to pay the costs of doing business associated with injuries in the workplace.[9]

Workman's compensation laws got insurance companies into the accident prevention field. They were able to interest business in substantial accident prevention programs because lower accident frequency and severity rates meant lower insurance premiums. Many firms thus discovered that safety is good business—an effective safety program so increases efficiency and decreases accident costs that cost savings outweigh the program's expenditures. For example, A. H. Yound, when vice-president of U.S. Steel, estimated that his company saved $117 million in a thirty-year period as a result of a safety program costing only $25 million. There were also examples where safety modifications of existing systems more than tripled output while eliminating safety hazards, or where safety redesign turned a woodworking department's operations around from a loss to a profit.[10]

Such examples, however, were not widespread enough to make a significant impact on the safety and health problem. The system of workman's compensation laws was criticized by a temporary National Commission on State Workman's Compensation Laws. In 1972, the Commission noted that

[7]*Ibid.*, p. 6.

[8]*Ibid.*, pp. 7–8.

[9]*Ibid.*, pp. 8, 9.

[10]J. V. Grimaldi, "Reducing Costs through Accident Prevention Engineering," *Mechanical Engineering*, June 1951, pp. 492–493.

only 22 of the 50 states met even half of the criteria suggested by the Labor Department. Its recommendations included the extension of coverage to all workers, increased benefit levels, removal of dollar and time limits on compensation, and fuller coverage of occupational diseases.[11]

State regulation was also attempted, but state laws varied widely in their stringency and coverage, and many were enforced only weakly. The weight of testimony at the congressional hearings on the subject of occupational safety and health established the bankruptcy of the state system of regulation. Among the numerous complaints were the failure of state laws to provide authority for entry into plants, grossly inadequate funding and staffing, advance notification to employers of an inspection, obsolete standards with little or no provision for updating them, and failure to furnish reports of inspection to employees affected.[12]

Then a coal-mine explosion in Farmington, West Virginia, in 1968 killed seventy-eight miners. This event, coupled with revelations of the extent of black-lung disease, prompted a national campaign for federal legislation which eventually resulted in the Federal Coal Mine Health and Safety Act of 1969. This experience of the coal miners was not lost on organized labor in other industries.[13]

> The tolerance with which workers endured the onerous conditions they were exposed to on the job was breaking down. The heat and noise, the dust and other contaminants that pervaded the environment of factory and foundry were being questioned. The risk of loss of limb or even loss of life itself was no longer regarded as an inevitable part of life's travail.
>
> The major element in the acquiescent attitude of workers had been their ignorance of the hazards they faced in the workplace. They were generally as unaware as were the American people of the threat to their lives posed by cigarette smoking and the myriad of pollutants emitted by automobiles and industrial processes. It was only when the results of scientific investigations entered the public consciousness that people began to change their attitudes. As knowledge of the harmful effects of toxic substances in man's environment spread, so did the determination grow among working people to put a halt to the practices which had made human guinea pigs of them in the workplace.[14]

Pressures mounted for a federal system of regulation covering all industries. The final impetus came from studies such as one by the National Safety Council in 1970 which estimated that more than 14,000 workers died on the job and another 2.2 million suffered disabling injuries each year as a result of accidents at work. The President's first report on OSHA estimated that there may be at least 100,000 deaths and 390,000 new cases of disabling diseases each year caused by exposure to such substances as asbestos, lead, silica, carbon monoxide, and cotton dust.[15] Supporters of federal regulation also

[11]Albert L. Nichols and Richard Zeckhauser, "Government Comes to the Workplace: An Assessment of OSHA," *The Public Interest*, No. 49 (Fall 1977), pp. 40–41.

[12]George Perkel, "A Labor View of the Occupational Safety and Health Act," unpublished paper presented at IRRA, Spring Meeting, 1972, p. 2.

[13]*Ibid.*, p. 1.

[14]*Ibid.*

[15]Fred K. Foulkes, "Learning to Live with OSHA," *Harvard Business Review*, Vol. 51, No. 6 (November–December 1973), p. 58.

cited what the House Committee on Education and Labor called the "on-the-job health and safety crisis." Injury rates had reversed their long-term downward trend and had been rising since the mid-1950s, so the report claimed. From 1960 to 1970, for example, the rate of accidents in manufacturing rose 26.7 percent, an increase explained only in part by cyclical economic factors and the changing composition of the labor force.[16]

The Occupational Safety and Health Act

Thus the federal government finally came to the workplace to deal with the safety and health problem in the form of the Occupational Safety and Health Act of 1970 (Williams-Steiger Act). The purpose of the act was "to assure so far as possible every working man and woman in the Nation safe and healthful working conditions and to preserve our human resources."[17] Congress outlined several specific means for OSHA to implement this mandate by giving it responsibility to:

- Encourage employers and employees to reduce hazards in the workplace and to implement new or improve existing safety and health programs;
- Establish "separate but dependent responsibilties and rights" for employers and employees for the achievement of better safety and health conditions;
- Establish reporting and recordkeeping procedures to monitor job-related injuries and illnesses;
- Develop mandatory job safety and health standards and enforce them effectively; and
- Encourage the States to assume the fullest responsibility for establishing and administering their own occupational safety and health programs, which must be "at least as effective as" the Federal program.[18]

At the time of its passage, OSHA covered every employer in a business engaged in interstate commerce that had one or more employees. The act did not affect workplaces covered under other federal laws such as the Coal Mine Health and Safety Act and the Federal Metal and Nonmetallic Safety Act. Federal, state, and local government employees were covered under separate provisions in the act for public employment. Reactions to this legislation were mixed.

> The enactment of the Occupational Safety and Health Act of 1970 was hailed by AFL-CIO President Meany as "a long step down the road toward a safe and healthy workplace." President Nixon called it a "landmark piece of legislation." The *Monthly Labor Review* went so far as to term it a "revolutionary program." On the other hand, Leo Teplow, formerly with the Iron and Steel Institute, in a memorandum written for the National Association of Manufacturers, described it as "a strange melange of Naderism and laborism."[19]

Administrative Structure. *Occupational Safety and Health Administration:* Located in the Department of Labor, this agency has legislative and execu-

[16]Nichols and Zeckhauser, "OSHA," p. 40.
[17]Occupational Safety and Health Act, Public Law 91-596.
[18]*All About OSHA*, U.S. Department of Labor, OSHA 2056, April 1976 (revised), pp. 1–2.
[19]Perkel, "Labor View," p. 1.

tive functions with respect to the federal safety and health program (see Exhibit 15.1). The major responsibilities of OSHA are to set and enforce standards related to safety and health in the workplace, work with the states in developing their own safety and health programs, and establish record-keeping requirements that employers are required to follow.

National Institute For Occupational Safety and Health: This agency is located in the Department of Health and Human Resources, and is the research arm of the program. NIOSH conducts research into safety and health-related problems, and recommends criteria to OSHA for consideration in setting of standards. It also undertakes education and training programs and performs work in the area of safety engineering.

EXHIBIT 15.1

Department of Labor
OCCUPATIONAL SAFETY AND HEALTH ADMINISTRATION
200 Constitution Avenue NW, Washington, D.C. 20210
Telephone: (202) 523-6091

Purpose: To develop and enforce worker safety and health regulations.

Regulatory Activity: This agency (1) sets standards to protect workers against safety and health hazards; (2) conducts workplace inspections to enforce these regulations and may issue citations and propose financial penalties for alleged violations; (3) approves, provides, and monitors half the funding for state-administered occupational safety and health programs; (4) requires employers to report workplace accidents that result in fatalities or the hospitalization of 5 or more workers; and (5) requires employers with 10 or more employees to keep and post in the workplace records of job injuries and illnesses.

Established: December 29, 1970

Legislative Authority:
   Enabling Legislation: Occupational Safety and Health Act of 1970 (84 Stat. 1590; P.L. 91-596)

   OSHA develops standards which supersede those issued under the following acts:
      Longshoremen's and Harbor Workers' Compensation Act of 1927 (44 Stat. 1444)
      Walsh-Healey Act of 1936 (49 Stat. 2036)
      Service Contract Act of 1965 (79 Stat. 1034; P.L. 89-286)
      Construction Safety Act of 1969 (83 Stat. 96; P.L. 91-54)

Organization: OSHA, an agency within the Department of Labor, is headed by an assistant secretary.

Note: OSHA regulations do not cover self-employed persons or any family-owned and operated farms and workplaces already regulated by other federal agencies. Federal agencies are not covered by OSHA workplace standards but must submit annual reports to OSHA on the status of their job safety and health programs.

Budgets and Staffing
(Fiscal Years 1971-1981)

	71	72	73	74	75	76	77	78	79	(Estimated) 80	81
Budget ($ millions)	n/a	n/a	37	69	90	109	127	147	155	185	208
Staffing	n/a	n/a	1699	1830	2471	2494	2717	2674	2855	2928	2928

From Ronald J. Penoyer, *Directory of Federal Regulatory Agencies,* 2nd ed. (St. Louis, Mo.: Washington University Center for the Study of American Business, 1980), p. 68. Reprinted with permission.

Occupational Safety and Health Review Commission: This commission is the judicial arm of the safety and health program (see Exhibit 15.2). It handles the appeals of employers on violations and penalties because of OSHA inspections. Because of its need to be objective, it was established as an independent agency.

Standard Setting. A safety or health standard has been defined as "a legally enforceable regulation governing conditions, practices, or operations to assure safe and healthful workplaces."[20] There are two types of standards on safety: horizontal regulations that apply to all industries and relate to such items as fire extinguishers, electrical groundings, railings, machine guards, and the like; and vertical provisions that apply to particular industry groups, such as the maritime industry and construction. Health standards relate to particular substances such as benzene, lead, or cotton dust that workers may come into contact with in one way or another. These standards are published in the Federal Register along with all amendments, corrections, insertions, or deletions involving standards.

Enforcement. The enforcement mechanism consists of inspections by OSHA safety and health officers. These inspectors visit business facilities to check compliance with the national safety and health standards that have been established. The inspector is concerned with what standards apply in a

---

EXHIBIT 15.2

OCCUPATIONAL SAFETY AND HEALTH REVIEW COMMISSION
1825 K Street NW, Washington, D.C. 20006
Telephone: (202) 634-7943

Purpose: To rule on contests initiated by employers or employees subsequent to a workplace inspection by the Occupational Safety and Health Administration (OSHA).

Regulatory Activity: The Commission acts as a court to rule on alleged job safety and health violations cited by OSHA that are contested by employers or employees after a workplace inspection.

Established: April 28, 1971

Legislative Authority:
Enabling Legislation: Occupational Safety and Health Act of 1970 (84 Stat. 1590)

Organization: This is an independent agency consisting of three commissioners appointed by the President with the advice and consent of the Senate, and 45 Administrative Law Judges in nine regional offices.

Budgets and Staffing
(Fiscal Years 1971-1981)

	71	72	73	74	75	76	77	78	79	(Estimated) 80	81
Budget ($ millions)	*	1	4	5	5	6	7	7	7	7	8
Staffing	10	121	188	188	172	175	181	171	171	179	179

*Less than $1 million

From Ronald J. Penoyer, *Directory of Federal Regulatory Agencies,* 2nd ed. (St. Louis, Mo.: Washington University Center for the Study of American Business, 1980), p. 44. Reprinted with permission.

---

[20]*All About OSHA,* U.S. Department of Labor, OSHA 2056, undated, p. 8.

given facility and whether the employer and employees are in compliance with these standards.

Obviously, not all the 5 million workplaces covered by the act can be inspected. OSHA simply does not have that much staff. Therefore, it has established a system of inspection priorities to give the worst situations attention before those where the safety and health conditions are likely to be better. These priorities have been established as follows:

- *Imminent Danger:* Imminent danger situations are given top priority. An imminent danger is any condition where there is reasonable certainty that a danger exists that can be expected to cause death or serious physical harm immediately or before the danger can be eliminated through normal enforcement procedures.

  If a compliance officer finds an imminent danger situation, he will ask for voluntary abatement of the hazard and removal of endangered employees from the area. If an employer fails to do so, OSHA, through the Regional Solicitor, can go to the nearest Federal District Court for appropriate legal action to correct the situation.

- *Catastrophes and Fatal Accidents:* High priority also is given to investigation of catastrophes, fatalities, and accidents resulting in hospitalization of five or more employees. Such situations must be reported to OSHA within 48 hours. Investigations are made to determine if OSHA standards were violated and to learn how to avoid recurrence of similar accidents.

- *Valid Employee Complaints:* Third priority is given to valid employee complaints of alleged violations of standards or of unsafe or unhealthful working conditions.

- *Special Emphasis Programs:* Next are OSHA's programs that focus upon particular dangers.

  In its first 3 years, OSHA conducted the Target Industry Program, which called for frequent inspections of five industries with injury rates that were more than double the national average: longshoring, meat and meat products, roofing and sheet metal, lumber and wood products, and manufacture of miscellaneous transportation equipment.

  In addition, special attention was given to the hazards of trenching and excavation work.

  Targets for special emphasis now are selected on a regional basis, based on the injury frequency rates of local industries.

  OSHA continues to emphasize the Target Health Hazards Program which focuses on five hazardous substances: asbestos, carbon monoxide, cotton dust, lead, and silica. These were selected because of broad employee exposure and the severity of the danger.

- *Random Inspections:* These inspections are conducted in establishments of all sizes and types, in all parts of the country.

- *Reinspections:* Establishments cited for alleged serious violations shall be reinspected to determine whether the situations have been corrected.[21]

The original act prohibited advance notice of inspections. This has since been changed by a court ruling (see next section) requiring search warrants. Once admitted, the compliance officer conducts a walkaround of the facility with a representative of both the employer and employees. The inspector takes notes and photographs of particular situations that may violate stand-

[21]*OSHA Inspections,* U.S. Department of Labor, OSHA 2098, June 1975, pp. 2–3.

ards. The employer's records of deaths, injuries, and illnesses are also checked for compliance. During the walkaround, employees may bring any conditions they believe to be a violation of standards to the attention of the compliance officer. After the walkaround is finished, the compliance officer discusses with the employer what he or she has seen and reviews probable violations. The officer then returns to his or her office and writes a report. The area director of OSHA or his or her superiors determine what citations will be issued and what penalties, if any, will be proposed. These are eventually mailed to the employer.

Violations. The workplace may, of course, be found in compliance with OSHA standards, in which case no citations will be issued or penalties imposed. If violations are found, citations may be issued and civil penalties proposed. In order of significance, these violations are placed in one of the following categories.

- *De Minimis:* A violation that has no direct or immediate relationship to job safety and health. A notice is issued but citations and proposed penalties are not.

- *Nonserious Violation:* A violation that has a direct relationship to job safety and health, but probably would not cause death or serious physical harm. A proposed penalty of up to $1,000 is discretionary. A penalty for a nonserious violation may be adjusted downward by as much as 50 percent, depending on the severity of the hazard, the employer's good faith (demonstrated efforts to comply with the Act), history of previous violations, and size of business. The resulting figure is also reduced an additional 50 percent on the assumption that the employer will correct the violation within the prescribed abatement period. If reinspection shows failure to abate, the same percentage of reduction is added to daily proposed penalties (up to $1,000 per day beyond the prescribed abatement date).

- *Serious Violation:* A violation where there is substantial probability that death or serious physical harm could result, and that the employer knew, or should have known, of the hazard. A proposed penalty of up to $1,000 is mandatory. A penalty for a serious violation may be adjusted downward by as much as 50 percent, based on the gravity of the violation, the employer's good faith, history of previous violations, and size of business.

- *Imminent Danger:* A violation where there is reasonable certainty that a danger exists that can be expected to cause death or serious physical harm immediately or before the danger can be eliminated through normal enforcement procedures. Should the employer fail to deal with the situation immediately, OSHA can apply to the nearest Federal District Court for appropriate legal action to correct the situation. Should OSHA decline to bring court action, the affected employees may sue the Secretary of Labor to compel court action. The operation or section of the workplace where the imminent danger exists can then be shut down by a temporary restraining order.[22]

Upon receipt of the citations and proposed penalties, the employer has fifteen working days to notify the area director, in writing (Notice of Contest), that he or she intends to contest the citation, penalty, or the time set for abatement. The area director then sends the case to the Occupational Safety and Health Review Commission. The Commission assigns the case to an administrative law judge, who eventually hears the case and issues a decision. The judge's decision may be reviewed by any member of the Commission, or

[22]OSHA 2056, April 1976 (revised), pp. 16, 22.

by the Commission itself, but such a review is not required. The final decision of the Commission may be further appealed to the U.S. Circuit Court of Appeals for the circuit in which the case arose. If the employer does not contest within the fifteen-day period, the OSHA action becomes a final order of the Review Commission and is not subject to further appeal or review.

Record-keeping. The OSHA Act of 1970 requires employers to prepare and maintain records of occupational injuries and illnesses. These records assist compliance officers in making inspections and investigations. They also provide the basis for a statistical program that produces reliable injury and illness incidence rates and other measures. This information is also believed to be helpful to employers in identifying many of the factors which cause injuries and illnesses in the workplace.

While the original legislation called for the maintenance of three forms, this has subsequently been changed to only two types of records.[23] The Log and Summary (OSHA No. 200) is provided to classify injury and illness cases and note their extent and outcome. The Supplementary Record (OSHA No. 101) is used for recording additional information about every recordable injury or illness. These records do not have to be sent to OSHA, but they must be maintained on the premises of the facility for five years after the year to which they relate. These records can be inspected or copied at any reasonable time by authorized federal or state government representatives. OSHA has also proposed a rule that would allow employees to see the list of accidents and illnesses at a workplace at any time.

Employer Responsibilities and Rights. Employers have certain responsibilities and rights under the Occupational Safety and Health Act. Some of the more important of these responsibilities and rights are listed below. Failure to fulfill many of the responsibilities can result in citations.

Employer Responsibilities
- Meet your general duty responsibility to provide a hazard-free workplace and comply with the occupational safety and health standards, rules, and regulations issued under the Act.
- Be familiar with mandatory OSHA standards and make copies available to employees for review upon request.
- Inform all employees about OSHA.
- Examine workplace conditions to make sure they conform to applicable safety and health standards.
- Remove or guard hazards.
- Make sure employees have and use safe tools and equipment (including personal protective equipment) and that such equipment is properly maintained.
- Use color codes, posters, labels, or signs to warn employees of potential hazards.
- Establish or update operating procedures and communicate them so that employees follow safety and health requirements for their own protection.
- Provide medical examinations when required by OSHA standards.
- Report to the nearest OSHA office, *within 48 hours,* the occurrence of any

[23]*Recordkeeping Requirements Under the Occupational Safety and Health Act of 1970,* U.S. Department of Labor, OSHA, 1978 (revised).

employment accident which is fatal to one or more employees or which results in the hospitalization of five or more employees.

- Keep OSHA-required records of work-related injuries and illnesses, and post the annual summary during the entire month of February each year. (This applies to employers with eight or more employees.)
- Post, at a prominent location within the workplace, the OSHA poster (OSHA 2203) informing employees of their rights and responsibilities. (In States operating OSHA-approved job safety and health programs, the State's equivalent poster and/or OSHA 2203 may be required.)
- Cooperate with the OSHA compliance officer by furnishing names of authorized employee representatives who may be asked to accompany the compliance officer during the inspection. (If none, the compliance officer will consult with a reasonable number of employees concerning safety and health in the workplace.)
- Not discriminate against employees who properly exercise their rights under the Act.
- Post OSHA citations of apparent violations of standards or of the general duty clause at or near the worksite involved. Each citation, or copy thereof, shall remain posted until the violation has been abated, or for 3 working days, whichever is longer.
- Abate cited violations within the prescribed period.

Employer Rights

- Seek advice and off-site consultation as needed by writing, calling, or visiting the nearest OSHA office. (OSHA will not inspect merely because an employer requests assistance.)
- Be active in your industry association's involvement in job safety and health.
- Request and receive proper identification of the OSHA compliance officer prior to inspection of the workplace.
- Be advised by the compliance officer of the reason for an inspection.
- Have an opening and closing conference with the compliance officer.
- File a Notice of Contest with the nearest OSHA area director within 15 working days of receipt of a notice of citation and proposed penalty.
- Apply to OSHA for a temporary variance from a standard if unable to comply because of the unavailability of materials, equipment, or personnel to make necessary changes within the required time.
- Apply to OSHA for a permanent variance from a standard if you can furnish proof that your facilities or method of operation provide employee protection that is at least as effective as that required by the standard.
- Take an active role in developing job safety and health standards through participation in OSHA Standards Advisory Committees, through nationally recognized standards setting organizations, and through evidence and views presented in writing or at hearings.
- Avail yourself, if you are a small business employer, of long-term loans through the Small Business Administration (SBA) to help bring your establishment into compliance, either before or after an OSHA inspection.
- Be assured of the confidentiality of any trade secrets observed by an OSHA compliance officer during an inspection.[24]

[24]OSHA 2056, April 1976 (revised), pp. 27–30.

Employee Responsibilities and Rights. OSHA does not cite employees for violations of their responsibilities, but each employee is expected to comply with all occupational safety and health standards and all rules, regulations, and orders issued under the act that apply to his or her own actions and conduct on the job. The employee also has many rights, some of which are listed below.

Employee Responsibilities

- Read the OSHA poster at the jobsite.
- Comply with all applicable OSHA standards.
- Follow all employer safety and health rules and regulations and wear or use prescribed protective equipment while engaged in work.
- Report hazardous conditions to the supervisor.
- Report any job-related injury or illness to the employer, and seek treatment promptly.
- Cooperate with the OSHA compliance officer conducting an inspection if he or she inquires about safety and health conditions in your workplace.
- Exercise your rights under the Act in a responsible manner.

Employee Rights

- Review copies of any of the OSHA standards, rules, regulations, and requirements that the employer should have available at the workplace.
- Request information from your employer on safety and health hazards in the area, on precautions that may be taken, and on procedures to be followed if an employee is involved in an accident or exposed to toxic substances.
- Request (in writing) the OSHA area director to conduct an inspection if you believe hazardous conditions or violation of standards exist in your workplace.
- Have your name withheld from your employer, upon request to OSHA, if you file a written and signed complaint.
- Be advised of OSHA actions regarding your complaint and have an informal review, if requested, of any decision not to make an inspection or not to issue a citation.
- File a complaint to OSHA within 30 days if you believe you have been discriminated against, discharged, demoted, or otherwise penalized because of asserting an employee right under the Act, and be notified by OSHA of its determination within 90 days of filing.
- Have the authorized employee representative where you work accompany the OSHA compliance officer during the inspection tour.
- Respond to questions from the OSHA compliance officer, particularly if there is no authorized employee representative accompanying the compliance officer.
- Observe any monitoring or measuring of hazardous materials and have the right of access to records on those materials, as specified under the Act.
- Request a closing discussion with the compliance officer following an inspection.
- Submit a written request to the National Institute for Occupational Safety and Health (NIOSH) for information on whether any substance in your workplace has potential toxic effects in the concentrations being used, and have your name withheld from your employer if you so request.
- Object to the abatement period set in the citation issued to your employer by writing to the OSHA area director within 15 working days of the issuance of the citation.

- Be notified by your employer if he or she applies for a variance from an OSHA standard, testify at a variance hearing, and appeal the final decision if you disagree with it.
- Submit information or comment to OSHA on the issuance, modification, or revocation of OSHA standards, and request a public hearing.[25]

Experience with the Federal Program

Coverage. There have been a few attempts to limit the coverage of OSHA throughout the years of its existence. Many of these attempts have focused on exemptions for small business, because many people believed that the inspection procedures and record-keeping requirements were particularly burdensome for these businesses. Finally, in late 1979, OSHA itself, under pressure from Congress, agreed to exempt businesses with ten or fewer employees in industries with good safety records from safety inspections. Forty-nine industries that had fewer than seven injuries or illnesses per 100 workers annually qualified for the exemption. This exemption would include, OSHA said, about 1.5 million establishments employing five million workers. The agency would still conduct health, as distinct from safety, inspections, and would still conduct safety inspections in response to employee complaints.[26]

The paperwork requirements for small business were also reduced by an OSHA ruling. Most employers with ten or fewer workers—3.4 million of the five million companies covered by job safety laws—were spared from keeping the employee accident and illness records originally required. They have to complete government forms only if a worker is killed and two or more are hospitalized.[27]

Such efforts, however, have not curbed congressional attempts to further limit OSHA's coverage. A bill that would exempt 90 percent of the nation's five million workplaces from regular OSHA inspections was introduced in 1978 for congressional consideration. Among those who introduced the bill was Senator Richard Schweiker (R., Pa.), who termed OSHA "probably the most despised federal agency in existence" and asserted that it has "failed to produce demonstrable benefits in workers' safety" during its existence. He said the bill would move OSHA "away from a regulatory policeman's role toward a cooperative partner in worker safety and health."[28]

Under the bill, employers with good safety records—as verified in state workers' compensation agency files—in any one year would be exempt from scheduled OSHA safety inspections during the next year. Employers who reported to the state agencies that they did not have any injuries would automatically be exempt. Other employers could apply for an exemption, which would be granted if they had not had any deaths in the preceding year

[25]*Ibid.*, pp. 30–32.

[26]"Some Small Companies Receive Exemptions on OSHA Inspections," *The Wall Street Journal*, December 26, 1979, p. 8.

[27]"U.S. Agency Ends Job-Safety Paper Work of Small Firms, Plans Cut for Large Ones," *The Wall Street Journal*, July 20, 1977, p. 7.

[28]"Senate Gets Bill Aimed at Curbing OSHA Rules," *The Wall Street Journal*, December 20, 1979, p. 6. See also "Restraining OSHA: It's Just a Matter of Time," *Business Week*, May 5, 1980, p. 110.

and only a limited number of injuries. The bill would still allow OSHA to conduct health inspections and investigate workplace accidents that caused death or serious injuries. The agency would also be free, with some limits, to conduct inspections based on complaints from employees, evidence of "imminent danger," or referrals from other inspectors. This system, supporters argue, would give employees an incentive to reduce injuries voluntarily and would force OSHA to direct its inspections to the most hazardous workplaces.

Standard-setting. Much of the hostility to OSHA that is behind the efforts to curb its power stems from the standard-setting process. Nichols and Zeckhauser criticize the way OSHA was structured on three grounds: (1) no attempt was made to analyze the problem of occupational safety and health in terms of likely causes and cures; (2) economic costs, which are a major consequence of any regulatory effort, were systematically excluded from being considered; and (3) serious thought has not been given to any approach other than direct regulation. These fundamental questions were ignored, they state, in the haste to set up a federal program to respond to what was perceived as a crisis situation. Given the way the program was set up, Nichols and Zeckhauser believe that most of OSHA's failings were predictable.[29]

With regard to the first point, some critics believe that the worker's own behavior, not the work environment, is the major cause of accidents. Thus the effort to set standards related to the work environment is misguided. If there is any truth to this view, efforts to improve supervision and training should be more effective in reducing accidents than capital-equipment regulations. Most accidents are probably a combination of worker behavior and the environment (lack of guards, etc.), but more research must be done to establish the true causes of most accidents, which would then provide a basis for developing an effective program to reduce them.[30]

The area of economic costs, the second point made by Nichols and Zeckhauser, is an important area that was overlooked in the legislation establishing the federal program. No economic impact statement or cost benefit analysis is required in the process of issuing regulations. Yet, safety and health regulations impose a substantial compliance cost on industry and the exclusion of any economic considerations in establishing regulations would seem to be a major omission that would eventually lead to repercussions, since regulations do affect productivity, contribute to inflation, and inhibit capital formation.

Finally, other approaches to the safety and health problem were not considered, such as the use of incentives to encourage employers to improve their safety and health records. The basic business of OSHA is setting and enforcing standards, many of them specifying in great detail the physical conditions of various aspects of the workplace. This form of intervention was adopted without looking at other methods that might be more effective. The command and control system that was adopted could be expected to provoke resistance, as it only further contributes to the adversarial relationship between business and government.

[29]Nichols and Zeckhauser, "OSHA," p. 42.

[30]See Joseph Barry Mason, "OSHA: Problems and Prospects," *California Management Review*, Vol. XIX, No. 1 (Fall 1976), pp. 21–28.

The history of OSHA with regard to standard setting is a lesson in how not to begin a regulatory program. Within one month of its creation, OSHA adopted, in wholesale fashion, about 4,400 consensus standards from previous federal regulations that were already in existence and from voluntary codes written by such organizations as the American National Standards Institute (ANSI). They had been written by safety experts and originally intended as no more than voluntary industry guidelines. Since many of these experts had little or no knowledge about production or costs, industry regarded many of the standards as unreasonable and ignored them. When OSHA made them legally binding, however, and backed them up with inspections and fines, many problems resulted.[31]

Some of these standards were trivial and unrelated to safety and health, such as the requirement that toilet seats be split and not round. Others were obsolete, such as the prohibition against ice in drinking water, which dated from the time ice was cut from polluted lakes. Still other standards were unnecessarily complex and difficult to understand, such as the 140 standards covering wooden ladders and the six pages devoted to fire protection equipment.[32]

These nit-picking regulations came in for severe criticism, and finally, in 1978, OSHA revoked 928 that were of little value in protecting safety and health. Included were standards requiring split-seat toilets, prescribing the type of wood to be used in portable ladders, and specifying the number of inches from the floor that portable fire extinguishers had to be mounted. The total number of regulations relating to ladders was reduced from ten pages to two. This process of revocation, however, took months of consultations, publications, and hearings, demonstrating that it is sometimes easier to establish regulations than get them off the books.[33]

Many of these consensus standards were adopted under pressure to do something quickly, and thus their relevance to safety and health was not reviewed. Some years later, however, they still constitute the majority of OSHA's standards. The process of establishing new standards is complex and lengthy. Most standards begin with a recommendation from NIOSH, which is then reviewed by an OSHA advisory committee. When proposed standards are finally issued in the Federal Register, many delays are caused by public hearings and court challenges by affected industries before a final standard can be issued.

The complexity of this process is well-illustrated by OSHA's attempt to focus more of its attention on the health aspects of the workplace and issue more health standards. By 1977, over 1,500 workplace chemicals had been identified as suspected carcinogens by scientists, but OSHA had issued final standards covering only 17 of these substances.[34] OSHA must proceed on a substance by substance basis in regard to health standards. This process is subject to all of the delays mentioned previously.

Various proposals have been made for classifying and regulating sus-

---

[31]Foulkes, "OSHA," p. 60.

[32]Nichols and Zeckhauser, "OSHA," p. 48.

[33]"Labor Department Revokes 928 Rules Covering Job Safety," *The Wall Street Journal*, October 25, 1978, p. 20.

[34]*The Budget for Fiscal Year 1981* (Washington, D.C.: U.S. Government Printing Office, 1980), p. 428.

pected carcinogens to speed up this process. Under a procedure proposed in 1980, OSHA would be required to publish a candidate list of substances suspected of being workplace carcinogens. These substances would eventually wind up in one of two regulatory categories—Category I, where the evidence is relatively conclusive, and Category II, where initial testing has shown a "suggestion" of carcinogenicity. For Category I substances, standards would be issued to reduce the exposure to the lowest feasible level through engineering controls. If a safe substitute exists, the carcinogen would be banned from the workplace entirely. For Category II substances, less comprehensive standards would be issued.[35]

OSHA hopes that such a procedure would clear away many of the regulatory questions that arise when the agency acts on a specific substance. These questions center mainly on the validity of animal testing, the existence of a safe exposure level, and the use of engineering controls (see box). Such a procedure as outlined above would restrict questions to whether the agency had correctly classified a particular substance and placed the appropriate limit on exposure.

Industry has been pressing for the use of cost-benefit analysis in setting standards, arguing that the law defines a standard as a regulation "reason-

---

The validity of animal testing is under attack in this area of occupational health as well as in the food safety area. The animals used in such tests are often fed such huge quantities of the suspect chemical that many people, including some scientists, conclude these tests are wholly unrealistic. Yet it would take great numbers of animals and more time to use more realistic procedures. Thus, in the absence of a better method, the dosage is increased to see the effects more readily.

Another basic problem is the unsettled question about safe exposure levels. The position of industry is that there are safe levels that can be established for most substances, below which exposure causes no harm; thus standards ought to be set at this level. OSHA argues that the law requires it to set health standards so as to ensure "to the extent feasible" that "no employee will suffer material impairment of health." If the best available evidence suggests there isn't any "safe level," then it must set the standard at the lowest feasible level.

The agency agrees that for particular individuals there may be thresholds of safe exposure for certain carcinogens. But the thresholds vary from person to person, OSHA argues, so that it is impossible to identify a safe threshold for entire populations. Research also indicates, OSHA says, that carcinogens may act in combination with each other to increase risk, and thus proper threshold levels cannot be set for any given substance.

A third issue is the use of engineering controls versus personal protection equipment. OSHA generally favors the use of engineering controls to reduce exposure to hazardous substance and noise in the workplace; industry favors use of protective equipment such as masks or earplugs. The cost differences can be substantial. The cost of engineering controls to reduce noise levels to 85 dB has been estimated at $18.5 billion. Personal protection equipment would cost only $43 million to achieve the same protection.

---

[35]Vicky Cahan and Charlene Canape, "A Cancer Policy neither Industry nor Labor Likes," *Business Week*, February 4, 1980, p. 76.

ably necessary or appropriate" to protect workers' health and safety. A standard that flunks a cost-benefit test is not reasonably necessary or appropriate, industry maintains. With regard to a proposed reduction in exposure to benzene, industry won a victory for its view, as a federal appeals court in New Orleans set aside the ordered reduction, ruling that OSHA cannot legally regulate occupational health hazards without using a cost-benefit analysis to "determine whether the benefits expected from the standard bear a reasonable relationship to the costs imposed." The Supreme Court, in a five-to-four decision, upheld the lower court ruling, but for mostly different reasons.[36] Only one judge, Lewis Powell, agreed with the lower court's reasoning. The other four upholding the ruling agreed that OSHA had failed to establish that the benzene rules were "reasonably necessary and appropriate" to remedy a "significant risk of material health impairment."

But the law neither requires nor permits cost-benefit analysis, argued OSHA under the Carter administration. To balance costs and benefits "squarely violates" the law's requirement to prevent impairment of health. The cost of regulation is only relevant when regulations are so onerous as to make compliance unfeasible. This view was upheld by another appeals court decision about cotton dust standards which rejected cost-benefit analysis and supported costly engineering controls to reduce exposure.[37] The Labor Department under the Reagan administration wants to review this standard utilizing cost-benefit analysis.

Thus OSHA got off to a terrible start in the standard-setting process. The use of consensus standards on such a broad scale without adequate screening or careful consideration was, in retrospect, a big mistake. But there are many unresolved issues in the standard-setting process, particularly with regard to health, that make it tremendously complex and lengthy. Many of these issues may have to be decided by the Supreme Court as it agrees to hear cases dealing with safety and health standards. There seems to be no conclusive scientific evidence to resolve some of these issues, given the current state of knowledge and medical technology. The law can also be interpreted differently in regard to the authority granted OSHA in its enabling legislation. These problems make the search for alternative methods of dealing with health and safety all the more important.

Enforcement. OSHA got off to a flying start in its enforcement program. In its first fiscal year, the agency made 32,700 inspections, issued 23,230 citations charging 102,860 violations, and proposed $2,300,000 in penalties.[38] While these figures sound impressive, the inspections represented only a small fraction of the total number of workplaces covered by the program. OSHA simply did not have enough inspectors to cover more workplaces. It became apparent that some kind of a priority system was needed to focus on the industries or companies where the more serious

---

[36]*Marshall v. American Petroleum Institute,* 581 F.2d 493 (5th Cir. 1978). See also "Court Battle over Benzene Safety Raises Issues of Weighing Agency Rules, Cost against Benefit," *The Wall Street Journal,* January 9, 1980, p. 44; and "Regulations Limiting Worker Exposure to Benzene Are Voided by High Court," *The Wall Street Journal,* July 3, 1980, p. 6.

[37]"A Court Gives OSHA Hope for More Clout," *Business Week,* November 12, 1979, pp. 42–43.

[38]Dan Cordtz, "Safety on the Job Becomes a Major Job for Management," *Fortune,* November 1972, p. 166.

problems existed. Ninety-five percent of all discretionary safety inspections are now targeted on larger workplaces and more hazardous industries. Comparable methods of targeting health inspections are currently being developed.[39]

In addition to not covering enough workplaces, the inspection system was also criticized because of the lack of trained enforcement personnel and because, in its early years, inspectors were trained to look for safety violations rather than health hazards. Very few industrial hygienists were employed by OSHA in its early years. Since that time, the quality of workplace safety and health inspections has been substantially improved through better use of the enforcement staff, 33 percent more training for OSHA compliance officers, and "crossover training" so that safety inspectors can also recognize health hazards.[40]

Finally, the inevitable constitutional challenge to the inspector's right to have unannounced access to private property came along. When an OSHA inspector tried to walk unannounced into the shop of Ferrol G. Barlow's shop in Pocatello, Idaho, the proprietor refused him entry. Barlow claimed that the inspector needed a search warrant; that the Fourth Amendment to the constitution prohibited unreasonable searches of private property. The Supreme Court eventually ruled that Barlow was legally correct, that employers can bar OSHA inspectors who do not have search warrants.[41]

This was not an undiluted victory for business, however, as the court released OSHA from having to show probable cause, as in criminal searches, to get the warrant. Also, the warrant need be obtained only if the employer refuses access to an inspector. The immediate effect of the ruling was not significant, as most businesses did not demand warrants because they believed OSHA would have no difficulty obtaining them. As of July 1978, only 1.5 percent of employers visited by inspectors since the May 23rd decision had demanded warrants before letting in the inspectors. The long-term effect may be more significant, however, as the American Conservative Union, for one, is encouraging more employers to demand warrants.[42]

Violations. As might be expected, the caseload of the Occupational Safety and Health Review Commission has increased over the years as more and more employers appealed the citations and penalties they were issued. This has, of course, necessitated the hiring of additional personnel, as these cases can be quite complex and lengthy. The right of OSHA to assess penalties administratively and commit the fact-finding to an administrative law court without trial by jury was challenged on the basis of the Seventh Amendment to the constitution. This amendment says that "in suits of common law" where the controversy involves more than $20, "the right of trial by jury shall be preserved." The Supreme Court did not uphold this challenge, claiming that the amendment was "never intended to establish the jury as the exclusive mechanism for fact finding in civil cases." Thus Congress was not prevented from committing new types of litigation to adminis-

[39]*The Budget for Fiscal Year 1981*, p. 428.
[40]*Ibid.*
[41]*Marshall v. Barlow's, Inc.*, 46 L.W. 4483 (1978).
[42]"Job Safety Inspectors Seldom Required to Get Warrants despite Justices' Ruling," *The Wall Street Journal*, July 17, 1978, p. 13.

trative agencies with special competence in the relevant field. In a footnote, the court also barred any challenge to OSHA's constitutionality through the Sixth Amendment, which grants the right to a jury trial in criminal proceedings.[43]

Employer Responsibilities and Rights. Looking at rights and responsibilities of employers and employees, it seems that the employer has more responsibilities than rights and that the employee has more rights than responsibilities. The Review Commission has generally upheld the legal position that employees cannot receive citations. Thus the employer has been held responsible for seeing that employees wear safety equipment (hard hats, ear plugs, and so on) and comply with other safety measures. Refusal by employees to comply has generally been considered an inadequate defense. Employers have been encouraged to treat enforcement of safety provisions as a condition of employment, that is, to make clear to employees that unless they comply with safety standards, they will be fired. Employers are subject to fines for unsafe practices even if there is no accident.

An interesting aspect of this issue of rights concerns the area of what might be called "inferred rights," rights that may be implied under a broad mandate to guarantee workers "hazard-free" workplaces. One such right recently debated concerned the right of employees to refuse to work in protest of allegedly hazardous working conditions. A case involving workers at Whirlpool Corporation went all the way to the Supreme Court. Two maintenance men, employed by this company, refused to walk out on a wire-mesh screen suspended high above the factory floor when ordered to do so by their superior. The company suspended them for six hours, docked their pay, and issued written reprimands.[44]

In the OSHA Act, Congress passed certain employee rights and provided that a worker could not be discharged or discriminated against for exercising them. The question is whether the right to refuse highly dangerous work was one of them. OSHA said that in addition to rights specifically enumerated, certain other rights exist by necessary implication. The company argued that if Congress had wanted to create such a right it would have done so, and to give workers the right to decide for themselves what is unsafe and reject assignments accordingly would open the door to mischief and abuse.

The Supreme Court unanimously upheld the right of workers to refuse, free from employer retaliation, to perform jobs they consider too dangerous. The regulation supporting this right "clearly conforms to the fundamental objective of the (OSHA) Act—to prevent occupational deaths and serious injuries," the Court said. Employees are legally protected when they refuse work of such a nature that a reasonable person under the circumstances then confronting the employee would conclude that there is a real danger of death or serious injury and there is insufficient time to eliminate the danger through resort to the regular enforcement channels.

---

[43]"Justices Uphold Right of Job Safety Unit to Set Penalties without Going to Court," *The Wall Street Journal*, March 24, 1977, p. 6. See also Michael A. Verespej, "OSHA's Power Reaffirmed," *Industry Week*, April 25, 1977, p. 54.

[44]Urban C. Lehner, "High Court Considers Workers' Right to Refuse Duties They See as Unsafe," *The Wall Street Journal*, January 10, 1980, p. 12.

The court made clear, however, that employers are under no legal obligation to pay workers who refuse to perform assigned tasks.[45]

Costs and Benefits

Before the Roundtable and Weidenbaum studies (see Chapter 9), there were numerous attempts to estimate the costs of the government's safety and health program. For example, in 1974, the National Association of Manufacturers surveyed its membership about the costs of meeting OSHA standards. The mean estimates of its membership ranged from $35,000 for firms with 100 or fewer employees to $4.7 million for those firms with over 5,000 employees.[46]

Another study that relied on business sources was completed by Dun's Review. This study estimated that compliance with OSHA standards would raise costs in many industries by 5 to 10 percent. It also cited estimates that OSHA compliance would cost the metal-stamping industry $6 million over a five-year period, and would add $2,000 to $3,000 to the cost of an average new home.[47]

Thus OSHA imposes substantial costs on business that vary a good deal by type of industry. The key question is, of course, whether the benefits being provided to workers and society exceed these costs, making the federal effort to regulate safety and health a worthwhile program. Without getting into the valuation of human life, the benefits that legitimately could be expected from the program include the following.

The greater productivity of those who would have sustained a job-related injury or illness in the absence of government regulation.

The greater enjoyment of life by those who thus avoided work-related disabilities.

The resources that would have had to be used in the treatment and rehabilitation of victims of work-related injuries or illnesses which were avoided.

The resources that would have had to be used to administer workmen's compensation and insurance, and to train those who would have been needed to replace the sick or disabled.

The reduction in the private efforts to increase occupational safety and health, which are replaced or reduced by the government's efforts.

The consequent decrease in damage to plant and equipment.

The savings that result from less disruption of work routines caused by accidents plus potential improvements in the morale and productivity of the workforce.[48]

For the first few years, no good data were available to show what impact the program was having. Since OSHA also made a change in the methods by which injury rate data were collected, it was impossible to make pre- and

---

[45]*Whirlpool v. Marshall,* 100 S. Ct. 883 (1980).

[46]Nichols and Zeckhauser, "OSHA," p. 56.

[47]*Ibid.*

[48]Murray L. Weidenbaum, *Business, Government, and the Public* (Englewood Cliffs, N.J.: Prentice-Hall, 1977), p. 66.

post-OSHA comparisons. By 1975, however, enough data had been collected to begin developing a record during the years OSHA had been in existence. The data for that year (1975) showed a drop in job-related deaths, injuries, and illnesses. While some argued that this drop reflected the high unemployment rates of 1975, which reduced the number of people working and hours worked, the Labor Department claimed that these figures were a positive indication of the success of national efforts to reduce such tragedies.[49]

Further declines appeared in 1976, but in 1977, the number of on-the-job fatalities among employers with 11 or more workers showed a sharp increase, 20 percent higher than the previous year. This kind of fluctuation raised some fundamental questions about the OSHA program and the meaning of the statistics. Did they actually reflect the efforts of government to reduce accidents and thus elucidate the failure of the regulatory effort? Or did they, as some argued, reflect such demographic factors as a young, inexperienced workforce more than the results of a regulatory program? The answers to these questions are complex and cast doubts on the ability to attribute changes in accident statistics to specific causes or programs.[50]

Alternatives

The difficulties that OSHA has experienced to date raise some fundamental questions about the whole program. As Nichols and Zeckhauser state: "An important question is whether the agency's failures have resulted simply from faulty execution (including the overly hasty adoption of thousands of consensus standards, excessive emphasis on safety relative to health, the inevitable start-up problems of any new agency, and, more controversially, the exclusion of economic considerations in all but extreme cases) or whether they were inherent in the basic approach taken: direct regulation through standards and inspections."[51] In any event, reducing injuries and illnesses in the workplace can result in a gain for everyone provided it is done effectively. Thus alternative methods to direct regulation deserve consideration.

One alternative is to make more information available to both employees and potential employees about the potential risks involved in working in a particular facility. Not only would information be provided about potentially dangerous substances a person might be exposed to and what steps were being taken to reduce exposure, but injury and illness data also could be made available. Some means would have to be developed to ensure that these data were accurate—perhaps some kind of auditing procedure. But if the data were accurate, the employees or candidates for employment could assess the risks involved against wage levels and other benefits provided by the company and make their decisions accordingly. This approach would thus stress the provision of relevant information and assumes that workers

[49]"Decline in Job Injuries Seen Linked to OSHA Effort," *Job Safety and Health*, January 1977, p. 5.
[50]"Accident Statistics that Jolted OSHA," *Business Week*, December 11, 1978, p. 62.
[51]Nichols and Zeckhauser, "OSHA," pp. 62–63.

would be intelligent enough to process this information. If safety and health were a serious concern of workers, companies with poor records and high risks either would have to pay more to attract workers or reduce the risks involved.

A newly developing discipline called risk-assessment could also be helpful in this approach. Perhaps a uniform method of assessing risk could be agreed upon, allowing comparisons between companies to be made on the basis of a single index number. Such a formal procedure could also help individual businesspeople and government policy-makers allocate resources where they will be more effective in reducing risk of injury or illness.

A performance-based approach, such as injury or exposure taxes, is also a possibility. An injury tax, for example, could be based on industrywide averages for accident frequency and severity rates or even on broader averages related to industries with comparable hazards. But however the reference standard is determined, employers who exceeded the standard would be taxed a substantial amount of money. These taxes would be tied to the actual performance of the company and would provide an incentive to improve the company's record. If the injury rate were not reduced, the prices of goods produced would have to rise to reflect the cost of the tax, thus shifting demand to goods produced under less hazardous conditions. Such an approach would also give employers the freedom to find the most efficient method of improving safety, as there would be no OSHA regulating conditions of production.[52]

Similarly, an exposure level to substances known to be harmful could also be set and taxes levied on a sliding scale of exposure above the standard. It would be necessary, of course, to set fee schedules for individual substances. This would be a subject of some debate and monitoring of exposure levels would still be required. But such an approach would again give an employer freedom to find the least expensive method of attaining the exposure level, taking the peculiarities of the industry and facility into account.[53]

This kind of performance-oriented approach would focus the effort where it should be focused, on the end result rather than on the actual conditions of the workplace, where the connection with safety and health is not altogether clear in most instances. To attain satisfactory performance, employers, not government agencies, would be required to devote more serious attention to improving performance rather than complying with safety standards, worrying about inspections, penalties, and similar items. The advantages of such a performance-based approach are summarized as follows:

> By providing appropriate incentives and then leaving decisions to the firm, efficiency is promoted in a number of ways: Regulatory impositions whose costs are well out of line with the benefits provided are avoided; variations among firms and industries in their costs and capabilities for achieving gains are automatically recognized; all possible methods for increasing workplace safety and health are pursued, including enhanced training, changed work practices, and new technologies; and pressure is maintained to achieve further gains.[54]

[52]*Ibid.*, pp. 64–67.
[53]*Ibid.*,
[54]*Ibid.*, p. 67.

324   OCCUPATIONAL SAFETY AND HEALTH

Options such as these have been considered by a presidential task force. Replacing the existing system of inspection and enforcement procedures with economic incentives is generally opposed by the labor unions, however. ✓ Typical is the statement by Steven H. Wodka, an official of the Oil, Chemical, and Atomic Workers International Union: "The only thing that has ever worked is strict enforcement, heavy fines, and stringent citations."[55]

Yet OSHA provides a lesson in how not to start a regulatory program. As stated by Nichols and Zeckhauser: "The chain of causality in the creation of OSHA ran from perceived crisis, through political pressure, to regulatory response. At no juncture did basic conceptual questions relating to market performance or failure, and the appropriate role for government to assume in response, play an important role in the debate. The lesson, a painful one for economists, is that however relevant or powerful economic concepts may be, they are likely to be ignored when political passions are strong."[56]

Questions for Discussion

1. What were the prevailing attitudes toward safety and health in the workplace during the early years of this century? What was the basis of these attitudes? How have these attitudes changed?
2. What are workman's compensation laws? What advantages did they have over the present system? Why didn't they work adequately in dealing with safety and health?
3. Identify the various factors behind the establishment of a federal safety and health program. Which, in your opinion, were most important? Was it inevitable that the federal government eventually intervene to regulate safety and health in the workplace?
4. Describe how the goals of the Occupational Safety and Health Act are to be accomplished. What are the functions of each piece of OSHA's administrative structure? Describe the inspection system. What problems exist with this kind of system?
5. Comment on employer and employee responsibilities and rights. Where does most of the burden fall? What are the most important rights employers have? What are the most important responsibilities of employees?
6. Should employers with good safety records be exempt from OSHA inspections? Would such a procedure increase the effectiveness of OSHA? In what ways?
7. What are the major problems with safety standards? What was the process by which OSHA adopted safety standards? What are the problems involved in setting health standards? Would some kind of a classification system work better?
8. Should cost-benefit analysis be used to set standards? Why or why not? Does the law require OSHA to do such analysis? How would you rule on this question?
9. Should OSHA be required to get search warrants? Did the court ruling requiring search warrants gut the enforcement program? Is the element of surprise important to effective enforcement?
10. What are "inferred rights" for employees? Has the Supreme Court opened up a Pandora's box with its recent ruling supporting a worker's right to refuse dangerous work free from employer retaliation?
11. Do the data on death, injuries, and illnesses actually reflect the effectiveness or ineffectiveness of the federal programs? If not, how would you measure the programs' effectiveness?

[55]"A New Set of Incentives to Make OSHA Work," *Business Week*, October 31, 1977, p. 36.
[56]Nichols and Zeckhauser, "OSHA," pp. 67–68.

12. Where did OSHA go wrong? Can its deficiencies be corrected? Are alternatives the only answer to improving safety and health in the workplace? Which alternative do you like best?

Suggested Reading

Accident Prevention Manual for Industrial Operations. National Safety Council, 7th ed., 1974.

Binford, Charles M., Fleming, Cecil S., and Prust, Z. A. *Loss Control in the OSHA Era.* New York: McGraw-Hill, 1975.

Bird, Frank E. *Management Guide to Loss Control.* Atlanta: Institute Press, 1974.

Boley, Jack W. *A Guide to Effective Industrial Safety.* Houston, Tex.: Gulf Publishing Co., 1977.

Gilmore, Charles L. *Accident Prevention and Loss Control.* American Management Association, 1970.

Hamilton, Alice. *Exploring the Dangerous Trades.* New York: Harper & Row, 1948.

Page, Joseph A. *Bitter Wages.* New York: Grossman Publishers, 1973.

Poulton, E. *The Environment at Work.* Springfield, Ill.: Charles C. Thomas, 1979.

Rothstein, Mark A. *Occupational Safety and Health Law.* St. Paul, Minn.: West Publishing Co., 1978.

Scott, Rachel. *Muscle and Blood.* New York: Dutton, 1974.

Simonds, Rollin H., and Grimaldi, John V. *Safety Management.* Homewood, Ill.: Richard D. Irwin, 1963.

Stellman, Jeanne M., and Daum, Susan M. *Work Is Dangerous to Your Health.* New York: Pantheon Books, 1973.

Wallick, Franklin. *The American Worker: An Endangered Species.* New York: Ballantine Books, 1972.

16

Consumerism

Consumerism is a movement designed to improve the rights and powers of consumers in relation to the sellers of products and services. It is a protest movement of consumers against what they or their advocates see as unfair, discriminatory, and arbitrary treatment. Consumerism is as old as business but has taken on new dimensions and thrusts in recent years. . . .

Consumerism does not mean that *caveat emptor*—let the buyer beware—is replaced by *caveat venditor*—let the seller beware. It does mean, however, that protecting the consumer is politically acceptable and that the government will survey consumer demands for better treatment and respond to them with new guidelines for and regulations over business.[1]

Consumerism is a broad and aggressive movement supported by consumers themselves, particularly consumer advocates, by many business organizations, and by the government. The movement was formed to see that the rights of consumers are respected and consequently that consumers are protected from a wide range of practices that can infringe upon these rights.

This chapter will focus on the rights of the consumer that need to be protected, and will examine the various activities of the government, consumer advocates, and business organizations themselves to protect these rights. First these activities will be looked at in historical perspective, and then examined from the standpoint of current consumer concerns.

History of Consumerism

Consumerism is not just a current phenomenon, as some people might suspect. Consumers obviously have been concerned about various aspects of

---

[1]George A. Steiner and John F. Steiner, *Business, Government, and Society: A Managerial Perspective* (New York: Random House, 1980), pp. 273–274. Quoted with permission.

the products they buy ever since the marketplace has existed. But in terms of the development of consumerism in this country, there are three distinct periods when something called a consumer movement can be identified. The concerns of the movements in each of these periods were different.[2]

Muckraking Era. Between 1879 and 1905, a number of bills were introduced into Congress to regulate the sale of food and drugs and protect consumers from the growing power of large business enterprises. However, these bills were apparently the work of a small group of consumer advocates, as both Congress and the public at large were rather apathetic about any public policy measures directed to protect consumers. This apathy, coupled with strong business opposition to the bills, meant that no action was taken on the consumer front during these years.

Then, in 1905, a book was published that changed the public's attitude dramatically. That book was Upton Sinclair's *The Jungle*, a sordid tale of conditions in the Chicago meat-packing industry. The original intent of the book may have been to focus on working conditions, as it told the story of an immigrant who came to this country to make his fortune. After some years of working long hours in unsafe and unhealthy conditions, however, he ended up on the "scrap heap" with his health broken and no money in his pocket. Thus ended the American dream.

What the public seized upon, however, were the conditions under which the food they were buying was produced and packaged. The book gave gruesome examples of the way meat was processed (see box). This book, more than any other single event, jolted the public out of its apathy and made the need for consumer protection apparent to many people. Congress responded by passing the following public policy measures.

- Pure Food and Drug Act (1906): Outlawed adulterations and misbranding of food and drugs sold in interstate commerce. This basic act has been amended many times since.
- Federal Meat Inspection Act (1907): Provided for federal inspection of meat sold in interstate commerce. Gave the Department of Agriculture power to inspect slaughtering, packing, and canning plants.
- Federal Trade Commission Act (1914): Designed to protect consumers from unfair methods of competition. Created the Federal Trade Commission to administer the act.
- Water Power Act (1920): Established the Federal Power Commission to protect consumers from public utility monopolies, making these monopolies subject to government regulation.

The focus of these efforts was to protect consumers from unsavory and unfair trade practices that were unknown to many people. The term "muckraking" is appropriate, as this movement was designed to expose these practices of business and build public support for public policy measures. This movement ended for all practical purposes before the depression, since prosperity for all became the order of the day, but the depression finally

[2]See Ralph M. Gaedeke, "The Movement for Consumer Protection: A Century of Mixed Accomplishments," *University of Washington Business Review* (Spring 1970), pp. 31–40.

THE JUNGLE

All of these were sinister incidents; but they were trifles compared to what Jurgis saw with his own eyes before long. One curious thing he had noticed, the very first day, in his profession of shoveler of guts; which was the sharp trick of the floor bosses whenever there chanced to come a "slunk" calf. Any man who knows anything about butchering knows that the flesh of a cow that is about to calve, or has just calved, is not fit for food. A good many of these came every day to the packing houses—and, of course, if they had chosen, it would have been an easy matter for the packers to keep them till they were fit for food. But for the saving of time and fodder, it was the law that cows of that sort came along with the others, and whoever noticed it would tell the boss, and the boss would start up a conversation with the government inspector, and the two would stroll away. So in a trice the carcass of the cow would be cleaned out, and the entrails would have vanished; it was Jurgis's task to slide them into the trap, calves and all, and on the floor they took out these "slunk" calves, and butchered them for meat, and used even the skins of them.

One day a man slipped and hurt his leg; and that afternoon, when the last of the cattle had been disposed of, and the men were leaving, Jurgis was ordered to remain and do some special work which this injured man had usually done. It was late, almost dark, and the government inspectors had all gone, and there were only a dozen or two of men on the floor. That day they had killed about four thousand cattle, and these cattle had come in freight trains from far states, and some of them had got hurt. There were some with broken legs, and some with gored sides; there were some that had died, from what cause no one could say; and they were all to be disposed of, here in darkness and silence. "Downers," the men called them; and the packing house had a special elevator upon which they were raised to the killing beds, where the gang proceeded to handle them, with an air of businesslike nonchalance which said plainer than any words that it was a matter of everyday routine. It took a couple of hours to get them out of the way, and in the end Jurgis saw them go into the chilling rooms with the rest of the meat, being carefully scattered here and there so that they could not be identified. When he came home that night he was in a very somber mood, having begun to see at last how those might be right who had laughed at him for his faith in America.

From Upton Sinclair, *The Jungle* (New York: New American Library, 1960), pp. 66–67. Reprinted with permission.

ended concerns of this kind because much of the public came to have other worries.

The Information Era. This era was again sparked by a book, called *Your Money's Worth* and written by Stuart Chase and F. J. Schlink. This book pictured the consumer as an "Alice in a Wonderland" of conflicting product claims and bright promises. It focused on advertising and packaging that inundated the consumer with information designed to sell a product rather than help the consumer make an intelligent decision. The consumer had no way to sort through all these conflicting claims and rosy promises to decide which could be believed and which were pure exaggeration.

The book made a plea for impartial product-testing agencies that had no vested interest in the product and thus could supply the consumer with objective information about the performance of the product that could be trusted. The 1930s, then, saw the development of independent consumer testing agencies, such as Consumers Union, that would test products and publish the results. In addition, some important public policy measures were also passed in the 1930s.

- Food, Drug, and Cosmetics Act (1938): Amended the earlier law by strengthening the definitions of adulteration and misbranding, and extended the scope of the law to cover cosmetics and therapeutic devices. Also established the Food and Drug Administration, with authority to seize products found unfit for consumption and prosecute persons or firms found in violation.
- Wheeler-Lea Act (1938): Amended the Federal Trade Commission Act of 1914 to give the FTC regulatory power over the advertising of food, drugs, cosmetics, and therapeutic devices.
- Wool Products Labeling Act (1939): Required labels on woolen goods to tell consumers the percentages of wool, reprocessed wool, and reused wool in the product.

The concern in this period was mainly with the provision of accurate and relevant information to consumers that could aid them in making intelligent and informed purchase decisions. The earlier concern about the quality of products, of course, continued, but the major focus was on advertising and labeling of products. The second World War marked the end of this particular consumer movement.

Continuing Consumer Concern. From the end of the Second World War until about 1965, there wasn't anything that could be clearly identified as a consumer movement. It was a period of widespread prosperity; consumers were being "blessed to death" with a proliferation of new products, and apparently were generally satisfied with the treatment they were getting. Nevertheless, there was a continuing concern about product quality and provision of information, as exemplified in the following public policy measures.

- Fur Products Labeling Act (1951): Stated mandatory specifications for the labeling, invoicing, and advertising of fur products.
- Flammable Fabrics Act (1953): Prohibited making clothing from highly flammable materials.
- Poultry Products Inspection Act (1957): Provided for government inspection of poultry products in interstate commerce.
- Textile Fiber Products Identification Act (1958): Required labels on clothing to show the percentage of textile fiber content and regulated the use of names for synthetic fibers. Also required the identification of the producer or distributor and country of origin.
- Food, Drug, and Cosmetics Act Amendments (1958): Further extended the Food and Drug Act to provide for regulation of food additives.
- Hazardous Substances Labeling Act (1960): Required warning labels on products used in households that were toxic, corrosive, irritating, or flammable.
- Food, Drug, and Cosmetic Act Amendments (1962): Known as the

Kefauver-Harris Drug Amendments, these amendments required pre-testing of drugs for effectiveness as well as safety and prescribed that drugs be labeled by the generic name.

Modern Consumer Movement. The modern consumer movement began in 1965 with the publication of another book, Ralph Nader's *Unsafe at Any Speed,* which eventually became a well-known book if not a best-seller. The book was critical about the safety of the Corvair automobile and indicted its producer, General Motors, for a lack of concern about automobile safety. The issue received national attention when it became public knowledge that General Motors had hired private investigators to follow Nader and investigate him while he was a witness for a Senate subcommittee. The president of General Motors, James Roche, apologized to Nader for these actions at a public hearing of the subcommittee. This apology, of course, received national television coverage and was very embarrassing to the company.

Not only did Nader receive instant publicity and notoriety because of this event, he also filed suit against General Motors and eventually settled out of court for $425,000, most of which was used to start his organization. Thus General Motors ironically helped Nader rise out of obscurity and financed his start in the public interest arena. This is not to suggest that without the General Motors incident a new consumer movement would never have begun. If it had not been Nader and automobile safety, it probably would have been someone else on some other issue.

The time was ripe for a new consumer movement to be concerned with a range of issues that grew out of a highly affluent population, a technologically sophisticated marketplace, and a society that in general had high expectations and aspirations for the fulfillment of higher needs. This modern consumer movement had no particular focus, as did the previous movements, but was concerned about a variety of issues related to the marketplace, including product safety, quality of products, reliability and product obsolescence, truth in advertising and packaging, uses of credit, completeness of information, product warranties, product liability, and other issues. This range of issues is exemplified in the consumer legislation that came pouring out of Congress in the latter half of the 1960s and early 1970s, most of which is listed below.

- Cigarette Labeling and Advertising Act (1966): Required labels on cigarette packages warning consumers about the dangers of smoking.
- Fair Packaging and Labeling Act (1966): Also known as the Truth-in-Packaging Act, this measure specified mandatory labeling requirements regarding identity and quantity of many household products.
- Child Protection Act (1966): Banned the sale of hazardous toys and articles intended for children.
- National Traffic and Motor Vehicle Safety Act (1966): Provided for a national safety program and the establishment of safety standards for motor vehicles.
- Wholesome Meat Act (1967): Required states to meet federal meat inspection standards and raised quality standards for imported meat.
- Flammable Fabrics Act Amendments (1967): Broadened the authority

of the federal government to set safety standards for flammable products including household products, fabrics, and materials.

- Consumer Credit Protection Act (1968): Also known as the Truth-in-Lending Act, this measure required full disclosure of the terms and conditions of finance charges for consumer loans and installment purchases.
- Wholesome Poultry Products Act (1968): Provided federal support for improving state-level poultry regulation.
- Radiation Control for Health and Safety Act (1968): Provided for mandatory control standards and recall of faulty electronic products.
- Child Protection and Toy Safety Act (1969): Broadened coverage of the Child Protection Act to include electrical, mechanical, and thermal hazards.
- Public Health Smoking Act (1970): Prohibited cigarette advertising on television and radio and required a revision of the warning label on cigarette packages.
- Amendments to the Federal Deposit Insurance Act (1970): Prohibited issuance of unsolicited credit cards, limited a customer's liability in case of loss or theft, regulated credit bureaus, and provided consumers with access to their credit files.
- Poison Prevention Packaging Act (1970): Authorized standards for child-resistant packaging of hazardous substances, such as drugs and medicine.
- Lead-Based Paint Elimination Act (1971): Provided assistance in developing and administering programs to eliminate lead-based paints.
- Consumer Product Safety Act (1972): Established a Federal Consumer Product Safety Commission, with the authority to create safety standards for consumer products and ban those products presenting an undue risk of injury to consumers.

Not only was Congress active in responding to consumer issues, the executive branch was active as well. President Kennedy delivered a special message to Congress calling for a broad range of legislative and administrative action to assist consumers. Kennedy directed that the Council of Economic Advisers create a Consumer's Advisory Council and that heads of federal agencies concerned with consumer welfare appoint special assistants to advise them on consumer issues. In addition, Kennedy enunciated what has since come to be called the consumer bill of rights (see box).

President Johnson built consumer representation more directly into the executive branch by appointing a Special Assistant for Consumer Affairs. President Nixon extended this concept by asking Congress in another special message to create a new Office of Consumer Affairs in the Executive Office of the President with a larger budget and greater responsibilities. Legislation was introduced in the 91st Congress to establish a new Department of Consumer Affairs, headed by a secretary with full cabinet rank. While this legislation did not pass, President Ford built consumer representation in every cabinet department as an alternative to the Consumer Protection Agency (see next section). Finally, President Carter issued Executive

THE CONSUMER BILL OF RIGHTS

President Kennedy first listed four rights of consumers that he believed needed protection: the right to safety, the right to a choice, the right to know, and the right to be heard. These rights were later supported by President Nixon. To these might be added a fifth right, the right to full value. Thus a complete consumer bill of rights contains the following:

1. The Right to Safety: The consumer has a right to be protected from dangerous products that might cause injury or illness as well as from the thoughtless actions of other consumers.
2. The Right to a Choice: The consumer has the right to be able to select products from a range of alternatives offered by competing firms.
3. The Right to Know: The consumer must have access to readily available, relevant, and accurate information to use in making purchase decisions.
4. The Right to Be Heard: The consumer must be able to obtain redress for injuries or damages suffered and have someone respond to legitimate complaints about abuses taking place in the market.
5. The Right to Value: The consumer has a right to expect a product to perform as advertised and meet the expectations that were created so that the consumer is getting full value for the money spent.

Order 12160 ordering all federal agencies to review their procedures to see that consumer interests are adequately addressed. The Order called for each agency to have a consumer staff, meaningful participation by consumers, informational materials for the public, adequate public access and complaint handling, and technical assistance to consumer organizations.

Government Agencies

Various agencies in the government have, of course, been a most active part of the consumer movement. Some new agencies were created during the modern consumer movement and additional responsibilities were given to some of the existing agencies. These agencies will be described in some detail because of the impact they have on businesses producing consumer products.

Federal Trade Commission. Established in 1914, the FTC was a product of Woodrow Wilson's philosophy toward consumers, which advocated policies of freeing them from monopolies and restoring competition.[3] Under Section 5 of the Federal Trade Commission Act, the agency was empowered to protect consumers against all "unfair methods of competition." With this mandate, the agency became involved in consumer-protection litigation as well as antitrust activities. The agency's consumer-protection authority, however, was restricted in 1931 by a Supreme Court decision which held that Section 5 did not reach trade practices, no matter how injurious to consumers, that did not injure competitors or the competi-

[3]Thomas G. Krattenmaker, "The Federal Trade Commission and Consumer Protection," *California Management Review*, Vol. XVIII, No. 4 (Summer 1976), p. 92.

tive process.[4] Seven years later Congress corrected this deficiency by amending Section 5 to give the agency authority for "unfair or deceptive acts or practices in commerce."

Thus empowered, the FTC has broader authority to regulate business than almost any other agency (see Exhibit 16.1). To protect the public against all "unfair methods of competition" and all "unfair or deceptive acts or practices in commerce" is a very broad mandate. To carry out its mandate, the FTC uses a variety of enforcement techniques to bring accused violators of laws under its jurisdiction into compliance. For example, the FTC can issue "cease and desist" orders for violations of the FTC Act to stop a business from continuing the proscribed conduct. Over the last few years, Congress has also given the FTC responsibility for the enforcement of a number of specialized consumer-protection statutes, including the Truth-in-Lending Act, the Truth-in-Packaging Act, and the Fair Credit Reporting Act. In addition, the agency can promulgate trade regulation rules that affect entire industries. An example of such a rule is an FTC proposal to ban the advertising of sugared products on children's television programs.

The agency is governed by a chairman and four other commissioners, all of whom are appointed by the President with the advice and consent of the Senate. The agency is organized into three major bureaus. The Bureau of Competition investigates and prosecutes antitrust cases. The Bureau of Consumer Protection is concerned with such consumer-protection activities as advertising practices, marketing abuse, credit practices, energy and product information, and product liability. The Bureau of Economics provides statistical information and economic analysis to the other bureaus. In addition, the agency has twelve regional offices engaged primarily in consumer-protection matters and coordinated by the Washington headquarters.

For much of its history, the FTC was not particularly active and did not present the threat to business that it has in recent years. It responded to many individual complaints but did not take much broader corrective action against the offending parties to change industry practice. The years from 1914 to 1969 have been characterized as years of neglect.[5] The commission became much more active in the 1970s because of the appointment of a more active chairman and an exposé written by the Nader organization. In the late 1970s, there was concern that the FTC was getting too active, and Congress took steps to block some of its trade regulations pertaining to advertising on children's television programs and the funeral industry. Talk about a legislative veto over all trade rules became widespread and was actually implemented when Congress reauthorized the agency in 1980.

Consumer Product Safety Commission. The CPSC was created by the Consumer Product Safety Act of 1972 to protect the public against unreasonable risks of injury associated with a wide range of consumer products. The background of this act was a National Commission study on product safety which found that 20 million Americans were injured severely enough each year because of product-related accidents to require medical treatment. Some 110,000 of these people were permanently disabled and 30,000 were killed, at a cost to the economy of more than $5.5 billion

[4]*Ibid.*, p. 93.
[5]*Ibid.*, pp. 94–95.

EXHIBIT 16.1 ———————————————————————————

FEDERAL TRADE COMMISSION
Pennsylvania Avenue at Sixth St. NW, Washington, D.C. 20580
Telephone: (202) 523-3625

Purpose: To ensure "vigorous, free and fair competition in the market place."

Regulatory Activity: The Commission has authority to act against and prevent: 1) general restraint of trade in interstate commerce; 2) false or deceptive advertising of consumer goods and other unfair or deceptive practices; 3) activities that tend to lessen competition or create a monopoly, such as price discrimination and certain mergers and acquisitions. The FTC also formulates its own "trade regulation rules," which have the force of law. When statutes are violated, it can issue a cease-and-desist order, conduct formal litigation, or seek civil penalties.

Established: 1914

Legislative Authority:
  Enabling Legislation: Federal Trade Commission Act of 1914 (38 Stat. 717), as
                amended (52 Stat. 111)

  The FTC also has responsibility for enforcement of the following acts:
    Clayton Act of 1914 (38 Stat. 730)
    Export Trade Act of 1918 (40 Stat. 516)
    Robinson-Patman Act of 1936 (49 Stat. 1526)
    Wool Products Labeling Act of 1940 (54 Stat. 1128)
    Lanham Trademark Act of 1946 (60 Stat. 427)
    Fur Products Labeling Act of 1951 (65 Stat. 175)
    Textile Fiber Products Identification Act of 1958 (72 Stat. 1717)
    Fair Packaging and Labeling Act of 1966 (80 Stat. 1269)
    Truth-in-Lending Act of 1969 (82 Stat. 146)
    Fair Credit Reporting Act of 1970 (84 Stat. 1521)
    Fair Credit Billing Act of 1974 (88 Stat. 1511)
    Magnuson-Moss Warranty—Federal Trade Commission Improvement Act of
      1975 (88 Stat. 2123)
    Hart-Scott-Rodino Antitrust Improvement Act of 1976 (90 Stat. 1383)
    Debt Collection Act of 1977 (91 Stat. 874)

Organization: The Commission became an independent administrative agency in 1951. It is headed by a five-member commission appointed to seven-year terms by the President with the advice and consent of the Senate.

Additional Responsibilities: The Commission also regulates various aspects of the consumer credit industry, including issuance of loans and credit cards and activities of credit reporting agencies and debt collection agencies; packaging and labeling of certain consumer commodities; and certain aspects of the fur and textile industries.

Budgets and Staffing
(Fiscal Years 1970-1981)

	70	71	72	73	74	75	76	77	78	79	(Estimated) 80	81
Budget ($ millions)	20	22	25	27	32	39	44	52	59	63	70	71
Staffing	1385	1385	1390	1530	1560	1569	1638	1668	1650	1665	1665	1665

From Ronald J. Penoyer, *Directory of Federal Regulatory Agencies,* 2nd ed. (St. Louis, Mo.: Washington University Center for the Study of American Business, 1980), p. 37. Reprinted with permission.

annually.[6] As with the background of OSHA, a crisis situation was believed to exist that demanded government attention. The solution to the crisis was again, as with OSHA, direct regulation.

The CPSC is another five-member commission headquartered in Washington, D.C., with fourteen field offices and testing laboratories around the country. The jurisdiction of the commission covers a broad range of consumer products, including ladders, swings, blenders, televisions, stoves, as well as stairs, ramps, windowsills, doors, and electrical wiring. The only consumer products not covered by the act are foods, drugs, cosmetics, automobiles, firearms, tobacco, boats, pesticides, and aircraft, all of which are regulated by other agencies. The agency was also given responsibility, like the FTC, for enforcing specific consumer legislation, including the Flammable Fabrics Act, the Refrigerator Safety Act, the Hazardous Substances Act, and the Poison Prevention Packaging Act[7] (see Exhibit 16.2).

The CPSC has the authority and responsibility to (1) develop and enforce uniform safety standards governing the design, construction, contents, performance, and labeling of all the consumer products under its jurisdiction, (2) ban consumer products deemed to be hazardous, (3) help consumers evaluate the comparative safety of products, (4) gather medical statistics and conduct research on product-related injuries, and (5) help to harmonize federal, state, and local product safety laws and enforcement.

Regarding its enforcement powers, the commission can order a manufacturer, wholesaler, distributor, or retailer to recall, repair, or replace any product that it determines in the course of its research to be unreasonably risky. Where the action is deemed to be justified because of the hazard involved, the commission can simply ban the product from being sold on the market. The fines involved range from $50,000 to $500,000, with a possible jail term of up to one year for violations. In addition, the act also requires manufacturers, wholesalers, distributors, or retailers to report within twenty-four hours the existence of any substantial product hazard that is known. The agency can then demand corrective action including refunds, recalls, dissemination of public earnings, and reimbursement of buyers for expenses they incur in the process. Over the course of its existence, the CPSC has adopted about a dozen mandatory standards for products ranging from swimming pool slides to matchbook covers, and has forced business to adopt several dozen voluntary standards. It has also banned some products and forced recalls of many others.

The Food and Drug Administration. The Food and Drug Administration (FDA), located in the Department of Health and Human Services, has been given the mandate to protect the public against impure and unsafe foods, drugs, and cosmetics, and to regulate hazards involved with medical devices and radiation. In addition to the basic Food and Drug Act of 1906, which has been amended many times since, the FDA has also been given responsibility for specific consumer legislation (see Exhibit 16.3).

The FDA's responsibility for drug regulation is carried out by the Bureau

[6]R. David Pittle, "The Consumer Product Safety Commission," *California Management Review*, Vol. XVIII, No. 4 (Summer 1976), p. 105.
. [7]*Ibid.*

EXHIBIT 16.2

CONSUMER PRODUCT SAFETY COMMISSION
1111 Eighteenth Street NW, Washington, D.C. 20207
Telephone: (301) 492-6590

Purpose: To protect the public against unreasonable risks of injury associated with consumer products.

Regulatory Activity: The Commission has authority: (1) to issue and enforce safety standards governing the design, construction, contents, performance, and labeling of more than 10,000 consumer products; and (2) to ban hazardous consumer products.

Established: October 27, 1972

Legislative Authority:
Enabling Legislation: Consumer Product Safety Act of 1972 (86 Stat. 1207; P.L. 92-573)

The Commission is responsible for the administration of four acts, which were under the jurisdiction of different agencies until 1972:
Flammable Fabrics Act of 1954 (67 Stat. 111; P.L. 83-88), as amended
Refrigerator Safety Act of 1956 (70 Stat. 953; P.L. 84-930)
Hazardous Substances Act of 1960 (74 Stat. 372; P.L. 86-613), as amended
Poison Prevention Packaging Act of 1970 (84 Stat. 1670; P.L. 91-601)

Organization: This independent agency is governed by a five-member commission, appointed for seven-year terms by the President, with the advice and consent of the Senate.

Products Regulated: ". . . any article or component part produced or distributed (i) for sale to a consumer . . . or (ii) for the personal use, consumption or enjoyment of a consumer . . ."

Products Exempted: Tobacco and tobacco products; motor vehicles and motor vehicle equipment; drugs; food; aircraft and aircraft components; certain boats; and certain other items.

Budgets and Staffing
(Fiscal Years 1973-1981)

	73	74	75	76	77	78	79	(Estimated) 80	81
Budget ($ millions)	*	19	34	38	40	40	39	45	44
Staffing	586	836	890	896	889	900	881	880	880

*Less than $1 million

From Ronald J. Penoyer, *Directory of Federal Regulatory Agencies,* 2nd ed. (St. Louis, Mo.: Washington University Center for the Study of American Business, 1980), p. 23. Reprinted with permission.

of Drugs, which administers rigid premarket testing procedures. No new drug in the country can be marketed until teams of physicians, pharmacists, chemists, and statisticians from the Bureau of Drugs have completed a thorough assessment. Firms wanting to place a new drug on the market must develop data to show that it is safe and effective and must also prove to the Bureau's satisfaction that adequate controls are provided to ensure proper identification, quality, purity, and strength of the new drug. The FDA now also requires pharmaceutical companies to monitor usage and side effects of drugs after they have been placed on the market. This procedure will

EXHIBIT 16.3 ——————————————————————————————

Department of Health and Human Services
FOOD AND DRUG ADMINISTRATION
5600 Fishers Lane, Rockville, Maryland 20857
Telephone: (301) 443-3170

Purpose: To protect the public against impure and unsafe foods, drugs, and cosmetics, and to regulate hazards involved with medical devices and radiation.

Regulatory Activity: The FDA (1) regulates, inspects, tests, sets standards for, and licenses the manufacture of biological products shipped in interstate or foreign commerce; (2) sets standards for, monitors the quality of, and regulates labeling of all drugs for human use; (3) develops regulations for the composition, quality, nutrition, and safety of foods, food additives, colors, and cosmetics, and inspects processing plants and marketing establishments; (4) sets standards for safe limits of radiation exposure; (5) evaluates the safety of veterinary preparations and devices; and (6) develops policy for and evaluates the safety, efficacy and labeling of medical devices.

Established: 1931

Legislative Authority:
　　Enabling Legislation: Agriculture Appropriation Act of 1931 (46 Stat. 392)
　　　　Food and Drug Act of 1906 (34 Stat. 768)
　　　　Food, Drug, and Cosmetic Act of 1938 (52 Stat. 1040) and the following amendments to it:
　　　　　　Food Additives Amendment of 1958 (72 Stat. 1788) (Delaney Amendment)
　　　　　　Color Additive Amendments of 1960 (74 Stat. 403)
　　　　　　Drug Amendments of 1962 (76 Stat. 704)
　　　　　　Medical Devices Amendments of 1976 (90 Stat. 539)
　　　　Fair Packaging and Labeling Act of 1966 (80 Stat. 1296)
　　　　Radiation Control for Health and Safety Act of 1968 (82 Stat. 1173)

　　FDA is also responsible for portions of:
　　　　Tea Importation Act of 1897
　　　　Filled Milk Act of 1923 (42 Stat. 1486)
　　　　Public Health Services Act of 1944 (58 Stat. 697)
　　　　Federal Hazardous Substances Act of 1966 (80 Stat. 1303)

Organization: This agency, located within the Department of Health and Human Services, is headed by a commissioner.

Budgets and Staffing
(Fiscal Years 1970-1981)

	70	*71*	*72*	*73*	*74*	*75*	*76*	*77*	*78*	*79*	*(Estimated)* *80*	*81*
Budget ($ millions)	68	85	105	143	165	201	218	245	276	300	309	314
Staffing	4152	4360	5431	6751	6116	6206	6362	7340	7483	7656	7654	7643

From Ronald J. Penoyer, *Directory of Federal Regulatory Agencies,* 2nd ed. (St. Louis, Mo.: Washington University Center for the Study of American Business, 1980), p. 59. Reprinted with permission.

strengthen the FDA's "postmarketing surveillance" system to discover defective products and have them removed from commercial channels and detect previously unsuspected adverse side effects of drugs.[8]

The FDA's responsibility for medical devices was given it by 1976 amendments to the Food and Drug Act. These amendments empower the

[8]"FDA Is Requiring Pharmaceutical Firms to Conduct Postmarketing Drug Survey," *The Wall Street Journal,* January 23, 1980, p. 12.

FDA to remove ineffective or unsafe medical devices from the market and requires extensive testing of new devices before they are approved for sale on the market. The amendments also require companies to report significant defects they discover and to inform physicians and patients of these problems, and to repair or replace, or refund money on, such defective products. The background to this extension of authority was many reports of faulty cardiac pacemakers, unsafe X-ray machines, inaccurate thermometers, and similar problems.

The responsibility of the FDA for food safety stems from amendments to the Food, Drug, and Cosmetic Act passed in 1958, which contain the famous Delaney Clause on food additives. These amendments gave the FDA authority to develop regulations for the composition, quality, nutrition, and safety of foods and food additives. Much of the current controversy about food safety centers on this Delaney Clause, which rigidly requires the FDA to prohibit the use of any food additive that is found to cause cancer in humans or animals (see next section). The FDA is also involved in developing rules on food labeling specifying ingredient and nutritional information to be provided for consumers.

The FDA also has responsibility for a food inspection system to inspect processing plants and marketing establishments. The agency has about 1,000 inspectors who work in cooperation with state inspectors. They look for good management practices (GMP), which mainly involve sanitation. Where unsanitary conditions exist that need attention, the FDA must turn the case over to a federal attorney for prosecution. The agency has no power to prosecute directly as do some other regulatory commissions.

The National Highway Traffic Safety Administration. NHTSA was created by the Highway Safety Act of 1970 to set safety standards for motor vehicles. The Energy Policy and Conservation Act and Clean Air Amendments of 1970 also gave it authority to set standards for fuel economy and emissions. The responsibilities of the agency include setting and enforcing mandatory average fuel economy standards for new motor vehicles, regulating the safety performance of new and used motor vehicles and their equipment, such as tires, and investigating auto safety defects and requiring manufacturers to remedy them (see Exhibit 16.4).

Regarding safety standards, the agency has focused on problems that statistics show pose the greatest hazards to motorists and pedestrians. Plans include requiring air bags or similar passive devices in new cars by 1984 to protect car occupants in frontal collisions, issuing rules to protect occupants in side-impact crashes, extending existing occupant rules for cars to light trucks and vans, recommending various braking improvements for cars and trucks, and developing rules to reduce exterior hazards, such as protrusions and edges, that injure pedestrians.

The agency can also order recalls for safety defects that are not covered by standards. The newspaper headlines are full of such recalls: GM IS RECALLING 598,000 VEHICLES; FORD MOTOR COMPANY SETS RECALL OF 123,000 CARS; CHRYSLER RECALLING ONE MILLION VOLARES AND ASPENS. These recalls cover a variety of defects from engine mounts, gas tanks, seat backs, faulty carburetors, and the like. Some companies find the power of the agency difficult to fight (see box), particularly when there is enough evidence to support the existence of a defect.

EXHIBIT 16.4

Department of Transportation
NATIONAL HIGHWAY TRAFFIC SAFETY ADMINISTRATION
400 Seventh Street SW, Washington, D.C. 20590
Telephone: (800) 424-9393

Purpose: To set standards for motor vehicle safety and for motor vehicle fuel economy, and to set federal standards for various state highway safety programs.

Regulatory Activity: This agency (1) sets and enforces mandatory average fuel economy standards for new motor vehicles; (2) regulates safety performance for new and used vehicles and their equipment, including tires; (3) investigates auto safety defects not covered by standards, and can require manufacturers to remedy such defects; (4) sets standards for auto bumpers, auto ratings (e.g. for crashes), and diagnostic auto inspections; (6) enforces the uniform national maximum speed limit; and (7) administers the federal odometer law.

Established: 1970

Legislative Authority

    Enabling Legislation: National Traffic and Motor Vehicle Safety Act of 1966 (80 Stat. 718), as amended
                            Highway Safety Act of 1966 (80 Stat. 731), as amended

NHTSA also carries out programs under the following acts:
    Clean Air Amendments of 1970 (84 Stat. 1700)
    Highway Safety Act of 1970 (84 Stat. 1793)
    Motor Vehicle Information and Cost Saving Act of 1972 (86 Stat. 947), as amended
    Energy Policy and Conservation Act of 1975 (89 Stat. 871)

Organization: This agency, within the Department of Transportation, is headed by an administrator.

Budgets and Staffing
(Fiscal Years 1970-1981)

	70	71	72	73	74	75	76	77	78	79	(Estimated) 80	81
Budget ($ millions)	32	45	72	77	77	75	62	82	89	114	119	160
Staffing	518	717	841	841	881	881	881	918	909	874	874	874

From Ronald J. Penoyer, *Directory of Federal Regulatory Agencies,* 2nd ed. (St. Louis, Mo.: Washington University Center for the Study of American Business, 1980), p. 74. Reprinted with permission.

Consumer Protection Agency

Another federal agency, usually called a Consumer Protection Agency, was almost created. This agency would have no regulatory functions, but its major function would have been to represent consumer interests before federal agencies and the courts. It would have had the authority to participate in formal and informal proceedings of other federal agencies and represent consumer interests in federal civil court proceedings involving review or enforcement of federal agency actions that substantially affected a consumer interest.

HOW NOT TO REACT TO A SAFETY CONTROVERSY

By Stuart A. Feldstein

U.S. industry has a lesson to learn from Firestone Tire & Rubber Co.: how not to react to a safety controversy. After 10 months of publicized debate, during which Firestone's reputation was bludgeoned, the company agreed on Oct. 20 to a tire recall so large it almost defies perspective. Involving up to 13.5 million tires, it is 34 times larger than the previous record, which Firestone also set when it offered in 1977 to take back 400,000 of the same model 500 radials now being recalled.

This time, Firestone will replace free some 7.5 million allegedly dangerous 500s purchased since September, 1975, and it will replace at half price up to 6 million additional older 500s. The cost will probably be more than $200 million, and it may cause Firestone to finish its fiscal year, ended Oct. 31, with a loss that might exceed $130 million.

A decision to fight. The recall did not have to happen the way it did, even if the tires are subject to failure, as government investigators suggest. Firestone almost certainly could have obtained the same settlement—or even a lesser one—with the National Highway Traffic Safety Administration last January or February, when that agency began complaining about the tires. Instead, the company chose to fight, claiming the tires were safe. It was during the battle, rather than at the outset, that additional revelations about the tires hardened NHTSA's position, as well as public opinion.

Firestone's defense at first seemed a courageous one, assuming the product was indeed free of fault. But as time passed, a series of well-publicized horror stories emerged about blowouts that killed or maimed motorists, along with disclosures of Firestone's own prior knowledge of the unusually high volume of its customers' complaints. Restoration of Firestone's reputation in the retail market is likely to cost more than the recalls. And Firestone, along with its competitors, will continue to feel side effects from the controversy. NHTSA, for example, has declared that because of the Firestone experience, it may try to do away with federal law allowing tire recalls to extend back only through three years of production.

It would seem reasonable that Firestone—of all companies—would have had the experience to deal with adversity. When the United Rubber Workers struck the tire industry for 140 days in 1976, it named Firestone as target for a consumer boycott and for bargaining an end to the dispute, in part because of poor relations between the union and Firestone beforehand.

In 1977, Firestone was immersed in hassles over a political slush fund of earlier years, and Robert P. Beasley, the company's chief financial officer at the time, was finally sentenced to prison for four years for stealing from the fund. When Firestone this year closed a tire plant in Switzerland to relieve European overcapacity, it engendered such hostility that the Swiss sent their ambassador in the U.S. to Firestone's headquarters to seek a reversal.

'Discontinued' tires. Yet Firestone last winter tried to suppress the results of a poorly administered NHTSA survey that seemed to indicate some people were having trouble with the 500s. The move provoked a major investigation of the matter. As a congressional subcommittee launched separate hearings, Firestone was declaring that the fuss was over a tire that had been discontinued 18 months earlier. The subcommittee found out Firestone manufactured 500s through April of this year.

In May, Firestone complained bitterly about a news story suggesting that 8% of the 500s had been returned by customers to dealers because of unhappiness with the product. But Firestone was later forced to disclose that its true adjustment rate for the 500 averaged 17.5% during the six years it was produced. That rate is higher by far than other companies experienced with their radials.

Firestone's long, sweltering summer was made hotter after an employee at corporate headquarters gave newsmen computer printouts of 1975 tests that showed a high failure rate among a small group of tires similar to the 500 and made as original equipment for General Motors Corp. Some Firestone-manufactured GM tires are now among those recalled.

Firestone Chairman Richard A. Riley still maintains that the tires are safe, and he says Firestone has been forced by adverse publicity to capitulate. That position may serve Firestone as it defends itself against about 150 lawsuits now pending over the 500. But when asked at a press conference if he was satisfied with the terms of the recall, Riley replied, "I'm not satisfied with losing anything, any time." That would appear to be the same attitude with which Firestone entered the dispute.

From *Business Week,* November 6, 1978, p. 65. Reprinted with permission.

The agency could also have initiated a lawsuit to review agency decisions if a substantial consumer interest were involved.

The agency could have appeared before the Interstate Commerce Commission, for example, and argued against a rate increase for long-distance movers. If the CPA was of the opinion that a decision by this agency that affected consumers was legally in error, it could seek a review of that decision in the federal courts. In addition to this representation function, the CPA was also to act as a clearinghouse for complaints of individual consumers against business enterprises.[9]

The first serious effort to create such an agency began in 1969. At one time, the bill creating the CPA had passed both houses of Congress, but not by enough of a margin to override the expected veto of President Ford. Thus the bill was not sent to the President during that session. With the inauguration of President Carter, hopes revived because he indicated support for the idea. By that time, however, the mood of the country and Congress had changed, and the bill was finally defeated in the House on February 8, 1978, by a 227 to 189 margin.[10]

Consumer Advocates

Another factor in consumerism is the independent groups and organizations that are active in raising consumer issues and supporting consumer causes. These groups are generally referred to as consumer advocates. While individual consumers can, of course, pursue their rights in a variety of ways, consumer groups have been formed over the years to pursue con-

[9]George Schwartz, "The Successful Fight against a Federal Consumer Protective Agency," *MSU Business Topics,* Vol. 27, No. 3 (Summer 1979), p. 46.
[10]*Ibid.,* p. 47.

sumer concerns in a more organized fashion. Some of the more important groups of this type are mentioned below.

Consumer Federation of America: Chartered in 1967, the CFA brings together about 200 organizations (mostly state and local consumer groups, labor unions, and rural electric cooperatives) with consumer interests. Its representatives lobby, testify at congressional hearings, and submit the federation's views on consumer topics to federal agencies.

National Consumer League: Originally concerned with labor isues, the league now deals with consumer issues as well by monitoring the actions of Congress and agencies of the federal government.

Consumers Union: Founded in 1936, CU is primarily a consumer information organization. It runs a large product-testing operation and publishes the results in *Consumer Reports* magazine. During the early 1970s, Consumers Union also became active in public interest litigation and consumer advocacy in government, an activity it has backed away from more recently.

Center for Auto Safety: Originally a Nader organization, the center pressures the automobile companies to make sure auto safety standards are followed. It also works with the industry and government in the development of new standards.

Conference of Consumer Organizations: Conducts seminars to promote a dialogue between consumer activists and businesses producing consumer products. Also helps in the formation of local consumer organizations.

The Nader Network: Includes many specialized organizations, such as the Center for the Study of Responsive Law, Congress Watch, Corporate Accountability Research Group, Public Interest Research Groups, and others (see Chapter 4).[11]

Business Reaction

The original response of business to the current consumer movement was largely negative. Business by and large opposed every piece of consumer legislation and feared that the costs of voluntary consumer programs would more than offset their public relations and marketing value. Much of this opposition was undoubtedly based on the different philosophies held by business, consumer advocates, and government about consumers and consumer behavior.

After losing so many battles in Congress, however, business gradually began to embrace the consumer movement and respond to it in a more constructive fashion. Some have at least adopted a posture of reasonable accommodation, others began to see a positive side to consumerism. Some of these accommodating actions included the following:

Consumer Research Institute: Founded by the Grocery Manufacturers Association, this organization studies consumer complaints and informs

[11]See Susan Gross, "The Nader Network," *Business and Society Review,* No. 13 (Spring 1975), pp. 5–15.

grocery manufacturers about those it decides are valid and widespread.

Cool-Line Service: Instituted by Whirlpool Corporation, this program offers customers a 24-hour, toll-free telephone service to call from anywhere in the country to ask about service or lodge a complaint. It highlighted the need for companies to develop a formal system to handle customer complaints and inquiries.

Better Business Bureau: This independent organization supported by business was revitalized in many respects, particularly in its ability to handle consumer complaints. Many BBBs offer a free arbitration service to settle small claims against business.

Consumer Appeals Board: Set up by Ford Motor Company, this panel was designed to hear the problems of Ford owners who, after exhausting all the usual complaint channels, still believed they had not been treated fairly. The board was composed of noncompany people including dealers, a state consumer activist, and a high-school vocational-technical teacher. General Motors set up a similar arbitration program.

Consumer Affairs Office: Many companies have created consumer affairs offices with varying responsibilities for the quality of products and consumers' satisfaction. These responsibilities may include handling consumer complaints and inquiries, dissemination of consumer information, monitoring company advertisements, providing input for product design, researching consumer satisfaction, developing warranties and guarantees, increasing product safety, overseeing product packaging and labeling, selecting suppliers, and improving quality control.[12] A professional organization called the Society of Consumer Affairs Professionals in Business (SOCAP) has been organized to promote professionalism among the executives who head these consumer affairs offices.

Important Consumer Issues

Many issues in the consumer area deserve attention, but they all cannot be covered in one chapter. What can be done is to highlight a few of the issues that are of current concern and describe them in some detail. The following issues seem to be in the headlines a good deal, and thus will be discussed from the standpoint of current public policy and the problems these policies are causing.

Food Safety. The controversy over food safety is taking place around the FDA's regulation of food additives, a term introduced into federal legislation in the 1958 amendments to the Food, Drug, and Cosmetics Act. Food additives are defined by the FDA as: "Substances added directly to food, or substances which may reasonably be expected to become components of food through surface contact with equipment or packaging materials, or even substances that may otherwise affect the food without becoming part of it."[13]

[12]Richard T. Hise et al., "The Corporate Consumer Affairs Effort," *MSU Business Topics*, Vol. 26, No. 3 (Summer 1978), p. 18.

[13]Thomas H. Jukes, "Current Concepts in Nutrition," *Medical Intelligence*, Vol. 297, No. 8 (August 1977), p. 427.

The 1958 food additives amendment contains the Delaney Clause (named after Congressman James Delaney of New York), which specifies that "no additive shall be deemed to be safe if it is found to induce cancer when ingested by man or animals, or if it is found, after tests which are appropriate for the evaluation of the safety of food additives to induce cancer in man or animals."[14] It should be noted that the clause does not apply to carcinogens that occur naturally in foods, it applies only to food additives. But food additives also can include packaging materials that can get into the food.[15]

Aside from the problem of the massive test doses used in animal testing, the Delaney Clause is always interpreted as meaning "zero tolerance" for additives that are discovered to induce cancer in humans or animals; that is, there is no threshold level below which carcinogens are safe. Theoretically, even one molecule could be hazardous. Given that laboratory techniques can now detect the presence of food additives in proportions as tiny as one part per billion (one part in a trillion is coming), some people believe that almost everything one eats can be shown to contain a confirmed or suspected carcinogen.

The current debate over food safety was touched off in March 1977 when the FDA disclosed that saccharin apparently could cause cancer and announced plans to ban its use as a food additive. Laboratory experiments in Canada had shown that when rats were fed the "maximum tolerable" dose of saccharin (the equivalent for humans of about 1,200 cans of diet soda per day) a larger than expected number of male rats got bladder cancer. Thus the FDA had no choice, under the Delaney Clause, but to ban the additive. The Canadian study was the final confirmation of a series of studies that had shown similar results.[16]

The FDA had previously banned other additives such as cyclamates, safrole, and red dye number two and other coloring agents under general provisions of the Food, Drug, and Cosmetics Act. What made the saccharin case different was that it was the only sugar substitute generally available. Thus the ban would have destroyed the $1.1 billion a year diet drink industry and deprived diabetics of their only source of sweetening. An unprecedented public outcry against the ban (the FDA received more than 100,000 comments) convinced Congress, in November 1977, to pass an 18-month moratorium.[17]

The moratorium legislation called for the National Academy of Sciences to study the question. They concluded, in November 1978, that saccharin was indeed a weak carcinogen, at least in rats. Therefore the sweetener must also be regarded as a potential, though probably feeble, human carcino-

---

[14]*Ibid.*, p. 428.

[15]"After acrylonitrile had been tentatively approved by the FDA in 1974, Monsanto built three plants to handle a big acrylonitrile bottle contract, but in 1977 the FDA withdrew approval of the plastic, having concluded that the material over the course of time did migrate into the liquid it contained, causing birth defects and perhaps cancer in test animals. Monsanto, left with 21 million useless Coca-Cola bottles on its hands, sent a brace of lawyers to litigate in an effort to get the ban lifted. A federal appeals court decision is due soon; meanwhile, Monsanto has mothballed two of the plants and sold the other." Walter McQuade, "Packagers Bear up under a Bundle of Regulations," *Fortune*, May 7, 1979, p. 182.

[16]"Saccharin: Where Do We Go from Here?" *FDA Consumer*, April 1978, p. 18.

[17]*Ibid.*, p. 17.

gen.[18] Weak, however, refers to the number of cases of cancer caused, not to the seriousness of the cancer. Cancer caused by a "weak" carcinogen, say some scientists, is no less deadly.[19] With this kind of inconclusive evidence and public pressure continuing for its use, when the moratorium did finally end in May 1979, the FDA chose not to revive the ban on saccharin. Once a safe substitute is found, however, it is likely to be banned very quickly.

A similar controversy has erupted over the use of nitrites, which combine with other compounds to form a class of substances called nitrosamines, some of which are believed to be potential carcinogens. Nitrites are used in curing meat, particularly bacon, and also occur naturally in vegetables and fruits. Nitrosamines are also found in most beer.

The controversy over food safety continues. The animal testing debate is not settled. Whether a safe threshold level exists has not been proven one way or the other. But scientists will continue to raise hard questions about both old and new additives that will have to be answered through public policy. Decisions must be made about where to draw the line between the desire of individuals for free choice and the collective need for protection when the choices are complex.[20] Perhaps the final word about food additives, however, is expressed in the following quote.

> The most injurious of all "food additives" is the additional food that is eaten after caloric needs have been satisfied. Overconsumption of food leads to obesity, which is a far greater danger to health than any of the food additives whose safety is now being questioned.[21]

Drug Regulation. The effects of drug regulation on the pharmaceutical industry are fairly well known, since regulation of drugs has been in existence for some time. Research has shown, for example, that the average time required for clinical study and agency approval increased from 2.7 years in 1966 to 6.6 years in 1973. The number of applications for clinical study fell to 41 in 1973, which was less than half the 85 that had been filed a decade earlier. The number of new drugs approved averaged 17 in the post-regulation period, compared with more than three times that amount in the five years before the Harris-Kefauver amendments were passed.[22]

The rate of return and research and development in the drug industry plummeted to about one-third the 1960 level. Drug companies are cutting back on basic research—the discovery of new and better drugs—and putting more money into product development. During the five-year period from 1972 to 1977, domestic research and development expenditures grew at an annual rate of only 2.3 percent, adjusted for inflation, while expenditures by United States companies abroad rose at an annual 19 percent rate.[23]

Finally, since 1960, the cost of discovering and developing a new drug rose eighteenfold, half of which has been attributed to FDA regulation.

[18]Tom Alexander, "Time for a Cease-Fire in the Food Safety Wars," *Fortune,* February 26, 1979, p. 94.

[19]"Saccharin," *FDA Consumer,* p. 20.

[20]*Ibid.,* p. 21.

[21]Jukes, "Concepts," p. 430.

[22]"The Hidden Cost of Drug Safety," *Business Week,* February 21, 1977, p. 80.

[23]*Ibid.,* p. 84. See also Jerome E. Schnee, "Regulation and Innovation: U.S. Pharmaceutical Industry," *California Management Review,* Vol. XXII, No. 1 (Fall 1979), pp. 23–31.

These costs have forced many smaller companies out of the market. Between 1957 and 1961, the four largest drug companies' share of innovational ouput amounted to 24 percent of the total industry's output. Between 1967 and 1971, the share of the four largest companies increased to 48.7 percent.[24]

Critics of drug regulation argue that these delays deny Americans the benefit of new drugs that are available in foreign countries with a shorter approval process. Thus the health of American people is being adversely affected rather than enhanced. Supporters of the FDA argue that approval delays actually protect Americans against possible hazardous drugs until the FDA is satisfied they are safe.

Proposals have been made to speed up the process. Some proposals would give the government power to approve breakthrough drugs before testing on them was completed. This approval could be granted in cases where lack of the drug could result in severe, life-threatening illness. Another proposal would allow approval of certain drugs for limited distribution, say only from a hospital or from people with special training and experience. Such limits could be used on a drug that otherwise would have been denied approval.

Regulation of Advertising. The Federal Trade Commission in recent years has adopted or considered adopting several new strategies to deal with deceptive practices in advertising. One such strategy is *affirmative disclosure,* which requires companies to tell the whole truth about their product. Nutrient labeling of food products would fall under this strategy. The idea is to provide consumers with more information on the theory that more is better. Another strategy is *ad substantiation,* which requires companies to back up their advertising claims with specific research data filed with the FTC before the ad is run. The FTC, for example, wanted proof from Ford Motor Company that its LTD was actually quieter than other cars that were more expensive. Similar proof was required of other companies.

Another strategy is that of *corrective advertising,* which is based on certain behavioral assumptions about the effects of advertising on consumers. Merely stopping a deceptive advertisement from being continued may not result in any decrease in the positive attitude that has been built up over time toward the product. Corrective advertising is needed, the FTC argues, to undo some of the positive effects of the ads and restore the market to the condition it was in before the deception took place. Some research on the effects of advertising tends to support these assumptions.[25]

The FTC asked for corrective advertising in such cases as Hi-C Fruit Drink, Profile Bread, Wonder Bread, Domino Sugar, Chevron F-310, and Listerine. In the latter case, the Supreme Court rejected the company's request for a review of the FTC order.[26] In a case involving Hawaiian Punch, the R. J. Reynolds Foods Company was asked to cease and desist alleged misrepresentations and also to disclose the true facts ("guaranteed to contain

---

[24]*Ibid.*, p. 82.

[25]See Harold H. Kassarjian, "Federal Regulation of Advertising," *Business and its Environment,* George A. Steiner, ed. (Los Angeles: UCLA Graduate School of Management, 1977), pp. 233–255.

[26]"High Court Rejects Warner-Lambert Bid to Review Order to Correct Listerine Ads," *The Wall Street Journal,* April 4, 1978, p. 2.

not less than 10 percent fruit juice") until such time as a substantial proportion of consumers were no longer misled into thinking that Hawaiian Punch contains major amounts of "seven natural fruit juices," that is, until a true process of unlearning, decay, or extinction *and* relearning successfully occurred. The commission apparently felt that consumers must be carefully exposed to the fact that what they learned earlier was in error, lest they continue to suffer from the misleading effects of that earlier "learning."

The concept of *counteradvertising* is based on similar behavioral assumptions. Under this strategy, public interest groups would have access to the public airwaves to present another side to all commercial messages that involve controversial issues, and to advertising that is silent about the negative aspects of the advertised product. An example of this strategy is the antismoking commercials that appeared on television when cigarette advertising was still permitted. This strategy has pretty well died out for the time being, however, because of inaction by the Federal Communications Commission, whose cooperation was necessary to implement the FTC proposal.

Product Safety. One key element in regulating product safety is the development of some kind of priority system by which to set standards. The CPSC did not make the same mistake as OSHA and adopt wholesale a set of previously written standards. Thus the agency must make some decisions about where to start developing standards for the 10,000 products under its jurisdiction.

To establish priorities, the CPSC relies on a Hazards Index, derived from a ranking of the severity of injuries and accident data from the National Electronic Injury Surveillance System (NEISS). This system provides aggregate frequency and severity data on accident cases from a sample of hospital emergency rooms. The total number of accidents associated with each product class are reported to the CPSC each month. For each product, the number of accidents causing a particular type of injury is multiplied by an index of the "mean severity" of that injury. These calculations are then summed up to produce a score for each product. The CPSC uses the rank ordering of products according to this score in deciding which products to regulate.[27] The CPSC also takes action on standards development on the basis of individual case information. Thus standards are set in response either to petitions from interested parties or to systematic data-gathering and evaluation activities within the agency itself.

The standard-setting process, however, is complicated and time consuming. The Consumer Product Safety Act constrains the ability of the CPSC to develop its own standards with a requirement that it look for other parties to develop safety standards which deal with the problems the CPSC has identified. The commission can maintain a scrutiny over this process, but its ability to do so is limited by financial and personnel resources. In many cases, it lacks the analytical resources to determine whether a proposed standard will actually solve the problem it has identified. The CPSC is also under a time limit to act within 30 days on a standard proposed by an offerer.[28]

[27]Nina Cornell, Roger Noll, and Barry Weingast, "Safety Regulation," *Business and its Environment,* George A. Steiner, ed. (Los Angeles: UCLA Graduate School of Management, 1977), p. 215.

[28]*Ibid.,* p. 222.

But not only are there problems with the agency process, there are also problems with the legislation on product safety. This legislation has been based on assumptions that are at variance with the procedures necessary for successful standards development. These assumptions are: "(1) that the essence of the safety problem is the presence of well-defined, clear-cut hazards to consumers and workers that can be avoided in a rather straight-forward fashion; (2) that identifying a reasonably effective way of prevent-ing them can be accomplished by a brief, cursory investigation; and (3) that the principal cause of inadequate product and occupational safety is bad acts by unethical businessmen."[29]

Some authors conclude that "in keeping with these assumptions, agencies are pushed to develop a large number of standards, with underlying jus-tifications that meet the relatively loose standards of proof required in ad-ministrative procedures, in a relatively short period of time."[30] Given these conditions, it is no wonder that an agency like the CPSC has difficulty setting standards for most hazardous products and spends its time on what seem to be frivolous hazards, such as matches and swimming pool slides. What is probably needed is a complete overhaul of the legislation dealing with product safety and the development of a sensible regulatory process (see box).[31]

Product Liability. In 1978, manufacturers and retailers paid an esti-mated $2.75 billion for product liability insurance, compared with an esti-mated $1.13 billion in 1975.[32] These soaring costs reflect a change in legal thinking regarding product liability. This change has been described as a shift from the old rule that manufacturers or sellers are liable for damages only when they have been negligent or unreasonably careless in relation to products, to a theory of strict liability, which holds a manufacturer or seller responsible for damages if a consumer is injured as a result of a product defect regardless of the degree of care exercised.[33]

Under the former theory, manufacturers would be held liable only if they failed to take reasonable steps to make the product safe for consumers who are likely to use the product. Under the latter theory, manufacturers could take every precaution in producing and distributing the product, but if it proves defective and injures consumers, they are strictly liable for damages. Thus the plaintiff's burden in proving a case has been considerably eased and more suits are being filed. Consumers seeking damages need not prove that the manufacturer was negligent or violated an express or implied warranty. All they need prove is that the product caused the injury. Even negligent use of the product by consumers is not always an effective defense for the manufacturer. Consumers who have improperly used products have nevertheless received sizable awards. The result of the liberalization of product liability laws has been cases like the following:

> To scent a candle, a teenager poured perfume made by Faberge Inc. over a lit wick. The perfume ignited, burning a friend's neck. Claiming that Faberge had

[29]*Ibid.*, p. 229.
[30]*Ibid.*
[31]*Ibid.*, p. 231.
[32]"The Devils in the Product Liability Laws," *Business Week*, February 12, 1979, p. 72.
[33]*Ibid.*

AN EXAMPLE OF GOOD STANDARD DEVELOPMENT

When targets are well chosen, safety regulatory agencies can be effective. The development of mandatory standards for baby cribs illustrates safety regulation at its best, and is instructive in that it demonstrates how a sensible regulatory process works.

In 1968, a Presidential commission discovered that the spacing between the slats of baby cribs was sufficiently wide that, under certain conditions, the entire body of a baby could slip between the slats until stopped by its skull. The baby would then strangle itself as it hung outside the crib.

The crib problem had two features. First, no one was collecting data in a fashion that would enable anyone—the government or the industry—to be aware of the problem, and accidents were too infrequent for the press and consumers to have become alerted to it. Second, once the problem was recognized, no one knew what kind of safety standard would deal with it effectively.

The problem was next addressed by the trade association of crib manufacturers. Without benefit of any systematic analysis, the manufacturers voluntarily adopted a standard of 3.25 inches between slats, down from 3.5 inches prior to the investigation by the President's Commission. Next the Bureau of Product Safety of the Food and Drug Administration—a precursor of the CPSC—commissioned a research project to measure the size of infants' buttocks as part of a larger project on various aspects of infant anthropometry. The study estimated that the buttocks of five percent of infants could be compressed by the pressure of their own weight to a diameter of 2.375 inches or less, nearly an inch smaller than the industry study. In April 1973, a mandatory spacing standard of 2.375 inches was adopted.

The key to the successful conclusion of the crib slat case was the role the FDA played in generating the information and analysis that made a rational design standard possible. The essence of the crib problem was the lack of understanding of the nature of the hazard by participants on both sides of the market. Once the FDA undertook to analyze the problem, the actual promulgation of mandatory standards was anticlimatic. Since the standards imposed essentially no costs on anyone and since the industry had already established procedures for voluntary adoption of crib slat spacing standards, the mandatory status of the federal standard was probably unnecessary once the basis for a rational standard had been established.

From Nina Cornell, Roger Noll, and Barry Weingast, "Safety Regulation," *Business and its Environment*, George A. Steiner, ed. (Los Angeles: UCLA Graduate School of Management, 1977), p. 229. Quoted with permission.

---

failed to warn consumers of the perfume's flammability, the friend won a $27,000 judgment. Despite its argument that there was no way to foresee that someone would pour perfume onto an open flame. Faberge lost its appeal.

In 1975 a paralyzed high school football player won a $5.3 million judgment against Riddell Inc., a maker of football helmets. A Miami jury came in with the verdict even though the helmet was never introduced at trial. Today, 14% of a Riddell helmet's cost is due to insurance, litigation, and settlements, before the Florida case, these factors cost 1%.[34]

These changes in the law and its interpretation have exposed manufacturers to unprecedented risks. Courts began to hold manufacturers liable

[34]*Ibid.*, pp. 72–73. Quoted with permission.

for the full life of their products and for "foreseeable" design defects that might not show up for years.[35] Ford Motor Company faced criminal charges of reckless homicide in its design of gas tanks for its Pinto cars, the first criminal action ever brought against an automaker. A guilty verdict in this case would have triggered other criminal charges against companies involved in product safety disputes.[36]

Because of these changes, many companies have been unable to afford product liability insurance and face risk of bankruptcy should they be hit with a product liability lawsuit. Reforms have been proposed to put some limits on the doctrine of strict liability, but the trend of thinking seems clear (see box). Managers must give increasing attention to adequate warnings about potential dangers in using products,[37] quality control systems to eliminate defective products, and product design to eliminate hazards by utilizing design safety concepts.[38]

Consumer Philosophies

It seems obvious, given all this activity by the federal government, consumer advocates, and even business itself, that the idea of consumers' rights being automatically protected by the marketplace is not accepted. The argument for consumer protection through public policy measures is based on the view that because the sellers in today's marketplace are much more powerful than consumers the balance of power must be restored by government protection or consumer groups. The market must be augmented by public policy measures to protect the rights of consumers. However, many different kinds of public policy measures are possible. The choice of specific policies depends on the particular philosophy one has regarding the consumer in today's marketplace. There are at least three ways to view the consumer, each of which has different policy implications.

Consumer Helplessness. This view holds that, on the one hand, today's consumer is subject to manipulation by large oligopolistic organizations in pursuit of higher profits. Since in most markets, power is exercised by a few large firms, these firms can dictate the terms of trade to consumers rather than bow to the forces of supply and demand. These organizations have the resources and ingenuity, it is believed, to control not only output and prices but also consumer demand. Consumer demand is manipulated by design of products, packaging, and advertising appeals so that buyers will take what the large firms produce. This view also holds that today's marketplace is so complex that the individual consumer finds it impossible to collect, evaluate, and understand all the information necessary to make good choices. Many consumers are either ignorant of what is good for them, it is believed, or too uninformed to make choices consistent with their best interests. They are not capable of protecting themselves.

[35]See "The Way to Ease Soaring Product Liability Costs," *Business Week*, January 17, 1977, p. 62.
[36]See "Who Pays for the Damage?" *Business Week*, January 21, 1980, p. 61.
[37]William L. Trombetta, "Products Liability: What New Court Rulings Mean for Management," *Business Horizons*, Vol. 22, No. 4 (August 1979), pp. 67–72.
[38]James P. Kuhn, "How to Manage Product Safety," *Industry Week*, April 22, 1974, pp. 53–59.

THE LANDMARK CASES IN PRODUCT LIABILITY

MacPherson vs. Buick Motor Co., **New York, 1916:** A manufacturer is liable for negligently built products that are "reasonably certain to place life and limb in peril," even though consumers do not buy directly from the manufacturer

Greenman vs. Yuba Power Products Inc., **California, 1963:** A manufacturer is strictly liable when he sells a product that proves to have a defect that causes injury

Larson vs. General Motors Corp., **U.S. Court of Appeals, 8th Circuit, 1968:** When faulty design of a product worsens an injury, a plaintiff may recover damages for the worsened part of the injury, even if the design defect did not cause the injury in the first place

Cunningham vs. MacNeal Memorial Hospital, **Illinois, 1970:** It is not a defense to claim that a product (in this case blood infected by hepatitis) could not be made safer by any known technology. This ruling of the Illinois Supreme Court, the only case in which judges squarely refused to consider "state of the art," was reversed by a state statute defining the selling of blood as a service

Cronin vs. J. B. E. Olson Corp., **California, 1972:** A product need not be "unreasonably dangerous" to make its manufacturer strictly liable for defective design

Bexiga vs. Havir Mfg. Co., **New Jersey, 1972:** If an injury is attributable to the lack of any safety device on a product, the manufacturer cannot base a defense on the contributory negligence of the plaintiff.

Berkebile vs. Brantly Helicopter Corp., **Pennsylvania, 1975:** Whether the seller could have foreseen a particular injury is irrelevant in a case of strict liability for design defect

Ault vs. International Harvester Co., **California, 1975:** Evidence that a manufacturer changed or improved its product line after the manufacture and sale of the particular product that caused an injury may be used to prove design defect

Micallef vs. Miehle Co., **New York, 1976:** Evidence that an injured plaintiff obviously knew of a danger inherent in using a product will not defeat his claim if the manufacturer could reasonably have guarded against the danger in designing the product

Barker vs. Lull Engineering Co., **California, 1978:** A manufacturer must show that the usefulness of a product involved in an accident outweighs the risks inherent in its design. In this radical ruling, the court shifted the burden of proof in design defect cases from plaintiff to defendant

From *Business Week*, February 12, 1979, p. 74. Reprinted with permission.

Thus the consumer is basically helpless, either subject to corporate power or overwhelmed by the complexities of the marketplace. Help is needed in the form of legislation designed to protect the consumer from unsafe products or fraudulent business practices, and set minimum standards of quality or performance for products. Consumer interest groups should focus their efforts on identifying unsafe products and deceptive practices and initiate appropriate political action through informational and lobbying campaigns at various levels of government. Business should increase its efforts to provide safer products and better instructions to consumers.

These policy measures based on the helpless consumer philosophy have the advantage of providing protection for all consumers regardless of their access to relevant information about particular products, their ability or willingness to use that information, their financial condition, or other relevant factors. If dangerous products or practices are kept off the market, society does not need to worry about the thoroughness or rationality of consumer decision-making.

These policies have the disadvantage, however, of requiring an intrusion into the free market system and placing restrictions on freedom of choice of both business and consumers. The design, contents, packaging, etc. of the products that come to market are dictated by government agencies and consumer advocates rather than by the marketplace. The people who draft the legislation and set the standards for acceptable products and practices may use substantially different criteria than consumers would use in deciding whether to buy such a product. There is a danger that the protectors will force values and criteria upon the protected that are not consistent with the latter's actual preferences.

The Consumer Self-Help Approach. A second view of the consumer holds that consumers have the native intelligence and willingness to make sound purchase decisions in their own best interests. However, the nature of today's marketplace, with rapid proliferation of products, the increasingly technical nature of products, and the confusing way much information is presented, means that the consumer has to make decisions about products with much less than perfect knowledge.

According to this view, government programs should be aimed at providing consumers with better market information directly, or forcing business firms to provide such information. Consumer groups should put their efforts into testing products and collecting and disseminating accurate product information. Business itself should provide more accurate, relevant, and understandable product and product-related information.

These policies are more consistent with a free market philosophy and are really aimed at making the market work better by providing more perfect information. Business firms should be more willing to voluntarily undertake programs consistent with this philosophy, thus reducing the need for government intervention. Consumer information programs are usually less costly to implement than other forms of consumer protection. Such policies also avoid the problem of restricting the consumer's freedom of choice. Instead of taking products off the market or banning them, these policies ensure that consumers are fully informed of the potential risks, and allow consumers to make their own choices.

One disadvantage of this approach is that it is often difficult to determine what is accurate and relevant information and in what form it would be most useful to consumers. There are many questions about how sophisticated consumers are in their ability to process information. The definition of what constitutes "deception" in advertising is debatable. Not much is known about how children are affected by product information. Thus much more research is needed into these areas to make this approach work successfully.

Another disadvantage of this approach is that it ignores the fact that many consumers seem unwilling or unable to make effective use of the information that is available. Environmental factors such as age, education, income level, and occupation affect the ability and willingness to use information. Many products are purchased habitually or routinely on the basis of past learning and brand loyalty. There are costs involved (such as time) in gathering and using information; it is not a free good to consumers. Many consumers make choices based on more "emotional" factors, such as convenience, friendliness of personnel, or social status, than on more "rational" factors, such as technical product information. Research is also needed into the environmental and personal factors that prevent consumers from using available information in making purchase decisions.

The Consumer Remedy Approach. This view holds that regardless of how many standards are developed and enforced and regardless of how much information is made available to consumers, some will continue to be victimized and have their rights violated. Because of the increased technical sophistication of today's products, there is an increased probability that something will go wrong after a purchase is made.

Policies that make it easier for consumers to obtain compensation for losses suffered in the marketplace after these losses occur are thus consistent with this philosophy. Government should pass legislation or initiate programs designed to make it easier and less costly for consumers to take action and obtain satisfaction for losses and grievances on their own initiative. Consumer groups can offer the services of people with expertise in dealing with the market and legal system to advise consumers and advocate their causes in attempting to gain satisfaction. Business can set up better systems to handle consumer complaints and inquiries and establish honest and fair methods to settle grievances.

These policies have the advantage of being realistic about the marketplace and human nature in assuming that risk and fraud will never be completely eliminated. They simply make it easier for consumers to be heard and obtain appropriate compensation for damages. An obvious disadvantage, of course, is that it is difficult to obtain compensation of any sort if one has been killed by a defective or unsafe product or because of insufficient information. Additionally, many people, such as the poor, aged, or minorities, may not have access to, be aware of, or be capable of taking advantage of such programs to obtain redress for their grievances. Broad exposure and help must be provided to these groups for the policies to work fairly.

The views that people hold about consumers and the marketplace at any given time are undoubtedly a mixture of all of these philosophies, and the policies adopted and advocated reflect this mixture. Nonetheless, it does seem that the dominant philosophy at the beginning of the current consumer movement was one of consumer helplessness with an emphasis on product bans, development of product safety standards, and similar measures. More recently, the provision of more information and education on how to use information seems dominant, consistent with the consumer self-help approach.

Something called a consumer education movement has been identified, which aims to teach consumers how to seek out, use, and evaluate consumer information so they can improve their ability to purchase and consume the products and services they deem most likely to enhance their well-being.[39]

[39]See Paul N. Bloom and Mark J. Silver, "Consumer Education: Marketers Take Heed," *Harvard Business Review*, Vol. 54, No. 1 (January–February 1976), pp. 32–42, 149–150.

This movement is evidenced by the many federal, state, and local consumer education programs that have been recently developed, by the efforts of such consumer groups as the Consumers Union to provide educational services to consumers, and by the increased efforts of business to educate consumers to use the information they make available. These efforts are based on the failure of the consumer information programs of earlier years and the recognition that purchasers need to know how to process information before it can be of value to them in a purchase decision.

The Future of Consumerism

A study commissioned by Sentry Insurance Company and conducted by the Marketing Science Institute and the opinion research firm of Louis Harris and Associates, Inc. concluded that the consumer movement is here to stay and is, in fact, growing stronger.[40] The consumers interviewed believed their shopping skills had gotten better, that product information and labeling had gotten better, and product safety had improved. Yet half the consumers felt they got a worse deal in the marketplace than ten years ago; more than half believed the quality of goods and services had gotten worse, products did not last as long as they did ten years ago, and that it was more difficult to get things repaired. The industries most frequently mentioned as doing a poor job in serving consumers were auto manufacturers, auto repair shops, the oil industry, used car dealers, hospitals, the medical profession, electric utility companies, credit loan companies, and the advertising industry. The survey also showed that the public was receptive to a variety of new initiatives in the consumer field. These ideas were presented in concept form without details on how they might be implemented or might work in practice.

1. A new federal government consumer protection agency.
2. A major convention to work out long-term policies in the consumer field.
3. Community bureaus to handle complaints against manufacturers, dealers, and salespeople.
4. A new independent testing center for evaluating the safety of potentially dangerous products.
5. The introduction of compulsory consumer affairs education in all high schools.
6. Corrective advertising by companies whose advertising is proven false or misleading.
7. A requirement that all large companies should employ a senior officer whose job it is to look after consumer affairs and consumer interests.
8. The appointment to the boards of all large companies of a public or consumer representative.[41]

The study also concluded that the business community was sharply out of step with the American public on consumer issues. Nongovernment con-

[40]*Consumerism at the Crossroads* (Concord, Mass.: Sentry Insurance Co., 1977).
[41]*Ibid.*, p. 77.

sumer activists were seen as most in touch with consumers and senior business managers as least in touch. Thus business can expect to be vigorously attacked by both consumer activists and elected representatives. The study recommended the following changes for business to consider.

- The study indicates need for three different kinds of change in the attitudes and perceptions of senior management based on better information about consumer needs, consumer attitudes and consumer expectations.
- The second step would be for very specific improvements of the kinds which consumers are demanding—safer products, better quality, better service, more reliable products, better guarantees and warranties, better complaint handling mechanisms, and so on.
- The third need is for better communication with the public about the steps which companies are taking to be responsive to and about the very real problem which business has in meeting consumer demands.[42]

Questions for Discussion

1. What was the focus of the first era of consumerism? How did the public policy measures passed by Congress address the issues raised?
2. What factors are behind the modern consumer movement? What is its focus? Why were there so many public policy measures coming from Congress?
3. Discuss the consumer bill of rights. How does the marketplace protect these rights? Why is there a need for government involvement?
4. Describe the powers of the various government agencies involved in protecting consumer rights. How do their functions differ? What rights do they protect?
5. Are you in favor of something like a Consumer Protection Agency? What would be its purpose? Why was the bill finally defeated after passing an earlier session of Congress? Will the idea be revived?
6. What are consumer advocates? What functions do they perform? Whose rights are they protecting? Should they be limited to specific kinds of activities?
7. Why was business so negative toward consumerism in its early years? Are there lessons to be learned here regarding business response to future social movements? What has business done in response to consumerism more recently?
8. Describe the food safety controversy. What is the Delaney Clause? Should it be amended? If so, how? What are the basic issues with respect to food safety that are unresolved?
9. What have been the effects of drug regulation? Is some kind of regulation necessary? Why or why not? What reforms would you suggest?
10. What is corrective advertising? What behavioral assumptions about the effects of advertising are behind this approach? Does this strategy make sense?
11. Why are product safety regulations so difficult to develop? What is the process by which they are developed? What reforms would be most helpful in your opinion?
12. Describe the changes in product liability. What impacts have these changes had on business? What are the reasons for this change in thinking? What responses can management make that are likely to be effective?
13. Describe the different consumer philosophies. Which one, if any, do you believe prevails today? What are the implications of your answer for business and management? What strategies would you propose that are consistent with this philosophy?

[42]*Ibid.*, p. v.

14. What is the future of consumerism? Will inflation change consumers' concerns? If so, how? Comment on the recommendations of the Sentry Insurance Company study. How would you implement these recommendations?

Suggested Reading

Aaker, David A., and Day, George S. *Consumerism: Search for the Consumer Interest.* New York: Free Press, 1974.

Andreasen, Alan R. *The Disadvantaged Consumer.* New York: Free Press, 1975.

Bishop, James, Jr., and Hubbard, Henry W. *Let the Seller Beware.* Washington, D.C.: The National Press, Inc., 1969.

The Challenge of Consumerism. New York: The Conference Board, 1971.

Creighton, Luch Black. *Pretenders to the Throne: The Consumer Movement in the United States.* Lexington, Mass.: Lexington Books, 1976.

Fornell, Claes. *Consumer Input for Marketing Decisions: A Study of Corporate Departments for Consumer Affairs.* New York: Praeger, 1976.

Goedeke, Ralph M., and Etcheson, Warren W. *Consumerism: Viewpoints from Business, Government, and the Public Interest.* San Francisco: Canfield Press, 1972.

Jones, Mary Gardner, ed. *Consumerism: A New Force in Society.* Lexington, Mass.: D.C. Heath, 1976.

Kinter, Earl W. *A Primer on the Law of Deceptive Practices.* New York: Macmillan, 1971.

Magnuson, Warren G., and Carper, Jean. *The Dark Side of the Marketplace.* Englewood Cliffs, N.J.: Prentice-Hall, 1968.

Nadel, Mark V. *The Politics of Consumer Protection.* New York: Bobbs-Merrill, 1971.

Nader, Ralph, ed. *The Consumer and Corporate Accountability.* New York: Harcourt Brace Jovanovich, 1973.

Nader, Ralph. *Unsafe at Any Speed: The Designed-in Dangers of the American Automobile.* New York: Grossman Publishers, 1972.

Sanford, David. *Who Put the Con in Consumer?* New York: Liveright, 1972.

Swartz, Edward M. *Toys That Don't Care.* Boston: Gambit, Inc., 1971.

Sturdivant, Frederick D., ed. *The Ghetto Marketplace.* New York: Free Press, 1969.

17

The Physical Environment: Issues and Concepts

Fifteen or so years ago, pollution and ecology were two terms rarely found in the lexicon of business. Today environmental survival and pollution abatement are major topics of the times and receive prominent exposure in the literature of business and economics. If any one issue provided the initial sustenance for social responsibility proponents, that issue was the effect of business operations and practices on the physical environment. Probably more words have been written on this subject than on most others of a business and social problems context.[1]

The physical environment (also called the natural environment) provides a number of services for human beings. Chief among them are that it provides a habitat in which plant and animal life can survive, and it contains resources that are usable in the production of goods and services. The physical environment contains, among other things, air, water, and land, without which life as we know it would be impossible. The physical environment is also called upon to provide resources that are used in the production process, whatever form that process might take.

Problems arise because the physical environment is also used as a place to dispose of waste material that results from the production of goods and

[1]Arthur Elkins and Dennis W. Callaghan, *A Managerial Odyssey: Problems in Business and its Environment* ©1978, 2/e, Addison-Wesley Publishing Company, Inc., Chapter 5, p. 173. Reprinted with permission.

services as well as from their consumption. Moreover, some resources are nonrenewable and are thus able to be completely exhausted at some point. Others, such as timber, are renewable, but conscious effort is generally needed to replace those renewable resources that are used. This replacement usually does not happen automatically, at least not fast enough to support a growing population.

This and the following chapter will focus on pollution of the physical environment that interferes with its ability to provide the first service that was mentioned, a habitat in which life can survive and flourish. The ability of the physical environment to serve as a gigantic garbage disposal depends on its dilutive capacity. Pollution occurs when the waste discharged into the environment exceeds its dilutive capacity—when air can no longer dilute the wastes dumped into it without harming the air itself; water can no longer absorb the wastes dumped into it without some fundamental change in the quality of the water;[2] and land cannot absorb any more waste material without producing harmful effects on land usage.

The amount of damage that results to a particular medium (air, water, land) varies by the type of pollutant, the amount of pollutant disposed of, and the distance from the source of pollution.[3] These damages, however, alter the quality of the environment and render it, to some degree, unfit to provide its normal services. Thus the air can become harmful for human beings to breathe, water unfit to drink, and land unfit to live on because of toxic wastes or radiation (see cartoon).

These damages are called negative externalities as far as the market system is concerned. They arise out of the transactions between producers and consumers in an industrial society, but are not normally factored into the prices of products. Before the advent of pollution control legislation, air and water in particular were treated as free goods available to anyone for dumping wastes. This caused no problem when the population was sparse, factories small, and products few in number compared to today. The environment's dilutive capacity was rarely exceeded and was perceived as infinite in its ability to absorb waste. Surely a vast body of water such as Lake Erie could never be "killed." Gradually however, changes in society began to cause serious pollution problems. The following factors were critical.

Population Growth and Concentration: More people means more manufactured goods and services to provide for their needs, which in turn means more waste material to be discharged into the environment. The concentration of people in urban areas compounds the problem. Eventually the dilutive capacity of the air, water, and land in major industrial centers becomes greatly exceeded and a serious pollution problem results.

Rising Affluence: As real income increases, people are able to buy and consume more goods and services, throw them away more quickly to buy something better, travel more miles per year using various forms of transportation, and expand their use of energy. In the process, much more waste material is generated for the society as a whole.

[2]Jerome Rothenberg, "The Physical Environment," *Social Responsibility and the Business Predicament,* James W. McKie, ed. (Washington, D.C.: The Brookings Institution, 1974), p. 194.
[3]*Ibid.*

**'The Air Is Deadly, The Water's Polluted And If You Try
To Crawl Into A Hole In The Ground, The Toxic Wastes
Will Get You'**

From *St. Louis Post-Dispatch*, February 20, 1980, p. 2E. Reprinted with permission.

Technological Change: Changes in technology have expanded the variety of products available for consumption, increased their quantity through increases in productivity, made products and packaging more complex, and raised the rate of obsolescence through rapid innovation. All of this has added to the waste disposal problem. In addition, the toxicity of many materials was initially unknown or not given much concern, with the result that procedures for the abatement of these pollution problems have lagged far behind the technology of manufacture.

Increased Expectations and Awareness: As society became more affluent, it could give attention to higher order needs. Thus expectations for a higher quality of life have increased, and the physical environment is viewed as an important component of the overall quality of life. One cannot fully enjoy the goods and services that are available in a hostile or unsafe environment. In addition, the people's awareness of the harmful effects of pollution increased due to mounting scientific evidence, journalistic exposé, and the attention given environmental problems by the media.

These forces combined about the mid-1960s to cause an environmental movement that sprang up from almost nowhere. Many of the energies that had gone into the civil rights movement were channeled into the environmental movement as the former waned. The result was a major public policy effort to control pollution and correct for the deficiencies of the market system in controlling the amount and types of waste discharged into the environment. These efforts have made a major impact on business and consumers alike and have caused technical and behavioral changes throughout society.

The Nature of Pollution and Control

There are various types of pollution, including air, water, solid waste, noise, and visual or aesthetic pollution. These various types and some of the causes are shown in Exhibit 17.1. Since these types of pollution and their causes are quite different, the policies to control them are also different. These policies will be discussed in detail in the next chapter. In general, however, four major types of policies or approaches have been adopted.

The first approach is one of requiring a comprehensive environmental evaluation of an activity before it is undertaken to ensure that all possible primary and secondary effects of the undertaking are examined and all alternatives considered before the activity is approved. An example of this approach is the environmental impact statement required of all federal agencies for projects that affect the environment. A second approach is the setting of pollution standards for specific types of pollutants. These standards set limits on the maximum allowable level of these pollutants that can be discharged. Violators who exceed these standards are fined. Air pollution is controlled in this manner. Another approach is to regulate industrial and municipal discharge activities through licensing procedures, granting these facilities permission to discharge pollutants or waste using certain broad types of technology available or by following certain procedures. Except for particularly hazardous substances, such as mercury, water pollution is con-

EXHIBIT 17.1 ────────────────────────────────

Factors Contributing to Pollution

Types	*Causes*
Air Pollution	Automobiles
	Incinerators
	Factory smokestacks
Water Pollution	Industrial waste
	Thermal pollution
	Municipal discharges
	Agrichemical and fertilizer runoff
Solid Waste	Industrial solids
	Household garbage
Noise	Jet aircraft
	Air compressors
	Motorcycles
	Power lawnmowers
	Snowmobiles
	Highway traffic
Aesthetic	Billboards
	Neon lights
	Telephone poles and wires
	Oil drilling rigs

trolled in this fashion. Finally, another approach examines substances before they are used to determine whether they are safe or whether they constitute such a hazard that their use needs to be limited or banned. The new toxic substances control legislation is an example of this technique.[4]

There are many objectives to pollution control. One is simply an aesthetic one: to improve the quality of the air so visibility is improved, to prevent pollution from blackening buildings, to reduce the foul odors from streams, rivers, or lakes, to reduce the level of noise so that normal conversations can be carried on, to hide offshore oil derricks behind structures that are more aesthetically pleasing.

Closely related to this objective is one of reducing the nuisance or inconvenience that pollution causes. Polluting a river or lake may make it unfit for fishing or swimming, which could cause some people a great amount of displeasure (see box). Pollution in the air can cause a certain amount of personal discomfort, such as eye irritation, that may not actually be a health hazard but is something people can definitely do without.

There are actual direct economic losses connected with pollution that its control can reduce. This can be something as mundane as the soiling of clothes, and thus a reduction of pollution can reduce cleaning and washing expenses. It is said, for example, that before the days of the renaissance in Pittsburgh, executives had to take an extra white shirt to work with them in

---

[4]Anthony D. Tarlock, "Environmental Law: What It Is, What It Should Be," *Environmental Science and Technology*, Vol. 13, No. 11 (November 1979), p. 1345.

The traditional approach echoes the theme that the business of business is business and that the firm has just as much right to use a stream, for example, as do fishermen and bathers. This type of argument, by the way, raises an interesting point put forth by many economists and is one worth pondering. All users of a resource create externalities. If a firm uses a stream to dump its waste chemicals, it is creating externalities for the swimmers and the fishermen who might also use the stream. On the other hand, the swimmers and the fishermen are creating externalities for the firm. The question to be answered on this puzzle is who creates greater externalities, the firm depriving the swimmers of their beach and the fishermen of their clear stream for trout flycasting, or the swimmers and fishermen depriving the firm of its cesspool. Off the top of the head, most people would indict the firm, since it is making a "mess" and messes rate lower on scales of values than clean activities. But, in economic terms, the stream may be making a more valuable contribution to society by being a sewer than it would be by being a recreation and food-producing unit. Generally, however, societal decisions are not made on economic bases alone, and the "other values" enter into the decision-making process through social and political avenues.

From Elkins and Callaghan, *A Managerial Odyssey: Problems in Business and its Environment,* © 1978, 2/e, Addison-Wesley Publishing Company, Inc., Chapter 5, pp. 177–178. Reprinted with permission.

the morning if they intended to go outside of the building for lunch. Other economic losses could result from damage to vegetation, livestock, or deterioration of buildings, particularly in cities such as Venice where many buildings are irreplaceable works of art.

Another objective of pollution control is to reduce the safety hazard that can exist due to lack of visibility. Poor visibility caused by pollution can constitute such a hazard for aircraft trying to land or take off and for automobiles. Accidents on the New Jersey turnpike, for example, have been attributed to the poor visibility caused by pollution from refineries and other industrial facilities in the area.

A very important objective of pollution control is to reduce the health hazards that pollutants cause. Cancer and heart and lung diseases have become the leading causes of death in our society, and a growing body of evidence links much of the occurrence of these diseases to the nature of the environment. Heart disease rates, for example, are known to be higher in areas of high air pollution, and although a direct cause may be difficult to prove, there is increasing belief that polluted air may aggravate preexisting heart conditions. The Environmental Protection Agency states that air pollution probably causes and certainly aggravates the following:

- Disease of the respiratory (breathing) system: nose, sinuses, throat, bronchial tubes, and lungs. All these organs have direct contact with breathed-in air.
- Diseases of the heart and blood vessels. Pollutants can pass through the lung membranes into the blood.
- Cancer, especially of the lungs. Airborne cancer-causing agents can

enter the body through the skin as well as the lungs and be carried by the blood to any organ.

• Skin diseases, allergies, eye irritation.[5]

Water pollution also poses hazards to human health. The possibility that asbestos fibers in the taconite tailings Reserve Mining Company was dumping into Lake Superior were a health hazard was an issue in this case, the longest of all environmental controversies. Extreme noise pollution over extended periods of time can cause loss of hearing. Hazardous waste disposal that is not properly accomplished can cause many problems if people build on old sites or if some of the chemicals leech into the drinking water. Finally, toxic substances pose health problems for those coming into contact with them. Some two million chemical compounds are known, and an estimated 25,000 new ones are developed every year. About 10,000 of these have significant commercial uses, and while most are probably safe, the toxicity of many is unknown.

Finally, a most significant objective of pollution control is simply to preserve the human race. Scientists have predicted, for example, that carbon dioxide buildup in the air throughout the world could cause global climate changes. By the year 2150, scientists predict, if fossil fuels continue as mainstays of the world energy supplies, the earth's average temperature would increase by six degrees centigrade with rises of three times that in polar regions. Such temperature rises could cause the following climatic changes:

• Warming of ocean waters, which would reduce the amount of sea ice, cause a rise in the sea level and move marine life toward the poles.

• An increase in the temperatures at the polar ice caps, which probably wouldn't melt them but would cause increased annual snowfall in Antarctica and Greenland. That would cause the ice to thicken, increasing stresses at the base of the ice caps which might result in slides of ice masses into the oceans. Melting of that ice might cause a rise in sea level of about five meters—over 16 feet—within 300 years.

• Poleward movement of agricultural zones. Higher altitudes would benefit from longer frost-free growing seasons, but summer temperatures might become too high for good crop production in existing farm belts. The corn belt in Iowa might move into Canada. . . . Rainfall on the earth also would increase.

• Deserts and semiarid regions would be severely altered, but it isn't clear if they would expand or contract or move toward or away from the poles.[6]

Such drastic changes could wipe out large parts of the civilized world and drastically alter the life style of others. Besides carbon dioxide buildup, acid rains are also causes of concern, as emissions from factories and other sources are carried by wind hundreds of miles and fall as acid rain or snow on areas or countries remote from the source. This has the effect of acidifying

[5]*Air Pollution and Your Health* (Washington, D.C.: Environmental Protection Agency, March 1979), p. 2.
[6]"Carbon Dioxide Buildup Could Cause Global Climate Changes, Study Warns," *The Wall Street Journal,* May 29, 1979, p. 7. Reprinted by permission of *The Wall Street Journal,* © Dow Jones & Company, Inc., 1979. All rights reserved.

bodies of water, forests, and cropland on a large scale. Again, large segments of the population could be threatened.[7]

Technology and Pollution

There is no doubt that technology is a major factor in pollution. One school of thought holds that technology is *the* major problem because it has been made to serve the traditional values of an economic society where growth in gross national product is a major national objective. The idea that more is better has meant that new technologies are introduced quickly into our society with relatively little attention given to either secondary or long-term effects on the environment. The goal is to exploit these technologies as quickly as possible to attain economic growth. Another contributing factor is the idea that there is a technological answer to everything, that most problems we face as a society have technological solutions. When technology is made to serve these values, problems are bound to occur, say the critics, as not enough thought is given to the effects of technology on the environment.

The solution, according to this way of thinking, is to make technology serve other values, to emphasize the quality of life more than the quantity of goods and services. Some people would like to see the country adopt a zero-growth policy, in which investment in new plants and equipment is allowed only to offset depreciation and obsolescence of existing plants and equipment. Phrases such as "decentralizing technologies" or "small is beautiful" are mentioned frequently as new strategies or approaches that would bring technology under control and minimize its adverse effects on the environment. An example is the installation of solar energy devices in every household and industrial facility to heat air and water and maybe even provide electrical power, doing away with the need for huge utilities that pollute the environment.

An opposing school of thought holds that economic growth is absolutely necessary to provide the money for the capital equipment that will eventually bring pollution under control. The money for pollution control will not be forthcoming in a no-growth economy, as people are not likely to change their life styles as drastically as the "small is beautiful" philosophy would require. The only solution, according to this way of thinking, is to continue the emphasis on growth so that the nation can afford the vast expenditures that pollution control requires. There is no solution to the environmental problem other than technological, and the country must have the economic wherewithal to develop new and more efficient technologies to control the pollution produced by an industrial society.

As in most controversies, the truth probably lies somewhere in between these opposing views. The middle ground in this controversy recognizes that the traditional sequence of technological development must be altered. The usual sequence of events goes something like this: (1) science discovers a new principle that has potential industrial applications; (2) industry develops a

[7]See "Acid from the Skies," *Time*, March 17, 1980, p. 88.

new technology based on this principle and introduces it into society; and (3) human beings are forced to adapt to whatever effects this new technology has on society. The problem is that as technology grows more and more complex and is introduced more rapidly, people find it more and more difficult to adapt to the secondary and long-term effects that many new technologies produce.

The middle ground recognizes that there are problems with the way technology is introduced into our society. Since economic growth is a primary objective, the business organization is the institution through which most new technologies are introduced into society. But a business institution asks only a limited set of questions when introducing technology, mostly related to feasibility (can it be done) and profitability (how much money can be made). These criteria need to be expanded to ask more questions about the effect any new technology will have on the environment. Thus the problem is not with technology per se, or with growth per se, but with the process by which new technology is introduced into society.

The National Environmental Policy Act

The National Environmental Policy Act, passed in 1969, is an attempt to expand the criteria for judging the feasibility of actions that affect the physical environment. The general purposes of the act are quite broad and include: (1) to declare a national policy that will encourage productive and enjoyable harmony between people and their environment, (2) to promote efforts that will prevent or eliminate damage to the environment and biosphere and stimulate people's health and welfare, and (3) to enrich the understanding of the ecological systems and natural resources important to the nation.[8] These purposes are amplified in the following declaration of a national environmental policy.

> The Congress, recognizing the profound impact of man's activity on the inter-relations of all components of the natural environment, particularly the profound influences of population growth, high-density urbanization, industrial expansion, resource exploitation and new and expanding technological advances, and recognizing further the critical importance of restoring and maintaining environmental quality to the overall welfare and development of man, declares that it is the continuing policy of the Federal Government, in cooperation with State and local governments, and other concerned public and private organizations, to use all practicable means and measures, including financial and technical assistance, in a manner calculated to foster and promote the general welfare, to create and maintain conditions under which man and nature can exist in productive harmony, and fulfill the social, economic and other requirements of present and future generations of Americans.[9]

To achieve the purposes of NEPA and accomplish the overall environmental policy set out in the preceding paragraph, the act declares that "it is the continuing responsibility of the federal government to use all practicable means, consistent with other essential considerations of national policy,

[8]National Environmental Policy Act of 1969, Public Law 91–190, Sec. 4321.
[9]*Ibid.*, Sec. 4331.

to improve and coordinate federal plans, functions, programs, and resources to the end that the Nation may":

(1) fulfill the responsibilities of each generation as trustee of the environment for succeeding generations;

(2) assure for all Americans safe, healthful, productive, and esthetically and culturally pleasing surroundings;

(3) attain the widest range of beneficial uses of the environment without degradation, risk to health or safety, or other undesirable and unintended consequences;

(4) preserve important historic, cultural, and natural aspects of our national heritage, and maintain, wherever possible, an environment which supports diversity and variety of individual choice;

(5) achieve a balance between population and resource use which will permit high standards of living and a wide sharing of life's amenities; and

(6) enhance the quality of renewable resources and approach the maximum attainable recycling of depletable resources.[10]

Finally, the act directs that all agencies of the federal government shall: (1) utilize a systematic, interdisciplinary approach that will ensure the·integrated use of the natural and social sciences and the environmental design arts in planning and in decision-making that may have an impact on people's environment; (2) identify and develop methods and procedures . . . that will ensure that presently unquantified environmental amenities and values may be given appropriate consideration in decision-making along with economic and technical considerations; and (3) include in every recommendation or report on proposals for legislation and other major federal actions significantly affecting the quality of the human environment, a detailed statement by the responsible official.[11]

Thus it appears that the bottom line of NEPA is this requirement that each federal agency prepare an environmental impact statement (EIS) in advance of each major action, recommendation or report on legislation that may affect the physical environment significantly. In this way, environmental concerns will be given systematic consideration along with economic and technical concerns, thus expanding the criteria upon which a decision is based. The primary purpose of the EIS is to disclose the environmental consequences of a proposed action, alerting decision-makers in the agency itself, the general public, and Congress and the President to the environmental risks involved. Such proposed actions may include new highway construction, harbor dredging or filling, nuclear power plant construction, large-scale pesticide spraying, new jet runways, bridge construction, and similar actions undertaken or approved by federal agencies.

An EIS is a very complicated document, running to hundreds and even thousands of pages on major projects. It is by nature an interdisciplinary document, requiring scientific and technical skills from many fields to prepare. The general content of the statement, as specified in NEPA, includes the following sections.

• A detailed description of the proposed action including information and technical data adequate to permit a careful assessment of environmental impact.

[10]*Ibid.*
[11]*Ibid.*, Sec. 4332.

- Discussion of the probable impact on the environment, including any impact on ecological systems and any direct or indirect consequences that may result from the action.
- Any adverse environmental effects that cannot be avoided.
- Alternatives to the proposed action that might avoid some or all of the adverse environmental effects, including analysis of costs and environmental impacts of these alternatives.
- An assessment of the cumulative long-term effects of the proposed action including its relationship to short-term use of the environment versus the environment's long-term productivity.
- Any irreversible or irretrievable commitment of resources that might result from the action or which would curtail beneficial use of the environment.[12]

This statement must be circulated for comment by the responsible agency at least 90 days before the proposed action and a final statement made public at least 30 days before the action. Thus citizens play an important role in the EIS process, a role that has been recognized by the courts. Citizens can sue federal agencies on environmental grounds for inadequacy of statements or other causes. Three years after the act was passed, more than 200 such cases were filed against federal agencies alleging violation of NEPA's section requiring the preparation of an environmental impact statement.[13]

The EIS is thus an attempt to introduce environmental criteria into the decision-making process of federal agencies. Such impact statements are not required of private business organizations except where federal permits are required. The experience with the EIS, however, is not good. The Council on Environmental Quality has issued guidelines for their preparation, but they are nonbinding on the agencies. The content of the EIS is primarily controlled by the agencies preparing them, which can lead to duplicate requirements when more than one agency is involved. The EIS has also been criticized as a bulky, useless effort that takes so long to prepare that it unnecessarily delays needed government projects.

To help resolve these problems, the administration proposed new regulations to streamline the EIS process. These regulations (1) limited the EIS to 150 pages, except in unusually complex cases where 300 pages would be allowed (some statements had run to more than 1,000 pages), (2) required that statements cover only important issues on a given project and cut down on lengthy background material, (3) allowed agencies to set deadlines for the issuance of statements by their staffs and outside consultants, (4) allowed federal agencies to adopt statements prepared by other agencies when the same project was involved, (5) required statements to identify the best alternative plan for a project from an environmental point of view, and (6) forced federal and state agencies to consult together closely, beginning in the early stages of a project, to avoid duplication of effort in preparing the statements.[14]

[12]*In Productive Harmony: A Brief Explanation of Environmental Impact Statements* (Washington, D.C.: Environmental Protection Agency, June 1976), p. 6.

[13]*In Productive Harmony: Environmental Impact Statements Broaden the Nation's Perspectives* (Washington, D.C.: Environmental Protection Agency, September 1972), p. 10.

[14]"President Proposes Streamlined Reports on Effect of U.S. Actions on Environment," *The Wall Street Journal*, June 8, 1978, p. 18.

Council on Environmental Quality

The National Environmental Policy Act also created the Council on Environmental Quality, a three-member body located in the executive office of the President (Exhibit 17.2). In general, the CEQ (1) evaluates all federal programs to see that they are consistent with the national policy on the environment, (2) advises and assists the President in environmental matters, and (3) develops national policies in the environmental area. Section 4344 of NEPA lists the following specific duties and functions of the council.

(1) to assist and advise the President in the preparation of the Environmental Quality Report required by section 4341 of this title;

(2) to gather timely and authoritative information concerning the conditions and trends in the quality of the environment both current and prospective, to analyze and interpret such information for the purpose of determining whether such conditions and trends are interfering, or are likely to interfere, with the achieve-

EXHIBIT 17.2 ──

COUNCIL ON ENVIRONMENTAL QUALITY
722 Jackson Place NW, Washington, D.C. 20006
Telephone: (202) 395-5770

Purpose: To administer the environmental impact statement process and to develop and recommend to the President policies for protecting and improving environmental quality.

Regulatory Activity: The CEQ is responsible for issuing regulations to federal agencies on the preparation of environmental impact statements required under the National Environmental Policy Act. It also (1) reviews and appraises federal programs affecting the environment; and (2) assists in coordinating national environmental programs.

Established: 1969

Legislative Authority:
Enabling Legislation: National Environmental Policy Act of 1969 (83 Stat. 852)
National Environmental Improvement Act of 1970 (84 Stat. 114)
Water Quality Improvement Act of 1970 (84 Stat. 94)

Organization: The Council, located within the Executive Office of the President, consists of three members appointed by the President with the advice and consent of the Senate. The Office of Environmental Quality within the Department of Housing and Urban Development provides staff for the Council.

Budgets and Staffing
(Fiscal Years 1971–1981)

	71	72	73	74	75	76	77	78	79	*(Estimated)* 80	81
Budget ($ millions)	1	2	2	2	3	3	4	1	4	4	3
Staffing	54	57	56	50	50	44	40	32	32	32	32

NOTE: Budget and staffing figures include the Office of Environmental Quality.

From Ronald J. Penoyer, *Directory of Federal Regulatory Agencies,* 2nd ed. (St. Louis, Mo.: Washington University Center for the Study of American Business, 1980), p. 25. Reprinted with permission.

ment of the policy set forth in subchapter I of this chapter, and to compile and submit to the President studies relating to such conditions and trends;

(3) to review and appraise the various programs and activities of the Federal Government in the light of the policy set forth in subchapter I of this chapter for the purpose of determining the extent to which such programs and activities are contributing to the achievement of such policy, and to make recommendations to the President with respect thereto;

(4) to develop and recommend to the President national policies to foster and promote the improvement of environmental quality to meet the conservation, social, economic, health, and other requirements and goals of the Nation;

(5) to conduct investigations, studies, surveys, research, and analyses relating to ecological systems and environmental quality;

(6) to document and define changes in the natural environment, including the plant and animal systems, and to accumulate necessary data and other information for a continuing analysis of these changes or trends and an interpretation of their underlying causes;

(7) to report at least once each year to the President on the state and condition of the environment; and

(8) to make and furnish such studies, reports thereon, and recommendations with respect to matters of policy and legislation as the President may request.[15]

The CEQ is thus responsible for administering the environmental impact statement process through the issuance of regulations to federal agencies regarding their preparation. Beyond this, however, the CEQ has no administrative authority for pollution control. Its approach is entirely preventive in nature. Another function of the CEQ is preparation of the Environmental Quality Report, an annual report on the state of the environment. The responsibility for this report is analogous to the Council of Economic Advisors and the Economic Report of the President.

Environmental Protection Agency

The other federal agency involved in protecting and enhancing the physical environment and one with much more sweeping authority over various aspects of pollution control is the Environmental Protection Agency (EPA). The EPA began on July 9, 1970, when President Nixon sent a reorganization plan to Congress that took fifteen units dealing with the environment from existing departments and agencies and relocated them in a new independent agency. The plan became effective on December 2, 1970, when the EPA officially opened its doors.

The EPA now has responsibility for pollution control in seven areas of the environment: air, water, solid waste, pesticides, toxic substances, radiation, and noise. Its general responsibilities in these areas include (1) the establishment and enforcement of standards, (2) monitoring of pollution in the environment, (3) conducting research into environmental problems and holding demonstrations when appropriate, and (4) assisting state and local governments in their efforts to control pollution (see Exhibit 17.3). The EPA

[15] Public Law 91-190, Sec. 4344.

EXHIBIT 17.3 —————————————————————————————————

ENVIRONMENTAL PROTECTION AGENCY
401 M Street SW, Washington, D.C. 20460
Telephone: (202) 755-0707

Purpose: To protect and enhance the physical environment.

Regulatory Activity: In cooperation with state and local governments, the agency controls pollution through regulation, surveillance, and enforcement in eight areas: air, water quality, solid waste, pesticides, toxic substances, drinking water, radiation, and noise. Its activities in each area include development of: (1) national programs and technical policies; (2) national emission standards and effluent guidelines; (3) rules and procedures for industry reporting, registration and certification programs; and (4) ambient air standards. EPA issues permits to industrial dischargers of pollutants and for disposal of industrial waste; sets standards which limit the amount of radioactivity in the environment; reviews proposals for new nuclear facilities; evaluates and regulates new chemicals and chemicals with new uses; and establishes and monitors tolerance levels for pesticides occurring in or on foods.

Established: 1970

Legislative Authority:
Enabling Legislation: Reorganization Plan No. 3 of 1970, effective December 2, 1970
The EPA is responsible for the enforcement of the following acts:
Water Quality Improvement Act of 1970 (84 Stat. 94)
Clean Air Act Amendments of 1970 (84 Stat. 1676)
Federal Water Pollution Control Act Amendments of 1972 (86 Stat. 819)
Federal Insecticide, Fungicide and Rodenticide Act of 1972 (86 Stat. 975)
Marine Protection, Research, and Sanctuaries Act of 1972 (86 Stat. 1052)
Noise Control Act of 1972 (86 Stat. 1234)
Provisions of the Energy Supply and Environmental Coordination Act of 1974 (88 Stat. 246)
Safe Drinking Water Act of 1974 (88 Stat. 1661)
Resource Conservation and Recovery Act of 1976 (90 Stat. 95)
Toxic Substances Control Act of 1976 (90 Stat. 2005)
Clean Air Act Amendments of 1977 (91 Stat. 685)
Clean Water Act of 1977 (91 Stat. 1566)

Organization: This independent agency, located within the Executive branch, is headed by an administrator.

Budgets and Staffing
(Fiscal Years 1970-1981)

	70	71	72	73	74	75	76	77	78	79	(Estimated) 80	81
Budget ($ millions)	71	125	455	527	629	850	772	718	885	1024	1084	1391
Staffing	n/a	n/a	7992	8492	9203	9203	9297	9550	10156	10153	11004	11226

NOTE: Budget figures exclude construction grants.

From Ronald J. Penoyer, *Directory of Federal Regulatory Agencies,* 2nd ed. (St. Louis, Mo.: Washington University Center for the Study of American Business, 1980), p. 27. Reprinted with permission.

is headquartered in Washington, D.C., with regional offices and laboratories located throughout the country (see Figures 17.1 and 17.2).

Benefits and Costs of Environmental Regulation

In its 1979 report, the CEQ claimed the nation's air quality was improving. Combined data from 25 major metropolitan areas showed that the number of unhealthy days declined by 15 percent between 1974 and 1977, while the number of very unhealthy days declined 32 percent. Data from about 50 of the most polluted counties in the United States showed that violations of ambient air quality standards between 1974 and 1977 either stayed constant or decreased. However, for 1977, the air in two of the 41 urban areas for which reliable data were available (New York and Los Angeles) still registered in the unhealthy range for more than two-thirds of the days of the year.[16]

The data did not show vast improvement in water quality since the early 1970s, but at least the situation was not getting worse. Between 1975 and 1978, there was little or no overall change in the level of six major water pollution indicators (fecal coliform, bacteria, dissolved oxygen, phosphorus, mercury, and lead.)[17] Table 17.1 shows that industry compliance with the water pollution reporting requirements ranged from 93 percent for fabricated metal products to 54 percent in the steel industry.

In this same report, the CEQ reported on the findings of an outside consultant who examined the existing benefit studies for air and water pollution control. This study found major divergences among estimates of air and water pollution control benefits. For example, the estimated health benefits of controlling air pollution from stationary sources ranged from $1.8 billion to $14.4 billion, even after adjustment in 1978 constant dollars and standardizing for a 20 percent improvement in air quality. Benefits from water pollution control ranged from $2.5 to $15.1 billion.[18]

Because of these variations, the study went a step further and selected a "most reasonable point estimate" (the single most likely value) for air and water pollution control benefits. Annual benefits realized in 1978 from measured improvements in air quality since 1970, the study said, could be reasonably valued at $21.4 billion. "Of this total, $17 billion represented reductions in mortality and morbidity, $2.0 billion reduced soiling and cleaning costs, $0.7 billion increased agricultural output, $0.9 billion prevention of corrosion and other materials damage, and $0.8 billion increases in property values."[19]

A reasonable point estimate was also developed for the total annual benefits to be enjoyed by 1985 as a result of the nation's water pollution control efforts. 1985 was chosen because it is the date by which the best available treatment technology is to be installed by industrial and municipal point sources. These benefits will amount to about $12.3 billion per year, the

[16]*Environmental Quality*, p. 17.
[17]*Ibid.*, pp. 75–78.
[18]*Ibid.*, p. 654.
[19]*Ibid.*, p. 655.

Figure 17.1. United States Environmental Protection Agency

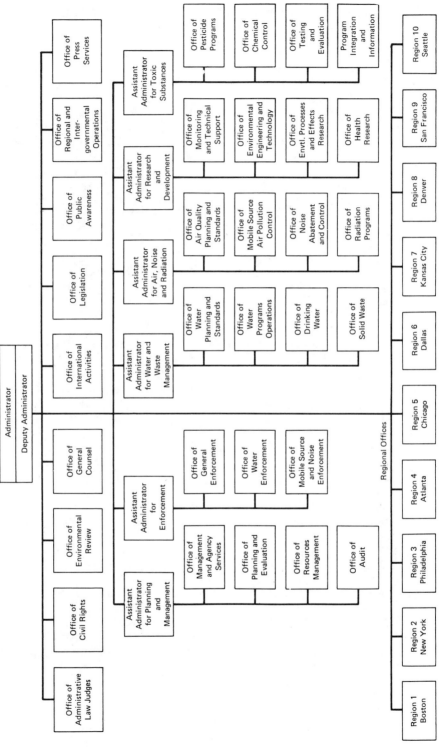

From *Finding Your Way through EPA* (Washington, D.C.: Environmental Protection Agency, August 1979), p. i (facing).

Figure 17.2. United States Environmental Protection Agency
Regional Organization

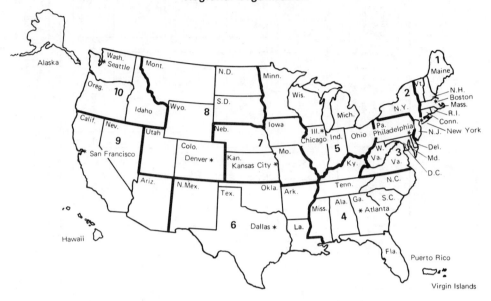

From *Finding Your Way through EPA* (Washington, D.C.: Environmental Protection Agency, August 1979), p. 25.

study estimated, with recreation benefits accounting for $6.7 billion, or about 54 percent of the total. This total does not include the health benefits that may result from the elimination of chemical contamination in drinking water.[20]

Table 17.2 shows the CEQ's estimates of incremental costs for the ten-year period from 1978 through 1987. This table shows that the cost of complying with all federal pollution control and environmental programs in 1978 was $26.9 billion. "Expenditures for federal air pollution programs totaled $16.6 billion in 1978, with $7.6 billion devoted to the control of mobile source air pollution (cars, trucks, buses, motorcycles, etc.) and another $5.0 billion for the control of air pollution from industrial point sources. Utilities, counted separately, were required to spend $2.8 billion for pollution abatement in 1978. Of the $16.6 billion in incremental costs for air pollution control in 1978, $7.5 billion was for capital costs, while $9.1 billion went to the operation and maintenance of air pollution control equipment."[21]

The difficulties inherent in cost-benefit analysis are considerable. As shown in Exhibit 17.4, intangible benefits defy economic analysis. How does one place an economic value on clearer and sunnier days? What is the economic value of improved visibility, less eye irritation, and the like? Nonetheless, the discipline of going through a cost-benefit analysis can be a benefit in and of itself, forcing policy-makers to think in these terms and

[20]*Ibid.*
[21]*Ibid.*, p. 665.

TABLE 17.1 **Industry Compliance**[a] **With Federal Water Pollution Reporting Regulations, 1977**[b]

SIC Code[c]	Industrial Category	Plants in Compliance	Plants Not in Compliance	Plants in Industry, Total	Percent Plants in Compliance
3400	Fabricated metal products	248	18	266	93
2600	Paper products	161	18	179	90
3200	Stone and concrete	89	15	104	86
2000	Food products	375	62	437	86
2200	Textiles	164	28	192	85
2800	Chemical products	480	83	563	85
2911	Petroleum refining	125	25	150	83
1000–1400	Mining	67	14	81	83
2821	Plastic materials	66	14	80	82
3300	Primary metal industries	147	40	187	79
2611, 2621	Pulp and paper mills	175	51	226	77
4911	Electric power plants	293	150	443	66
3312	Steel plants (blast furnaces)	51	44	95	54

[a]Compliance here means that industries report effluent levels to EPA each quarter. It does not necessarily imply that they have reduced their effluents to the limit required by their permit.

[b]Data compiled June 9, 1977 from the Permit Compliance System (PCS) Source Inventory and the *Quarterly Noncompliance Report.*

[c]Standard Industrial Classification Code.

Source: Council on Environmental Quality, *Environmental Quality* (Washington, D.C.: U.S. Government Printing Office, 1979), p. 138.

move away from the "health at any price" philosophy embodied in much of the legislation.

Alternatives to Pollution Control

The resources devoted to pollution control are not inconsiderable, making it reasonable to ask whether environmental goals might be met more efficiently than the existing system of standards. Two of the most popular alternatives to present environmental policy are the use of effluent charges or marketable permits, both offering economic incentives to business for pollution control.

Under a system of effluent charges, polluters would be charged a predetermined fee for every unit of pollution they discharged. This charge would provide an inducement for polluters to reduce their pollution, an inducement that would vary, of course, with the amount of the per-unit effluent charge. For every unit of pollution eliminated, that much less would be paid in pollution charges. Firms would be acting in their own self-interest under a system that forces them to internalize pollution costs that were previously borne externally by society. They could continue to pollute and

TABLE 17.2 **Estimated Increment Pollution Abatement and Environmental Quality Expenditures, 1978–87** [a] (Billions of 1978 Dollars)

	1978			1987			Cumulative (1978–87)			
	Operation and Maintenance	Annual Capital Costs [b]	Total Annual Costs	Operation and Maintenance	Annual Capital Costs [b]	Total Annual Costs	Capital Investment	Operation and Maintenance	Capital Costs [b]	Total Costs
Air Pollution										
Public	0.9	0.3	1.2	2.0	0.8	2.8	4.6	13.7	5.5	19.2
Private										
Mobile	4.3	3.3	7.6	5.1	9.3	14.4	59.6	45.0	66.4	111.4
Industrial	2.3	2.7	5.0	3.7	5.2	8.9	28.6	44.1	38.6	82.7
Utilities	1.6	1.2	2.8	6.5	4.8	11.3	26.4	37.5	28.1	65.6
Subtotal	9.1	7.5	16.6	17.3	20.1	37.4	119.2	140.3	138.6	278.9
Water Pollution										
Public	1.5	3.0	4.5	2.1	5.0	7.1	17.2	16.6	46.7	63.3
Private										
Industrial	2.1	1.6	3.7	5.7	4.6	10.3	28.0	38.9	30.4	69.3
Utilities	1.2	0.8	2.0	1.8	1.2	3.0	3.9	16.0	10.1	26.1
Subtotal	4.8	5.4	10.2	9.6	10.8	20.4	68.5	71.5	87.2	158.7
Solid Waste										
Public	NA	NA	NA	0.5	0.3	0.8	NA	3.5	2.2	5.7
Private	NA	NA	NA	1.2	0.6	1.8	NA	8.8	4.7	13.5
Subtotal	NA	NA	NA	1.7	0.9	2.6	NA	12.3	6.9	19.2
Toxic Substances	0.1	NA	NA	0.3	NA	0.3	NA	2.2	NA	2.2
Drinking Water	<.05	<.05	<.05	0.4	0.4	0.8	NA	2.9	2.7	5.6
Noise	<.05	<.05	<.05	0.6	1.0	1.6	4.8	2.5	4.1	6.6
Pesticides	<.05	<.05	<.05	0.1	<.05	0.1	NA	0.4	<.05	0.4
Land Reclamation	NA	NA	NA	0.8	NA	0.8	NA	6.0	NA	6.0
Total	14.0	12.9	26.9	30.8	33.2	64.0	192.5	238.1	239.5	477.6

NA = Not Available

[a]Incremental costs are those made in response to federal environmental legislation beyond those that would have been made in the absence of that legislation.

[b]Interest and depreciation.

Source: Council on Environmental Quality, *Environmental Quality* (Washington, D.C.: U.S. Government Printing Office, 1979), p. 667.

EXHIBIT 17.4 ───────────────────────────────

Improving Air Quality Yields Both Economic and Intangible Benefits and Costs

Benefits		Costs	
Category	*Example*	*Category*	*Example*
Improvements in human health	Decreased morbidity	New abatement equipment	Sulfur-removing scrubbers
Increased productivity of ecological systems	Lessened damage to plants and animals	Modifying existing technology	Automobile emissions controls
Enhancement of recreational opportunities	More clear and sunny days	Operations and maintenance	Additional energy costs
Reduction of adverse impacts on household and industrial production	Lowered cleaning costs	Process and design changes	Aircraft engine redesign
Quality of life	Improved visibility, less eye irritation, reduction of noxious odors	Plant shutdowns	Temporary or permanent unemployment
		Administration, implementation, and enforcement costs	Monitoring costs

From Lester B. Lave and Eugene P. Seskin, "Health Benefits Exceed by 70% Costs to Control Stationary Source Air Pollution," *Chemical and Engineering News,* April 23, 1979, p. 40. Reprinted with permission.

pay to do so, or undertake pollution control efforts, deciding on the most efficient technology to be employed. "High-cost" firms with respect to pollution control might find it more expensive to eliminate their discharge, and thus would choose to continue to pollute, paying the charges. The "low-cost" firms would find it more beneficial to install pollution control technology. Thus considerable savings might accrue to society where there are great differences in abatement costs between polluters, as compared to the existing system which requires identical percentage reductions from all polluters.[22]

The marketable rights or permit system involves determining the maximum permissible total discharge of a given pollutant that would be allowed over a region. Permits to discharge some fraction of this total would then be auctioned off to the highest bidders. Firms most likely to enter this market would be those whose production necessitates a certain amount of pollution, yet individuals or groups who value clean air and water could also enter the market to buy up rights and in effect take them off the market. Only those holding permits for specific pollutants would be allowed to discharge them. These permits could be bought either in the original auction or from firms or other groups and individuals who had so acquired them.

[22]*Ibid.*, p. 672.

The value of these rights would be determined through an exchange process. The market for pollution rights would work much the same as the stock market. Firms would have an incentive to search for pollution-free methods of production to avoid the cost of acquiring permits. Those that could reduce or eliminate pollution for less than the cost of the permits would do so, while those firms that could not would have to buy them in order to operate. Thus the marketable rights approach also tends to obtain reductions from low-cost polluters and minimizes the cost of pollution control to society.[23] Exhibit 17.5 shows how this process would work with a reduction in the cost to society. To some extent, this system of marketable rights already

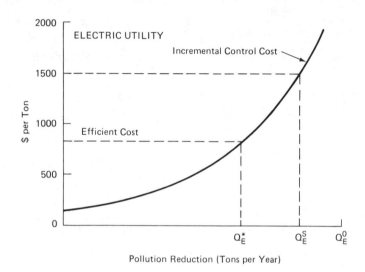

Pollution Reduction (Tons per Year)

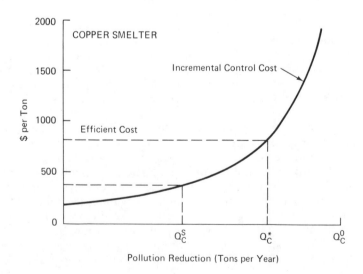

Pollution Reduction (Tons per Year)

[23]*Ibid.*, pp. 672–673.

THE PHYSICAL ENVIRONMENT: ISSUES AND CONCEPTS

EXHIBIT 17.5

Utility Could Buy SO₂ Emission Rights Under Marketable Rights System

How would a system of marketable rights work? Imagine that a copper smelter and an electric power plant are built side by side, and that the amounts of sulfur dioxide removal are given by Q_C and Q_E, respectively, in the figures. The cost of removing an incremental ton of SO_2 in this location to meet federal standards (Q_C^S and Q_E^S) is $1500 for utilities and $400 for smelters.

If each plant were given this standard as a marketable right—equal to $Q_C^0 - Q_C^S$ for the copper smelter, and $Q_E^0 - Q_E^S$ for the utility (where Q_C^0 and Q_E^0 are the values for zero pollution, that is, complete pollution removal)—the utility would buy some of the copper smelter's right. This would require the smelter to tighten its controls to an SO_2 emission level below that required by its standard—that is, by $Q_C^* - Q_C^S$—and allow the utility to raise its level to Q_E^*.

Since the total costs of control are equal to the area under each incremental control cost curve, costs to the public would be reduced by an amount equal to the difference between the marked area under the utility curve and the marked area under the copper curve. But total emissions would be unchanged.

From Robert W. Crandall, "Environmental Control Is Out of Control," *Chemical and Engineering News,* April 23, 1979, p. 32. Reprinted with permission.

exists in the EPA's offset policy, which requires reduction in pollution in nonattainment areas in order for new polluting facilities to be built.[24]

Theoretically, these systems offer great promise and one might hope for their early implementation. In practice, however, it might not be possible to reap all the savings these methods offer. Among the difficult questions that would have to be answered concerning their use are the following.

- How great are the savings such systems might actually provide? Are treatment costs among polluters really so very different? Cannot the existing regulations differentiate among such sources when limits are assigned under the standards-and-enforcement approach?

- How difficult is it to set a just charge that accurately reflects pollution costs and thereby achieves the desired level of water or air quality? How will polluters actually respond to charges at various levels? What would be the effect of varying the charge suddenly if it was discovered to be too high or low?

- Do adequate source-monitoring devices exist so that it can be determined whether a polluter is paying his appropriate effluent charge? (Note that accurate monitoring is required under a standards-and-enforcement approach, as well.) Could marketable permits be purchased as a tool to drive competitors out of business? Could polluters form a cartel to keep the price of pollution permits artificially low?[25]

Conclusion

The environmental movement has become institutionalized. What was in the 1960s a movement characterized by moral outrage over the way the environment was being treated, in the 1970s became institutionalized into a

[24]See Bruce Yandle, "The Emerging Market in Air Pollution Rights," *Regulation,* July/August 1978, pp. 21–29.

[25]*Environmental Quality,* p. 674.

comprehensive system of laws and regulations to protect the environment. Whether overregulation exists with respect to the environment is a relevant question, but there is also no way to turn back the clock. The 1970s, according to Barbara Blum, Deputy Administrator of the EPA, "marked the beginning of what can be called a worldwide revolution with regard to environmental and related consumer matters."[26] Human beings have realized that in order to survive they must reach a workable accommodation with the physical environment.

> Environmental legislation passed in the past few years, as well as the most recent amendments to the original air and water laws, ask that we now get to the root of environmental and related public health problems without diminishing our efforts to prune the most noxious branches. We are on the threshold of accepting the fact that the manner in which our society conducts its private and its public business has far-reaching health, economic and social implications and bears fundamentally on the essential integrity of ecological systems upon which we depend for life itself. We are beginning to understand that how we do things is as important as what we do. We are beginning to acknowledge that it is environmental and public health folly to continue to think we can deal adequately with toxic substances after they have been produced, and economic folly to continue to consign valuable natural resources to the trash heap of environmental mismanagement while the world's supplies continue to dwindle.

> We are on the threshold of a new era in environmental protection. An era in which the after-the-fact economic and environmental folly that has too often characterized our handling of environmental problems until now must give way to an emerging imperative for before-the-fact resource management and public health protection. The times call for new patterns of interaction among all levels of government, the assumption of key responsibilities by industry, and for meaningful public awareness and participation in all the major activities mandated by environmental legislation.[27]

Questions for Discussion

1. What services does the physical environment provide for human beings? Which of these services are most important? Where are trade-offs between the different services involved?
2. What is pollution? What factors have contributed to a pollution problem in this country? Are these factors still important today? What implications does your answer have for the environmental movement?
3. Distinguish between the different methods of pollution control. Give examples of each method. Is one method best, in your opinion, for all types of pollution or is some kind of a mix the best strategy as far as public policy is concerned?
4. How is technology related to pollution? Describe the environmentalist and economic point of view with respect to technology. With which school of thought do you identify most closely? Why? What is the middle ground in this controversy?
5. What is an environmental impact statement? How does an EIS help attain the objectives of the National Environmental Policy Act? Describe the specific content of an environmental impact statement.
6. What is the difference between the Council on Environmental Quality and the

[26]*On the Threshold of a New Environmental Era* (Washington, D.C.: Environmental Protection Agency, April 1978), p. 2.
[27]*Ibid.*, pp. 3–4.

Environmental Protection Agency? For what purposes was each agency created? Which agency is of most concern to business? Why?

7. Does cost-benefit analysis make sense as a way to make decisions on environmental policy? Why or why not? Is it possible to quantify all the costs and benefits in the same terms so a direct comparison of costs with benefits can be made? Is it necessary?

8. Describe the most popular alternative methods of pollution control. What are the advantages and disadvantages of each method? What advantages do they have over the present system? If you had to choose one method to implement, which would you choose? Why?

Suggested Reading

Barbaro, Ronald, and Cross, Frank L., Jr. *Primer on Environmental Impact Statements.* Westport, Conn.: Technomic Publishing Co., 1973.

Canter, Larry W. *Environmental Impact Assessment.* New York: McGraw-Hill, 1977.

Commoner, Barry. *The Closing Circle.* New York: Knopf, 1971.

Dorfman, Robert, and Dorfman, Nancy, eds. *Economics of the Environment,* 2nd ed. New York: W. W. Norton & Co., Inc. 1977.

Edel, Matthew. *Economics and the Environment.* Englewood Cliffs, N.J.: Prentice-Hall, 1973.

Kapp, K. William. *The Social Costs of Private Enterprise.* New York: Schocken Books, 1971.

Kneese, Allen V. *Economics and the Environment.* New York: Penguin Books, 1977.

———, and Schultz, Charles L. *Pollution, Prices, and Public Policy.* Washington, D.C.: Brookings Institution, 1975.

Leonard, H. Jeffrey, Davies, J. Clarence III, and Binder, Gordon. *Business and Environment: Toward Common Ground.* Washington, D.C.: The Conservation Foundation, 1977.

Nagel, Stuart S. *Environmental Politics.* New York: Praeger, 1974.

Oelschlaeger, Max. *The Environmental Imperative: A Socio-Economic Perspective.* Washington, D.C.: University Press of America, 1977.

Saunders, Peter John Williams. *The Estimation of Pollution Damage.* Manchester, England: Manchester University Press, 1976.

18

Public Policies to Control Pollution

The fervor of the late sixties and early seventies has evolved into the environmental institutions of the seventies and eighties. Environmentalists today carry calculators instead of picket signs. Demonstrating housewives are now Presidents of the Lung Association or the League of Women Voters. Law students wearing sweatshirts and sneakers now carry legal briefs in fine leather cases—and those briefs have established a truly astounding docket of precedent setting environmental decisions.

Perhaps most significant, the street leaders on Earth Day have become the institutional leaders of today. In fact, many of them are now EPA administrators wondering why the environmentalists are shouting at them.[1]

After NEPA came a whole series of public policy measures aimed at protecting the environment and conserving energy and other natural resources. While NEPA itself is an example of the first type of pollution control mentioned at the beginning of the previous chapter, the concern in this chapter is with the other three types of pollution control: setting of standards, licensing, and determining the safety of substances before they are used. These methods will be examined by looking at each of the environmental areas for which the EPA has responsibility.

Air Pollution

There are many natural sources of air pollution, including wind-blown dust, pollen, and other aero-allergens, smoke and gases from forest or grass fires, gases and odors from swamps and marshes, fog, volcanic ash and gases,

---

[1]Douglas M. Costle, *The New Environmentalists* (Washington, D.C.: Environmental Protection Agency, 1979), pp. 2–3.

natural radioactivity, and ozone from lightning. Air pollution existed before the advent of modern industrial societies. But the artificial sources of pollution that come from industrial processes are the concern of public policy to control. Six pollutants were initially identified by the EPA in 1971 as being the most pervasive of artificial pollutants and in need of immediate reduction and control. These six are sulfur oxides, particulates, carbon monoxide, ozone, nitrogen oxides, and hydrocarbons. In 1978, lead was added to the list of harmful pollutants. The nature and health effects of these pollutants are varied (see box).

PRINCIPAL KINDS OF AIR POLLUTION, THEIR SOURCES AND EFFECTS

Here are brief descriptions of the air pollutants for which EPA standards have been set, their principal sources, and summaries of the adverse effects of each on human health.

Sulfur oxides are gases that come from the burning of sulfur-containing fuel, mainly coal and oil, and also from the smelting of metals and from certain industrial processes. They have a distinctive odor. Sulfur dioxide (SO_2) comprises about 95 percent of these gases, so scientists use a test for SO_2 alone as a measure of all sulfur oxides.

As the level of sulfur oxides in air increases, there is an obstruction of breathing, a choking effect that doctors call pulmonary flow resistance. The amount of breathing obstruction has a direct relation to the amount of sulfur compounds in the air. The effect of sulfur pollution is enhanced by the presence of other pollutants, especially particulates and oxidants. That is, the harm from two or more pollutants is more than additive. Each augments the other, and the combined effect is greater than the sum of the parts would be.

Many types of respiratory disease are associated with sulfur oxides: coughs and colds, asthma, bronchitis, and emphysema. Some researchers believe that the harm is mainly due not to the sulfur oxide gases but to other sulfur compounds that accompany the oxides: sulfur acids and sulfate salts.

Particulates are solid particles or liquid droplets small enough to remain suspended in air. They include dust, soot, and smoke—particles that may be irritating but are usually not poisonous—and bits of solid or liquid substances that may be highly toxic.

Particulates are measured all together by filtering all the particles from a known amount of air and weighing them. The EPA standard for particulates gives only a rough indication of the health hazard, since it does not separate toxic particles from those that are merely annoying. Research is under way to find quick, economical methods of measuring various kinds of particles and also their sizes. The smaller the particles, the more likely they are to reach the innermost parts of the lungs and work their damage.

The harm may be physical: clogging the lung sacs, as in anthracosis, or coal miners' "black lung" from inhaling coal dust; asbestosis or silicosis in people exposed to asbestos fibers or dusts from silicate rocks; and byssinosis, or textile workers' "brown lung" from inhaling cotton fibers.

The harm may also be chemical: changes in the human body caused by chemical reactions with pollution particles that pass through the lung membranes to poison the blood or be carried by the blood to other organs. This can happen with inhaled lead, cadmium, beryllium, and other metals, and with certain complex organic compounds that can cause cancer.

Many studies indicate that particulates and sulfur oxides (they often occur

---

together) increase the incidence and severity of respiratory disease.

Carbon monoxide (CO) is colorless, odorless, poison gas formed when carbon-containing fuel is not burned completely. It is by far the most plentiful air pollutant. EPA estimates that more than 102 million metric tons of CO are spewed into the air each year in the United States. (A metric ton is 1,000 kilograms, or about 2,200 pounds.)

Fortunately this deadly gas does not persist in the atmosphere. It is apparently converted by natural processes to harmless carbon dioxide, in ways not yet understood, fast enough to prevent any general buildup. But it can reach dangerous levels in local areas, as in city-street canyons with heavy auto traffic and little wind. More than 75 percent of the CO emitted comes from road vehicles.

Clinical experience with accidental CO poisoning has shown clearly how it affects the body. When the gas is breathed, CO replaces oxygen in the red blood cells, reducing the amount of oxygen that can reach the body cells and maintain life. Lack of oxygen affects the brain, and the first symptoms are impaired perception and thinking. Reflexes are slowed, judgement weakened, and a person becomes drowsy. An auto driver breathing high levels of CO is more likely to have an accident; an athlete's performance and skill drop suddenly. Lack of oxygen then affects the heart. Death can come from heart failure or general asphyxiation, if a person is exposed to very high levels of CO.

Ozone is a poisonous form of pure oxygen and the principal component of modern smog. Until recently EPA called this type of pollution "photochemical oxidants." The name was changed because ozone was the only oxidant actually measured and by far the most plentiful.

Ozone and other oxidants—including peroxyacetal nitrates (PAN), formaldehydes, and peroxides—are not emitted into the air directly. They are formed by chemical reactions in the air from two other pollutants, hydrocarbons and nitrogen oxides. Energy from sunlight is needed for these chemical reactions, hence the term photochemical smog, and the daily variation in ozone levels, increasing during the day and decreasing at night.

Ozone is a pungent-smelling, faintly bluish gas. It irritates the mucous membranes of the respiratory system, causing coughing, choking, and impaired lung function. It aggravates chronic respiratory diseases like asthma and bronchitis and is believed capable of hastening the death, by pneumonia, of persons in already weakened health. PAN and the other oxidants that accompany ozone are powerful eye irritants.

It is an irony of nature that a form of pure oxygen can be so harmful. Regular oxygen (O_2, two atoms to the molecule) gives life to all animals and most plants; ozone (O_3, three atoms) is poisonous.

Note: Ozone in the air we breathe should not be confused with the so-called "ozone layer" in the stratosphere. The stratosphere begins at an altitude of seven to ten miles, depending on the latitude and the season of the year. Ozone in this thin air absorbs a large part of the sun's ultraviolet radiation. Scientists believe that some human actions—for instance, supersonic aircraft flights and the release of fluorocarbon gases from spray cans—could cause a permanent reduction in stratospheric ozone. This could increase the ultraviolet radiation reaching the earth, raising the incidence of human skin cancer and probably affecting the earth's climate and ecological systems in unpredictable ways. The high ozone layer seems to be maintained by natural processes, mainly by the sun's radiation. Lightning discharges are the principal natural source of ozone in the lower atmosphere.

Nitrogen oxides. When any fuel is burned at a high enough temperature—above 650°C (1,200°F)—some of the abundant nitrogen in the air will react too, forming poisonous, highly reactive gases called nitrogen oxides. Nitrogen dioxide (NO_2) is the most plentiful of these and the one measured to indicate all. It is a suffocating, brownish-colored gas and a strong oxidizing agent, quick to react with water vapor to form corrosive nitric acid.

Principal sources of nitrogen oxide emissions are electric utility and industrial boilers (56%) and auto and truck engines (40%).

Occupational health studies have shown that nitrogen oxides can be fatal at high concentrations. At lower levels, they can irritate the lungs, cause bronchitis and pneumonia, and lower respiratory infections like influenza. However, the principal harm to people seems to come not from nitrogen oxides directly but from the oxidants they help to form by uniting in sunlit air with hydrocarbons to make ozone and other ingredients of photochemical smog.

NO_2 has been difficult to measure in the ambient air. The first sampling and analysis methods turned out to be unreliable and were withdrawn as official methods in 1973. After extensive testing a reliable monitoring technique was approved in 1976.

Hydrocarbons are unburned fuels in gaseous or vapor form. Gasoline, for example, is a mixture of many kinds of hydrocarbons, each containing more than twice as many hydrogen atoms as carbon atoms linked together in molecules of many different sizes and patterns.

Unlike sulfur and nitrogen oxides, the vast family of hydrocarbons is not measured by testing for a single compound. Indeed, the simplest hydrocarbon, methane (CH_4) that occurs in swamps, coal mines, and natural gas, is excluded by the official testing method; only more complex hydrocarbons that are highly reactive are measured.

Most of the estimated 28 million metric tons of hydrocarbons emitted each year in the United States come from gasoline vapors that escape burning in auto engines, either evaporating from the tank or fuel lines or going out the tail pipe. Other large sources are gasoline stations, handlers, and transporters; industries that use solvents; and users of paint and drycleaning fluids.

At the levels usually found in ambient air, hydrocarbons, as a class of compounds, may have no direct effect on human health. In a confined space, of course, they could cause asphyxiation by displacing the air, and some, like benzene, can be hazardous in themselves. A major problem with hydrocarbons stems from the oxidants they help to form by reacting with nitrogen oxides in sunlight.

Lead. Particles of this metal or its compounds enter the air from auto exhaust (tetraethyl lead, an anti-knock agent in gasoline) and from industries that smelt or process the metal. About 90% of all airborne lead is from autos.

Lead is absorbed into the body and accumulates in bone and soft tissues. Its most pronounced effects are on the blood-forming, nervous, and kidney systems, though it may also affect other body functions. Young children are especially susceptible to lead poisoning.

The ambient air standard for lead was adopted by EPA in 1978, seven years after the other six standards.

From *Air Pollution and Your Health* (Washington, D.C.: Environmental Protection Agency, March 1979), pp. 7–11.

The total amount of pollution in the air over the United States at any given time adds up to hundreds of millions of tons. Table 18.1 shows the total emissions over a seven-year period of the five most pervasive pollutants. The amount of these pollutants spewed into the air each year averages around 200 million metric tons (a metric ton is about 2,200 pounds), nearly a ton for

TABLE 18.1 **Estimated Pollutant Emissions in the United States 1970 Through 1977 (Millions of Metric Tons)**

Year	Suspended Particles		Sulfur Oxides		Nitrogen Oxides		Hydro-carbons*		Carbon Monoxide		Total
1970	22.2	11%	29.8	15%	19.6	9%	29.5	15%	102.2	50%	203.3
1971	20.9	10%	28.3	14%	20.2	10%	29.1	15%	102.5	51%	201.0
1972	19.6	10%	29.6	14%	21.6	11%	29.6	14%	103.8	51%	204.2
1973	19.2	10%	30.2	14%	22.3	11%	29.7	14%	103.5	51%	204.9
1974	17.0	9%	28.4	15%	21.7	11%	28.6	15%	99.7	50%	195.4
1975	13.7	7%	26.1	14%	21.0	11%	26.9	15%	96.9	53%	184.6
1976	13.2	7%	27.2	14%	22.8	11%	28.7	15%	102.9	53%	193.8
1977	12.4	6%	27.4	14%	23.1	12%	28.3	15%	102.7	53%	193.9

*Volatile hydrocarbons only; methane and other nonreactive compounds omitted so far as possible. *National Air Quality, Monitoring, and Emission Trends Report, 1977. EPA, December 1978.*

Source: *Cleaning the Air: EPA's Program for Air Pollution Control* (Washington, D.C.: Environmental Protection Agency, June 1979), p. 4.

every man, woman, and child in the country.[2] Table 18.2 shows the source of these pollutants for 1977, the latest year for which figures are available. A glance at this table shows clearly that certain kinds of sources predominate for different types of pollution. The internal combustion engine (autos and trucks), for example, accounted for 83 percent of carbon monoxide emissions. Stationary fuel burning (power, heating) accounted for 82 percent of sulfur oxide emissions.

Recent public policy measures designed to reduce air pollution date from the Air Pollution Act of 1955, which authorized the Public Health Service to undertake air pollution studies through a system of grants. This act created

TABLE 18.2 **Estimated Pollutant Emissions by Source, 1977 (Millions of Metric Tons)**

Source	Suspended Particles		Sulfur Oxides		Nitrogen Oxides		Volatile Hydro-carbons		Carbon Monoxide	
Transportation (autos, trucks)	1.1	9%	0.8	3%	9.2	40%	11.5	41%	85.7	83%
Combustion (power, heating)	4.8	39%	22.4	82%	13.0	56%	1.5	5%	1.2	1%
Industrial processes	5.4	43%	4.2	15%	0.7	4%	10.1	36%	8.3	8%
Solid waste (incinerators)	0.4	3%			0.1		0.7	2%	2.6	3%
Miscellaneous (fires, solvents)	0.7	6%			0.1		4.5	16%	4.9	5%
Total	12.4		27.4		23.1		28.3		102.7	

National Air Quality, Monitoring, and Emissions Trends Report, 1977. EPA, December 1978.

Source: *Cleaning the Air: EPA's Program for Air Pollution Control* (Washington, D.C.: Environmental Protection Agency, June 1979), p. 5.

[2]*Cleaning the Air: EPA's Program for Air Pollution Control* (Washington, D.C.: Environmental Protection Agency, June 1979), pp. 3–4.

the first federally funded air pollution research activity. The Clean Air Act of 1963 replaced the 1955 act, and was aimed at the control and prevention of air pollution. It permitted legal steps to end specific instances of air pollution and authorized grants to state and local governments to initiate control programs. The 1965 Amendments to the Clean Air Act (called the National Emissions Standards Act) gave the federal government authority to curb motor vehicle emissions and set standards which were first applied to 1968 model vehicles. The Air Quality Act of 1967 required the states to establish air quality regions with the standards for air pollution control and implementation plans for their accomplishment. The Clean Air Act Amendments of 1970 provided the legal basis for a new system of national air quality standards to be set by the federal government and called for a roll-back of auto pollution levels. In the Clean Air Act Amendments of 1977, new deadlines were set for the attainment of air quality standards.

Thus the public policy approach to pollution control is many-faceted. To control ambient air quality, the EPA sets primary and secondary standards for the seven pollutants mentioned earlier. The primary standards concern the minimum level of air quality that is necessary to keep people from becoming ill and are aimed at protecting human health. The secondary standards are aimed at the promotion of public welfare and the prevention of damage to animals, plant life, and property generally. These standards are based on scientific and medical studies that have been made of the pollutant's effects. Table 18.3 shows the current standards that are in effect.

TABLE 18.3 **National Quality Standards for Ambient Air***

Pollutant	Averaging Time	Primary Standards (health)	Secondary Standards (welfare, materials)
Particulates	annual	75 ug/m³	60 ug/m³
	24-hour	260 ug/m³	150 ug/m³
Sulfur dioxide	annual	80 ug/m³ (.03 ppm)	
	24-hour	365 ug/m³ (.14 ppm)	
	3-hour	—	1300 ug/m³ (.5 ppm)
Carbon monoxide	8-hour	10 mg/m³ (9 ppm)	same as primary
	1-hour	40 mg/m³ (35 ppm)	
Hydrocarbons (nonmethane)	3-hour (6-9 am)	160 ug/m³ (.24 ppm)	same as primary
Nitrogen dioxide	annual	100 ug/m³ (.05 ppm)	same as primary
Ozone	1-hour	240 ug/m³ (.12 ppm)	same as primary
Lead	3-month	1.5 ug/m³ (.006 ppm)	

*In micrograms or milligrams per cubic meter—ug/m³ and mg/m³—and in parts per million—ppm.

Source: Cleaning the Air: EPA's Program for Air Pollution Control (Washington, D.C.: Environmental Protection Agency, June 1979), p. 10.

As can be seen, the primary and secondary standards for some of the seven pollutants are the same.

Since air pollution problems vary from place to place throughout the country, a regional concept was adopted for air pollution control through the establishment of 247 air quality control regions. These air quality control regions were useful units for management and control as each region had individual problems and individual characteristics of pollution control. An air quality control region is defined by the EPA "as an area with definite pollution problems, common pollution sources, and characteristic weather."[3]

The states were given responsibility for drawing up plans to attain the standards for the air quality control regions within their boundaries. The primary standards were to be attained by mid-1975 as required by the 1970 Clean Air Act. When that deadline came, however, only 69 of the 247 air quality control regions were in compliance with all the antipollution standards then in existence. Sixty regions failed the standards for particulates, 42 for sulfur dioxide, 74 for ozone, 54 for carbon monoxide, and 13 for nitrogen dioxide. Such cities as Los Angeles, Chicago, and Philadelphia violated the standards for all pollutants. Some interesting headlines appeared in the newspapers when these goals were not attained, such as "AIR TO BE ILLEGAL—BUT BREATHE ANYWAY."

Obviously some adjustments had to be made. These were finally worked out in the 1977 amendments. Under these amendments, the primary standards are to be attained as expeditiously as possible but not later than 1982, with extensions until 1987 for two pollutants most closely related to transportation systems (carbon monoxide and ozone). Each state is also required to draw up specific plans for bringing what is called each nonattainment region up to standard and for maintaining the purity of air in regions that already meet the standards. These plans have to contain the following information:

- An inventory of pollution sources: each power plant, factory, or other stationary source of pollutant emissions, with careful estimates of how much of each kind of pollutant is emitted each year
- Data on "mobile sources"—such as motor vehicles—including the number of vehicles, miles traveled, and emission estimates per year based on these studies
- Specific enforceable proposals for reducing both stationary and mobile emissions according to a reasonable schedule, with target dates for attaining each stage of reduction
- Assurance that the state has the legal power to carry out the plan through local legislation and enforcement authority.[4]

The 1977 amendments strengthened efforts to maintain air quality in regions where the air is already cleaner than the standards allow. Three kinds of regions were defined. A Class I region includes all national parks and wilderness areas and may include further areas named by the states. In

[3]*Ibid.*, p. 9.
[4]*Ibid.*, pp. 10–11.

these regions, no additional sulfur or particulate sources are permitted. In Class II areas, some industrial development is permitted up to a specified level. Class III areas can have about twice as much pollution from new sources, sometimes even up to the minimum federal standards. Any potential new pollution sources in these regions must obtain a permit before operating and meet a number of other conditions, such as using the best available control methods.

For nonattainment areas, the EPA has adopted an offset policy. New industrial development is permitted as long as offsetting reductions are made from existing sources for the pollutants to be emitted by the new facilities. These existing sources must reduce their emissions more than enough to compensate for new sources of pollution. An example of this policy cited by the EPA was in Oklahoma City, where several oil firms agreed to put floating tops on large storage tanks to reduce hydrocarbon emissions so General Motors could build an automobile plant there.[5]

Stationary sources of air pollution, as distinguished from ambient air quality, are also controlled. Typical stationary sources are power plant and factory smokestacks, industrial vents for gases and dust, coke ovens, incinerators, burning dumps, and large furnaces. The state plans required by the 1977 amendments must inventory these sources and determine how they should be reduced to bring the regions into conformance with ambient air quality standards.

The law currently makes the EPA set emission limits for certain designated pollutants for selected categories of industrial plants and for those that are substantially modified. In addition, in 1981, the EPA set standards for all major stationary new sources. These limits are called "new source performance standards" and are specific to each industry. These standards set the maximum amount of each kind of pollutant that can be emitted from a new plant's stacks for each unit of the plant's production. In 1979, the EPA adopted a new policy toward stationary sources of pollution called the bubble concept. This policy gives business more flexibility in meeting EPA standards (see box).

For mobile sources of air pollution, the EPA sets standards for automobile, truck, and aircraft emissions. A near disaster was averted in 1977, when Detroit was producing 1978 model cars that were not in compliance with the standards for carbon monoxide and nitrogen oxides that were to go into effect that year. The auto industry claimed that the technology did not exist to meet these standards and asked for a relaxation that was finally granted, but not until a substantial number of cars had been produced for inventory. The primary standards for carbon monoxide and ozone, as mentioned earlier, have been further relaxed by the 1977 amendments.

The final part of the public policy program to control air pollution is the setting of hazardous emission standards. While all air pollutants are regarded as hazardous to some degree, some are considered so dangerous to human health that they are limited individually. Presently such limitations apply to any discharge of asbestos, beryllium, mercury, and vinyl chloride. These substances have strict limits as to the amount that can be emitted into

[5]*Ibid.*

the atmosphere. Other substances are also being considered for this category of control.

Water Pollution

The major sources of water pollution are (1) organic wastes from urban sewage, farms, and industries, (2) sediments from agriculture, construction, and logging, (3) biological nutrients, such as phosphates in detergents and nitrogen in fertilizers, (4) toxic substances from industry and synthetic chemicals such as those found in pesticides, plastics, and detergents, (5) acid and mineral drainage from open-pit and deep-shaft mining, and (6) runoff containing harmful chemicals and sediment drained from streets and parking lots.[6]

[6]*Setting the Course: Clean Water* (Washington, D.C.: National Wildlife Federation, undated), p. 5.

There are both point and nonpoint sources of water pollution. Point sources are places where polluting substances enter the water from a discernible, confined, and discrete conveyance such as a sewer pipe, culvert, tunnel, or other channel or conduit. Point sources are those that come from industrial facilities and municipal sewage systems. Pollutants can also wash off, run off, or seep from broad areas of land. These are called nonpoint source pollutants. Common pollutants of the latter type are sediment eroded from soil exposed during construction of buildings and pesticides and fertilizers washed off cropland by rainwater.[7]

Public policy measures to control these sources of pollutants began with the Rivers and Harbors Act of 1899, which prohibited discharge of pollutants or refuse into or on the banks of navigable waters without a permit. The next public policy measure on water pollution was the Oil Pollution Act of 1924, which prohibited the discharge of refuse and oil into or upon coastal or navigable waters of the United States.

Modern efforts to control water pollution began with the Water Pollution Control Act of 1948, which declared that water pollution was a local problem and required the U.S. Public Health Service to provide information to the states that would help them coordinate research activities. The Water Pollution Control Act of 1956 contained enforcement provisions by providing for a federal abatement suit at the request of a state pollution control agency. The Water Pollution Control Act Amendments of 1961 broadened federal jurisdiction and shortened the process of enforcement by stating that where health was being endangered, the federal government did not have to receive the consent of all the states involved.

The Water Quality Act of 1965 provided for the setting of water quality standards that were state and federally enforceable. These became the basis for interstate water quality standards. This act also created the Water Pollution Control Administration within the Department of Health, Education and Welfare. The Clean Water Restoration Act of 1966 imposed a fine of $100 per day on a polluter who failed to submit a required report. Finally, the Water Quality Improvement Act of 1970 prohibited discharge of harmful quantities of oil into or upon the navigable waters of the United States or their shores. It applies to offshore and onshore facilities and vessels. The act also provided for regulation of sewage disposal from vessels.

The current system of water pollution control was established by the Federal Water Pollution Control Act Amendments of 1972, which mandated a sweeping federal-state campaign to prevent, reduce, and eliminate water pollution. This law proclaimed two general goals for the United States: (1) to achieve wherever possible by July 1, 1983, water that is clean enough for swimming and other recreational uses, and clean enough for the protection and propagation of fish, shellfish, and wildlife; and (2) by 1985, to have no discharges of pollutants into the nation's waters. These goals were to be attained by the following provisions.[8]

1. The act required three phases of nationally uniform industrial effluent limitations. By July 1, 1977, existing industries were to have reduced their pollutant discharges to the level attainable by using the "best

[7]*Ibid.*, pp. 4, 5.

[8]*A Guide to the Clean Water Act Amendments* (Washington, D.C.: Environmental Protection Agency, November 1978), pp. 1–2.

practicable" water pollution control technology (BPT) determined by averaging the pollution control effectiveness achieved by the best plants in the industry. By July 1, 1983, the law required existing industries to reduce their pollutant discharges even more by using the "best available" pollution control technology (BAT), based on the best pollution control procedures economically achievable. New source performance standards (NSPS) were to be achieved immediately when a new source commenced operation. The act defined new source as "any source the construction of which is commenced after the publication of proposed regulation which will be applicable to such source, if such standard is thereafter promulgated."

2. The act established a National Pollutant Discharge Elimination System (NPDES), which required permits for all point sources of pollution, providing the first major direct enforcement procedure against polluters. Under the system, it is illegal for any industry to discharge any pollutant into the nation's waters without a permit from EPA or from a state that has an EPA approved permit program. When issued, the permit regulates what may be discharged (see box) and the amount of each identified pollutant from a facility. The discharger must monitor its wastes and report on discharges, and comply with all applicable national effluent limits and with state and local requirements that may be imposed. If a plant cannot comply immediately, the permit contains a compliance schedule of firm dates by which the pollutants will be reduced or eliminated.

WHAT'S A POLLUTANT?

It's illegal under the 1972 Federal Water Pollution Control Act to discharge pollutants into the Nation's waters except under an NPDES permit.

Pollutants covered by this permit requirement are: Solid waste, incinerator residue, sewage, garbage, sewage sludge, munitions, chemical wastes, biological materials, radioactive materials, heat, wrecked or discarded equipment, rock, sand, cellar dirt, and industrial, municipal, and agricultural wastes discharged into water.

Excluded from the NPDES permit program are: Discharges of sewage from vessels; pollutants from vessels or other floating craft in coastal or ocean waters; discharges from properly functioning marine engines; water, gas, or other material injected into oil or gas wells, or disposed of in wells during oil or gas production, if the State determines that ground or surface water resources will not be degraded; aquaculture projects; separate storm sewer discharges; and dredged or fill material.

Discharges excluded from the NPDES permit system are covered by other pollution control requirements.

From *Toward Cleaner Water* (Washington, D.C.: Environmental Protection Agency, 1974), p. 5.

---

3. The act continued and expanded the water quality standards program initiated under earlier legislation. Water quality standards previously established by states for interstate waters remained in effect unless they were not consistent with the previous legislation. The states also had to adopt water quality standards for intrastate waters and submit them to the EPA for approval.

4. The act required special controls over severely toxic pollutants, by establishing a formal rule-making process under which the EPA was to identify toxic pollutants and issue effluent standards for control of these substances on a pollutant-by-pollutant basis rather than by industrial categories.

5. The act required national effluent limitations for municipal dischargers, and provided for an expanded federal program of financial assistance to local governments for planning and construction of wastewater treatment works.

6. Finally, the act required comprehensive river basin and regional water quality planning for both point and nonpoint sources of pollution, a provision which set in motion major planning initiatives in all states.

This act was amended by the Clean Water Act of 1977, which made over fifty changes in the 1972 law. The most important from a business point of view was a change in the classification system of industrial pollutants and the establishment of new deadlines. This change resulted in a much greater emphasis on the control of toxic pollutants. These new categories and their deadlines are described below.[9]

Conventional Pollutants: These include BOD (biological oxygen demand), suspended solids, fecal coliforms, pH (acidity) and other pollutants so designated by the EPA. Industry is to have installed the "best conventional" technology (BCT) by July 1, 1984 to control these pollutants.

Toxic Pollutants: The 1977 amendments specify an "initial list" of toxic substances to which EPA may add or subtract. Industry is to have installed the "best available" technology (BAT) by July 1, 1984, or not later than three years after a substance is placed on the toxic pollutant list, to control toxic substances.

Nonconventional Pollutants: This category includes "all other" pollutants, that is, those not classified by the EPA as either conventional or toxic. The treatment required is the "best available" technology (BAT) by July 1, 1984, or within three years of the date the EPA established effluent limitations, but no later than July 1, 1987. A modification of these requirements is available under certain circumstances.

Nonpoint sources of pollution are regulated under Section 208 of the Clean Water Act. These nonpoint sources of pollution are a much more difficult problem to control. They generally cannot be collected and treated in some fashion, but can only be reduced by greater care in the management of water and land resources. Examples of nonpoint sources of pollution are the following:

- Urban stormwater: water running off buildings and streets, carrying with it oil, grease, trash, salts, lead, and other pollutants.
- Agricultural runoff: rain washing fertilizers, pesticides, and topsoil into water.
- Construction runoff: earth washed into streams, rivers, and lakes from erosion.

[9]*Ibid.,* p. 6.

- Acid mine drainage: water seeping through mined areas.
- Forestry runoff: water washing sediments from areas where the earth has been disturbed by logging and timber operations.[10]

Section 208 requires that states and localities establish programs to control nonpoint source pollution. In contrast to point sources of pollution where uniform national standards have been developed, state and local governments have been assigned the major burden and responsibility for developing nonpoint source pollution controls. The reason for this approach is that soil conditions and types, climate, and topography (which are primary determinants of nonpoint source pollution) vary throughout the country. Identifying Best Management Practices (BMPs) is one of the most important tasks in 208 planning. These are the techniques that will be used to control pollution. The EPA defines BMPs as:

> a practice or combination of practices that is determined by (a designated planning agency) after problem assessment, examination of alternative practices, and appropriate public participation to be the most effective, practicable (including technological, economic and institutional considerations) means of preventing or reducing the amount of pollution generated by nonpoint sources to a level compatible with water quality goals.[11]

The Clean Water Act requires that citizens must be involved in 208 planning. Such participation is a right and not just a privilege. Citizens should have access to all information about the development of the plan and should be consulted on all important planning decisions. The EPA will provide guidance documents to state and local 208 agencies and review their work to ensure that the control programs are adequate to attain clean water.[12] The 208 planning process is shown in Figure 18.1.

Pesticides

The pesticide problem is one of the best examples in history of being between a rock and a hard place. Pests destroy crops worth billions of dollars each year, and with a steadily expanding population and a decrease in arable land, the world must use pesticides to control these pests and maintain high crop yields. There is no other way, with existing technology, to raise crops on the scale that is required.

Yet in poisoning pests, human beings may also be poisoning themselves. Questions have been raised about the health hazards posed by the use of pesticides. Douglas M. Costle, administrator of the EPA, says, "In the past we willingly accepted claims that pesticides have no long-term effect on humans. Neither EPA nor industry is in a position to make such reassurances honestly."[13]

One of the first to point out these dangers was Rachel Carson. In her book

[10]*Clean Water and Agriculture* (Washington, D.C.: Environmental Protection Agency, January 1977), pp. 2–3.
[11]*Setting the Course: Clean Water,* p. 13.
[12]*Ibid.,* p. 7.
[13]Allen A. Boraiko, "The Pesticide Dilemma," *National Geographic,* Vol. 157, No. 2 (February 1980), p. 150.

Figure 18.1

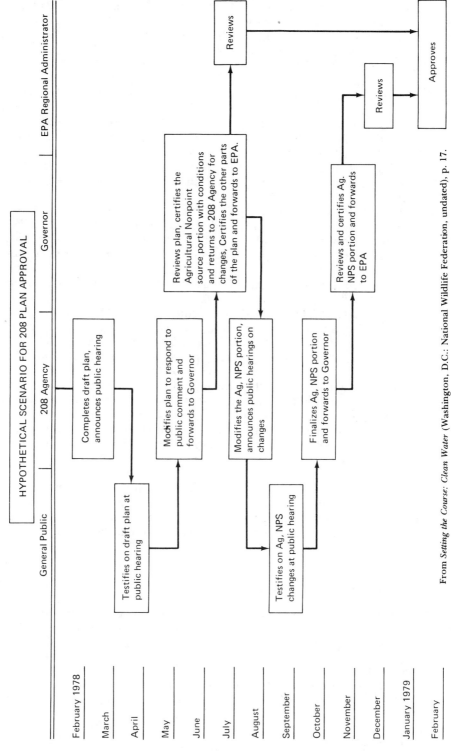

HYPOTHETICAL SCENARIO FOR 208 PLAN APPROVAL

From *Setting the Course: Clean Water* (Washington, D.C.: National Wildlife Federation, undated), p. 17.

Silent Spring, information about the dark side of pesticide use was presented to the public. Before this, pesticides were by and large seen as an unqualified benefit, but after her book, fear began to spread throughout society that pesticides were unmanageable poisons. Federal pesticide regulation was toughened and enforcement responsibility transferred from the Department of Agriculture, which promoted chemical pest control, to the EPA. The use of DDT was banned in 1972, and fifteen other pesticides have been suspended or banned since that time.[14]

Pesticides are regulated by the Federal Insecticide, Fungicide, and Rodenticide Act (FIFRA) of 1947. This act assigned EPA the responsibility for protecting human health from any commercially available product used to kill germs, insects, rodents, and other animal pests, as well as weeds and fungi. These products cannot be sold until they are first registered with the agency.[15]

Amendments to the act in 1972 required the EPA to reregister the 35,000 pesticides previously registered and already on the market. The EPA was required to do a cost-benefit analysis on these products. If this analysis revealed that a particular product posed an unreasonable risk to human health or the environment when weighed against its benefits to agriculture and society, it had to be removed from the marketplace or restrictions placed on its use.[16]

These amendments, however, required the EPA to proceed on a product-by-product basis, even though many of them have similar chemical properties. Further amendments to FIFRA in 1978 allowed the EPA to take a "generic" approach to registering pesticides. Using this approach, the agency will be able to make one regulatory decision for an entire group of pesticides that have similar chemical ingredients rather than looking at them separately. It is estimated that the agency will thus have to consider fewer than 1,000 active ingredients of the 35,000 different commercial products on the marketplace. Standards will be set for these 1,000 ingredients, and products will be registered according to whether they measure up to these standards.[17]

Under the EPA's pesticide program, more than a million private users, mostly farmers, and 150,000 commercial applicators have been trained and certified in the safe use of pesticides. This program trains people in the proper use, handling, storage, and disposal of pesticides. Only such certified users are allowed to use pesticides that have a "restricted use only" classification.[18]

Toxic Substances

Control of toxic substances is an example of the approach to pollution control that examines substances before they are used to determine whether they are safe or whether their use should be limited or banned. There are

[14]*Ibid.,* p. 151.
[15]*1978 Report: Better Health and Regulatory Reform* (Washington, D.C.: Environmental Protection Agency, February 1979), p. 29.
[16]*Ibid.*
[17]*Ibid.*
[18]*Ibid.,* p. 30.

two million known chemical compounds, 30,000 of which are in substantial commercial use. Some 1,000 new chemicals are put into production each year and thus into the environment. Before the Toxic Substances Control Act (TSCA), previous laws that dealt with these substances authorized the government to act only after widespread exposure and possibly serious harm had already occurred. The major concept underlying TSCA is that the government has the authority to act before a substance can harm human health or the environment—the substance is, in effect, guilty until proven innocent.

TSCA encompasses an estimated 70,000 chemicals manufactured for commercial purposes and the several million research and development chemicals. The entire chemical industry was put under comprehensive federal regulation for the first time, as the law applies to virtually every facet of the industry—product development, testing, manufacturing, distribution, use, and disposal. In addition, importers of chemical substances are treated as domestic manufacturers, thus extending EPA's control to certain aspects of the international chemical trade.[19]

The initial impact of TSCA was in the area of inventory reporting. The act required the EPA to compile and publish an inventory of chemical substances manufactured, imported, or processed in the United States for commercial purposes. This inventory was compiled from reports that manufacturers, importers, processors, or users of chemical substances were required to prepare and submit to the agency.[20]

There were two reporting periods for this inventory. During the first, which ended May 1, 1978, most manufacturers and importers were required to report. From this information, the EPA compiled an initial inventory of chemical substances, which is available to manufacturers.[21] Thirty days after its publication, the premanufacture notification provisions of TSCA, which require notification to the EPA in advance of manufacture or importation, became effective for companies intending to manufacture or import (in bulk form), for a commercial purpose, a chemical substance that had not been identified on the initial inventory.

A second, 210-day, reporting period began June 1, 1979, ending December 31, 1979, which resulted in the publication of a revised inventory. During this period, importers of chemical substances, as part of mixtures or articles, and companies who have only processed or used (since January 1, 1975) a reportable chemical substance that did not appear on the initial inventory, reported such substances for inclusion on the revised inventory. This revised inventory was published in July 1980. Since then, the EPA has added new chemical substances to the inventory after they have satisfied the premanufacture notification provisions of the act.

After publication of the initial inventory, the premanufacture provisions of TSCA went into effect. These provisions require a manufacturer who has developed a new chemical not on the inventory list to submit a notice to the EPA at least 90 days before beginning manufacture or importation of a

---

[19]*Ibid.*, p. 21.

[20]Environmental Protection Agency, Office of Toxic Substances, *Reporting for the Chemical Substance Inventory* (Washington, D.C.: 1977), p. 1.

[21]See *Directory of TSCA Local Resource Centers* (Washington, D.C.: Environmental Protection Agency, May 1979).

new chemical substance for commercial purposes other than in small quantities solely for research and development. The information that has to be given the EPA includes the following:

1. A description of the new chemical substance, including the chemical identity, molecular structure, and the common or trade name.
2. The estimated total amount to be manufactured and processed.
3. The proposed categories of use.
4. The estimated amount to be manufactured and processed for each proposed category of use.
5. The manner and methods of distribution in commerce and disposal.
6. The estimated amount of the substance for each manner and method of distribution in commerce and disposal.
7. Direct and indirect exposure of humans and of ecological populations, including exposure levels, as a result of manufacture, processing, distribution in commerce, use, and disposal of the chemical substance.
8. Releases to the air, land, and water (including emissions, effluents, and other discharges), whether intentional or unintentional.
9. Assessments of risks to health and the environment resulting from the manufacture, processing, distribution in commerce, use, and disposal of the chemical substance.
10. Safeguards, controls, and other measures to be used to limit exposure.
11. Descriptions and other information concerning related chemical substances and mixtures, including by-products, coproducts, impurities, and degradation products.
12. Descriptions of mixtures and articles which contain or may contain the new chemical substance.[22]

In addition to this information, the submitter must append any test data in his possession or control and descriptions of other data concerning the health and environmental effects of the substance. The EPA encourages, but does not require, the submitter to follow the premanufacture testing guidelines the EPA has published. In any event, all test data are to be submitted regardless of their age, quality, or results.[23]

The administrator of the EPA has a number of options available to him or her after receipt of this information, such as extending the 90-day premanufacture review period for an additional 90 days for good cause or initiating no action within the 90-day period because the chemical is deemed not to present a hazard to health or the environment.

If a hazard is believed to exist, however, the administrator may issue a proposed order to take effect on the expiration of the notification period to prohibit or limit the manufacture, processing, distribution in commerce, use, or disposal of such substance or to prohibit or limit any combination of such activities. This action can be taken for either of the following two reasons.

1. The information available to the Administration is insufficient to permit a reasoned evaluation of the health and environmental effects of a chemical

[22]Appendix I to Premanufacture Notification Draft Guideline, *Chemical Regulation Reporter* (Washington, D.C.: The Bureau of National Affairs, Inc., 1978), p. 1124.
[23]*Ibid.*, p. 1123.

substance and in the absence of sufficient information to permit such an evaluation, the manufacture, processing, distribution in commerce, use, or disposal of such substance, or any combination of such activities, may present an unreasonable risk of injury to health or the environment.

2. Such substance is or will be produced in substantial quantities, and such substance either enters or may reasonably be anticipated to enter the environment in substantial quantities or there is or may be significant or substantial human exposure to the substance.[24]

If a total ban on the substance is not necessary, the administrator can issue further directives regarding regulation of the substance. He or she can set concentration levels, limit the use of the chemical, require warnings or instructions on its use, require public notice of risk or potential injury, or regulate methods of disposal. If the administrator has reason to believe the method of manufacture rather than the chemical itself is at fault, he or she may order the manufacturer to revise quality control procedures to the extent necessary to remedy whatever inadequacies are believed to exist.[25]

In addition to these premanufacture notification provisions, another section of TSCA affects chemical usage. The act empowers the EPA administrator to require manufacturers or processors of potentially harmful chemicals to conduct tests on these chemicals. The need for such testing must be based on the following criteria.

1. The chemical may present an unreasonable risk to health or the environment, or there may be substantial human or environmental exposure to the chemical.
2. There are insufficient data and experience for determining or predicting the health and environmental effects of the chemical.
3. Testing of the chemical is necessary to develop such data.[26]

This section applies to all chemical substances already in existence. An interagency committee has been established by the act to assist the administrator to determine chemicals that should be tested, but his or her actions are not limited to these recommendations by the committee. This committee may designate, at any one time, up to 50 chemicals from its list of recommended substances for testing (see box). Within one year, the administrator must either initiate testing requirements for these designated chemicals or publish in the Federal Register his or her reasons for not initiating such requirements.[27]

Hazardous Waste Disposal

One of the most serious problems facing the nation is the problem of hazardous waste disposal. The full extent of the problem has yet to be adequately measured, but a report to the EPA in January 1979 estimated that there may be 32,000 to 50,000 disposal sites in the United States containing hazardous wastes. Of these sites, anywhere from 1,200 to 2,000

[24]U.S. Congress, *Toxic Substances Control Act*, p. 2015.
[25]*Ibid.*, pp. 2020–2021.
[26]Environmental Protection Agency, *The Toxic Substances Control Act*, p. 2.
[27]*Ibid.*, p. 3.

A TOXICS SAMPLER

The following information is taken from "Hazardous Substances" (EPA, November 1978), a report produced by the four federal agencies that have predominant responsibility to regulate toxic and hazardous materials—EPA, CPSC, FDA and OSHA. These selected substances were among a number identified by the agencies for priority investigation and possible regulatory action:

Acrylonitrile (AN)—a substance used in making acrylic fibers, synthetic rubbers and plastics. AN is a highly toxic material that may also be a human carcinogen and a teratogen.

Arsenic—a chemical used mainly in various pesticides and in the manufacture of glass. It is a notorious poison that in small amounts can cause dermatitis, muscular paralysis, and damage to the liver and kidneys. It is also a suspect human carcinogen and teratogen.

Asbestos—a mineral used in making such products as roofing, insulation, certain cement pipe, flooring, packing and gaskets, friction materials, coating, plastics, textiles and paper. Concern exists about asbestos in air, food and drinking water because it has caused cancer of the lung, abdominal cavity lining, intestinal tract and other organs among exposed workers and their immediate families.

Benzene—a chemical octane booster in gasoline, also used in the manufacture of numerous other chemicals. It has causd leukemia and chromosomal damage among exposed workers.

Beryllium—a light metal used in the manufacture of rockets and airplanes, ceramic parts and household appliance circuitry. It may cause fatal lung disease. Long-term exposure may lead to heart problems, enlarged liver and spleen, kidney stones and cancer.

Cadmium—a heavy metal used mainly in electroplating but also in certain plastics, pigments and other products. It may cause kidney damage and emphysema. It is also a suspect carcinogen, teratogen and mutagen.

Chloroform and Chlorinated Solvents—Compounds used in numerous chemical processes and in dry cleaning and degreasing operations. The solvents may pose health hazards in aerosol sprays, paints, certain cleaners and pesticides. Health effects include depression of the central nervous system and heart functions, liver problems and possibly cancer.

Chromates—metal derivatives used in paints and pigments, fungicides, wood preservatives and corrosion inhibitors. These compounds are human irritants and corrosives, have caused skin ulcers and kidney inflammation in people and may be cancer agents. Chromates are also toxic to fish and other animals.

Coke oven emissions—smoke and fumes released by heating coal to produce coke for the iron and steel industry. These emissions have caused lung cancer and other illnesses among coke workers.

EDB—used mainly as an additive in leaded gasoline but also as a pesticide, a solvent and as an intermediate industrial chemical. EDB may cause cancer, reproductive damage and mutated genes.

Ethylene oxide—roughly 2.1 billion kilograms of this chemical are used each year mainly to produce auto antifreeze and other chemical compounds and also to sterilize medical equipment. ETO is a human mutagen and causes testicular damage. It is also an eye and respiratory tract irritant and skin blistering agent.

Mercury—a heavy metal used in electrical apparatus, in the preparation of other chemicals, in medicines and pharmaceutical products, paints and pesticides. Depending on the form of mercury, this metal can cause severe nervous system damage and kidney destruction.

PBBs—a flame retardant compound no longer made in the United States but accidentally mixed with animal feed in 1973 causing possible human illness and the destruction of thousands of farm animals.

PCBs—fire-resistant fluids no longer made in the United States but still widely used to insulate heavy duty electrical equipment. PCBs are suspect human cancer agents that also may cause nerve, skin and liver damage. They are widespread and long-lasting contaminants.

From *A Toxics Primer* (Washington, D.C.: League of Women Voters Education Fund, 1979), pp. 10–11. Reprinted with permission.

may pose significant risks to human health or the environment. Most of these dumps are still being used, but 500 to 800 are most likely abandoned.[28]

The Love Canal incident provides a horror story in how not to manage disposal of hazardous wastes. Love Canal, located in Niagara Falls, New York, was an uncompleted, abandoned nineteenth-century waterway. It had been used as an industrial dump site since the 1930s, and in 1947 was purchased by Hooker Chemical and Plastics Company to dispose of drums of toxic chemical wastes. The site was covered and sold to the Niagara Falls Board of Education in 1953, who proceeded to build an elementary school and a playing field on the site. Part of the site was also sold to a developer who built several hundred homes on the periphery of the old canal.[29]

In 1976, after some years of unusually heavy rains and snow, the chemicals began seeping into basements of the houses. The canal itself overflowed and chemicals that had leaked from the decayed drums entered the environment. In August 1978, the New York State Department of Health declared the Love Canal area "a grave and imminent peril" to the health of those living nearby. Investigations were conducted into complaints about an abnormal number of miscarriages, birth defects, cancer, and a variety of other illnesses. Eleven different actual or suspected carcinogens, including the dreaded dioxin, were found among the many chemicals leaching into the air, water, and soil. Air monitoring equipment found pollution levels ranging as high as 5,000 times the maximum safe level. Finally, President Carter declared Love Canal a disaster area, making federal disaster relief aid available to the residents, and signed an emergency order under which the federal government and New York State will share the cost of relocating the area families.[30] The total costs of this problem will not be known for many years, but as of July 1979:

- Two hundred and sixty-three families had been evacuated; two hundred and thirty-six homes had been purchased by the state; a thousand additional families had been advised to leave their homes;
- Housing values had dropped to nil;

[28]U.S. Council on Environmental Quality, *Environmental Quality* (Washington, D.C.: U.S. Government Printing Office, 1979), p. 174.
[29]*Ibid.*, p. 177.
[30]*Ibid.*, pp. 176–177.

- Almost $27 million had been appropriated by municipal, state, and federal agencies for providing temporary housing, closing off the contaminated area, and containing the leachate (including digging a trench, installing a drain pipe to catch the leachate, and covering the canal with a clay cap to seal it); and

- Nine hundred notices of claims had been filed against Niagara Falls, Niagara County, and the Board of Education for a total of more than $3 billion in damages to health and property, and other suits had been filed against Hooker Chemical Company.[31]

These health dangers did not come to light until 23 years after the dump site was closed. The crucial question for society is how many more such "time bombs" exist in the country (see box). The EPA estimates that only about 10 percent of hazardous wastes are being disposed of in a manner that would comply with regulations yet to be adopted. The majority of toxic wastes are being disposed of in nonsecure ponds, lagoons, or landfills. Others are being incinerated in a manner that pollutes the air or does not completely detoxify the waste residues.[32]

Hazardous wastes are regulated by the Resource Conservation and Recovery Act of 1976, which, when fully implemented, will provide cradle-to-grave control of hazardous waste material, from point of production through the point of disposal. Those who produce wastes will have to obtain a permit to manage them on their own property. When shipping them to a treatment, storage, or disposal facility, they will have to provide a manifest containing basic information about the waste material. All treatment, storage, and disposal operations will be required to meet minimum standards to protect public health and the environment.[33]

The cost estimates to meet these regulations vary widely. The EPA estimated that the 17 industries most affected would have to spend $750 million annually to meet the proposed regulations. Concurrently they were spending only $155 million per year for hazardous waste management. The Manufacturing Chemists Association, surveying its 63 member companies, estimated the cost at nearly $300 million annually. The cost of cleaning up existing dumps is even more staggering. Estimates have varied from $28.4 billion to as high as $55 billion. No public agency or private corporation has enough money to clean up these inactive dumps.[34] Various proposals have been made to tax industry annually to create a federally run "superfund" that would be used for cleanup of both chemical spills and dump sites. Such a "superfund" was created by Congress in late 1980 for cleaning up abandoned hazardous waste dumps.

Noise Pollution

Noise is a subtle pollutant. The damage done by air and water pollution is right before our eyes in contaminated water, oil spills, dying fish, and in smog that clouds the air and burns the eyes. Noise, however, leaves no visible

---

[31]*Ibid.*, p. 177.
[32]*Ibid.*, p. 182.
[33]*Better Health and Regulatory Reform*, p. 16.
[34]*Environmental Quality*, pp. 182–183.

• In Lowell, Mass., 1 billion gallons of mixed toxic waste stored in 15,000 rotting drums and tanks was discovered at a closed waste dump only one-quarter of a mile from inhabited homes. Among the wastes were flammable solvents, chlorinated hydrocarbons, plating and etching wastes, and solvent distillation residue sludges. Local pollution of soils, ground water, and air had resulted from spills and leaks of the wastes. Earlier, while the dumpsite was still active, improper discharges of untreated materials into sewers, causing back-ups 1 mile away, had caused health problems for sewer workers and led to complaints by workers in neighboring firms. The waste dump operator, the Silresim Company, had since gone bankrupt, leaving the chemical dump behind. Massachusetts was forced to appropriate $1.5 million to remove the wastes.

• In Gray, Maine, trichloroethane, which is classified as a carcinogen by the National Cancer Institute, was found in the ground water aquifer under the East Gray section of the town, apparently due to storage and operations by an oil tank cleaning firm, the McKin Company. The company was closed down by the city in September 1977, but 16 polluted wells had to be sealed, and for some time 750 families were forced to rely on trucked water. Since then, the town has had to extend the municipal water system to affected areas, at a cost to the taxpayers of $600,000.

• In Hardeman County, Tenn., 40 families near a rural landfill drank from wells polluted with such pesticides as endrin, dieldrin, aldrin, and heptachlor. The Velsicol Chemical Company had used a neighboring 300-acre site from 1964 to 1972 for shallow burial of 300,000 55-gallon drums of pesticide production residues. Residents have complained of a wide variety of ailments including liver and urinary tract problems, dizziness, nausea, and rashes. They have filed a $2.5 billion suit against Velsicol; meanwhile, they have had to hook into the water system of nearby Toone, Tenn., at a cost of $200,000.

• Near Montague, Mich., toxic wastes disposal from another Hooker Chemical Company plant have polluted surface and ground waters. The wastes include mirex (a pesticide), chloroform, carbon tetrachloride, and other chlorinated hydrocarbons. A contaminated plume 2,000 feet wide extends 1 mile from the disposal site to White Lake, a major recreational finger lake of Lake Michigan. Onsite disposal of drums containing toxic wastes and lagoon disposal of brine sludges ceased in 1978, but the site is still used for deep-well injection of brines. The state has sued Hooker Chemical to force cleanup of the site, a job estimated to cost between $200 and $300 million.

From U.S. Council on Environmental Quality, *Environmental Quality* (Washington, D.C.: U.S. Government Printing Office, 1979), p. 179.

evidence, although it can pose a hazard to our health and well-being. It has been estimated that 20 to 25 million people—about one in ten people in the United States—are exposed to noises of such duration and intensity that they can cause a permanent reduction in their ability to hear. Of these, 10 to 15 million are estimated to be workers exposed to excessive noise on the job.[35] There is growing evidence that noise is also linked to other health problems such as heart disease, high blood pressure, and disturbances of the digestive and respiratory systems.[36]

[35]*Ibid.*, p. 534.
[36]See *Noise: A Health Problem* (Washington, D.C.: Environmental Protection Agency, August 1978).

Noise is measured by use of a decibel scale. This scale measures sound pressure or energy according to international standards. The decibel scale is logarithmic; therefore a small increase in decibels represents a great increase in intensity. Every ten-decibel increase represents a tenfold increase in physical intensity and approximately a doubling in loudness as perceived by people. The reason for such a scale is that the human ear is sensitive over such a wide range of acoustic energy that the numbers had to be compressed for convenience and practicality.[37]

Noise emanates from many different sources. Transporation noise, industrial noise, and noise from construction activities are some of the worst offenders. The effects of noise on human beings varies with the decibel level and distance from the source, as well as duration and other variables. Exhibit 18.1 shows the decibel level of some common sounds and gives some approximate indication of the effect on hearing.

EXHIBIT 18.1

Sound Levels and Human Response

Common Sounds	Noise Level (dB)	Effect
Carrier deck jet operation Air raid siren	140	Painfully loud
	130	
Jet takeoff (200 feet) Thunderclap Discotheque Auto horn (3 feet)	120	Maximum vocal effort
Pile drivers	110	
Garbage truck	100	
Heavy truck (50 feet) City traffic	90	Very annoying Hearing damage (8 hours)
Alarm clock (2 feet) Hair dryer	80	Annoying
Noisy restaurant Freeway traffic Man's voice (3 feet)	70	Telephone use difficult

[37]*Noise and Its Measurement* (Washington, D.C.: Environmental Protection Agency, February 1977).

Air conditioning unit (20 feet)	60	Intrusive
Light auto traffic (100 feet)	50	Quiet
Living room Bedroom Quiet office	40	
Library Soft whisper (15 feet)	30	Very quiet
Broadcasting studio	20	
	10	Just audible
	0	Hearing begins

This decibel (dB) table compares some common sounds and shows how they rank in potential harm to hearing. Note that 70 dB is the point at which noise begins to harm hearing. To the ear, each 10 dB increase seems twice as loud.

From *Noise and Its Measurement* (Washington, D.C.: Environmental Protection Agency, February 1977), p. 2.

The federal noise program was formally established under Title IV of the Clean Air Amendments of 1970, which directed the EPA to conduct a "full and complete investigation and study of noise and its effect on public health and welfare and to report the findings to Congress within one year." That report provided the basis of the first noise control legislation in the United States, the Noise Control Act of 1972. Under this act, the EPA was mandated to:

• Identify major sources of noise;
• Regulate those identified sources;
• Propose aircraft noise standards to the FAA;
• Label noisy products;
• Engage in research, technical assistance, and dissemination of public information;
• Coordinate all federal noise control efforts.[38]

In 1978, the Noise Control Act was amended with the Quiet Communities Act to encourage the development of noise control programs on the community and state level. These amendments provided a necessary link between the federal program and noise control activities at the local level. This

[38]*Noise Control Program* (Washington, D.C.: Environmental Protection Agency, April 1979), p. v.

effort was begun in 1977, when the EPA launched its first Quiet Communities Program (QCP) research and demonstration project in Allentown, Pennsylvania. This was a pilot project to demonstrate the application of the best available techniques for local noise control. Its emphasis was on total community involvement and action, aided by EPA guidance and fiscal support.[39]

For noise standards for newly manufactured products, the EPA identified ten products as major noise sources: medium and heavy trucks, motorcycles, buses, garbage trucks, wheel and crawler tractors (used in construction), portable air compressors, jack hammers, rock drills, power lawnmowers, and truck refrigeration units. Table 18.4 shows the status of regulations for these major noise sources.

The EPA shares with OSHA the responsibility for regulation of occupational noise. In 1974, OSHA proposed a maximum permissible daily exposure level of 90 decibels for an eight-hour period. The EPA concluded the 90 dB was not adequately protective and under its authority, given by the Noise Control Act of 1972, recommended that OSHA adopt a more stringent standard of 85 decibels for an eight-hour period as well as a 3-decibel

TABLE 18.4 **Federal EPA Product Regulations (Noise Emission Limits on Newly Manufactured Products)**

	1976	1977	1978	1979	1980	1981	1982	1983
Portable air compressors	F		E	E				
Medium and heavy trucks	F		E				S	
Wheel and crawler tractors		P		Fa				Ea
Garbage trucks (truck-mounted solid waste compactor)			P		F	Ea	Sa	
Buses—school city intercity			P		Fa	Ea		
Motorcycles				P	Fa	Ea		
Identified as Major Noise Sources: truck-transport refrigeration units, power lawnmowers, pavement breakers, and rock drills								
Under Consideration: light vehicles, tires, chain saws, construction equipment								

P = proposed.
F = final regulations issued.
E = rule goes into effect.
S = more stringent noise limits go into effect.
aProjected dates.

Source: Council on Environmental Quality, *Environmental Quality* (Washington, D.C.: U.S. Government Printing Office, 1979), p. 560.

[39]*Ibid.*, p. 3.

"equal energy" rule for trading off duration for intensity (a higher decibel level for a shorter period of time). Both agencies advocate the use of engineering controls to meet these standards instead of hearing protectors, believing the latter to be an inferior alternative. This makes compliance with occupational noise standards considerably more expensive.[40]

Questions for Discussion

1. Describe the current system of air pollution control. What is ambient air quality? How does this differ from stationary sources of air pollution? What methods of control are used in each situation?
2. Describe the "bubble concept" in controlling stationary sources of air pollution. Is this a more sensible policy than regulating stack by stack? Does it give business more flexibility?
3. What is the difference between point and nonpoint sources of water pollution? Which is easier to control? Why? Describe the way point sources of water pollution are currently controlled.
4. Name some nonpoint sources of pollution. Describe the system by which these sources are controlled. Is this a workable system as far as you are concerned? What are best management practices? Where do they fit into the system?
5. What are toxic substances? How is the Toxic Substances Control Act going to control these substances? What impact is this system likely to make on business in general and the chemical industry in particular?
6. What is hazardous waste material? How are these materials going to be controlled? What is the likely impact on business organizations? What industries will be most affected?
7. Describe how noise is measured. How does noise pollution differ from most other pollutants? What mandates were given the EPA by the Noise Control Act of 1972? What has been done so far in this area of noise regulation?
8. Comment on the public policies to control pollution described in this chapter. Are they necessary? Have they been effective? Would some of the alternatives mentioned in the previous chapter be more effective?

Suggested Reading

Brace, Paul. *Glossary of the Environment*. New York: Praeger, 1977.

Brown, Michael. *Laying Waste: The Poisoning of America by Toxic Chemicals*. New York: Pantheon Books, 1980.

Goldman, Marshall I., ed. *Controlling Pollution: The Economics of a Cleaner America*. Englewood Cliffs, N.J.: Prentice-Hall, 1967.

Greenberg, Michael P., and Belnay, Glen. *A Primer on Industrial Environmental Impact*. New Brunswick, N.J.: Rutgers University Press, 1979.

Hite, James C., et al. *The Economics of Environmental Quality*. Washington, D.C.: American Enterprise Institute, 1972.

Rohrlick, George F., ed. *Environmental Management: Economic and Social Dimensions*. Cambridge, Mass.: Ballinger, 1976.

Sax, Newton Irving, ed. *Industrial Pollution*. New York: D. Van Nostrand, 1974.

Sive, Mary R. *Environmental Legislation: A Source Book*. New York: Praeger, 1976.

---

[40]*Environmental Quality*, p. 562.

PART FOUR

Management Responses to Public Policy Issues

19

Management Philosophy and Public Policy: Social Responsibility and Responsiveness

The traditional economic model of business operations has served business well. Business needs to make no apology for its profound role in bringing economic plenty to many parts of the world. The job that business has done ranks high among civilization's all-time achievements. If conditions have changed, however, then the old model may not apply precisely the way it applied in the past. In a dynamic world businessmen are not going to solve tomorrow's problems with yesterday's theories.[1]

How shall a manager think about his or her responsibilities to society? What philosophical framework makes sense with regard to public policy issues? What conceptual framework will be most useful in helping a manager develop effective responses to changes in the environment? These questions are important because it is out of a general philosophy or theory of management and its responsibilities that specific corporate practices and policies are developed. The purpose of the next two chapters is to discuss recent thinking about management and its broader responsibilities to society.

[1] © 1976 by the Regents of the University of California. Reprinted from *California Management Review*, Volume XIX, No. 1, pp. 14–15 by permission of the Regents.

Corporate Social Responsibility

While the concept of corporate social responsibility may have had its origins in the 1930s as some scholars suggest,[2] the concept came into its own, so to speak, during the 1960s as a response to the changing social values of society. While there are many definitions of social responsibility (see box), in general it means that a private corporation has responsibilities to society that go beyond the production of goods and services at a profit—that a corpora-

---

DEFINITIONS OF SOCIAL RESPONSIBILITY

Insofar as the changing public mood applies to business, it is insisting upon a greater social conscience, social concern, and social responsibility. The idea of social responsibility is that decision-makers are obligated to take actions which protect and improve the welfare of society as a whole along with their own interests. The net effect is to enhance the quality of life in the broadest possible way, however the quality of life is defined by society. In this way harmony is achieved between business's actions and society's wants. The businessman acts in a manner that will accomplish social benefits along with the traditional economic gains which the firm seeks. He becomes concerned with social outputs as well as economic outputs, and with the total effect of his economic and institutional actions on society.

> From Keith Davis and Robert L. Blomstrom, *Business and Society*, 3rd ed. (New York: McGraw-Hill, 1975), pp. 6–7.

It [social responsibility] refers to the obligations of businessmen to pursue those policies, to make those decisions, or to follow those lines of action which are desirable in terms of the objectives and values of our society.

> From Howard R. Bowen, *Social Responsibilities of the Businessman* (New York: Harper & Row, 1953), p. 6.

When people talk about social responsibilities they are thinking in terms of the problems that arise when corporate enterprise casts its shadow on the social scene, and of the ethical principles that ought to govern the relationships between the corporation and society.

> From Richard Eells and Clarence Walton, *Conceptual Foundations of Business* (Homewood, Ill.: Richard D. Irwin, 1961), pp. 457–458.

The idea of social responsibilities supposes that the corporation has not only economic and legal obligations, but also certain responsibilities to society which extend beyond these obligations.

> From Joseph W. McGuire, *Business and Society* (New York: McGraw-Hill, 1963), p. 144.

The social responsibility of business encompasses the economic, legal, ethical, and discretionary expectations placed on organizations by society at a given point in time.

> From Archie B. Carroll, "A Conceptual Model of Corporate Social Performance," College of Business Administration, University of Georgia, 1979, Working Paper No. 79-055, p. 9.

---

[2]See William C. Frederick, "From CSR_1 to CSR_2: The Maturing of Business and Society Thought," Graduate School of Business, University of Pittsburgh, 1978, Working Paper No. 279, p. 1.

tion has a broader constituency to serve than that of stockholders alone. Corporations relate to society through more than just the marketplace and serve a wider range of human values than the traditional economic values implied in the primary purpose of a corporation as an economic institution.

The concept of corporate social responsibility means that corporations have a responsibility to help society solve some of its most pressing social problems, many of which the corporation helped cause, by devoting some of its resources (human, financial, capital) to the solution of these problems. Some of the most common social problems have been identified as cleaning up pollution, providing equal job opportunities to minorities and women, producing safe, quality products, promoting safety and health in the workplace, responding to problems in the immediate community, hiring and training disadvantaged people, and promoting minority economic development.

The concept of social responsibility involves a change in the terms of the contract between business and society. It presents a challenge to the belief that maximizing private profit also maximizes public benefits. Any institution in society is created to perform certain functions that society wants accomplished. The old contract between business and society was based on the view that economic growth was the source of all progress, social as well as economic. The engine of growth was considered to be the drive for profits by competitive private enterprise. According to the old contract, business had a basic economic mission to produce goods and services and perform other economic functions, and in so doing it was making its maximum contribution to society.

The new contract between business and society is based on the view that economic growth has some detrimental side effects that impose social costs on certain segments of society or on society as a whole. The pursuit of economic growth and profits does not necessarily lead to social progress. In many cases it has led instead to a deteriorating physical environment, discrimination against certain groups in society, poverty for some groups, urban decay, and other social ills. The new contract between business and society involves the alleviation of these social costs of business out of a sense of social responsibility. The new contract does not invalidate the old, it simply adds new terms or additional clauses to that contract. Figure 19.1 depicts these old and new contracts and distinguishes between economic and social inputs and outputs. The new contract includes a responsibility for both economic and social outputs.

Arguments in Favor of Social Responsibility. Many arguments have been advanced to support this concept of social responsibility. One argument is simply that if public expectations of business have changed, business has no choice but to accommodate itself to these changes. An institution is allowed to exist only because it performs a useful function in society, and business's charter can be amended or revoked at any time if it fails to live up to society's expectations. Thus if business wants to continue in existence, it must respond to changes in society and do what society demands. If society wants business to respond to social values, it must do so or be threatened with extinction.

Another argument in support of social responsibility is that profit maximization should be seen over a longer time period than it has been in

Figure 19.1. The Contract Between Business and Society

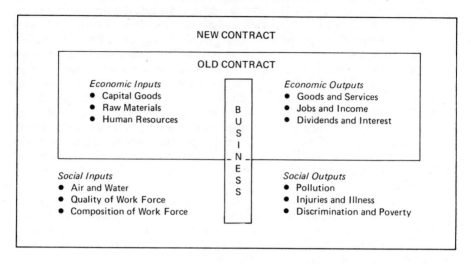

the past. While expenditures to help solve social problems may reduce short-run profits, it is in the long-run self-interest of business to produce environmental conditions that are favorable for business survival and operation. Thus enlightened self-interest dictates a business concern for social problems—it cannot hope to remain a viable institution in a deteriorating society.

> Enlightened self-interest thus has both carrot and stick aspects. There is the positive appeal to the corporation's greater opportunities to grow and profit in a healthy, prosperous, and well-functioning society. And there is the negative threat of increasingly onerous compulsion and harassment if it does not do its part in helping to create such a society. . . . Inasmuch as the business community as a whole has an initial stake in a good, well-functioning society, it can be argued that the stockholder's interest in the long-run is best served by corporate policies which contribute to the development of the kind of society in which business can grow and prosper.[3]

A third argument is that business will gain a better public image by being socially responsible. If the values of society have indeed changed, a company that is responsive to these changes should be more favorably thought of than one that is not responsive. This should mean more customers, more sales of products, better employees, better stock market performance, and easier access to capital markets to raise funds for expansion.

One of the most powerful arguments for social responsibility is simply that by being socially responsible business may be able to avoid government regulation. This argument is based on the belief that social issues or expectations go through some sort of evolutionary sequence, such as that shown in Exhibit 19.1. According to this argument, if business does not respond properly to a change in social expectations, the expectations will be picked

[3]Committee for Economic Development, *Social Responsibility of Business Corporations* (New York: CED, 1972), pp. 29–30.

EXHIBIT 19.1 ────────────────────────────────────

The Evolutionary Sequence of Societal Expectations of Business Performance

Without a proper business response . . .	Business options	The example of civil rights
Societal Expectations of today become . . .	Semi-autonomous	Late 1950s
Political issues of tomorrow . . .	Defensive	1960 platforms (both parties)
Legislated requirements the next day . . .	Compliance	1964 Civil Rights Act
And litigated penalties the day after that . . .	Pay penalties (ordered or negotiated)	1974 backlog: 100,000 EEOC cases

From Ian Wilson, "What One Company Is Doing About Today's Demands on Business," *The Changing Role of Business in Society*, George A. Steiner, ed. (Los Angeles: UCLA Graduate School of Management, 1976), p. 20. Reprinted with permission.

up by the political system and find their way into legislation that, if passed, will result in regulation to force compliance on business or the payment of penalties in case of violations. As an issue moves through this sequence, the options for business are narrowed to where they become almost nonexistent. Thus the trick for business is to get involved in an issue in the early stages of its development, and if business can make a proper response that effectively meets societal expectations, government regulation may be avoided altogether.

There is also the argument that business has enormous resources that would be useful in solving social problems. Business has managerial talent, expertise in many technical areas, and physical and financial resources, all of which can be very useful in helping to alleviate society's problems. Business is also known for its innovational ability and its concern for efficient use of resources, which are also useful assets in the social realm. Thus business ought to be encouraged or perhaps even required to try its hand at solving social problems.

The idea that social problems can be turned into profitable opportunities is an especially intriguing one for some businesspeople. A few corporations claim this argument as their justification for social involvement (see box). They build plants in ghetto areas, for example, not necessarily out of a moral sense of doing good, but out of a more practical business sense of exploiting a profit-making opportunity. A lot of wasted talent in these areas can be put to good use in making products. Certain companies might also claim that enough useful products can be recovered from waste material to make a pollution control program a profitable endeavor.

Finally, there is the moral argument that business has an obligation to help solve social problems because it helped create or at least perpetuate them in the first place. Business causes pollution, it creates unsafe workplaces, it helps perpetuate discrimination through its hiring and promotion practices.

> What is required is a fundamental change in which business takes the initiative and provides the leadership for planning and managing the implementation of programs meeting these needs—in cooperation with government, labor unions, universities, churches and all other major segments of society. The major problems of our society are massive, and massive resources are required for their solution. The best approach is to view them with the strategy in mind that they can be profitable business opportunities with an appropriate sharing of cost between business and government. Where the resources for solving problems are beyond those of a single company, as most are, they should be pooled through cooperative projects or joint venture companies.
>
> From *Social Responsibility Report* (Minneapolis, Minn.: Control Data Corporation, 1978), p. 1.

Therefore business has a moral responsibility to deal with these negative impacts on society, rather than leaving them for someone else to solve. Many social problems are the direct result of business operations and these are quite properly the social responsibility of business.

Arguments Against Social Responsibility. Despite these supporting arguments, the concept of social responsibility has some serious problems, raised by those who do not support the concept wholeheartedly. One such problem is simply the matter of definition. S. Prakash Sethi has written that social responsibility "has been used in so many different contexts that it has lost all meaning. Devoid of an internal structure and content, it has come to mean all things to all people."[4] This diversity and fuzziness has left concerned citizens, businesspeople, scholars, and public policy-makers confused.

This definitional problem exists at both the conceptual and operational levels, but at the latter level it becomes a particularly crucial problem as corporations try to be specific about their social responsibilities. How shall a corporation's resources be allocated to help solve social problems? With what specific problems shall the corporation concern itself? What priorities should be established? What goals or standards of performance should be developed? How much money should be spent? What technology should be employed? What measures are appropriate to determine adequate performance?

There is no market mechanism to answer these questions about resource allocation. The market does not work in allocating resources for the provision of public goods and services. Preferences or desires for public goods and services are not revealed through market behavior and thus the market offers little or no information to the manager that is useful in making decisions about solving social problems. For most corporations, there is no money to be made in pollution control, affirmative action programs, hiring the disadvantaged, or other social efforts. A way to measure long-run profits or the profits that might result from an improved corporate image have not yet been developed.

In the absence of a market mechanism, management could presumably

---

[4]S. Prakash Sethi, "Dimensions of Corporate Social Responsibility," *California Management Review,* Vol. 17, No. 3 (Spring 1975), p. 58.

make these operational decisions on their own according to whatever criteria they deem appropriate. This, however, raises the accountability problem. Milton Friedman poses a crucial question: what right do managers of *private* corporations have to determine *public* policy for their organizations?[5] Friedman argues that when managers assume the right to make decisions about social investment they are involved in the realm of public decision-making without being subject to any of the guidelines or limitations imposed by the market. Nor are they subject to any democratic political process as a check on their decision-making. Businesspeople would in effect be imposing taxes on the public by using stockholders', consumers', and employees' money for a public purpose. Furthermore, they would be making the decisions on how these funds should be spent. They would thus be spending someone else's money for a social interest and exercising governmental (political) power without any definite criteria for them to follow. This leaves the public with nothing more than businesspeople's claim that their actions are in the public interest—a claim that has no clear meaning and thus cannot be challenged by the public whose interests are at stake. Social responsibility would, therefore, mean whatever managers want it to mean and represents

> an invasion into the public domain by managers who are not selected through any public process, are not subject to annual reviews provided by elections, are not forced to engage in public dialogue with their constituents, are not required to justify the expenditures of corporate funds (involuntary taxes) before a budget committee of the Congress, and need not balance competing interests before coming to their decisions.[6]

Without some kind of accountability a corporation's decisions can be arbitrary. A corporation may make philanthropic grants or hire disadvantaged people and incur extra costs for training. But the corporation, or more precisely its managers, would be deciding what causes are worthy of support and what people should be singled out as disadvantaged and deserving. Since these activities are most likely consistent with their own values, corporate responsibility advocates would probably be satisfied with these corporate actions. But what if corporations tried to defend foreign payments on the grounds that this action was socially responsible behavior in the host country? Would advocates be happy with this action? The point is that corporate power used in this manner is not accountable and is not to be trusted. It is dangerous to assume that corporate managers know what is best for society, yet the social responsibility doctrine encourages nonelected corporate executives to impose their tastes and preferences on the society as a whole.

Related to this view of social responsibility is the argument that if business does take over activities that traditionally have been considered within the domain of other institutions or individuals, it might substantially increase its power and influence over the other members and institutions of our society and become a monolothic institution, being all things to all people. Such a

[5]Milton Friedman, "The Social Responsibility of Business Is to Increase Its Profits," *New York Times Magazine,* September 13, 1970, pp. 122–126.
[6]F. A. Hayek, "The Corporation in a Democratic Society," *Management and Corporations, 1975* (New York: McGraw-Hill, 1960), p. 106.

concentration of power in one institution would lead to a breakdown of pluralism and pose a threat to individual freedoms (see box).[7]

Employing the standard self-interest assumption common to economic analysis, it can be seen that social responsibility would indeed be a popular idea among corporate executives, as apparently it is. It is, for whatever reasons, an opportunity to increase the power of corporate decision-makers. Just as with virtually all other goods, more power is usually preferred to less. As was noted earlier, such power carries with it few restrictions. In essence, the doctrine of corporate social responsibility suggests that corporate executives do what politicians have not done and offers fewer constraints to promote more responsive behavior. The implication of this logic must be that corporate executives are simply better persons than our current (or past) public servants. If this is indeed true, great steps toward more responsive government can be made by replacing current politicians with corporate executives.

If, on the other hand, corporate leaders are not fundamentally different from other men, the acceptance of the social responsibility doctrine implies even more autonomy for "public" decision-makers than is currently possible. Such an arrangement should result in even more resources directed toward those uses which benefit the corporate leaders or special interest groups than is observed under existing arrangements. Furthermore, cooperation among corporate executives to facilitate efficient social investment would enhance their opportunities to form cartels and further other efforts to restrict competition.

From Gerald D. Keim and Roger E. Meiners, "Corporate Social Responsibility: Private Means for Public Wants?" *Policy Review*, No. 5 (Summer 1978), pp. 91–92.

Another argument against corporate social responsibility posed by Milton Friedman is that he believes the sole responsibility of a corporation is to the shareholders. The manager of a corporation, according to Friedman, is only a salaried employee of the owners, and is legally and ethically bound to earn the highest return on their investment while staying within the rules of the game. Thus managers must abide by the principles of profit maximization. They have no legal or moral right to pursue any other objectives, social or otherwise.[8]

Some people question the ability of business to solve social problems. Businesspeople, by and large, have no experience in dealing with such problems. There is no reason to believe they will be any more effective, or even as effective, as other institutions that have more experience and expertise in dealing with these kinds of problems. There is not enough incentive for them to pursue social goals with the same vigor with which they pursue private goals, which would stimulate them to develop the necessary expertise and to gain needed experience.

Private efforts, it is argued, will be more efficient because corporations have demonstrated great efficiency in pursuing private goals. Unfortunately, such

[7]Theodore Levitt, "The Dangers of Social Responsibility," *Harvard Business Review*, Vol. 36, No. 5 (September–October 1958), pp. 41–50.
[8]Friedman, "Social Responsibility," pp. 122–126.

efficiency observed in the pursuit of private goals cannot necessarily be transferred to efforts directed toward public or social goals. The organizational structure of the corporation which delivers efficient production of private goods and services cannot be expected to pursue social goals with the same efficiency simply because the incentives for doing so are absent.[9]

Another argument against social responsibility is that this term is fundamentally a moral concept, and it is difficult if not impossible for organizations to respond to the moral imperatives inherent in such a concept. People can have moral responsibilities, but not organizations, which are structured to attain certain practical objectives and are basically amoral in their operations. A moral concept such as social responsibility does not apply to organizations such as corporations.

Finally, it is argued that the concept of social responsibility is a subversive doctrine that would undermine the principles upon which a free enterprise system is based. For managers to be held accountable for the use of corporate resources to solve social problems, people affected by these decisions would have to be represented at some point in the decision-making process. This could mean, for example, that consumers, minorities, women, environmentalists, and so on, would all have to be represented on the board of directors. Such a diversity of interests means that decision-making in the corporation would be political rather than being based on economic criteria. The former is how a socialistic economy operates. Social responsibility thus subverts the principles of a free enterprise economy.

> The view has been gaining widespread acceptance that corporate officials and labor leaders have a social responsibility that goes beyond serving the interests of their stockholders or their members. This view shows a fundamental misconception of the character and nature of a free economy. In such an economy, there is one and only one social responsibility of business—to use its resources and engage in activities designed to increase its profit so long as it stays within the rules of the game, which is to say, engages in open and free competition, without deception or fraud. . . . Few trends could so thoroughly undermine the very foundations of our free society as the acceptance by corporate officials of a social responsibility other than to make as much money for their stockholders as possible. This is a fundamentally subversive doctrine.[10]

Corporate Social Responsiveness

A new philosophy began to emerge during the beginning of the 1970s that sought a way around these difficulties. The concept of corporate social *responsiveness* began to be heard in academic circles more frequently, and while initially it may have appeared that only semantics was involved, it gradually became clear that the shift from responsibility to responsiveness was much more substantive. Corporate social responsiveness has been defined by William C. Frederick as follows.

[9]Gerald D. Keim and Roger E. Meiners, "Corporate Social Responsibility: Private Means for Public Wants?" *Policy Review*, No. 5 (Summer 1978), p. 83.
[10]Milton Friedman, *Capitalism and Freedom* (Chicago: University of Chicago Press, 1962), p. 133.

> Corporate social responsiveness refers to the capacity of a corporation to respond to social pressures. The literal act of responding, or of achieving a generally responsive posture, to society is the focus. . . . One searches the organization for mechanisms, procedures, arrangements, and behavioral patterns that, taken collectively, would mark the organization as more or less capable of responding to social pressures.[11]

The beginning of this philosophy is attributed to Professor Raymond Bauer and his colleagues at Harvard Business School, most notably Robert Ackerman, who began a line of research focusing on internal corporate responsiveness to social problems. Out of that research came the development of a conceptual model that outlined three stages of the internal response process of corporations: awareness, commitment, and implementation (Exhibit 19.2).

In the first phase, the chief executive officer recognizes a social problem to be important. This awareness is marked by several activities. Initially, the chief executive officer may begin to speak out on the issue at meetings of industry and trade associations, stockholders, and civic groups. He or she becomes active in organizations and committees involved in studying the problem and influencing opinion about policy approaches. He or she may also commit corporate resources to special projects, such as ghetto plants, waste recovery facilities, and training centers. Finally, the CEO perceives the need for an up-to-date company policy, which he or she takes pains to communicate to all managers in the organization. However, responsibility for implementing the policy is assigned as a matter of course to the operating units as part of their customary tasks performed in running the business. While this approach fails to provoke acceptable action or achievement with respect to the problem in most cases, the major outcome of this phase is at least a sense of enriched purpose and an increased awareness of social problems.[12]

The key event heralding the beginning of phase two is the appointment of a staff specialist reporting to the chief executive officer or one of his or her senior staff. The staff specialist coordinates the corporation's activities in response to a social problem, helps the chief executive officer perform his or her public duties, and ensures that the corporation's response to the problem is implemented throughout the organization. The specialist begins to gather more systematic information on the company's activities relating to the problem and matches this data with his or her assessment of environmental demands. This is the beginning of an internal data system and a systematic manner of assessing and interpreting the environment to management. The specialist also mediates between operating divisions and external organizations, including government agencies that are pressuring the corporation.[13]

Eventually, however, it is discovered that the appointment of a staff specialist still fails to elicit the corporate response envisaged in corporate policy. The staff specialist's attempts to force action on the corporation are

---

[11]Frederick, "From CSR₁ to CSR₂," p. 6.

[12]Robert W. Ackerman, "How Companies Respond to Social Demands," *Harvard Business Review*, Vol. 51, No. 4 (July–August 1973), p. 92.

[13]*Ibid.*, pp. 92–93.

EXHIBIT 19.2

Ackerman/Bauer Model of Corporate Responsiveness

Phases of Organizational Involvement

Organizational Level	Phase 1			Phase 2			Phase 3		
Chief Executive	Issue:	Policy problem		Issue:	Obtain knowledge		Issue:	Obtain organizational commitment	
	Action:	Write and communicate policy		Action:	Add staff specialists		Action:	Change performance expectations	
	Outcome:	Enriched purpose, increased awareness							
Staff Specialists				Issue:	Technical problem		Issue:	Provoke response from operating units	
				Action:	Design data system and interpret environment		Action:	Apply data system to performance measurement	
				Outcome:	Technical and administrative learning				
Division Management							Issue:	Management problem	
							Action:	Commit resources and modify procedures	
							Outcome:	Increased responsiveness	

- *Phase I*—social concerns exist but are not specifically directed at the corporation.
- *Phase 2*—broad implications for the corporation become clear but enforcement is weak or even nonexistent.
- *Phase 3*—expectations for corporate action become more specific and sanctions (governmental or otherwise) become plausible threats.

From R. Ackerman and R. Bauer, *Corporate Social Responsiveness: The Modern Dilemma* (Reston, Va.: Reston Publishing Co., 1976), p. 128. Reprinted with permission of Reston Publishing Co., Inc., a Prentice-Hall Co., 11480 Sunset Hills Rd., Reston, Va. 22090.

alien to the decentralized mode of decision-making within most corporate organizations. The staff specialist becomes overburdened with moderating conflict within the organization and crisis-by-crisis involvement. But at least a good deal of technical and administrative learning is accomplished in this phase.[14]

In the third phase, top management sees the organizational rigidities to be more serious than previously acknowledged. They cannot be waved away with a policy statement nor can they be overcome with a staff specialist. Instead, the whole organizational apparatus has to become involved. In this phase, the CEO attempts to make the achievement of a social policy objective a goal for all managers in the organization by institutionalizing the policy. This attempt involves modifying procedures of the company related to the setting of objectives, reward systems, performance measurement, and similar procedures.[15]

The initial research by Bauer and Ackerman triggered other models of the corporate response process. For example, S. Prakash Sethi also developed a three-stage model that defined corporate behavior as social obligation, social responsibility, and social responsiveness. In the first stage, social obligation, the corporation seeks legitimacy by meeting legal and economic criteria only. The corporation believes it is accountable only to its stockholders and strongly resists any regulation of its activities. In the second stage, social responsibility, the corporation searches for legitimacy by recognizing the limited relevance of meeting only legal and economic criteria, and accepts a broader set of criteria for measuring corporate performance that includes a social dimension. Management considers groups other than stockholders that might be affected by its actions and is willing to work with these outside groups for good environmental legislation. In the third stage, social responsiveness, the corporation accepts its role as defined by the social system, and recognizes that this role is subject to change over time. Furthermore, it is willing to account for its actions to other groups, even those not directly affected by its actions, and assists legislative bodies in developing better legislation. Thus business becomes an active supporter as well as promoter of environmental and social concerns.[16] This three-stage model and its relationship to various dimensions of corporate behavior is shown in Exhibit 19.3.

More recently, James Post and his colleagues at Boston University have developed another three-phase model of the response process that is a hybrid version of the other models (Exhibit 19.4). They generalize from these models and describe a process in which the corporation initially responds to issues in an ad hoc fashion, followed by a stage in which external issues are incorporated into the decision processes of the firm, and finally, a stage in which sensitivity to these issues is institutionalized into the reward and evaluation systems of the organization.[17]

[14]*Ibid.*, p. 93.

[15]*Ibid.*, pp. 93–95.

[16]Sethi, "Dimensions," pp. 58–64.

[17]James E. Post, "The Internal Management of Social Responsiveness: The Role of the Public Affairs Department," paper presented at a seminar on "The Corporation in Society: Planning and Management of Corporate Responsibility," held at the University of Santa Clara, Santa Clara, California, October 31–November 2, 1979, p. 23.

From these examples, it can be seen that corporate social responsiveness deals with how corporations respond to social problems. The important questions in this philosophy are not moral, related to whether a corporation should respond to a social problem out of a sense of responsibility, but are more pragmatic and action-oriented, dealing with the ability of a corporation to respond and what changes are necessary to enable it to respond more effectively.

EXHIBIT 19.3

A Three-State Schema for Classifying Corporate Behavior

Dimensions of Behavior	State One: Social Obligation Proscriptive	State Two: Social Responsibility Prescriptive	State Three: Social Responsiveness Anticipatory and Preventive
Search for legitimacy	Confines legitimacy to legal and economic criteria only; does not violate laws; equates profitable operations with fulfilling social expectations.	Accepts the reality of limited relevance of legal and market criteria of legitimacy in actual practice. Willing to consider and accept broader—extralegal and extramarket—criteria for measuring corporate performance and social role.	Accepts its role as defined by the social system and therefore subject to change; recognizes importance of profitable operations but includes other criteria.
Ethical norms	Considers business value-neutral;managers expected to behave according to their own ethical standards.	Defines norms in community related terms, i.e., good corporate citizen. Avoids taking moral stand on issues which may harm its economic interests or go against prevailing social norms (majority views).	Takes definite stand on issues of public concern; advocates institutional ethical norms even though they may be detrimental to its immediate economic interest or prevailing social norms.
Social accountability for corporate actions	Construes narrowly as limited to stockholders, jealously guards its prerogatives against outsiders.	Construes narrowly for legal purposes, but broadened to include groups affected by its actions; management more outward looking.	Willing to account for its actions to other groups, even those not directly affected by its actions.
Operating strategy	Exploitative and defensive adaptation. Maximum externalization of costs.	Reactive adaptation. Where identifiable internalize previously external costs. Maintain current standards of physical and social environment. Compensate victims of pollution and other corporate-related activities even in the absence of clearly established legal grounds. Develop industry-wide standards.	Proactive adaptation. Takes lead in developing and adapting new technology for environmental protectors. Evaluates side effects of corporate actions and eliminates them prior to the action's being taken. Anticipates future social changes and develops internal structures to cope with them.
Response to social pressures	Maintains low public profile, but if attacked, uses PR methods to upgrade its public image; denies any deficiencies; blames public dissatisfaction on ignorance or failure to understand corporate functions; discloses information only where legally required.	Accepts responsibility for solving current problems; will admit deficiencies in former practices and attempt to persuade public that its current practices meet social norms; attitude toward critics conciliatory; freer information disclosures than state one.	Willingly discusses activities with outside groups; makes information freely available to public; accepts formal and informal inputs from outside groups in decision making. Is willing to be publicly evaluated for its various activities.
Activities pertaining to governmental actions	Strongly resists any regulation of its activities except when it needs help to protect its market position; avoids contact; resists any demands for information beyond that legally required.	Preserves management discretion in corporate decisions, but cooperates with government in research to improve industry-wide standards; participates in political processes and encourages employees to do likewise.	Openly communicates with government; assists in enforcing existing laws and developing evaluations of business practices; objects publicly to governmental activities that it feels are detrimental to the public good.

Legislative and political activities	Seeks to maintain status quo; actively opposes laws that would internalize any previously externalized costs; seeks to keep lobbying activities secret.	Willing to work with outside groups for good environmental laws; concedes need for change in some status quo laws; less secrecy in lobbying than state one.	Avoids meddling in politics and does not pursue special-interest laws; assists legislative bodies in developing better laws where relevant; promotes honesty and openness in government and in its own lobbying activities.
Philanthropy	Contributes only when direct benefit to it clearly shown; otherwise, views contributions as responsibility of individual employees.	Contributes to noncontroversial and established causes; matches employee contributions.	Activities of state two, *plus* support and contributions to new, controversial groups whose needs it sees as unfulfilled and increasingly important.

EXHIBIT 19.4

The Evolution of Internal Responsiveness

Stage	Characterized by . . .
I	Ad Hoc Responses to External Issues
II	Awareness of External Issues Is Incorporated into Decision Processes (Strategic Planning, Manpower) of Firm
III	Responsiveness to Public Issues Is Institutionalized in Reward and Management Evaluation Systems of the Organization

From James E. Post, "The Internal Management of Social Responsiveness: The Role of the Public Affairs Department," paper presented at a seminar on "The Corporation in Society: Planning and Management of Corporate Responsibility," held at the University of Santa Clara, Santa Clara, California, October 31–November 2, 1979, p. 23. Reprinted with permission.

One of the advantages of the social responsiveness philosophy is its managerial orientation. The concept ignores the philosophical debate about responsibility and obligation and focuses on the problems and prospects of making corporations more socially responsive. One of the reasons for research into corporate response patterns is to discover those responses that have proven to be most effective in dealing with social problems.[18]

The corporate social responsiveness approach also lends itself to more rigorous analytical research to discover patterns of response and focuses on specific techniques, such as environmental scanning or the social audit, to improve the response process. Such research can also discover how management can best institutionalize social policy throughout the organization. Such questions can be investigated as what organizational structures are most appropriate, whether top management commitment is crucial, what changes in the reward structure improve the corporation's response to social problems, what role the public affairs department should play in the re-

---

[18]Frederick, "From CSR$_1$ to CSR$_2$," p. 6.

sponse process, and how social policy can be best formulated for the organization as a whole.[19]

Despite these advantages, however, the notion of corporate social responsiveness still has many problems, some of which are the same as those that plagued the social responsibility concept. The concept of corporate social responsiveness does not clarify how corporate resources shall be allocated for the solution of social problems. Companies respond to different problems in different ways and to varying degrees. But there is no clear idea as to what pattern of responsiveness will produce the greatest amount of social goods and services for society. The philosophy of responsiveness does not help the company decide what problems to get involved in and what priorities to establish to produce social betterment. Thus it provides no better guidance to management than does social responsibility.[20]

On the one hand, the concept seems to assume that social pressures exist and that business must respond to them, placing business in a passive role of simply responding to a society that actively expresses its wishes. But social responsiveness provides no moral or even practical reason for business to get involved in social problems. It does not provide any foundation for social responsiveness, and by ignoring this question offers no specific guidance to either society or management on the best strategies or policies to be adopted to produce social betterment.[21]

On the other hand, the concept seems to suggest that management itself, by determining the degree of social responsiveness and the problems it will respond to, decides the meaning of social responsiveness and what social goods and services shall be produced. The concept of social responsiveness contains no explicit value theory and advocates no specific set of values for business to follow in making social responses. If management is left to follow its own values in making these decisions, the same problem of accountability plagues both the concept of corporate social responsibility and corporate social responsiveness.[22]

Questions for Discussion

1. Does every manager have a philosophy regarding business and its responsibilities to society? How is such a philosophy formed? Why is it important?
2. Define the basic meaning of the concept of social responsibility. What common elements are found in all the definitions offered in the text? Why did corporate social responsibility become an issue in the 1960s?
3. What specific kinds of responsibilities are usually referred to by the term corporate social responsibility? Isn't a firm being socially responsible by producing goods and services at a profit? Why is this not enough?
4. What does it mean to say that the terms of the contract between business and society have changed? Where would one look to find the terms of the new contract? How does it differ from the old contract?
5. Discuss the arguments in favor of corporate social responsibility. Which are most

[19]*Ibid.*, pp. 12–13.
[20]*Ibid.*, p. 14.
[21]*Ibid.*
[22]*Ibid.*, pp. 14–16.

powerful or persuasive, in your opinion? Which, if any, do you regard as bogus arguments?

6. Can business avoid government regulation by being socially responsible? Why or why not? With respect to what specific issues that are now regulatory matters might it have avoided regulation? How would this happen?

7. Examine the arguments against the social responsibility of business. Are there any that you personally agree with? Why or why not? Which do you regard as invalid arguments?

8. Is there an accountability problem with corporate social responsibility? How can this problem be solved? Does social responsibility lead to socialism, as Milton Friedman claims?

9. How does corporate social responsiveness differ from corporate social responsibility? Why do you think this shift has taken place in academic thinking?

10. What are the advantages of a responsiveness approach? What are its disadvantages? On the whole, do you believe the concept of corporate social responsiveness represents a theoretical advance in business-society relationships?

11. Does the concept of corporate social responsiveness avoid the major problems associated with the concept of corporate social responsibility? Why or why not?

12. Are either of these concepts adequate to provide a realistic and relevant philosophy for management in the latter years of the twentieth century and beyond? If your answer is no, what would you suggest as an alternative?

Suggested Reading

Ackerman, Robert W. *The Social Challenge to Business.* Cambridge, Mass.: Harvard University Press, 1975.

———, and Bauer, Raymond. *Corporate Social Responsiveness: The Modern Dilemma.* Reston, Va.: Reston Publishing Co., 1976.

Berle, Adolf A. *Power without Property.* New York: Harcourt Brace Jovanovich, 1959.

———. *The Twentieth Century Capitalist Revolution.* New York: Harcourt Brace Jovanovich, 1954.

———, and Means, Gardiner C. *The Modern Corporation and Private Property.* New York: Macmillan, 1932.

Blake, David H., Frederick, William C., and Meyers, Mildred S. *Social Auditing: Evaluating the Impact of Corporate Programs.* New York: Praeger, 1976.

Bowen, Howard R. *Social Responsibilities of the Businessman.* New York: Harper & Row, 1953.

Cavanagh, Gerald F. *American Business Values in Transition.* Englewood Cliffs, N.J.: Prentice-Hall, 1976.

Chamberlain, Neil W. *Remaking American Values: Challenge to a Business Society.* New York: Basic Books, 1977.

Davis, Keith, Frederick, William C., and Blomstrom, Robert W. *Business and Society: Concepts and Policy Issues,* 4th ed. New York: McGraw-Hill, 1980.

Eells, Richard. *The Meaning of Modern Business.* New York: Columbia University, 1960.

———, and Walton, Clarence. *Conceptual Foundations of Business.* Homewood, Ill.: Richard D. Irwin, 1961, 1969.

Friedman, Milton. *Capitalism and Freedom.* Chicago: University of Chicago Press, 1962.

Heald, Morrell. *The Social Responsibilities of Business: Company and Community, 1900–1960.* Cleveland, Ohio: Case-Western Reserve, 1970.

Klein, Thomas A. *Social Costs and Benefits of Business.* Englewood Cliffs, N.J.: Prentice-Hall, 1977.

Preston, Lee E., ed. *Research in Corporate Social Performance and Policy.* Greenwich, Conn.: JAI Press, 1978.

Research and Policy Committee of the Committee for Economic Development. *Social Responsibilities of Business Corporations.* New York: Committee for Economic Development, 1971.

Steiner, George A. *Business, Government, and Society: A Managerial Perspective,* 3rd ed. New York: Random House, 1980.

Sturdivant, Frederick D. *Business and Society: A Managerial Approach,* Rev. ed. Homewood, Ill.: Richard D. Irwin, 1981.

20

Management Philosophy and Public Policy: Public Responsibility

The absence of effective leadership for the business community on many public policy questions—in consensus building and in dealing with other groups and governments—means that business enterprises forfeit almost entirely to politicians. The rapid expansion of government regulations in recent years and specifically government's penchant for rigid, bureaucratic "command and control" regulations, even when ineffective or counterproductive, have arisen in part from a lack of coherence and consensus within the business community about more constructive choices for achieving social purposes.[1]

Neither the concept of corporate social responsibility nor the concept of corporate social responsiveness provides an adequate philosophical framework or theory for management to understand the changing role of business in society and respond to those changes appropriately. Serious problems of definition and accountability, as pointed out in the previous chapter, render these concepts inadequate to provide clear guidance for management in responding to issues of public concern.

[1]John T. Dunlop, "The Concerns: Business and Public Policy," *Harvard Business Review*, Vol. 57, No. 6 (November-December 1979), p. 86. Copyright © 1979 by the President and Fellows of Harvard College; all rights reserved.

The Social Policy Process

To make this point more clearly, it might be instructive to take a close look at what a socially responsible and responsive corporation would look like and to discuss each element of the response process. The structure of such a corporation is depicted on the right hand side of Exhibit 20.1. This part of the exhibit depicts a corporation that is structured to respond to social issues and incorporate them into its operating strategy.

Society is composed, as described in Part Two of this book, of people with ideals, values, ideologies, and ethical standards, all of which are eventually translated into a set of expectations that a society has for itself and for the major institutions in that society. Institutions are expected to respond to the expectations of society, and if an institution's performance does not meet these expectations, a gap develops between expectations and performance, and pressures begin to build around specific issues of concern to the public.

A key part of being a socially responsible or responsive corporation is to have a environmental forecasting and scanning process to be able to track public expectations and determine how much pressure is building on specific issues so the corporation can decide whether it needs to change its performance and do a better job of responding. A socially responsible and responsive corporation must learn to anticipate public issues that are of major concern so that it can attempt to make an effective response to them before too much pressure builds and the issues become politicized. Once this happens, management loses a great deal of discretion and its responses will most likely become defined by government legislation and regulation.

Once these expectations and issues are identified, some high level group within the corporation must formulate the corporation's policy on the issues of major concern to the organization. This group must look at the broad array of issues that have been identified as being on the public agenda, analyze their impact on the corporation to develop some notion about priorities, determine whether the corporation can respond to them effec-

EXHIBIT 20.1

Response Processes

Society
(Ideals—Values—Ideologies—Expectations)

The Public Policy Process	*The Social Policy Process*
• Legislation	• Environmental Forecasting
• Regulation	• Social Policy Formulation
• Enforcement	• Social Policy Implementation 1. Top Management Commitment 2. Staff Functions 3. Operating Departments
• Litigation	• Social Performance Measurement and Reporting

tively (does it have the resources), and decide how many and what kinds of resources should be allocated to the problem. A number of questions need to be answered at this stage (see Figure 20.1), and they are most appropriately answered at the very top levels of the company. This can be done by a social policy committee of the board, a top management committee, or whatever. But some high level group with authority must determine the social policy for the corporation as a whole.

Then comes the stage of implementing the policy. The first element in this stage is top management commitment. The rest of the employees must perceive that top management is seriously committed to the social policy set for the company or implementation is not likely to get off the ground. This stage also involves staff who have expertise in certain areas, such as pollution control or affirmative action, and can provide advice and guidance to both top management and operating management on social issues in their domain. Then comes the need to actively involve the operating departments in implementing the policy in their day-to-day operations—improving safety conditions, hiring more minorities, or whatever is called for. The best way to do this is simply to change the reward system for the operating departments, so that the rewards employees, including operating management, receive do not depend solely on meeting the corporation's basic economic mission but on meeting the company's social policy goals as well.

The last stage of a socially responsible and responsive corporation is instituting some system of social performance measurement and reporting. This system has two basic goals: it provides the means of measuring the performance of individual managers and departments so they can be rewarded appropriately, and it provides the basis for measuring the performance of the company as a whole, which can be reported to society and thus provide accountability. The corporation would be reporting to society how well it had utilized its resources to meet public expectations about the provision of social goods and services.

Serious problems arise at each stage of this structure. Environmental forecasting is not a very well-developed technique for identifying social trends and issues and may never become so, at least in the immediate future. People's tastes and preferences for social goods and services cannot be measured with precision. Certain trends and issues can be identified, but by the time they are major enough to be seen by a scanning process, the value of an anticipatory posture may already have been lost, as the issues have undoubtedly already become politicized. A more scientific approach to identifying people's preferences for social goods and services may not work as well as a political approach.

Judgments must be made about those issues that are identified as being of concern to the corporation. These judgments must be made by the body that sets social policy for the corporation as a whole in the same way judgments are made about product development, plant expansion, and similar economic decisions. These latter decisions, however, are part of the basic economic purpose for which a corporation was created, and are legitimate management decisions. The provision of what are in effect public goods and services, however, is not part of a corporation's basic economic purpose. In most cases, the allocation of resources to provide public goods and services will interfere with the corporation's basic economic mission. What right do

Figure 20.1. Decision-Making Flow Chart

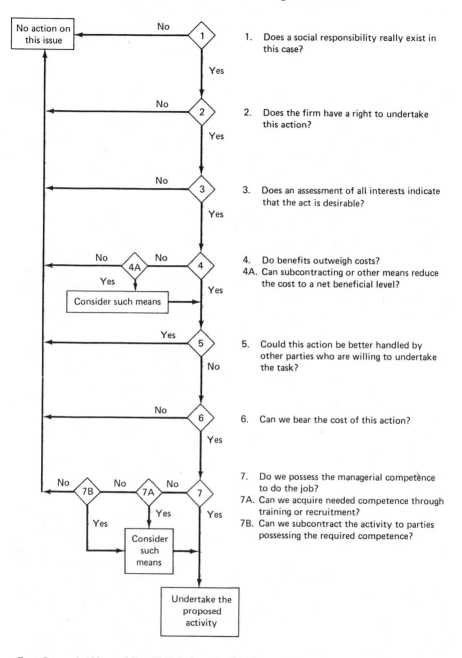

From Ramon J. Aldag and Donald W. Jackson, Jr., "A Managerial Framework for Social Decision Making," p. 34, *MSU Business Topics*, Spring 1975. Reprinted by permission of the publisher, Division of Research, Graduate School of Business Administration, Michigan State University.

managers of private, profit-making corporations have to make these kinds of decisions? From whence comes the legitimacy for managers of private organizations to decide public policy for society as a whole? To whom are they accountable for the use of resources? What criteria outside of their own values can they use to guide them in these decisions? At this stage questions of definition and accountability are most crucial.

At the implementation stage, the problem is one of organizational schizophrenia. How can managers and employees respond to two different reward systems at the same time, especially when they are often in conflict with each other? How are trade-offs going to be determined at the operating levels and a general social policy be translated into specific decisions about plants and equipment or employee hiring and firing? At this level the difficulty becomes most apparent of changing a business organization so that. it can simultaneously perform two different functions and pursue two major sets of goals that are often in conflict.

The problems of social performance measurement and reporting again are formidable. As will be discussed in Chapter 23, there are a variety of methods, both proposed and in use, to measure and report on corporate social performance. There is at present nothing even approaching a commonly agreed upon or generally accepted set of social accounting principles. Business is horrified by the idea of developing any kind of a common index by which to compare the social performance of companies. Attempts in this area are fraught with problems, and despite some years of efforts, little progress has been made.

Some people would argue that these criticisms of a socially responsible and responsive corporation are too severe. Environmental forecasting, it could be argued, may improve to the point where it can be an effective tool for most corporations in anticipating issues. Some degree of legitimacy may be found for management's right to make public policy decisions. Some means may even be worked out to respond to two different reward systems. And progress may be made along the front of social measurement and reporting.

Besides these arguments, it is a fact that corporations have responded to some social problems on their own and have built plants in disadvantaged areas, hired disadvantaged people, started minority purchasing programs, and engaged in other such activities with little or no government involvement. Corporations have been ranked according to their social responsibility efforts and awards given to those judged as having made outstanding efforts in certain social problems.[2]

But the viewpoint that permeates this entire book is very skeptical that anything like a truly socially responsible or socially responsive corporation will ever evolve, that, on its own, can effectively respond to a wide range of public issues so as to avoid government intervention. Corporations are limited in their ability to respond to social problems. The basic reason for this view is simple. Business is an economic institution that was designed to function as part of an economic system. Its ability to respond to public issues

[2]See Milton R. Moskowitz, "Choosing Socially Responsible Stocks," *Business and Society Review*, No. 1 (1972), pp. 71–75; "Industry Rates Itself," *Business and Society Review*, No. 1 (1972), pp. 96–99; "The 1975 Good Guys: 13 Companies Win Awards for Corporate Social Responsibility," *Business and Society Review*, No. 16 (Winter 1975–76), pp. 19–27.

on its own and provide public goods and services is severely limited. Efforts to reform the corporation to make it more responsible or responsive are generally not very successful.

If a firm unilaterally engages in social action that increases its costs and prices, it will place itself at a competitive disadvantage with other firms that do not engage in social action. Such action to solve social problems is not feasible in a competitive system unless all competitors pursue roughly the same policy on these problems. Since collusion among competitors is illegal, the only way such concerted action can occur is when some other institution, such as government, makes all competitors engage in the same activity or pursue the same policy.

> . . . [E]very business . . . is, in effect, "trapped" in the business system that it has helped to create. It is incapable, as an individual unit, of transcending that system. . . . [T]he dream of the socially responsible corporation that, replicated over and over again, can transform our society is illusory. . . . Because their aggregate power is not unified, not truly collective, not organized, they [corporations] have no way, even if they wished, of redirecting that power to meet the most pressing needs of society. . . . Such redirection could only occur through the intermediate agency of government rewriting the rules under which all corporations operate.[3]

The Public Policy Process

There is a very good reason why most public issues have gone the route depicted in the left-hand side of Exhibit 20.1, which shows the basic structure of government's response to the changing ideals, values, ideologies, and expectations of society. This response of government to public issues is inevitable, and no amount of corporate reform along the lines of corporate social responsibility or corporate social responsiveness is going to eliminate government involvement. Like it or not, government is the appropriate body to formalize and formulate public policy for society as a whole.

The process of legislation, regulation, enforcement, and litigation is the process through which most public policy on the corporation has been formulated and implemented. Identification of issues is made by politicians as they assess the needs of society and become aware of the concerns of their constituencies. Bills may be introduced in Congress, and if passed by both the House and Senate and signed by the President, become law. Policy is formulated and priorities established through the political process. Implementation is carried out by the regulatory agencies, as most legislation that affects business involves some new regulatory functions. Additional responsibilities may be given to an existing agency, or perhaps a new agency may be created. Regulation involves some kind of an enforcement mechanism to ensure compliance, and where noncompliance is discovered, litigation with the agency itself and eventually through the regular court system may be the result.

This is the route all significant public issues, such as equal opportunity, pollution control, workplace safety and health, product safety, toxic sub-

---

[3]Neil W. Chamberlain, *The Limits of Corporate Responsibility* (New York: Basic Books, 1973), pp. 4, 6.

stance control, and hazardous waste disposal, have traveled. Public policy measures related to these and other issues have significantly changed the role of business in society and complicated the management task enormously. Yet in the social responsibility and social responsiveness literature the focus is still on corporate reform, stressing obligations or methods by which the corporation can be made more responsive to public concerns through internal changes. Meanwhile, the public policy process continues to churn out more legislation and regulations that shape business behavior, and this process, which is in great need of reform, goes relatively unnoticed.

Problems with the public policy process are many and significant. The links between elected public officials and their constituencies could be improved. To the extent that government is remote from the average citizen, the legislation that is passed by Congress could represent more the values of the legislators themselves or the values of a small number of people who belong to interest groups that can exert political pressure far out of proportion to what their numbers would suggest, rather than the values of the larger body of people the politicians are supposed to be representing.

There are many problems at the regulatory stage, the most serious of which are related to the adverse economic impacts made by regulations that force very costly and inefficient methods of compliance on business. The enforcement stage involves negative incentives—penalties and fines—that have inherent problems. Litigation forces business into an adversary role where any kind of cooperative effort to work out a compromise solution that is best for all parties concerned is well-nigh impossible. Finally, there is no formalized and comprehensive method of measuring progress toward public policy goals and reporting regularly on this progress, or lack thereof, to the society as a whole.

Despite these problems, however, the important point to be made is that this process is a legitimate process for formulating public policy for corporations and for society. The public policy process is sufficiently representative of society as a whole and accountable to society through the election process and other means. Government, then, is the major institutional force in the public policy process because it has a legitimate right to allocate resources for the production of public goods and services and formulate public policy for corporations in response to changing public expectations.

> Society can choose to allocate its resources any way it wants and on the basis of any criteria it deems relevant. If society wants to enhance the quality of air and water, it can choose to allocate resources for the production of these goods and put constraints on business in the form of standards. . . . These nonmarket decisions are made by those who participate in the public policy process and represent their views of what is best for themselves and society as a whole. . . . It is up to the body politic to determine which market outcomes are and are not appropriate. If market outcomes are not to be taken as normative, a form of regulation which requires public participation is the only alternative. The social responsibility of business is not operational and certainly not to be trusted. When business acts contrary to the normal pressures of the marketplace, only public policy can replace the dictates of the market.[4]

[4]Rogene A. Buchholz, "An Alternative to Social Responsibility," pp. 12–16, *MSU Business Topics*, Summer 1977. Reprinted by permission of the publisher, Graduate School of Business Administration, Michigan State University.

The Principle of Public Responsibility

A management philosophy that seeks to incorporate broader responsibilities to society and provide a theoretical foundation for appropriate responses to public policy issues as they arise must recognize the limitations of business to respond to these issues on its own, and the legitimate right of government to formulate public policy on issues that affect the whole or major segments of society. This view represents what many believe is a realistic assessment of business's responsibility to society and prescribes an appropriate role for business to play in the solution of some of our most pressing social problems. That role is one of working with government and other groups to solve these problems out of a sense of public responsibility.

The principle of public responsibility was first enunciated by Lee Preston and James Post in a book called *Private Management and Public Policy.* The two fundamental questions about management's responsibility to society that they attempted to deal with were: (1) "what is the appropriate scope of private management responsibility within society—how far is the managerial unit supposed to go in anticipating and attempting to deal with social needs and problems, and (2) within the defined scope, what are the criteria of appraisal and evaluation?"[5]

The problem management faces, according to Preston and Post, is defining the specific limits and consequences of managerial social involvement in a particular situation and deciding what, if anything, to do about them. As a basis for resolving this problem, Preston and Post suggested the principle of public responsibility. This principle was intended to define the functions of organizational management within the specific context of public policy. It explicitly states that public policy is, along with the market mechanism, the source of guidelines and criteria for management behavior.

Within this principle there are certain primary involvements determined by the specialized functional role of the organization. This specialized role defines the firm's nature and social purpose, and provides the basis for exchange relationships between it and the rest of society. Secondary involvements include all those relationships, activities, and impacts of the organization that are ancillary or consequential to its primary involvement activities.

The principle of public responsibility states that the organization should analyze and evaluate pressures and stimuli coming from public policy in the same way it analyzes and evaluates market experience and opportunity. The public policy process is the means by which society as a whole articulates its goals and objectives, and directs and stimulates individuals and organizations to contribute to and cooperate with them. Appropriate guidelines of behavior are to be found in the larger society, not in the personal vision of managers or in the special interest of groups.

To implement this principle management must scan the environment, develop a set of techniques or procedures that can be used to make and carry out decisions resulting from this new perspective, and also develop techniques for evaluation and control. Scanning requires the organization (1) to

[5]Lee E. Preston and James E. Post, *Private Management and Public Policy* (Englewood Cliffs, N.J.: Prentice-Hall, 1975), p. 4.

identify the extent of its involvement in society, (2) to discover relevant social issues and public policy goals, and (3) to develop ideas for implementation techniques and responses. This leads to cognizance, reporting, participation, and experimentation.

Preston and Post claim that this principle of public responsibility overcomes the defects of social responsibility by defining the scope of management concern in terms of primary and secondary involvement. This principle also recognizes the public policy process as the source of goals and priorities for management activities not mediated by the market.[6]

The philosophy of management that makes most sense in responding to the changing role of business in society is one of public responsibility, a concept that implies business's willingness to become more actively involved in public issues, even those that are not necessarily directly related to the immediate self-interest of the company but that are of major concern to society. Involvement in public issues means the development of a capacity to identify and research public issues, the willingness to debate these issues in the public arena, and the ability to work with other groups in society, particularly government, that have other ideologies and other incentives, to solve these problems.

Some of the most important social problems facing the country are inflation, unemployment, energy, pollution control, poverty, health and safety issues related to both employees and products, hazardous waste disposal, and water shortages. Obviously these problems cannot be managed effectively by any one business corporation alone or even a coalition of businesses, should such coalitions be allowed by the antitrust laws. Nor can these problems be solved by government alone—the deficiencies of government in fighting inflation, adopting realistic regulations, and developing and implementing a comprehensive energy program are all too painfully apparent. What these problems call for is a new kind of business-government relationship—some call it a partnership, others cooperation—that is different from the traditional adversarial relationship that has existed in the country. Energy and unemployment, for instance, are broad issues affecting the whole of society and approaches to these problems have to be worked out as matters of public policy involving business, government, and other institutions as appropriate (see box).

Many business leaders recognize the importance of this principle of public responsibility and are advocating that business managers become more active in the political process and work more closely with government and other groups to help shape public policy. Acceptance of this principle involves acceptance of a public as well as a private role for management. Typical of such attitudes on the part of business leaders are the following quotes.

Executives are realizing that the day is gone when the spot at the top of an organization chart permitted a private life style. A generation or two in the past, you could get by in business by following four rules: stick to business, stay out of trouble, join the right clubs, and don't talk to reporters. Some of us may yearn for that bygone era, but we have to take life as it comes—and today's executive is more often in the midst of the fray. CEO's are now to be found tramping through the corridors in Washington and the state capitals, testifying, talking with elected

[6]*Ibid.* pp. 94–105.

A great many reporters, scholars, and critics of business have assumed and asserted for a long time that business and government enjoy a very close rapport; but our observation has been that, whatever that rapport may or may not have been in the past, business today is extremely suspicious of and hostile toward government. And, as business distrusts government, government distrusts business. In each case, this distrust is based largely on misconceptions regarding the roles and performance of the other party. This is a bad situation because many of the problems that our society will have to face require increased cooperation between government and business; this will be essential if the nation is to solve persistent problems of economic growth and stability, to end high employment and inflation, to reduce the social and international tensions that result from economic inequality and poverty, to check and reverse urban decay, to avert threats to the natural and social environment of an expanding industrial system, to accomplish the rebuilding of a healthy and decent social order in which business institutions, as well as those of government, can regain public respect.

One of the most striking findings of our study, we think, was the distrust that business feels not only toward the government but toward the democratic process itself. This is a latent cause of much that has gone wrong in business's public standing.

Business cannot solve that problem or achieve its own objectives unless it accords to other groups the respect business seeks for itself.

Strikingly, businessmen today seem remarkably pessimistic about the future of the capitalist system. The only group that is even more convinced that we are witnessing the twilight of capitalism is the Marxists. The loss of faith by businessmen in the compatibility of capitalism and democracy could be a self-fulfilling prophecy.

There is obviously no simple formula that business can follow to regain public respect and understanding. What corporate executives need to accept is that they have two major roles to play: one in directing and managing the affairs of their companies, the other in recognizing and responding intelligently to the expectations and needs of the broad society. If they neglect the second role, or despise it, they will get themselves and their organizations into deep trouble and deeper public disrepute, as some have already done.

The resulting extremely adverse public reaction has driven the leaders of business thinking toward acceptance of a new concept of the role of business in society—a concept that is far broader than the earlier ideology which held that the sole aim of the corporation was to produce a profit.

We have called the new creed "the consent doctrine"—the recognition of the public's participation in shaping business policy and business actions. Businessmen must recognize that they play their role, exercise their considerable power, subject to the consent of the public.

But this consent doctrine does not, in my view, imply a merely accommodating or passive role for business. Rather, business should seek to contribute actively, by its own performance, its policy advice, and its cooperation with other groups, to the solution of the grave problems that trouble society today and will affect it tomorrow. Businessmen must learn to look ahead and help government do what the individual corporation cannot do: tackle the broad, long-range problems that lie beyond the reach and grasp of the individual firm. In contributing to the broad social welfare, business will regain respect for itself, and for other participants in the democratic process.

From Leonard Silk, "Business in the Public Forum," *Challenge*, Vol. 19, No. 5 (November–December 1976), p. 55. Quoted with permission.

representatives and administrative aides, pleading cases in the agency offices and occasionally in the White House. Reporters are learning the names of businessmen and finding that many more of them have their doors open.[7]

. . . I want to add my own conviction that business executives must participate personally in the formation of public policy. This is not something we can delegate to our trade associations. We must study the issues, develop constructive positions, and then speak out—in public forums, in Congressional testimony, in personal contacts with our representatives in government. This is an unavoidable responsibility of business leadership today, for companies large and small.[8]

I think we must put behind us the low-profile stance that so many in business have adopted. Too many of us have left the responsibility for government to others. We've had the attitude of "We're too busy with our jobs." I feel that if we want to maintain our jobs and if we want to restore growth and vitality to our businesses, we must participate in the governmental process. We must join in the public policy debate . . . a debate that holds our future in its resolution.[9]

Public policy is too important and too complex to be left up to government alone. Many of the adverse economic consequences of much public policy formulated in the 1960s and 1970s might have been avoided if business had taken public policy more seriously and had been more active in the political process. Business has a great deal of technical and managerial expertise to bring to bear on the solution of public issues. But the approach has to be one of problem solving, not manipulation of government for strictly business interests. This approach presents new challenges to business and requires managers to acquire new knowledge. It requires a basic understanding of business's public responsibility to participate in the public policy process and help solve more directly the nation's economic and social problems.

Fran Steckmest, public affairs consultant for Shell Oil Company, calls an executive who is skilled in the public policy process a "public policy corporate executive." This type of executive deals effectively with the public policy dimension of business as an integral factor in managing the corporation. The public policy corporate executive recognizes that the day of the cloistered executive has passed, and has the knowledge, skills, experience, and attitudes for this new role.[10] Steckmest describes the qualifications that are needed to operate effectively in the public policy arena as follows.

Knowledge: A basic understanding of the U.S. social, economic and political systems, including history, structure, institutions and processes; an understanding of current and emerging social, economic and political issues impacting corporations and society; familiarity with the principles and techniques for public policy analysis; and an understanding of basic attitudes and viewpoints of the leadership of significant institutions and interest groups.

Skill: Ability to apply the foregoing knowledge in planning, day-to-day decision-

[7]Irving S. Shapiro, "The Process: Business and Public Policy," *Harvard Business Review,* Vol. 57, No. 6 (November-December 1979), p. 100.

[8]Reginald Jones, "The Legitimacy of the Business Corporation," General Electric Company, An Executive Speech Reprint, 1977, p. 4.

[9]Robert L. Mitchell, "Reason and Participation: The Road to Better Government-Business Interaction," remarks to the 3rd International Conference of the National Petroleum Refiners Association, San Antonio, Texas, April 3, 1978, p. 11.

[10]F. W. Steckmest, "Career Development of the 'Public Policy Corporate Executive,'" *Public Affairs Review,* 1981, p. 2.

making and particularly in communicating effectively under the varying circumstances required in the public policy process; e.g., person-to-person, small meetings, speeches, legislative testimony, and press, television and radio interviews.

Experience: Participation in the public policy process; e.g., analysis of public policy issues and formulation of corporate positions; explaining public issues and positions by speeches, legislative testimony and TV/radio appearances; and interaction with counterparts in government, the media, academia, unions and public interest groups. Participation in the political process; e.g., activity on behalf of a political party or advocacy group; election campaign work, or service as an elected or appointed official.

Attitude: Personal commitment to sustain and improve the U.S. system of political democracy and capitalist economy. Also, as William S. Sneath, Chairman of the Union Carbide Corporation advises: "Corporate participation in the public policy process requires conduct which engenders credibility and trust; recognition that there is no perfect public policy; and understanding that the process works by balancing interests and the corporate goal must be to strengthen—not dominate—the system."[11]

Underscoring the need for this type of executive with a philosophy of public responsibility, Steckmest goes on to say that CEOs "who do not recognize the social and political role of the corporation or are reluctant to play their role in public affairs . . . forfeit their opportunity to influence or cope more effectively with the business environment. . . . The result . . . is increased isolation of the CEO from public contact, decreased sensitivity to changing public attitudes, and misinterpretation or over-reaction to new issues—too late to change the course of the now-mature issue, but with ample time to inflict page one damage on the corporation's reputation, largely by presenting a corporate image of insensitivity or inflexibility concerning the issue."[12] These words apply not only to the chief executive officer, but to all managers whose work is affected by public policy.

THE CORPORATE CHIEFS' NEW CLASS

By Marshall Loeb

Irving Shapiro, a charter member, calls them the class of the '70s. They are the unique and rather brotherly band who became chief executives of some of America's largest corporations in the past decade, and by many measures they have changed the nation as much as did the clamorous '60s kids. These corporate chiefs are activists in society and politics, for they know that no company is an island; none can prosper for long if the country is unsound.

Now, quite a few leaders of the class of the '70s are about to make their valedictory. "We are all getting close to retirement age," says Shapiro, 63, who in 15 months has to leave the chairmanship of Du Pont, the chemicals colossus. "It will be a challenge for companies to produce the same kind of group in the 1980s."

But what a band they have been. In the inner circle is Shapiro, son of Lithuanian immigrants (Father was a pants presser, Mother a sweatshop gar-

[11]*Ibid,* p. 7. Quoted with permission.
[12]*Ibid.,* pp. 5–6.

ment worker), who got a law degree on loans from the University of Minnesota, and says, "I've always wanted to be sure that I didn't take more from the system than I was putting back." There is Shapiro's friend Reg Jones, a British-born intellectual, who has been similarly motivated to repay the society in which he climbed to become chairman of General Electric. And Citicorp's Walter Wriston, imbued with public commitment by his father, a university president who was also a high Government adviser. And AT&T's former Chairman John deButts, the courtly North Carolinian, who cherishes the Southern tradition of public service. And many more.

Together and separately they lobby U.S. Presidents and Congressmen and city councilors to adopt laws that would promote jobs for deprived minorities and investment for capital-starved companies. They often recruit each other for public-interest projects, major and modest. When Manhattan College, a Catholic institution, needed money recently, its fund-raising load was carried by GM's Thomas Aquinas Murphy, DeButts and Shapiro. A few months earlier the same three men, a neatly balanced ticket, did the same thing for Yeshiva University, a Jewish institution. They and others are prime movers of the Business Roundtable, which has replaced some more regressive groups as the premier public policy arm of corporate America. A few years ago, his peers selected Irv Shapiro to head the Roundtable. When Shapiro, who is a Jew, a Democrat and a lawyer, was chosen in 1974 as chairman of Du Pont, which had been led by Christian, Republican, financial and technical men, it seemed that almost any American could hope to become chief of almost any U.S. company.

While managing a $12.6 billion-a-year U.S. firm, Shapiro appears to spend almost as much time in Washington as in Wilmington, Del. He persuaded business chiefs and the B'nai B'rith to accept a sensible compromise U.S. policy for dealing with the Arab boycott of Israel. He travels the country making speeches laden with proposals to stimulate U.S. technology by giving inventors more patent protection and to improve the judicial system by increasing the number of judges and more closely scrutinizing their performance.

"It is startling how much corporate America has changed," says Shapiro. "In the past, businessmen wore blinders. After hours, they would run to their club, play golf with other businessmen, have a martini—and that was about it. They did not see their role as being concerned with public policy issues. In a world where Government simply took taxes from you and did not interfere with your operations, maybe that idea was sensible. In today's world, it is not. I'm much more interested in what Russell Long thinks than what some businessman thinks. And you can find out from Russell Long very simply what he thinks."

Yet sometimes a small concern nags at Shapiro. "I worry that businessmen may lose perspective and get greedy, pressing for their own self-interest." Then he is reassured when he looks at some newer people who are rising in companies. Says Shapiro: "Most of the new chiefs understand the outside world, and they can deal with policy issues in America and abroad. If I were choosing a chief executive, I would not be overly concerned with his education or specific background. I would ask if he relates to the larger world, or if he knows how to produce widgets but cannot do anything else."

In Shapiro's view, the most important problem facing the new class of business leaders, the class of the '80s, will be to find jobs for unemployed city blacks and Hispanics. Industry simply will have to apply more of its brain power and resources to that American dilemma. "Business and labor and government will have to come together to tutor and train perhaps half a million kids for jobs."

He sees new coalitions forming. Business schools and schools of government will link together because their interests are so close. Government may wisely choose to exploit more of the talents of business people. "We have to have

something like the Manhattan Project. The Government ought to tap eight or
ten very able people and tell them it is their public duty to drop what they are
doing and help carry out a program to make fuels from coal and shale. We
ought to be putting people like Reg Jones and John deButts and Exxon's Cliff
Garvin to work in Washington."

Shapiro has no false hopes that businessmen will be loved. "Except in
wartime, business is never going to be a popular force in this country. Our goal
should be to create an arm's-length but nonadversary relationship between
business and Government. Business is a means to an end. It's not an end in
itself. There is not much point in being a businessman if you're not going to
accomplish something that benefits society."

Questions for Discussion

1. Describe the various elements of the process of social policy-making for corporations. Are there any elements you would add or stress more than the author has?
2. What problems exist with each of these elements or stages? How serious are these
   problems? Do you agree with the author's overall criticism of this process? Why or
   why not?
3. Are there severe limitations on a corporation's ability to be socially responsible or
   responsive? Do these limitations render the concepts of social responsibility and
   responsiveness inadequate to provide a management philosophy that is relevant
   for the rest of the twentieth century and beyond? Should they be abandoned in
   favor of some other philosophy?
4. Why have most public issues gone the public policy process route? Is government
   the legitimate institution to formalize and formulate public policy for society as a
   whole? Why or why not? How else is public policy made in society? Is the impact on
   the corporation of these other policies as significant as the ones adopted by
   government?
5. Where does the public policy process need reform? What priorities would you
   establish for reform efforts? How would you go about promoting these reforms?
6. What is the principle of public responsibility? How does it differ from the concepts
   of social responsibility and responsiveness? What are the implications of public
   responsibility for the role of management in today's world?
7. Discuss the article by Leonard Silk. What changes are advocated in corporate
   structure and behavior? Is there a need for a new relationship between business
   and government? What form should this relationship take?
8. Examine the qualifications Steckmest proposes for the "public business executive." Has your business school education thus far given you any of this knowledge, skills, experience, or attitudes? What changes, if any, would you propose for
   the curriculum at your school to prepare you for this role of a "public business
   executive"?

Suggested Reading

Carroll, Archie B., ed. *Managing Corporate Social Responsibility*. Boston: Little Brown,
   1977.
Chamberlain, Neil W. *The Limits of Corporate Responsibility*. New York: Basic Books,
   1973.

Madden, Carl H. *Clash of Culture: Management in an Age of Changing Values.* Washington, D.C.: National Planning Association, 1972.

Perrow, Charles. *The Radical Attack on Business.* New York: Harcourt Brace Jovanovich, 1972.

Preston, Lee E., and Post, James E. *Private Management and Public Policy.* Englewood Cliffs, N.J.: Prentice-Hall, 1975.

21

Changes in Corporate Structure and Behavior

Like a hall of mirrors in which one's every move is both monitored and mimicked, virtually every major department of the typical corporation in the United States has one or more counterparts in a federal agency that controls or strongly influences its internal decision making. . . . In addition to the more obvious types of corporate responses to government intervention . . . a variety of internal adjustments are taking place. Each major corporate function is undergoing an important transformation: reacting to government actions, trying to anticipate or obviate further government activity, or attempting to alter that external environment.[1]

The changes that public policy has made on the corporate form of organization and its behavior are extensive. The corporation has had to adapt itself to its changing role in society as manifested primarily in the increasing amount of government regulation. The need for a management philosophy to be consistent with the public policy dimension is one thing, but the need to adapt the internal corporate organization and its behavior is quite another. As the environment of business changes, the business organization itself has to change to survive, if for no other reason. Some of the major changes that have taken place will be discussed in this chapter as examples of responses the corporation has made to cope with the impact of public policy.

Changes in Corporate Structure

The first series of changes to be discussed relates to corporate structure. While structure, of course, is not entirely separate from behavior, (structure

[1]Murray L. Weidenbaum, *The Future of Business Regulation: Private Action and Public Demand* (New York: AMACOM, a division of American Management Associations, 1979), pp. 34–35. Quoted with permission.

and behavior are in some sense a function of each other), for purposes of discussion it is useful to consider each of these two aspects separately. The structure of a corporation refers more to its internal organization and the impact public policy has made on this organization.

Public Issues Management. Many corporations have developed or are developing an internal expertise in managing public issues of importance to the company. This expertise is generally referred to as "public issues management." This term does not mean that the company expects to manage a public issue in a society-wide sense. What it does mean is that the company manages its response to a public issue the same way it manages other aspects of the business.

This expertise helps the company manage its way through public issues, coordinates the company's response to public issues, and, in some cases, sees that broader environmental concerns that give rise to public policy issues are incorporated into the strategic plan of the business. This expertise also assists the various functional areas in addressing public issues and attempts to internalize an awareness of the public policy dimension throughout all levels of management. This latter task involves, among other things, providing learning experiences for management on the importance and potential impact public policy can make on the corporation.

The structural changes related to this development of public issues management include a change in the public relations function or the growth of a public affairs department in some corporations. In some cases, the title of public relations has been changed to public affairs; in other cases, public relations is now considered to be a subdivision of public affairs; and in still other companies, public affairs and public relations are entirely separate departments. Some companies have also established community or urban affairs departments.

Obviously, companies have handled this change differently, but the major thrust of these developments is a change in the way business relates to the public. The old emphasis on public relations, which implied relations with the press and was most likely a one-way communication from business to the public, is simply not enough to deal with the new demands being forced on business by government and other groups in the public realm.

Related to this change in public relations or public affairs is the growth of Washington offices, both in numbers of people employed for this function and the influence these offices now wield in the total corporate structure. The Washington office is the "eyes, ears, and mouth" of the corporation in the nation's capital. Its primary function has changed from a concern with winning government contracts to a concern with legislative and regulatory matters that have impact on business. Its roles have become intelligence gathering and issue tracking—to gather information about public issues that are at various stages of development and interpret these issues to management. In this sense, the Washington office acts as sort of an intermediary between the federal government and corporate headquarters. Its job is also, of course, to assist in other aspects of issues management, particularly in the development of strategies to make the company's position known to the proper people in the federal government.

These changes imply that public issues are being taken much more seriously than was evident in the old public relations function. Involved in this structural change is a real concern for doing one's homework on public issues so the organization can effectively participate in the formulation of public policy. The concept of public issues management and the different aspects of this development are discussed thoroughly in the next chapter.

Public Responsibility Committees. Another structural change is the development of public responsibility committees at the board level. The board of directors represents the interests of shareholders and thus must be concerned with the impact of public policy on the corporation and its prospects for success in the marketplace. This change reflects the impact that a broader constituency has been making on the corporate organization. These committees have such responsibilities as the following:

1. Identify the major constituencies—both internal and external—who normally judge the behavior and performance of the corporation; examine what they expect of the corporation's performance socially and environmentally.
2. Recommend specific issues for board and management consideration, and determine their relative priority.
3. Recommend corporate policy to respond to the priority issues.
4. Consider and recommend potential new areas of public policy and potential impacts on the corporation.
5. Examine and report to the full board on corporate attitudes toward the needs and concerns of the major constituencies of the corporation.
6. Recommend where duties and responsibilities lie throughout the company with respect to the priority public policy issues.[2]

Some of the areas that a public responsibility committee concerns itself with include affirmative action, community relations, pollution, product quality and safety, occupational safety and health, charitable contributions, and government relations. The public responsibility committee can devote more time and consideration to these issues than can the full board. The issues can then be discussed thoroughly at the board level along with the more traditional business concerns. The committee is also in a better position to monitor corporate performance in these areas than is the full board of directors. Through its actions, a public responsibility committee can indicate to all employees that top management is dedicated to public responsibility and can help spread this philosophy throughout the organization (see box at top of next page).[3]

The public responsibility committee can serve as a kind of audit committee when composed entirely of outside directors. Executives of the company concerned with affirmative action or pollution can be called before the committee to report on their activities. The committee can then report on these matters to the full board. Some companies have both a public responsibility committee at the board level to identify trends and issues and a management committee to deal with specific responses of the company (see box at bottom of next page).

A study completed by the Center for Research in Business and Social

---

[2]Michael L. Lovdal, Raymond A. Bauer, and Nancy H. Treverton, "Public Responsibility Committees of the Board," *Harvard Business Review*, Vol. 55, No. 3 (May-June 1977), pp. 40–41. Copyright © 1977 by the President and Fellows of Harvard College; all rights reserved.
[3]*Ibid.*, p. 41.

Policy at the University of Texas at Dallas found that in 1979, ninety companies had such committees at the board level, a 95 percent increase over the
forty-six companies that reported such committees in existence in 1977.[4]
The top 200 corporations of the sample on which the study was based
accounted for 60 percent of the public responsibility committees while
constituting only 26.9 percent of the total population. Large corporations
are clearly the leaders in establishing these committees.

Twenty-seven different designations were used as names for these committees. These designations are grouped in Table 21.1 into seven different
classifications. The most popular classifications were the public policy committee or social responsibility committee categories. The public policy committee classification included such titles as public interest, public policy,
public issues, public affairs policy, human resources and public policy, and
public policy and consumer affairs. The social responsibility committee
classification included such titles as public responsibility, social responsibility, and social responsiveness.[5]

[4]S. Prakash Sethi, Bernard J. Cunningham, and Patricia M. Miller, *Corporate Governance: Public
Policy-Social Responsibility Committee of Corporate Board: Growth and Accomplishment* (Dallas: University of Texas Center for Research in Business and Social Policy, 1979), p. 49.
[5]*Ibid.*, p. 8.

overriding mission: to effect changes in the policies and operations of the bank that ensure optimum responsiveness while balancing the diverse needs of the bank's constituencies.

Public Policy Committee

The Public Policy Committee is composed of six outside directors and two inside directors with the Chairman of the Social Policy Committee serving as the secretary. It meets monthly, and its function is to advise management and monitor performance. This involvement of the Board of Directors underscores for employees at all levels the bank's commitment to corporate responsibility, and it provides an objective assessment of performance by independent directors.

Social Policy Committee

The Social Policy Committee is at the heart of the bank's corporate responsibility process. Ten senior bank officers, representing a cross section of line and staff units, sit on the committee. It meets at least once a month, providing the link that transforms issues into policy decisions and ultimately into line management responsibilities. This committee seeks to make those changes in the bank's policies and practices which are necessary to ensure that the bank's operations reflect the values of its core constituencies and the expectations of the public at large.

Social Policy Department

The Social Policy Department's primary function is to provide advocacy for constituency concerns. This unit also provides staff support to both the Social and Public Policy Committees.

The department has three sections, each focusing on a different aspect of the bank. The Retail Section deals with issues affecting consumers, small businesses, and California communities. Members of this group are concerned mainly with the operations of the bank's statewide network of branches. The Wholesale Section addresses issues of international scope and works closely with the bank's World Banking Division. The Administration/Corporate Section handles issues pertaining to the bank's administrative units—for example, Personnel—and works with subsidiaries of BankAmerica Corporation in establishing their own corporate responsibility systems.

All three sections provide management and the board with early identification and analysis of social issues and trends, ascertain their relevance to the bank, and develop recommendations for changes in the way the bank conducts its business. The department also monitors performance in areas where line management responsibility already exists; for example, consumer publications, customer relations, equal employment opportunity, disclosure, shareholder relations, minority purchasing, and corporate giving. Finally, this unit ensures that dialogue is maintained with core constituencies and serves as a clearinghouse for constituency concerns, public expectations, and the social impact of the bank's operations.

From Bank of America Corporate Responsibility Report, *Community and the Bank 1979*, pp. 46–47. Reprinted with permission.

These public responsibility committees recorded the largest increase in size between 1977 and 1979 when compared with other board committees and are the largest board committees in terms of membership (Table 21.2). In 1979, the average public responsibility committee had 4.9 members, with

TABLE 21.1 **Classification of Names Used by Corporations to Designate Their Public Policy-Social Responsibility Committees**

Type of Name	Percent of Corporations Using It
Public Policy Committee	44.5
Social Responsibility Committee	33.3
Contributions Committee—General	8.9
Contributions Committee—Education	1.1
Conflict of Interest/Ethics	6.7
Corporate Conduct/Principles	4.4
Public and Government Relations	1.1
	100.0

Source: S. Prakash Sethi, Bernard J. Cunningham, and Patricia M. Miller, *Corporate Governance: Public Policy-Social Responsibility Committee of Corporate Board: Growth and Accomplishment* (Dallas: University of Texas Center for Research in Business and Social Policy, 1979), p. 7. Reprinted with permission.

TABLE 21.2 **Average Size of Various Board Committees**

Committee	Average Size 1977	1979
Audit Committee	4.0	4.1
Compensation Committee	4.5	4.3
Nominating Committee	4.8	4.3
Public Policy-Social Responsibility Committee	4.3	4.9

Source: S. Prakash Sethi, Bernard J. Cunningham, and Patricia M. Miller, *Corporate Governance: Public Policy-Social Responsibility Committee of Corporate Board: Growth and Accomplishment* (Dallas: University of Texas Center for Research in Business and Social Policy, 1979), p. 11. Reprinted with permission.

90 percent of the companies having committee sizes between three and seven members.[6] Outside directors tended to constitute the largest proportion of the membership of these committees, with the most popular backgrounds of these outsiders being that of industrialist (32.4 percent) and academician (14.4 percent).[7]

Specialist Functions. Another structural change is the growth of specialist functions within corporate organizations. These functions have been developed because of the need to comply with government regulations on such areas as the physical environment, safety and health, pensions, and affirmative action—areas where there are now people other than lawyers who know the regulations, whose job it is to see that the company is in compliance, and who handle the information requirements that regulations involve. In some cases, for example, corporations have established a new vice-presidential position of environmental affairs, often linked with health

[6]*Ibid.,* p. 10.
[7]*Ibid.,* p. 50.

and safety, which implies a rather sizable staff that concerns itself with these matters. One could look at this development as the growth of counterpart or shadow groups within corporations that mirror the regulatory agencies themselves.

Interlake Inc., for example, a producer of steel and powdered metals in Oak Brook, Illinois, reports that its environmental staff has grown to 40 people. A vice-president of the company spends about 95 percent of his time on environmental matters and states that his advice is sought on all company activities that affect the environment. *Business Week* states that this case is not unusual. "Increasingly, corporations are upgrading the status and responsibilities of their environmental managers. Their staffs and budgets are being enlarged, and many are gaining more clout with top management."[8]

These environmental experts have the responsibility of studying the rules issued by the Environmental Protection Agency and determining what a company must do to be in compliance. They point out where new projects, for example, will violate environmental laws, which could result in construction delays or complete shut-down of the project. Advice from environmental experts has helped other companies save money by redesigning products or manufacturing processes to be less polluting.[9]

The same kind of response has been made in the health and safety area. Figure 21.1 depicts a typical worker protection system in the chemical industry. The system includes worker and area monitoring for hazardous levels of dangerous substances and chemical analysis and toxicology studies related to these substances that, along with medical checkups of the workers themselves, are analyzed by a computer, which then form the basis of process design and safety training. The successful operation of such a system requires many safety and health workers. The number of industrial hygienists in the chemical industry, for example, has tripled in the last ten years. But they are only part of an interdisciplinary approach to worker safety. and health. The typical team consists of a variety of experts including industrial hygienists, physicians, toxicologists, and engineers.[10]

The same phenomenon has occurred in other areas of government regulation, such as equal opportunity and consumer products. Groups of experts make sure that the company is in compliance with equal opportunity laws and develop affirmative action plans if the company is a government contractor. Consumer affairs offices have been developed to handle consumer complaints and determine that the company is in compliance with food safety regulations. These specialist functions employ many highly paid people and have significant impact on corporate decision-making.

Changes in Corporate Behavior

The changes in corporate behavior that have resulted from the impact of public policy are as significant as those in corporate structure. These behavioral changes refer to changes in the roles or activities of specific people

8"The New Corporate Environmentalists," *Business Week*, May 28, 1979, p. 154.

9*Ibid.*, pp. 154–155.

10"Protecting Chemical Workers," *Time*, April 28, 1980, pp. 82–83.

Figure 21.1. Worker Safety Protection System

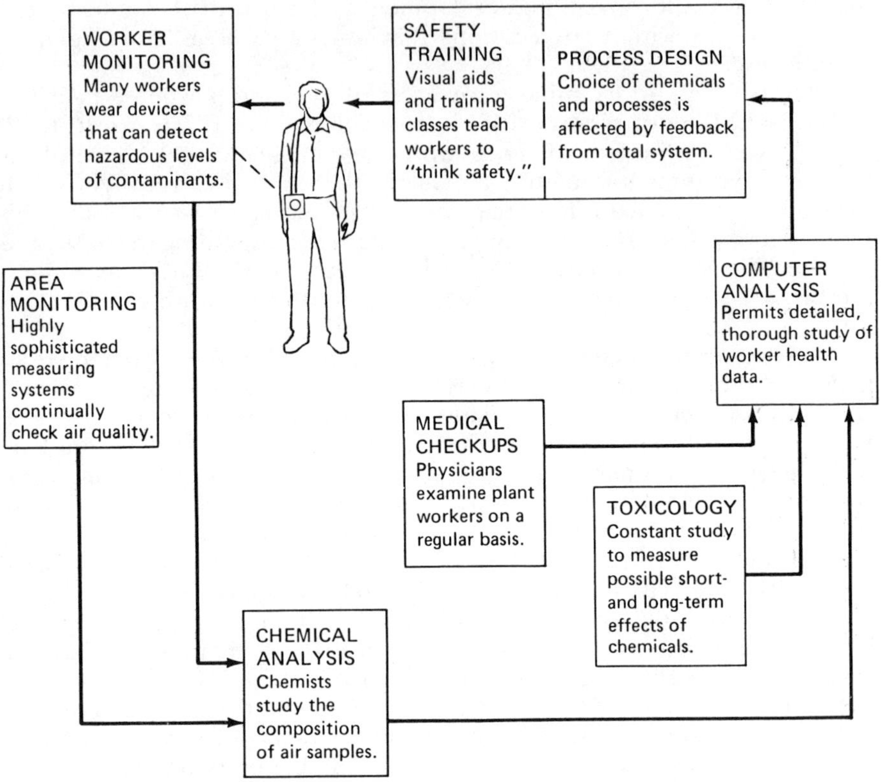

From "Protecting Chemical Workers," *Time*, April 28, 1980, p. 83. Reprinted with permission of the Chemical Manufacturers Association.

in the organization or changes in the activities of the entire organization. Many such changes could be mentioned here, but only four major ones will be discussed, because of their particular significance.

Top Management Involvement. There is no doubt that public policy concerns have penetrated into the ranks of top management. This penetration has resulted in top management's changed attitudes and behavior regarding the importance of the public policy dimension. The first chapter highlighted the amount of time the top management of Olin Corporation was spending on the public policy issues confronting that corporation. The CEOs of other companies have been spending a great deal of time relating to constituent groups normally considered external to the company, doing things like testifying before Congress, speaking out on public issues, and talking with public interest group leaders. Many top executives now realize that the success of their business may be tied up with their ability to deal successfully with these external constituencies, particularly the government. Business cannot be run in a vacuum anymore.

A Conference Board survey of 185 CEOs, published in 1976, showed that

103 of these executives were spending at least one-fourth of their time dealing with external matters and an additional 72 as much as half of their time (Table 21.3). Even more significant was the fact that 92 percent of these CEOs said they were spending more time on external relations than they were three to five years previous to the study (Table 21.4). The author's own survey, completed in 1979, showed that the amount of time the CEOs spent on external matters ranged from 20 to 75 percent, with an average of 40 percent. The most frequently mentioned figure (mode) was 50 percent.[11] These figures show the importance of public policy and external constituencies to top management.

The roles the CEO plays, according to the Conference Board study, include (1) the personification of the company, (2) policy-maker, and (3)

TABLE 21.3 **How Much of the Chief Executive's Time Is Spent on External Relations?**

Percent of Time	Number of CEO's
0 percent	0
1-25 percent	103
26-50 percent	72
51-75 percent	6
76-100 percent	0
Total	181*

*The total does not add up to the 185 chief executives polled. Two did not answer this question; one said the percent varies according to the occasion; one is too new in the job to estimate.

Source: Phyllis S. McGrath, *Managing Corporate External Relations: Changing Perspectives and Responses* (New York: The Conference Board, 1976), p. 49. Reprinted with permission.

TABLE 21.4 **Is the Chief Executive Spending More Time on External Relations Now Than Three to Five Years Ago?**

	Number	Percent
More time	171	92%
Less time	2	1%
About the same	12	6%

Source: Phyllis S. McGrath, *Managing Corporate External Relations: Changing Perspectives and Responses* (New York: The Conference Board, 1976), p. 49. Reprinted with permission.

[11]Rogene A. Buchholz, *Business Environment/Public Policy: Corporate Executive Viewpoints and Educational Implications* (St. Louis, Mo.: Washington University Center for the Study of American Business, 1980), p. 17.

everything to a limited degree. The chief executive officers see themselves as the principal external representatives of the company; their actions and words must at all times reflect the policies of the company. They must therefore speak before the largest and most important groups and handle the *key* contacts with all the various publics (top government officials, major stockholders, and so on).[12]

As policy-makers, the CEOs either initiate corporate policy on important public issues or provide the "broad thematic guidance" to policy and make the major decisions on critical public issues. The CEOs are also involved in everything else related to public policy, along with the expertise the company may have in public issues management. The CEO initiates policy, endorses external programs, sets the personal tone, and makes major public statements. The staff handles the normal day-to-day activities that can be accomplished under established policy and philosophy.[13]

The various publics to which the CEO relates are shown in Table 21.5, along with frequency of involvement. Relations with government heads the list, which includes presenting company statements at congressional committee hearings and before regulatory agencies. Investor relations includes making presentations to major meetings of analyst societies as well as playing the leading part in the annual stockholder meeting. Membership on boards of trustees of colleges and universities and meeting with public interest group leaders are typical activities in the third category. Relations with the media is a very important role that CEOs are taking more and more seriously. Participation in associations like the Business Roundtable is a very important activity for many CEOs, given the impact such organizations can

TABLE 21.5 **The Role of the Chief Executive with the External Publics**

Public	Number of Times Cited by 185 Chief Executives*
Government relations	124
Investor relations	74
Relations with special interest groups (consumers, customers, minorities, etc.)	52
Media relations	25
Business and professional associations membership	21
Community and civic affairs	20

*Figures are not totaled because many chief executives mentioned more than one role.

Source: Phyllis S. McGrath, *Managing Corporate External Relations: Changing Perspectives and Responses* (New York: The Conference Board, 1976), p. 51. Reprinted with permission.

---

[12]Phyllis S. McGrath, *Managing Corporate External Relations: Changing Perspectives and Responses* (New York: The Conference Board, 1976), p. 50.
[13]*Ibid.*

have on public policy. Finally, community involvement can include supporting charitable causes, commitment to youth projects, and involvement with
other aspects of community life.[14]

The CEO is involved with many more aspects of the external environment
than just the traditional ones of shareholders and customers. This amounts to
a major behavioral change of the top management of a corporation. Many
CEOs have become quite sophisticated in their understanding of the external environment, and through experience and hard work have managed to
acquire many of the skills and attitudes necessary for handling external
relations effectively. When supported by a well-organized public issues
management staff that can spend time researching public issues and thinking through company responses, the CEOs' effectiveness in the public policy
arena can be greatly enhanced.

Personal Liability of Management. Another effect that public policy has
had on top management is the impact of new thinking about accountability
on the shield that traditionally protects managers from individual accountability for corporate acts of lawlessness and negligence. The risks executives
face under federal law alone have increased dramatically because of public
policy measures. Penalties for violations of antitrust laws were recently
increased (see Chapter 11). The Foreign Corrupt Practices Act carries
with it stiff fines for foreign payments (see Chapter 6). Add to that the
penalties associated with the newer forms of social regulation, the enforcement powers of states, and the fact that many of the new laws allow private
companies and individuals to file suits to collect damages, and it can readily
be seen that the potential for involvement in litigation is enormous (see
Exhibit 21.1).

The traditional view of top management accountability was to shield
executives from unlawful acts of subordinates. Only when they were directly
involved in wrongdoing was there a possibility of incarceration. Beginning in
the late 1970s, however, Congress, state legislators, regulatory agencies, and
the courts began to insist that top executives accept personal responsibility
for the actions of every individual within the organization. According to S.
Prakash Sethi, this new view of liability covers health, safety, and environmental violations involving general public welfare about which the
executive may have no personal knowledge. As evidence of this trend, Sethi
cites the following examples.

- The President of a Philadelphia-based supermarket chain, Acme Markets Inc.,
  was convicted in 1973 of violating the Federal Food and Drug Act and fined
  $250 after inspectors found evidence of rat infestation at a warehouse in
  Baltimore. The U.S. Supreme Court upheld his conviction in 1975. (*United States
  v. John R. Park*, 421 U.S. 658, 1975)

- Four managers of American Chicle and an executive of its parent company,
  Warner-Lambert, were charged with manslaughter and criminally negligent
  homicide after six workers were killed and 55 others injured in an explosion and
  fire at a Long Island City chewing gum plant in 1976. A New York State judge
  dismissed the case earlier this year, but the state intends to appeal.

- The manager of an H.J. Heinz Co. plant in Tracy, California, received a

[14]*Ibid.*, pp. 51–52.

EXHIBIT 21.1

The Risk Executives Face Under Federal Law

Agency	Year enforcement began	Complaint may name individual	Maximum individual penalty	Maximum corporate penalty	Private suit allowed under applicable statute
Internal Revenue Service	1862	Yes	$5,000, three years, or both	$10,000, 50% assessment, prosecution costs	No
Antitrust Div. (Justice Dept.)	1890	Yes	$100,000, three years, or both	$1 million, injunction, divestiture	Yes
Food & Drug Administration	1907	Yes	$1,000, one year, or both for first offense; $10,000, three years, or both thereafter	$1,000 for first offense; $10,000 thereafter; seizure of condemned products	No
Federal Trade Commission	1914	Yes	Restitution, injunction	Restitution, injunction, divestiture, $10,000 per day for violation of rules, orders	No
Securities & Exchange Commission	1934	Yes	$10,000, two years, or both	$10,000, injunction	Yes
Equal Employment Opportunity Commission	1965	No		Injunction, back pay award, reinstatement	Yes
Office of Federal Contract Compliance	1965	No		Suspension, cancellation of contract	Yes
Environmental Protection Agency	1970	Yes	$25,000 per day, one year, or both for first offense; $50,000 per day, two years, or both thereafter	$25,000 per day, first offense; $50,000 per day thereafter; injunction	Yes
Occupational Safety & Health Administration	1970	No*	$10,000, six months, or both	$10,000	No
Consumer Product Safety Commission	1972	Yes	$50,000, one year, or both	$500,000	Yes
Office of Employee Benefits Security (Labor Dept.)	1975	Yes	$10,000, one year, or both; barring from future employment with plan; reimbursement	$100,000, reimbursement	Yes

*Except sole proprietorship

Date: BW

From "The Law Closes in on Managers," *Business Week*, May 10, 1976, p. 113. Reprinted with permission.

six-month suspended sentence and probation after being cited by California Food and Drug authorities for unsanitary working conditions in his plant.

• A Minneapolis municipal judge ordered Illinois-based Lloyd A. Fry Roffling Co. to select one of its executives to serve a 30-day jail term for the plant's violations of city air pollution standards. The sentence was rescinded because of a legal technicality.[15]

These and other examples lead Sethi to conclude that courts are rejecting the traditional view of executive liability and placing more and more blame at the top. "The new presumption is that a vigilant executive will make certain that subordinates are staying within the law. If those subordinates fail, it is proof that the executive was not properly vigilant. Thus, the executive's criminal liability accrues solely from the fact that he holds a responsible position in the corporation."[16]

The executives' favored status with respect to criminal penalties is thus changing. Tighter controls must be developed, as in the Olin case mentioned in the first chapter, to ensure compliance with government regulations. Managers must be aware of the laws that apply to corporate behavior and must also be sure their subordinates will not unwittingly get them in trouble. This litigious potential demands more attention from top management and could result in the following effects on society and the economy.

> An indiscriminate use of harsh penalties could, for instance, cause considerable damage to the social fabric by aggravating conflict between business and government. It also could adversely affect economic well-being by retarding corporate performance and economic growth. Increased personal liability may make executives more cautious about introducing new products and services into the marketplace. Indeed, there is some evidence already that increased regulatory requirements and the rapid increase in the volume of damage suits filed against corporations have led marketers to withhold new products.[17]

The federal criminal code is currently being rewritten, and one provision being considered of interest to management is the creation of a new kind of federal felony called "reckless endangerment." Under this concept, a company or executive who violates federal health or safety regulations so seriously that "he places another person in danger of imminent death or serious bodily injury" could be prosecuted. This provision would apply to such laws as the Federal Mine Safety and Health Act, the Food, Drug, and Cosmetics Act, and the Occupational Safety and Health Act. Under a "reckless endangerment" prosecution, penalties would be much more severe than just being found in violation of the act itself.[18]

Management Training Programs. All levels of management must be aware of the public policy dimensions of the corporate functions for which they have responsibility. The front office must be replaced as the only place where public policy issues are seriously considered. The public policy dimension must somehow be diffused throughout the organization and be-

---

[15]S. Prakash Sethi, "Who Me?: Jail as an Occupational Hazard," *The Wharton Magazine*, Vol. 2, No. 4 (Summer 1978), pp. 19–20.

[16]*Ibid.*, p. 22.

[17]*Ibid.*, p. 26.

[18]"A Threat to Crime-Code Reform," *Business Week*, January 28, 1980, pp. 106, 108.

come a part of every manager's modus operandi. Perhaps the reason top management has to spend so much time on public policy matters and is being held more accountable for subordinates' actions is because concern for these matters has not been widely diffused throughout the organization and has not become a routine and accepted part of business planning and operation. Companies' educational programs have increasingly included a public policy content to educate managers in how to handle external relations more effectively. These educational efforts include the following.

- Internal management development programs that have environmental concerns as part of the curriculum.
- Company-developed and -operated continuing education programs in Washington, D.C., to teach management employees how government functions.
- Company publications or internal management monographs devoted in part or in whole to public issues of concern to the company.
- Educational programs dealing with legislative issues of concern to the company, designed to stimulate grass-roots political activity.
- Attendance at outside institutes or university seminars and conferences dealing with environmental or public policy matters.
- Participation in advanced management programs at colleges and universities where public policy material constitutes at least part of the content.
- Attendance at programs and seminars in Washington, D.C., to learn about government.
- Management retreats and seminars, some of which are devoted to environmental issues where many outside speakers are invited.
- Participation in professional societies or industry and trade associations.
- Participation in the President's Interchange Program—an exchange of executives between business and government.
- Involving employees and managers in creating social programs or in developing social policy for the company.
- Service by employees on a foundation advisory committee helping to make decisions about charitable contributions.
- Regular management meetings at which public issues are discussed— these meetings become something of an educational process, particularly for new managers.
- Faculty forums where university faculty are invited to discuss public issues with younger managers for a two- or three-day period.

The variety of these efforts is impressive and provides further evidence of the impact public policy is making on business. There seems to be a good deal of this educational activity going on at present and more such activities are planned for the future. Further efforts of this kind are needed to make external relations a part of routine business matters and decision-making. Thorough acquaintance with the environment in which business functions and public policy issues of concern to the company are a vital part of a manager's education and development.[19]

The Paperwork Impact. The cost of compliance with federal government regulations is a matter of increasing concern to business and industry. A highly visible aspect of the cost of compliance is the paperwork that regulation involves. The Federal Paperwork Commission, which was formed to study the paperwork cost for society as a whole, estimated that the paperwork costs imposed on private industry alone are approximately $25 to $32 billion per year. The ten thousand largest firms are estimated to have spent between $10 and $12 billion on paperwork, or an average of more than $1 million each,[20] and to have filled out more than 10 billion sheets of paper a year.[21]

The amount of paperwork is, of course, directly related to the degree of government involvement in the economy. Prior to 1930, the government imposed minimal paperwork burdens on business organizations. During the New Deal period and World War II, government intervention in the economy increased because of the need to finance the war effort and regulate the economy with price controls and rationing. Along with this increase in government intervention went an increase in paperwork. This increase continued with the advent of social regulation, jumping from $1.2 billion in 1950 to $30 billion in 1975.[22]

WHAT THE REGULATORS WANT. As the federal government establishes new agencies and programs, its requests for information from business and industry increase in number and in kind. These requests for information can be categorized according to the type of information they seek.

Statistical Information. Most of this information is requested by the Bureau of the Census, but the International Trade Commission, the Bureau of Labor Statistics, and the Bureau of Economic Analysis might also be involved. A typical report of this type is the Annual Survey of Manufacturers, a yearly summary of plant operations filed with the Bureau of the Census.

Financial Information. This type of information is requested primarily by the Federal Trade Commission and the Securities and Exchange Commission. The new Line of Business Report, which was granted court approval despite a challenge by more than 200 companies, requires that specific financial data about a company's lines of business be reported. The FTC will use this information to determine whether some lines of business are anti-competitive. The SEC, among others, requires the Annual Report General Form, better known as the 10K.

Personnel and Benefits. Information about salaried and hourly pension plans now has to be supplied to the government because of the Employee Retirement Income Security Act. Often affirmative action plans have to be

[19]Buchholz, *Corporate Executive Viewpoints*, pp. 23–25.

[20]U.S. Commission on Federal Paperwork, *Final Summary Report* (Washington, D.C., 1977), p. 5.

[21]Testimony of Thomas J. McIntyre, cochairman, Commission on Federal Paperwork, before Senate Committee on Government Operations, May 3, 1976.

[22]National Archives and Records Service, General Services Administration, as reported in U.S. Commission on Federal Paperwork, "Study of Federal Paperwork Impact on Small and Large Businesses" (an internal draft prepared by the staff of the Commission of Federal Paperwork), July 1977, p. 10.

prepared and filed by companies having government contracts above a certain amount. Both types of information are requested by the Department of Labor. Annual statistics on the employment of minorities and women in various occupational categories are requested by the Equal Employment Opportunity Commission.

Environmental Information. What information is required will vary, of course, according to the industry. Most commonly, information about air pollution, water pollution, waste disposal, and drinking water usage will be required. But if the company manufactures chemicals that government agencies consider to be toxic, it will eventually be required to report on an ongoing basis detailed scientific data for all new chemicals that are developed. Agricultural chemicals are further regulated by the Federal Insecticide, Fungicide, and Rodenticide Act of 1972, which deals with the use, testing, and sale of pesticides. Numerous reports have to be filed for each product of this type the company makes. These include requests for a label, experimental use permits, requests for new uses of an old chemical, and reports pertaining to plant shipments.

Safety and Health Information. Information about occupational injuries and illnesses is required by the Occupational Safety and Health Administration. While no forms have to be filed on a periodic basis, records on the safety and health of the workforce must be maintained at each plant or workplace of a company.

Energy Information. More and more information about energy usage is being required by the new Department of Energy. Companies must disclose domestic natural gas reserves and domestic crude oil purchases, make energy conservation reports, and the like.

THE COSTS OF PAPERWORK. Complying with these requests costs the company and the economy as a whole. Not all the costs are immediately obvious, and some of them, such as direct reporting costs, are astonishingly high.

Direct Reporting Costs. This category includes the cost of employee time devoted to filling out reports, computer expense, the hiring of consultants, lawyers, accountants, or other professionals to prepare or review reports, and overhead costs including secretarial support, postage, rent, heat, light, supplies, and the like. Most of these costs are variable and depend on the frequency with which the report has to be completed and sent to a federal agency. They are also incremental.

Even though the information the government wants may already exist on some company report, numbers cannot simply be copied onto the federal forms. Information from many different company reports may have to be gathered to completely fill out a single federal form. Then, too, the information may have to be aggregated or disaggregated. Finally, there may be some necessity for interpreting exactly what information is needed.

Start-Up Costs. Start-up costs begin with determining exactly what information is required by a federal agency. The explanation accompanying the information request may be vague and require some discussion, interpretation, or even travel to government offices.

The information requested may not be readily available on existing reports or computer files if it is different from the information the company normally requires for its own operations. A new system may have to be designed and installed to supply the information on an ongoing basis. People may have to be trained to fill out the forms and supply the right information.

Compliance with the new Toxic Substances Control Act provides a current example of a start-up cost. The act requires the EPA to compile and publish an inventory of chemical substances manufactured, imported, or processed in the United States for commercial purposes. Any substance not on this list will then be considered a new chemical subject to premanufacture notification requirements. This inventory will be compiled from inventories that manufacturers, importers, processors, or users of chemical substances are required to prepare and submit to the agency.

This inventory reporting is entirely a start-up cost and can be expensive to a company since it involves many professional people, such as chemists. A large chemical company spent $598,000 in 1977–1978 to provide its inventory to the EPA.[23]

Avoidance Costs. Avoidance costs are expenses incurred in attempting to avoid disclosing information to the federal government. These could include the costs of lobbying efforts to support or oppose legislation introduced in Congress, attempts to change the ruling of an agency to avoid having to disclose certain types of information, legal counsel on some disclosure requirement, research into the implications and feasibility of an information request, or advertising and public relations involved in influencing public opinion. These avoidance costs are most often incurred when new areas of regulation or new reports are being considered. The legal expenses incurred in challenging the Line of Business Report and the Corporate Patterns Report mounted by over 200 corporations are good examples of avoidance costs.

TABLE 21.6 **Annual Paperwork Cost by Type of Information for a Large Corporation**

Type of Report	Employee Hours	Annual Cost	Number of Reports	Cost per Report*	Percent of Total
Statistical	3,309	$ 99,270	59	$ 1,682	2.7%
Financial	4,422	136,960	18	7,609	3.8%
Personnel and Benefits	5,269	158,070	13	12,159	4.4%
Environmental	36,800	1,104,000	15	73,600	30.9%
Safety and Health	18,800	564,000	—	—	15.7%
Energy	11,492	344,760	40	8,619	9.6%
Agricultural Chemicals	37,600	1,128,000	—	—	31.4%
Miscellaneous	1,811	54,330	7	7,761	1.5%
Totals	119,503	$3,589,390	152	$111,430	100.0%

*This cost is determined per individual report, no matter how often it is filed.

Source: Rogene A. Buchholz, "Corporate Cost for Compliance with Government Regulation of Information," *Government Regulation of Accounting and Information.* A. Rashad Abdel-khalik, ed. (Gainesville, Fla.: University Presses of Florida, 1980), p. 34. Reprinted with permission.

[23]Reported in Rogene A. Buchholz, "Corporate Cost for Compliance with Government Regulation of Information," *Government Regulation of Accounting and Information,* A. Rashad Abdel-khalik, ed. (Gainesville, Fla.: University Presses of Florida, 1980).

TABLE 21.7 **Annual Cost of Reports Filed with Federal Government Agencies**

	Cost	Percent of Total
Department of Agriculture	$ 720	—
Department of Commerce		
Bureau of the Census	47,250	1.3%
Bureau of Economic Analysis	9,960	0.3
Office of Export Administration	1,140	—
Department of the Interior		
Bureau of Mines	5,040	0.2
Geological Survey	30,960	0.9
Other	1,320	—
Department of Labor		
Bureau of Labor Statistics	12,270	0.4
Occupational Safety and Health Administration*	564,000	15.7
Other	132,420	3.7
Department of Energy	315,120	8.8
Department of the Treasury		
Bureau of Alcohol, Tobacco and Firearms	42,180	1.2
Federal Reserve Bank	1,410	—
Internal Revenue Service	17,100	0.5
Other	1,200	—
Cost Accounting Standards Board	750	—
Environmental Protection Agency	2,232,000	62.2
Equal Employment Opportunity Commission	25,650	0.7
Federal Trade Commission	44,050	1.2
General Services Administration	450	—
International Trade Commission	20,250	0.6
Renegotiation Board	11,700	0.3
Securities and Exchange Commission	72,450	2.0%
Totals	$3,589,390	100.0%

*OSHA complies with government regulations by maintaining records rather than by filing reports. The cost of maintaining these records appears here.

Source: Rogene A. Buchholz, "Corporate Cost for Compliance with Government Regulation of Information," *Government Regulation of Accounting and Information,* A. Rashad Abdel-khalik, ed. (Gainesville, Fla.: University Presses of Florida, 1980), p. 35. Reprinted with permission.

Legal Exposure. As more and more information is requested by the federal government, the legal risk increases. Many of the forms filed with government agencies have to be signed by responsible corporate officials who are certifying the accuracy of the information. Honest mistakes or irresponsibility may involve the official and the corporation in litigation, the costs of which may be enormous. Such legal exposure is likely when information requirements are ambiguous or when subjective estimates are required.

Secondary Costs. These costs include such factors as the loss of productivity that may result from paperwork requirements, the increased construction costs resulting from inflation while the paperwork is completed on a new project, the investment disincentive that is involved in disclosing proprietary information on a new product to a government agency where it may be leaked to the company's competitors, and the negative effects on innovation that delays caused by paperwork might bring about. These costs, while extremely difficult to measure and quantify, may be the most serious of all and may be many times the total of all the other costs taken together.

COMPANY EXAMPLE. The author recently completed a detailed study of the direct reporting costs incurred during the 1977 calendar year by a large chemical company headquartered in the United States. A summary of these costs, broken down by type of report, is shown in Table 21.6. Table 21.7 shows how much of the total cost went to satisfy the requirements of each government agency involved.

The total time required by this company to fill out federal forms came to 119,503 employee hours. If each employee works 1,880 hours per year, this total represents the equivalent of 64 full-time employees involved in fulfilling information requests from the federal government.

The total cost of approximately $3.5 million represented .07 percent of sales for that company in 1977, and 1 percent of profits—a cost of $45 per employee. If each of the top 200 companies spends $3.5 million, the cost of compliance is $700 million. And this $3.5 million figure includes only the direct reporting costs incurred in complying with regulation by the federal government. The paperwork cost imposed by state and local governments was beyond the scope of this study.

The great majority of the direct reporting cost is in the new areas of regulation: safety and health, energy, equal opportunity, pension programs, and the environment. Table 21.8 shows that 92 percent of the total direct reporting cost is attributable to these areas. The costs of statistical and financial reporting are not a significant percentage of the total.

TABLE 21.8 **Percentage of Direct Reporting Cost Attributable to New Areas of Regulation***

Safety and Health	15.7%
Energy	9.6
Equal Opportunity	2.0
Pensions	2.4
Environmental	62.3
	92.0%

*Statistical and financial reporting account for the remaining 8 percent.

Source: Rogene A. Buchholz, "Reducing the Cost of Paperwork," Business Horizons, Vol. 23, No. 1 (February 1980), p. 87. Reprinted with permission.

It is also clear that a tremendous amount of money is being spent to clean up the environment and control environmental problems. Fully 62.3 percent of the total paperwork cost for the company studied was attributable to information required by environmental regulations.

Questions for Discussion

1. What is public issues management? Is there a better term that could be used to describe this concept? What corporate functions does it include?
2. Describe the responsibilities of a public responsibility committee of the board. Do you believe this kind of committee is necessary for a business organization in today's environment? Why or why not?
3. What are shadow counterparts of the regulatory agencies? What functions do they perform in the corporation? How do they affect decision-making? Give some specific examples.
4. Why does top management spend so much time dealing with external matters? Is this inevitable, given the current environment of business? Could more of the CEOs' responsibility in this regard be diffused throughout the organization?
5. Describe the potential legal risk that executives face today. What changes have taken place with respect to the accountability of executives? What are some reasons for these changes?
6. Is the trend toward more executive liability for corporate wrongdoing likely to continue? How does this make you feel about being a manager? What impact is this trend likely to have on business and the economy?
7. How can management training programs help diffuse a public policy dimension throughout the organization? Of all those efforts mentioned, which do you believe are likely to be most effective? Which would you recommend for your company?
8. Why has the paperwork burden on corporations increased? What types of information have to be supplied to the federal government? What are the costs of this paperwork?
9. Where has paperwork made the greatest impact on the corporation? Is all this paperwork necessary to make public policy decisions? What can be done to bring it under control?
10. Stepping back and looking at the whole picture, how would you describe the impact public policy has made on the corporation? Is it significant? Nothing to worry about? Insignificant? What further impact, if any, can you foresee in the future?

Suggested Reading

Brown, James K. *The Business of Issues: Coping with the Company's Environments.* New York: The Conference Board, 1979.

Buchholz, Rogene A. *Business Environment/Public Policy: Corporate Executive Viewpoints and Educational Implications.* St. Louis, Mo.: Washington University Center for the Study of American Business, 1980.

Goldshmid, Harvey J., ed. *Business Disclosure: Government's Need to Know.* New York: McGraw-Hill, 1979.

McGrath, Phyllis. *Managing Corporate External Relations: Changing Perspectives and Responses.* New York: The Conference Board, 1976.

———. *Redefining Corporate-Federal Relations.* New York: The Conference Board, 1979.

Weidenbaum, Murray L. *Business, Government, and the Public.* Englewood Cliffs, N.J.: Prentice-Hall, 1977.

22

Public Issues Management

Issue management is a program which a company uses to increase its knowledge of the public policy process and enhance the sophistication and effectiveness of its involvement in that process.[1]

The concept of public issues management grows out of the public responsibility of a corporation. The term implies that corporations have a responsibility to become involved with public issues and develop policies on these issues comparable to the way policy is developed on traditional business concerns. The need to take public issues seriously becomes more apparent as public policy makes more significant impacts on corporate structure and behavior.

Public issues management does not mean, as stated in the previous chapter, that corporations are going to manipulate public policy or manage a public issue in regard to society as a whole. It simply refers to the process by which a company's response to a public issue is managed. The term focuses on the management of responses to public issues and recognizes that a corporation has a responsibility to help formulate public policy that will ✓ affect it as well as other segments of the business community and the society.

The overall response corporations make to public issues can take one of four major forms (Exhibit 22.1). A reactive response fights every public issue that affects the corporation and opposes any change in corporate structure or behavior that public policy would make, much as business did in the late 1960s with consumer legislation. No attempt is made to anticipate public issues or develop a constructive response.

---

[1]*The Fundamentals of Issue Management* (Washington, D.C.: Public Affairs Council, 1978), p. 1. Quoted with permission.

EXHIBIT 22.1

Corporate Responses to Public Issues

Reactive	Accommodative	Proactive	Interactive
Fighting Change	Adapting to Change	Influencing Change	Adjusting to Change

An accommodative response is to simply adapt to the changes made by public policy as best as possible and go about one's business. There is no attempt to fight or influence change in any manner. Legislation and regulation are simply accepted and accommodated in the corporate system with the appropriate structural and behavioral changes.

The proactive response recognizes the impact public policy can make on the corporation and may involve some kind of mechanism to anticipate those public issues that will affect the corporation most significantly. But rather than fighting change or simply accommodating to the changes a public issue may demand, the proactive response attempts to influence change by changing the environment out of which the issue arises to prevent change from becoming necessary or at least to minimize the effects of a particular public issue on the corporation.

The interactive response recognizes the legitimacy of public policy as a process through which public expectations are expressed and the fact that business and society are related to each other complexly. This complexity involves the use of different strategies by the corporation to adjust to changing public expectations. As stated by James Post, a professor at Boston University: "Sometimes action is taken to influence public opinion; at other times, to change corporate behavior. The two prerequisites for successfully using the interactive approach are a management commitment to anticipating external change and a willingness to adjust the corporation's normal operations to minimize the gap between performance and expectations. When consistently applied over time, an interactive approach tends to produce goals that the company and the public can accept."[2]

The latter response is where public issues management comes into play most effectively, as an interactive corporation manages its response to a public issue comparable to the way it manages other parts of the business. The interactive corporation tries to get a reasonably accurate agenda of public issues that it should be concerned with, analyzes the elements of these issues, and develops constructive approaches to these issues, which it attempts to implement in the public policy arena and in its own structure and behavior.

Many business leaders and academics recognize the importance of developing a public issues management system (see box). Some believe that the very survival of business and the business system is at stake and that business must develop better and more constructive responses to public issues than it has in the past or be faced with a further loss of credibility.

[2]James E. Post, "Public Affairs and Management Policy in the 1980s," *Public Affairs Review* (Washington, D.C.: Public Affairs Council, 1980), p. 8.

According to David L. Shanks, Director of Corporate Public Relations and Advertising at Rexnard Corporation, proper management of public issues has many benefits, both protective and opportunistic. Public issues management (1) allows management to select issues that will have the greatest impact on the corporation, (2) allows "management of" instead of "reaction to" issues, (3) inserts relevant issues into the strategic planning process, (4) gives the company ability to act in tune with society, (5) provides opportunities for leadership roles, and (6) protects the credibility of business in the public mind.[3]

WHAT'S AT STAKE: SURVIVAL, SOME SAY

"The increasing rate of change in all aspects of the environment and the expectation that future organizations will be more complex and more dependent on their environments indicate that, to survive, organizations must conduct environmental analysis."
> —Excerpted from Eli Segev, "How to Use Environmental Analysis in Strategy Making," *Management Review,* March, 1977, pp. 4–5.

"It is hard to find a reasonably informed person today who is not aware that the rate of change all around us has become not only inconvenient, uncomfortable, disconcerting or confusing, but outright dangerous with respect to the future of whole countries, socioeconomic systems, and certainly some private corporations—if not private enterprise as such."
> —Peter Gabriel, "Managing Corporate Strategy to Cope With Change," *Conference Board Record,* March, 1975, p. 57.

"In a world of uncertainties, where change is the one thing we can count on, businesses need the ability to anticipate and adapt successfully to change in both matters of public policy and their own market pursuits. Through a better understanding of public-policy genesis and development, organizations should be able to foresee public-policy changes and be responsive to them. Such an approach enables change—that is the key concept, *change*—to be accommodated with minimal disruption."
> —Graham Molitor, 1977, (For full citation, see footnote 3, Chapter 2.)

"The modern frontiers of professional management—corporate planning and external affairs—are those areas in which change is occurring most rapidly, where the least is known, where the most speculation occurs and where the opportunities for imaginative executive leadership are greatest. . . . The manner in which organizations of all types, and large business corporations in particular, respond to commercial and social complexity is fundamental to their institutional legitimacy and their survival."
> —James Post, "The Challenge of Managing under Social Uncertainty," *Business Horizons,* August 1977, pp. 51–52.

"Business leaders are going to have to learn to think politically in a politicized economy.

"We will have to do it because there are so many public policy issues that affect business and its ability to meet the needs and expectations of the people. Inflation, energy, technology, foreign trade and investment, taxation, capital formation, job formation—all these are issues of vital importance to America's

---

[3]James K. Brown, *The Business of Issues: Coping with the Company's Environments* (New York: The Conference Board, 1979), p. 72.

future. But the voices speaking out for a sensible, economically sound approach to these issues are very few indeed. Business leaders these days are trying to make themselves heard, and I think we are making some honest headway. But we will not get the serious attention of the Congress until we have the vocal backing of a solid constituency.

"That is why we must raise these issues with our employees, our customers, our shareowners and others who have a direct, personal stake in the success of American business. They and their families number in the millions. Their potential as a base of support for sound policy is enormous. But we are not going to have their support unless we work for it as a politician works for it—earning their trust, discussing the issues, demonstrating how they are personally affected, and asking them, directly and persuasively, for their wholehearted support."

　　—Reginald H. Jones, chairman of the General Electric Company, in a speech delivered to the Wharton Club of Washington, D.C., May 17, 1978.

From James K. Brown, *The Business of Issues: Coping with the Company's Environments* (New York: The Conference Board, 1979), p. 4. Reprinted with permission.

The Nature of Public Issues

The term "public issues management" implies that there is something called a public issue that is distinct from, say, an issue that emerges out of a traditional business function that is more or less private. A public issue can be defined as a public policy question that can be acted on by affected corporations, and either is, or is likely to be, the subject of proposed government action.

Public issues can be categorized according to type, that is, the way business is likely to be affected. An *operational* issue affects one or more, but not all, corporate units. For example, a public issue may affect only manufacturing or marketing, or may affect only certain geographic regions. A *corporate* issue affects the corporation as a whole, such as corporate governance or public disclosure of information. Finally, a *societal* issue affects the environment in which business functions. Such issues as national economic planning and income transfer programs would fall in this category.[4] More examples of each of these types of issues are shown in Exhibit 22.2.

Another way to categorize public issues is according to timing. A *current* issue is currently being debated or otherwise acted on in local, state, or federal government institutions. An *emerging* issue is a public policy question with three essential characteristics: (1) its definition and contending positions are still evolving, (2) it is likely to be the subject of government action in the next three to five years, and (3) it can be acted on by affected corporations.[5] Finally, a *strategic* issue is important in the long-range planning cycle of the corporation, as such an issue concerns the future role of the corporation in society.[6]

[4]Fran Steckmest, "Some Definitions and Examples of Public Policy Issues," presented at the Public Affairs Council Workshop, Washington, D.C., May 16–17, 1978.

[5]*The Fundamentals of Issue Management*, p. 3.

[6]Steckmest, "Definitions and Examples."

EXHIBIT 22.2 ———————————————————————————

Example of the Three Types of Emerging Issues

I. Operational

- Waste Oil Disposal
- Transportation Accidents Involving Chemicals
- Industry—Agriculture Competition for Water Supply
- Traffic Congestion in a Plant Area

II. Corporate

- Federal Chartering
- Corporate Governance
- Corporate Public Disclosure
- Legal and Ethical Behavior

III. Societal

- Political/Governmental Issues

    Congressional Reform
    National Economic Planning
    Election Campaign Financing Reform
    Openness in Government
    Reform of the Initiative Process

- Personal Rights and Entitlements Issues

    Personal Privacy
    "On-the-Job Constitutional"
    Sexual Preference
    A Job
    Housing
    Health Care
    Freedom from Risk
    Restitution for Losses

From F. W. Steckmest, "Some Definitions and Examples of Public Policy Issues," presented at the Public Affairs Council Workshop, Washington, D.C., May 16–17, 1978. Reprinted with permission.

The notion of a time frame for issues suggests that public issues have a life cycle. Issues in the *latent* phase are not being discussed very widely, if at all, yet they lie just below the surface of a more extended discussion ready to emerge at an appropriate time. The civil rights issue was a latent issue for many years, and emerged in the 1960s because the time was ready and conditions right for some kind of change. The raising of the retirement age was a latent issue that emerged full-blown almost overnight, but could have been predicted by closely watching demographic trends and economic conditions.

The discussion phase can take many different forms. Reasoned discourse among academics on a public issue is one form of discussion. News stories on television or in print are another type of discussion. Protests and mass demonstrations are also a form of discussion, as is debate on the floor of Congress. At this stage the issue is brought before the public, so to speak, and placed on the public agenda and becomes politicized. If the issue affects business, there is most likely some kind of a gap between public expectations and corporate performance that can be closed by a change in corporate behavior. This change will most likely be forced or encouraged by the government through the political process.

In the *institutional* phase, the issue has matured. Legislation has been passed or corporate behavior has changed sufficiently, if the issue lends itself to this approach, so that legislation is not needed. Thus the issue has become institutionalized in business and/or government. If legislation has been passed, probably regulations will also be issued. This legislation and ensuing regulations may be challenged in the courts. The issue at this stage is largely a legal or technical matter.

As argued in Chapter 7, corporate governance has been a latent issue for years because of the conflict of values between a democratic society and how a private corporation is governed. The issue emerged in the 1970s perhaps partly in response to abuses of corporate power, but also because of other changes in society. The issue is currently being discussed in academia, government, business, and other circles. Some legislation has been passed to force more corporate disclosure, and corporations have responded to the issue with changes in the board of directors. But the issue has not, as yet, fully matured, and the final outcome of the discussion phase is not yet clear.

The concept of a public issue life cycle is important because different corporate strategies are called for at different stages. The options that are open to business for some kind of an interactive response are different at each stage, making necessary a "fit" between the life cycle stage and the response of the corporation. The development of an appropriate strategy is the purpose of a public issues management system.

Public Issues Management System

The management of public issues involves a series of stages or steps that, taken as a whole, constitute a public issues management system. Exhibit 22.3 shows the various stages of a typical system of this kind that was put together from the sources indicated in the exhibit itself.

The first stage is one of identifying those trends and issues of interest to the corporation. This task involves developing some kind of a forecasting system to discover and track trends in public expectations and identify specific issues that are likely to affect business as early in their life cycle as possible. This stage of public issues management will be more fully discussed later in the chapter.

Once issues have been identified, their potential impact on the corporation must be evaluated. The reason for this evaluation is to set some priorities for corporate responses. The corporation cannot respond to every public issue—it probably does not have the resources—nor can it respond to every issue in the same manner. Priorities must be set according to the potential impact of the issue on the corporation, the corporation's ability to respond, and other factors, such as the issue's probability of occurrence. The corporation must assess whether the issue is operational, corporate, or societal, whether it is current, emerging, or strategic, and whether it is in the latent, discussion, or institutional phase.

The next stage involves basic analysis and research on issues of highest priority. For this task, involvement of a public affairs staff devoted to public issues research is important. Involvement of functional areas—such as manufacturing when environmental issues are concerned or personnel when the issue is minority hiring—is also crucial. Outside sources can also be

EXHIBIT 22.3

Public Issues Management System

I. Identifying Public Issues and Trends in Public Expectations
   - Developing forecasts of trends and issues
   - Tracking trends and issues that are developing
   - Identifying those of interest to the corporation

II. Evaluating Their Impact and Setting Priorities
   - Assessment of impact and probability of occurrence
   - Assessment of corporate resources and ability to respond
   - Categorization of issues along relevant dimensions
   - Preparation of issue priorities

III. Research and Analysis
   - Ensuring that priority issues receive staff coverage
   - Involving functional areas where appropriate
   - Using outside sources of information

IV. Position Development
   - Development of position options
   - Recommended position
   - Management decision

V. Strategy Development
   - Analysis of strategy options
   - Management decision
   - Integration with overall business strategy

VI. Implementation
   - Dissemination of agreed-upon position and strategy
   - Development of tactics consistent with the overall strategy
   - Development of alliances with external organizations
   - Linkage with internal and external communication networks

VII. Evaluation
   - Assessment of results by staff
   - Management evaluation
   - Modification of implementation plans
   - Additional research

Adapted from Donald J. Watson, "The Changing Political Environment of Business," paper presented at the Conference on Business and Its Changing Environment, UCLA, July 31, 1978; *The Fundamentals of Issue Management*, p. 2; and Ian Wilson, "Characteristics of Futures Research," material prepared for Conference on Business Environment and Public Policy, Washington University Center for the Study of American Business, July 8–13, 1979.

used at this stage, particularly consulting organizations, academia, or research centers such as the American Enterprise Institute for Public Policy Research or the Center for the Study of American Business.

At this stage, the corporation must do its homework and perform quality research on public issues comparable to the kind of effort devoted to technological issues in research and development laboratories. The development of a good priorities list is essential, as a corporation cannot do a thorough job of research and analysis on every public issue that is identified. The intent of this stage is not only to more thoroughly analyze the potential impact an issue can make on a corporation, but also to analyze the different positions or strategies that can be taken on the issue. The result is an analysis of the basic elements of an issue, including the pros and cons of different positions or strategies.

Emerging from this research and analysis phase is the development of different options that can be taken on an issue along with a recommended position that can be presented to management for consideration. The recommended position must reflect the best thinking of the corporation and be based on solid research rather than a hastily put together reaction that will most likely not work in the corporation's best interests. Management must eventually decide to go along with the recommendation or adopt one of the other options.

Once this decision is made, strategy must be determined. The basic strategic decision is whether the position chosen calls for modification of corporate behavior to close the gap between public expectations and corporate performance, whether an attempt should be made to influence the environment by changing public expectations or legislation, or whether a mixture of both strategies should be attempted. A decision must also be made as to whether the company wants to adopt a high or low profile on the issue. Finally, a strategic choice must be made whether to lead public expectations, to attempt to close the gap and meet them but no more, or whether on a given issue the company can afford to lag behind public expectations and allow a gap between expectations and performance to continue (Figure 22.1).

Management again must make a decision about these strategy options, and choose a basic strategy on a public issue integrated with the overall business strategy of the company's basic economic mission.

The choice of an overall strategy must then be disseminated to the appro-

Figure 22.1. Patterns of Corporate Responsiveness

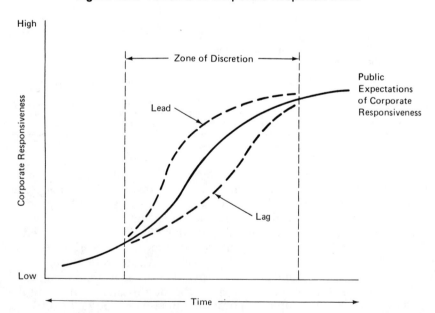

From Robert W. Ackerman and Raymond A. Bauer, *Corporate Social Responsiveness: The Modern Dilemma* (Reston, Va.: Reston Publishing Co., 1976), p. 39. Reprinted with permission of Reston Publishing Co., Inc., a Prentice-Hall Co., 11480 Sunset Hills Rd., Reston, Va. 22090.

priate people in the company who are responsible for implementation. They must develop specific tactics for changing corporate behavior, influencing public opinion, changing the thinking of public policy-makers, developing a court case—whatever tactics are consistent with the strategy chosen. If other parties, such as a trade association, are involved, alliances must be built during this stage and action taken. Lobbying tactics must be developed and carried out if attempts at legislative influence are appropriate.

Finally, linkages with internal and external communications networks must be developed as needed. For example, if grass-roots lobbying is called for this must be communicated to the grass-roots network for it to be activated. If a change in the way a company produces a product to reduce ecological damage is appropriate, this must be communicated to the plant personnel who are in a position to make the necessary changes. External communications involves informing the public about what the company is doing to meet public expectations or engaging in a debate about the issue itself.

Finally comes the all-important stage of evaluation. The tactics that are implemented must constantly be evaluated to ascertain whether they are achieving results. Some kind of evaluation system must be developed to determine whether the public issues management effort is a success. This evaluation is extremely difficult. How much credit, for example, can any single corporate effort be given for the defeat of a bill in Congress? Or if the bill passed when the objective was to defeat it, was this the fault of a single corporate lobbying effort? How can changes in public opinion be measured and attributed to a specific advocacy advertising program? What is the impact of a corporate economic education program?

These are very complex questions, and yet without some kind of evaluation by both the staff involved in public issues management and management itself, one is operating in the dark, so to speak. The process of evaluation is important because the implementation tactics may have to be modified in light of the evaluation or additional research performed to develop different positions.

All through this public issues management system there are a number of key decisions that have to be made. Figure 22.2 shows these decisions in the form of a flow-chart. The actual decisions and outputs of each stage are shown in the boxes. This exhibit shows the "flow" of an issue through the public issues management system.

Environmental Forecasting and Planning

The first law of forecasting: Forecasting is very difficult, especially if it's about the future.

When presenting a forecast: Give them a number or give them a date, but never both.

A forecaster's best defense is a good offense, so: If you have to forecast, forecast often. But: If you're ever right, never let 'em forget it.

From Edgar R. Fiedler, "The Three Rs of Economic Forecasting—Irrational, Irrelevant and Irreverent," *Across the Board*, Vol. XIV, No. 6 (June 1977), pp. 62–63.

Figure 22.2. Flow-chart of Public Issues Management

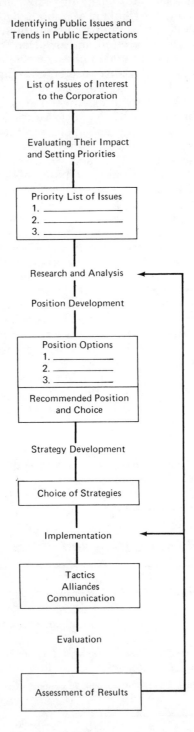

Identifying Public Issues and
Trends in Public Expectations

List of Issues of Interest
to the Corporation

Evaluating Their Impact
and Setting Priorities

Priority List of Issues
1. _____
2. _____
3. _____

Research and Analysis

Position Development

Position Options
1. _____
2. _____
3. _____

Recommended Position
and Choice

Strategy Development

Choice of Strategies

Implementation

Tactics
Alliances
Communication

Evaluation

Assessment of Results

One of the most important elements in successful public issues management is the development of an ability within the corporation to forecast those public issues in the environment that will have an impact on the corporation. The earlier an issue can be identified in its life cycle, the more options business has open to it and the better chance business has to develop an effective response. Thus forecasting and planning are linked. The forecast must be incorporated into the planning process to have any value to the corporation. The strategic plans of the company must reflect all factors in the environment that impinge on the corporation, not just the more traditional economic and technological factors.

This is not to suggest that effective forecasting will enable a corporation to plan a response to public issues that will avoid government involvement altogether. As stated in earlier chapters, the view that corporations can respond unilaterally to every social issue to meet public expectations is naive. But forecasting of issues can enable a corporation to be more interactive in helping to formulate public policy and change its performance, rather than being reactive and opposing every new piece of legislation or public demand, or accommodative in simply adapting itself to whatever legislation and regulation eventuates.

The need for forecasting social and political factors has become a must for many companies. Some have been confronted with a number of embarrassing situations that could have been avoided with a little forethought. Ignoring social and political trends has cost other companies a good deal of money because they have been forced to respond to public pressure or burdensome government regulation. In some cases, the very survival of the company may be at stake. The following examples illustrate the problems that can occur by ignoring social and political factors in the environment.

> General Motors Corp. and other auto makers paid dearly for failing to recognize early enough that Ralph Nader's objection to the Corvair model was a forerunner of a broad-based consumer movement for safer products and tougher liability standards. Similarly, by ignoring early warnings from environmentalists, hundreds of manufacturers were forced to retrofit plants with pollution-control gear that could have been incorporated more cheaply in the original plant design. More recently, Nestle Company faced a worldwide boycott of its producers after it seemingly ignored the public outcry against its marketing of infant formula in underdeveloped countries where it was a far too expensive substitute for mother's milk.[7]

Perhaps some attempt at definitions is in order before discussing the concepts and methods of environmental forecasting and planning. Forecasting can be simply defined as the attempt to predict some future event or condition as a result of rational study and analysis of data that are believed to be pertinent.[8] Thus forecasting, in this sense, is not an intuitive guess about the future but is rather an educated guess based on actual data and analysis that provide evidence of future trends and perhaps even events.

Strategic planning can be defined as "that activity which specifies for a business a course of action that is designed to achieve long-term objectives in

---

[7]"Capitalizing on Social Change," *Business Week*, October 29, 1979, p. 105.

[8]*Webster's New Collegiate Dictionary* (Springfield, Mass.: G. & C. Merriam Co., 1974), p. 449.

the light of all major external and internal factors, present and future."[9] This definition, according to Ian Wilson of General Electric Company, places no restrictions on the scope of objectives or courses of action, such as limiting them to financial or marketing strategies. The definition implies that strategies are needed for the totality of a business's relationship to the environment, including political strategies and strategies for dealing with emerging social issues.[10]

Conceptual Basis for Environmental Forecasting. Forecasting and planning are nothing new to business, of course, but traditionally these activities have been limited to the economic and technological environments (Figure 22.3). Economic forecasting at the macro level includes projections of future gross national product, consumption and investment expenditures, productivity projections, inflation, and balance of payments. The purpose of this level of forecasting is to get some idea of the general economic conditions with which business will be faced in the immediate future. For this purpose, many corporations subscribe to one or more of the econometric models that are available, sometimes adapting them to their own purposes.

Economic forecasting at the micro level involves forecasting related to the specific markets in which the company sells products, either mature markets that have been in existence for some time, markets that are newly developing, or potential markets the company may be considering. The purpose of this forecasting is to be more specific about the sales of particular products the company is already producing or considering. Micro forecasting also

Figure 22.3. Traditional Environmental Forecasting

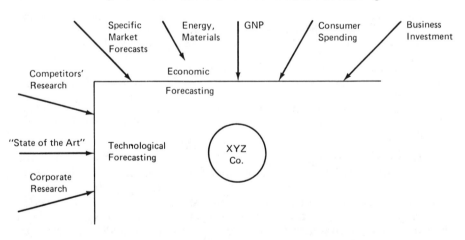

From Ian H. Wilson, "Socio-Political Forecasting: A New Dimension to Strategic Planning," *Michigan Business Review*, Vol. XXVI, No. 4 (July 1974), p. 19. Reprinted with permission.

[9] Ian H. Wilson, "Reforming the Strategic Planning Process: Integration of Social Responsibility and Business Needs," *The Unstable Ground: Corporate Social Policy in a Dynamic Society*, S. Prakash Sethi, ed. (Los Angeles: Melville Publishing Co., 1974), p. 250.
[10] *Ibid.*

involves financial forecasts about the availability of money and credit to support the operations of the company.

Technological forecasting is concerned with state-of-the-art developments in products and processes, trying to predict where new technological breakthroughs are likely to happen that will significantly alter corporate planning. Forecasts of completion dates for company research and development projects are also a part of this area, as well as attempts to assess competitors' technical competence and development activities.[11]

The traditional approach to environmental forecasting has been two-sided, based on the assumption that all other factors are equal. But the 1960s and 1970s taught many business organizations that all other things were not equal, and that it was precisely the social and political environments that were giving business the most trouble and affecting its profits and very survival. Ian Wilson, one of the early pioneers for a broader approach, proposed a four-sided model for environmental forecasting, including the political and social environments in addition to the economic and technological ones (Figure 22.4).[12]

Forecasting the political environment involves, in its broadest sense, some assessment of business-government relations as a whole. For example, a crucial question is whether the traditional adversarial relationship is likely to continue or whether the long-term trend of business-government relations

Figure 22.4. The Four-Sided Model

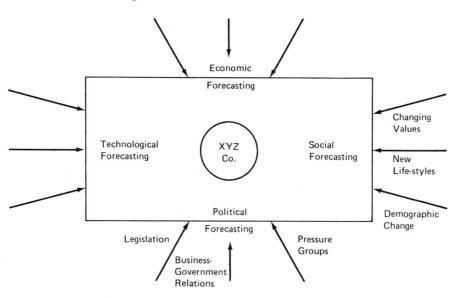

From Ian H. Wilson, "Socio-Political Forecasting: A New Dimension to Strategic Planning," *Michigan Business Review*, Vol. XXVI, No. 4 (July 1974), p. 20. Reprinted with permission.

[11]*Ibid.*, p. 247.
[12]*Ibid.*, pp. 247–248.

is tending more toward cooperation or at least a peaceful coexistence. The answer to this basic question has significant implications for the kind of political strategies a business adopts. More specific forecasting of the political environment involves keeping track of legislation being considered by Congress, the stage of the political process legislation is in, what the likely outcome will be, and keeping aware of the various political pressures being applied by interest groups on issues of concern to the corporation.

The social environment is much more difficult to forecast, but such a forecast at least involves some attempt to predict major value changes in society that may give rise to new concerns and demands that will affect the corporation or the business system as a whole. Forecasting the social environment also means predicting whether current lifestyles are likely to continue or whether some major changes are probable. Finally, demographic trends are also important to follow, as shifts in population with respect to age or regional location can have major effects on the corporation.

An adequate forecasting system must include at least these four major environmental elements. It is not enough to focus on economic and technological aspects alone. Changes in government regulation and social expectations can affect profits as much as changes in technology or general economic conditions. Social and political forecasting is more and more becoming a part of the corporate scene.[13]

Principles of Environmental Scanning. The first stage in implementing this forecasting framework is the design of an environmental scanning system. The purpose of a scanning system is to monitor current events that are taking place in the business environment and forecast future trends that are likely to affect business. Events can be defined as important specific occurrences in the different environments in which business functions. Such an event is the passage of legislation to raise the mandatory retirement age from 65 to 70, an event that took place in the political environment. A trend can be defined as a general tendency or course of events, that is, a whole series of events that seems to be tending in a certain direction. The aging of the population in the 1970s is an example of a trend in the social environment that built up pressure for a change in the retirement age.

After developing the four-sided forecasting framework, Wilson goes on to enunciate certain principles that he believes should guide the scanning effort. The scanning system should be holistic in its approach—the economic, technological, social, and economic environments should not be seen as separate or distinct from each other. The system should also be iterative in its operation, be designed to deal with alternative futures, provide for contingency planning, and be an integral part of the decision-making process of the corporation. Wilson elaborates on these points as follows.

1. It must be holistic in its approach to the business environment, i.e. it should view trends—social, economic, political, technological—as a piece, not piecemeal. Ecology and general systems theory both point to the maxim that "everything is related to everything else"; and Jay Forrester has demonstrated the dangers of applying linear, segmented thinking to analysis of any closed, complex system—a corporation, a city or a society—with its dynamic, inter-

---

[13]"Capitalizing on Social Change," pp. 105–106.

acting parts and constantly operating feedback-loops. The scanning system should, therefore, be comprehensive in its scope and integrative in its approach (cross-impact analyses and scenarios are remarkably useful techniques in this regard).

2. It must also be continuous, iterative in its operation. In a fast-changing world, it makes little sense to rely on one-shot, or even periodic, analyses of the environment. Only constant monitoring, feedback and modification of forecasts can be truly useful. Carrying on the radar analogy, I call this a "cybernetic pulsing through the future."

3. The system must be designed to deal with *alternative futures.* In an uncertain environment we can never truly know the future, no matter how much we may perfect our forecasting techniques. It is highly misleading, therefore, to claim (or believe) that an early warning system can predict the future. What it can do—and do effectively, if well designed—is to help us clarify our assumptions about the future, speculate systematically about alternative outcomes, assess probabilities, and make more rational choices.

4. It should lay heavy stress on the need for *contingency planning.* This is a necessary corollary to the preceding point. In fact, there is (or should be) a strong logical connection in our thinking among uncertainty, alternatives and contingencies: the three concepts are strongly bound together. In the final analysis, of course, after considering alternatives, we have to commit to a plan of action based on our assessment of the most probable future. But those lesser probabilities—even the "wild card" scenarios—should not be neglected, for they represent the contingencies for which we should also, in some degree, plan. A commitment to contingency planning is, it seems to me, the essence of a flexible strategy.

5. Most important, the environmental scanning system should be an *integral part of the decision-making* system of the corporation. Speculation about alternative futures makes no real contribution to corporate success if it results merely in interesting studies. To contribute, it must be issue-oriented and help make today's decisions with a better sense of futurity: but it can do this *only* if the planning and decision-making system is designed to include the requirements of such monitoring and early warning.[14]

Sources of Environmental Information. One method of categorizing the sources for gathering information in the scanning process for the social and political environments is shown in Exhibit 22.4. According to this scheme, sources are categorized into internal and external, and personal and impersonal within each of these categories. Internal sources refer to those within the corporation itself while, of course, external sources refers to those outside the organization. Personal sources means the use of people as sources, while impersonal refers to the use of reports or studies.

The chief executive officer is an obvious source of environmental information, especially if he or she is politically involved and thus knows something about the current political scene in Washington or at the state level. Because of time pressures, the CEO cannot be part of a continual scanning process, but if the right questions are asked when time is available, the CEO can be a good source of information. When the CEO brings up an issue, it is very likely to be of concern to the company.

---

[14]Ian H. Wilson, "Environmental Scanning and Strategic Planning," *Business Environment/Public Policy: 1979 Conference Papers,* Lee E. Preston, ed. (St. Louis, Mo.: AACSB, 1980), pp. 160–161. Quoted with permission.

The board of directors is another good source of information, especially when there is a public responsibility committee whose job it is to be concerned about such matters. Information about the political environment, such as legislation or regulation being considered, ought to be readily available from a corporation's Washington office. Other executives and managers are another good source of information. They can be polled directly or asked to be part of a more sophisticated process such as a Delphi exercise. Finally, staff specialists who are involved in regulatory areas can supply information about their particular area of concern.

Impersonal internal sources include management reports and memoranda that may deal with issues in the political and social environments, accounting reports that show how resources are being allocated, and planning reports and budgets that show how much money is going to be spent on pollution control, for example, pointing out the importance of that issue to the future of the company as assessed by those who put the budget together.

With regard to external personal sources, the use of outside consultants in a very useful source of information about emerging social and political issues. These outside consultants frequently conduct research for the company to measure the effectiveness of a particular program in dealing with an issue of concern to a constituency of the corporation.

Conferences are a good place to pick up environmental information and one finds a good many corporate executives attending conferences like the Annual Meeting of the Academy of Management. Executives and managers of other companies may be good sources of information, as are government officials in various positions. The information from these sources must be screened carefully, however, as it is more likely to be biased than information from other sources. Finally, representatives of public interest groups can be consulted on their current concerns, which they often are willing to express quite readily.

Impersonal external sources include reports from the general business and trade associations, such as the Business Roundtable, which publishes studies analyzing various aspects of the environment. Government publications are an obvious source of scanning information, particularly congressional hearings on such subjects as corporate governance or antitrust reform. The Federal Register, of course, contains regulations that affect business, both regulations being proposed and those issued in final form. Finally, the Census Reports contain demographic information about population trends.

Newspapers and magazines are an important source of information. Some companies and industries have a rather elaborate system for monitoring these sources. The American Council of Life Insurance, for example, has a Trend Analysis Program that depends on the efforts of over 100 volunteer monitors who work for member companies. These volunteers regularly scan one or more publications from a list of close to 100 publications, and abstract any article in their assigned area that meets the following criteria: (1) the article involves an event or an idea that is indicative of either a trend or discontinuity in the environment, and (2) it contains implications for the long-range concerns of society and the life insurance business. These abstracts are analyzed six times a year by an abstract analysis committee and may eventually find their way into a trend report for member companies.[15]

Trade and technical journals are another source of information. Some companies have a full-time employee who does nothing but monitor trade journals. Special counseling and reporting services can be useful sources of information. Finally, the publications of public interest groups must not be overlooked, especially those that are known to be influential in political circles.

There seems to be no end to sources of information for the political and social environments. Some means must be developed to organize these sources into a useful framework for analysis. Some of these sources will obviously be more important than others, and it is best to have the entire picture in mind when making these judgments. The next step in the forecasting and planning process is deciding what to do with all this scanning information. How can all this information be put together in a forecast that is useful for planning?

---

[15] James K. Brown, *The Business of Issues: Coping with the Company's Environments* (New York: The Conference Board, 1979), pp. 22–25.

The Forecasting and Planning Relationship. There are two approaches, according to Wilson, in developing a forecast of the future (see Figure 22.5). One can take all this scanning information and try to predict long-term trends; take a leap into the future, so to speak, and develop alternative scenarios. Then one can work backwards, through a process of deductive reasoning, to develop hypotheses on the implications of these various futures for the corporation in the immediate present. The other approach is to focus on the specific events themselves and continue to monitor them, and then, through a process of inductive reasoning, create a future five years hence based on these events.[16]

These two approaches should be seen as complements to each other rather than as alternative methods of forecasting. Environmental scanning can contribute to both long-term macro forecasts and short-term micro analyses. The purpose of either approach is to identify emerging issues in sufficient time to allow an interactive response by the corporation. To be useful for planning, however, the issues that have been identified as being of concern to the corporation must be ranked or somehow prioritized. The corporation cannot concern itself with everything, but most focus its efforts on those issues that are likely to have the greatest impact.

One method of prioritizing issues is to lay out the issues in a matrix arrangement (Figure 22.6). The issues have to be analyzed by the forecasting group with the help of management and decisions made about the probability of their occurrence—that they will be significant enough to enough segments of society to be placed on the public agenda—and their potential impact on the specific company. Once placed in the appropriate cell of the matrix, the issues can then be categorized into high, medium, and low

Figure 22.5. Approaches to Forecasting

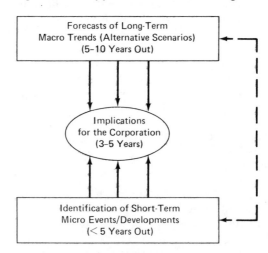

From Ian Wilson, "Characteristics of Futures Research," materials prepared for Conference on Business Environment and Public Policy, Washington University Center for the Study of American Business, July 8–13, 1979, p. 2. Reprinted with permission.

[16]Wilson, "Scanning and Planning," pp. 159–160.

Figure 22.6. Issues Priority Matrix

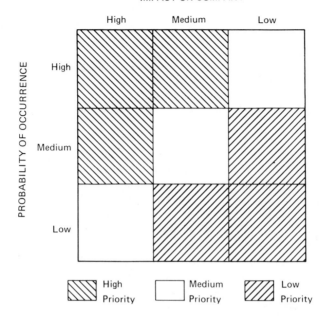

Adapted from James K. Brown, *The Business of Issues: Coping with the Company's Environments* (New York: The Conference Board, 1979), p. 32. Reprinted with permission.

priority. Those issues falling into the top left-hand portion of the matrix should receive immediate management attention, those in the middle are not as crucial but still need attention, and those falling in the lower right-hand corner can be put on the back burner for the time being. This assessment, however, must be done periodically, as conditions change quite rapidly at times. The key to this method, of course, is a correct analysis of the issues according to the two dimensions of the matrix. For this analysis, techniques such as probability analysis, trend impact analysis, cross-impact analysis, and simulation modeling may be useful.

There are less sophisticated methods of prioritizing issues, of course, that use rather broad definitions of categories (see box). But regardless of the method used, the outcome should be some listing of issues in a priority scheme (Exhibit 22.5) that can be useful for planning. These priorities can then be factored into the planning process of the corporation along with economic and technological priorities to develop a holistic plan that incorporates the four major environments in which the corporation functions.

The Structure of Public Issues Management

Structure as well as process is important in the area of public issues management, as both are related to how well a company manages its response to public issues. The various structural elements in public issues management can be discussed under the general headings of external affairs and government relations.

External Affairs. The term "external affairs" refers to the more general approach a corporation takes toward structuring its relations with the external environment. This term includes government relations, but because of its critical importance, government relations will also be discussed separately. The function of an external affairs unit is to relate the corporation to its various external constituencies, because it is these constituencies that are concerned about public issues and how a corporation responds to them.

External Publics of the Corporation. There are various external publics to which a corporation must relate, including the federal government, customers, the financial community, stockholders, the media, the local community, and local government. Table 22.1 shows how some external relations executives themselves ranked the importance of these constituencies. Not surprisingly, the relationship with the federal government came out on top, reflecting the increasing importance of Washington in influencing business behavior. It is interesting to note that stockholders ranked lower than the media, reflecting the importance of devoting time and effort to media relations. The media convey information about business and have a tremendous impact on public opinion, making it an important constituency.

The stockholders are an important constituency to some corporations as far as public issues are concerned. They can be mobilized to help implement a company's position on a public issue. For example, in 1976, Dart Industries requested support from stockholders on the issues of tax reform and oil company divestiture. The company conducted a random survey of 1,052 of

EXHIBIT 22.5

Sears' Agenda of Public Issues

Issues with Direct Impact on the Company

First Priority	*Second Priority*	*Third Priority*
Equal Employment Opportunity	Equal Pay	Postal Service
Social Security	Profit Sharing/Stock Ownership/Capital Gains	Product Usage: Codes and Restrictions
Minimum Wage	Pensions	Flame Retardency
Employee Health Care	Corporate Taxes	Raw Material Pricing and Access
Credit Income/Financing/Interest Costs	Worker's Compensation	Environmental Protection
FTC Requirements	Unemployment Compensation	Retirement Policies
Product Liability	Labor Law	OSHA
Warranty Requirements	Transportation Regulations	Product Restrictions
	International Trade Policy	Privacy
	Product Safety	Copyright Laws
	Labeling and Packaging Specifications	Disclosure
	Product Specifications	Corporate Governance
	Energy Requirements	Metric Changeover
	Franchise Regulations	Sex/Violence on TV
	Energy Costs	
	Electronic Funds Transfer	
	Electronic Communications Regulation	
	Credit Practice Regulations	
	Federal/State Legislative/Regulatory Conflicts	
	Advertising Regulations	

Issues with Indirect Impact on the Company

Fourth Priority

National Energy Program	Government Subsidy of Business/Cities	Food Policy
Full Employment	Housing Policy	Public Confidence in Institutions
Inflation	Immigrants	National Planning
Government Spending/Deficit	Welfare Reform	Plaintiffs Access to the Courts
Monetary Policy	Water Conservation	White Collar and Corporate Crime

From Robert E. Barmeier, "The Role of Environmental Forecasting and Public Issues Analysis in Corporate Planning," *Business Environment/Public Policy: 1979 Conference Papers,* Lee E. Preston, ed. (St. Louis, Mo.: AACSB, 1980), p. 158. Reprinted with permission.

the 8,591 stockholders who had been mailed letters to evaluate the effectiveness of the effort. Of the 146 people who responded to the survey, 55 said they had taken a position on both the tax reform and divestiture issue, 49 said they had taken a position on one of the issues, and 42 said they had acted on neither issue. These results were encouraging enough for the company to continue the program.[17]

[17]Phyllis McGrath, *Action Plans for Public Affairs* (New York: The Conference Board, 1977), pp. 21–24.

TABLE 22.1 **How 147 External Relations Executives Rank Their Corporations' Publics[1]**

Public	Ranked by Importance to the Company
Federal Government	1
Customers	2
Financial community	3
The media	4
Stockholders	5
Local government	6
Community	7
Other	8

[1]Employees, while unquestionably a public of any company, are not included for consideration in this report because the material relates only to *external* publics.

Source: Phyllis McGrath, *Managing Corporate External Relations: Changing Perspectives and Responses* (New York: The Conference Board, 1976), p. 9. Reprinted with permission.

Organization of External Affairs. There are many ways to organize external affairs, as evidenced by corporate organizational charts. The functional units generally include government relations, media relations, stockholder relations, institutional investor relations, customer relations or consumer affairs, and community relations.[18] However, two general patterns of organizing these functions emerge from the diversity. One pattern is to have no dominant executive below the level of chief executive to whom all of the external relations functions report. The other pattern is to have one executive below the level of CEO who is responsible for all the various functions of external affairs. Typical models of these two patterns are shown in Figure 22.7. Most corporate organizations of external affairs are hybrids of these two approaches.

The External Relations Executive. Various dimensions of the external relations executive were explored in a Conference Board study of 156 such executives. Table 22.2 shows the titles that these people had in their respective companies. The use of public affairs as a title has almost captured first place over public relations. Dissatisfaction with the title of public relations includes the following reasons: (1) public relations is traditionally identified as media relations, (2) public relations is identified with corporate image building, (3) public relations has lost credibility in business and elsewhere, and (4) the new scope of the function requires a more appropriate title.[19] This trend toward the use of public affairs as a title will probably continue, as the difference between this title and public relations appears to be substantive and not just a matter of semantics. The title of public affairs implies

[18]Phyllis McGrath, *Managing Corporate External Relations* (New York: The Conference Board, 1976), p. 22.
[19]McGrath, *External Relations,* p. 47.

Figure 22.7

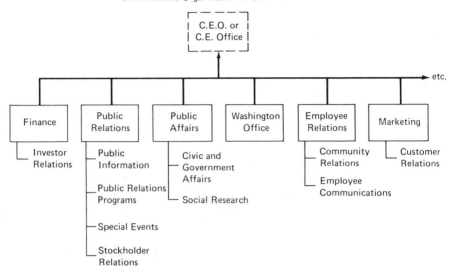

Decentralized Organization of External Affairs

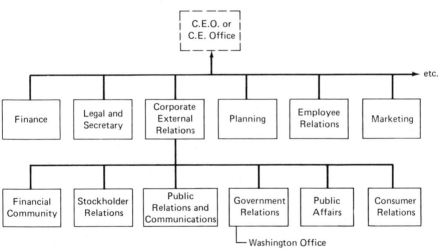

Centralized Organization of External Affairs

From Phyllis McGrath, *Managing Corporate External Relations: Changing Perspectives and Responses* (New York: The Conference Board, 1976), pp. 24–25. Reprinted with permission.

more than just communications and seems more appropriate for the function of public issues management.

The background of the external relations executive was most likely to be, as shown in Table 22.3, public relations or journalism. As the importance of public policy increases, however, many executives believe that this traditional source of external relations executives is no longer adequate. This

TABLE 22.2 **Title of the External Relations Executive[1]**

Functional Title	Number of Executives
Public relations	47
Public affairs	45
Corporate communications	17
Corporate relations	13
Corporate affairs	8
Public relations and advertising	5
External affairs	3
Public affairs and corporate relations	1
Public affairs and corporate affairs	1
External relations	1
Total	141

[1]Based on companies that have a coordinated external relations staff and use functional designations.

Source: Phyllis McGrath, *Managing Corporate External Relations: Changing Perspectives and Responses* (New York: The Conference Board, 1976), p. 46. Reprinted with permission.

TABLE 22.3 **Background of the External Relations Executive**

Background	Number of Executives
Public relations and journalism	76[a]
Operations or general business	21
Law	18
Marketing	17
Government work or corporate government relations	8
Advertising	7
Economics and finance	7
International operations	4
Science and engineering	4
Other	6
Total	170*

[a]Eighteen of these gained their experience with public relations counseling firms.
*The other six executives did not provide background information.

Source: Phyllis McGrath, *Managing Corporate External Relations: Changing Perspectives and Responses* (New York: The Conference Board, 1976), p. 53. Reprinted with permission.

background again emphasizes communications skills, which are only a part of the external relations function. There is a need for people with a depth of understanding of environmental concerns and with a knowledge of public issues and the public policy process, so that public issues can be managed effectively. This need has implications for the curriculum of business schools.[20]

[20]See Rogene A. Buchholz, *Business Environment/Public Policy: Corporate Executive Viewpoints and Educational Implications* (St. Louis, Mo.: Washington University Center for the Study of American Business, 1980), pp. 42–45.

The external relations executive typically has three major roles, according to the Conference Board study. These roles include (1) advice or counsel, (2) service, and (3) control (see box). Table 22.4 shows the relative importance of these roles with respect to the various publics served by the external relations function. On the whole, there is a fairly consistent balance between these roles across most of the external publics.

---

1. Advice or Counsel. In this role, the external relations executive acts as an "internal consultant" to other operating and functional units, as well as for the chief executive. The external relations executive advises other company executives on the best way to handle questions, issues and problems which relate to the company's external publics.

2. Service. In this capacity, the external relations executive conceives, conducts and carries out programs relating to the various corporate publics, and provides this service for operating units and for the corporation as a whole.

3. Control. The third role of the external relations executive is involvement in formulation of policy and guidelines that determine the corporation's relations with its various publics, as well as monitoring the implementation of such policy and guidelines.

From Phyllis McGrath, *Managing Corporate External Relations: Changing Perspectives and Responses* (New York: The Conference Board, 1976), pp. 54–55. Quoted with permission.

Thus the external relations function is different across organizations, as are, of course, most organizational functions. But the external relations function is newer, perhaps making it more susceptible to diversity. However, the trend is definitely toward an increase in the importance of this function consistent with the growing importance of public policy to corporations. A professionalization of the field is taking place, as exemplified in a statement of ethical guidelines for external relations professionals (see box).

TABLE 22.4 **The Three-Part Role of the External Relations Executive in Relation to the Most Frequently Cited Publics**

External Public	Counsel or Advice	Service	Control
Media	127	135	114
Federal Government	124	106	89
Government—state and local	119	99	83
Individual stockholders	105	115	74
Financial community	109	115	73
Customers	110	97	60
Community	127	116	89
Special interest groups:			
Ecologists	20	18	12
Consumers	16	14	9
Women and minorities	17	10	10
Educational institutions	13	14	10
Industry associations	8	9	6
Total mentions	895	848	629

Source: Phyllis McGrath, *Managing Corporate External Relations: Changing Perspectives and Responses* (New York: The Conference Board, 1976), p. 56. Reprinted with permission.

A STATEMENT OF ETHICAL GUIDELINES FOR BUSINESS PUBLIC AFFAIRS PROFESSIONALS

A. The PUBLIC AFFAIRS PROFESSIONAL maintains professional relationships based on honesty and reliable information, and therefore:

1. Represents accurately his or her organization's policies on economic and political matters to government, employees, shareholders, community interests, and others.
2. Serves always as a source of reliable information, discussing the varied aspects of complex public issues within the context and constraints of the advocacy role.
3. Recognizes diverse viewpoints within the public policy process, knowing that disagreement on issues is both inevitable and healthy.

B. The PUBLIC AFFAIRS PROFESSIONAL seeks to protect the integrity of the public policy process and the political system, and therefore:

1. Publicly acknowledges his or her role as a legitimate participant in the public policy process and discloses whatever work-related information the law requires.
2. Knows, respects and abides by federal and state laws that apply to lobbying and related public affairs activities.
3. Knows and respect the laws governing campaign finance and other political activities, and abides by the letter and intent of those laws.

C. The PUBLIC AFFAIRS PROFESSIONAL understands the interrelation of business interests with the larger public interests, and therefore:

1. Endeavors to ensure that responsible and diverse external interests and views concerning the needs of society are considered within the corporate decision-making process.
2. Bears the responsibility for management review of public policies which may bring corporate interests into conflict with other interests.
3. Acknowledges dual obligations—to advocate the interests of his or her employer, and to preserve the openness and integrity of the democratic process.
4. Presents to his or her employer an accurate assessment of the political and social realities that may affect corporate operations.

Public Affairs Council
Committee on Professionalism

Charles S. Mack, Chairman	Gordon D. MacKay
Richard A. Edwards	Horace E. Sheldon
Robert J. Grimm	F. Clifton White
	May 1979

From Charles S. Mack, "Ethics and Business Public Affairs," *Public Affairs Review* (Washington, D.C.: Public Affairs Council, 1980), p. 28. Reprinted with permission.

Government Relations. Because of its importance and growth, the government relations function deserves to be treated separately. The data in Figure 22.8, based on a 1979 Conference Board survey of 389 government relations executives, show the increase in government relations activity at the federal level both in terms of what had happened in the previous three years and what was believed would happen three years into the future.

Ninety-two percent of these government relations executives said the

Figure 22.8. Increase in Activity Over the Past Three Years and Anticipated Change in the Next Three Years

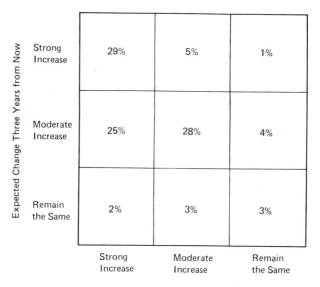

From Phyllis McGrath, *Redefining Corporate-Federal Relations* (New York: The Conference Board, 1979), p. 3. Reprinted with permission.

concern of their companies with and involvement in federal government relations had increased over the past three years. Of these executives, 56 percent described this increase as strong. The same percentage of executives (92 percent) believed that government relations activity would increase over the next three years and 35 percent believed this would be a strong increase.[21]

Seventy-one percent of these government relations executives said that the strongest factor behind this growth was the impact of government regulations and legislation. Another 9 percent credited a reassessment of corporate policy and 4 percent pointed to changes in top management. The remaining 16 percent offered a variety of other explanations.[22] From this information, the Conference Board study reached the following conclusion:

> Government relations is gaining greater status within the organization, as government relations executives report direct involvement in the decision-making process of their companies. More and more chief executives are emphasizing the importance of this function and are taking a more direct, personal role in it. So, too, are other senior executives, and those in charge of technical areas, R and D, personnel, finance, and so on throughout the management team.[23]

[21]Phyllis McGrath, *Redefining Corporate-Federal Relations* (New York: The Conference Board, 1979), pp. 2–3.
[22]*Ibid.*, p. 1.
[23]*Ibid.*, p. 2.

Regarding the organization of the government relations function, of the 389 companies that participated in the Conference Board Study, 73 percent had a separate unit dealing with government relations. The existence of these separate units depended on the size of the company. Only 53 percent of those companies reporting up to $250 million in sales had a government relations department. But among respondents with sales of $10 billion or more, 90 percent reported they had a separate department.[24]

The existence of these units by industry grouping was also studied. Industries that have been regulated for years by the old-style industry regulation (utilities, communications, transportation) head the list. But industries such as food, petroleum, chemicals and drugs, and lumber and paper, which have been affected by food safety and drug regulations and energy and environment regulations, are also high on the list.

The government relations function can be physically positioned in either or both of two major locations. It can be located at headquarters, at the Washington office of the company, or at both places. The Conference Board study showed that the headquarters location was most preferred by the 285 companies having a separate government relations function. The following list shows these preferred locations, including some that deviate from the more traditional pattern.

- 94 have only a headquarters unit
- 56 have only a Washington office
- 104 have both a headquarters unit and a Washington office
- 16 have a subunit in the general counsel's department
- 7 have a headquarters unit and a subunit in the general counsel's department
- 4 have a Washington office and a subunit in the general counsel's department
- 4 have some "other" organizational arrangement.[25]

Reporting relationships and titles of unit heads vary with the location. When there is a headquarters unit only, the unit head usually reports directly to the CEO or president of the company. The most prevalent titles are vice-president, director, manager, or counsel. The same reporting relationship is most prevalent when there is a Washington office only, that is, the unit head reports directly to the CEO or president. The most prevalent title is vice-president, but director is also common, and there are a few managers.[26]

When units are located in both Washington and headquarters, the Washington office can report to the headquarters executive, the headquarters unit and the Washington office can report to the same executive, or each unit can report to a different executive. Titles differ, and sometimes vice-presidents report to vice-presidents, or vice-presidents report to directors, and so forth. Figure 22.9 shows the most prevalent reporting relationships for these various unit locations.

The background of the government relations executive is varied. Most of

[24]*Ibid.*, p. 56.
[25]*Ibid.*, p. 57.
[26]*Ibid.*, pp. 60–61.

Figure 22.9. Prevalent Reporting Relationships

HEADQUARTERS UNIT AND WASHINGTON OFFICE

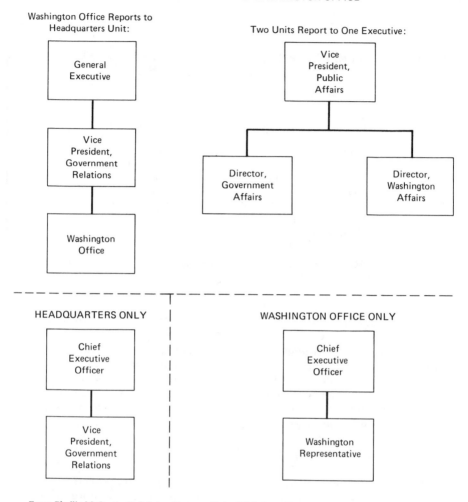

From Phyllis McGrath, *Redefining Corporate-Federal Relations* (New York: The Conference Board, 1979), p. 62. Reprinted with permission.

them are lawyers, public affairs or communications specialists, or have had experience in government. Other are academicians or people who have worked for trade associations, or people who have come up through the ranks of the company.[27]

The type of person who heads the government relations unit reflects the company's government relations philosophy. For a communications-oriented company that views government relations as getting the company's message across to legislators, the unit head is likely to have a communications

[27]*Ibid.*, p. 63.

background. Companies concerned more with regulatory matters are likely to have a lawyer in this position.[28] The staff of the government relations unit also reflects a variety of disciplines (see box), indicating that the function actually calls for a combination of talents.

DISCIPLINES REPRESENTED ON THE GOVERNMENT RELATIONS STAFF (IN ORDER OF FREQUENCY)

Washington	Headquarters
Law	Law
Government Relations	Public Relations-Communications
Business	Business
Public Relations-Communications	Government Relations-Public Affairs
Technical	Political Science
Government	Economics
Other (including marketing and international)	Government

From Phyllis McGrath, *Redefining Corporate-Federal Relations* (New York: The Conference Board, 1979, p. 65. Reprinted with permission.

The government relations function is concerned with three areas of government, legislative, executive, and regulatory, and involves activities at all of these levels. Strategies for legislative relations include Washington contact and grass-roots programs as well as political action committees. Maintaining contact with the executive branch requires someone with Washington experience who may still have contacts, or someone who has an interest in developing them. Working through organizations such as the Business Roundtable is a successful strategy for executive branch relations. Maintaining regulatory relations involves more legal work, but also increasingly involves technical people who are brought in from company headquarters to provide detailed technical information for the regulators. This information can be critical to getting the kind of regulations that the company can live with and successfully incorporate in its operations.[29]

Contacting government officials, including lobbying and social contact, is an important activity. The government relations function, particularly a Washington office, assists other people in the company when they lobby and testify before Congress or regulatory agencies. Another set of activities relates to internal communications—keeping key people in the corporation informed about legislative and regulatory developments of interest to the company. One of the basic day-to-day responsibilities of government relations is to monitor public policy developments that may have an impact on the company's operations.[30]

[28]*Ibid.*
[29]*Ibid.*, pp. 5–7.
[30]*Ibid.*, pp. 10–24.

While this discussion has focused on government relations on the federal level, government relations at the state level is also important to many corporations. Some companies have as part of the government relations function a subunit that deals with state and local government relations.[31]

Finally, government relations is in some sense the job of everyone who is part of the corporation, not just that of the government relations unit. Because of importance of public policy, there is a constant flow of corporate people into Washington to testify, meet with government officials, contact the staff of legislators or regulatory agencies, and attend meetings on governmental matters.[32]

The executive who plays the most critical role in the company's total government relations effort is, of course, the CEO. The CEO is the best person to meet with high-level government officials and help motivate staff, stockholders, and others by putting his or her stamp of approval on PACs, grass-roots programs, and similar strategies. Table 22.5 shows the different government relations activities of the CEO and the frequency of CEO involvement in these activities. The Conference Board study also indicates that CEO commitment and support of government relations is increasing, reflecting the increasing importance of public policy to corporations.[33]

Evaluating the Public Issues Management Effort

Evaluating the public issues management effort, both external affairs and government relations, at best, as the Conference Board points out, poses a conundrum. Evaluation is important as a basis for future planning and

TABLE 22.5 **Government Relations Activities of the Chief Executive Officer**[1]

Activity	Number of Mentions
Spokesperson for the company	334
Active in peer group efforts	300
Personal contact with key legislators	277
Personal contact with executive branch	206
Spokesperson for the industry	195
Presents testimony	130
Personal contact with regulatory agencies	129
Other	82

[1]The list of activities in the survey was not an open-ended one, therefore the number of mentions is greater than the number of companies in the sample because respondents were permitted to check more than one activity.

Source: Phyllis McGrath, *Redefining Corporate-Federal Relations* (New York: The Conference Board, 1979), p. 76. Reprinted with permission.

[31]McGrath, *Action Plans*, pp. 34–40.
[32]McGrath, *Corporate-Federal Relations*, p. 70.
[33]*Ibid.*, pp. 74–77.

budgeting regarding the effort. Yet using either a management by objectives approach or a results-oriented evaluation can be very frustrating, so much so that many companies simply abandon the evaluation effort entirely. There are no reliable yardsticks, many executives believe, with which a company can measure the effectiveness of its public issues management effort. Some even believe that there is no need to evaluate the effort, since it is a job that simply must be done regardless of the results.[34]

> As is the case with many other staff functions whose impact on corporate profits is not immediately evident, external relations does not readily lend itself to measurement. This general difficulty is compounded in the case of external relations by the multitude of influences outside of management's sphere of control that can and do affect the issues and publics that corporate external relations programs are aimed at. In most areas, "results achieved," whether good or bad, cannot be attributed to corporate actions alone.[35]

Corporations that do evaluate the effort generally use one of two approaches: (1) evaluation on the basis of set objectives, or (2) evaluation on the basis of activities carried out. Regarding the first approach, the two objectives of public issues management most frequently mentioned were to improve business credibility and develop a positive corporate image. The former is the most global objective, as the restoration of public trust usually refers to not just one company or even one industry, but to the total business community. The attainment of a positive corporate image relates to the degree of public acceptance of the company.[36] The following are among some of the results looked for in accomplishing this objective.

- Accurate and objective coverage by the media.
- The ability to conduct the regular business of the corporation without interference, and the continued growth of the company.
- A sound environment for advancing the marketing and investment objectives of the company.
- Some perceptible degree of change in external attitudes to the company.
- Some degree of success in anticipating problems; a minimum of surprises from the company's publics.[37]

Judgment about attainment of these objectives is based on informal or formal feedback. Informal feedback includes the feedback a CEO gets when he or she comes into contact with business peers, from other people who are not part of the business community, and even from family and friends. Senior management also obtains feedback from employees, customers, educators, and government officials. The opinion survey is most frequently used to obtain formal feedback. Industrial companies conduct surveys to determine whether or not the company's message is reaching its targeted publics.[38] Some companies develop an elaborate procedure for the use of opinion surveys for evaluation (see box).

[34]McGrath, *External Relations*, pp. 68–69.
[35]*Ibid.*, p. 64.
[36]*Ibid.*
[37]*Ibid.*, p. 65.
[38]*Ibid.*, pp. 65–66.

A major utility conducts a three-pronged approach to public opinion polling. First, the company subscribes to all of the available political and public opinion measuring services. Second, once a year, the public relations department conducts a public overview survey of its own. This survey measures customer satisfaction, asking a sampling of customers questions not only concerning the quality of the product, but whether or not the customer thinks the company is a good corporate citizen. At the same time, an internal survey is conducted to find out how employees perceive and react to messages from senior management. The third aspect consists of dozens of special studies done each year, relating to whatever issues or problems are topical. Because the unit operates with a small staff, most of this survey work is conducted by outside polling firms.

From: Phyllis McGrath, *Managing Corporate External Relations* (New York: The Conference Board, 1979), p. 66. Quoted with permission.

Evaluation on the basis of activities focuses on what the public issues management group is doing. This evaluation can get as specific as measuring the number of contacts with legislators, the number of internal communications issued, or the number of people involved in the grass-roots lobbying program. Meeting budgeted forecasts is an activity measure used in some corporations.[39]

Basic to the problem of evaluation is the question of what constitutes success in public issues management. A study of success in external affairs based on information from external affairs executives showed that the level of perceived success was highest for customer and stockholder relations, two areas that organizations traditionally have monitored. Environmental affairs was ranked lowest because it is a more recent concern for management and may also be more complex.[40]

The formulation of objectives and policies was found to have a positive correlation to perceived success in external affairs, even though only 57 percent of the respondents indicated their companies had established such policies and objectives. Over 72 percent of the firms had a formal evaluation mechanism, however, suggesting that many firms are evaluating their external affairs effort without formal objectives. Again, the existence of an evaluation procedure was linked to a higher level of perceived success.[41] Thus evaluation and setting of objectives may be important factors in the process, at least as far as perceived success of the public issues management effort is concerned.

Questions for Discussion

1. Define the term "public issues management." Does this use of the term "management" differ from its use in other contexts? If so, how?

[39]*Ibid.*, pp. 66–67.
[40]W. Harvey Hegarty, John C. Alpin, and Richard A. Cosier, "Achieving Corporate Success in External Affairs," *Business Horizons,* Vol. 21, No. 5 (October 1978), p. 68.
[41]*Ibid.*, pp. 70–72.

2. Describe the difference between a reactive, accommodative, proactive, and interactive response. Which response pattern would you recommend for corporations? Why?
3. How important do you think public issues management is to corporations? Is it crucial to their survival? Is it crucial to survival of the free enterprise system?
4. What is a public issue? Describe the different ways public issues can be categorized. Give some examples of issues that are in each of the different categories.
5. Describe the life cycle of a public issue. Do you find the three-phase model outlined in the text useful? How can you tell where an issue is in its life cycle? Give examples of issues in each phase. What other models of a public issues life cycle can you suggest?
6. Trace the flow of an issue through the public issues management system described in the text. Where are the crucial points in this process? Where do key decisions have to be made?
7. How important is environmental forecasting to a company? How are forecasting and planning linked? Define both concepts.
8. Describe the four-sided planning model. Name some specific factors in the economic, technological, political, and social environments that it is important for corporations to know about. Are there any other environments you would include in this forecasting model?
9. Discuss the principles that Wilson enunciates for environmental scanning. Are these principles realistic and appropriate? Are there any that strike you as more important than the others?
10. Discuss the various sources of environmental information outlined in the text. Which sources, if any, seem to be most important? Are there any sources you would add to this list? Would you categorize them differently?
11. Discuss the different approaches to prioritizing issues of concern to a company mentioned in the text. Is it necessary to get very sophisticated in this process? Why or why not? Which system would you recommend for your company?
12. What are the various external constituencies of a corporation? How would you relate to each of these constituencies? Think in terms of specific programs and organizational structure.
13. Do you favor a centralized approach to external affairs or a decentralized approach? Would you have an executive below the level of CEO responsible for all the various functions of external affairs or would you have no such executive? What are the advantages and disadvantages of each approach? Is there an optimum structure?
14. What title do you prefer for the external relations executive? What is the difference between public relations and public affairs? Why is public relations as a title falling into disfavor? Is it no longer appropriate to describe the function? Why or why not?
15. What is the customary background of the external relations executive? Is this background adequate? What would you suggest as an alternative?
16. How has government relations grown? What are the reasons behind this growth? What are your projections about future growth in government relations?
17. What activities does government relations perform? How important are these activities to the corporation? What does it mean to say that government relations is a part of everyone's job in the corporation?
18. Describe the different ways of evaluating the public issues management effort. Is evaluation possible? What are the problems? What method do you prefer?

Suggested Reading

Ackerman, Robert W., and Bauer, Raymond A. *Corporate Social Responsiveness: The Modern Dilemma.* Reston, Va.: Reston Publishing Co., 1976.

Aguilar, Francis Joseph. *Scanning the Business Environment.* New York: Macmillan, 1967.

Andrews, K. *The Concept of Corporate Strategy.* Homewood, Ill.: Dow-Jones Irwin, 1971.

Ansoff, H. I. *Corporate Strategy.* New York: McGraw-Hill, 1965.

Brown, James K. *This Business of Issues: Coping with the Company's Environments.* New York: The Conference Board, 1971.

Lawrence, P., and Lorsch, J. *Organizations and Environment.* Cambridge, Mass.: Harvard University Press, 1967.

Lorange, P., and Vancil, R. *Strategic Planning Systems.* Englewood Cliffs, N.J.: Prentice-Hall, 1977.

McGrath, Phyllis. *Action Plans for Public Affairs.* New York: The Conference Board, 1977.

———. *Managing Corporate External Relations: Changing Perspectives and Responses.* New York: The Conference Board, 1976.

———. *Redefining Federal Corporate Relations.* New York: The Conference Board, 1979.

MacMillan, I. C. *Strategy Formulation: Political Concepts.* New York: West, 1978.

Pfeiffer, Jeffrey, and Aalancik, Gerald R. *The External Control of Organizations.* New York: Harper & Row, 1978.

Post, James E. *Corporate Behavior and Social Change.* Reston, Va.: Reston Publishing Co., 1976.

Rothschild, W. E. *Putting It All Together.* New York: American Management Association, 1976.

Steiner, G. A. *Top Management Planning.* New York: Macmillan, 1969.

23

Social Measurement and Reporting

. . . That what we measure provides an insight into what kind of a person—or a firm—or a nation—we are. After all, people naturally keep track of the things that are most important to them. . . . The things we measure, how we measure them, the form in which we record and analyze the data, and to whom we disclose it, not only tell much about us but are also likely to have a considerable effect on the way we act.[1]

This chapter focuses on the development of a methodology for measuring performance in social areas (equal opportunity, occupational safety and health, pollution control) and the design of an appropriate reporting format for performance based on these measures. The need to measure performance should be obvious. Without some means of determining whether or not goals are being attained, a corporate entity or the nation as a whole have no way of knowing how efficiently resources are being allocated. These resources could be wasted without much of anything being accomplished. Performance measurement is crucial to management of resources. The reporting question involves the notion of accountability—to whom is the corporation or the government accountable in the use of resources and thus who deserves to know how well goals are being attained? What reporting format is most appropriate to convey the important information to a constituency that is interested in how well resources are being allocated and goals attained?

The need for a new measurement and reporting system in most of the public policy areas covered in the previous chapters should also be obvious.

[1]Eli Goldston, *The Quantification of Concern: Some Aspects of Social Accounting* (Pittsburgh, Pa.: Carnegie-Mellon University, 1971), pp. 15–16. Quoted with permission.

The traditional financial reports of a corporation tell us nothing about the performance of a safety program or how many women and minorities have been hired in the last fiscal year and what percentage they constitute of either the total workforce of the company or particular occupational categories. The national income accounts tell us nothing about the effectiveness of the government's pollution control program. The gross national product figures, for example, which are an aggregation of all the goods and services produced in the country, does not differentiate between goods that were produced under polluting conditions and goods that have been produced to reduce pollution.

Thus an important goal of public policy is the development of appropriate methodologies to measure performance in social areas, and the publication of these figures in a meaningful and relevant fashion to the appropriate constituencies. This area of social measurement and reporting will be discussed at two levels: (1) the micro level, the level of the firm, where the development of the social audit will be discussed, and (2) the macro level, or the perspective of society as a whole, where the use of social indicators will be examined.

The Social Audit

The social audit is an attempt by an individual corporation to measure its performance in an area where it is making a social impact, whether it is the impact being made on the company's workforce of an affirmative action program, the impact of a safety and health program on the health and safety of its employees, the impact of an environmental control program on the surrounding community, or the impact of a consumer affairs program on consumers themselves.

The social audit is an attempt to identify, measure, evaluate, report, and monitor the effects a corporation is having on society or on certain segments of society that are not covered in the traditional financial reports.

The term "social audit," however, deserves some explanation. The word "audit" has a precise meaning in accounting terminology, referring to an "attest" function performed by an independent accounting group attesting that the corporation's financial records are accurate and conform to generally accepted accounting principles. The audit in social audit, however, does not refer to this attest function, but to the various attempts that corporations have made or proposals that have been advocated for the measurement and reporting of corporate social performance.

Problems of Social Auditing. The definition of a social audit mentioned previously states the five tasks of social auditing: identification, measurement, evaluation, reporting, and monitoring. None of these tasks is easy. They involve some difficult conceptual and technical problems that require answers, however primitive the state of the art may be at the time.

Identification, for example, involves a fundamental decision on whether a corporation is going to adopt a comprehensive approach to the social audit and attempt to measure the total social impact it is having on society, or whether it is going to take a piecemeal approach and measure only specific programs or areas of the company that are believed to have the most significant social impact. The comprehensive approach is a very ambitious undertaking, involving a nontraditional approach to the corporation and its relationship to society, the development of some kind of methodology to measure the social impact of all corporate activities on society, and an evaluation as to whether the total impact is positive or negative. The next section will show some examples of this type of audit.

If the piecemeal approach is adopted, a corporation is faced with making choices about which areas are most important and deserve attention. Some areas, for most corporations, are fairly standard, such as equal opportunity, pollution control programs, and safe and healthful working conditions for employees. But beyond these fairly standard areas, the issue of identification gets fuzzy. Should a corporation audit consumer complaints about product quality? Is job satisfaction an important aspect of the quality of life that deserves to be audited? If the corporation is involved in South Africa, should this aspect of its operations receive attention? Is the ethical performance of corporate executives important to measure in some fashion? What about the corporation's minority purchasing program or charitable contributions?

The list of social impact areas a corporation could audit is almost endless. But the line has to be drawn somewhere. Most likely it will be drawn by corporate executives on the basis of their particular interests or their perceptions of constituent concerns, or on the basis of some kind of survey performed by the corporation to find out what their constituents are interested in knowing.[2]

Measurement is even more difficult. First, should the audit be based on the use of multiple measures or a single measure? The advantages of a single measure, such as dollars and cents, is obvious. One can then come up with a bottom line figure representing total social impact that can be compared with past years' performance (if the comprehensive approach is used) or that can be used to compare the performance across various social areas (if the piecemeal approach is used) to determine where resources are being used most efficiently and where the most socially beneficial impact is being made.

However, is the use of a single measure realistic? Can a common denominator be found to express the performance in such different areas as affirmative action and pollution control? Do not these social areas involve apples and oranges (and bananas and pineapples), so that despite the drawbacks, multiple measures appropriate to each area are the only realistic possibility? Again, examples of both approaches will be presented in the next section.

Secondly, should the measures be input- or output-oriented, that is, should they be based on inputs to a social area (pollution control expenditures, purchases from minority firms) or on the actual outputs of these expenditures (reduction in pollution, economic health of minority businesses)? Input measures are probably easiest to develop, but do they really measure performance? To take a specific example, the amount of money a corporation contributes to charitable causes is easy to measure. But is this really a measurement of performance? Would not a more relevant performance measurement be to ascertain the social impact these contributions were

[2]Raymond A. Bauer and Dan H. Fenn, Jr., "What Is a Corporate Social Audit," *Harvard Business Review*, Vol. 51, No. 1 (January-February 1973), pp. 40–41.

making on improvement of education, improvement in the quality of life in the disadvantaged community, or wherever else these contributions were going?

Evaluation is equally difficult. Once some measures are developed, what do they mean? What are appropriate benchmarks against which to measure performance? Where government standards exist, such as pollution standards, the problem may be solved. Many believe, however, that these standards should be treated as minimums as far as performance is concerned, not as standards for judging the success of a particular program.[3]

In the equal opportunity area, measures of minorities employed can be judged against percentages of minorities in the relevant population. Comparisons can be made across occupational categories to determine where discrepancies in the hiring or promotion of women and minorities exist. But in most areas, the standards for measuring success are vague or nonexistent. What constitutes a successful minority purchasing program? How many consumer complaints have to be received before product quality can be judged to be poor? Where is the dividing line between good and bad ethics of corporate executives?

Another interesting question regarding evaluation is whether the corporation should be evaluated solely on what it has done in the social area, or whether a corporation should also be evaluated on its corporate social inactivity—social impacts that it should have dealt with but did not for one reason or another. This is a kind of opportunity cost concept. Should the corporation be penalized for not doing what it should have done in dealing with social problems as well as receiving credit for those things it has done?

Reporting involves the question of whether to go public with social information or whether to use the data collected only for internal purposes. The latter purpose is laudable because management can use performance information in assessing corporate social performance and make appropriate decisions about the most effective use of corporate resources. Keeping the information internal also protects the corporation from being unfairly or unjustly criticized for its social performance or lack thereof by corporate critics.

But shouldn't the corporation be accountable to the public, particularly its shareholders, on the use of resources to accomplish social goals? Isn't the accountability basically the same as the financial accountability to shareholders embodied in the annual report? Doesn't the public have a right to know, in this case, that makes reporting an obligation?

Another question related to reporting is the usefulness of social information to the public. Where no common measures or reporting format exists, it is difficult, if not impossible, to compare the social performance of different firms. Even if an investor wanted to take social information into account when buying stock, it would be difficult to make judgments about corporations on this dimension. Any suggestion to develop a common index by which to compare the social performance of corporations has met with strong opposition from business.[4]

[3]*Ibid.*, p. 41.

[4]See Report of the Task Force on Corporate Social Performance, U.S. Department of Commerce, *Corporate Social Reporting in the United States and Western Europe* (Washington, D.C.: U.S. Government Printing Office, 1979), pp. v–viii.

Finally, monitoring involves a follow-up operation. A one-time social audit would seem to be an ineffective way to measure a corporation's social performance. Society changes, technology changes, government regulations change; what was once a satisfactory level of performance may prove to be inadequate at a later date. A corporation must commit itself to periodic social audits, and establish the data base and expertise within the company to perform this monitoring. "Continued systematic monitoring of social performance of both the overall organization's efforts as well as that of individual divisions or managers keeps alive and operational the organization's original commitment and protects its investment in any given action that has important social consequences."[5]

Types of Social Audits. There are many different approaches to the social audit, each of which has distinct advantages and disadvantages. These approaches are inventory, program management, cost or outlay, process audit, cost-benefit technique, and social indicator. Many of these approaches are actually used by corporations, others are simply proposals. They will be discussed in turn, with examples presented where possible.

Inventory Approach. The inventory approach is simply a listing and brief description of corporate social programs that a corporation has developed to help solve social problems. Sometimes this listing appears on a page or two of the annual report (see Exhibit 23.1). At other times, special booklets may be published describing the company's community activities or its charitable contributions.[6] The description may or may not contain quantitative information about costs or results, but the informality of this approach makes it difficult to systematically compare different costs and results to evaluate performance, and impossible to compare different companies. It is not very useful to management in evaluating performance of particular programs or to external constituencies in evaluating the total social performance of the company.

Program Management Approach. The program management approach again focuses on specific social programs the company has developed rather than total social impact of the corporation, but is a more systematic effort to identify costs and evaluate achievements than the inventory approach. This approach is essentially an extension of a traditional management audit to social programs.

The example shown in Exhibit 23.2 (Social Responsibility Program Statement) is broken down into specific social programs, such as job safety and community involvement. The resources committed to each program are shown (money, personnel, or physical property), and where possible are expressed in dollars. The last column (effect on human behavior and/or environment) is an attempt to measure the results of the program. This column would be most useful to management in comparing results with resources committed to get some idea of how efficiently resources are being utilized, and to compare the results with the actual objectives that may have been set by management.

This approach seems to be of most use for the management of social

---

[5]David H. Blake et al., *Social Auditing: Evaluating the Impact of Corporate Programs* (New York: Praeger, 1976), pp. 4–5.

[6]See *Participation* (Los Angeles: Atlantic Richfield Company, Public Affairs Department, 1975).

EXHIBIT 23.1 ───────────────────────────────────

The Inventory Approach

Corporate Responsibility

Along with a number of well-defined financial goals and targets. Multifoods has a corporate objective which challenges the Company to expand its awareness of growing social and environmental responsibilities and to increase its ability to act effectively.

The accomplishment of this goal has many measurements, and substantial progress was made in this area in fiscal 1978.

Equal Employment Opportunity

Total worldwide employment grew some 3 percent to 8,133 during the year. Overall minority employment in the United States rose from 10.5 percent to 11.3 percent. At the same time, the percentage of minority employees in management rose from 3.8 to 3.9 percent, and the number of women in managerial and administrative positions rose from 9.2 to 9.9 percent. The Company plans to aggressively pursue its affirmative action commitment through the hiring, training and promotion of qualified minority and women job candidates.

Corporate Contributions

During the year Multifoods sought out innovative programs through which it could direct funds from its Corporate Contributions Program. In its home state of Minnesota, for instance, Multifoods underwrote the cost of the newspaper production and distribution of the script of the CBS Special, "The Defection of Simas Kudirka." Approximately 100,000 secondary school students took part in this reading enrichment program. Total payments from the Contributions Program reached a record $652,000 in fiscal 1978.

Environmental Control

Multifoods continues to keep abreast of environmental controls and regulations. The businesses in which Multifoods is involved do not have major pollution problems. The Company during the year improved its various environmental systems and controls and continues in compliance with current governing standards.

Energy Conservation

Multifoods for the last four years has conducted an on-going and effective program to reduce energy consumption. Each division continues to develop improved programs and become more energy efficient. Several key locations have reduced their average energy usage by as much as 15 percent.

Loaned Executives

The Company, along with the great majority of business and labor organizations in the United States, has long been concerned with the need to improve productivity.

In light of this concern Multifoods was quick to respond to a call for a loaned executive for a year to the American Productivity Center, organized in Houston under the direction of Jackson Grayson, former chairman of the Wage and Price Commission.

In addition, Multifoods supplied loaned executives to the United Way and the National Alliance of Businessmen. Many other officers and employees are active volunteers in various civic, educational, community and business organizations.

Code of Conduct

In all countries in which it operates plants or buys or sells products, it is the practice of Multifoods to conduct its business in compliance with the laws of those countries. The pursuit of good corporate citizenship is spelled out in a published Code of Conduct, and it is the individual responsibility of each employee to comply with the procedures established by the Code.

From *Social Responsibility Disclosure: 1978 Survey* (Cleveland, Ohio: Ernst & Ernst), p. 62. Reprinted with permission.

EXHIBIT 23.2

Social Responsibility Program Statement

Program	Committed Resources	Effect on Human Behavior and/or Environment
Human resources		
Company medical plan	$___Health insurance contribution	___Number of employees covered
		___Claims paid during year
Job safety program	$___Expended for noncompulsory safety equipment	___Injuries/1,000 man-hours
	___Man-hours spent on safety seminars and instruction	___Ratio of employee injuries to industry average
	___Suggestions adopted	
Leisure and recreation	$___	___Employees participants in softball league
	$___Land value	___Man-hour usage of company athletic facilities
Education	___Employees participating in company courses of instruction	___Employees successfully completing company courses of instruction
	$___Tuition paid	___Credit hours financed at colleges or universities
		___Degrees awarded to employee participants in tuition reimbursement program
Physical resources		
Company recycle program	___Man-hours spent on special studies	___Tonnage recycled
		___Ratio of waste/final output
		___Energy usage/final output
Land reclamation program	$___	___Ratio of reclaimed/damaged land
Product or service contributions		
Product safety	$___	___Product safety innovations implemented
	___Product research man-hours	
Packaging reduction	$___	___Reduction in tons of nonrecyclable packaging
	___Product research man-hours	___Tons of product or packaging recycled
Community involvement		
Local business development	$___Funds contributed	___Businessmen receiving free consulting
	$___Loans to minority	
	$___Business averaging	___Workers trained and removed from welfare
	___Man-hours spent training unemployed	
Community fund	$___Contributions	
	___Man-hours devoted to lecture on United Fund activities	___Percentage of employees contributing fair share

From C. H. Brandon and J. P. Matoney, Jr., "Social Responsibility Financial Statement," *Management Accounting*, November 1975, p. 33. Reprinted by permission.

programs. It does not seem to be very useful for external reporting. No standards exist against which to judge whether too much or too little has been invested in these programs. This approach is also of little value in the selection of priorities, since it evaluates individual social programs in a vacuum. The report does not include an estimate of the needs and demands of communities matched to the particular capabilities and limitations of an individual business. Performance is related mainly to the objectives set by management. Relatively little information is provided about the impact of a program on a particular social problem of concern to the community or society at large.

The Process Audit. The process audit is like the program management and inventory approaches in that it focuses on specific social programs, but it provides more information about those programs. As originally formulated by Bauer and Fenn of the Harvard Business School, the process audit consists of four steps or phases. The questions that are relevant to each of these phases are shown in Exhibit 23.3, which is an application of the process audit technique to an educational contributions program.

1. An assessment of the circumstances under which each social program being audited came into being.

2. An explication of the goals of the program—a statement of what the program is intended to accomplish.

3. The rationale behind the activity, specifying how the goals are to be attained.

4. Describe what is actually being done as opposed to what the rationale says ought to be done.[7]

The goal of such an audit, according to Bauer and Fenn, "is to assemble the information that will make it possible for a person to intelligently assess the program, to decide whether he agrees with its goals, to decide whether the rationale is appropriate to the goals, and to judge whether the actual implementation promises to attain these goals satisfactorily."[8] It is obvious that this approach is again primarily management-oriented and suffers from many of the same disadvantages of the program management approach as far as external reporting is concerned.[9]

EXHIBIT 23.3

The Process Audit as Applied to an Educational Contributions Program

Phase I: History and Background of Program
1. How long has the company given educational contributions?
2. By what methods have these contributions been given?
3. How much and in what areas have these contributions been given?
4. What has been the organizational history of educational contributions?

Phase II: Program's Objectives
1. What are the objectives of the various categories of educational contributions?
2. Is there an overall objective to educational contributions? If so, what is it?
3. How were these objectives determined and by what criteria?
4. Are these objectives periodically evaluated? If so, how?

Phase III: Program's Operations
1. How is the program organized?
2. What is its current budget?
3. How was this budget determined and what criteria were used?
4. How is the program's budget allocated and what criteria are used?
5. What special managerial skills and/or managerial difficulties are involved in this program?
6. Is the management of this program evaluated? If so, how?

Phase IV: Summary Evaluation
1. Are the actual grants made consistent with its stated objectives?
2. According to the company's overall objectives, are changes needed in the program's objectives or operations? If so, what are these changes?

[7]Bauer and Fenn, "Social Audit," p. 47.

[8]*Ibid.*

[9]See Blake et al., *Social Auditing,* for an extensive discussion of the process audit and some specific applications of the technique.

The Cost or Outlay Approach. This approach, as the name suggests, focuses on the costs or other outlays that are associated with a given social program. There is also some attempt made to determine whether the amounts involved are appropriate. A specific proposal for an audit of this type, called a Socio-Economic Operating Statement, was made by David F. Linowes, a CPA from a New York accounting firm.[10]

This SEOS would be prepared periodically along with a business organization's profit and loss statement and balance sheet. It would consist of a tabulation of those expenditures a business made voluntarily (not required by law or union contract) that were aimed at three areas: (1) improving the welfare of employees, (2) improving conditions of the environment, and (3) improving safety of the products the company makes. Offset against these expenditures would be negative charges for the cost of social actions that have been brought to the attention of management, but that management chose not to respond to. These detriments consist of the cost of those actions that are of such a nature that a "reasonably prudent and socially aware" business management would have responded favorably.

The Linowes proposal attempts to measure more of the total social impact of a company, both positive and negative, by introducing the opportunity cost concept. While recognizing a certain degree of subjectivity in the preparation of this report, Linowes suggests that the SEOS should be prepared by an interdisciplinary group within the company and formally audited by an outside independent interdisciplinary team headed by a CPA. In addition, Linowes offers the following guidelines to help classify socioeconomic items to be included on the report.

> If a social beneficial action is required by law, but is ignored, the cost of such item is a "detriment" for the year. The same treatment is given an item if postponed, even with government approval. Similarly, if a socially beneficial action is required by law and is applied earlier than the law requires, it is an improvement. (In an inflationary period this might mean a saving of money for the company and could be categorized as a contingent asset.)

> A pro-rata portion of salaries and related expenses of personnel who spent time in socially beneficial actions or with social organizations is included as an "improvement."

> Cash and product contributions to social institutions are included as "improvements."

> Cost of setting up facilities for the general good of employees or the public—without union or government requirement—is an includable "improvement."

> Neglecting to install safety devices which are available at a reasonable cost is a "detriment."

> The cost of voluntarily building a playground or nursery school for employees and/or neighbors is a plus on the exhibit. Operating costs of the facility in each succeeding year are also includable.

> Costs of relandscaping strip mining sites, or other environmental eyesores, if not otherwise required by law, are listed as improvements on the SEOS exhibit.

---

[10]David F. Linowes, "An Approach to Socio-Economic Accounting," *The Conference Board Record*, Vol. IX, No. 11 (November 1972), pp. 58–61. See also David F. Linowes, *Strategies for Survival* (New York: AMACOM, 1973).

Extra costs in designing and building unusually attractive business facilities for beauty, health and safety are includable "improvements."[11]

An example of an SEOS is shown in Exhibit 23.4. As can be seen, the statement has a "bottom line" figure that shows the amount of total socio-economic contribution or deficit for a given year. This figure can be compared to the figure from other companies in the same industry, provided they use the same format and follow the same guidelines. Statements of the same company can be compared over several years to see the general directions in which a company is moving in its social involvement.

Problems with this approach, however, make its usefulness limited. Efforts to allocate the costs of various functions between social programs and day-to-day business operations could prove troublesome. The incremental approach (voluntary actions only would appear on the statement) could also prove troublesome because of the many government regulations that apply to corporate activities. There is also no way to overcome the subjectivity introduced by using the opportunity cost concept for social detriments. Where does one draw the line as to what a "reasonably prudent socially aware" business management would have done? Finally, measuring just the costs ignores the benefits that are accruing either to the corporation or to society, an important piece of information to both management and the public.

The Cost-Benefit Approach. The cost benefit technique also attempts to measure the total social impact of a corporation, but not just those activities that are voluntarily undertaken. The cost-benefit approach tries to tally up aggregate social costs and benefits of all corporate activities as they affect society. The reporting model should systematically reflect the value of all resources consumed by the entity, including resources that are free to the consuming entity (noninternalized costs or external diseconomies) and the value of all benefits produced, including those providing no compensation to the producing entity (external economies). To determine whether the entity was a net benefit or cost to society, the values would have to be expressed in a common denominator (dollars and cents).[12]

The vantage point of a cost-benefit audit, according to Ralph Estes, is that of society looking toward the entity. This is different from the vantage point of traditional financial accounting, which reflects the viewpoint of the firm looking out toward society (see Figure 23.1). From the former vantage point, the benefits to society would be measured by the values or utilities received by society (which may differ from the amount paid to the entity) while costs would reflect the full detriments to society (not only those for which the entity pays).

An example of a cost-benefit audit based on this model is shown in Exhibit 23.5, which illustrates the different vantage point of this report.[13] Environmental improvements, for example, which would normally be considered as costs to the company, are benefits to society in this report. Pay-

---

[11]*Ibid.*, p. 59.

[12]Ralph Estes, *Corporate Social Accounting* (New York: Wiley Interscience, 1976), pp. 92–95.

[13]See Clark C. Abt, *The Social Audit for Management* (New York: AMACOM, 1977), pp. 258–264, for another example of a cost-benefit type of social audit.

EXHIBIT 23.4

XXXX CORPORATION
Socio-Economic Operating Statement
for the Year Ending December 31, 1971

I *Relations with People:*
   A. *Improvements:*

1. Training program for handicapped workers	$ 10,000	
2. Contribution to educational institution	4,000	
3. Extra turnover costs because of minority hiring program	5,000	
4. Cost of nursery school for children of employees, voluntarily set up	11,000	
Total Improvements		$ 30,000

   B. *Less: Detriments*

1. Postponed installing new safety devices on cutting machines (cost of the devices)		14,000
C. Net improvements in People Actions for the Year		$ 16,000*

II *Relations with Environment:*
   A. *Improvements:*

1. Cost of reclaiming and landscaping old dump on company property	$ 70,000	
2. Cost of installing pollution control devices on Plant A smokestacks	4,000	
3. Cost of detoxifying waste from finishing process this year	9,000	
Total Improvements		$ 83,000

   B. *Less: Detriments*

1. Cost that would have been incurred to relandscape strip mining site used this year	$ 80,000	
2. Estimated costs to have installed purification process to neutralize poisonous liquid being dumped into stream	100,000	$180,000
C. Net Deficit in Environment Actions for the Year		($97,000)*

III *Relations with Product:*
   A. *Improvements:*

1. Salary of V.P. while serving on government Product Safety Commission	$ 25,000	
2. Cost of substituting lead-free paint for previously used poisonous lead paint	9,000	
Total Improvements		$ 34,000

   B. *Less: Detriments*

1. Safety device recommended by Safety Council but not added to product		22,000
C. Net improvements in Product Actions for the Year		$ 12,000*
Total Socio-Economic Deficit for the Year		($69,000)
Add: Net Cumulative Socio-Economic Improvements as at January 1, 1971		$249,000
Grand Total Net Socio-Economic Actions to December 21, 1971		$180,000

*The starred items are summed to obtain the Total Socio-Economic Deficit for the year 1971.

From David F. Linowes, "An Approach to Socio-Economic Accounting," *The Conference Board Record,* Vol. IX, No. 11 (November 1972), p. 60. Reprinted with permission.

Figure 23.1. The Estes Social Performance Model of Reporting Viewpoints

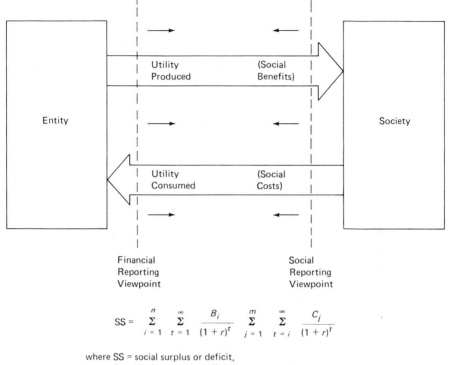

$$ SS = \sum_{i=1}^{n} \sum_{t=1}^{\infty} \frac{B_i}{(1+r)^t} \quad \sum_{j=1}^{m} \sum_{t=i}^{\infty} \frac{C_j}{(1+r)^t} $$

where SS = social surplus or deficit,
B_i = the ith social benefit,
C_j = the jth social cost,
r = an appropriate discount rate,
t = time period in which benefit or cost is expected to occur

From Ralph Estes, *Corporate Social Accounting* (New York: Wiley Interscience, 1976), pp. 93–94. Reprinted by permission.

ments for goods and services, which are normally considered to be revenues to the company, are actually costs from a society's point of view.

That this kind of social audit is an ambitious undertaking should be obvious. Its usefulness lies in its ability to develop realistic cost estimates for all the line items on the report. This could be extremely difficult in the areas of discrimination, work-related injuries and illness, and environmental damage, among others. All cost benefit studies in social areas suffer from this difficulty of valuing social benefits and costs in economic terms. The values assigned to these items, however, would undoubtedly make the difference as to whether a firm was a net cost or benefit to society.

The Social Indicator Approach. This approach to social auditing has two steps. The first is to perform an external audit of community well-being through the use of social indicators (see next section). This audit provides a corporation with some objective data on what community needs are and which of those needs are most pressing. The second step is to measure internal corporate activities that are related to the community indicators.

An example of this kind of audit is the one performed by the First

EXHIBIT 23.5

THE PROGRESSIVE COMPANY
Social Impact Statement for the Year Ended December 31, 19x1

Social Benefits
Products and services provided		$xxx	
Payments to other elements of society			
Employment provided (salaries and wages)	$xxx		
Payments for goods and other services	xxx		
Taxes paid	xxx		
Contributions	xxx		
Dividends and interest paid	xxx		
Loans and other payments	xxx	xxx	
Additional direct employee benefits		xxx	
Staff, equipment, and facility services donated		xxx	
Environmental improvements		xxx	
Other benefits		xxx	
Total Social Benefits			$xxx

Social Costs
Goods and materials acquired		$xxx	
Buildings and equipment purchased		xxx	
Labor and services used		xxx	
Discrimination			
In hiring (external)	$xxx		
In placement and promotion (internal)	xxx	xxx	
Work-related injuries and illness		xxx	
Public services and facilities used		xxx	
Other resources used		xxx	
Environmental damage			
Terrain damage	$xxx		
Air pollution	xxx		
Water pollution	xxx		
Noise pollution	xxx		
Solid waste	xxx		
Visual and aesthetic pollution	xxx		
Other environmental damage	xxx	xxx	
Payments from other elements of society			
Payments for goods and services provided	$xxx		
Additional capital investment	xxx		
Loans	xxx		
Other payments received	xxx	xxx	
Other costs		xxx	
Total Social Costs			xxx
Social Surplus (Deficit) for the Year			$xxx
Accumulated Surplus (Deficit) December 31, 19x0			xxx
Accumulated Surplus (Deficit) December 31, 19x1			$xxx

From Ralph Estes, *Corporate Social Accounting* (New York: Wiley Interscience, 1976), p. 96.
Reprinted with permission.

National Bank of Minneapolis. The major advantage of this approach is the measurement of corporate activities in relation to community needs and the impact this can have on the planning process (Figure 23.2). The external audit measures actual social conditions in the community. Based on this audit, an objective assessment can be made of social priorities. The internal audit will tell the company how well its own activities are meeting these needs, and plans can be made to make appropriate adjustments in corporate actions if necessary. Thus corporate social actions need not be based on the whims or interests of management, but on hard data about the real social conditions in the community.

Purposes of Social Auditing. Despite this variety in methods of measurement and reporting, the social audit can serve some useful purposes or objectives. One important purpose is to provide information to management and to the outside world about the impact of business on society. This impact can be positive or negative, and of varying magnitude, but without some kind of measurement and reporting, however crude, there is no way of knowing much of anything of a systematic nature about these impacts. The social audit can help to clarify both for management and external audiences the nature and magnitude of corporate activities that have social significance.[14]

A second purpose of the social audit is to provide a basis for accountability for the social consequences of corporate activities. This accountability can be either from lower levels of management to top management or from the corporation as a whole to society at large. Social auditing can provide the evaluation of corporate activities on the basis of social as well as economic performance. It is hoped that good social performance would be rewarded by promotion or public acclaim, and that the converse would also be true. Thus performance and accountability are linked, but social measurement and reporting are needed to provide this linkage.[15]

A third purpose is the use to which the social audit can be put by the management of corporations. The information contained in a social audit could be used to broaden the basis of "normal" management decisions. Specifically, the social audit would (1) allow a corporation to assess existing performance in regard to a host of public policy measures, (2) enable a corporation to measure, evaluate, and reward the performance of managers who have been given the responsibility for achieving public policy objectives, (3) provide an informational base for the integration of public policy objectives into long-range business planning, and (4) provide a means for assessing future performance with regard to high-priority public policy objectives.[16]

Figure 23.2. Social Decision-making Process

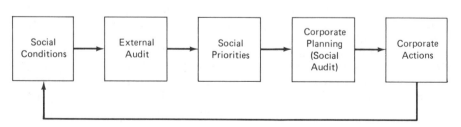

[14]Report of the Task Force on Corporate Social Performance, p. 87.

[15]*Ibid.*, p. 88.

[16]*Ibid.*, p. 113.

In summary, without social measurement and reporting by corporations there can be no assurance of progress toward public policy goals, no evaluation of the relative cost-effectiveness or efficiency of alternative methods of dealing with social impact, no comparison among or between companies and industries to determine what is possible, what is standard, and what should be corrected, and no criteria for corporate decision-making in the interests of attaining public policy objectives.

Social Indicators

The use of social indicators is a macro approach to social measurement and reporting, involving an attempt to measure social aspects of a community or an entire society. Social indicators are direct measures of one or more aspects of the quality of life in a given region or society that should be capable of observation over a period of time, thus providing time-series data for comparison. The specific definition of a social indicator is something of a controversy. According to Kenneth Land of the Russell Sage Foundation:

> There is little agreement on the defining characteristics of social indicators beyond the notions that (1) social indicators are time-series that allow comprehension over an extended period, and (2) social indicators are statistics that can be disaggregated or crossclassified by other relevant characteristics.[17]

Land suggests that the term "social indicator" refers to social statistics that are components in a social system (including sociopsychological, economic, demographic, and ecological components) or of some particular segment or process thereof, can be collected and analyzed at various times, and can be aggregated or disaggregated to levels that are appropriate to specifications of the model.[18]

Thus a social indicator is an aggregate or representative welfare measure that indicates the extent to which some goal of general interest to a community or society has been achieved. The indicator can be obtained by aggregating other statistics into a meaningful summary statistic or by selecting from some properly defined set of statistics one series whose movements are reasonably representative of all the rest. The major problems in the use of social indicators are in determining (1) what social statistics are relevant to the indicator, and (2) how to weigh the various statistics to arrive at a summary indicator.

Perhaps these attempts at defining the term "social indicator" will become more clear by looking at a specific example. Exhibit 23.6 shows a summary listing of the indicators that were first proposed for the external audit of the First National Bank of Minneapolis, mentioned in the previous section. The first step in using the social indicator approach is to define the term "quality of life" and decide on a set of components or accounts that, taken together, comprise the various elements of life that people think are important to their well-being. The criteria used to decide on these components for the First

[17]Kenneth C. Land, "On the Definition of Social Indicators," *The American Sociologist,* Vol. 6, No. 4 (November 1971), p. 322.
[18]*Ibid.*

EXHIBIT 23.6

Proposed Components and Standards for
Annual Social-Environmental Audit

Components (Accounts)	Standards
1. Job Opportunities	Percent of persons unemployed.
	Percent of persons who have changed jobs in the last five years.
	Percent of population employed.
	Percent of skilled jobs without people to fill them.
2. Pleasing and Healthy Physical Environment	Amount of pollution in the air measured against established standards.
	Amount of pollution in the water measured against established standards.
	Visual appearance of the area as judged by an urban environment committee on the basis of their own criteria.
	Percent of land dedicated to highway use.
	Percent of land preserved for parks and open space use.
3. Suitable Housing	Percent of substandard dwelling units.
	Number of communities with zoning ordinances permitting low and moderate income housing.
	Number of new housing starts in past year.
	Average number of persons per dwelling unit.
4. Good Health	Percent of infant mortalities.
	Life expectancy.
	Per capita incidence of heart disease.
	Venereal disease rate.
5. Adequate Income Levels	Percent of households earning less than $5,000 a year.
	Percent of households earning less than $10,000 a year.
	Number of people on various forms of public assistance and annual net gains or losses for public assistance case loads.
6. Quality Education	Percent of high school graduates.
	Percent of high school dropouts.
	Percent of high school graduates going to college.
	Percent of high school students taking national comparative tests who score better than national averages.
7. A Safe Society	Number of violent crimes per 10,000.
	Number of misdemeanors per 10,000.
	Number of felonies per 10,000.
	Percent of core city and suburban persons who feel safe walking the streets at night in their neighborhood.
8. A High Level of Citizen Participation	Percent of eligible persons voting in city elections.
	Number of persons in city-wide civic groups or numbers of persons in neighborhood associations.
	Percent of persons over 21 donating to the United Fund.

9. Widespread Cultural Activity	Number of persons visiting:
	  a) Guthrie Theatre
	  b) Walker Art Center
	  c) Minneapolis Institute of Arts
	  d) Minnesota Orchestra
	  e) St. Paul Arts and Sciences Center
	  f) Civic and semi-professional theatres.
	Number of community art exhibitions and concerts.

10. Adequate Transportation	Number of automobiles registered in metropolitan area. Percent of persons using public buses for daily transportation to work. Percent of one-passenger cars driving into downtown area in rush hours.

Reprinted from Todd Otis, "Measuring Quality of Life in Urban Areas," *Evaluation*, Fall 1972, p. 37, by permission of the copyright holder, Minneapolis Medical Research Foundation.

Minneapolis audit included the following: (1) the area was considered to be important by most people, (2) it could objectively be shown to be important, (3) it was guaranteed as a basic right regardless of whether it was supported by the majority, (4) it was at least potentially subject to influence by public or private social policies, and (5) enough data were available to at least attempt a measurement.

Using these criteria, the components shown in Exhibit 23.6 were developed. For the income component, both perceived and objective importance were taken as self-evident, since money is a basic unit of trade and essential for material survival. An adequate income is increasingly considered to be a right, and many government resources have been devoted to guaranteeing adequacy. In addition, well-defined and accepted measures are available.

Employment was of similar importance. It is accepted as a basic means of survival, and many resources are used to maximize job opportunities. But work has also been shown to be basic to self-esteem. Moreover, employment is increasingly considered a right. Health is of at least equal concern, since it, too, is essential for physical survival, and to fully participate in and enjoy life. Again, massive public outlays demonstrate its importance.

Public safety is important both physically and psychologically. People obviously can be harmed physically by crime and accidents, but there is also a disadvantage to living in fear of crime, even if one is not directly affected by it. Housing fulfills the basic need for shelter. Bad housing can cause health and sanitation problems, and excessive costs for housing can affect a family's quality of life in other areas. In addition, basic questions of discrimination and access are involved.

In a complex, postindustrial society, education is becoming increasingly important for adaptation to change and for skill training. Society has made elementary and secondary education mandatory, and some form of higher education is increasingly necessary to land a good job, although its role is being questioned. Participation is a less tangible quality-of-life component. It is less necessary in a basic survival sense, but as basic needs are met, a sense of belonging becomes more important. Many people believe participation is one of the best indicators of community health. Participation is essential to the operation of a democracy, and is obviously beneficial for other community activities.

A good physical environment is essential to good health; the link between pollution and illness has been established by many studies. But people also consider an aesthetically pleasing environment to be an important part of the quality of life. Transportation is a basic necessity for getting from one place to another. But the type of transportation used by society can have profound effects on other quality-of-life areas, such as pollution. Culture, like participation, might be considered a "frill" by some people, but it is an important component of civilized societies, and the arts are considered an important part of the area's quality of life.

Once these components have been decided upon, the actual social indicators must be found that will provide some measure of these various aspects that make up the quality of life for a region. Statistics must be discovered that provide an "indication" of the status of a particular component. In Exhibit 23.6, it was decided, for example, that the amount of pollution in the air and water would provide some indication of what kind of pleasing and healthy physical environment existed. The percentage of substandard housing units in the area would indicate something about the quality of housing, the number of crimes would relate to a safe society, and so forth. Criteria have also been developed for the selection of these indicators. The following is a representative list of such criteria.

1. Must be able to be quantified and expressed in some unit, such as dollars.

2. Must be relevant to the component and readily available.

3. Must have some predictive value to be used in extrapolating trends.

4. Must be unique and mutually exclusive, so that no two components contain the same indicator.

5. Must be unambiguous so that anyone can get the same answer.

6. Must be verifiable and meet rules of evidence.

7. Must be reliable over time.

8. Must be result-oriented where possible, as opposed to input-oriented.

9. Must be objective, although subjective measures about people's feelings of safety, for example, are sometimes useful.

10. Must show an absence of skewing by extraneous events.

Not every social indicator study includes the same components or the same indicators. Experts differ on which are most relevant and useful. The components and indicators used in the 1973 Office of Management and Budget report are different from other reports, for example. It is difficult to find indicators that are relevant and available to all the various components of life that people believe are important.

Albert Biederman did an interesting study in 1966 by taking the 81 specific national goals set forth by the President's Commission on National Goals in 1960 and attempting to find published statistics relevant for evaluating progress toward each of these goals.[19] In examining the four major statistical series that existed in 1962 (The Statistical Abstract of the United

[19]*Goals for Americans: Report of the President's Commission on National Goals* (Englewood Cliffs, N.J.: Prentice-Hall, 1960).

States, Historical Statistics of the United States, Economic Indicators, and Health, Education, and Welfare Trends), Biederman was able to find statistics relevant for evaluating only 59 percent (48 out of 81) national goals. The fewest statistics were available (Table 23.1) for goals dealing with the status of the individual, democratic processes, arts and sciences, technological change, and hiring conditions. Many more statistics were available for the economic, education, and health and welfare areas.[20]

Social indicators can serve a number of purposes. They can be used to evaluate existing social policies and programs where economic measures are not relevant. They can be used to measure and evaluate the secondary social effects of economic policies or technological change. They can help policymakers set priorities when developing public policies to deal with social problems. And finally, social indicators can help to identify emerging social problems, enabling preventive actions to be taken before such problems reach crisis proportions.

Extent of Social Measurement and Reporting

Since 1971, Ernst and Ernst have conducted an annual survey of the extent and nature of what they call social responsibility disclosure in the annual reports of the Fortune 500 industrial companies. The 1978 survey was expanded to include an evaluation of the Fortune 50 Life Insurance Companies and 50 Commercial Banks as well. The highlights of the 1978 survey are shown below.[21]

TABLE 23.1 **Availability of Indicators Relevant to National Goals Formulated by President's Commission in 1960**

Goal Areas	No. of specific goals	No. of goals to which some indicator is relevant	No. of goals to which no indicator is relevant
The Individual	6	3	3
Equality	3	2	1
Democratic Process	11	5	6
Education	5	5	0
Arts & Sciences	8	2	5
Democratic Economy	9	4	5
Economic Growth	9	9	0
Technological Change	5	1	4
Agriculture	5	4	1
Living Conditions	10	2	8
Health & Welfare	10	10	0
Total	81	48	33

Source: Albert D. Biederman, "Social Indicators and Goals," *Social Indicators,* Raymond H. Bauer, ed. (Cambridge, Mass.: MIT Press, 1966), p. 88. Reprinted with permission.

[20] Albert D. Biederman, "Social Indicators and Goals," *Social Indicators,* Raymond H. Bauer, ed. (Cambridge, Mass.: MIT Press, 1966), pp. 68–153.

[21] *Social Responsibility Disclosure: 1978 Survey* (Cleveland, Ohio: Ernest & Ernst), pp. 1–6.

SOCIAL MEASUREMENT AND REPORTING

Industrials

The percentage of companies including SR information in their annual reports decreased slightly in the 1978 Survey to 89.2% from 91.2% the previous year. In particular, there was a reduction in the number of companies including information in the categories of Environment, Human Resources, Community Involvement, and Products while the number of disclosures pertaining to Energy and Fair Business Practices showed an increase [Table 23.2]. Almost 50% of the Fortune 500 firms consistently reported on social performance for the five-year period ending March 31, 1978 [Figure 23.3].

Coincident with the slight decline in the number of disclosing companies was a decrease in the number of firms quantifying their disclosures. In 1977, 52% of all industrials surveyed, and 59% of those making SR disclosures supplemented their disclosure with either monetary or nonmonetary quantification, in comparison with the 55% and 60% respectively, reported for 1976. Not unexpectedly, the number of quantified disclosures related to the Environment, Human Resources and Community Involvement categories showed a decrease consistent with the overall decline in those categories.

Although the number of companies making SR disclosures showed a decline, a greater number of pages were devoted to them. The 1978 Survey identified approximately 250 pages of SR disclosure, compared with the 196 reported in 1977. The average number of pages devoted to SR information, per disclosing company, increased from .43 to .56 pages, making 1977's average page count greater than that of any other year in the Survey's history. The percentage of disclosing companies devoting more than one page of the annual report to SR information increased from 11% to 16% while the percentage of companies using less than one-half page decreased from 73% to 67% [Table 23.3].

SR disclosures were located throughout the annual reports with a majority in the general body. However, the number and percentage of companies disclosing this information in the President's letter significantly decreased [Table 23.4].

Commercial Banks

Ninety-four percent of the Fortune 50 Commercial Banks made SR disclosures. Fair Business Practices, Human Resources, and Community Involvement were the topics receiving the most attention.

TABLE 23.2 **Summary of SR Disclosures by General Category**

| | Companies Disclosing | | | |
| | 1977 | | 1976 | |
Category	No.	%	No.	%
Environment	252	57	269	59
Energy	263	59	239	52
Fair Business Practices	328	74	316	69
Human Resources	211	47	235	52
Community Involvement	147	33	181	40
Products	145	33	198	43
Other Disclosures	108	24	89	20

Source: Social Responsibility Disclosure: 1978 Survey (Cleveland, Ohio: Ernst & Ernst), p. 3. Reprinted with permission.

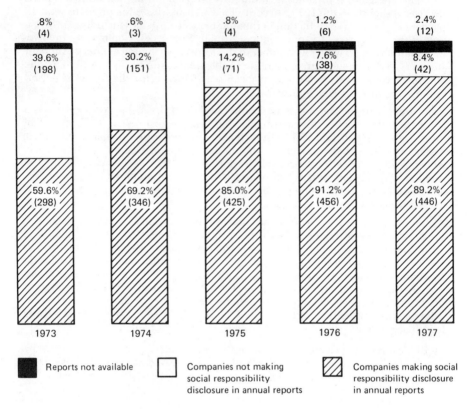

Figure 23.3. Fortune 500 Companies Making Social Responsibility Disclosure (Based on the 1973-1977 Fortune 500 Listings)

	1973	1974	1975	1976	1977
Reports not available	.8% (4)	.6% (3)	.8% (4)	1.2% (6)	2.4% (12)
Companies not making	39.6% (198)	30.2% (151)	14.2% (71)	7.6% (38)	8.4% (42)
Companies making	59.6% (298)	69.2% (346)	85.0% (425)	91.2% (456)	89.2% (446)

■ Reports not available   □ Companies not making social responsibility disclosure in annual reports   ▨ Companies making social responsibility disclosure in annual reports

From *Social Responsibility Disclosure: 1978 Survey* (Cleveland, Ohio: Ernst & Ernst), p. 3. Reprinted with permission.

TABLE 23.3 **Number of Pages Devoted to SR Disclosure**

	Companies			
	1977		1976	
Number of Pages	No.	%	No.	%
.01–.25	226	51	234	51
.26–.50	71	16	100	22
.51–.75	39	9	47	10
.76–1.00	38	8	26	6
Greater than 1.00	72	16	49	11
Total	446	100	456	100
Average	.56		.43	

Source: Social Responsibility Disclosure: 1978 Survey (Cleveland, Ohio: Ernst & Ernst), p. 5. Reprinted with permission.

TABLE 23.4 **Location of SR Disclosure**

Location in Annual Report	Companies Making Disclosure In Each Location			
	1977		1976	
	No.	%	No.	%
President's letter to shareholders	171	38	209	46
Separate section of annual report in some way devoted to SR. (This need not be a major section of the annual report, but, at a minimum, a paragraph heading relating to an aspect of social responsibility)	177	40	181	40
Other section of the annual report (general body of the report), e.g., financial highlights, new product development, captions of photographs, discussion of lines of business, financial statements	431	97	438	96
Separate booklet sent to shareholders together with annual report	6	1	7	2

Source: Ernst & Ernst, *Social Responsibility Disclosure: 1978 Survey,* p. 6. Reprinted with permission.

The average number of pages devoted to SR disclosure was .43. However, at least eight banks reported SR information outside the annual report by publishing an additional booklet specifically devoted to social responsibility.

Forty percent of the disclosing banks provided quantified disclosure. Community Involvement was the category in which the largest number of monetary disclosures were made while nonmonetary disclosures were most often made in the category of Fair Business Practices.

Life Insurance Companies

Eighty-eight percent of the life insurance companies provided SR information in their annual reports. Disclosing companies devoted an average of .50 pages to SR information with the highest number being 3.25 pages.

Extensive disclosure was provided on Fair Business Practices, Human Resources, and Community Involvement. In particular, the topic of employee training was frequently mentioned.

Forty-eight percent of the disclosing life insurance companies provided quantified information. The greatest number of monetary disclosures were in the category of Community Involvement while most of the nonmonetary disclosures were in the area of Human Resources.

These figures, however, can be misleading. Most companies in the United States do little more than pay lip service to the idea and do not report much social information. An average of .56 pages is not very much and only 16 percent of the Fortune 500 companies devote more than a page to social responsibility disclosure. Some of these efforts are quite extensive, such as the 60-page Public Interest Report published by General Motors. The social audit, however, seems to be used much more widely in Western Europe, especially in West Germany and France, where the law requires corporations to report certain kinds of social information.[22]

The use of social indicators, at least on a national level, is not nearly so extensive. One of the first attempts to obtain statistical information about American society as a whole was made by President Hoover's Research Committee on Social Trends, appointed in 1929. Their report, called *Recent Social Trends in the United States,* correctly anticipated a number of social trends, but plans to update and review it annually were scrapped during the depression.

Interest in social indicators did not again appear until the 1960s, as the Democratic administrations under Presidents Kennedy and Johnson focused increasing attention on the nation's social problems. During this period, three individuals in the academic world added their voices to the social indicator movement. Bertram Gross of Wayne State University developed proposals for a "Social State of the Union" report as part of a larger "Social Systems Model."[23] At the Russell Sage Foundation, Eleanor B. Sheldon published *Indicators of Social Change: Concepts and Measurements* in 1968.[24] Finally, Harvard sociologist Daniel Bell, as chairman of the Commission on the Year 2000 and a participant in the Commission on Automation, Technology, and Economic Progress, developed a model for a "System of Social Accounts," to serve as a model balance sheet for social progress.[25]

The government itself again became interested in social indicators when the Secretary of HEW under President Johnson appointed a panel on social indicators charged with studying the feasibility of a social report. The final product of the Social Indicator Panel was a document entitled *Toward a Social Report,* which was published by HEW in 1969.[26] While stating that data for a complete social report did not exist, the report assembled existing indicators and urged further study. Four years later, in 1973, the Office of Management and Budget put out *Social Indicators,* a report designed to update and improve upon the earlier HEW report.[27] But it was not the complete and systematic social report that many had hoped for. This report was updated and published again four years later.[28] Since then, there has been no comprehensive, systematic effort at social measurement and reporting at the national level.

---

[22]See "When Businessmen Confess Their Social Sins," *Business Week,* November 6, 1978, pp. 175–176.

[23]Bertram M. Gross, "The State of the Nation: Social Systems Accounting," *Social Indicators,* Raymond Bauer, ed. (Cambridge, Mass.: MIT Press, 1966), p. 154.

[24]Eleanor B. Sheldon et al., *Indicators of Social Change: Concepts and Measurements* (New York: Russell Sage Foundation, 1968).

[25]Daniel Bell, "The Idea of a Social Report," *The Public Interest,* Spring 1969, p. 72.

[26]U.S. Department of Health, Education and Welfare, *Toward a Social Report* (Washington D.C.: U.S. Government Printing Office, 1969).

[27]Office of Management and Budget, *Social Indicators 1973* (Washington, D.C.: U.S. Government Printing Office, 1973).

[28]U.S. Department of Commerce, *Social Indicators 1976* (Washington: D.C.: U.S. Government Printing Office, 1977).

Questions for Discussion

1. Why is it necessary to measure social performance? What issues are involved in the social reporting question? What is the difference between the two levels of social measurement and reporting?
2. Define the social audit. Is the use of the term "audit" in this connection correct? Why or why not? What term would you use to refer to social measurement and reporting at the micro level?
3. List the different tasks involved in a social audit. Then list the problems that exist for each of these tasks. How would you resolve these problems if you were assigned the job of developing a social audit for your company?
4. Describe the different types of social audits. What are the advantages and disadvantages of each type? Which type comes closest to meeting all the criteria you established in the previous question?
5. Which of these types would be most useful from a management point of view? Why? Which would be more useful to the external publics of business?
6. Which social audit is most realistic? Which is most practical? What do you think of the cost benefit approach? Does this approach make sense from either a management or society point of view? Why or why not?
7. List the purposes of a social audit. Which do you think are most important? Which of the types that were described in the text would have the best chance of accomplishing these purposes?
8. Define the term "social indicator." What does a social indicator indicate? What components or accounts would you choose to measure the quality of life in the community or region where you live?
9. Describe the criteria for selecting a social indicator. Take a few of the indicators in Exhibit 23.6 and analyze them in terms of how well they fit the criteria.
10. What purposes do social indicators serve? What did First Minneapolis National Bank use them for? Of what use could they be to government policy-makers?
11. Does the social audit appear to be widely used by corporations in this country? Why or why not? What are the reasons the social audit seems to be used more widely in Western Europe?
12. What is the history of the use of social indicators in the United States? Considering the amount of attention given to social problems by the federal government, why have they not been used more extensively? Do you think social indicators will be used more in the future?

Suggested Reading

Abt, Clark C. *The Social Audit for Management.* New York: AMACOM, 1977.

American Institute of Certified Public Accountants. *Measurement of Corporate Social Performance.* New York: AICPA, 1977.

Bauer, Raymond. *Social Indicators.* Boston: Massachusetts Institute of Technology Press, 1966.

————, and Dan H. Fenn, Jr. *The Corporate Social Audit.* New York: Russell Sage Foundation, 1972.

Blake, David H., Frederick, William C., and Myers, Mildred S. *Social Auditing: Evaluating the Impact of Corporate Programs.* New York: Praeger, 1976.

Corson, John J., and Steiner, George A. *Measuring Business Social Performance: The Corporate Social Audit.* New York: Committee for Economic Development, 1974.

Dierkes, Meinholf, and Bauer, Raymond A. *Corporate Social Accounting.* New York: Praeger, 1973.

Estes, Ralph W. *Accounting and Society.* Los Angeles: Melville, 1973.

Goldston, Eli. *The Quantification of Concern: Some Aspects of Social Accounting.* Pittsburgh, Pa.: Carnegie-Mellon University, 1971.

Gordon, Lawrence A., ed. *Accounting and Corporate Social Responsibility.* Lawrence: University of Kansas, 1978.

Johnson, Harold L. *Disclosure of Corporate Social Performance: Survey, Evaluation, and Prospects.* New York: Praeger, 1979.

Linowes, David F. *Strategies for Survival:* New York: AMACOM, 1973.

Report of the Task Force on Corporate Social Performance, U.S. Department of Commerce. *Corporate Social Reporting in the United States and Western Europe.* Washington, D.C.: U.S. Government Printing Office, 1979.

Seidler, Lee J., and Seidler, Lynn L. *Social Accounting: Theory, Issues and Cases.* Los Angeles: Melville, 1975.

Sheldon, Eleanor B., et al. *Indicators of Social Change: Concepts and Measurements.* New York: Russell Sage Foundation, 1968.

U.S. Department of Commerce. *Social Indicators 1976.* Washington, D.C.: U.S. Government Printing Office, 1977.

Wilcox, Leslie D., et al. *Social Indicators and Societal Monitoring. An Annotated Bibliography.* New York: Elsevier Scientific Pub. Co., 1973.

24

The Future of Business and Public Policy

> By its nature, a farseeing look at the future is less important for the answers it purports to give than for the questions it raises. Among the questions raised by this report:
> —Will government intervention finally drain the entrepreneurial energy of American business, or will business deflect this trend by learning how to combine profits with self-regulation?
> —Will corporations be allowed to grow as large as they must to hold their own against foreign competitors and to fulfill the social goals demanded of them?
> If this report succeeds in raising those questions, and others of equal importance, it will have served its purpose.[1]

The problem that public policy poses for business and business management can be seen at two levels. At the macro level, the problem is one of providing society with public goods and services in a manner that does not unduly interfere with the ability of the productive apparatus of society to provide private goods and services efficiently. The major questions at this level involve the relationships of business and society as a whole—particularly the business-government relationship—and the use of regulation as a means to force business into providing public goods and services such as clean air and water. Will regulation of business increase or decrease, and will alternatives be seriously explored?

The micro problem of public policy is how a private, profit-making institution can incorporate the public policy dimension into its operations

---

[1]"The Future: How U.S. Business Will Change in the Next 50 Years." Reprinted from the September 3, 1979 issue of *Business Week* by special permission, (c) 1979 by McGraw-Hill, Inc., New York, NY 10020. All rights reserved.

and integrate public policy concerns with traditional business policy concerns into a total management strategy. This integration involves, as discussed in the latter chapters of this book, a philosophy of public responsibility and the development of a public issues management function to incorporate this philosophy into day-to-day corporate operations. One major question at this level concerns the future of management education in relation to this public policy dimension, a future to which it is hoped this book contributes.

Business and Society

Underlying the importance of public policy to management is the changing role of business in society. This change is part of a newly evolving social-political-economic order that is taking place in American society, based on new ideas and values about the nature of life and the goals worth pursuing. The basic value question concerns the wealth of a nation, to use the title of Adam Smith's book. What is it that makes a society wealthy? How is wealth defined?

During the mercantilist era the wealth of a nation was considered to be located in the amount of gold or silver it had in its treasury. Thus nations tried their best to maintain a favorable balance of trade, and sought to colonize the new world. These colonies fitted nicely into this system by providing raw materials for the mother country and a market for finished goods, adding to the wealth of the producing nation. Public policy measures had to be passed to discourage development of manufacturing on a large scale in the colonies themselves.

This order came to an end with the rise of capitalism, particularly as it developed in this country. The wealth of a nation, Adam Smith argued, was tied up in the amount of goods and services its people could produce. Government should keep its hands off this economic mechanism and let it operate efficiently to increase the wealth of society. The emphasis was placed on the business institution to provide these goods and services and on the measurement of gross national product as an indication of how much wealth was being created.

This emphasis on private goods and services, however, caused problems in the social realm that eventually had to be alleviated by public policy measures. Unemployment, pollution, poverty, discrimination, unsafe products and workplaces, all became social problems of sufficient magnitude to deserve the allocation of significant amounts of the nation's resources. The pursuit of wealth in the sense of a focus on private goods and services is changing to more of a balance with public goods and services. These public goods and services emphasize other aspects of the quality of life, a term that is increasingly being used to refer to the aspirations of American society. Thus it might not be incorrect to say that the emerging economic-political-social order sees the wealth of a nation tied up with the quality of life that can be provided its citizens (Exhibit 24.1).

Improving the quality of life involves the provision of both private and public goods and services. The full enjoyment of private goods and services depends on a healthy environment that is maintained by public goods and

EXHIBIT 24.1 ─────────────────────────────

The Wealth of a Nation

Type of System	Basic Orientation
Mercantilism	Gold Stock
Capitalism	Goods and Services
?	Quality of Life

services. Expensive clothes become soiled in a dirty environment. Wastes not disposed of properly are risks to human health. Cities become dangerous places in which to live because of racial tensions. Government has grown in importance and size to deal with these public policy problems and business is no longer such a dominant institution. Consequently, economic values are no longer so dominant either. Society does not always shape itself to the economy, but the economy is being forced to adjust to other values primarily through the process of regulation.

This is the basic reality that business has to live with and that managers of private institutions have to take into account. The future holds many challenges to business management that arise out of this changing relationship between business and society. As shown in Figure 24.1, society consists of a people with ideas, values, and expectations of what they want out of life and the goals they believe are worth pursuing. These change over time, as a brief overview of the history of American society will show. Based on these ideas, values and expectations, society forms institutions, which are more or less formalized procedures by which society tries to fulfill its expectations. Business is one such institution created to provide the society with material goods and services to enhance the material standard of living. These institutions use the resources that society has available to perform their missions.

At the present time, business is caught in a squeeze between society's changing ideas, values, and expectations, which have defined new roles for business to perform in addition to its basic economic mission, and resource shortages. Because of these shortages and the increasing cost of raw materials, business finds it harder to fulfill its basic economic mission to the satisfaction of the American people, let alone its newly defined social and political roles. Given these conditions, it is no wonder that business has lost credibility in American society and has been inundated with a series of new public policy directives.

Figure 24.1

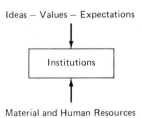

Ideas — Values — Expectations

Institutions

Material and Human Resources

Business-Government Relations

One of the most crucial questions about the future of business and public policy concerns the relationship between business and government. The adversarial relationship, as described in Chapter 8, is considered by many academics and businesspeople as no longer viable for dealing with the problems the nation faces (see box).

What is also needed is a new premise about the right and proper relationship between business and government. For a long time the two have been circling around each other like gladiators in combat, blocking and parrying each other's moves. That may amuse some of the spectators, but too often it results in poor government policies and lousy business decisions. We get programs grounded in vindictiveness rather than practicality, and all the while, enormous amounts of energy are being put into adversarial politicking that could more properly be used to resolve the nation's real problems. . . . What the nation needs from business and government is an understanding that neither one of those institutions has a monopoly on intelligence or probity, or the wisdom to prescribe all by itself for the public welfare.

From Irving S. Shapiro, "The Process: Business and Public Policy," *Harvard Business Review*, Vol. 57, No. 6 (November-December 1979), p. 98. Copyright © 1979 by the President and Fellows of Harvard College; all rights reserved.

The Committee for Economic Development, for example, has proposed a business-government partnership that involves acceptance of the fact that high priority public policy goals can be reached only through a massive cooperative effort of government, industry, labor, and education. On business-government relations in particular, the CED states that each has its own roles to perform in the formulation and solution of public policy problems.[2]

Government's basic role is to determine the nation's goals through the political process. This responsibility is derived from the constitution, which charges the federal government to preserve the common good by making, interpreting, and enforcing the norms of society. These norms, which include society's goals, ought to govern social, economic and political life in such a way that, in pursuing self-interest, no individual or group of individuals will be allowed to work against the national good. Related to its normative responsibilities are a number of other governmental functions. These include setting priorities, developing strategies and programs, and creating conditions for carrying out the work effectively and efficiently.

Within a national goals and priorities framework, business has a significant part to play in the actual implementation of social programs. With its profit-and-loss discipline, it is a proven instrument for getting society's work done. As an incentive for social consciousness and good citizenship, government must create the market conditions that will induce business enterprises to apply their operational capabilities to those public tasks they can

---

[2]Committee for Economic Development, *Social Responsibilities of Business Corporations* (New York: Committee for Economic Development, 1971), pp. 57–58.

carry out more efficiently than other institutions. "Government at all levels," says the CED, "seems likely to function best as a market creator, systems manager, and contractor of social tasks rather than as an actual operator of every kind of public service."[3]

> Thus the incentive for profit is the only practicable way of unleashing the power and dynamism of private enterprise on a scale that will be effective in generating social progress. Social consciousness and good citizenship, while important prerequisites, cannot realistically be expected by themselves to bring business resources to bear on the country's social problems on the massive scale that is needed. To achieve this, government must create the market conditions that will induce business enterprises to apply their operational capabilities to those public tasks they can carry out more efficiently than other institutions.[4]

The incentives that government can use to get business involved in solving social problems include contracts, cash subsidies, loans, credit guarantees, insurance, and tax benefits. In providing such incentives the government becomes the visible hand that replaces the invisible hand to achieve the public good.

This proposal offers business a carrot rather than a stick approach to getting involved in social problems, and is patterned after the way decisions are presently made regarding national defense. This approach recognizes the formal involvement of government as planner, a role that only an entity that is representative of society as a whole can play. Many believe that only in some such manner can truly public goals be determined and a policy shaped for the nation as a whole.

Gerald R. Proust, writing in the *Conference Board Record*, argues that society is moving toward a more coordinated, forecasted, planned development characteristic of a postindustrial society. This movement implies an increasing centralization and politicization of economic as well as social decision-making. Government will increasingly act as coordinator of fundamental decisions affecting all economic institutions. The degree to which business will have an impact on this decision-making process in the future is contingent on its ability to become an integral part of the public policy process. The business leaders of today and tomorrow must be able to work within the political process, representing the interests of business and at the same time understanding the effect of corporate decisions on society. Thus business must provide leadership on public policy questions.[5]

> The absence of effective leadership for the business community on many public policy questions—in consensus building and in dealing with other groups and governments—means that business enterprises forfeit almost entirely to politicians. The rapid expansion of government regulations in recent years and specifically government's penchant for rigid, bureaucratic "command and control" regulations, even when ineffective or counterproductive, have arisen in part from a lack of coherence and consensus within the business community about more constructive choices for achieving social purposes.[6]

[3]*Ibid.*, p. 52.

[4]*Ibid.*, p. 51.

[5]Gerald R. Proust, "Corporate Social Strategy in a Post-Industrial World," *The Conference Board Record*, Vol. XII, No. 9 (September 1975), pp. 32–36.

[6]John T. Dunlop, "The Concerns: Business and Public Policy," *Harvard Business Review*, Vol. 57, No. 6 (November-December 1979), p. 100. Copyright © 1979 by the President and Fellows of Harvard College; all rights reserved.

In terms of a specific policy mechanism that would enable government to more adequately fulfill its partnership responsibilities with business, Vice-President Walter Mondale proposed some years ago The Full Opportunity and National Goals and Priorities Act.[7] This bill contained two titles, the first of which established the opportunity for all Americans to live in decency and dignity, and declared this goal to be a continuing responsibility of the federal government, consistent with the primary responsibilities of state and local governments.

The bill was patterned after the Employment Act of 1946 and called for the creation of a Council of Social Advisers in the Executive Office of the President, and for the development of an annual Social Report of the President to be transmitted to Congress no later than February 15 of each year. Through these means, the enormous potential of the social sciences could be given the kind of direction and visibility needed to assist the executive in making, administering, and evaluating public policy.

The second title of the bill would establish within Congress an Office of Goals and Priorities Analysis, which would be the counterpart for Congress of the Council of Social Advisers. Its function would be to submit an annual report to Congress setting forth goals and priorities of needs, costs, available resources, and program effectiveness. This national priorities report could include the following:

1. An analysis, in terms of national priorities, of the programs in the annual budget submitted by the President and in the Economic and Social Reports of the President.

2. An examination of resources available to the nation, the foreseeable costs and expected benefits of existing and proposed federal programs, and the resource and cost implications of alternative sets of national priorities.

3. Recommendations concerning spending priorities among federal programs and courses of action, including the identification of those programs and courses of action that should be given greatest priority and those that could more properly be deferred.[8]

This office would enable Congress to become better informed, since it would have its own source of information on social issues, along with that information collected by the executive branch as published in the Social Report of the President.

Furthermore, it was hoped that the creation of such a policy planning mechanism would lead to a more efficient and rational allocation of resources, particularly in the utilization of the private sector in the implementation of social policy. It would encourage Congress to recognize that the primary type of incentive for involving business in social programs ought to be contractual or in the form of subsidies reflected in the expenditure side of the federal budget rather than in the form of special tax incentives. This is the case because the budgetary process is subject to legislative and public scrutiny and is increasingly being accompanied by performance evaluation to determine how well the intended objectives are met (see box).

[7]U.S. Congress, Senate, *Full Opportunity and National Goals and Priorities Act*, S. 5, 93rd Congress, 1st Session, 1973.

[8]U.S. Congress, Senate, *Full Opportunity and National Goals and Priorities Act*, S. 5, Report 93-324 to accompany S. 5, 93rd Congress, 1st session, 1973, p. 2.

FULL OPPORTUNITY AND NATIONAL GOALS AND PRIORITIES ACT

- Establishes the President's Council of Social Advisers comparable in the social sphere to the Council of Economic Advisers in the economic area.
  a. Gather timely and authoritative information and statistical data and analyze and interpret them.
  b. Appraise the various social programs and activities of the federal government.
  c. Recommend to the President the most efficient and effective way to allocate federal resources.
- Requires the President to submit an annual Social Report to Congress, the social counterpart to his Economic Report.
  a. Detail the overall progress and effectiveness of federal efforts toward implementing the policy of the act.
  b. Review state, local, and private efforts to this end.
  c. Present current and foreseeable needs, programs, and policies and recommendations for legislation.
- Creates a joint committee of Congress called the Office of Goals and Priorities Analysis comparable to the Joint Economic Committee of Congress.
  a. Analyze the Economic and Social Reports of the President in terms of national priorities.
  b. Examine the resource and cost implications of alternative sets of national priorities.
  c. Recommend spending priorities among federal programs and courses of action.

For businesses' responsibility in such a partnership, the concept of voluntarism might be a useful approach. The essence of a viable partnership is not only a rational formulation of public policy objectives, but also voluntary and willing compliance. The use of appropriate incentives will help, but some government leaders believe that voluntarism is the key to successful implementation of public policy objectives. To avoid the kind of regulation we have today, the regulated will have to do their own enforcement on a larger scale in responding to public policy objectives and measuring performance of these objectives.[9]

The Future of Regulation

There will be continued pressure for additional regulation of business, particularly from public interest groups. The recent Big Business Day should remind everyone that these groups have not ceased their efforts to further increase government control over the corporation and regulate it in the public interest, a term with some obvious problems of definition. These groups are advocating more regulation of corporate governance (federal chartering, public interest directors, and the like), splitting up large com-

[9]"A Pervasive Government and Voluntary Regulation," *Business Week*, September 3, 1979, pp. 201–203.

panies or at least preventing mergers of large companies to reduce what they perceive as unaccountable corporate power, and the creation of new agencies, such as the agency for consumer advocacy that for the moment seems dormant, but may indeed reappear. Business cannot sit back and think it has won the regulatory war by preventing any new regulatory areas from appearing recently and now needs to only fight a few battles in specific areas of already existing regulation.

But even assuming that Congress does not pass any legislation in the next few years that creates whole new areas of regulation, legislation that has already been passed, but not yet fully implemented (toxic substances, hazardous waste disposal) will keep new regulations coming for some years to come. These areas are just now receiving increasing attention from the administration and interest groups who are pressuring the regulatory agencies to implement the legislation already passed. Murray Weidenbaum had this to say on the future of the chemical industry and regulation.

> Five years from today, every company in the chemical industry will be far more closely regulated than it is today. Five years from today, the chemical industry is also likely to take first place honors as the most closely regulated industry in America. Five years from today is 1984.
>
> Unfortunately, those are forecasts that I can make with great confidence. That is so because the future rise in regulation is not dependent on Congress passing any new laws. My forecasts solely take account of the vast amounts of regulation that is in the pipeline—that is, the laws passed by the Congress in recent years for which the implementing regulations have not yet been fully developed and promulgated.[10]

With regard to regulatory reform, the legislative veto or some variation of this idea seems to be getting a great deal of recent attention. Congress recently gave final approval to a $225 million, three-year authorization for the Federal Trade Commission, but did not give the agency a blank check. The bill restricts the agency's investigation of the insurance industry, "unfair" television advertisements aimed at children, and bars the agency from enforcing antitrust laws against agricultural cooperatives, and from cancelling registered trademarks on the grounds that they have become generic names. The bill also gives Congress the right to veto any new rules of the agency.

Another example of congressional oversight is a bill introduced by Senator Richard Schweiker (R-Pa). called the Occupational Safety and Health Improvement Act (S. 2153), which would exempt 90 percent of the nation's workplaces from OSHA safety inspections. These and similar initiatives reflect Congress's desire to exert more direct control over regulatory agencies, a trend that some believe will continue for the immediate future.[11]

A variation of this kind of congressional oversight is the establishment of a Regulatory Policy Board (S. 2147), which would replace President Carter's Regulatory Council and the Regulatory Analysis Review Group. The RPB would consist of a member of the Council of Economic Advisers, the chair-

---

[10]Murray L. Weidenbaum, "Looking Forward (?) to 1984," *The Point Is: A Summary of Public Issues Important to the Dow Chemical Company,* No. 13, February 29, 1980, p. 1.

[11]*Major Regulatory Initiatives during 1979: The Agencies, the Courts, the Congress* (Washington, D.C.: American Enterprise Institute, 1980), p. 46.

man of the Administrative Conference, the director of the Office of Management and Budget, plus the heads of three executive agencies and three independent agencies designated by the president. Its functions would be to (1) publish a semiannual calendar of all major rules under consideration by the agencies, (2) monitor agency compliance with regulatory analysis requirements of the act, and (3) select each year for interagency review the initial regulatory analyses of up to 20 major rules which, if promulgated, would have the most significant economic impact.

In September 1979, Senator Dale Bumpers introduced an amendment to the Federal Courts Improvement Act (S. 1477) to revise the provisions of the Administrative Procedures Act that prescribes the scope of judicial review of federal administrative agency action. This Bumpers amendment would, among other things, eliminate any presumption on judicial review that an agency's regulations are valid, require the agencies to show that their jurisdictional authority over a particular matter is either expressly provided in or clearly implied by their enabling statutes, and would continue the reviewing court's obligation to ensure that the agency has complied with all applicable procedural requirements.

Soon after taking office, President Reagan established a Presidential Task Force on Regulatory Relief, chaired by the Vice-President and including as members the Secretary of the Treasury, the Attorney General, the Secretary of Commerce, the Secretary of Labor, the Director of the Office of Management and Budget, the Assistant to the President for Policy Planning, and the Chairman of the Council of Economic Advisors. The major purposes of the task force are to review new proposals by regulatory agencies in the executive branch, assess regulations already in effect, and oversee the development of legislative proposals as appropriate. The task force is to be guided by the following principles: (1) federal regulations should be initiated only when there is a compelling need; (2) alternative regulatory approaches (including no regulation) should be considered and the approach selected that imposes the least possible burden on society consistent with achieving the overall statutory and policy objectives; and (3) regulatory priorities should be governed by an assessment of the benefits and costs of the proposed regulations.

These efforts at regulatory oversight, either by Congress, a special board or task force, or the courts are a mixed blessing for business. If the oversight body is probusiness, the results, for the most part, are likely to be acceptable to business. But this assumption cannot be true for all times and places, as the composition of these bodies will change over time. The regulatory power still remains in government; it is not dissolved or given to business. The most likely result of these efforts is further politicization of the regulatory process, with more delays and uncertainty than exists at present.

Alternatives to regulation, or deregulation, may be the only feasible long-run solution to the problems that the regulatory process poses for business and society. The other reform measures seem only short-term solutions that have limited prospects for success. They leave the regulatory process itself basically intact, a process that may be so inherently flawed that it needs to be scrapped in favor of alternatives. The regulatory process continues the adversarial relationship between business and government, a relationship the society may no longer be able to afford, and it involves the use of a command and control system to force changes in behavior, a process that is not consistent with the incentive approach used in the marketplace.

This does not imply that government has no role to play in setting objectives and seeing that they are attained. It may be in the best position to set standards related to occupational safety and health, for example, but they should be performance standards, not standards dealing with equipment specifications or other details of the workplace. Performance standards could also be set for the other areas of social regulation. Then the government could provide incentives as described previously, to encourage attainment of the standards or let the marketplace itself induce changes in business behavior. Such an approach involves a degree of cooperation between business and government in setting realistic and attainable performance standards and business's willingness to admit the legitimacy of social objectives. But alternatives to regulation would allow business much greater degrees of freedom in efficiently attaining social objectives, a goal that would obviously benefit society as a whole.

Questions for Discussion

1. What is the difference between a micro and a macro view of business and public policy? What questions about the future of business and public policy are important at each of these levels?
2. What does the phrase "quality of life" mean? How does the provision of economic goods and services relate to this concept? What noneconomic dimensions are important to the quality of life in our society?
3. Do you agree with the author's rather sweeping generalizations about the wealth of nations? Why or why not? What implications does your answer have for the future of business-society relations?
4. Describe the partnership model proposed by the Committee for Economic Development. Do you agree with the role that is prescribed for government? What would you change, if anything? Is this proposal a viable alternative to the adversarial relationship?
5. What does it mean to say that business must provide leadership on public policy questions? What is likely to be the result if it does not? How can business fulfill this leadership role? How does voluntarism relate to leadership?
6. Explain the major provisions of the Mondale bill (The Full Opportunity and National Goals and Priorities Act). Would the structure this bill contains produce more effective and rational public policies from government? Why or why not? Why do you think this bill never passed Congress?
7. What does the future of regulation look like? What implications does your answer have for your first job in business and your future management career? What reform measures would you like to see adopted? What is your assessment of the probabilities that these reform measures will be adopted in the near future?

Suggested Reading

The Changing Expectations of Society in the Next Thirty Years. Washington, D.C.: AACSB/EFMD, 1979.

Commission on Population Growth and the American Future. *Population and the American Future.* Washington D.C.: U.S. Government Printing Office, 1972.

Ewald, William R., Jr., ed. *Environment and Change: The Next Fifty Years.* Bloomington: Indiana University Press, 1968.

Kahn, Herman. *The Future of the Corporation.* New York: Mason & Lipscomb, 1974.

Kahn, Herman, and Bruce-Briggs, B. *Things to Come: Thinking about the Seventies and Eighties.* New York: Macmillan, 1972.

———, and Wiener, A. *The Year 2000.* New York: Macmillan, 1967.

Management in the XXI Century. Washington, D.C.: AACSB/EFMD, 1979.

Morris, DuBois S., Jr., ed. *Perspective for the 70's and 80's: Tomorrow's Problems Confronting Today's Management.* New York: National Industrial Conference Board, 1970.

Perloff, Harvey S., ed. *The Future of the U.S. Government: Toward the Year 2000.* Englewood Cliffs, N.J.: Prentice-Hall, 1971.

Theobald, Robert. *An Alternative Future for America Two: Essays and Speeches.* Chicago: Swallow, 1968.

———. *Futures Conditional.* New York: Bobbs-Merrill, 1971.

Index

Cambridge Survey Research Center, 75
Campaign contributions, 190–98
Carbon dioxide, 364
Carcinogens, 317–18
Carlson v. Coca-Cola Co., 208
Carr, Albertz Z., 82–84
Carson, Rachel, 394–95
Caterpillar Tractor Co., 162
Center for Auto Safety, 343
Center for Research in Business and Social
    Policy, 446–48
Center for the Study of American Business,
    158, 162
Chandler, Alfred, 28–29
Charles River Associates, 164
Chemical Facts of Life, 182–83
Chicago Board of Trade v. United States,
    210
Chilton, Kenneth W., 162
Chrysler Corporation, 134–38
Churchill and Shank, 297
Citizen sovereignty, 24
City Venture Corporation, 243
Civil Aeronautics Board, 151, 170
Civil Rights Act, 275–76
Clayton Act, 32, 207–8
Clean Air Act, 387–89
Clean Water Act, 393
Cobbs, John, 137–39
Commission on Federal Paperwork, 164
Committee for Economic Development, 6,
    526
Comparable worth, 291–92
Competition:
    maintenance of, 33–34
    nature, 28, 221
Comprehensive Employment and Training
    Act, 233–34, 236
Concentration, 31
Conference Board, 214, 251, 450–53, 488
Conference of Consumer Organizations,
    343
Conglomerate merger, 212
Consumer affairs offices, 344
Consumer Federation of America, 343
Consumerism:
    bill of rights, 333
    definition, 327
    executive branch, 332–33
    future, 355–56
    history, 327–33
    issues, 344–51
    legislation, 328–32
    philosophies, 351–55
Consumer Product Safety Act, 332
Consumer Product Safety Commission, 153,
    334–37, 348–49
Consumer Protection Agency, 340–42
Consumer Research Institute, 343–44
Consumer sovereignty, 18
Consumers Union, 343
Contributory negligence, 304

Control Data Corporation, 241–43, 416
Cool-Line service, 344
Coopers and Lybrand, 97
Corporate governance:
    definition, 102–3
    and disclosure, 112–14
    and employees, 111
    and institutions, 109–11
    and management, 106–7
    and shareholders, 103–6
Corporations:
    economic power, 206
    formation, 30–31
Corrective advertising, 347–48
Corrupt Practices Act, 192
Cost-effectiveness analysis, 172
Costle, Douglas M., 394
Council of Economic Advisors, 141
Council on Environmental Quality, 368–
    70, 372, 374
Council of Social Advisors, 528–29
Counter advertising, 348
Current Population Surveys, 254

*Daniel McAleer and Local #2350, Com-
    munications Workers of America v.
    American Telephone and Tele-
    graph Co.,* 286
Data Resources, Inc., 166
deButts, John D., 7
Delaney clause, 339, 345
Demsetz, Harold, 219
Denison, Edward, 164
Depression, 35–37
Deregulation, 170
Disadvantaged, 233–37
Disclosure, 112–14
Discrimination, 229
    handicapped, 294
    nature of, 272–74
    other, 295–97
    religious, 293–94
Domhoff, William G., 51–52
Dow Chemical Co., 165
Drucker, Peter, 218
Drug regulation, 346–47
Dunlop, John T., 168
Dun's Review, 322
DuPont Company, 213

Economic concentration:
    aggregate, 213–15
    market, 215–17
Economic education, 184
Economic management, 39–40
Economic planning:
    arguments against, 145–46
    arguments for, 145

public policy skills, 9–12
  speaking out on issues, 177–78
  training programs, 455–56
Marketable rights, 377–79
Market system:
  elements, 15–19
  operating principles, 19
Marshall v. American Petroleum Institute,
  318
Marshall v. Barlow's Inc., 320
McDonald v. Santa Fe Trail Transportation Co., 285
McKean, Roland, 91
Means, Gardiner C., 104–5, 109, 134–39, 148, 214
Metzenbaum, Howard M., 112
Middle-class, 50
Miller, James C. III, 169
Minority business, 237–39, 243–44
Minority Enterprise Small Business Investment Corporation, 238
Minority purchasing program, 239–41
Mobil Oil Corporation, 180–81
Molander, Earl, 91, 98–100
Mondale, Walter, 528
Monopoly, 211
Monsanto Corporation, 182–83
Mythic/Epic cycle, 78–80

Nader network, 343
Nader, Ralph, 43, 54–55, 75, 120, 167, 331, 334, 473
National Academy of Sciences, 345
National Alliance of Businessmen, 6
  development, 234–35
  financing, 235
  operation, 235–36
  results, 237
National Association of Manufacturers, 185, 322
National Association of Purchasing Management, 94
National Consumer League, 343
National economic planning, 44
National Environmental Policy Act, 366–68
National Highway Traffic and Motor Vehicle Safety Act, 331
National Highway Traffic Safety Administration, 153, 166, 339–40, 341–42
National Industrial Recovery Act, 41
National Institute for Occupational Safety and Health, 308, 317
National Labor Relations Board, 41, 153
National Minority Purchasing Council, 238, 240
National Pollutant Discharge Elimination System, 392
National Safety Council, 306

Nestle Company, 473
New Deal, 37, 39
New York Stock Exchange, 109
Nichols and Zeckhauser, 316, 323, 325
Noise Control Act, 405
Noise pollution, 402–7
Noise standards, 406
Northern Pacific Ry. v. United States, 206

Occidental Petroleum Corp., 5
Occupational hazards, 304
Occupational Safety and Health Act, 307
Occupational Safety and Health Administration, 153, 307–8
  alternatives, 323-25
  costs and benefits, 322–23
  coverage, 315–16
  employees, 314–15
  employers, 312–13, 321–22
  enforcement, 309, 319–320
  noise, 406
  record-keeping, 312
  standards, 309, 316–19
  violations, 311, 320–21
Occupational Safety and Health Review Commission, 309, 311, 320
Office of Federal Contract Compliance Programs, 277, 281
Office of Management and Budget, 515
Office of Minority Business Enterprise, 238
Offset policy, 379, 389
Okun, Arthur, 90, 248, 262–63, 268
Olasky, Marvin, 266
Oligopoly, 206
Olin Corporation, 3–5
Organization of Petroleum Exporting Countries, 44–45

Paglin, Morton, 253–56
Paperwork:
  company study, 461
  costs, 458–61
  impact, 457–61
  types, 457–58
Pattern or practice cases, 288–90
Pesticides, 394–96
Physical environment, 358
Planning, 142–46
Plattner, Marc, 266
Pluralism, 52–59
Political Action Committees:
  contributions, 193–97
  definition, 193
  growth, 192
  operation, 193
  organization, 194
  rules and limitations, 192–93

Saccharin, 345
Sargent, Alice G., 297
Schweiker, Richard, 530
Sears Roebuck and Company, 295, 298
Securities Exchange Act, 88
Securities and Exchange Commission, 112, 114, 151
  and foreign payments, 84, 86–87
  investor responsibility, 119
  proxy rules, 117
Selekman, Benjamin and Sylvia, 90
Self-interest, 17
Sentry Insurance Company, 355
Sethi, S. Prakash, 416, 422, 453
Shapiro, Irving S., 439–41
Shared monopoly, 212
Shareholders:
  activist, 117–20
  and corporate governance, 103–6
  resolutions, 117–20
Sheehan, Robert, 107
Sherman Act, 32, 206–7
  penalties, 208
  violations, 210–11
Silk, Leonard, 437
Sinclair, Upton, 328–29
Small and Independent Business Protection Act, 212
Smith, Adam, 18, 78
Smoot-Hawley Tariff, 37
Social Audit, 499–512
  cost-benefit, 507–9
  definition, 499
  problems, 499–502
  purposes, 511–12
  types, 502–11
Social change, 78–80
Social decision-making, 431
Social indicators, 512–16
  definition, 512
  usage, 520
Social measurement and reporting, 516–20
Social movements, 42–43, 76–77
  definition, 76
  stages, 77
  types, 77
Social performance measurement, 430
Social policy, 429–33
Social regulation:
  nature of, 152
  pressures for, 152
  reasons for, 153
Social reporting, 430
Social responsibility, 6, 15, 43
  arguments against, 416–19
  arguments for, 413–16
  definition, 412–13
Social Responsibility Program Statement, 504
Social responsiveness:
  advantages, 424

definition, 420
problems, 425
Socio-Economic Operating Statement, 506–7
South Africa, 4, 118
Specialist function, 448–49
Standard Oil Company, 32, 209
State chartering, 121–22
Steckmest, Fran, 438–39
Steiner, George A., 8
Stigler, George, 223
Strategic planning, 473–74
Subsidies, 132
Sullivan, Leon, 116
Sunset legislation, 171
Superfund, 402

Tariffs, 132
Task Force on Regulatory Relief, 172, 531
Tax credits, 133
Teachers Insurance and Annuity Association, 119
Teamsters v. U.S. (T.I.M.E.–D.C., Inc.), 288
Technology:
  and corporate governance, 111
  and economic concentration, 221
  and pollution, 365–66
  progress, 69
  and values, 65–66
Technostructure, 111
Temporary National Economic Committee, 38
Tennessee Valley Authority, 139
Testing, 292–93
The Managerial Revolution Reassessed, 108
The Modern Corporation and Private Property, 109
The process audit, 504–5
The Visible Hand, 28–29
Thompson, Arthur A., 219
Tillman Act, 191
Tocqueville, Alexis de, 53
Tombari, Henry, 9–10
Top management:
  accountability, 453–55
  public, 452
  public policy involvement, 450–53
  public policy roles, 451–52
Towey, James F., 3, 5
Townsend, Robert, 116
Toxic pollutants, 393
Toxic substances, 5, 396–99, 400–401
Toxic Substances Control Act, 397
Trans World Airlines v. Hardison, 293
Treasury Department, 87
Trust, 31

DATE DUE